W9-CHN-708

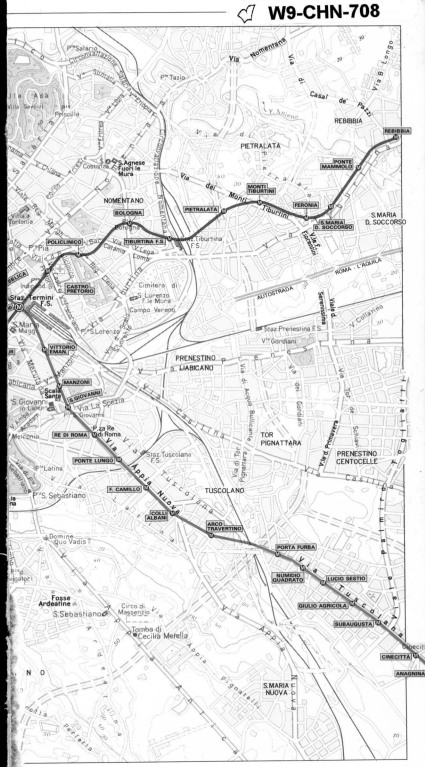

Founded on the left bank of the Tiber, Rome has straddled the river since the Imperial age. From antiquity to the 19th century, when the *muraglioni* (high embankments) were constructed, frequent flooding forced the Romans to build dikes, dredge the riverbed, and build numerous bridges to connect the two banks. These included ancient structures such as the Pons Sublicius (the oldest on record), the Pons Aemilius (the first stone bridge) and the Pons Aelius (the forerunner of the Ponte Sant'Angelo). The newest bridges are the Ponte Duca d'Aosta (opposite the Foro Italico) and the Ponte Principe Amadeo.

THIS IS A BORZOI BOOK
PUBLISHED BY ALFRED A. KNOPF, INC.

Copyright © 1994 Alfred A. Knopf, Inc., New York

*Originally published in France by Nouveaux-Loisirs, a subsidiary of
Gallimard, Paris, 1994. Copyright © 1994 by Editions Nouveaux-Loisirs*

*Endpapers cartography and street maps of Rome from page 516 to 541 originally printed in
Guide d'Italia: Roma © Touring Club Italiano, Milan 1993.
Reprinted with permission of TCI.*

Rome. English
Rome / [Gallimard editions].
p. cm.-- (Knopf guides)
Includes bibliographical references and index.
ISBN 0-679-75067-3 : $25.00
1. Rome (Italy.) -- Guidebooks.
I. Gallimard (Firm) . II. Title
III. Series
DG804.R6829213 1994
914.5'63204929 -- dc20
CIP 94-5868

First American Edition

NUMEROUS SPECIALISTS AND ACADEMICS HAVE CONTRIBUTED TO THIS GUIDE:
AUTHORS: Noëlle de la Blanchardière, Pascale de la Blanchardière, Marie-Paule
Boutry, Massimo Bray, Catherine Brice, Filippo Coarelli,
Clarisse Deniau, Jean-Louis Fournel, Stéphane Guégan, Antonio del Guercio,
Etienne Hubert, Vincent Jolivet, Grégory Leroy, Jean-Louis Marlroux,
Christian Michel, Claudia Moatti, Daniel Nony, Corinne Paul, Simone Pelizzoli,
Guido Prola, Mauro Quercioli, Laure Raffaëlli, Nathalie Salis, Raffaele Simone, Livia Tedeschini.
ILLUSTRATORS: Caterina d'Agostino, Michèle Bisgambiglia, Anne Bodin,
Pierre Boutin, Nicolette Castle, Jean Chevallier, Paul Coulbois, François Desbordes, Hugh Dixon,
Sandra Doyle, Claire Felloni, William Fischer, Eugene Flurey, Eric Gillion, Hubert Goger, Laurent
Gourdon, Jean-Marie Guillou, Perrine Henri, Jean-Benoit Héron, Olivier Hubert, Pierre de Hugo,
Roger Hutchins, Jean-Michel Kacédan, Bruno Lenormand, Philippe Lhez, Philippe Mignon,
Jean-Pierre Pontcabare, Pierre Poulain, Claude Quiec, Jean-Claude Sénée,
Jean-Louis Serret, Mike Shœbridge, Jean-Michel Simier, Pascal Robin,
Catherine Totem, Tony Townsend, Riccardo Tremori, John Wilkinson.
PHOTOGRAPHERS: Araldo de Luca, Antonello Idini, Marzio Marzot,
Gabriella Peyrot

WE WOULD ALSO LIKE TO THANK:
Dominique Fernandes, Françoise Gaultier, Pierre Gros, Jean Héritier, Catherine Metzger, Claire Sotinel,
Florence Valdès-Forain, École Française de Rome

WE WOULD LIKE TO GIVE SPECIAL THANKS TO:
Russel Baker, Malcolm Bell (American Academy in Rome), Caroline Harbouris, Paola Lanzara (Orto
Botanico), Giovanni Lussu. Francesco Porseo and Derek Wilson

TRANSLATED BY LOUIS MARCELIN-RICE AND KATE NEWTON;
PRACTICAL SECTION TRANSLATED BY SÉBASTIEN MARCELIN-RICE
EDITED AND TYPESET BY BOOK CREATION SERVICES, LONDON.
PRINTED IN ITALY BY EDITORIALE LIBRARIA.

ROME

KNOPF GUIDES

CONTENTS

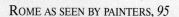

In 1477 the market which for decades had been held in Piazza del Campidoglio and the adjacent streets was moved to Piazza Navona, where it remained and operated every day until 1869. In acquiring the equivalent function of a Piazza del Comune or a Piazza del Duomo, from the 15th century Piazza Navona became the true heart of Rome.

"I was in Rome in 1791. At the time, the city still had 166,000 inhabitants,... everything...had an air of grandeur and opulence. Today I entered Rome by the same route, and instead of horses and carriages it was filled with flocks of sheep, oxen, and half-wild horses; behind, black-eyed shepherds herded them along."

F. Lullin de Châteauvieux

Ponte Rotto

Ponte Cestio

THE FORUM

THE COLISEUM

THE VATICAN

THE PANTHEON

PIAZZA NAVONA

THE QUIRINAL

IL TRIDENTE

VIA APPIA

TRASTEVERE

▲ ROME

1. ROME 2. VIA APPIA ANTICA 3. OSTIA ANTICA 4. LIDO DI OSTIA 5. LAGO DI BRACCIANO 6. MONTI SABATINI 7. LAGO DI BOLSENA 8. VITERBO 9. ORVIETO 10. MONTI SABINI

11. Terni 12. Abbazzia di Farfa 13. Monti Reatini 14. Monti Carseolani 15. Tivoli 16. Villa Adriana 17. Palestrina 18. Colli Albani 19. Lago di Nemi 20. Lago di Albano

HOW TO USE THIS GUIDE

(Sample page shown from the guide to Venice)

The symbols at the top of each page refer to the different parts of the guide.

- ■ **NATURAL ENVIRONMENT**
- ● **KEYS TO UNDERSTANDING**
- ▲ **ITINERARIES**
- ◆ **PRACTICAL INFORMATION**

The itinerary map shows the main points of interest along the way and is intended to help you find your bearings.

The mini-map locates the particular itinerary within the wider area covered by the guide.

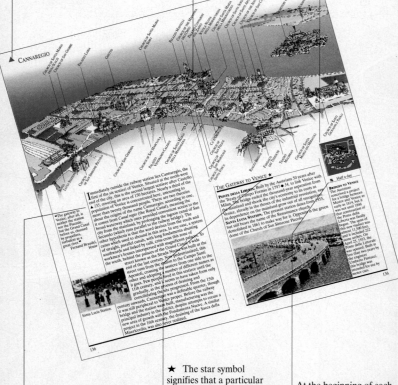

●▲■◆

The symbols alongside a title or within the text itself provide cross-references to a theme or place dealt with elsewhere in the guide.

★ The star symbol signifies that a particular site has been singled out by the publishers for its special beauty, atmosphere or cultural interest.

At the beginning of each itinerary, the suggested means of transport to be used and the time it will take to cover the area are indicated:

- ⇥ By boat
- 🚶 On foot
- 🚲 By bicycle
- ⊕ Duration

THE GATEWAY TO VENICE ★

PONTE DELLA LIBERTÀ. Built by the Austrians 50 years after the Treaty of Campo Formio in 1797 ● *34,* to link Venice with Milan. The bridge ended the thousand-year separation from the mainland and shook the city's economy to its roots as Venice, already in the throes of the industrial revolution, saw

🚶 Half a day

BRIDGES TO VENICE

NATURE

THE TIBER

EEL
So common that the city's last professional
fishermen make their living from eels.

Nicknamed "*il Biondo Tevere*" ("the Blond
Tiber") because of the silt that tinges its waters,
the river, now channeled between embankments, is still a
natural space that shelters a wide range of fish (including carp,
rudd, and eels) and birds (among them cormorants, kingfishers
and various kinds of gulls). On the other hand, there is very
little vegetation apart from the occasional clump of greenery
that the attentive observer wandering along the riverbanks will
notice, where willows or poplars have spontaneously reappeared
on abandoned land.

It was only at the end of the 19th century
that embankments were built in Rome to
channel the Tiber.

MALLARD
A few couples nest regularly on the little
islands in the river.

LITTLE GREBE
These can be seen in winter, especially near
Ponte Sant'Angelo.

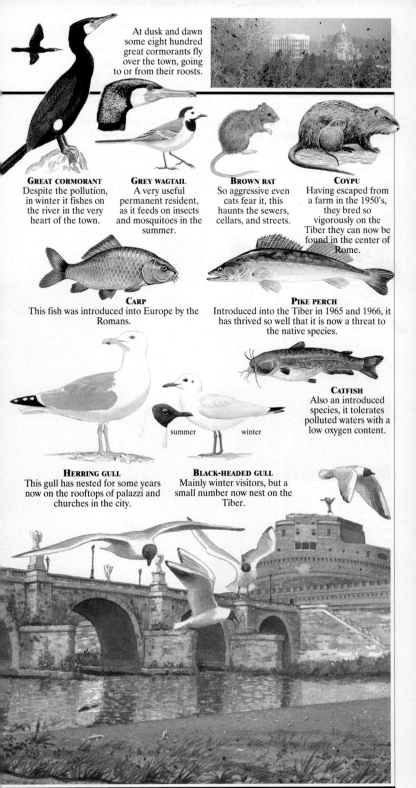

At dusk and dawn some eight hundred great cormorants fly over the town, going to or from their roosts.

GREAT CORMORANT
Despite the pollution, in winter it fishes on the river in the very heart of the town.

GREY WAGTAIL
A very useful permanent resident, as it feeds on insects and mosquitoes in the summer.

BROWN RAT
So aggressive even cats fear it, this haunts the sewers, cellars, and streets.

COYPU
Having escaped from a farm in the 1950's, they bred so vigorously on the Tiber they can now be found in the center of Rome.

CARP
This fish was introduced into Europe by the Romans.

PIKE PERCH
Introduced into the Tiber in 1965 and 1966, it has thrived so well that it is now a threat to the native species.

CATFISH
Also an introduced species, it tolerates polluted waters with a low oxygen content.

HERRING GULL
This gull has nested for some years now on the rooftops of palazzi and churches in the city.

BLACK-HEADED GULL
Mainly winter visitors, but a small number now nest on the Tiber.

summer   winter

17

THE FLORA AND FAUNA OF THE RUINS

SICILIAN LIZARD
Also known as "the lizard of the ruins", it sometimes
feeds on the remains of tourists' picnics.

The archeological sites all over Rome are protected
environments favorable to the development of unusual flora and
fauna. Common plant species such as the fig tree and the caper
bush (indigenous to the rocks of the Mediterranean) flourish
side by side among the ruins. Orchids also frequently grow
there. A number of bird species find a choice refuge in ancient
Rome.

LITTLE OWL
Particularly common in
the forums, where it hunts
rodents.

HOOPOE
Sometimes nests on
the Palatine, but is
being disturbed by
the flow of tourists.

BLACK REDSTART
These birds build
their nests among the
ruins, away from
tourists.

Cats are without
doubt the most
commonly found
mammals in the
forums.

The Forum is one of
the best places to
find original flora
and fauna, firmly
established in the
walls and among
the ruins.

GREEN LIZARD
This large, relatively uncommon lizard eats
insects and sometimes fledglings too.

JACKDAW
Nests in the Coliseum, but is now less common as it is being driven out by crows.

BLUE ROCK THRUSH
A few couples of this superb species nest in the Coliseum and in the tallest ruins of the forums.

CISALPINE SPARROW
This Italian variety of house sparrow can be identified by its brown skullcap.

KESTREL
Nests in bell towers and ruins, where it even hunts bats.

CAPER
This thorny bush with pretty white flowers grows on walls and in crevices between stones.

FIG
Common in the forums. It bears fruit at the end of the summer.

SPLEENWORT
This small fern grows mainly in the cracks between the blocks of stone in the forums.

WALL PELLITORY
Abundant at the foot of walls, this plant swiftly overruns neglected spots.

F. Desbordes

BUTTERFLY ORCHID
This magnificent orchid is found during April on all dry and chalky ground.

"Ruin-of-Rome" – a tiny and aptly named plant.

■ VILLA DORIA-PAMPHILI

EUROPEAN POND TORTOISE
This reptile can occasionally be observed in the villa's largest lake, resting on half-submerged branches.

Since antiquity the Romans have been masters of the art of designing superb gardens and country villas, though many of them have been swallowed up by the city. Rome's public parks are an example of these Italian-style gardens where allées, squares, and flowerbeds, bordered by yew, box, or evergreen oak, alternate with groves of such exotic trees as cedars or palms, or with islands of wilder vegetation whose fauna is every bit as interesting as that around various ponds and lakes.

Despite its well-kept Italian-style gardens, the Villa Doria-Pamphili offers shelter to wild flora and fauna that have adapted remarkably well to urban conditions.

RED FOX
At dusk foxes sometimes come to scavenge in the larger parks, but are not very common.

HEDGEHOG
Being shy creatures, hedgehogs only come out at night to hunt for insects and earthworms.

MOORHEN
These birds nest in thick vegetation around the ponds and lakes of Villa Doria-Pamphili.

NUTHATCH
With great agility it creeps down tree trunks, head first.

NARROW-LEAVED CEPHALANTHERA
In May and June this discreet orchid flowers in shady places.

VIOLET BIRDS'-NEST ORCHID
A large orchid that grows in sunny patches of undergrowth on poor soil.

MAGPIE
Never far from man, the magpie population is increasing, especially in Rome's villas.

GREY HERON
Herons visit the small lakes of the Villa Doria-Pamphili in winter to fish.

SPIDER ORCHID
This lovely orchid, which blooms from the month of April, grows on very chalky soil.

PURPLE ORCHID
Twenty-nine species of orchid are found in Rome. This one is fairly common.

EVERGREEN OR HOLM OAK
Unlike other oaks, this tree keeps its leaves all year round.

■ THE PINETO

Even today the Pineto still serves as grazing land for sheep, at the very gates of Rome.

The Pineto owes its name to the copses of umbrella pines planted on its heights. It stretches along a valley hollowed out by water, the Valle d'Inferno, to the nearby hills a few minutes from the heart of the city. This protected site gives a fairly accurate idea of the original natural environment of Rome. In fact the city developed in a transitional zone, something between a strictly Mediterranean environment, characterized by forests of evergreen trees, and that of the hills farther inland forested with deciduous trees.

EUROPEAN BEE-EATER

This lovely bird has nested in the Pineto for many years. It makes its nest at the bottom of a tunnel hollowed out in sandy soil.

PHILLYREA LATIFOLIA

This bush grows in the sunny Mediterranean scrubland known as the *macchia* or maquis.

MYRTLE

The flowers give off a most distinctive sweet scent.

TREE HEATHER

This tall heather thrives on the flinty soil of the *macchia*.

SARSAPARILLA

This "creeper" clings to plants or bushes in order to grow.

ARBUTUS

The fruits, which ripen in the fall, are sometimes used to make a liqueur.

BARRED WOODPECKER

It often builds its nest in crevices in the trunks of dead poplars.

TAWNY OWL

It hoots in September and October to establish its territory.

RED ADMIRAL

This butterfly migrates seasonally. It is most in evidence in Rome in the fall.

GREEN TOAD

The damp valley that traverses the Pineto provides an ideal habitat for this toad.

PRAYING MANTIS

These insects are often seen in sunny meadows at the end of the summer, when they lay their eggs.

■ THE TREES OF ROME

YEW
In gardens yew, like box, is sometimes "sculpted" into geometrical shapes or animal forms.

A large number of popes, princes, and great men have sought to leave a reminder of their power in the city by planting trees chosen from among the most exotic or majestic species. Nevertheless, in Rome it is difficult to distinguish between self-sown trees and ones that have been planted.

CYPRESS
Planted by Michelangelo in the Baths of Diocletian when he worked there on the Basilica of Santa Maria degli Angeli.

ORANGE TREE
The orange tree planted by St Dominic at the Basilica of Santa Sabina on the Aventine is almost 1,000 years old.

PLUM TREE
One of Garibaldi's soldiers died at the foot of the plum tree in Villa Glori.

JUDAS TREE
This is supposed to be the kind of tree on which Judas hung himself after betraying Jesus.

Palm trees were often planted to complement Liberty (Art Nouveau) architecture.

BAY
The bay tree in the gardens of the Farnesina was donated by the poet Pascarella in 1934.

EUROPEAN OAK
Torquato Tasso and St Philip Neri rested in the shade of the "Quercia del Tasso" ▲ 365.

UMBRELLA PINE
Also called Italian pine or "pine-kernel pine", this is the king of trees in Rome. It has been associated with the Roman countryside since antiquity. Over the centuries it has inspired countless painters, as well as Ottorino Respighi's orchestral suite *The Pines of Rome*.

24

THE HISTORY OF ROME

Foundation rites.

ROME'S ORIGINS AND THE AGE OF THE KINGS

THE END OF THE 2ND MILLENNIUM
There is evidence of exchanges between the Mycenaean world and the shores of Italy.

ABOUT 800 BC
The beginning of the Etruscan civilization in Tuscany.

Romulus and Remus.

ABOUT 750 BC
The Greeks found Cumae (in Campania).

ABOUT 600 BC
Marseilles founded by the Greeks, and Capua by the Etruscans.

499 BC
Roman victory over the Latins at Lake Regillus.

Stele dedicated to Romulus (right).

494 BC
Secession of the plebs; creation of tribunes of the people.

396 BC
The Etruscan city of Veii captured by the Romans.

390 BC
The Gauls briefly take possession of Rome.

THE LEGEND. Fleeing Troy, Aeneas, son of Aphrodite and the mortal Anchises, reached the delta of the Tiber in the land of the Latins. He married Lavinia, the daughter of their king, and founded Lavinium. Romulus and Remus were born from the union of the Vestal Virgin Rhea Silvia with the god Mars. The twins, flung into the Tiber by their great-uncle, a usurper, were washed up at the foot of the Palatine Hill, where they were suckled by a she-wolf and discovered by shepherds. When they grew up they founded Rome, on April 21, 753 BC: Romulus plowed a furrow to mark out the sacred precinct of the newly founded town and in a quarrel killed Remus, who had jeeringly jumped over it. Shortly afterward he had the Sabine women kidnapped to provide wives for his companions. From 616 there was a succession of three

Etruscan kings (Servius Tullius and the two Tarquins). In 509, after the expulsion of Tarquinius Superbus (Tarquin the Proud), the Republic came into being, with annually elected magistrates called consuls and a temple dedicated to Jupiter, Juno and Minerva on the Capitoline Hill.

ARCHEOLOGY. In the 8th century BC villages covered the hills surrounding the marshy hollow of the Forum. Around the end of the 7th century they gradually gave way to a city that had Latin as its language, Latin gods (Jupiter, Mars and Quirinus) and a temple on the citadel of the Capitol, dominating the Forum. However, it was the Etruscans who turned it into in a town with walls, sewers, aristocratic dwellings and public institutions (including sacred laws, a senate and an army). At the beginning of the 5th century their domination faded, and Rome no longer participated in Mediterranean exchanges.

A POWERFUL ITALIAN REPUBLIC

Pyrrhus.

THE CONQUEST OF THE PENINSULA. Rome took control of the Latins and loosened the grip of the Etruscans. It then exerted pressure in the direction of Campania, with war after war against the Samnites, and eventually had to face the elephants of Pyrrhus, King of Epirus, who had answered the call of the Greeks, alarmed by the advance of Rome. With a multitude of treaties of alliance and by annexing territories, founding colonies and building strategic roads, Rome ensured its hegemony over the Italian peninsula.

PATRICIANS AND PLEBEIANS. The patricians claimed to be the descendants of the first senators and wanted to keep for themselves the right to be magistrates (praetors or consuls)

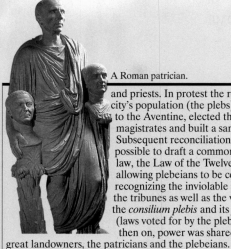

A Roman patrician.

and priests. In protest the rest of the city's population (the plebs) withdrew to the Aventine, elected their own magistrates and built a sanctuary. Subsequent reconciliations made it possible to draft a common code of law, the Law of the Twelve Tables, allowing plebeians to be consuls and recognizing the inviolable power of the tribunes as well as the validity of the *consilium plebis* and its *plebiscita* (laws voted for by the plebs). From then on, power was shared by the great landowners, the patricians and the plebeians.

323 BC
Death of Alexander the Great.

295 BC
The Romans conquer the Gauls, the Etruscans, and finally the Samnites at Sentinum.

272 BC
The Romans capture Tarentum.

THE CONQUEST OF THE WORLD AND THE CIVIL WARS

THE DOMINATION OF THE MEDITERRANEAN. This took place over two centuries, and Rome often preferred client-states to provinces under direct administration. The Punic wars, at the expense of Carthage, led to the conquest of Sicily, Sardinia and Corsica, then the Iberian peninsula, and finally part of North Africa. The Gauls of the Po plain were forced

Hannibal in Italy (center).

264–241 BC
First Punic War.

219–202 BC
Second Punic War. Scipio Africanus defeats Hannibal.

192–188 BC
Wars in Greece and Asia.

to submit; then the other Gauls, conquered by Julius Caesar, who advanced as far as the Rhine and the North Sea. On the other side of the Adriatic, Rome quelled the Greek world, wiping out the kingdoms of Alexander's successors.

SOCIAL TENSIONS. Rome changed radically during the 1st century. Its religion was enriched with new cults. Latin became a literary language and a national theater was founded. But above all, the conquests brought a flow of money and slaves into Italy. The rich increased their properties, while small landowners lost their land and moved to the towns. The senators were intent on retaining their power, challenged as they were by the *equites* (knights), by other great landowners and by the *publicani* (tax farmers administering the resources of the State). In the army, to which Marius had admitted proletarians, the legionaries began to show greater loyalty to their generals than to the State. Burdened by increasingly heavy taxes, the Italian provinces under Rome's control obtained Roman citizenship after rebelling in 91 to 88 BC. The political unity of Italy was henceforth achieved.

146 BC
Destruction of Carthage (end of Third Punic War) and Corinth.

The Senate.

81–79 BC
*Sulla's dictatorship.
He reforms the
constitution.*

THE DEATH OF THE REPUBLIC. The end of the Republic witnessed the development of two factions within the ruling class: the *optimates* (the conservative aristocrats) and the *populares* ("friends of the people"), who championed reforms which they obtained in an atmosphere of violence. Nevertheless, the senatorial government dealt successfully with the slaves' revolt led by Spartacus and with Catilina's conspiracy. But after Sulla, who twice marched on Rome, political authority was seized by the generals: in 60 BC Pompey, Crassus and Julius Caesar joined forces in a triumvirate that monopolized power. After conquering Gaul, Caesar crossed the Rubicon, marched on Rome, assumed dictatorial powers, and eliminated Pompey and his supporters. His assassination, on March 15, 44 BC, sparked another civil war: Mark Antony and Octavian (the future Augustus) defeated the tyrannicides Brutus and Cassius before becoming bitter enemies. Octavian's naval victory at Actium over Antony and Cleopatra enabled him to seize power and to annex Egypt. By 30 BC the whole of the Mediterranean had become Roman.

Caesar's murder.

73–71 BC
Spartacus' revolt.

63 BC
*Cicero's consulship.
The Catiline
conspiracy.*

THE MAJESTY OF THE "PAX ROMANA"

27 BC
*Octavian becomes
Augustus.*

ABOUT 30 AD
Crucifixion of Jesus

47 AD
*The census shows six
million Romans.*

THE JULIO-CLAUDIAN DYNASTY. In forty-five years of power Augustus laid the foundations for the government of the Roman Empire for four centuries. Forums, aqueducts and temples were built, in addition to other public works. Police and fire brigades and food-distribution facilities were organized in the city, and legions were dispatched to the frontiers. The last great conqueror Augustus vanquished the peoples of the Alps and extended the Empire as far as the right bank of the Danube, though he failed to keep Germany. Tiberius consolidated the Imperial autocracy during his painstaking reign of twenty-two years. Italians and people in the provinces converted to the cult of the emperor, thus demonstrating their loyalty to a regime that had brought peace to the Mediterranean world. Thanks to Caligula and his successors the games became a State institution – to the delight of the Roman plebs, who also benefited from distribution of free food. Under

*Augustus of Prima
Porta.*

*A votive shield
(centre).*

SENATVS
POPVLVSQVEROMAN
IMPCAESARIDIVIFAVG
COSVIIIDEDITCLVPEV
VIRTVTISCLEMENTIA
IVSTITIAEPIETATISERG
DEOSPATRIAMQVE

64 AD
Great fire of Rome.

68–69 AD
*The last revolts of the
Gauls.*

Claudius, the port of Ostia was enlarged in order to improve the capital's food supply. After a devastating fire Nero embarked on town planning on a vast scale, a trend that lasted fifty years and culminated in the building of Trajan's Forum ▲ *165*.

PEACE IN THE 2ND CENTURY.

After Augustus until the time of Septimius Severus new provinces were created, but from London to Arabia most of these were former client-states. This transformation frequently encountered harsh resistance, especially in Judaea. Although the conquests continued under Trajan with his annexation in 107 of Dacia on the right bank of the Danube, Hadrian had to give up Mesopotamia in 117. Antagonism between the Empire's two cultures was lessened thanks to this Greek-loving emperor, and a number of the Greek elite were included in the Imperial administration. By Caracalla's Edict of 212AD Roman citizenship, previously granted to the notables of the cities and tribes and to the auxiliary soldiers, was finally granted to all free men throughout the Empire.

FIERCE RESISTANCE TO THE BARBARIANS.

In the same period the Empire passed from the offensive to the defensive. Encouraged by interior crises, the army chose emperors such as Maximinus the Thracian, a common soldier brought to power in 235. However, despite a series of epidemics and several rebellions, the Empire remained prosperous and its government stable. The millennium of Rome was celebrated in 248 by Philip the Arab. Then, in 260 Valerian was captured by the Parthians. Despite pressure from the barbarians, the Romans' sense of solidarity, together with Gallienus' genius, enabled them to stem the advance of the Visigoths as far as Greece. But a miscellany of rival generals succeeded him, and eventually in 293 Diocletian attempted to divide up the Imperial power between two Augustuses and two Caesars.

THE CHRISTIAN EMPIRE.

This tetrarchy did not last. In 313, to his own advantage, Constantine started to build a bureaucratic monarchy based on divine right, endowed with a well-organized religion, Christianity, and a new capital, Constantinople. Within a century State paganism vanished, despite its restoration under the Emperor Julian (361–3). The soldier-emperors returned, and on the death of one of them, Theodosius, in 395 the division of the Empire became final. In 406 the Rhine front gave way under pressure from the Suevi and the Vandals. In 410 Rome was sacked by the Visigoths, and in 455 by the Vandals. Puppet emperors succeeded one another in the Western Empire, which was devastated by the barbarians. Germans and Romans formed alliances to repel Attila's Huns, who attempted to invade first Gaul and then Italy. Finally in 476 Odoacer, King of the Heruli, deposed the Emperor of the West, Romulus Augustulus (right), and recognized the fictitious authority of the Emperor of Constantinople. The Western Empire had ceased to exist.

79 AD
Eruption of Vesuvius destroys Herculaneum and Pompeii.

132–5 AD
Revolt of Judaea.

161–80 AD
Marcus Aurelius repels invasions by the Parthians and Marcomanni.

274 AD
Construction of the Aurelian Wall.

303–4 AD
The last major persecutions of Christians.

325 AD
The Council of Nicaea.

330 AD
Foundation of Constantinople.

Rome attacked by the Goths.

391 AD
Theodosius bans pagan worship.

THE MAKING OF THE HOLY ROMAN EMPIRE

FROM THE FALL OF THE EMPIRE TO POPE GREGORY THE GREAT. When the last Emperor of the West was overthrown, Rome was still the most important metropolis in the western world. It emerged barely recognizable from the war (535–55) waged by Justinian, Emperor of Byzantium, who sought to assert Imperial authority over Italy. But from 568 the peninsula was partially lost to the Lombard invasion. In Rome there were rapid changes: the Senate, the last vestige of the ancient order, disappeared. Pope Gregory the Great (590–604) took control, in place of the amorphous Byzantine regime, and laid the foundations of the popes' temporal power.

Gregory I the Great.

476
Odoacer deposes the Emperor of the West in Ravenna.

554
Justinian asserts Byzantine authority in Italy, with Ravenna as its capital.

751
Resumption of Lombard expansion. End of the Ravenna exarchate.

962
Otto the Great, King of Germany, is crowned Emperor.

Charlemagne crowning his son.

CAROLINGIAN SUPPORT. The Lombard threat led the Pope to form an alliance with the Franks. The pontiff claimed the territories of Rome and Ravenna. Charlemagne recognized his power, and by having himself crowned in Rome restored the city's prestige as the ideal center of the Christian West.

1075–1122
The War of the Investitures is ended by the Concordat of Worms.

NOBILITY, POPE AND EMPEROR. A long period followed during which the city came under the sway of the great Roman feudal and noble families – the dukes of Spoleto (9th century), the Theophylacts, the Crescentii, then the counts of Tusculum (9th to 10th centuries) – who profited from the weakening of the Carolingians and then from the crisis of pontifical authority and the absence of the Germanic Holy Roman Emperors. In the 11th century a conflict flared up between the Pope and the Emperor. In 1075 Gregory VII referred to a decree banning the Empire's interference in the affairs of the Church, which he intended to reform. In 1084 the Emperor Henry IV responded: he besieged Rome and abducted him. Robert Guiscard, summoned by the Pope, repelled the Emperor and partially destroyed Rome.

THE AGE OF THE COMMUNE

1154–83
Wars between Frederick Barbarossa and the communes. Recognition of the rights of the communes by the Peace of Constance.

1266
Charles d'Anjou establishes an Angevine kingdom in southern Italy.

THE FIRST STEPS. In 1143 a popular revolt against the Pope led to the creation of a Senate independent from the Church and the nobility; thus a commune emerged that was soon to find an ardent champion in Arnaldo da Brescia. The Emperor Frederick Barbarossa had this ringleader executed and restored to the Pope his sovereignty over Rome, which formally recognized the commune.

STRUGGLES BETWEEN LAY AND CHURCH AUTHORITIES. After a flourishing period for the commune in the early 13th century, the post of the only senator in Rome created in 1191 was granted to Charles d'Anjou (1263), before the position

Pope Gregory XI
returning to Avignon.

became a papal appendage. The failure of the Crusades made Rome the Christians' first holy town. But the exile of the popes to Avignon soon began (1309–77). The town's institutions benefited by their banishment. However, as in the previous century, Rome continued to be torn by the feuds between two noble families, the Orsini and the Colonna. Inspired by the myth of Republican Rome, between 1347 and 1354 Cola di Rienzo ● *XV* endeavored to restore the Republic and took very severe measures against the nobility. The Pope had scarcely returned to Rome when the great schism of the West (1378–1417) undermined his power and caused war to break out throughout the Church's territory. Rome was left in the hands of Ladislas of Durazzo.

1340
Beginning of the Hundred Years War.

Cola di Rienzo.

1348
The Black Death in Europe.

THE RENAISSANCE

RESTORATION OF PAPAL AUTHORITY. The year 1420 marked the return of the sovereign pontiffs to Rome. During their absence the city had fallen into decline. It was unhealthy, short of food and depopulated. The popes transformed this decaying city into a capital worthy of their mission and reimposed their authority. The commune of the people, the nobility, and pontifical power: these were the poles of Roman political life for three centuries. The popes opted for an anti-commune policy that provoked violent reactions during the 15th century and installed a bureaucracy capable of governing the city directly. The Pope and the College of Cardinals headed a complex administration (the Curia) consisting of five councils. The great families vied to join it, while their nepotism led the popes to keep key posts for their own relations. Alexander VI was even tempted to carve out a State in central Italy for his son, Cesare Borgia.

A PERIOD OF SPLENDOR. A policy of large-scale building was initiated at the end of the 15th century. For two centuries Rome, whose population was increasing, became a vast building site. The pontifical court was the main center of humanist culture, and the town welcomed the great Renaissance artists. The popes of the day (Alexander VI, Julius II, Leo X, Clement VII) became great princes who took part in the alliances of Italy's wars, encouraging France

1453
The Turks capture Constantinople.

1454
Peace of Lodi between the great Italian States.

1494
Charles VIII sets out to conquer the Kingdom of Naples: start of the Wars of Italy.

Pope Julius II.

1517
Beginning of the Lutheran Reformation.

1530
Charles V is consecrated Emperor in Bologna.

or its adversaries in turn. The Sack of Rome ● *36* (1527) seemed likely to put an end to this splendor. But the pontificate of Paul III and preparations for the Council of Trent restored Rome's cultural and political importance.

The Sack of Rome
(left).

1545–63
The Council of Trent. Counter-Reformation.

THE COUNTER-REFORMATION

1559
Treaty of Cateau Cambrésis: France relinquishes Italy.

THE ALL-POWERFUL PAPACY AND THE FRAGILITY OF THE STATE. Nevertheless, the disruption created by Protestantism in the Christian world and the transfer of the great trading centers from the Mediterranean to the Atlantic and Northern Europe forced Rome to somewhat reduce its universal ambitions. The Pontifical State owed its survival less to real strength than to the logic of the Counter-Reformation, which found a powerful ally in the Spanish monarchy. But the Pope reigned as a king, and the Curia saw its role in local affairs increase. The former cooperation between the aristocracy and the high-ranking clergy lasted until the end of the 17th century – leaving little room for the bourgeoisie, who therefore asserted their position in other capitals.

POVERTY AND GRANDEUR. The popes – especially Sixtus V (left), Paul V and Urban VIII, who between them commissioned many of Rome's Baroque treasures – pursued an active policy of promoting the arts. Patronage encouraged culture while censure stifled it. Opulence and misery rubbed shoulders in this densely populated town: aristocrats, prelates and powerful foreigners measured their prestige according to the number of poor who knocked at their doors and the quantity of servants and peasants they employed.

TO THE NAPOLEONIC AGE

1618–48
The Thirty Years War.

1702–12
The War of the Spanish Succession.

1796–7
Napoleon's Italian campaign.

1799
The Austrians occupy much of the peninsula.

1800–1
French victory at Marengo. The Peace of Lunéville puts the peninsula back under French hegemony.

IMMOBILISM AND CONFORMITY. Clement XI seemed for a time to wish to involve the Pontifical State in the War of the Spanish Succession. But the military and political impotence of the Holy See obliged it to remain neutral. Cut off from mainstream European politics, Rome was forced to content itself with its religious, artistic and archeological prestige.

THE NAPOLEONIC HURRICANE. The French Revolution and its repercussions were to revive political life. In 1798 the French occupied the town. A Roman republic was born, and the Pope was exiled. On his return to Rome in 1800, he accepted all the arrangements. In 1808 French troops again occupied Rome and dismantled the former administration. The following year, his temporal power abolished, the Pope was again forced into exile. Finally on May 24, 1814, he regained the Papal States, and in 1815 the Congress of Vienna restored their former frontiers.

FROM THE RESTORATION TO ITALIAN UNITY

1806
Napoleon proclaimed Emperor of Rome. Proclamation of the Kingdom of Italy.

1814
The fall of the Empire.

Pius IX (right).

THE FIRST WAR OF INDEPENDENCE. Political liberalism, patriotic aspirations and social claims made headway in the first half of the 19th century. In the revolutionary outburst of 1848 temporary governments flourished in several Italian cities, including Rome. For two years it seemed that Pius IX wished to be the spokesman for these new aspirations. However, he recalled his troops

Giuseppe Garibaldi.

involved in the First War of Independence and left his State. On February 9, 1849, Mazzini's supporters proclaimed the abolition of temporal power and the Roman Republic. In reply, France intervened in the Pope's favor and occupied Rome.

ROME BECOMES THE CAPITAL.

In 1859, at the end of the Second War of Independence, the new Kingdom of Italy extended to within a few miles of Rome. France occupied the city, blocking the Roman question, and Garibaldi twice tried in vain to take it. Finally, when the French troops were evacuated, the Piedmontese entered the city on September 20, 1870. Annexed by plebiscite on October 2, Rome was proclaimed the capital of the kingdom.

1848
Revolutions in Europe. First War of Italian Independence. Defeat by the Austrians.

1860
The King of Piedmont is declared King of Italy.

The first Italian flag.

1861
Proclamation of the Kingdom of Italy.

FROM UNITY TO THE PRESENT DAY

THE RISE OF FASCISM IN ROME.
Having inherited an extremely weak economy in 1870, the new capital experienced various difficulties until World War One, despite the laws in its favor introduced by the Giolitti government. The Fascist government, which assumed power two years after the March on Rome, was to bring about both a rhetorical rehabilitation of the Eternal City and a reconciliation with the Church by signing the Lateran Treaty, thus putting an end to dissension between the Church and the State.

1915
Italy enters the war on the side of the Allies.

The March on Rome (center).

1924
The Assassination of Matteotti.

1924–43
The Fascist regime.

1933
Hitler comes to power in Germany.

1946
The first Italian Republic.

FROM WORLD WAR TWO TO TODAY.
The Fascist government abandoned the city as soon as the armistice was declared on September 8, 1943. Caught between its status as an open city and the Nazi occupation, Rome's inhabitants began intense underground activity, and the city served as one of the two headquarters of the National Liberation Committee until June 1944. The signing of the Treaty of Rome (1957), the Holy Years (1950 and 1975) and the Olympic Games (1960) brought Rome into the limelight. This city where the service sector is so dominant has been a victim of its own sudden growth: it lacks basic amenities and exists in a state of urban chaos, which the municipality has been unable to remedy despite efforts made since 1975.

Pope John XXIII.

33

In 509 BC a revolution rid Rome of its kings and established a government that entrusted the State to the Senate and the Roman people, as well as to a body of magistrates. The oligarchic Republic continued until the end of the 1st century AD, despite the expansion of the City-State and the birth of a gigantic empire. In 27 BC power passed into the hands of a single man, the *princeps* or Emperor. The Roman Empire remained undivided until the 4th century AD. Subsequently, due to the threat of barbarian invasions, a division of authority was imposed – which led to the collapse of the Western Empire in 476, while in the East the Byzantine State was asserting itself.

"PROVOCO"
"I appeal to the people" was the ritual formula that a citizen (on the left) condemned to death by a magistrate (center) had to pronounce in Republican times to place himself under the protection of the people.

The augurs, recognizable by their sacred crook (the *lituus*), interpreted the omens (*auspicae*) before any public act, such as elections or war.

THE COMITIUM
An approximate reconstruction. The layout of the Comitium admirably reflected the political institutions of the Republic. The Curia housed the sessions of the Senate, which possessed great authority. Assemblies of the people (*populus*) were held on the circular tiers of steps; although theoretically sovereign, they were only permitted to gather to vote when summoned by the superior magistrates. Finally, the magistrates (consuls, praetors, tribunes of the people, etc.) harangued the crowd from the *rostra* ▲ 140, which faced the Curia.

THE CENSUS OF CITIZENS
Under the Republic this took place every five years. First the father of the family (standing on the left) declared his assets. Then he was assigned his status in the social and military hierarchy (second scene). A religious ceremony accompanied by a sacrifice concluded the process.

> "IN THIS CONSTITUTION…EVERYTHING WAS ORGANIZED IN SUCH AN EQUITABLE MANNER THAT IT WAS IMPOSSIBLE TO SAY WHETHER THE REGIME WAS ARISTOCRATIC, DEMOCRATIC OR MONARCHIC."
>
> POLYBIUS

The emperor was known as *Augustus* (to indicate his moral authority) and *imperator* (commander-in-chief). He was also invested with *tribunicia potestas* (the power exercised by a tribune of the people). Finally he was *pontifex maximus* (high priest), as shown in this relief depicting Marcus Aurelius making a sacrifice.

THE VOTE
From the 1st century BC Romans voted in writing. On this *denarius* coin one citizen, standing on the bridge (booth), is placing his voting slip in an urn, while another leans forward to receive his slip.

Diocletian was the first to conceive of dividing the Empire in two parts, each to be governed by an Augustus and a Caesar. The tetrarchy was to reestablish the unity of the State, as symbolized by this sculpture from Venice. This system was finally adopted only in the 4th century.

On May 6, 1527, Charles V's army, commanded by the Constable of Bourbon and consisting mostly of unpaid Lutheran *landsknechte* from Germany, besieged the ramparts of the Borgo, entered Trastevere and crossed the Tiber by the Ponte Sisto. The Pope barricaded himself inside Castel Sant'Angelo. As in 410 AD, Rome was put to the sack. According to Lutheran propaganda, the sins of the new Babylon were thus expiated. The whole of Christendom was stunned by this traumatic event.

More than four thousand people, including the Constable of Bourbon, lost their lives in combat and during the siege.

THE LOOTING
For several weeks the city was systematically plundered by the troops.

THE PEACE TREATY
In Madrid, Emperor Charles V feigned regret over the conduct of his troops by not holding victory celebrations, but he knew full well how to reap the profits and only agreed to meet Clement VII to sign a peace treaty on June 20, 1529, in Barcelona.

THE POPE IN CASTEL SANT'ANGELO
On June 6, 1527, the Pope capitulated and agreed to pay a very high ransom, but the Spaniards kept him prisoner in Castel Sant'Angelo until December 8. In spite of the plague that was decimating both the inhabitants and the army, the destruction of the city continued for six months.

THE GRAFFITI
Frescoes and the walls of palazzi still bear traces of the soldiers' graffiti ▲ 360.

Tu es Petrus et super hanc petram aedificabo ecclesiam meam … Tibi dabo claves caelorum ("You are Peter and on this rock I will build my Church … I will give you the keys of the kingdom of heaven," *Matthew* 16:18–19). As Peter's successor, the Pope is the basis of the community of believers, the head of the Roman Church (*Ecclesia romana*). Originally he was aided by deacons (who administered the charitable works of the Church), the parish priests of Rome and the bishops of the suburbicarian dioceses (Ostia, Albano, Palestrina, Frascati, Sabina and Porto). These prelates, who were the Pope's close advisers, constituted the original College of Cardinals, which since the 12th century has had the task of electing the Pope. As successors to the apostles, the bishops (*episcopoi*) used to be elected by the religious community; today they are appointed by the Pope.

CARDINAL
Appointed by the Pope to assist in governing the Church.

BISHOP
"Prophet, pontiff and pastor", responsible for the Christians in a diocese.

PRIEST
Ordained by the bishop, who invests him with his powers. He assists the bishop in his tasks, particularly in administering the sacraments.

THE POPE
Elected in conclave by the cardinals, he heads the community of believers.

WOMEN'S ORDERS
Nuns who dedicate themselves to the Christian life are today active in the field of health care and education in missions in the Third World.

THE REGULAR CLERGY
In the monastic tradition they follow a Rule established by a founder. The Cistercian shown here belongs to the Order founded by St Bernard in 1098.

Despite the endless destruction it suffered, Rome never stopped producing innumerable masterpieces that were to influence European thought, arouse passions and fashions, provoke debate and research. Through medieval guide books, the *Mirabilia Urbis*, and the research of collectors and artists that opened the way to archeology, one discovers a real defiance of the passage of time.

THE DOMUS AUREA ▲ *174*

At a time when explorers were discovering new worlds, feverish excavations were being carried out in Rome. Some ambitious projects date from that period (including the archeological map begun by Raphael), and important discoveries were made. One of these was the Domus Aurea, entirely decorated with "grotesques" that were to have a major influence on Renaissance artists. Nero's palace contained innumerable sculptures, one of which was the *Laocoön*, discovered in 1506. It illustrates the story in the second book of the *Aeneid*, where a priest from Troy and his children are suffocated by two of Apollo's serpents. Julius II had this remarkable group moved to the Octagonal Courtyard of the Vatican ▲ *224*.

A CHANGE OF MENTALITY

Until the end of the 18th century excavations had sought mainly to discover buried treasure; from that time archeological digs focused on unearthing ruins, and even on restoring large complexes. The French played a considerable role in these developments. They funded numerous digs and created a variety of institutions, with directors such as Canova, Giuseppe Valadier and the Prefect of Tournon. Napoleon associated himself with efforts to embellish the city by opening the Pincio promenade.

TOWARD SCIENTIFIC ARCHEOLOGY

In the 19th century some great research institutions were started, like the Institute for Archeological Correspondence, created in 1829, whose aspirations are symbolized in this engraving.

SUBTERRANEAN ROME

When De Rossi rediscovered the catacombs ▲ *324* and founded Christian archeology, there was a revival of religious fervor.

THE FIRST HISTORY OF ART

Johann Joachim Winckelmann came to Rome in 1755 to be Cardinal Albani's librarian. This Prussian with a passion for antiquity maintained that "the only way to achieve art is to imitate the Ancients". Inspired by this neoclassical principle, he established a chronology of ancient works of art that became a seminal source for art historians.

Religious ceremonies were once again celebrated in the underground basilicas, attracting thousands of pilgrims. Pius IX is seen here visiting the Crypt of the Popes ▲ *326*.

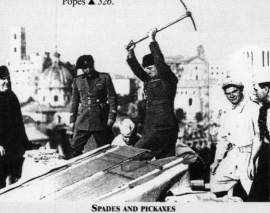

SPADES AND PICKAXES

Seeing themselves as the heirs to the Roman Empire, the Fascists exalted archeology. Their desire to renew the capital also destroyed it: ancient Rome vanished under "the pickaxe of the regime".

Dante expressed harsh views on the Roman language in the 14th century: he condemned it as the ugliest form of Italian speech, to be classed as a *tristiloquium*, meaning a sordid and common language. According to the poet, this was due to the character of the people, as revealed in their habitual use of the familiar "tu" form of address rather than the more polite "voi". In spite of this judgment, it was during the 14th century that one of the finest literary monuments to medieval Roman was written: the anonymous chronicle of the life of the tribune Cola di Rienzo ● *XV*. This extraordinarily

powerful narrative is an irreplaceable example of "first phase" Roman, when it was dominated by the linguistic forms of central Italy.

Origins

Latin was spoken locally in Rome before it became the language of a huge state. It died when the civilization that disseminated it went into decline. By the end of the Empire the Latin spoken in the city had already undergone profound changes. The classical forms had already given way to the popular ones (low Latin) that were to lead to the so-called "vulgar" romance languages. Thus in a 9th-century church one reads graffiti used as reminders to the priests, such as: *Non dicere ille secrita a bboce* ("Do not repeat secrets out loud"). Two centuries later, a graffiti commentary was added to a picture of one of St Clement's miracles in the beautiful basilica that bears his name ▲ *193*; the commentary is in vulgar Latin with deeply plebeian

expressions, but the saint speaks on in classical Latin! "Romanesco" (the dialect of Rome) was already fixed in the 13th century, when the first literary texts began to appear. At that time it possessed the unmistakable characteristics of a central-southern Italian dialect. One finds, for instance, *quanno* for *quando* (when) with the *nd* = *nn* assimilation typical of central and southern Italy.

Florentine versus Roman

The 15th century saw the start of the most important linguistic process to have taken place in Rome since the decline of Latin. This process, known as the *seconda fase* ("second phase") or "Tuscanization" of the Roman language, was to distinguish it from the other dialects of the region. The phenomenon was partly due to the growing prestige of the Florentine language and partly to the arrival in Rome of intellectuals and officials from Tuscany (among them Leon Battista Alberti, Enea Silvio Piccolomini and Pietro Bembo). Since many of them became members of the Curia, which was the cradle of all the most important cultural activity in Rome, Vatican documents from then on tended to be written in Tuscan or at least strongly imbued with it. Furthermore, the Sack of Rome in 1527 ● *36* marked the start of a major linguistic upheaval: already the home of many foreigners, the city was now overrun by refugees. It is estimated that in 1550 about 75 percent of Rome's population consisted of immigrants or children of immigrants. This situation helped the Florentine language to become the one used by the nobles. Rome thus lost the opportunity of giving a single language base to the whole of Italy.

Rome, the open city

The presence of many foreigners is still one of Rome's characteristics. Throughout the 20th century residents from the provinces have flooded into Rome, especially from central and southern Italy, and the Roman language is no longer

perceived as a dialect. A large number of newspapers and magazines are produced in Rome, national television and radio are an important presence, and the cinema has made use of many Roman actors – such as Alberto Sordi, Vittorio Gassman, Anna Magnani, Aldo Fabrizi and Marcello Mastroianni, to name but a few. All these factors have contributed to making Roman speech less of a dialect and to the introduction of Roman expressions into current Italian usage. If you look at the works of Giuseppe Gioacchino Belli, Carlo Pascarella and Trilussa (Carlo Alberto Salustri) ▲ *363* – the three greatest Roman-dialect poets, whose writings range from the beginning of the 19th century to the first half of the 20th – you will notice the progressive Italianization of their language. However, this has not prevented the survival of specifically Roman forms of speech and the development of a strictly local dialect, popularly called Romanaccio, spoken by the humbler classes. To give you an idea of it, *abbiamo* (we have) is *amo* in Romanaccio; *facciamo* (we make or do) is *famo*; *diciamo* (we say) is *dimo*; and *quello stupido* (that idiot) becomes *quoo stupido*.

THE GREAT ROMAN WRITERS

The greatest exponent of the use of Roman dialect in literature was Giuseppe Gioacchino Belli (1791–1863), who wrote more than two thousand sonnets. These form a prodigious fresco of the life of the humbler people of Rome and constitute an exceptional documentation of the Roman dialect of the time. Other Italian authors have successfully used Romanaccio, the most important and famous of these being Pier Paolo Pasolini (1922–75) and Carlo Emilio Gadda (1893–1973).

ANNA MAGNANI

Although when she made her début in the theater her strong personality attracted attention, Anna Magnani (1908–73) was only "discovered" by the Roman cinema in 1934. It then took her twelve years to achieve stardom, with Roberto Rossellini's *Roma, città aperta* (1945). Working with directors such as Visconti, Pasolini, Renoir and Cukor, she became without question one of the greatest Italian film actresses. The crowning reward of her career came with the Oscar she received in 1956 for her role in *The Rose Tattoo*.

VICOLO R VIII
DEI
CHIODAROLI

> **"**Most of all, I love watching the Roman urchins in the poor streets. Sprawling in dark doorways, young mothers are overrun by swarms of children, like tranquil bitches who let their sharp-toothed puppies play and fight all over them. The most beautiful are the most serious, with their luxuriant curly hair and long eyelashes, and a disdainful mouth above a small, mischievous chin.**"**
>
> Colette, *Nocturnes*

ROMANESCO AND ITALIAN

Today Romanesco (the Roman language) is so widespread that it has deeply penetrated the Italian language, enriching it with a great number of words – such as *palazzinaro* (real-estate speculator), *benzinaro* (service-station attendant), *tassinaro* (taxi driver), *ragazzo/ragazza* (boy/girlfriend), *ragazzino* (child), *fasullo* (bogus, fake), *malloppo* (loot), *bustarella* (money offered as a bribe) and *fregarsene* (not to give a damn about something). Most of the swear words and strong language in modern Italian came from Romanesco – starting with *stronzo* (turd) – and mainly spread via the cinema. Although the cosmopolitan character of the population of modern Rome has reduced the usage of Roman dialect in everyday life, popular songs have helped ensure its partial survival.

PLACE NAMES

The Roman dialect has often given places nicknames: the dome of St Peter's, for example, is currently dubbed *er cupolone*; Piazza della Rotonda (in front of the Pantheon) is called *a ritonna*; and the Palazzo di Giustizia is *er palazzacio*. In the historic center of Rome the street names of entire neighborhoods still recall the traditions and terminology of the Middle Ages – among them Via dei Chiavari (locksmiths' street), Via dei Giubbonari (tailors' street), Via dei Capellari (hatters' street), Via dei Pettinari (wool carders' street), Via dei Sediari (chair makers' street) and Via dei Coronari (goldsmiths' street).

FAMILY NAMES

Among typical Roman names, Proietti indicates a foundling in the family long ago; Orsini a link with the noble family of that name; Sargenti or Sargentini a military rank; Sbardella the job of ostler or groom; and Solfanelli a connection with an ancient craft that no longer exists.

GIAMBATTISTA PIRANESI

VIEWS OF ROME

Although in most of his writings he described his profession as "Venetian architect", Giambattista Piranesi (1720–78) was above all the author of engravings that glorified ancient Rome and, to a lesser extent, the modern city. This passionate champion of the supremacy of Roman art over Greek magnifies Rome in his impressive engravings with a pronounced contrast between light and shade. His "views" (often seen from below) and his diminutive figures give the monuments a vastness that is sometimes totally unrelated to reality. His scenes are nevertheless very precise, and he imposed a new vision of Rome on several generations.

The bust of Piranesi sculpted in ancient-Roman style by his friend Polanzani in 1750 shows him bare-chested and with short hair. The only building in Rome by the *Venetus architectus* (Venetian architect) is the church of the Knights of Malta, Santa Maria del Priorato ▲ *180*.

THE FRONTISPIECE
This plate served as the frontispiece to *Vedute di Roma*, engraved between 1745 and Piranesi's death, just after his famous *Prisons* and at the same time as the *Caprices*, whose inspiration is very similar. At the heart of the composition is a statue of Rome set on the summit of the Capitol ▲ *130*, missing an arm and surrounded by scattered fragments of sculpture and architecture. Even in ruins, Rome preserves an undeniable grandeur that testifies to its past magnificence: this is the omnipresent message of Piranesi's work.

This plate shows the column as it was before
the 20th-century excavations, still flanked by
houses and dominated by the Church of the
Santissimo Nome di Maria. The minute
figures looking up at it and on the balcony
give it a monumental scale.

This magnificent imaginary view served as the
frontispiece of the third volume of *Antichità romane*
(1756). It was not Piranesi's concern to portray
reality, nor even to suggest an archeological
reconstruction, but to demonstrate his faith in the
splendor of Rome.

THE FORUM ▲ *136*

This view of the Forum is less distorted by
perspective than most of Piranesi's works. It
shows what a fascinating area this must have
been to walk in, with its columns and partially
buried triumphal arches. The quarter pulled
down by Mussolini is on the left.

When Piranesi drew it, the Coliseum had just
been saved from destruction by Benedict XIV,
who turned it into a shrine commemorating
the Christian martyrs. Numerous models of
the Coliseum existed in the 18th century,
which facilitated this bird's-eye view.

G I Soldati Pretoriani
H Sedie a la Gioventù
  ri sitinenti si Ciu
K Sederano le Donne
L Scale per salir sop.
  la Toidea
M Cappellette e Croc
N Manca la Cornice
O Avanti Pi Stuchi
  a 2. II

VEDUTA dell'Isola Tiberina. A Auanzi delle Sostruzioni del Tempio d'Esculapio, e sú parte di essa la Poppa della nave di Travertino simbolica di quella, che condusse il Serpe da Epidauro. B Effigie d'Esculapio. C Chiesa di S. Bartolomeo. D Ponte antico

In this engraving Piranesi sought to give an impression of what the island in the Tiber used to be like, rather than to depict its actual state with precision. He emphasizes the remains of the ancient decorations that made the island look like a ship.

● ROMAN INSCRIPTIONS

In all the towns of classical antiquity a multitude of inscriptions (honorific, legal, religious, funerary, etc.) vied for the attention of passersby. Engraved on stone or bronze, they mostly relied on a repertory of formulas (hence the abundance of abbreviations) and were intended to keep the public memory alive.

1 = I	15 = XV
2 = II	19 = XIX
3 = III	20 = XX
4 = IIII, IV	40 = XL
5 = V	50 = L
6 = VI	80 = LXXX
7 = VII	90 = XC
8 = VIII	100 = C
9 = IX	500 = D
10 = X	1000 = M

1678 = MDCLXXVIII

ABBREVIATIONS
AUG.: Augustus
COS.: Consul
CENS.: Censor
IMP.: Imperator
P.P.: Pater Patriae (Father of the Nation)
TRIB. POT.: Tribunicia potestas (tribunician power)
F.: Filius (son of)
S.P.Q.R.: Senatus Populusque Romanus
S.C.: Senatus consultum (decree of the Senate)
B. VIX.: Bene vixit (he had a good life).

INSCRIPTION ON THE ARCH OF TITUS
"The Senate and the Roman People to the divine Titus Vespasian Augustus, son of the divine Vespasian." The word "divine" indicates that the Emperor was already dead when this arch was dedicated to him.

INSCRIPTION ON THE BASE OF TRAJAN'S COLUMN
▲ 166
"The Senate and the Roman People to the Emperor Trajan Nerva, Caesar, son of the divine Nerva, Augustus, Germanicus (conqueror of the Germans) Dacicus (conqueror of the Dacians), Pontifex Maximus (supreme pontiff), invested for the seventeenth time with tribunician power, acclaimed Emperor for the sixth time, Consul for the sixth time, Father of the Nation. This indicates the height of the hill before it was leveled by these works."

This engraving by the Belgian Nicolaus Van Delft reproduces, with some errors and additions, several of the inscriptions on the base of the obelisk that was found in 1586 and re-erected in Piazza di San Giovanni in Laterano ▲ *196*.
Above: "Sixtus V, Pontifex Maximus (supreme pontiff), for the absolutely invincible Cross, near the Basilica of San Giovanni in Laterano" ▲ *198*.

In the center: "Sixtus V Pont[ifex] Max[imus]."
Below : "Flavius Constantius (and not Constantine as this copy falsely indicates), son of Constantine Augustus, dedicated (D[onum] Dedit) to the Senate and the Roman People (S.P.Q.R.) the obelisk that was taken from its site (Karnak) by his father and which had lain for a long time in Alexandria. He put it on a ship of an astonishing size, with three hundred oarsmen, and transported it with difficulty over the sea and along the Tiber to Rome to erect it in Circus Maximus."

COLA DI RIENZO

Cola di Rienzo (1313–54) used his knowledge of antiquity to incite the Roman people to rebel against the nobles. In 1346 he found a bronze plaque on which was engraved the law attributing Imperial powers to Vespasian. He displayed this text, explained it to the people, and cried "Romans, see how great was the magnificence of the Senate who conferred the Empire upon him!" His statue (1887) by Girolamo Massimo, with its base resembling a collage of ancient marble pieces and fragments of inscriptions, was inspired by this story.

● PAPAL COATS OF ARMS

PAPAL COATS OF ARMS
The popes, who were great connoisseurs of architecture, had their family coats of arms engraved in stone – among them the Barberini bees (Urban VIII) ▲ *292*, the Farnese irises (Paul III) ▲ *244* and the Peretti lion (Sixtus V).

CLEMENTE VII	PAOLO III	GIULIO III	MARCELLO II	PIO IV
1523 — 1534	1534 — 1549	1550 — 1555	1555 — 1555	1559 — 1565

S. PIO V	GREGORIO XIII	SISTO V	URBANO VII	GREGORIO XIV
1566 — 1572	1572 — 1585	1585 — 1590	1590 — 1590	1590 — 1591

INNOCENZO IX	CLEMENTE VIII	LEONE XI	PAOLO V	GREGORIO XV
1591 — 1591	1592 — 1605	1605 — 1605	1605 — 1621	1621 — 1623

URBANO VIII	INNOCENZO X	ALESSANDRO VII	CLEMENTE IX	CLEMENTE X
1623 — 1644	1644 — 1655	1655 — 1667	1667 — 1669	1670 — 1676

B. INNOCENZO XI	ALESSANDRO VIII	INNOCENZO XII	CLEMENTE XI	INNOCENZO XIII
1676 — 1689	1689 — 1691	1691 — 1700	1700 — 1721	1721 — 1724

BENEDETTO XIII	CLEMENTE XII	BENEDETTO XIV	CLEMENTE XIII	CLEMENTE XIV
1724 — 1730	1730 — 1740	1740 — 1758	1758 — 1769	1769 — 1774

PIO VI	PIO VII	LEONE XII	PIO VIII	GREGORIO XVI
1775 — 1799	1800 — 1823	1823 — 1829	1829 — 1830	1831 — 1846

PIO IX	LEONE XIII	S. PIO X	BENEDETTO XV	PIO XI
1846 — 1878	1878 — 1903	1903 — 1914	1914 — 1922	1922 — 1939

PIO XII	GIOVANNI XXIII	PAOLO VI	GIOVANNI PAOLO I	GIOVANNI PAOLO II
1939 — 1958	1958 — 1963	1963	1978 — 1978	1978

ARTS AND TRADITIONS

Rome had its share of oracles as well as ghosts, and in troubled times certain statues even began to "talk". It became customary, under the cover of nightfall, to post mocking epigrams, pamphlets and satires criticizing the government on these "talking statues". This practice, of Venetian origin, found fertile soil in the papal city, which was hardly renowned for its tolerant attitudes.

PASQUINADES
In the 16th century Aretino (1492–1556) had been forced to flee the city because of his satirical sonnets, or "pasquinades", written on the occasion of the election of the new pope. In the 18th century crimes of opinion were still severely punishable by the law, and one of Benedict XIII's edicts threatened "the death penalty, the confiscation of assets and the vilification of the name…of anyone who…writes, prints or distributes…libels of the kind known as pasquinades". However, the death penalty was rarely applied.

PASQUINO AND OTHERS
Several ancient statues were used for the posting of libels. Such was the fate of Pasquino (right) ▲ 279, who gave his name to these dissenting tracts but is in reality a fragment from a group depicting Menelaus and Patroclus. The Abate Luigi, thus named due to his resemblance to a ridiculous deformed sacristan of the Church of the Sudario, is actually a portrait of a Roman consul, magistrate or orator; and Marforio (above) is a representation of a river god.

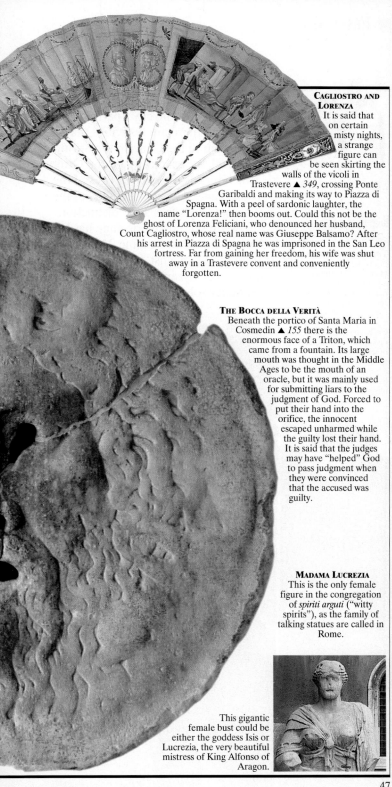

CAGLIOSTRO AND LORENZA

It is said that on certain misty nights, a strange figure can be seen skirting the walls of the vicoli in Trastevere ▲ *349*, crossing Ponte Garibaldi and making its way to Piazza di Spagna. With a peel of sardonic laughter, the name "Lorenza!" then booms out. Could this not be the ghost of Lorenza Feliciani, who denounced her husband, Count Cagliostro, whose real name was Giuseppe Balsamo? After his arrest in Piazza di Spagna he was imprisoned in the San Leo fortress. Far from gaining her freedom, his wife was shut away in a Trastevere convent and conveniently forgotten.

THE BOCCA DELLA VERITÀ

Beneath the portico of Santa Maria in Cosmedin ▲ *155* there is the enormous face of a Triton, which came from a fountain. Its large mouth was thought in the Middle Ages to be the mouth of an oracle, but it was mainly used for submitting liars to the judgment of God. Forced to put their hand into the orifice, the innocent escaped unharmed while the guilty lost their hand. It is said that the judges may have "helped" God to pass judgment when they were convinced that the accused was guilty.

MADAMA LUCREZIA

This is the only female figure in the congregation of *spiriti arguti* ("witty spirits"), as the family of talking statues are called in Rome.

This gigantic female bust could be either the goddess Isis or Lucrezia, the very beautiful mistress of King Alfonso of Aragon.

47

THE ROMAN CARNIVAL
For some it derives from the Saturnalia of antiquity or from the feasts dedicated to Sol Invictus of the late Empire. For others it is simply linked to the Christian calendar. It disappeared at the end of the 19th century when freedom of expression was stifled because of social unrest.

Even in the papal city, alongside Christian feasts like that of the city's patrons St Peter and St Paul, there are festivities that bear no relation to the Church: the Spring Festival, for example, and the Ottobrata, which recalls the ancient rites of the grape-harvest season. In many of the Eternal City's feasts the distinction between sacred and profane has become blurred; thus while June 24 is the Feast of St John the Evangelist, to whom Rome owes its primacy over Byzantium, it is also the feast of the summer solstice.

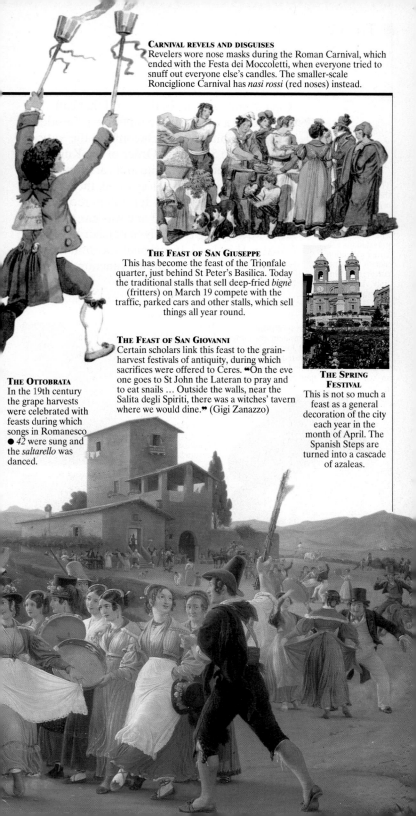

CARNIVAL REVELS AND DISGUISES
Revelers wore nose masks during the Roman Carnival, which ended with the Festa dei Moccoletti, when everyone tried to snuff out everyone else's candles. The smaller-scale Ronciglione Carnival has *nasi rossi* (red noses) instead.

THE FEAST OF SAN GIUSEPPE
This has become the feast of the Trionfale quarter, just behind St Peter's Basilica. Today the traditional stalls that sell deep-fried *bignè* (fritters) on March 19 compete with the traffic, parked cars and other stalls, which sell things all year round.

THE FEAST OF SAN GIOVANNI
Certain scholars link this feast to the grain-harvest festivals of antiquity, during which sacrifices were offered to Ceres. *"On the eve one goes to St John the Lateran to pray and to eat snails … Outside the walls, near the Salita degli Spiriti, there was a witches' tavern where we would dine."* (Gigi Zanazzo)

THE OTTOBRATA
In the 19th century the grape harvests were celebrated with feasts during which songs in Romanesco ● *42* were sung and the *saltarello* was danced.

THE SPRING FESTIVAL
This is not so much a feast as a general decoration of the city each year in the month of April. The Spanish Steps are turned into a cascade of azaleas.

● THE ORDER OF MALTA

The eight points of the Maltese cross represent the eight Beatitudes. Also, eight powerful European states presided over the Order's creation, namely Provence, Auvergne, France, Italy, Aragon, England, Germany and Castile.

Rome is the only city in the world that can claim to be a capital three times over. Besides being the capital of Italy, it contains the Vatican State and the Sovereign Order of the Knights of Malta. Created to welcome and care for pilgrims arriving in the Holy Land, the Order of Hospitalers of St John of Jerusalem received papal recognition in 1113 and was given the task of defending the Holy Sepulcher by Calixtus II in 1120. Its original vocation thus became overlaid by a military function, like that of other orders of knighthood.

FROM JERUSALEM TO RHODES
First established in Jerusalem, the Order was transferred to St John of Acre in 1187. After being defeated by the Sultan of Egypt, it left the Holy Land and settled in Cyprus in 1290, then moved to Rhodes, which it captured in 1310.

FROM RHODES TO MALTA
Chased from Rhodes by Sultan Suleiman's Turks, in 1523 the Order petitioned the Pope for a new base and was granted Malta. This was confirmed in 1530 by a treaty between the Pope and Charles V. The Order exercised sovereignty over the island for several centuries.

FROM MALTA TO ROME
In 1798 Napoleon seized the island without opposition on his way to Egypt. Lacking a home, the Order moved to Russia and then various places in Italy before settling in Rome in 1834.

"IT TAKES A PIRATE AND A HALF TO BEAT A PIRATE!"
This was the rallying cry of the Order of the Knights of Malta, who reacted blow by blow to the Moorish and Turkish offensives. In fact, their methods and objectives were similar to those of the Barbary Coast pirates.

| 25 TARI | 8 SCUDI | 15 GRANI | 375 GRANI |

✠ SOVRANO MILITARE ORDINE DI MALTA ✠
POSTE MAGISTRALI

SOVRANO MILITARE ORDINE DI MALTA
POSTE MAGISTR[...]   10 SCUDI

A SOVEREIGN STATE
Although it has given up all hope of recovering its rule over Malta, since 1962 the Sovereign Order of Malta has succeeded in re-establishing stable and recognized institutions. Its headquarters at No. 68 Via Condotti and its property on the Aventine ▲ *180* are extraterritorial. Like the Vatican, the Order issues its own stamps and mints its own coins; it also has a diplomatic service and issues its own passports. Branches of the Order exist in some ninety countries.

A SYMBOLIC CURRENCY
The monetary system of the Order of Malta is founded on the scudo, which is worth 12 tari or 240 grani. The Order mints coins of gold, silver and bronze. At present two gold coins of 10 scudi each are worth approximately 380,000 Italian lire, and a collection consisting of one 2 scudi silver piece plus one bronze 10 grani coin costs about 30,000 lire.

51

The Pope is the Bishop of Rome and as successor to St Peter he is the head of the Christian community. He is assisted in this capacity by the Sacred College of cardinals (which elects and advises him), together with the Roman Curia, which embraces the Vatican's entire governmental organization. This includes the Congregations (like ministries, responsible for important issues), law courts (since the Pope has episcopal jurisdiction over all baptized Catholics), secretariats, commissions and other institutions.

THE TIARA
This is the most obvious symbol of papal sovereignty. The long white stole worn by the Pope is also a symbol of his power.

PAPAL AUDIENCES
The Pope grants a general audience to pilgrims every Wednesday. This is held in the Papal Audience Hall built by Pier Luigi Nervi in 1974. Every Sunday at noon the Pope recites the Angelus and addresses all those present in Piazza San Pietro from a window in the apostolic palace. In the summer he does the same from a window of his summer residence in Castel Gandolfo.

THE "URBI ET ORBI" BLESSING
It is from the great central loggia of St Peter's that the Pope grants his blessing "Urbi et Orbi" (to the city and to the world).

HOLY YEARS
The Holy Door, the one on the extreme right of the five doors of the four major basilicas, is only opened every twenty-five years for the duration of the Holy Year (1975, 2000 and so on).

THE "FISHERMAN'S RING"
At the pontifical enthronement, the master of ceremonies presents the Pope with the *piscatorio* (the "fisherman's ring"). The name of the ring alludes to the primacy granted, according to St John's Gospel, to St Peter, who had been a fisherman.

THE "SEDIA APOSTOLICA GESTATORIA"
This chair, which most probably dates from the 5th century and symbolizes the spiritual and the material supremacy of the head of the Church, was still used in 1978 by Pope John Paul I. In the past, the Pope used to make his way from the Sistine Chapel to St Peter's seated on this chair, preceded by the College of Cardinals and the pontifical court.

ELECTING A POPE
When the College of Cardinals goes into conclave to elect a new pope, they cast four votes a day. Only the smoke rising from the Sistine Chapel, where the voting takes place, provides an indication of the results. Black smoke means that no candidate has received the necessary two-thirds majority; white smoke indicates that a new pope has been elected.

"HABEMUS PAPAM"
The president of the Sacred College proclaims the election of a pope by pronouncing the hallowed formula "*Habemus papam*". Not long after, the new pontiff appears clad in white. His consecration takes place a few days later.

Today restoration work is based on scientific research. Sophisticated technologies are used to determine the state of preservation of a work of art and to discover the techniques that were used in creating it. Observations are carefully classified and analyzed by computers. After restoration, the details of the operation are recorded. All this data is filed for future reference in case further restoration is required at a later date. Methods such as these have been used for the many restoration operations carried out in Rome in recent years.

MARCUS AURELIUS' STATUE

Set in the middle of a busy piazza, this statue had been exposed to all the insidious effects of pollution, and its structure had been weakened by oxidation, corrosion, rain and vibrations. In addition, it had been damaged by earlier attempts at restoration.

Its recent restoration was carried out by the Istituto Centrale del Restauro. First, various analyses, including a thermal scan to determine degree of condensation, were carried out. Its cleaning was a very delicate process because of the layer of gold leaf. Corrosive substances and particles deposited by the atmosphere had to be removed. Because of gold's incompatibility with anticorrosive treatments, the statue had to be protected by a film of acrylic resin before being placed in a protective glass case.

Before frescoes can be restored, chemical testing is required. Color samples are needed in order to determine which pigments were originally used, and to discover what parasitical materials have been deposited on the surface of the painting.

THE SISTINE CHAPEL Layers of greasy dust, soot from candles used in ceremonies and especially a film of animal glue had altered and seriously darkened the colors. Furthermore, certain figures had been retouched when this varnish was applied to protect them. Finally, the infiltration of rainwater from the roof had left whitish saline deposits on the ceiling. The restoration, carried out by Vatican experts, was undertaken when it was discovered that microclimatic variations were contracting the varnish in such a way that it was lifting the painted surface in certain places. The operations were minimal; in fact the main work consisted in cleaning the frescoes, for which the solvent AB 57 was used. The frescoes have now been restored to their original colors.

FONTANA DI TREVI The fountain was suffering from static problems due to the materials from which it was made, and also from general degradation associated with a highly polluted environment (such as ingrained dirt and disintegration due to polluting agents).

In particular, it was covered with calcium deposits and algae formations. After general strengthening and cleaning work (sandblasting and ultrasound), plus localized biocidal cleansing, it was equipped with a water processing unit.

Roman cuisine combines the country cooking of Lazio and the Abruzzi region with popular culinary traditions featuring pasta, fresh and dried vegetables, salt cod, offal and pork. Although some of the recipes of antiquity have been handed down (mainly dishes blending sweet and savory flavors), the character of Roman cooking is largely due to the use of condiments (garlic, herbs and spices), sometimes combined with *pecorino* (a sharp sheep cheese), which give a delightful texture, taste and smell to even the simplest dishes.

2. Remove the toughest leaves and cut off the stems.

3. Using a small sharp knife, pare the artichokes into a conical shape.

7. Season them again with a little salt, and let them simmer uncovered over a low flame. When they are half done, turn the artichokes onto their sides.

6. Place the artichokes prepared in this way on their bases in a pan or dish. Cover with the glasses of water (according to the number of artichokes) and half a glass of olive oil.

> **"A COUNTRY'S CUISINE IS THE ONLY RELIABLE PROOF OF ITS CIVILIZATION."**
>
> MARCEL ROUFF

INGREDIENTS
2 small artichokes per person, lemon juice, salt, pepper, garlic, *mentuccia* (fresh peppermint), 2 glasses of water, half a glass of olive oil.

1. Wash the peppermint and chop the garlic finely.

4. Trim the tips into a point and rub the artichokes all over with a little lemon juice to prevent them from discoloring.

5. Spreading the leaves of the artichokes slightly, insert the salt, pepper, garlic and peppermint leaves between them.

8. When they are cooked, serve them upright in a dish. If the liquid in which they have cooked has not thickened sufficiently, reduce it over a gentle flame. Serve them hot or cold, according to taste, accompanied by a white Castelli wine such as Frascati, Colli Albani or Velletri.

SWEETMEATS
Mostaccioli, panpepato and *pangiallo* are traditional cakes made with dried fruit, nuts and honey, primarily for the Christmas season.

Around the Pantheon and the Borgo Pio there are lots of small shops specializing in ecclesiastical clothing, rosaries and religious souvenirs.

SAMBUCA
A liqueur with an aniseed taste. Romans often float a coffee bean on the surface and light it for added flavor.

JEWISH PASTRIES
A delicious combination of candied fruit, raisins and marzipan, these are only found in the patisseries of the Ghetto.

CASTELLI WINES
The vineyards of the Colli Albani, to the southeast of Rome, produce delicious white wines, the best known being Frascati.

NEWSPAPERS IN ROME
Il Messaggero has a daily column in Romanesco (*Avventure in città*). Do not miss the Thursday edition of *La Repubblica*, which has a supplement (*Trovaroma*) listing the cultural events of the week to come.

"FIACCOLE"
On festive occasions these little lights flicker on Roman monuments.

ARCHITECTURE

The town around 1490.

The population of Rome has varied considerably – from a million in the 1st century AD, to 30,000 after the Sack of Rome, to more than three million today – and the size and shape of its inhabited area have not ceased to fluctuate. The town has survived the ravages of history with admirable continuity: the fourteen "regions" of Augustus' time formed the basis for the medieval and modern *rioni* (quarters), and the ancient aqueducts still feed its fountains.

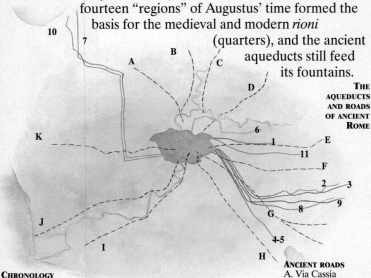

THE AQUEDUCTS AND ROADS OF ANCIENT ROME

CHRONOLOGY OF THE AQUEDUCTS
1. Aqua Appia, 312 BC
2. Anio Vetus, 272 BC
3. Aqua Marcia, 144 BC
4. Aqua Tepula, 125 BC
5. Aqua Iulia, 33 BC
6. Aqua Virgo, 19 BC
7. Aqua Alsietina, 2 BC
8. Aqua Claudia, 38–52 AD
9. Anio Novus, 38–52 AD
10. Aqua Traiana, 109 AD
11. Aqua Alexandriana, c. 226 AD

ROMAN AQUEDUCTS
"The aqueducts bring so much water to Rome … that almost every house has a great number of tanks, tubes and pipes." So wrote Strabo, the geographer, during the time of Augustus. At the beginning of the 2nd century AD their total capacity amounted to about 250,000 cubic gallons per day.

ANCIENT ROADS
A. Via Cassia
B. Via Flaminia
C. Via Salaria
D. Via Nomentana
E. Via Tiburtina
F. Via Prenestina
G. Via Latina
H. Via Appia
I. Via Ostiense
J. Via Portuense
K. Via Aurelia

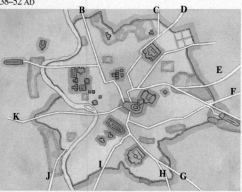

LEISURE AND ENTERTAINMENT IN ANCIENT ROME
As the political role of the people diminished, the emperors organized more facilities where leisure time could be spent, including porticos (covered walks), baths, and buildings where games were held (circuses, theaters, amphitheaters, stadiums, odeons, etc.).

MEDIEVAL ROME

During the late Middle Ages, with the decrease in population, a major part of the area within the Aurelian Wall fell into disuse. The Vatican, fortified in 854, became the political and religious center. From the 10th century to the end of the 13th century, the inhabited area was concentrated around the Tiber as well as the Forum. In the 14th century catastrophes and epidemics decimated the population, but it soon increased again due to a surge of immigration.

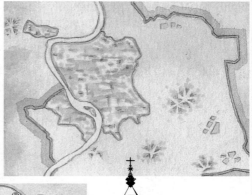

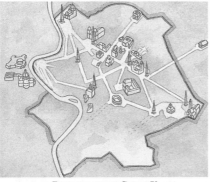

BUILDING UNDER SIXTUS V

The Pope had new palaces and religious buildings erected, constructed important roads such as the Via Felice, and created vast squares decorated with columns, fountains and obelisks.

THE TOWN PLANNING OF SIXTUS V

During the five years of his pontificate, with Domenico Fontana as his chief architect, Sixtus V (1585–90) implemented a huge urban plan which was to make Rome Europe's first modern city.

ROME THE CAPITAL

1870: When Rome became the capital, there were only 200,000 inhabitants.
1910: Its new role accelerated building activity. The city spread mainly eastward, and the popular neighborhood of Testaccio sprang up in the south.
1930: Rome's expansion gathered momentum. Suburbs developed far from the center, isolated in the countryside.
1960: The great parks were now the only areas free from buildings.

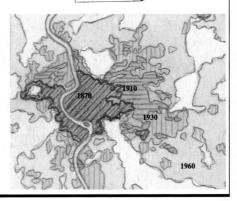

61

Roman architecture relied for a long time on the assembly of large quadrangular blocks, but masonry characterized by the difference between its facing materials and its internal composition appeared at an early date. The fill, or *opus caementicium*, made of rubble mixed with lime mortar, was highly resistant but rather ungainly. At first it was faced with *opus incertum*; then with *opus reticulatum*, which was soon replaced by *opus testaceum*, a brick facing rapidly adopted for all Roman walls.

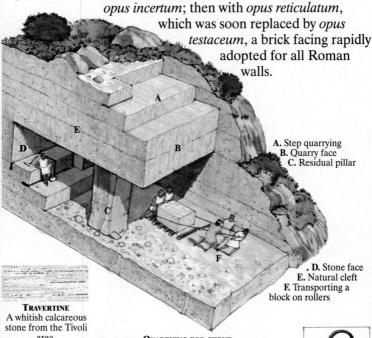

A. Step quarrying
B. Quarry face
C. Residual pillar
D. Stone face
E. Natural cleft
F. Transporting a block on rollers

TRAVERTINE
A whitish calcareous stone from the Tivoli area.

TUFA
A compound of volcanic rocks of varying colors.

QUARRYING FOR STONE
Once the soil covering the rock had been stripped away, the quarrymen scored the rough outline of the blocks on the stone so that, while it was being extracted, it could be hewn into the shape and size required by the architect.

A ROMAN LEWIS

HOIST
A winch operated by a lever was used to lift and position stones.

TECHNIQUES FOR TRANSPORTING AND POSITIONING THE BLOCKS
1. Tenons (projections) were left on the face of the stone so ropes could be attached.
2. Small cavities were carved symmetrically in the blocks so they could be lifted by GRIPS.
3. A dovetail cavity was sunk into the top of the block so a LEWIS could be inserted.

TOOLS

The funerary reliefs reproduced above show builders' tools (compasses, set square, sledgehammer, chisel, plumbline, cutter, etc.) and stone masons preparing blocks.

BRICKS

Standard square bricks were designed for the facing of *opus caementicium* walls. Lines were scored on them to facilitate their division into facing elements. Each one, depending on its size, could be divided into two, four, eight or eighteen triangular facing bricks.

BRICK COLUMNS

The Romans even used bricks to build columns. They sometimes gave the columns a fluted appearance, and often coated them with stucco.

STAMPS

Roman tile and brick manufacturers marked their products by stamping the damp clay with a seal before it was fired. From the end of the 1st century AD and throughout the 2nd century the most common stamp was in the shape of a *lunula* (crescent).

LIME KILNS

These were in the shape of a flattened cone built on a circular base. Above the combustion chamber

stood a cone of heat-resistant bricks, with vents, over which the lime clay was placed. The kilns were fed with firewood and dry grasses through an opening in the base of the combustion chamber.

Quick lime

Slaked lime

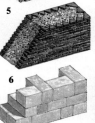

OPUS
1. Caementicium
2. Incertum
3. Quasi reticulatum
4. Reticulatum
5. Testaceum
6. Quadratum

OPUS MIXTUM
A. Corner reinforcements of large stone quoins.
B. Corner reinforcements of brick wall.
C. Brick wall with a travertine door frame.

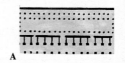

A

The major achievements of architecture in imperial Rome – diversifying forms and expanding the volume of interiors – are inseparable from the progress made in the design and construction of arches, vaults and cupolas. The most significant advance was the introduction of vaults built in *opus caementicium*, together with the increased use of *opus testaceum*, which gave these vaults a strength and flexibility that allowed for unprecedented boldness. Once freed from the constraints of a system relying on rhythmic supports (columns and pillars), ancient classical architecture was able to create structures that contained the seeds of all the future developments of Christian and Islamic architecture.

AN ARCHED BAY IN THE TABULARIUM
▲ *141*
This is one of the first examples of a rhythmic system to have a long-lasting effect. The vaulted architecture assumes the weight-bearing functions, while the noble order of the colonnade is used decoratively. Later this type of façade was frequently used for theaters and amphitheaters.

CROSS-SECTION OF THE BASILICA OF MAXENTIUS
As this section shows, the skylight with "thermal" windows (the arches of which echo those of the vaults) is supported by buttresses.

THE BASILICA OF MAXENTIUS ▲ *145*
This building pushed the expertise acquired by architects and engineers in the construction of the vast halls of Imperial baths to its limits. It demonstrates the complete break with the traditional use of freestanding columns to form galleries or peristyles. Unity of space conceived as a whole replaced the juxtaposition of naves separated by rhythmic supports, which had been a feature of previous basilicas. Its luxurious decoration in *opus sectile* (multicolored marble paving and paneling) has now disappeared. All that remains of its ornamental elements are the deep coffers of the exedras.

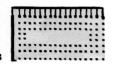

B

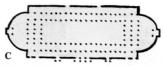

C

D

THE ANCIENT BASILICAS

In the time of Augustus the system used for the Tabularium was adopted for the façades of the monumental Aemilia ▲ *136* (**A**) and Julia ▲ *141* (**B**) basilicas. The central nave of the Basilica Ulpia ▲ *165* (**C**), the largest ever built, was covered by a strong timbered roof; vaults constructed in *opus caementicium* spanned the full width of its great lateral exedras.

These were reinforced with metal struts embedded in the masonry.

The Basilica of Maxentius (**D**) exploited the full potential of the concrete vault: its inner volume, freed from the constraint of rows of columns, was able to expand into a vast area with exedras.

a

THE SUPPORT

A temporary support for vaults and arches was needed during construction. Consisting of at least two semicircular wooden frames strengthened with struts and trusses, the support would receive stone blocks or bricks (**a**), or poured cement and rubble (**b**).

1

2

THE ARCHITRAVE AND THE ARCHIVOLT

From the 3rd century BC the Romans had been building weight-bearing arches using the classical architrave (**1**). This technique was soon to be replaced by the archivolt (**2**), which rapidly found an application in buildings of all types.

EXEDRA
Semicircular apse or portico, with seating.

LATERAL EXEDRA
Used to buttress the pillars subject to lateral pressure from the main vault.

b

CROSS-SECTION OF THE BATHS OF CARACALLA ▲ *319*

This section reveals the structural affinity between Roman baths, Imperial reception halls and basilicas, although designed for very different purposes. They were all built according to a similar principle of weight distribution, due to the introduction of cement vaults and cupolas in the 2nd century AD.

● BUILDINGS FOR ENTERTAINMENT

Gladiator and animal fight.

The buildings of ancient Rome used for spectacles can only be understood if one is aware of the religious and social functions of the games or performances they were designed for. These included theatrical representations, gladiatorial combats and chariot races, and most of them already existed in Rome before buildings were designed specifically for them. Although there had been dramatic art in Rome since the 3rd century BC, theaters as such were only built at the end of the Republic.

AMPHITHEATERS

These were a typically Roman invention. The elliptical (or nearly elliptical) shape of the arena enabled a vast crowd of spectators to watch a number of different gladiatorial combats taking place at the same time.

STRUCTURE

The eighty radial walls, the walkways, the stairs, the balcony, the half columns and the external arcades together serve as a shell for the enormous spread of the *cavea* (stone steps).

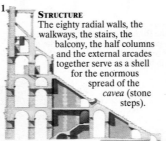

SEATS

The building contains two semicircular ranges of seats or *maeniae* facing each other ("*theatrum*", like its Greek equivalent, means a place for spectators to sit).

THE COLISEUM OR FLAVIAN AMPHITHEATER

▲ 170. This is the largest amphitheater to have been built in the Roman world. Travertine pillars alternating with arches provide a solid frame for its walls made of brick, stone blocks and concrete. The carved blocks were assembled without mortar and secured with metal fixings. The whole structure is made up of nearly identical modules (**A**) erected side by side.

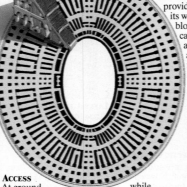

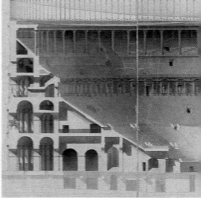

ACCESS

At ground level, arcades provided access to the different sections of the *cavea* (tiers of steps) allocated to the various social classes (**A**). In addition, movement inside the Coliseum was regulated by a complex network of ramps and corridors, while compulsory routes to reach assigned seats determined the entrance to be used. The "games" were thus an opportunity for Roman society to demonstrate its sense of hierarchy and cohesion.

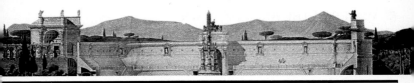

CIRCUSES

These were less costly structures than amphitheaters, and their technical requirements were more modest. The Circus Maximus and Circus Flaminius fulfilled an important role in the Rome of the 4th and 3rd centuries BC due to their link with the triumphal rituals.

CROSS-SECTION AND PLAN OF THE CIRCUS OF MAXENTIUS ▲ *328*
Circuses were built with a long, low central wall, the *spina* ▲ *178*, around which the chariots raced. Each end was marked by a turning point known as a *meta*.

THEATERS

Roman theaters were modeled on theaters of the Hellenistic period in Sicily and southern Italy. But whereas the Greek theaters were left open, facing the natural landscape, with their *cavea* resting on the slope of a hill, Roman ones were enclosed buildings erected on architectural substructures with monumental stage fronts.

STAGE FRONT AND CROSS-SECTION OF POMPEY'S THEATER ▲ *248*

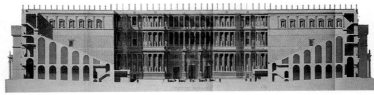

3

OUTER WALLS

In amphitheaters and theaters the external façade of the *cavea* consisted of superimposed arcades framed by engaged columns and separated by friezes.

4

The three lower levels of the Coliseum's façade are made up of (from the bottom) Tuscan Doric, Ionic and Corinthian columns. The fourth level is blind and is decorated with pilasters.

PLAN OF THE COLISEUM
These drawings show the internal and external structure.

PLAN OF MARCELLUS' THEATER ▲ *157*
The *cavea* of Roman theaters never went beyond a semicircle.

In Imperial times, Marcellus' theater served as a model for theaters in the Western Provinces.

The control and regular distribution of water to large cities was one of Rome's most remarkable urban innovations. Nothing brought a more radical modification to lifestyles than the abundance of running water in towns, with all the public and private infrastructures this implied. Roman engineers were not the inventors of aqueducts, but the challenges Rome had to face in order to harness sometimes quite remote water sources gave rise to the construction of some remarkable buildings.

"CASTELLUM DIVISORIUM" (WATER TOWER)
This enabled water to be distributed within the town. A circular basin was constructed to receive the water, through a grating, from the aqueduct. Lead piping carried the water from the basin to different parts of the town.

PIPES
Water pipes were generally made out of lead sheets rolled around a caliber and welded with a lead seal secured by a strip of clay. The Roman architects Vitruvius and Frontinus established precise standards for their calibration.

BATHS
In the *tepidaria* and *caldaria* the floor and the bottom of the swimming pools were supported by small terracotta pillars around which air heated by an oven could circulate. This space was called the *hypocaustum*. Beneath the marble facing of the walls a very thick coating of cement covered rectangular ceramic piping (*tubuli*), which served as vents for hot air or steam.

CROSS-SECTION OF AN AQUEDUCT

From the spring (*sorgente*) to the *castellum divisorium*, raised sections with arches alternated with underground sections. The latter could be maintained and examined through inspection vents (*lumina*) at regular intervals. Settling sumps (*piscinae liminariae*) allowed the water of the *specus*, as the channel of the aqueduct was called, to be purified before it reached the town. Steep dips in the terrain were traversed by means of siphons, but generally the aim was, wherever possible, to avoid supplying water under pressure.

A. *Sorgente* (spring)
B. *Lumina* (inspection vents)
C. *Piscina liminaria* (settling sump)
D. *Sifone rovescio* (siphon)
E. *Castellum divisorium* (water tower)

PUBLIC FOUNTAINS

These were rarely more than 260 feet apart, so that no one ever lived more than 130 feet away from one. The lead supply pipe came up through a stone fixed in the sidewalk and flowed into a basin made of stone slabs set in the street.

"DOMUS"

This Pompeian *domus* is a good example of a sophisticated house with an *atrium* and a peristyle laid out as a garden.

"INSULA"

This *insula* ▲ *410* in Ostia is one of the most remarkable examples of a large multistoried apartment building with a staircase that opens on to a central courtyard with arcades. It has the unusual feature of a thermal bath connected to it for the use of residents.

THE DISPOSAL OF WASTE WATER

Not all Roman towns had a network of underground sewers. In Rome the main sewer, the *cloaca maxima* ▲ *156*, which is very ancient, remained an open sewer for a long time. It permitted all the water in the city to be drained into the Tiber.

It was situated opposite a public fountain and possessed an *impluvium* (1), or cistern, for the collection of rainwater. Some houses were even equipped with running water and had a decorative fountain in the peristyle (2).

THE TROPHIES OF MARIUS
These figures displayed reproductions of arms and armor stripped from Rome's enemies as a symbol of victory.

In Rome, as in all the great cities of the Empire, the religious buildings gave the urban landscape a sense of order and hierarchical significance. They were the richest and most diverse buildings in the whole array of ancient monuments. Triumphal arches, which were another characteristic of Roman towns, stood at each of the key points in the metropolis. Great mausoleums also adorned the city, commemorating the emperors as if they were Hellenistic sovereigns.

ETRUSCAN TEMPLES
The most ancient temples belonged to the Italo-Etruscan tradition, of which the venerable Temple of Jupiter Capitolinus ▲ *128* was the best example. Three halls of worship (*cellae*) opened onto a deep portico with widely spaced columns.

ROUND TEMPLES
The Temple of Hercules ▲ *155* in the Forum Boarium is the oldest instance in Rome of an entirely Greek design (the *tholos periptera*).

QUADRANGULAR TEMPLES OF HELLENIC ORIGIN
These made use of all the Greek architectural resources in an essentially decorative form, as can be seen in the Temple of Portunus ▲ *155*.

TRIUMPHAL ARCHES
The most striking examples of these symbols of Rome's military supremacy have three bays, like the Arch of Constantine ▲ *169*. This displays all the traditional signs of solemnity: the bays are framed by Corinthian columns on pedestals, a high attic crowns the whole structure, and every available space is decorated with reliefs.

A. Plan of the Temple of Jupiter Capitolinus.

B. Plan of the Temple of Portunus.

C. Plan of the Temple of Venus and Rome.

D. Plan of the Temple of Hercules.

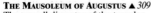

THE MAUSOLEUM OF AUGUSTUS ▲ 309
The overall diameter of the tumulus was about 285 feet. It had three levels: a vast cylindrical podium planted as a "sacred forest", the cylindrical drum of the mausoleum itself surrounded by a colonnade, and finally a truncated pyramid erected on the top, supporting a colossal statue of the Emperor. The door leading into the mausoleum was framed by two obelisks.

THE "CELLAE"
Porphyry, polychrome marbles and gilded coffers adorned the *cellae*.

THE TEMPLE OF VENUS AND ROME ▲ 146
This double sanctuary was made up of two temples placed back to back along a longitudinal axis. It was the largest religious building in the Graeco-Roman world.

THE PLAN OF THE PANTHEON
The vast rotunda is preceded by a great quadrangular portico (*pronaos*) with sixteen majestic columns.

THE INTERIOR OF THE PANTHEON ▲ 264
The monumental rigor of this building is due to the harmonious juxtaposition of two simple geometrical figures: the cylinder and the hemisphere.

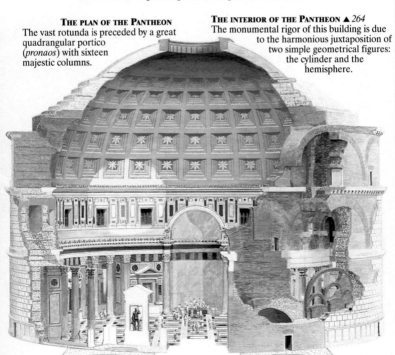

● MEDIEVAL TOWERS AND DWELLINGS

During the 11th and 12th centuries the Roman nobility developed an architectural idiom that combined fortifications, towers and ramparts with dwellings. Palaces, surrounded by the houses of relatives and servants, and towers (the military scope of which soon became merely emblematic), were the homes of the grandees until the end of the Middle Ages.

CASA DEI CRESCENZI
This house was built in the 11th century by Nicolo di Crescenzio with a view to "reviving the ancient setting of Rome", as an inscription set above the door proclaims. It is a good example of the reuse of classical architectural and decorative materials and elements within the medieval, domestic, architectural idiom.

TORRE ANGUILLARA ▲ *356*
This 13th-century tower in Trastevere was rebuilt around 1455. Its crenelations are the product of a 19th-century restoration.

THE TOMB OF CECILIA METELLA
▲ *330* Certain tombs on the Via Appia were used as foundations for medieval fortifications.

THE FORTIFICATION OF THE MAUSOLEUM
The Tomb of Cecilia Metella is a vast two-floored structure. In 1299 it was turned into a gigantic dungeon by Pietro Caetani. The Ghibelline crenelations were added at that time. However, its spacious balcony and broad windows make this fortress less severe.

TORRE DELLE MILIZIE ▲ 168
This very tall tower, the symbol of "Roma turrita", was erected at the beginning of the 13th century on the ruins of Trajan's market. The 1348 earthquake destroyed its upper floors.

TORRE DEI CAPOCCI
This was built in the 13th century as a part of one of the largest fortified complexes, using building materials and bricks from

A MEDIEVAL TOWN HOUSE
The house standing at No. 14 Via dell'Atleta (a delightful street in Trastevere ▲ 353) is one of the best examples of Roman medieval architecture. Its brick and tufa-rubble façade is adorned with a loggia with a twin arcade supported by marble columns, while above, a frieze of smaller ogival arches rests on travertine corbels.

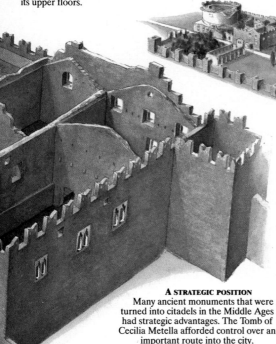

PLAN OF THE FORTIFIED COMPLEX
The Tomb of Cecilia Metella was surrounded by a rectangular wall originally buttressed by sixteen protruding quadrangular guard towers. It extended over both sides of the Via Appia, which it controlled. The layout of the buildings within these battlements indicates the degree to which the highway had been "privatized", with the castle on one side of the road and its chapel, San Nicola da Bari, on the other.

A STRATEGIC POSITION
Many ancient monuments that were turned into citadels in the Middle Ages had strategic advantages. The Tomb of Cecilia Metella afforded control over an important route into the city.

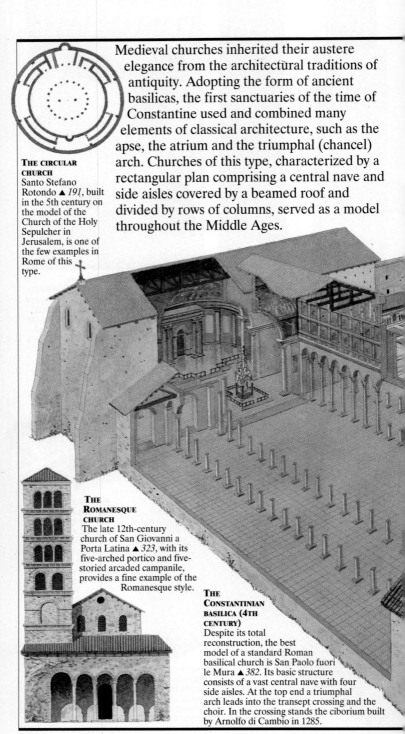

Medieval churches inherited their austere elegance from the architectural traditions of antiquity. Adopting the form of ancient basilicas, the first sanctuaries of the time of Constantine used and combined many elements of classical architecture, such as the apse, the atrium and the triumphal (chancel) arch. Churches of this type, characterized by a rectangular plan comprising a central nave and side aisles covered by a beamed roof and divided by rows of columns, served as a model throughout the Middle Ages.

THE CIRCULAR CHURCH
Santo Stefano Rotondo ▲ *191*, built in the 5th century on the model of the Church of the Holy Sepulcher in Jerusalem, is one of the few examples in Rome of this type.

THE ROMANESQUE CHURCH
The late 12th-century church of San Giovanni a Porta Latina ▲ *323*, with its five-arched portico and five-storied arcaded campanile, provides a fine example of the Romanesque style.

THE CONSTANTINIAN BASILICA (4TH CENTURY)
Despite its total reconstruction, the best model of a standard Roman basilical church is San Paolo fuori le Mura ▲ *382*. Its basic structure consists of a vast central nave with four side aisles. At the top end a triumphal arch leads into the transept crossing and the choir. In the crossing stands the ciborium built by Arnolfo di Cambio in 1285.

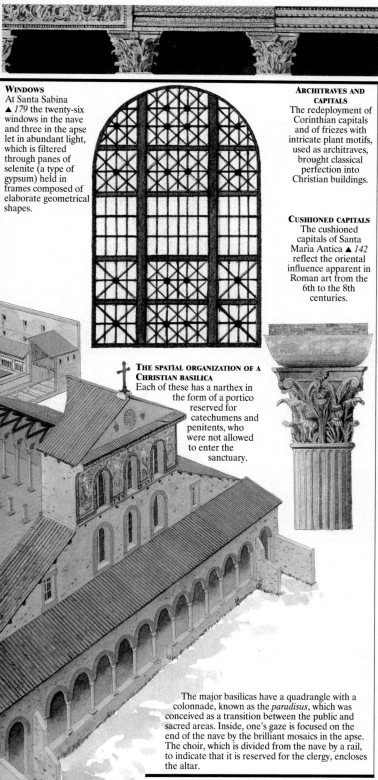

WINDOWS
At Santa Sabina ▲ 179 the twenty-six windows in the nave and three in the apse let in abundant light, which is filtered through panes of selenite (a type of gypsum) held in frames composed of elaborate geometrical shapes.

ARCHITRAVES AND CAPITALS
The redeployment of Corinthian capitals and of friezes with intricate plant motifs, used as architraves, brought classical perfection into Christian buildings.

CUSHIONED CAPITALS
The cushioned capitals of Santa Maria Antica ▲ 142 reflect the oriental influence apparent in Roman art from the 6th to the 8th centuries.

THE SPATIAL ORGANIZATION OF A CHRISTIAN BASILICA
Each of these has a narthex in the form of a portico reserved for catechumens and penitents, who were not allowed to enter the sanctuary.

The major basilicas have a quadrangle with a colonnade, known as the *paradisus*, which was conceived as a transition between the public and sacred areas. Inside, one's gaze is focused on the end of the nave by the brilliant mosaics in the apse. The choir, which is divided from the nave by a rail, to indicate that it is reserved for the clergy, encloses the altar.

PAVEMENTS. Rich geometrical patterns surround disks of porphyry sliced from the shafts of ancient columns.

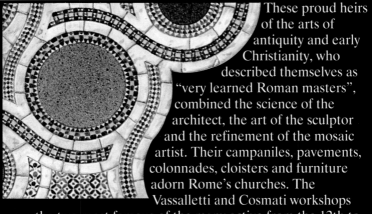

These proud heirs of the arts of antiquity and early Christianity, who described themselves as "very learned Roman masters", combined the science of the architect, the art of the sculptor and the refinement of the mosaic artist. Their campaniles, pavements, colonnades, cloisters and furniture adorn Rome's churches. The Vassalletti and Cosmati workshops were the two most famous of the many active from the 12th to the 13th century in the expressive, elegant and refined decorative art form known as the "Cosmatesque".

THE EPISCOPAL THRONE OF SAN LORENZO FUORI LE MURA ▲ *381*

This throne, designed in the 13th century for the Pope as Bishop of Rome, is a symbol of the papacy's political theology. Instead of very explicit symbolic motifs, it aims at rich decorative and chromatic effects. The great central disk resembling a nimbus evokes sanctity, while the three-lobed design above it exalts the theocratic ideas dear to Pope Innocent IV.

DETAIL OF INLAID FRIEZE IN THE CLOISTER OF SAN PAOLO FUORI LE MURA

Polychrome decorations, geometrical designs and mosaics emphasize the architectural features, which glitter with marble, porphyry and serpentine taken from the ruins of antiquity.

COLUMNS FROM THE CLOISTER OF SAN PAOLO FUORI LE MURA

The Roman marble cutters explored every possibility in the decoration of columns, ranging from the rectilinear to the twisted and entwined, enhancing their rhythm with inlaid patterns.

THE CLOISTER OF SAN PAOLO FUORI LE MURA ▲ 382

This cloister, probably designed by one of the Vassalletti, is among the great architectural and decorative achievements of the 13th century in Rome. Each of its four galleries consists of four or five arcades separated by pilasters topped by a pseudo-Corinthian capital.

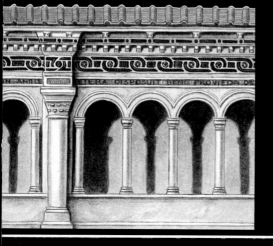

CARVED MARBLE PASCHAL CANDELABRA
Numerous religious objects were also

COUNTER-REFORMATION ARCHITECTURE

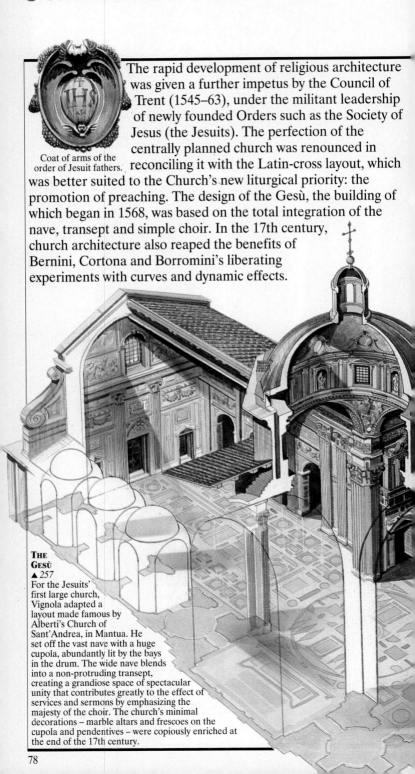

Coat of arms of the order of Jesuit fathers.

The rapid development of religious architecture was given a further impetus by the Council of Trent (1545–63), under the militant leadership of newly founded Orders such as the Society of Jesus (the Jesuits). The perfection of the centrally planned church was renounced in reconciling it with the Latin-cross layout, which was better suited to the Church's new liturgical priority: the promotion of preaching. The design of the Gesù, the building of which began in 1568, was based on the total integration of the nave, transept and simple choir. In the 17th century, church architecture also reaped the benefits of Bernini, Cortona and Borromini's liberating experiments with curves and dynamic effects.

THE GESÙ
▲ 257
For the Jesuits' first large church, Vignola adapted a layout made famous by Alberti's Church of Sant'Andrea, in Mantua. He set off the vast nave with a huge cupola, abundantly lit by the bays in the drum. The wide nave blends into a non-protruding transept, creating a grandiose space of spectacular unity that contributes greatly to the effect of services and sermons by emphasizing the majesty of the choir. The church's minimal decorations – marble altars and frescoes on the cupola and pendentives – were copiously enriched at the end of the 17th century.

A	B	C
Renaissance	Counter-Reformation	Baroque

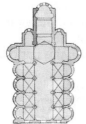

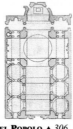

B. SANT'IGNAZIO
▲ *261* The layout and façade of the Gesù were virtually copied when this church was constructed in 1650. Only its lavish decorations distinguished it from its model, built in the austere spirit of the Counter-Reformation, before the innovations of the 17th century.

C. SANT'ANDREA DEL QUIRINALE ▲ *296*
In this small elliptical church Bernini developed elegant dynamic effects by means of contrasting curves and the tension created by his use of limited space.

A. SANTA MARIA DEL POPOLO ▲ *306*
This church's ground plan in the shape of a Latin cross and its façade divided into three sections reflect the internal layout of a nave with two aisles, reminiscent of the pure Renaissance style of Santa Maria Novella in Florence, the façade of which was designed by Alberti in 1458.

THE FAÇADE OF THE GESÙ
In the rational tradition of the early Renaissance, Giacomo della Porta's façade, with its two levels linked by consoles, reflects the interior layout of the church. Three doors open into the single nave. The lateral sections contain chapels. This particular feature is echoed on the first level by the grouping of the pilasters and the projection of the columns supporting the main door's double pediment. The longitudinal axis is thus emphasized.

PROFILE OF A COUNTER-REFORMATION FAÇADE
Unlike later, Baroque churches, the Gesù has a flush façade with only slight projections.

THE PANTHEON ▲ 264
This cupola (2nd century BC) became the model for the "concrete vault". The extrados (outer surface) serves as a complete covering.

While Bernini and Borromini shared the same classical and Renaissance background and pursued a similar goal in seeking to give life to the principles of composition, they differed in their manner of interpreting these traditions – the one theatrical and the other architectural.

The cupola, or dome, was the essential element in the new challenges of religious architecture and underwent unprecedented variations in this period.

THE CUPOLA OF SANT'IVO
The drum supports a stepped cupola surmounted by a lantern at the apex of powerful ribs. A spiral enhances the upward movement.

SANT'IVO DELLA SAPIENZA ▲ 272
In Borromini's masterpiece, begun in 1642, the dynamic tension generated by the contrasting concave and convex surfaces is brought to a climax. Externally the hexagonal drum appears even more powerful because it inverts the design of the façade, whose curve is extended by the two arcades of the courtyard. Inside, six apses facing each other in pairs, in accordance with the building's interplay of contrasts, reveal the star-shaped ground plan.

The papal emblems of the *monti* decorate the parapet of the façade.

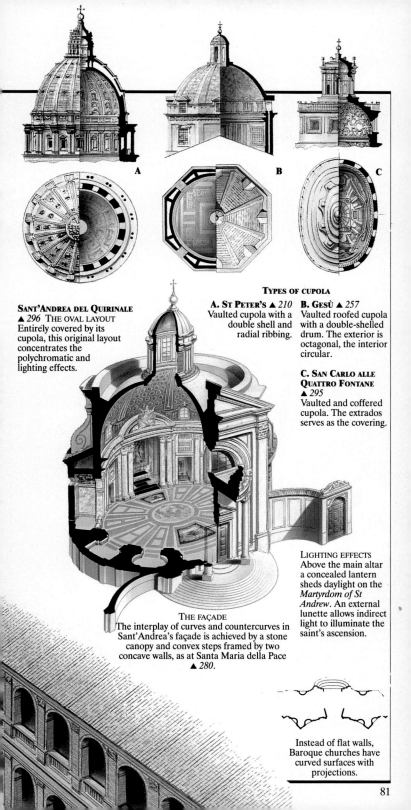

TYPES OF CUPOLA

A. ST PETER'S ▲ *210*
Vaulted cupola with a double shell and radial ribbing.

B. GESÙ ▲ *257*
Vaulted roofed cupola with a double-shelled drum. The exterior is octagonal, the interior circular.

C. SAN CARLO ALLE QUATTRO FONTANE ▲ *295*
Vaulted and coffered cupola. The extrados serves as the covering.

SANT'ANDREA DEL QUIRINALE ▲ *296* THE OVAL LAYOUT
Entirely covered by its cupola, this original layout concentrates the polychromatic and lighting effects.

LIGHTING EFFECTS
Above the main altar a concealed lantern sheds daylight on the *Martyrdom of St Andrew*. An external lunette allows indirect light to illuminate the saint's ascension.

THE FAÇADE
The interplay of curves and countercurves in Sant'Andrea's façade is achieved by a stone canopy and convex steps framed by two concave walls, as at Santa Maria della Pace ▲ *280*.

Instead of flat walls, Baroque churches have curved surfaces with projections.

81

THE ART OF "TROMPE L'ŒIL"

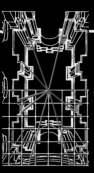

Preparatory cartoon showing the *trompe l'oeil* effect on a squared surface, with a central vanishing point.

In the 17th century many Roman ceilings were covered with princely apotheoses, celestial glories and *quadrature* (painted architectural elements). Cupolas reveal Baroque cloud formations that sweep architecture, paintings and sculptures up into their luminous vortex. One of the most spectacular masterpieces of this art of illusion, the absolute mastery of the rules of perspective, is the Church of Sant'Ignazio ▲ *261*, where Andrea Pozzo painted a *trompe l'oeil* cupola and, in the nave, a magnificent fresco in which earthly architecture seems to reach heavenly heights.

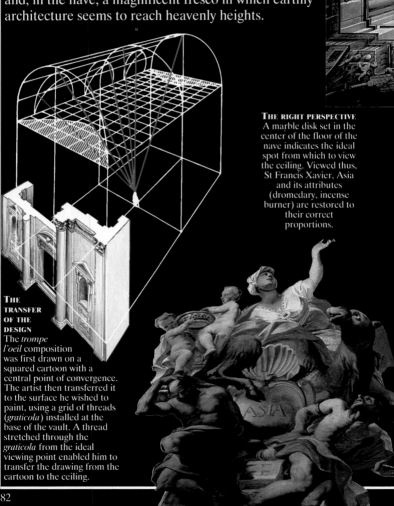

THE RIGHT PERSPECTIVE
A marble disk set in the center of the floor of the nave indicates the ideal spot from which to view the ceiling. Viewed thus, St Francis Xavier, Asia and its attributes (dromedary, incense burner) are restored to their correct proportions.

THE TRANSFER OF THE DESIGN
The *trompe l'oeil* composition was first drawn on a squared cartoon with a central point of convergence. The artist then transferred it to the surface he wished to paint, using a grid of threads (*graticola*) installed at the base of the vault. A thread stretched through the *graticola* from the ideal viewing point enabled him to transfer the drawing from the cartoon to the ceiling.

"I HAVE RESOLVED TO DRAW ALL LINES CONVERGING ON A SINGLE POINT: THE GLORY OF GOD."

ANDREA POZZO

GENERAL VIEW OF THE CEILING
The swarms of figures in this composition could only be included thanks to the false architectural perspective, which blends naturally into this sublime apotheosis of the Jesuit Missionary Order.

THE PROJECTION OF A CIRCLE
One might perhaps guess that to create the illusion of perfect circles Pozzo had to paint vertical ovals, and that the seemingly gigantic columns are only a few inches tall.

DISTORTED VISION
If you move away from the ideal viewpoint, all this beauty becomes distorted and seems to be in danger of an eternal fall.

Bernini (1598–1680) defined unity as the harmony of opposites, rather than as static composition. Because they shared a common theatrical purpose, different arts came together in his conception of architecture to create a dramatic effect that demanded the faithful participate as spectators. Indeed his aim was to convince people of the truth of the Faith and the grandeur of Rome by making full use of the ambiguities produced by a rhetorical ordering of space, light and figurative elements.

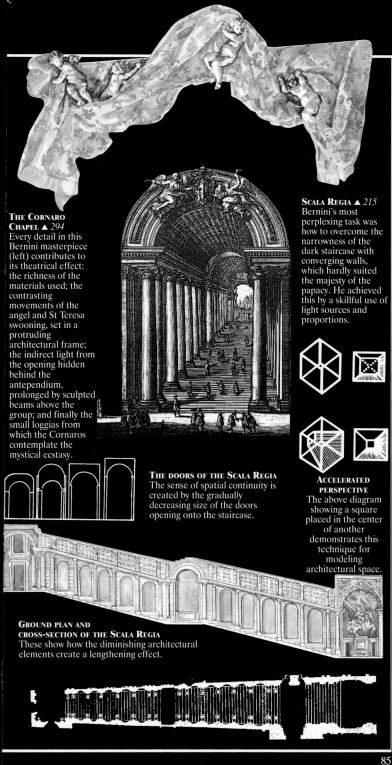

THE CORNARO CHAPEL ▲ 294
Every detail in this Bernini masterpiece (left) contributes to its theatrical effect: the richness of the materials used; the contrasting movements of the angel and St Teresa swooning, set in a protruding architectural frame; the indirect light from the opening hidden behind the antependium, prolonged by sculpted beams above the group; and finally the small loggias from which the Cornaros contemplate the mystical ecstasy.

SCALA REGIA ▲ 215
Bernini's most perplexing task was how to overcome the narrowness of the dark staircase with converging walls, which hardly suited the majesty of the papacy. He achieved this by a skillful use of light sources and proportions.

ACCELERATED PERSPECTIVE
The above diagram showing a square placed in the center of another demonstrates this technique for modeling architectural space.

THE DOORS OF THE SCALA REGIA
The sense of spatial continuity is created by the gradually decreasing size of the doors opening onto the staircase.

GROUND PLAN AND CROSS-SECTION OF THE SCALA REGIA
These show how the diminishing architectural elements create a lengthening effect.

Following the example of the popes, during the Renaissance Roman nobles and cardinals began to build grandiose palaces that were symbols of the power they wielded in the city. Not all of these possess the austere grandeur of Palazzo Farnese – their principal model – but from the 15th to the 17th centuries they generally followed a similar layout: a quadrilateral building with a central *cortile* (courtyard) surrounded by a gallery with arcades. Their façades testify to the rigorous approach of Roman architects.

THE CANCELLERIA ▲ *249* . The highly rational character of this masterpiece of Renaissance architecture (1483–1513), long thought to have been designed by Bramante and whose proportions respect the Golden Section, should not make one overlook its innovative elements, such as the use of corner bay extensions to maximize the building's horizontal potential.

THE CLASSICAL ORDERS ▲ *94*
In the courtyard of Palazzo Farnese the three classical orders, Doric, Ionic and Corinthian, are displayed in the superimposed arcades as in the Coliseum. Precise proportional ratios govern these architectural features.

Doorway, by the architect Serlio (1475–1554), making use of the Golden Section.

PALAZZO FARNESE ▲ *244*
Modeled on the Florentine tradition, Antonio da Sangallo's design featured a quadrangular ground plan and an austere façade without columns, adorned only by alternating window pediments and moldings. Inside, on the other hand, the vestibule with high coffered vaulting and the original elevation of the courtyard (1513–46) recall the architecture of ancient Rome.

PALAZZO SPADA ▲ 246

THE STUCCOWORK ON THE FAÇADE OF PALAZZO SPADA
The exuberant ornamental effects contrast with the rigorous classicism of the façade's overall design. The Mannerist richness of these stucco decorations (1556–60) is possibly the first Roman emulation of de Rosso's inventive moldings at Fontainebleau.

PALAZZO SPADA ▲ *246*
The façade of this palazzo, built at the very beginning of the Counter-Reformation period, has a strictly classical design with bossage decorations between the *piano nobile* and the attic.

BAROQUE WINDOW
The dynamics of this window by Carlo Maderno in Palazzo Barberini are due to the interplay of light and shade and to a hint of perspective worthy of Bernini.

THE LAYOUT OF PALAZZO FARNESE
The main entrance leads to an inner courtyard, from which a grand staircase provides access to the *piano nobile*. The reception rooms are on this floor. The ground floor rooms are reserved for household services, while the upper floors and the loggia contain the living quarters.

ATTIC WINDOW IN PALAZZO BARBERINI
▲ *291*. This early work by Borromini includes all the elements of his mature style: the dynamics of the details create a strange tension in a window that has an otherwise classical design.

The villa, which had been a major feature of classical architecture, came into its own again in Florence a little before 1500. But it was in Rome, inspired by ancient examples such as Hadrian's Villa and Pliny's descriptions, that the ideal constructions of the humanist period were built. Bramante's Belvedere, Raphael's Farnesina and Villa Madama and Vignola's Villa Giulia and Villa Caprarola were designed as refined places of *otium*, or contemplative leisure, and were soon imitated all over Europe. Their terraces, loggias and belvederes provided viewpoints from which to gaze at an exalted vision of Nature with which Man felt in perfect harmony.

THE CORTILE DEL BELVEDERE IN THE VATICAN (C. 1505)
This courtyard ▲ *214* was designed as a terraced garden. Its lowest level could be used for a variety of entertainments, particularly aquatic jousting tournaments.

THE FARNESINA (1509–11)
▲ *360* Built for Agostino Chigi by Peruzzi, a Tuscan who did not share Bramante's and Raphael's passion for archeology, this became one of the Farnese properties. It was one of Rome's first suburban Renaissance villas.

GROUND PLAN OF THE FARNESINA
The loggia with two projecting wings and the division between winter reception rooms facing south and other living rooms facing north, as well as the painted *trompe l'oeil* perspectives overlooking vast landscapes, were all standard in subsequent villas.

VILLA D'ESTE (1560–c. 1570) ▲ *392*
Like many other villas, this one stands on the slope of a hill, all the better to dominate its wonderful gardens and to view the entire western horizon. The steepness of the ground also ensured a constant water supply to the fountains and offered the visitor, who originally entered the property from below, a carefully stage-managed approach to the building. The walk through these enchanting gardens, quite unlike traditional geometrical parterres, was conceived as a journey of discovery, with innumerable paths winding through coppices, grottoes and nymphaeums.

VILLA MEDICI (C. 1570–6) ▲ *315*
This was built on the site of the gardens of Lucullus for Cardinal Ricci di Montepulciano and was later embellished by Cardinal Ferdinando de' Medici. Today's inner façade was originally the villa's main entrance. Its principal features are its grandiose porch loggia, overlooking the gardens, and the abundance of classical decorations, which make it look like a Roman triumphal arch.

THE SITE OF VILLA D'ESTE
The steep slope of the hill determined both the internal layout of the buildings and the landscaping of the gardens, in a spirit characteristic of the transition from the Renaissance to the Baroque. Many travelers, from Montaigne to Liszt, praised this villa's charms.

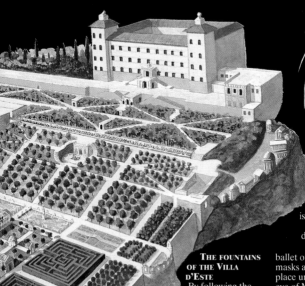

DIANA OF EPHESUS
This copy of a classical statue from the Farnese collection, portraying the goddess of nature, is the key element in one of the Villa d'Este's fountains.

THE FOUNTAINS OF THE VILLA D'ESTE
By following the paths criss-crossing the gardens (the only way to go) visitors will discover the Fontana dell'Organo Idraulico and the Rometta ("little Rome") fountain. This ballet of water, greenery, masks and statues takes place under the watchful eye of Mother Earth, with her thousand breasts, in a blend of learned classical iconographic references to the myth of Hercules, the legendary founder of the Este family, and to the garden of the Hesperides.

It was not until the French occupation, in 1808, that the neoclassical style established itself in Rome. Later, with the build-up to the unification of Italy in 1861, or even before, a debate began over the "national style", which led to a period of eclecticism and a revival of earlier architectural idioms. The neo-Renaissance style rapidly came to the fore in both private and public buildings, while "Liberty" (Italian Art Nouveau) also became popular and Neoclassicism survived in a rather ponderous and bastardized form. Cast iron and glass, however, was rarely used in the architecture of the city.

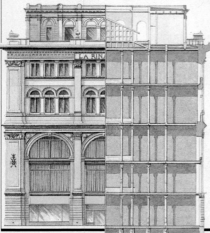

PIAZZA DEL POPOLO AND THE PINCIO (1813–20)
Giuseppe Valadier (1762–1839), the great neoclassical architect of Rome, was responsible for terracing the Pincio ▲ *316* and for the layout of the two semicircular areas of Piazza del Popolo ▲ *306*.

THE BOCCONI BUILDING (RINASCENTE) ▲ *267*
The façade of this neo-Renaissance building (1886) highlights the use of glass. Inside, cast-iron columns support the various floors, which overlook a vast central space, in conformity with the conventional design of European department stores.

GALLERIA SCIARRA (1883) ▲ *301*
The design of this *galleria* of shops, with its Liberty frescoes influenced by Pompeian and pre-Raphaelite paintings, had to overcome the problem of how to provide light. Its architect, Giulio de Angelis, made use of cast-iron structures to lighten the whole ensemble and support a glazed roof.

TESTACCIO ▲ *184*

In this popular area built at the beginning of the 20th century, the apartment blocks lining the streets were given large open courtyards. The idea was to allow air to circulate around the blocks and to relieve the solid monotony of the façades.

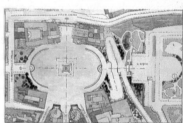

The layout of Piazza del Popolo and the Pincio as they are today.

THE VITTORIANO (1885–1911) ▲ *160*

This weighty symbol of post-Unification monumental architecture is a supreme example of the mixture of styles prevailing at the end of the 19th century. Basically a neoclassical project, it has its roots in the Hellenistic tradition, as much through its use of white marble as through its grandiose composition of colonnades and steps, recalling the altar in Pergamon or the temple in Praeneste ▲ *402*. A rather heavy neo-Realist statue of the king was added before the completion of the planned sculpted decorations, which are much more in the symbolist vein.

The Vittoriano's appearance earned it the nickname of "the typewriter".

Fascist architecture has a dual nature. Mussolini's regime was a blend of the most modern trends with a nostalgia for Rome's glorious past. Both rationalism and historical references were therefore encouraged in architecture by the Fascists, who saw them as a means of pleasing everyone. The return to classical antiquity was suited to the staging of mass rallies, while the rationalist style seemed ideal for housing developments and functional buildings. It is from the rationalist movement that most postwar architecture evolved.

SAN PIETRO E PAOLO, EUR (1937–41) ▲ *388*
✝ This church with strictly geometrical volumes, built by Arnaldo Foschini, is designed in the shape of a Greek cross and was modeled on the churches of the Renaissance. Its vast dome (over 235 feet), decorated with coffers and resting on a drum with *oculi*, is a reference to the styles of classical antiquity.

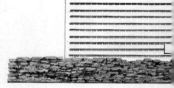

PALAZZO DELLA CIVILTÀ DEL LAVORO, EUR (1939) ▲ *387*
This is one of the finest monuments of the rationalist school designed for the Universal Exhibition of 1942 ▲ *386*. It was built by the architects Giovanni Guerrini, Ernesto Bruno La Padula and Mario Romano.

THE FACING
Its reinforced-concrete structure consists of five floors with rectangular bays supported by pillars. It is faced with a succession of false travertine arches, whose rhythmic repetition was intended to evoke that of the Coliseum ▲ *170*.

FASCIST SCULPTURE
With typical Fascist overstatement this group recalls the classical theme of the Dioscuri (Castor and Pollux) with their mounts.

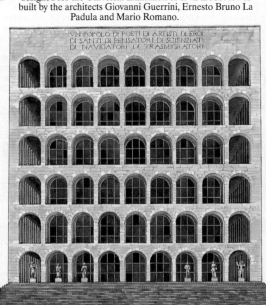

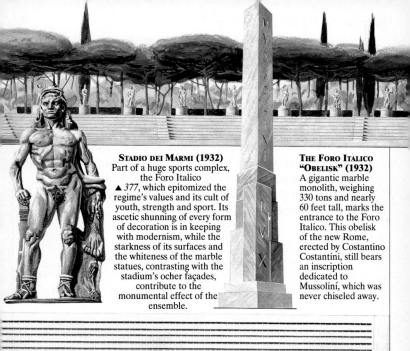

STADIO DEI MARMI (1932)
Part of a huge sports complex, the Foro Italico ▲ 377, which epitomized the regime's values and its cult of youth, strength and sport. Its ascetic shunning of every form of decoration is in keeping with modernism, while the starkness of its surfaces and the whiteness of the marble statues, contrasting with the stadium's ocher façades, contribute to the monumental effect of the ensemble.

THE FORO ITALICO "OBELISK" (1932)
A gigantic marble monolith, weighing 330 tons and nearly 60 feet tall, marks the entrance to the Foro Italico. This obelisk of the new Rome, erected by Costantino Costantini, still bears an inscription dedicated to Mussolini, which was never chiseled away.

STAZIONE TERMINI (1938–50) ▲ 338
The rebuilding of Rome's main station spanned the Fascist period and the postwar years. It provides a good illustration of the transition of architectural styles during this period of political change. The two rigid lateral buildings with false arches faced in Travertine were the first to be built, and evoke the paintings of Giorgio De Chirico▲ 387 in no uncertain way. The grandiose main hall (opened in 1950), on the other hand, is striking because of the dynamic use of materials in its powerfully ribbed undulating roof.

PALAZZETTO DELLO SPORT (1956–8)

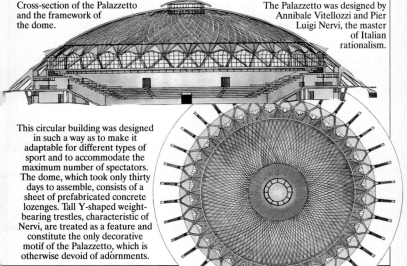

Cross-section of the Palazzetto and the framework of the dome.

The Palazzetto was designed by Annibale Vitellozzi and Pier Luigi Nervi, the master of Italian rationalism.

This circular building was designed in such a way as to make it adaptable for different types of sport and to accommodate the maximum number of spectators. The dome, which took only thirty days to assemble, consists of a sheet of prefabricated concrete lozenges. Tall Y-shaped weight-bearing trestles, characteristic of Nervi, are treated as a feature and constitute the only decorative motif of the Palazzetto, which is otherwise devoid of adornments.

● THE CLASSICAL ORDERS

 2

 3

 4

 5

Using an architecture of columns, the Greeks developed the Doric, Ionic and Corinthian styles, which provided aesthetic solutions to every kind of building. In Rome during the 1st century BC Vitruvius formulated a theory concerning the classical orders at a time when the development of the arch and the vault had reduced columns to a more decorative function. These styles and their variants were destined to become the basic orders of western architecture.

SUPERIMPOSED ORDERS

In all periods the orders were always superimposed in the same sequence. From the bottom: Doric or Tuscan (**1** and **2**), Ionic (**3**), Corinthian (**4**) and Composite (**5**).

Doric capital with ovolo molding.

II. ENTABLATURE

1. Architrave: smooth in the Doric style, but divided into three bands or *fasciae* in the Ionic and Corinthian.
2. Taenia (fillet).
3. Frieze: (left to right)
– Ionic, sometimes omitted from the entablature, sometimes plain.
– Doric, always consisted of alternating metopes (**a**) and triglyphs (**b**), each crowned by a mutule and anchored under the taenia by a *regula* with *guttae*.
– Corinthian, could be adorned with figurative motifs (**c**), animals or plants.
4. Cornice.

I. PEDIMENT AND ROOF

1. Tympanum. **2.** Raking cornices.
3. Bases for gable and angle *acroteria*: these often took the form of sculptures.

I. PEDIMENT

II. ENTABLATURE

III. COLUMNS

Columns have three parts: the base (**a**), the shaft (**b**), which can be smooth or fluted, and the capital (**c**). Their proportions and decorations vary according to the order they belong to:
1. Doric (normally has no base).
2. Tuscan Doric (with a base).
3. Ionic.
4. Corinthian.
5 and **6.** Composite.

III. COLUMNS

IV. SUBSTRUCTURE

1. Bases flanking steps. **2.** Podium: unlike the Greeks, the Romans generally erected temples on massive stone platforms.

ROME
AS SEEN
BY PAINTERS

B oth a painter and
an architect, Gian
Paolo Panini
(c. 1693–1765), was
one of the most
representative artists
of the 18th century.
Like many of his
contemporaries, he
used painting as a
means to show reality:
cities, palaces, the
private apartments of
the nobility and the
dwellings of the
common people. In his
*Galleries of Views of
Ancient Rome* (1) and
Galleries of Views of

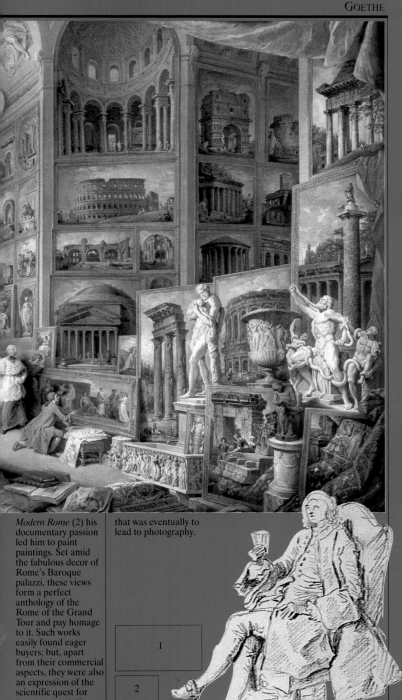

Modern Rome (2) his documentary passion led him to paint paintings. Set amid the fabulous decor of Rome's Baroque palazzi, these views form a perfect anthology of the Rome of the Grand Tour and pay homage to it. Such works easily found eager buyers; but, apart from their commercial aspects, they were also an expression of the scientific quest for true representation that was eventually to lead to photography.

1

2

Even when he decided to portray a real place, as in this *View of the French Academy in Rome* (1), GUSTAVE MOREAU (1826–98) never forgot his overriding artistic aim: to suggest more than the visible. Built up in monochrome masses, the various parts of this picture (trees, flowerbed, buildings) amount to a "vision" rather than a "view". A very well known place, painted many times, thus acquires a certain mystery, which the time of day chosen by Moreau – a gentle twilight – accentuates and makes more magical.

Although as a writer Goethe (1749–1832) offers a totally romantic idea of Rome and Italy, during his visit to Rome in 1784 he admired David's *The Oath of the Horatii*, a pictorial manifesto of neoclassicism. In contrast, David's *The Pyramid of Caius Cestius in Rome* (2) – a nocturnal view of a strangely eerie and exotic place – clearly belongs to the poetry of the ruins which Mantegna had already explored in the 15th century and which the Romantics made their own.

Corot

With *The Coliseum seen from the Farnese Gardens* (1), painted in 1826, Jean-Baptiste Corot (1796–1875) reveals the very essence of his art, in which natural light combines with a geometry free from cumbersome narrative detail. This picture, with its complex composition, has a classical clarity: beyond the foliage in the foreground the view stretches to the distant horizon, visible behind the broken circle of the Coliseum.

Before becoming a Futurist, Giacomo Balla (1871–1958) was a Divisionist, like so many other artists of his generation. At the beginning of the 20th century he painted *The Villa Borghese* many times (2) in pointillist style. In this evocative view, the last echoes of 19th-century art combine with a framework influenced by photography.

"THE DOME OF ST PETER'S 'IS SILHOUETTED AGAINST THE PUREST TINT OF AN ORANGE SUNSET, WHILE OVERHEAD A FEW STARS BEGIN TO APPEAR IN THE SKY'."

STENDHAL

Corot's long sojourns in Italy did not fail to influence certain Italian painters at the beginning of the 19th century. This was demonstrated in particular by their abandonment of documentary views in favor of a freer and more basic treatment of a mass of structural forms, devoid of anecdotal secondary detail. Ippolito Caffi (1809–66) was one of the artists who succeeded in making the most of Corot's lesson. Caffi painted several Roman landscapes, including this *View of Rome from the Pincio Gardens*, which is suffused with a romantic atmosphere to a greater degree than most of his works. Nevertheless, the twilight composition, in which the suggestion of ghostly figures contrasts with the distant reddish silhouette of St Peter's seen against the flaming sky of the sunset, is no less faithful to the new ideas that Corot's example inspired.

The colors of Rome, red in particular, fired Yves Brayer (1907–90) with enthusiasm. His spontaneous gouaches and more carefully studied oil paintings made him an ironic witness of Roman life in the 1930's, as this picture of *German Seminarians on the Ponte Sant'Angelo* shows.

YVES BRAYER
ROME 1934

ROME
AS SEEN BY
WRITERS

REMINDERS OF THE PAST

ANCIENT RUINS

Visitors to Rome are constantly struck by the echoes of history resounding in the stones of the city. Michel Eyquem de Montaigne (1533–92), the French moralist and essayist, visited Rome at a time when the physical evidence of the Roman Empire was often stumbled upon by builders digging the foundations for new buildings.

❝It would often happen to one digging deep in the earth to come upon the capital of a lofty column which still stood on its base far below; and builders were wont to seek for their erections no other foundations than some mass of ancient masonry, or on arches such as are commonly seen in that of old the road all the way from Rome to Ostia ran past the habitations of men. Amongst other ruins we saw, about midway and on our left, a very beautiful tomb of a Roman prætor with an inscription quite perfect thereon. In Rome, the ruins, as a rule, only manifest themselves to us by the massive solidity of their construction. The ancients built thick walls of brick, and these they lined either with strips of marble or some other white stone, or with a kind of cement, or with thick tiles set thereupon. This outside crust, on which the inscriptions were written, has almost everywhere been ruined by the lapse of years, wherefore we have now but little knowledge as to all these matters. Inscriptions still remain where the walls were originally built in solid fashion. The approaches to Rome in almost every case have a barren and uncultivated look, whether through the unfitness of the soil for cultivation, or whether, as seems more likely, through the absence of husbandmen and handicraftsmen in the city. On my journey hither I met divers troops of villagers from the Grisons and Savoy on their way to seek work in the Roman vineyards and gardens, and they told me they gained this wage every year. The city is all for the court and the nobility, every one adapting himself to the ease and idleness of ecclesiastic surroundings. There are no main streets of trade; what there are would seem small in a small town, palaces and gardens take up all the space.❞

MICHEL EYQUEM DE MONTAIGNE, *THE JOURNAL OF MONTAIGNE'S TRAVELS IN ITALY BY WAY OF SWITZERLAND AND GERMANY IN 1580 AND 1581*, JOHN MURRAY, LONDON, 1903

CLASSICAL ANTIQUITY

William Beckford (1560–1844), the traveler, collector and English member of parliament, perceived in Rome a fanciful atmosphere in which spirits from classical antiquity still run free.

❝A spring flowed opportunely into a marble cistern close by the way; two cypresses and a pine waved over it. I leaped out, poured water upon my hands, and then, lifting them up to the sylvan Genii of the place, implored their protection. I wished to run wild in the fresh fields and copses above the Vatican, there to have remained, till fauns might peep out of the concealments, and satyrs begin to touch

their flutes in the twilight; for the place looks still so wonderous classical, that I can never persuade myself, either Constantine, Attila, or the Popes themselves, have chased them all away. I think I should have found some out, who would have fed me with milk and chesnuts, have sung me a Latian ditty, and mourned the woeful changes which have taken place, since their sacred groves were felled, and Faunus ceased to be oracular. Who can tell but they would have given me some mystic skin to sleep on, that I might have looked into futurity? Shall I ever forget the sensations I experienced, upon slowly descending the hills, and crossing the bridge over the Tyber, when I entered an avenue between terraces and ornamented gates of villas, which leads to the Porto del Popolo? and beheld the square, the domes, the obelisk; the long perspective of streets and palaces opening beyond, all glowing with the vivid red of sun-set? You can imagine how I enjoyed my beloved tint, my favourite hour, surrounded by such objects.**

WILLIAM BECKFORD, *THE GRAND TOUR OF WILLIAM BECKFORD*,
PENGUIN BOOKS, LONDON, 1986

THE SACK OF ROME

The autobiography of Benvenuto Cellini (1500–71) is an extraordinarily vivid account of the events of his time. In the following passage he describes the sack of Rome by the Imperialist army under Constable of Bourbon in 1527.

**Having got into the castle in this way, I attached myself to certain pieces of artillery, which were under the command of a bombardier called Giuliano Fiorentino. Leaning there against the battlements, the unhappy man could see his poor house being sacked, and his wife and children outraged; fearing to strike his own folk, he dared not discharge the cannon, and flinging the burning fuse upon the ground, he wept as though his heart would break, and tore his cheeks with both his hands. Some of the other bombardiers were behaving in like manner; seeing which, I took one of the matches, and got the assistance of a few men who were not overcome by their emotions. I aimed some swivels and falconets at points where I saw it would be useful, and killed with them a good number of the enemy. Had it not been for this, the troops who poured into Rome that morning, and were marching straight upon the castle, might possibly have entered it with ease, because the artillery was doing them no damage. I went on firing under the eyes of several cardinals and lords, who kept blessing me and giving me the heartiest encouragement. In my enthusiasm I strove to achieve the impossible; let it suffice that it was I who saved the castle that morning,

and

107

brought the other bombardiers back to their duty. I worked hard the whole of that day; and when the evening came, while the army was marching into Rome through the Trastevere, Pope Clement appointed a great Roman nobleman named Antonio Santacroce to be captain of all the gunners. The first thing this man did was to come to me, and having greeted me with the utmost kindness, he stationed me with five fine pieces of artillery on the highest point of the castle, to which the name of the Angel specially belongs. This circular eminence goes round the castle, and surveys both Prati and the town of Rome. The captain put under my orders enough men to help in managing my guns, and having seen me paid in advance he gave me rations of bread and a little wine, and begged me to go forward as I had begun. I was perhaps more inclined by nature to the profession of arms than to the one I had adopted, and I took such pleasure in its duties that I discharged them better than those of my art. Night came, the enemy had entered Rome, and we who were in the castle (especially myself, who have always taken pleasure in extraordinary sights) stayed gazing on the indescribable scene of tumult and conflagration in the streets below. People who were anywhere else but where we were, could not have formed the least imagination of what it was. I will not, however, set myself to describe that tragedy, but will content myself with continuing the history of my own life and the circumstances which properly belong to it. **99**

THE LIFE OF BENVENUTO CELLINI,
TRANS. JOHN ADDINGTON SYMONDS, MACMILLAN, LONDON 1925

Around the Colosseum
The city's history impressed itself most forcefully on American novelist Theodore Dreiser (1871–1945) as he wandered around the Colosseum.

66Being new to Rome, I was not satisfied with what I had seen, but struck forth again ... only to find myself shortly thereafter and quite by accident in the vicinity of the Colosseum.... It was exactly as the pictures have represented it – oval, many-arched, a thoroughly ponderous ruin. I really did not gain a suggestion of the astonishing size of it until I came down the hill, past tin cans that were lying on the grass – a sign of the modernity that possesses Rome – and entered through one of the many arches. Then it came on me – the amazing thickness of the walls, the imposing size and weight of the fragments, the vast dignity of the uprising flights of seats, and the great space now properly cleared, devoted to the arena. All that I ever knew or heard of it came back as I sat on the cool stones and looked about me.... It was a splendid afternoon.... Small patches of grass and moss were detectable everywhere, growing soft and green between the stones. The five thousand wild beasts slaughtered in the arena at its dedication, which remained as a thought from my high-school days, were all with me. I read up as much as I could, watching several workmen lowering themselves by ropes from the top of the walls, the while they picked out little tufts of grass and weeds beginning to flourish in the earthy niches. Its amazing transformations from being a quarry for greedy popes by whom most of its magnificent marbles were removed, to its narrow escape from becoming a woolen-mill operated by Sixtus V, were all brooded over here. It was impossible not to be impressed by the thought of the emperors sitting on their especial balcony; the thousands upon thousands of Romans intent upon some gladiatorial feat; the guards outside the endless doors, the numbers of which can still be seen, giving entrance to separate sections and tiers of seats; and the vast array of civic life which must have surged about. I wondered whether there were vendors who sold sweets or food and what their cries were in Latin. One could could think of the endless procession that wound its way here on gala days. Time works melancholy changes.**

THEODORE DREISER, *A TRAVELLER AT FORTY*,
GRANT RICHARDS, LONDON, 1914

THE GRANDEUR OF ROME

THE CATACOMBS OF SAN SEBASTIANO

The churches of Rome tend to inspire feelings of awe; in the case of Lady Anna Miller (1741–81) this was transformed into panic when she had an unfortunate accident. She describes the incident here in a letter to a friend written during her visit in 1770–71.

**The catacombs are the vastest, and the most noted in the neighbourhood of Rome. We explored them accompanied by a ragged ill-looking fellow, whose business is to sweep the church, and shew these silent mansions of the dead.... We were provided with little wax candles, and descended the stair-case, each carrying a lighted *Bougie* ... Having, at length, reached the bottom, after no very agreeable descent, we found ourselves in a labyrinth of very narrow passages, turning and winding incessantly; most of these are upon the slope, and, I believe, go down into the earth to a considerable depth. They are not wider than to admit one person at a time but branch out various ways like the veins in the human body; they are also extremely damp, being practised in the earth, and caused our candles to burn blue. In the side niches are deposited the bodies (as they say) of more than seventy-four thousand martyrs. These niches are mostly closed by an upright slab of marble, which bears an inscription descriptive of their contents. Several are also buried under these passages, whose graves are secured by iron grates. We followed our tattered guide for a considerable time through the passages; at last he stopt, and told M —— if he would go with him to a certain *Souterrain* just by, he would shew him a remarkable catacomb. At that moment I was staring about at the inscriptions, and took it for granted that M —— was really very near, but after some moments I asked the footman who was standing at the entrance if he saw his master; he replied in the negative, nor did he hear any voice: this alarmed me; I bid him go forward a little way, and that I would wait where I was, for I feared losing myself in this labyrinth in attempting to get out, not knowing which way they had turned. I waited a little time, and finding the servant did not return, called out as loud as I could, but, to my great disappointment, perceived that I scarce made any noise; the sound of my voice, from the dampness of the air, or the lowness of the passages, remaining (as it were) with me. I trembled all over, and perceived that my *Bougie* was near its end; I lighted another with some difficulty, from the shaking of my hands ... but figure to yourself the horror that seized me, when, upon attempting to move, I perceived myself forcibly held by my clothes from behind, and all the efforts I made to free myself ineffectual. My heart, I believe, ceased to beat for a moment, and it was as much as I could do to sustain myself from falling down upon the ground in a swoon. However, I summoned all my resolution to my aid, and ventured to look behind me, but saw nothing. I then again attempted to move, but found it impracticable.... I made more violent efforts, and in struggling, at last discovered, that there was an iron grate, like a trap-door, a little open behind me, one of the pointed bars of which had pierced through my gown, and held me in the manner I have related. I soon extricated myself, and walking forward, luckily in the right path, found M —— who was quietly copying an inscription, the guide lighting him, and the servant returning towards me with the most unconcerned aspect imaginable.❞

LADY ANNA MILLER, *LETTERS FROM ITALY IN THE YEARS 1770 AND 1771*,
EDWARD AND CHARLES DILLY, LONDON, 1776

TRANSFORMATION

The character Dorothea Brooke, in "Middlemarch" by George Eliot (1819-80) has a disastrous honeymoon in Rome but still feels strongly moved by the city itself.

❝Ruins and basilicas, palaces and colossi, set in the midst of a sordid present, where all that was living and warm-blooded seemed sunk in the deep degeneracy of a superstition divorced from reverence; the dimmer but yet eager Titantic life gazing and struggling on walls and ceilings; the long vistas of white forms whose marble eyes seemed to hold the monotonous light of an alien world: all this vast wreck of ambitious ideals, sensuous and spiritual, mixed confusedly with the signs of breathing forgetfulness and degradation, at first jarred her as with an electric shock, and then urged themselves on her with that ache belonging to a glut of confused ideas which check the flow of emotion. Forms both pale and glowing took possession of her young sense, and fixed themselves in her memory even when she was not thinking of them, preparing strange associations which remained through her after years. Our moods are apt to bring with them images which succeed each other like the magic-lantern pictures of a doze; and in certain states of dull forlornness Dorothea all her life continued to see the vastness of St. Peter's, the huge bronze canopy, the excited intention in the attitudes and garments of the prophets and evangelists in the mosaics above, and the red drapery which was being hung for Christmas spreading itself everywhere, like a disease of the retina.❞

GEORGE ELIOT, *MIDDLEMARCH*, LONDON, 1871-2

ST PETER'S

Charles Dickens (1812–70) was impressed by the pomp and pageantry of High Mass at St Peter's.

❝On Sunday, the Pope assisted in the performance of High Mass at St. Peter's. The effect of the Cathedral on my mind, on that second visit, was exactly what it was at first, and what it remains after many visits. It is not religiously impressive or affecting. It is an immense edifice with no one point for the mind to rest upon; and it tires itself with wandering

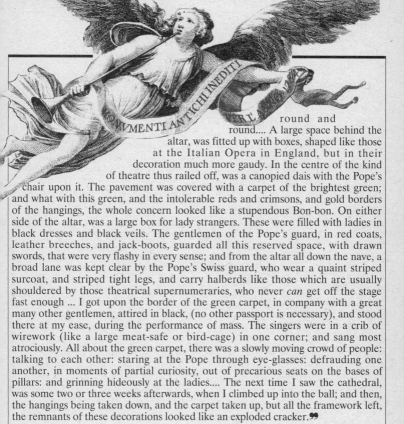

round and round.... A large space behind the altar, was fitted up with boxes, shaped like those at the Italian Opera in England, but in their decoration much more gaudy. In the centre of the kind of theatre thus railed off, was a canopied dais with the Pope's chair upon it. The pavement was covered with a carpet of the brightest green; and what with this green, and the intolerable reds and crimsons, and gold borders of the hangings, the whole concern looked like a stupendous Bon-bon. On either side of the altar, was a large box for lady strangers. These were filled with ladies in black dresses and black veils. The gentlemen of the Pope's guard, in red coats, leather breeches, and jack-boots, guarded all this reserved space, with drawn swords, that were very flashy in every sense; and from the altar all down the nave, a broad lane was kept clear by the Pope's Swiss guard, who wear a quaint striped surcoat, and striped tight legs, and carry halberds like those which are usually shouldered by those theatrical supernumeraries, who never *can* get off the stage fast enough ... I got upon the border of the green carpet, in company with a great many other gentlemen, attired in black, (no other passport is necessary), and stood there at my ease, during the performance of mass. The singers were in a crib of wirework (like a large meat-safe or bird-cage) in one corner; and sang most atrociously. All about the green carpet, there was a slowly moving crowd of people: talking to each other: staring at the Pope through eye-glasses: defrauding one another, in moments of partial curiosity, out of precarious seats on the bases of pillars: and grinning hideously at the ladies.... The next time I saw the cathedral, was some two or three weeks afterwards, when I climbed up into the ball; and then, the hangings being taken down, and the carpet taken up, but all the framework left, the remnants of these decorations looked like an exploded cracker. 99

CHARLES DICKENS, *PICTURES FROM ITALY,*
CHAPMAN AND HALL, LONDON, 1846

THE SISTINE CHAPEL

Stendhal (1783–1842), the writer otherwise known as Henri Beyle, was less impressed by his experience of mass, this time in the Sistine Chapel.

66I am just come from the celebrated *Capella Sestino:* I was present at the Pope's mass, and was in one of the best places to the right, behind Cardinal Gonsalvi. I heard all those famous sopranos of the *Sestino*, never was *charivari* more disgusting; it is the most offensive noise I have heard for ten years. For two hours, that this mass lasted, I passed one and a half in ceaseless astonishment, feeling myself, examining myself, to discover whether I was not ill, or in interrogating my neighbours. Unluckily, they were almost all English, to whom music is a mere dead letter; my interrogations were addressed to their feelings, they answered me by passages from Dr. Burney. 99

STENDHAL, *ROME, NAPLES AND*
FLORENCE IN 1817,
HENRY COLBURN,
LONDON, 1818

A MONSTER CHURCH

It was not so much the grandeur as the size of St Peter's that overwhelmed the narrator of "The Innocents Abroad" by Mark Twain (1835–1910). The book is a humorous account of a naive American tourist traveling round the Mediterranean, and it established Twain's reputation as a leading wit of his day.

❝Of course we have been to the monster Church of St. Peter, frequently. ... When we reached the door, and stood fairly within the church, it was impossible to comprehend that it was a *very* large building. I had to *cipher* a comprehension of it. I had to ransack my memory for some more similes. St. Peter's is bulky. Its height and size would represent two of the Washington capitol set one on top of the other – if the capitol were wider; or two blocks or two blocks and a half of ordinary buildings set one on top of the other. St. Peter's was that large, but it could and would not look so. The trouble was that everything in it and about it was on such a scale of uniform vastness that there were no contrasts to judge by – none but the people, and I had not noticed them. They were insects. The statues of children holding bases of holy water were immense, according to the tables of figures, but so was every thing else around them. The mosaic pictures in the dome were huge, and were made of thousands and thousands of cubes of glass as large as the end of my little finger, but those pictures looked smooth, and gaudy of color, and in good proportion to the dome. Evidently they would not answer to measure by. Away down toward the far end of the church (I thought it was really clear at the far end, but discovered afterward that it was in the centre, under the dome,) stood the thing they call the *baldacchino* – a great bronze pyramidal frame-work like that which upholds a mosquito bar. It only looked like a considerably magnified bedstead – nothing more. Yet I knew it was a good deal more than half as high as Niagara Falls. It was overshadowed by a dome so mighty that its own height was snubbed. The four great square piers or pillars that stand equidistant from each other in the church, and support the roof, I could not work up to their real dimensions by any method of comparison. I knew that the faces of each were about the width of a very large dwelling-house front, (fifty or sixty feet,) and that they were twice as high as an ordinary three-story dwelling, but still they looked small. I tried all the different ways I could think of to compel myself to understand how large St. Peter's was, but with small success. The mosaic portrait of an Apostle who was writing with a pen six feet long seemed only an ordinary Apostle.❞

MARK TWAIN, *THE INNOCENTS ABROAD*, HARTFORD, CONNECTICUT, 1869

LIFE IN ROME

LODGINGS

Lady Mary Wortley Montagu (1689–1762) lived in France and Italy with her ambassador husband for almost twenty-three years and wrote many letters back to her friends and family in England. This extract comes from a letter of October 22, 1740, to the Countess of Pomfret.

66DEAR MADAM, – I flatter myself that your ladyship's goodness will give you some pleasure in hearing that I am safely arrived at Rome. It was a violent transition from your palace and company to be locked up all day with my chambermaid, and sleep at night in a hovel; but my whole life has been in the Pindaric style. I am at present settled in the lodging Sir Francis Dashwood recommended to me. I liked that Mr. Boughton mentioned to me . .. much better; 'tis two zechins per month cheaper, and at least twenty more agreeable; but the landlord would not let it, for a very pleasant reason. It seems your gallant knight used to lie with his wife; and as he had no hopes I would do the same, he resolves to reserve his house for some young man. The only charm belonging to my present habitation is the ceiling, which is finer than that of the gallery; being all painted by the proper hand of Zucchero, in perfect good preservation. I pay as much for this small apartment as your ladyship does for your magnificent palace; 'tis true I have a garden as large as your dressing-room. I walked last night two hours in that of Borghese, which is one of the most delightful I ever saw.99

THE LETTERS AND WORKS OF LADY MARY WORTLEY MONTAGU,
ED. BY LORD WHARNCLIFFE, RICHARD BENTLEY, LONDON, 1837

ROME IN DECAY

In the same year, 1740, Horace Walpole (1717–97) wrote from Rome to his friend Robert West that he found the city and its nobility to be in a state of decay and impecunity.

66I am very glad that I see Rome while it yet exists; before a great number of years are elapsed, I question whether it will be worth seeing. Between the ignorance and poverty of the present Romans, every thing is neglected and falling to decay; the villas are entirely out of repair, and the palaces so ill kept, that half the pictures are spoiled by damp.... The Cardinal Corsini has so thoroughly pushed on the misery of Rome by impoverishing it, that there is no money but paper to be seen. He is reckoned to have amassed three millions of crowns. You may judge of the affluence the nobility live in, when I assure you, that what the chief princes allow for their own eating is a testoon a day; eighteenpence: there are some extend their expense to five pauls, or half a crown: Cardinal Albani is called extravagant for laying out ten pauls for his dinner and supper. You may imagine they never have any entertainments: so far from it, they never have any company. The princesses and duchesses particularly lead the dismallest of lives. Being the posterity of popes, though of worse families than the ancient nobility, they expect greater respect than my ladies the countesses and marquises will pay them; consequently they consort not, but mope in a vast palace with two miserable tapers, and two or three monsignori, whom they are forced to court and humour, that they may not be entirely deserted.99

HORACE WALPOLE, *LETTER TO RICHARD WEST*, 1740

"DIRTY CREATURES"

Another critical view of Romans appears in a letter from Tobias Smollett (1721–71), written in 1765. The English novelist, poet and journalist published a collection of his letters under the title of "Travels through France and Italy". It is an acerbic work which earned him the nickname "Smelfungus" from his contemporaries.

❝Nothing can be more agreeable to the eyes of a stranger, especially in the heats of summer, than the great number of public fountains that appear in every part of Rome, embellished with all the ornaments of sculpture, and pouring forth prodigious quantities of cool, delicious water, brought in aqueducts from different lakes, rivers, and sources, at a considerable distance from the city. These works are the remains of the munificence and industry of the antient Romans, who were extremely delicate in the article of water: but, however, great applause is also due to those beneficent popes who have been at the expence of restoring and repairing those noble channels of health, pleasure, and convenience. This great plenty of water, nevertheless, has not induced the Romans to be cleanly. Their streets, and even their palaces, are disgraced with filth. The noble Piazza Navona, is adorned with three or four fountains, one of which is perhaps the most magnificent in Europe, and all of them discharge vast streams of water: but notwithstanding this provision, the piazza is almost as dirty as West Smithfield, where the cattle are sold in London. The corridores, arcades, and even staircases of their most elegant palaces, are depositories of nastiness, and indeed in summer smell as strong as spirit of hartshorn. I have a great notion that their ancestors were not much more cleanly. If we consider that the city and suburbs of Rome, in the reign of Claudius, contained about seven millions of inhabitants, a number equal at least to the sum total of all the souls in England; that great part of antient Rome was allotted to temples, porticos, basilicæ, theatres, thermæ, circi, public and private walks and gardens, where very few, if any, of this great number lodged; that by far the greater part of those inhabitants were slaves and poor people, who did not enjoy the conveniencies of life; and that the use of linen was scarce known; we must naturally conclude they were strangely crouded together, and that in general they were a very frowzy generation. … What seems to prove, beyond all dispute, that the antient Romans were very dirty creatures, are these two particulars, Vespasian laid a tax upon urine and ordure, on pretence of being at great expence in clearing the streets from such nusances; an imposition which amounted to about fourteen pence a year for every individual; and when Heliogabalus ordered all the cobwebs of the city and suburbs to be collected, they were found to weigh ten thousand pounds. This was intended as a demonstration of the great number of inhabitants; but it was a proof of their dirt, rather than of their populosity. I might likewise add, the delicate custom of taking vomits at each other's houses, when they were invited to dinner, or supper, that they might prepare their stomachs for gormandizing; a beastly proof of their nastiness as well as gluttony.❞

TOBIAS SMOLLETT, *TRAVELS THROUGH FRANCE AND ITALY*, OXFORD UNIVERSITY PRESS, 1907

THE SCENTS OF ROME

Hester Piozzi (1741–1821) married an Italian musician in 1784 amid much opposition from friends and family. Her opinion of Romans was not high, however, and she agrees with Smollett about the odor of the city.

66Nothing can equal the nastiness at one's entrance to this magazine of perfection [the Barberini Palace]; but the Roman nobles are not disgusted with all sorts of scents, it is plain. These are not what we should call perfumes, indeed, but certainly *odori* – of the same nature as those one is obliged to wade through before Trajan's Pillar can be climbed. That the general appearance of a city which contains such treasures should be mean and disgusting, while one literally often walks upon granite and tramples red porphyry under one's feet, is one of the greatest wonders to me in a town of which the wonders seem innumerable; that it should be nasty beyond all telling, all endurance, with such perennial streams of the purest water liberally dispersed and triumphantly scattered all over it, is another unfathomable wonder; that so many poor should be suffered to beg in the streets when not a hand can be got to work in the fields, and that those poor should be permitted to exhibit sights of deformity and degradations of our species, to me unseen till now, at the most solemn moments, and in churches where silver and gold and richly-arrayed priests scarcely suffice to call off attention from the squalid miseries, I do not try to comprehend. That the palaces which taste and expense combine to decorate should look quietly on while common passengers use their noble vestibules, nay stairs, for every nauseous purpose; that princes, whose incomes equal those of our Dukes of Bedford and Marlborough, should suffer their servants to dress other men's dinners for hire, or lend out their equipages for a day's pleasuring, and hang wet rags out of their palace-windows to dry, as at the mean habitation of a pauper, while, looking in at those very windows, nothing is to be seen but proofs of opulence and scenes of splendour, will not undertake to explain. Sure I am that whoever knows Rome will not condemn this *ébauche* of it.99

HESTER PIOZZI, *GLIMPSES OF ITALIAN SOCIETY IN THE 18TH CENTURY*,
SEELEY AND CO., LONDON, 1892

SENSORY PLEASURES
In the 20th century, the air in Rome is full of exhaust fumes but there are many sensory pleasures in store for the visitor, according to William Sansom (1912–76), the English travel writer and novelist.

66Although the traffic in Rome is still so loud that a large aeroplane can be seen passing apparently soundless above, it is not as bad as it was in the era of the scooter and moto; you can still tell what that was like by crossing to the poorer quarter of Trastevere where the scooter tends to survive both in bulk and at speed. Every year, in fact, more Italians own cars; and thus does the traffic get slower and quieter. Huge motionless phalanxes are formed. Meanwhile, through the gas of motorised curses and petrol vapour, we can still get a glimpse of a Barberini bee or two, or of the once avant-garde motifs of a Borromini church; and escape into small and inexpensive restaurants where sucking-lamb with rosemary is a dream (how we all, and the bambino-loving Italians, love eating babies) and where a single wood-strawberry irradiates a whole fruit salad. Alas to report that the Taverna Margutta, friend for years of painters true and false, has now become an antique shop: but oldtimers like Ranieri, the Caffè Greco, and the Casina Valadier with its splendid view over this golden-brown city pimpled with a rich fungus of domes – these continue.The present drive is still towards Trastevere, where Roast Umbrian Pigling and Giant Tyrrhenian Shrimps (not-too-grown-up port and prawns) in a gas-lit atmosphere may well be eaten. One of the troubles about Rome is that the wealth of sight-seeables is so great you cannot take bus or taxi between them, or you would miss one or the other. The only thing is to walk. After a day of the papal renaissance and baroque, and of the great ancient walls of brick which being of brick often look as though they are not ruins but being built now by builders gone on strike – all one desires is a bidet of *caffè granita* to bathe the feet in. **"**

WILLIAM SANSOM, *GRAND TOUR TODAY*,
HOGARTH PRESS, LONDON, 1968

PIGEONS AND RATS
The Italian novelist Italo Calvino (1923–85) writes in his novel "Palomar" about the city's wildlife.

" 'Shoo! Shoo!' Mr Palomar rushes on to the terrace to drive away the pigeons, who eat the leaves of the gazania, riddle the succulent plants with their beaks, cling with their claws to the cascade of morning-glories, peck at the blackberries, devour leaf by leaf the parsley planted in the box near the kitchen, dig and scratch in the flowerpots, spilling dirt and baring the roots, as if the sole purpose of their flights were devastation. The doves whose flying once cheered the city's squares have been followed by a degenerate progeny, filthy and infected, neither domestic nor wild, but integrated into the public institutions and, as such, inextinguishable. The sky of Rome has long since fallen under the dominion of the over-population of these lumpen-fowl, who make life difficult for every other species of bird in the area and oppress the once free and various kingdom of the air with their monotonous, moulting, lead-gray livery.

Trapped between the subterranean hordes of rats and the grievous flight of the pigeons, the ancient city allows itself to be corroded from below and from above, offering no more resistance than it did in the past to the barbarian invasions, as if it saw not the assault of external enemies but the darkest, most congenial impulses of its own inner essence.

The city has also another soul – one of the many – that lives on the harmony between old stones and ever-new vegetation, sharing the favors of the sun. **"**

ITALO CALVINO, *MR PALOMAR,* TRANS. WILLIAM WEAVER,
SECKER & WARBURG, LONDON, 1985

AEDILIS · FAMILIA · GLADIATORIA · PVGNABIT
POMPEIS · PR · K · IVNIAS · VENATIO · ET · VELA ·

VISITING ROME

EXPENSES

Tobias Smollett here gives advice to 18th-century visitors to the city.

❝Having given our names at the gate, we repaired to the dogana, or custom-house, where our trunks and carriage were searched; and here we were surrounded by a number of servitori de piazza, offering their services with the most disagreeable importunity. Though I told them several times I had no occasion for any, three of them took possession of the coach, one mounting before and two of them behind; and thus we proceeded to the Piazza d'Espagna, where the person lived to whose house I was directed. Strangers that come to Rome seldom put up at public inns, but go directly to lodging houses, of which there is great plenty in this quarter. The Piazza d'Espagna is open, airy, and pleasantly situated in a high part of the city immediately under the Colla Pinciana, and adorned with two fine fountains. Here most of the English reside: the apartments are generally commodious and well furnished; and the lodgers are well supplied with provisions and all necessaries of life. But, if I studied œconomy, I would choose another part of the town than the Piazza d'Espagna, which is, besides, at a great distance from the antiquities. For a decent first floor and two bed-chambers on the second, I payed no more than a scudo (five shillings) per day. Our table was plentifully furnished by the landlord for two and thirty pauls, being equal to sixteen shillings. I hired a town-coach at the rate of fourteen pauls, or seven shillings a day; and a servitore di piazza for three pauls, or eighteen-pence. The coachman has also an allowance of two pauls a day. The provisions at Rome are reasonable and good, the vitella mongana, however, which is the most delicate veal I ever tasted, is very dear, being sold for two pauls, or a shilling, the pound. Here are the rich wines of Montepulciano, Montefiascone, and Monte di Dragone; but what we commonly drink at meals is that of Orvieto, a small white wine of an agreeable flavour.❞

TOBIAS SMOLLETT, *TRAVELS THROUGH FRANCE AND ITALY*,
OXFORD UNIVERSITY PRESS, 1907

SIGHTSEEING

William Beckford worried about the number of sights to be seen in Rome and despaired of doing them justice.

❝I absolutely will have no antiquary to go prating from fragment to fragment, and tell me, that were I to stay five years in Rome, I should not see half it contained. The thought alone, of so much to look at, is quite distracting, and makes me resolve to view nothing at all in a scientific way; but straggle and wander about just as the spirit chuses. This evening it led me to the Coliseo, and excited a vehement desire in me to break down and pulverize the whole circle of saints' nests and chapels, which disgrace the arena. You recollect, I dare say, the vile effect of this holy trumpery, and would join with all your heart in kicking them into the Tyber. A few lazy abbots were at their devotion before them; such as would have made a lion's mouth water; fatter I dare say, than any saint in the whole martyrology, and ten times more tantalizing. I looked first, at the dens where wild beasts used to be kept, to divert the magnanimous people of Rome with devastation and murder; then, at the tame cattle before the altars. Heavens! thought I to myself, how times are changed! Could ever Vespasian have imagined his amphitheatre would have been thus inhabited? I passed on, making these reflections, to a dark arcade, overgrown with ilex. In the openings which time and violence have made, a distant grove of cypresses discover themselves; springing from heaps of mouldering ruins, relieved by a clear transparent sky, strewed with a few red clouds. This was the sort of prospect I desired, and I sat down on a shattered frieze to enjoy it … Next, directing my steps to the arch of Constantine, I surveyed the groups of ruins which surrounded me. The cool breeze of the evening played in the beds of canes and oziers, which flourished under the walls of the Coliseo: a cloud of birds were upon the wing to regain their haunts in its crevices; and, except the sound of their flight, all was silent; for happily no carriages were rattling along. I observed the palace and obelisk of Saint John of Lateran, at a distance; but it was too late to take a nearer survey; so returning leisurely home, I traversed the Campo Vaccino, and leaned a moment against one of the columns which supported the temple of Jupiter Stator. Some women were fetching water from the fountain hard by, whilst another group had kindled a fire under the shrubs and twisted fig-trees, which cover the Palatine hill. Innumerable vaults and arches peep out of the vegetation. It was upon these, in all probability, the splendid palace of the Cæsars was raised. Confused fragments of marble, and walls of lofty terraces, are the sole traces of its antient magnificence. A wretched rabble were roasting their chesnuts, on the very spot, perhaps, where Domitian convened a senate, to harangue upon the delicacies of his entertainment. **99**

THE GRAND TOUR OF WILLIAM BECKFORD,
PENGUIN BOOKS, LONDON, 1986

MAJESTY

In 1818 the English poet Percy Bysshe Shelley (1792–1822) left England to settle in Italy. The following extract is from a letter to Thomas Love Peacock in December 1818.

66I have seen the ruins of Rome, the Vatican, St. Peter's, and all the miracles of ancient and modern art contained in that majestic city. The impression of it exceeds anything I have ever experienced in my travels.… We visited the Forum and the ruins of the Coliseum every day. The Coliseum is unlike any work of human hands I ever saw before. It is of enormous height and circuit, and the arches built of massy stones are piled on one another, and jut into the blue air, shattered into the forms of overhanging rocks. It has been changed by time into the image of an amphitheatre of rocky hills overgrown by the wild olive, the myrtle, and the fig-tree, and threaded by little paths, which wind among its ruined stairs and immeasurable galleries.… The interior is all ruin. I can scarcely believe that when encrusted with Dorian marble and ornamented by columns of Egyptian granite, its effect could have been so sublime and so impressive as in its present state. It is open to the sky, and it was the clear and sunny weather of the end of November in this climate when we visited it, day after day. **99**

LETTERS OF PERCY BYSSHE
SHELLEY, EDITED BY R.
INGPEN, LONDON, 1909

17TH-CENTURY ROME

The influence of the 17th century should not be overlooked by visitors to Rome, according to Edith Wharton (1862–1937), the American novelist and short-story writer.

❝It might be well for the purist to consider what would be lost if the seventeenth-century Rome which he affects to ignore were actually blotted out. The Spanish Steps would of course disappear, with the palace of the Propaganda; so would the glorious Barberini palace, and Bernini's neighbouring fountain of the Triton; the via delle Quattro Fontane, with its dripping river-gods emerging from their grottoes, and Borromini's fantastic church of San Carlo at the head of the street, a kaleidoscope of whirling line and ornament, offset by the delicately classical circular cortile of the adjoining monastery. On the Quirinal hill, the palace of the Consulta would go, and the central portal of the Quirinal (a work of Bernini's), as well as the splendid gateway of the Colonna gardens. The Colonna palace itself, dull and monotonous without, but within the very model of a magnificent pleasure-house, would likewise be effaced; so would many of the most characteristic buildings of the Corso – San Marcello, the Gesù, the Sciarra and Doria palaces, and the great Roman College. Gone, too, would be the Fountain of Trevi, and Lunghi's gay little church of San Vincenzo ed Anastasio, which faces it so charmingly across the square; gone the pillared court-yard and great painted galleries of the Borghese palace, and the Fontana dei Termini with its beautiful group of adjoining churches; the great fountain of the piazza Navona, Lunghi's stately façade of the Chiesa Nuova, and Borromini's Oratory of San Filippo Neri... But even those who remain unconverted, who cannot effect the transference of artistic and historic sympathy necessary to a real understanding of seventeenth-century architecture, should at least realize that the Rome which excites a passion of devotion such as no other city can inspire, the Rome for which travellers pine in absence, and to which they return again and again with the fresh ardour of discovery, is, externally at least, in great part the creation of the seventeenth century.❞

EDITH WHARTON, *ITALIAN BACKGROUNDS*,
MACMILLAN & CO., LONDON, 1905

OFF-SEASON

John Cheever (1912–82) recommended visiting Rome out of season – but cautioned readers to take an umbrella.

❝I still cook breakfast in my underwear in this Palace of Justice or Haunted Public Library and at nightfall the combination of dim-lamps and Roman gin makes me feel very peculiar. The gin is terrible. They make it in Torino. The city seems mercurial and while it is lovely in the sun with the fountains sparkling it looks, in the rain, like that old movie-shot: European Capital On Eve Of War. Everyone carries a wet umbrella, there are anxious crowds around every news stand, the consulate ante-rooms are full of Egyptian evacuees asking for news or mail, and the atmosphere of anxiety and gloom is dense. Then the sun comes out and everything seems fine. This place isn't much good for entertaining because you can't HEAR anybody or else they echo. I pretend to work in the mornings and visit ruins in the afternoon. Castel San Angelo is my favorite but I like the Forum which is very near here. It's a good time of year for sight-seeing because we seem to be the only tourists left. Now and then you run into a cluster of determined Germans but they are infrequent and seem autumnal and a little sad like the honking of geese. The art galleries are empty and so dark that you can walk for a mile without picking out the shape of a foot.**99**

THE LETTERS OF JOHN CHEEVER, SIMON & SCHUSTER, NEW YORK, 1988

TOMBS

Bernard Berenson (1865–1959), the American art historian and philosopher, recommends a visit to Santa Maria del Popolo. The following diary entries were written on November 7, 1952, and October 31, 1950.

66An hour in Santa Maria del Popolo. Poked about in corridors, sacristies, closets, as well as in the church itself. What variety! Early and late Renaissance tombs, two of them done by the incumbent in his lifetime. They knew better than to trust their heirs. Choir with ceiling by Pinturicchio at his best, and tombs by Andrea Sansovino anticipating schemes adopted later by Michelangelo for the sepulchre of Julius II at San Pietro in Vincoli. The chapel with frescoes by Pinturicchio again at his best; the recumbent bronze by Vecchietta, the two Caravaggios placed in such a way as to suggest that those who ordered them did not think too highly of them. The charming Jonah in the Chigi Chapel delighted me again. But what impressed me most this time was the tomb of an Odescalchi lady, who died at twenty-two in her third childbirth, made in 1772 or thereabouts. That such a masterpiece, rivalling the best Chinese art for expression of energy in leaves, in the eagle, the tree trunk, the sweep of the drapery, not to speak of the colour, had been done so late, only just before the collapse into the 'art nouveau' which we know as 'Empire', amazed me.**99**

66 I first came to Rome in the autumn of 1888 and spent the following months on my feet from early morning till bedtime....Except for [a] group of artists I knew nobody, nor did it occur to me to want to know anybody. Looking was enough and reading, but mostly looking. Here, as in Paris and London, I lived more inwardly than outwardly, although I was active enough. What went on inside me, not always perceived by me, counted as real and satisfactory.**99**

BERNARD BERENSON, *THE PASSIONATE SIGHTSEER*,
THAMES & HUDSON, LONDON, 1960

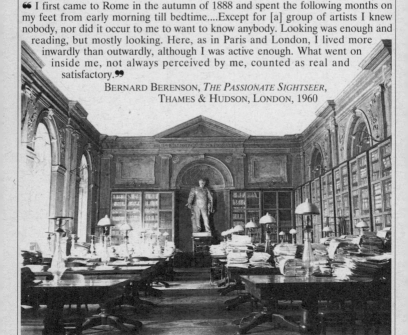

ITINERARIES

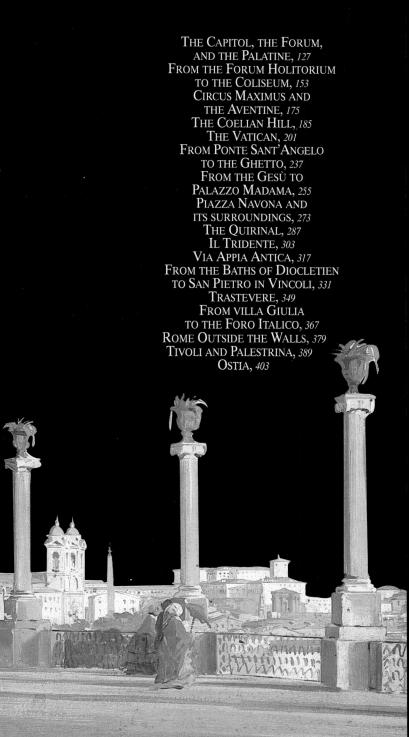

▲ Rome seen from the Janiculum.

▲ Via della Conciliazione.

The Palazzo della Civiltà del Lavoro in EUR. ▼

▲ Ponte Vittorio Emanuele II.

▲ The Coliseum.

The Fountain of Neptune in Piazza Navona. ▼

▲ An ice-cream shop in Trastevere.

▲ Metro sign.   Monks and nuns at the Vatican. ▼

▲ Market stall near Campo de' Fiori.

▲ The Campo de' Fiori flower market.   Carabinieri. ▼

▲ Via Appia Antica.

The colors of Rome. ▼

▼ Ecclesiastical clothes shop at the Vatican.

THE CAPITOL, THE FORUM AND THE PALATINE

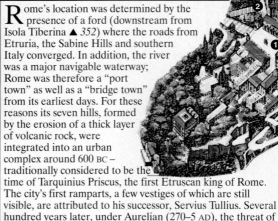

THE TARPEIAN ROCK
Tarpeia was seduced by King Titus Tatius, who besieged the Capitol after the rape of the Sabine women ▲ *177*. She offered to

open the gates of the citadel in exchange for his favors. Tatius feigned consent, but once inside got his soldiers to crush her to death with their shields. The rock from which traitors were hurled to death was thus called the Tarpeian Rock.

Rome's location was determined by the presence of a ford (downstream from Isola Tiberina ▲ *352*) where the roads from Etruria, the Sabine Hills and southern Italy converged. In addition, the river was a major navigable waterway; Rome was therefore a "port town" as well as a "bridge town" from its earliest days. For these reasons its seven hills, formed by the erosion of a thick layer of volcanic rock, were integrated into an urban complex around 600 BC – traditionally considered to be the time of Tarquinius Priscus, the first Etruscan king of Rome. The city's first ramparts, a few vestiges of which are still visible, are attributed to his successor, Servius Tullius. Several hundred years later, under Aurelian (270–5 AD), the threat of barbarian invasions made the construction of new fortifications necessary; large sections of his 12-mile wall have been preserved.

THE CAPITOL (CAMPIDOGLIO)

The hill has two crests separated by a depression (the Asylum), which is now Piazza del Campidoglio. On the northern summit the *arx* ("fortress"), a kind of fortified refuge, was dominated by the Temple of Juno Moneta, standing near the Tarpeian Rock (or Saxum). On the southern summit stood the Temple of Jupiter Capitolinus, the largest temple in Rome, reputedly founded by Tarquinius Priscus though only inaugurated at the beginning of the Republic. Some vestiges of its foundations can still be seen beneath the Palazzo dei Conservatori, while under the Palazzo Senatorio there are remains of the Temple of Veiovis, a very ancient evil deity. Other gods had sanctuaries on the hill, but almost nothing is left of these. Apart from its religious function, the Capitol was the center of political power; part of the state archives were kept in the Tabularium, which dominated the Forum. The Capitol was also the center for the most important ceremonies, such as the investiture of the consuls on January 1, and above all the Triumph. This supreme honor, given to generals under the Republic and later to the emperors, was the occasion for a long procession leading to the steps of the Temple of Jupiter. The Capitol's importance has endured throughout the history of Rome. In the Middle Ages the Tabularium, which had been fortified by Rome's powerful noble families, became the seat of the new Roman Senate. This hill houses the main municipal institutions, and it has been a center for Roman art since the 16th century.

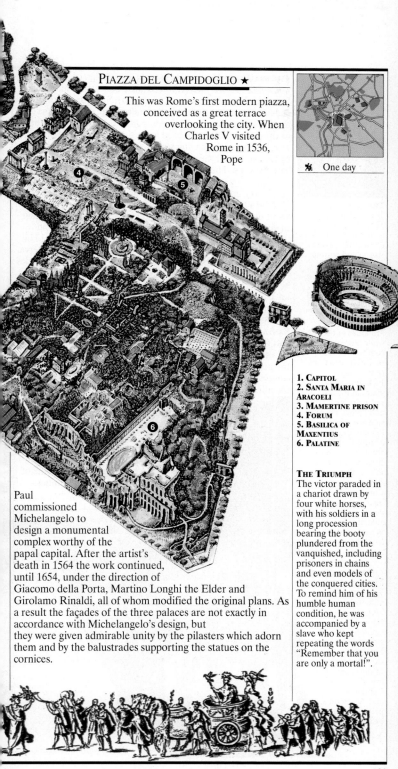

PIAZZA DEL CAMPIDOGLIO ★

This was Rome's first modern piazza, conceived as a great terrace overlooking the city. When Charles V visited Rome in 1536, Pope

✻ One day

1. **Capitol**
2. **Santa Maria in Aracoeli**
3. **Mamertine prison**
4. **Forum**
5. **Basilica of Maxentius**
6. **Palatine**

THE TRIUMPH
The victor paraded in a chariot drawn by four white horses, with his soldiers in a long procession bearing the booty plundered from the vanquished, including prisoners in chains and even models of the conquered cities. To remind him of his humble human condition, he was accompanied by a slave who kept repeating the words "Remember that you are only a mortal!".

Paul commissioned Michelangelo to design a monumental complex worthy of the papal capital. After the artist's death in 1564 the work continued, until 1654, under the direction of Giacomo della Porta, Martino Longhi the Elder and Girolamo Rinaldi, all of whom modified the original plans. As a result the façades of the three palaces are not exactly in accordance with Michelangelo's design, but they were given admirable unity by the pilasters which adorn them and by the balustrades supporting the statues on the cornices.

THE STEPS
The *cordonata*, Michelangelo's monumental stairway, leads to the piazza. Its top and bottom are adorned with pairs of ancient statues. Egyptian basalt lions from the Temple of Isis in the Campus Martius crown the twin fountains at the base, while marble Roman copies of Greek figures from a temple in the Circus Flaminius stand guard at the top, representing Castor and Pollux. On either side are the two marble Trophies of Marius that came from Piazza Vittorio Emanuele II ▲ 340. Finally there are two statues of Constantine, flanked by milestones (the columns used on all Roman roads to indicate distances from the Forum) from the Via Appia.

THE STATUE OF MARCUS AURELIUS
This remarkable equestrian statue was long thought to represent Constantine and stood at the Lateran throughout the Middle Ages. It was brought to the Capitol in 1538 and placed on a pedestal designed by Michelangelo.

THE STATUE OF MARCUS AURELIUS. The design of the piazza was almost entirely determined by the equestrian statue of Emperor Marcus Aurelius (161–80 AD). Since its restoration ● *54* at the end of the 1980s it stands in one of the rooms of the Capitoline Museum. This has altered the overall harmony of the piazza, because it used to be the focal point of both the oval pattern of the paving stones and the trapezium formed by the façades of the palaces.

THE PALACES. The PALAZZO SENATORIO stands at the back of the piazza. Its left wing incorporates the tower of Martin V (1417–31), and the right wing one of Boniface IX's (1389–1404) towers. The façade is aligned with the central Torre dei Longhi (1582) and Michelangelo's twin converging flights of steps. In front of the steps statues of the Nile and the Tiber from the Baths of Constantine on the Quirinal Hill stand on either side of an ancient porphyry statue of Minerva, transformed into the goddess Rome. The symmetrical façades of the PALAZZO DEI CONSERVATORI (on the right), rebuilt between 1564 and 1576, and the CAPITOLINE MUSEUM (on the left), built between 1603 and 1655, conceal buildings of very different dimensions. (Go up the short flight of steps to the right of the Capitoline Museum).

SANTA MARIA IN ARACOELI ★. According to legend the Virgin and Child appeared to the Emperor Augustus, who then built an altar (*ara*) here. In the 13th century the Franciscans built the present church, which became the official church of the *comune* of Rome. Above the door is a beautiful mosaic of the Cavallini school portraying the *Virgin and Child*. At the end of the Black Death, in 1348, the Roman people built the steep monumental flight of marble steps in front of the church, which is dedicated to the Virgin Mary. The church served as the burial place of many members of noble Roman families, whose carved

tombstones are embedded in a fine Cosmatesque ● 76 pavement dating from the 13th to 14th century. Not to be missed is the Chapel of San Bernardino di Siena (first on the right), decorated with splendid frescoes by Pinturicchio around 1486. Rome's most venerated statue of the Child Jesus (15th century) is preserved in a small chapel beside the sacristy. (Descend the Via del Campidoglio, to the right of the Palazzo Senatorio, to enjoy a magnificent view of the Forum and the Palatine Hill. Returning to the other side of the Palazzo Senatorio, go down the steps toward the Forum).

THE TULLIANUM OR MAMERTINE PRISON. The Church of San Giuseppe dei Falegnami, which has a travertine façade dating from the beginning of the Imperial period, is built over a Roman dungeon consisting of two rooms. The circular hole in the stone floor of the upper room was originally the only access to the prison below. This was where prisoners of State, such as Jugurtha and Vercingetorix, were incarcerated and strangled; but the medieval legend claiming that St Peter was imprisoned here is unfounded.

SANTI LUCA E MARTINA. In 1588 the Church of Santa Martina was given to the Accademia di San Luca ▲ 299, and thus acquired the name of the patron saint of the arts. The discovery of the body of St Martin during restoration work in 1634 by Pietro da Cortona, the "prince" of the academy, excited the interest of Pope Urban VIII and his nephew, Cardinal Francesco Barberini. The two prelates therefore commissioned him to build a new church on the site of the old one. Despite its sober decoration, this is one of Rome's finest 17th-century churches. It was designed in the form of a Greek cross, but its façade was widened to the same breadth as the transept. (The entrance to the Forum is in Via dei Fori Imperiali.)

In the courtyard of the Palazzo dei Conservatori stand fragments of a colossal statute of Constantine found at the Basilica of Maxentius ▲ 145 in 1487. The head measures 8½ feet, the foot 6½ feet.

THE LEGEND OF THE "SANTO BAMBINO"
This statue of the Child Jesus, said by some to be made of olive wood from the Garden of Gethsemane and believed by others to be the work of a saint, is endowed with miraculous powers. In Rome beautiful children are still referred to as "*bello come il pupo dell'Aracoeli*" (pretty as the Aracoeli babe).

131

The Museo Capitolino – the oldest museum in Europe – and the Palazzo dei Conservatori, with its various sections (the Sale dei Conservatori, Museo del Palazzo dei Conservatori, Braccio Nuovo, Museo Nuovo and Pinacoteca), contain rich collections of classical antiquities as well as some major European paintings from the 16th and 17th centuries.

CONSTANTINE
This colossal head (8 feet 6 inches high) from the Basilica of Maxentius belonged to a seated figure of the Emperor (325–6 AD).

FUNERARY STELE
In Greece it was customary to adorn tombs with stelae depicting the deceased in the company of a friend or relative. Such is the role of the young girl holding a bird belonging to the deceased in this 5th-century fragment.

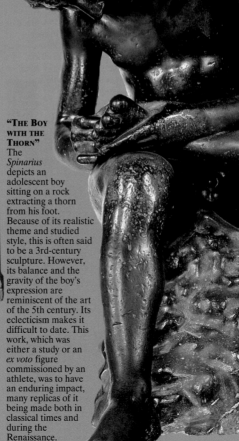

"THE BOY WITH THE THORN"
The *Spinarius* depicts an adolescent boy sitting on a rock extracting a thorn from his foot. Because of its realistic theme and studied style, this is often said to be a 3rd-century sculpture. However, its balance and the gravity of the boy's expression are reminiscent of the art of the 5th century. Its eclecticism makes it difficult to date. This work, which was either a study or an *ex voto* figure commissioned by an athlete, was to have an enduring impact, many replicas of it being made both in classical times and during the Renaissance.

BUST OF COMMODUS
The artist applied great technical virtuosity in portraying the emperor who, at the end of his reign, saw himself as Hercules. This bust bearing the emblems of the "Conqueror of the World" (the lion skin and club) seems to float weightlessly above two cornucopias, borne by Victories, surmounting a celestial globe.

"BUST OF JUNIUS BRUTUS"
Ivory-and-glass inlays give a lifelike look to the eyes of this 3rd-century head (erroneously identified as that of L. Junius Brutus, Rome's first consul), supported on a modern bust. The calm, strict facial expression nevertheless corresponds to the ideal image of a man of the Roman Republic.

THE WOLF OF THE CAPITOL
This bronze from the early 5th century BC portrays the animal totem of Rome and illustrates one of the city's best-known legends. Its naturalism combines with a keen abstract sensitivity: the dilated nostrils, the wide-open eyes and the three furrows on the forehead convey a strong sense of realism, whereas the rest of the body is highly stylized. The twins, Romulus and Remus, were Renaissance additions.

"The Triumph of Bacchus"
Among the works painted by Pietro da Cortona around 1620 for his patron, the Marchese Sacchetti, this is probably the one most clearly influenced by Titian's *Bacchanals* – a series of paintings that da Cortona had admired when they were acquired by Cardinal Ludovisi.

"The Dying Gaul"
Hellenistic art was prone to the representation of certain ethnic types, such as the Galatian warriors with rough features and thick bushy hair that the sculptors of Pergamon, in Asia Minor, excelled in depicting. This wounded Gaul, with his poignant expression, corresponds exactly to the dominant style of the 3rd century BC. The statue was discovered in the gardens of Villa Ludovisi.

"THE CAPITOLINE VENUS"
This figure of a goddess surprised while
bathing, from the 2nd century AD, is one of
the many works derived from the famous
Aphrodite of Cnidus sculpted by
Praxiteles in the 4th century BC.

"ST JOHN THE BAPTIST"
Caravaggio probably painted this work
between 1600 and 1603. Leonardo da
Vinci had already portrayed John the
Baptist as a disturbing adolescent in his
painting that now hangs in the Louvre,
but Caravaggio here removes every
religious aspect from the theme. It is no
doubt one of the works he painted using
a live model in a dark studio lit only by a
lamp hanging from the ceiling.

"DOVES DRINKING"
This mosaic panel ▲ *397* from Hadrian's villa is
a copy of a motif from a famous mosaic by
Sosias of Pergamon. It reveals how persistent
the taste for Hellenistic art was in ancient
Rome.

"It appears that the Forum was still in its full splendor in the 7th century, but that in 1084…these buildings were… completely in ruins … Subsequently the Forum became a cattle market and came to be known by the vile name of

The formation of the Forum valley was due to the erosion of a bank of volcanic tufa by a stream named the Velabrum, which meandered between the Palatine and Capitoline hills toward the Tiber. Used as a necropolis in the Iron Age (10th to 9th century BC), this marshy area was drained at the beginning of the rule of the Etruscan kings, when Tarquinius Priscus is said to have channeled the waters of the Velabrum in order to implement a series of public works, the most important being the city's huge sewer, the *cloaca maxima* ● 69. Rome then began to develop on this site, which remained its political, administrative and religious center until the end of the Republican period. During the Middle Ages, when the population

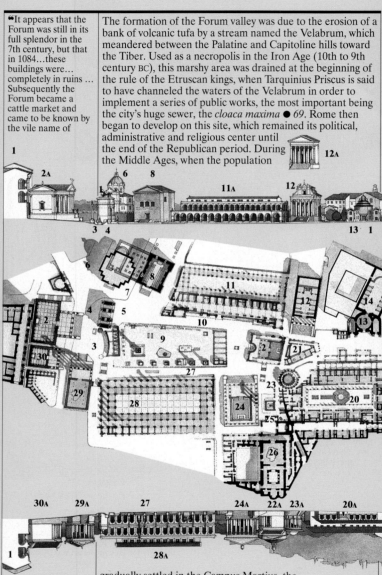

gradually settled in the Campus Martius, the Forum – although strewn with debris – came to be used as grazing land for cattle and acquired the name of *Campo Vaccino* ("the cattle field"). It was not until the 19th century that archeologists began to unearth the half-buried ruins, digging sometimes as deep as 65 feet.

Campo Vaccino, which it retained up to the time of the excavations ordered by Napoleon."
Stendhal, *Promenades dans Rome*

BASILICA AEMILIA

This ancient basilica was a large covered space, divided into aisles, that provided shelter during the rainy season for the

Forum's principal activities: legal, political and economic. Later, Christian churches were built according to this design. The basilica was founded by the censors Marcus Aemilius Lepidus and Marcus Fulvius Nobilior. After restorations funded by the Aemilii family, under Augustus it was given the form we see today. On the eastern side there is a dedication to Augustus' grandson, which reads "Lucius Caesar, prince of youth". The basilica was burned down in 410 AD, but was restored, for the last time,

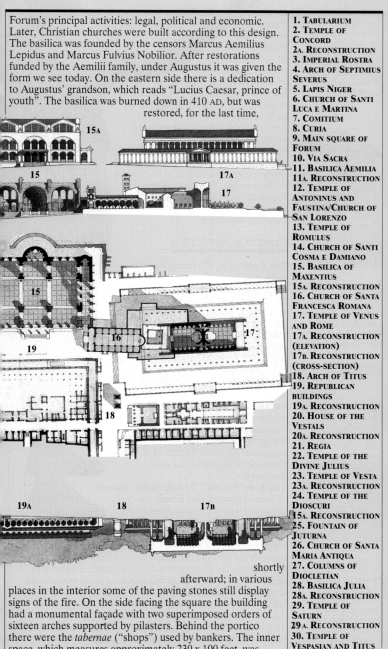

1. TABULARIUM
2. TEMPLE OF CONCORD
2A. RECONSTRUCTION
3. IMPERIAL ROSTRA
4. ARCH OF SEPTIMIUS SEVERUS
5. LAPIS NIGER
6. CHURCH OF SANTI LUCA E MARTINA
7. COMITIUM
8. CURIA
9. MAIN SQUARE OF FORUM
10. VIA SACRA
11. BASILICA AEMILIA
11A. RECONSTRUCTION
12. TEMPLE OF ANTONINUS AND FAUSTINA/CHURCH OF SAN LORENZO
13. TEMPLE OF ROMULUS
14. CHURCH OF SANTI COSMA E DAMIANO
15. BASILICA OF MAXENTIUS
15A. RECONSTRUCTION
16. CHURCH OF SANTA FRANCESCA ROMANA
17. TEMPLE OF VENUS AND ROME
17A. RECONSTRUCTION (ELEVATION)
17B. RECONSTRUCTION (CROSS-SECTION)
18. ARCH OF TITUS
19. REPUBLICAN BUILDINGS
19A. RECONSTRUCTION
20. HOUSE OF THE VESTALS
20A. RECONSTRUCTION
21. REGIA
22. TEMPLE OF THE DIVINE JULIUS
23. TEMPLE OF VESTA
23A. RECONSTRUCTION
24. TEMPLE OF THE DIOSCURI
15A. RECONSTRUCTION
25. FOUNTAIN OF JUTURNA
26. CHURCH OF SANTA MARIA ANTIQUA
27. COLUMNS OF DIOCLETIAN
28. BASILICA JULIA
28A. RECONSTRUCTION
29. TEMPLE OF SATURN
29A. RECONSTRUCTION
30. TEMPLE OF VESPASIAN AND TITUS
30A. RECONSTRUCTION

shortly afterward; in various places in the interior some of the paving stones still display signs of the fire. On the side facing the square the building had a monumental façade with two superimposed orders of sixteen arches supported by pilasters. Behind the portico there were the *tabernae* ("shops") used by bankers. The inner space, which measures approximately 230 x 100 feet, was divided into four aisles by "African" marble columns that supported the roof. Where the entrance used to stand, one can see a bas-relief illustrating the origins of Rome, which decorated the basilica in the 1st century BC.

THE CURIA

Slabs of marble and stucco decorated the main façade of Julius Caesar's Curia, which replaced the Curia Hostilia, destroyed by fire in 52 BC.

THE BAS-RELIEFS OF THE CURIA

The incomplete relief on the left shows the cancellation of fiscal debts. The citizens' records were burned

in the Emperor's presence. The relief on the right (above) shows the institution of the *alimenta*, whereby the interest from agricultural loans to landowners was distributed to poor children. These scenes are set in the Forum and so provide a rare contemporary image of it.

Near the steps of the basilica, to the west, there is a circular marble base which is all that remains of the SANCTUARY OF VENUS CLOACINA, built over the Forum's opening to the *cloaca maxima* ● *69* ▲ *136*. In the Argiletum (the street that separates the basilica and the Curia) stood the famous little TEMPLE OF JANUS, one of the oldest Roman deities, whose two-headed statue was placed in the middle of this passage. The doors of this sanctuary, of which nothing remains, were left open at times of war and closed in peacetime.

COMITIUM AND CURIA

THE COMITIUM. Mirroring Republican institutional principles ● *34*, the Comitium provided circular step-seating for the people who gathered to hear the speeches of legislators. They spoke from a platform known as the Rostra which, in commemoration of the naval victory at Antium (338 BC), was decorated with the bronze figureheads (*rostra*) seized from the vanquished fleet. On the opposite side of the Comitium was the Curia, one of the Senate's meeting places. With the end of the Republic, when electoral meetings were moved to the Campus Martius and Caesar's construction work began, this group of buildings became gradually less important. Between 54 and 44 BC the old Curia Hostilia and Rostra were destroyed.

THE LAPIS NIGER. The only visible remains of the old Comitium is a black marble pavement with a white marble border. The Roman author Festus mentions the *niger lapis ad Comitio* ("the black stone of the Comitium") as a funerary place, associated with the death of Romulus. Digs beneath the paving have revealed ruins from the 6th century BC, including an altar, part of a column, and a fragment of stone with an archaic Latin inscription in boustrophedonic script (running alternately from left to right and from right to left), which appears to have been the ritual and sacrificial rules of a sanctuary dedicated to Vulcan.

THE CURIA. The Senate could hold meetings in any temple, but its official seat was the Curia. The large brick building between the Argiletum and the Comitium is the Curia Julia, built by Julius Caesar in order to replace the old one and also to suit the design of his own forum, which Augustus inaugurated in 29 BC. Its present appearance is due to restorations carried out by Diocletian after a fire in 283 AD.

The two bronze panels that were removed to make the main doors of the Lateran Basilica ▲ *198* in the 17th century date from this period, as does the marble paving. Transformed into the Church of Sant'Adriano during the 7th century, the Curia was once again restored in 1930. Its dimensions (approximately 70 feet high, 60 feet wide and 90 feet long) correspond to the proportions recommended by Vitruvius ● *94*, the famous architect of the Augustan period. The grandiose interior has a flat ceiling (today's wooden structure is modern). On the left and right there are three low, wide steps on which seats for three to six hundred senators were arranged. Between the two doors at the back there is a large podium, from which the assemblies were directed. Its base was probably adorned with a statue of Victory, placed there by Octavian before he became the Emperor Augustus. The two bas-reliefs illustrating Trajan's Imperial munificence were found in the middle of the Forum; they date from the early 2nd century AD.

AT THE FOOT OF THE CAPITOL

THE ARCH OF SEPTIMIUS SEVERUS. Built in 203 AD, this arch is nearly 70 feet high. On both sides identical monumental inscriptions dedicate it to the Emperor Septimius Severus and his son Caracalla; the fourth line, which was erased and rewritten, gave the name of Septimius' other son, Geta, assassinated by his brother after their father's death. The bases of the columns illustrate the salient events of two victorious campaigns in the Middle East, including Roman soldiers carrying off Parthian prisoners.

SEPTIMIUS SEVERUS (193–211 AD) Born in Africa, he married a Syrian noblewoman, Julia Domna. They had two sons, Caracalla and Geta.

SEPTIMIUS' ARCH Of the numerous bas-reliefs that feature on this arch, two splendid panels over the minor arches record the most memorable moments from Septimius' Parthian expeditions: the Roman army departs, the Emperor speaks, enemy cities are captured… In the center of the major arch stands Mars, surrounded by winged Victories with the four seasons at their feet.

AT THE FOOT OF THE CAPITOL
The achievement of this magnificent reconstruction made between 1865 and 1866 was its appreciation of the spatial relationship between the monuments, virtually stacked together, with the Arch of Septimius Severus and the temples of Concord, Vespasian and Saturn dominated by the massive Tabularium.

THE IMPERIAL ROSTRA. After the Comitium was demolished ▲ *138*, new semicircular Rostra were built at the northwest end of the Forum and inaugurated by Mark Antony between 45 and 44 BC, not long before Julius Caesar's death. A rectilinear structure was later added by Augustus, no doubt in an attempt to obliterate the memory of his former rival and of the purges of 43 AD during which the heads of those executed, including Cicero's, were displayed there. At the end of the Rostra that is nearest to the arch there is a circular brick base known as the *umbilicum urbis* ("the navel of the city"), which symbolized the center of Rome. At the other end of the hemicycle are the remains of the *milliarium aureum*, a small monument erected by Augustus to mark the ideal point of convergence of the Imperial highways and to measure distances from Rome.

TEMPLE OF SATURN. Erected in the earliest Republican times, around 498 BC, this temple served as Rome's state treasury and records office (*aerarium*). It was completely rebuilt in 42 BC at Munatius Plancus' request, and was again restored after being damaged in Carinus' fire in 283 AD. The anniversary of the temple's dedication was accompanied by the unbridled merrymaking of the Saturnalia, around December 17. On this date, which marked the end of the solar year, social roles were inverted and slaves were served by their masters.

PORTICO OF THE DEI CONSENTES. In 1834 the remains of a portico with columns were discovered in front of an edifice consisting of eight rooms built in brick. It was probably part of the monument that housed the gilded statues of the *dei consentes*. These deities, six male and six female, may date back to the twelve gods that the Etruscans believed Jupiter consulted. Alternatively they may have been the Roman version of the Greek *dodekatheon*: Jupiter, Neptune, Mars, Apollo, Vulcan, Mercury, Juno, Minerva, Diana, Venus, Vesta and Ceres.

THE TEMPLE OF VESPASIAN AND TITUS. This temple dedicated to Vespasian and the Divine Titus (it was customary to worship emperors as gods after they died) was restored under Septimius Severus and Caracalla. Its façade had six columns. All that remains are three marble Corinthian columns supporting a fragment of the architrave, on which the inscription [*R*]*estituer*[*unt*] and a bas-relief showing instruments of sacrifice can be seen. The temple was faced with white marble.

THE TEMPLE OF CONCORD. Founded by Camillus in 367 BC to commemorate the end of the struggle between the plebeians and the patricians, under the Republic this temple was frequently used for meetings of the Senate. Between 7 BC and 10 AD it was restored by Tiberius thanks to booty plundered from the Germans. It contained many works of art, and in Imperial times became a sort of museum.

THE CENTRAL PART OF THE FORUM

PHOCAS' COLUMN AND THE LACUS CURTIUS. The paving of the Forum we see today is dated by a large, partially restored inscription near Phocas' Column that reads: *L. Naevius Surdinus pr*[*aetor*] (9 BC). This column, which stands on a stepped pedestal in front of the Rostra, was dedicated to the Byzantine Emperor Phocas in 608 AD and was the last commemorative monument to be built in the Forum. Slightly to the east is a circular base with a central opening known as the Lacus Curtius. This has given rise to several legends and was originally considered to be the place where the Sabine chief Mettus Curtius was swallowed up, together with his horse, during the legendary Sabine-Roman conflict. Although the original bas-relief on Greek marble illustrating the story is now in the Capitoline Museum, a cast of it can be seen.

BASILICA JULIA. Between Vicus Jugarius and Vicus Tuscus foundation stones and fragments of columns show the position of the Basilica Julia, built by Julius Caesar and Augustus on the site of the Basilica Sempronia (founded by the father of the Gracchi in 170 BC). Although Diocletian had it restored in the 3rd century, the repeated sacking of Rome left almost nothing of this ancient building. Even the brick pillars we see today are 19th-century reconstructions.

THE TABULARIUM
At the end of the Forum one can still see the enormous tufa substructure of the Tabularium, surmounted by a gallery of arches framed by Doric pillars.

CASTOR AND POLLUX
The *equites* (knights) regarded the Dioscuri as their patrons and regularly celebrated their feast on July 15.

Cicero delivered his fourth tirade against Catilina in the Temple of Concord in 63 BC.

The Temple of the Dioscuri.

THE FOUNTAIN OF JUTURNA
The nymph Juturna was famous for her beauty. To show his love for her, Jupiter

THE TEMPLE OF THE DIOSCURI. To the east of the Vicus Tuscus there are three Corinthian columns belonging to the Temple of the Dioscuri (Castor and Pollux), whose cult spread to Rome from Greece at the beginning of the 5th century BC. According to the legend, during the Battle of Lake Regillus (499 BC) between the Romans and the Latins, two mysterious horsemen led the Romans to victory. Soon afterward the same two figures were seen taking their horses to drink at the Fountain of Juturna – then, having proclaimed the Roman victory, they disappeared. The Roman people recognized them as the Dioscuri. Their temple was built in the 5th century BC and restored by Tiberius.

THE FOUNTAIN OF JUTURNA. Before the building of the Aqua Appia, Rome's first aqueduct, the Roman population drew water from the Tiber, wells and a few rare springs. The most important of these was at the foot of the Palatine Hill. It was deified as Juturna, the sister of the Dioscuri, who like all water goddesses was believed to have healing properties. At the center of its square marble-faced basin stood a rectangular pedestal, which supported the statue of the Dioscuri found lying in pieces in the basin. The sculptured group can now be seen in the Forum's antiquarium. Not far away is a small temple dedicated to Juturna. Behind the fountain was the *statio aquarum* (the "aqueduct office"), which was transferred to the Campus Martius in 328 AD.

THE ORATORY OF THE FORTY MARTYRS. This room, dating back to Trajan's times, was transformed into an oratory by the addition of an apse. On the rear wall a fresco, probably painted in the 8th century AD, portrays the martyrdom of forty Christian soldiers during Diocletian's persecutions at the end of the 3rd century.

DOMITIAN'S BUILDINGS AND THE CHURCH OF SANTA MARIA ANTIQUA. An important group of buildings stands to the south of the Fountain of Juturna: a portico facing the Forum, shops on the Vicus Tuscus,

granted her immortality and gave her power over the springs of Latium. Virgil cast her as the "divine sister of Turnus", the enemy of Aeneas, and describes her role in the conflict between them. Another legend makes her the wife of Janus and mother of Fontus, the god of springs.

and a large brick hall originally covered by a vault. To the east, other rooms adjoin a covered ramp leading to the Imperial palaces of the Palatine. This complex was long thought to have been a monumental porch belonging to the palaces, but it is more likely to have been the Athenaeum, a sort of university created by Hadrian. The CHURCH OF SANTA MARIA ANTIQUA was built here in the 6th century; its wall paintings dating from the 8th century, applied in different layers, are a unique source of information on Rome in the early Middle Ages. The oldest paintings to be seen date from the period of Pope John VII (705–7), who resided in the Imperial palace. To the south of this church are the remains of the HORREA AGRIPPIANA, grain stores built by Agrippa, Augustus' friend and son-in-law. The CHURCH OF SAN TEODORO is also in this area, although its entrance is just outside the Forum.

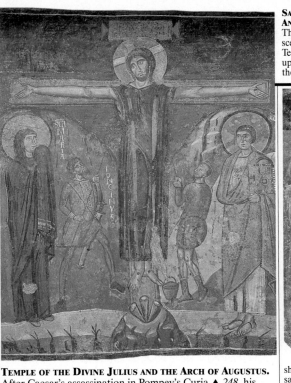

Santa Maria Antiqua.
The left aisle has scenes from the Old Testament in the upper section, while the scenes below

Temple of the Divine Julius and the Arch of Augustus.
After Caesar's assassination in Pompey's Curia ▲ *248*, his body was brought to the Forum and cremated. A column with the inscription *Parenti patriae* ("To the father of the nation") and a temple, dedicated by Augustus in 29 BC, were erected on this spot. This was the first posthumous deification in Rome, but all that has survived of the temple are parts of the podium and of the tribune built in front of it to display the figureheads of Anthony and Cleopatra's fleet, defeated by Octavian at Actium in 31 BC. Beside the temple lie the scant remains of the Arch of Augustus. This had three openings and is almost certainly the monument built by the Senate in 29 BC to commemorate the victory at Actium.

The Regia. The construction of the "Royal house" is attributed to Numa Pompilius ● *26*, the second king of Rome, who is said to have used it as his residence. It included the House of the Vestals and the building reserved for the *rex sacrorum*, a title which in early Republican times conferred the priestly attributes of the ancient kings. Later it became the residence of the *pontifex maximus*, Rome's

show Christ and the saints. Only a few fragments of the right aisle's murals can still be seen. They include a niche with a *Virgin and Child*, and the apse with a *Crucifixion* above and *Christ Giving His Blessing* below; on his right is Pope Paul I (757–67). San Teodoro.

TEMPLE OF ANTONINUS AND FAUSTINA
The temple's transformation into a church saved it from destruction. Its fine façade, with steps and cipollino columns, has been preserved. The *cella*'s magnificent frieze, featuring griffins and ornate candelabra (see top of facing page), recalls the temple's funerary vocation.

highest priestly functionary. After a fire and two reconstructions in the early years of the Republic, it acquired the appearance it was to keep throughout Imperial times.

THE TEMPLE OF VESTA AND THE HOUSE OF THE VESTALS ★. The temple of the goddess Vesta stands in front of the Regia. This sanctuary and the House of the Vestals were designed as a single unit, the Atrium Vestae. A substitute for the royal hearth (perceived as symbolizing all others and representing the permanence of the State), the Temple of Vesta housed the city's sacred fire. Tending this fire was originally the task of the king's daughters, but under the Republic the duty was conferred upon six specialized priestesses known as Vestals. They had to be from patrician families and were selected for this function at the age of six. They were obliged to keep their virginity throughout the time of their priesthood, which lasted for thirty years. The penalty for breaking this vow was to be buried alive in the Campus Sceleratus on the Quirinal Hill (their accomplice merely suffered flagellation in the Comitium ▲ *138*). The temple also housed the "pledges" of the permanence of Rome's universal empire said to have been brought from Troy by Aeneas. The most important of these was the Palladium, an archaic effigy of Minerva reputed to preserve the city that possessed it. The present ruins of the temple, entirely made of brick, date from the end of the 2nd century, as do those of the House of the Vestals. This was a vast building several floors high, with rooms overlooking a rectangular courtyard, itself adorned with three basins and surrounded by statues of the greatest Vestals.

THE OTHER SIDE OF THE VIA SACRA

The Via Sacra was the Forum's most ancient thoroughfare, and its most prestigious. The triumphal parades of victorious generals used it to reach the Temple of Jupiter on the Capitol. **TEMPLE OF ROMULUS.** This small domed temple was dedicated to Maxentius' son Romulus ▲ *329*, who died and was deified in 309 AD. Later it was used as the vestibule to the Church of Santi Cosma e Damiano ▲ *168*. The temple was originally erected at street level, but archeological digs in the last century exposed its foundations.

ornements de la frise

TEMPLE OF ANTONINUS AND FAUSTINA ★. This large temple, transformed into the Church of San Lorenzo in Miranda in the Middle Ages, is easily identifiable due to the monumental inscription on its architrave. In 141 AD Antoninus Pius erected it in memory of his wife, Faustina, who had died and been deified that same year. His own name was added to the dedication when he died in 161 AD.

THE ARCHAIC NECROPOLIS. In 1902, to the right of the temple, the remains of a necropolis were discovered, with forty-one Iron Age tombs. The oldest type consisted of a circular pit enclosing tomb furniture and an urn containing cremated remains. Shaped like a hut, the urn was quite a realistic representation of an Iron Age dwelling ▲ *148*. The later tombs were for the burial of bodies. Objects found in the necropolis are displayed in the Antiquarium of the Forum ▲ *147*.

BASILICA OF MAXENTIUS AND CONSTANTINE. This was one of the most grandiose monuments in Imperial Rome. Begun under Maxentius in 306 AD and completed under Constantine in 312, it covered nearly 65,000 square feet. The barrel vaulting of the huge central nave, 115 feet high, was supported by three immense cross-vaults resting on eight piers. These formed adjacent transepts covering the two lower side aisles, each in turn divided into three great vaulted niches. The roofing was made of gilded bronze tiles, which were reused in the 7th century for the roof of St Peter's. The central transept to the north, which can still be seen today, ended with an apse and was the Emperor's law court. A magnificent entrance with a portico supported on four porphyry columns opened to the south, providing access from the Via Sacra up a central flight of steps. The interior decoration of the basilica consisted of multicolored marble inlays on the walls and floors, gilded stucco coffering on the ceilings, marble and porphyry columns against the walls, and numerous statues that have now disappeared. During the Renaissance the Basilica of Maxentius served as a model and source of inspiration for many architects, including Bramante in his plans for the new St Peter's.

A view from the Forum (below), and the paving stones of the Via Sacra.

THE BASILICA OF MAXENTIUS
Known for a long time as the Temple of Peace, this ruin was identified by the archeologist Nibby at the start of the 19th century when it was freed of the rubble that partly covered it. Only one wing is still standing; the rest of the building was probably destroyed by an earthquake, perhaps the one in 1349 that damaged the Coliseum ▲ *170* and the Torre dei Conti ▲ *168*.

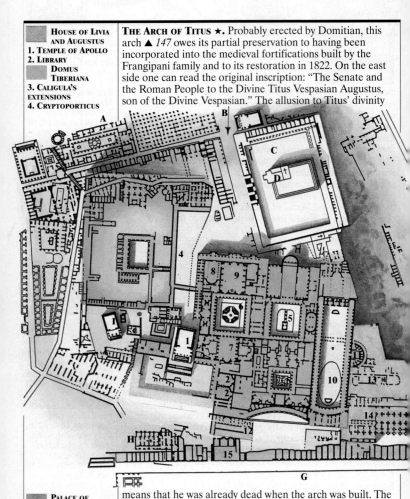

HOUSE OF LIVIA AND AUGUSTUS
1. TEMPLE OF APOLLO
2. LIBRARY
DOMUS TIBERIANA
3. CALIGULA'S EXTENSIONS
4. CRYPTOPORTICUS

PALACE OF DOMITIAN
5. PERISTYLE OF DOMUS AUGUSTANA
6. PERISTYLE OF DOMUS FLAVIA
7. CENATIO JOVIS
8. BASILICA
9. AULA REGIA
10. DOMITIAN'S STADIUM
11. TRIBUNE
12. PAEDAGOGIUM
SEVERIAN BUILDINGS
13. BATHS
14. DOMUS SEVERIANA
15. DOMUS PRAECORUM

THE ARCH OF TITUS ★. Probably erected by Domitian, this arch ▲ *147* owes its partial preservation to having been incorporated into the medieval fortifications built by the Frangipani family and to its restoration in 1822. On the east side one can read the original inscription: "The Senate and the Roman People to the Divine Titus Vespasian Augustus, son of the Divine Vespasian." The allusion to Titus' divinity means that he was already dead when the arch was built. The bas-relief in the center of the arch shows Titus being carried off to heaven on the back of an eagle. The small relief of the frieze on the eastern side illustrates the victory of Vespasian and Titus (who was his eldest son) over the Jews in 71 AD.

THE TEMPLE OF VENUS AND ROME. This was originally the site of the gigantic statue of Nero that stood in front of the *atrium* of the Domus Aurea ▲ *174*. The Emperor Hadrian had to use twenty-four elephants to move this bronze colossus ▲ *171* to its pedestal beside the Coliseum before he could build the temple. Hadrian himself is supposed to have designed this inspired edifice; however, it is said to have displeased a leading architect, Apollodorus of Damascus, to such an extent that his outspoken criticisms cost him his life. Dedicated in 135 AD, the temple consisted of two symmetrical *cellae*, back to back, divided by a central wall, so that "Rome" faced the Forum and Venus faced the Coliseum. The idea of attributing divinity to a city was inspired by a Hellenistic practice already current in Rome since the 2nd century BC.

THE ANTIQUARIUM OF THE FORUM. In the setting of the former Convent of Santa Francesca Romana one can see the most important archeological finds from the Forum, which include objects from the archaic necropolis ▲ *145* and fragments of a marble relief from the Basilica Aemilia ▲ *136* illustrating the myths concerning the origins of Rome.

THE PALATINE ★

With its lawns and umbrella pines, the Palatine is still one of the most enchanting parts of the city.

THE CRADLE OF ROME. Its central position made this hill the most obvious spot for human settlement. According to legend it was settled at a very early date by a Greek colony from Pallantion, in Arcadia, led by their king, Evander. In the *Aeneid* Virgil mentions the Arcadians that Hercules and later Aeneas are said to have met in this place. During the Republic the hill became the residential quarter of Rome's ruling classes. Augustus' decision to live on the Palatine was of great importance for its future: after him all the emperors chose to reside here, including Tiberius (whose palace was enlarged by Caligula and Domitian), Nero, the Flavians (who built the Domus Flavia and Domus Augustana) and Septimius Severus. Consequently the name Palatium (Palatine) came to mean the palace as well as the hill. During the Middle Ages the Frangipani family established their fortified dwelling here as a refuge for the popes. In the 16th century Vignola built the Farnese family sumptuous gardens (part of which have survived), adorned with fountains, aviaries and works of art. It was thanks to this great family that the first excavations of Domitian's palace were undertaken in the 18th century, before those financed by Napoleon III.

MYTHS AND CULTS. The Feast of the Palilia was held on April 21, the anniversary of the city's foundation. The other important feast on the Palatine was the Lupercalia, when there was a procession from the *lupercal*, the cave on the Tiber side of the hill where according to tradition the she-wolf suckled Romulus and Remus, the legendary founders of Rome. It also involved a purification and fertility ritual in which *luperci* (wolf priests) raced around the hill, clad in the skins of the goats they had sacrificed. As they ran, they wielded shreds of the sacrificed animals, which were supposed to bring fertility to the land and to anyone they touched, especially women. Several other cults originated and flourished on the Palatine, including those of Apollo and Cybele. (Proceed up the Clivus Palatinus to the eastern corner of the hill, passing the Farnese Gardens on your right.)

"Before Jupiter was born the Arcadians already lived in their land, and this people must be older than the moon.**"**

Ovid

THE ARCH OF TITUS
Two large marble bas-reliefs inside the arch illustrate scenes from Titus' triumphal parade. The one to the south shows a procession about to pass through the Triumphal Gate; the items carried include the seven-branched candelabra and silver trumpets plundered from the Temple in Jerusalem. In the relief to the north Titus is shown advancing in his four-horse chariot, preceded by the lictors. The goddess Rome holds the horses by their bridles while Victory crowns the Emperor; allegorical figures representing the Senate and the Roman people follow behind.

AROUND THE HOUSE OF LIVIA

THE HOUSE OF ROMULUS. This is where Romulus is said to have lived, in a hut near the spot where Augustus later chose to build his own house. In 1948 excavations revealed traces of Iron Age dwellings: three hut bases carved in the tufa of the hill and protected by a small drainage trench. Between these sites and Livia's house two archaic water cisterns were found, one of them particularly well preserved.

A funerary urn in the shape of an archaic hut. The three hut bases unearthed in 1948 belonged to dwellings of this type; the largest measures 16 feet on its longest side. Wooden posts, which supported the walls and roof, stood in post holes like the ones that can still be seen.

THE TEMPLE OF THE MAGNA MATER. One of the most significant events in the religious crisis that accompanied the Second Punic War against Hannibal was the adoption in 204 BC of the cult of Cybele, the Great Mother. The center of her cult was at Pessinus, in northern Asia Minor, where her image, an amorphous black stone (possibly a meteorite), was said to have fallen from heaven. Its introduction to Rome was due to the consultation of the Sibylline books, a compilation of Greek and Etruscan oracles and prophecies related to the cult of Apollo and brought to Rome by Tarquinius Superbus. The temple was only completed in 191 BC. Its remains are to be seen between the site of the archaic huts and the *tabernae* of the Domus Tiberiana, where there is a statue of the goddess (right).

THE TRANSPORTATION OF THE GODDESS CYBELE
The sacred image of Cybele (the black stone) was brought to Rome by sea. During the feast days of the goddess (the Ludi Megalenses), held once a year around April 4, many plays were performed. It was on such occasions that some of the best works of Plautus and Terence were produced.

THE HOUSE OF LIVIA. To the east of the statue of Cybele is a group of houses dating from the end of the Republic. One of these is probably the part of Augustus' house reserved for his wife, Livia. It was excavated by Pietro Rosa in the middle of the 19th century under Napoleon III's patronage. A sloping corridor leads into a rectangular patio enclosed by pillars. The *tablinium* and two adjacent rooms have very fine "second style" wall paintings dating from around 30 BC. In front of the entrance a painting portraying Polyphemus and Galatea has now almost completely faded. In another room one of the walls is soberly decorated with a festoon of fruit and foliage, while above it scenes of life in Egypt are depicted against a yellow background. All the rooms of the house were paved with simple black-and-white mosaics.

THE HOUSE OF LIVIA ★
The right wall of the *tablinium* is the best preserved. The painted surface is divided into three sections by Corinthian columns. The central panel of the mural portrays Io, watched over by Argos, who has just been freed by Mercury. It is probably a copy of a famous painting by Nikias.

THE HOUSE OF AUGUSTUS. The historian Suetonius states that Augustus purchased the house of the orator Hortensius in 36 AD and later added many other buildings. The smaller

rooms to the west appear to have been the living quarters, while the apartments to the east that surround the large central hall were most probably used for official functions.

THE TEMPLE OF APOLLO. This was believed to be the Temple of Jupiter Victor until it was definitively identified in 1956. All that remains are the stone base of the temple, traces of its marble pavement and fragments of Corinthian capitals. According to tradition, Augustus is said to have had the temple built within the precinct of his house between 36 and 28 BC. The Emperor regarded Apollo – the god of order, light and youth – as his personal protector, attributing his victory over Mark Antony in 31 BC to him. This faith in the Greek god was further exemplified by his staging of the Secular Games in 17 BC and by the sumptuous decoration of this temple, which was entirely built of Luni marble. Three Greek sculptors, Scopas, Kephisodotos and Timotheos, were commissioned to make the statues of the deities Apollo, Diana and Leto. It was in the base of the statue of Apollo that the Sibylline books were later deposited, preserved until then in the Temple of Jupiter Capitolinus. This relocation had the effect of making Augustus' own home virtually the religious center of the city, a notion that was further reinforced when the Emperor had a statue and altar of Vesta transferred there as well.

THE DOMUS TIBERIANA. The first Imperial palace to be conceived as such from the time of its construction was that of Tiberius, the successor of Augustus. It extended over the area between the Temple of Cybele and the slopes leading down to the Forum. In the 16th century this section of the Palatine was turned into the Farnese gardens. The area so far excavated includes eighteen rooms on the south side, an oval basin (which may have been a fish tank) and the long cryptoporticus, an underground gallery where one can see the remains of murals, fragments of mosaic pavements and part of a stucco ceiling with Cupids, the original of which is now in the Palatine's antiquarium ▲ *151*. To the right, a later wing of this gallery leads to the Domus Augustana ▲ *150*. Caligula enlarged the palace in the direction of the Forum, and Domitian had it rebuilt.

The walls of the Temple of Apollo were adorned with painted terracotta panels. The subtle use of color is characteristic of the Augustan period.

Palaces gradually replaced the older buildings on the western slopes of the Palatine, transforming the appearance of the hill.

THE PALACE OF DOMITIAN

DOMUS FLAVIA. Until the end of the Empire, this palace was the official residence of the emperors. Its construction, directed by the architect Rabirius, started at the beginning of Domitian's reign and was only completed in 92 AD. At the center of the Domus Flavia an enormous rectangular peristyle surrounds a great octagonal fountain. Sumptuous rooms open onto it from all sides. To the north is the Aula Regia (throne room), given this name by 18th-century archeologists because of its impressive size. This was where the Emperor gave public audiences. Gigantic statues in colored marble stood in the niches. The apse was where the Emperor appeared with great majesty in the role of *dominus et deus*, as Domitian was the first to want to be called. To the west of the *aula* is the basilica, a slightly smaller rectangular hall with a nave and two aisles culminating in a deep apse, which was probably the Emperor's council chamber. A smaller room to the east is arbitrarily referred to as the *lararium*. Beneath it was discovered the most interesting Republican house in Rome, the HOUSE OF THE GRIFFINS (so called because of a stucco decoration featuring two griffins). Finally, to the south of the peristyle there is a large hall that still has most of its rich marble pavement, which was raised on a *hypocaustum* so that it could be heated. This was no doubt the grandiose dining hall known as the Cenatio Jovis.

THE DOMUS AUGUSTANA. This was the emperors' private residence. The northern end was built around a large peristyle adorned with an ornamental basin; in the center of this, on a high podium, was a little temple that could be reached by means of a bridge. On the south side the ground floor (which is much lower than the rest of the palace) is laid out around a square courtyard that opened via a huge exedra onto the Circus Maximus ▲ *177*. The upper floor, which is badly preserved and over-restored, is of a complex design and includes rooms of a more modest size.

THE HOUSE OF THE GRIFFINS ★
The most interesting paintings (c. 100 BC) found here are now in the Antiquarium of the Palatine ▲ *151*, together with those from the Aula Isiaca (a house discovered under the basilica).

The Septizodium, which was destroyed by Sixtus V.

Reconstruction of the palace's façade overlooking the Circus Maximus (left). A watercolor of it painted in 1886 (above).

Part of the basilica of the Domus Flavia.

HELIOGABALUS (218–22AD)
High priest of a sun-god cult, he came to power at the age of fourteen but was soon deposed and murdered because of his cruelty.

THE STADIUM. This edifice in the shape of a circus, surrounded by a portico on two levels, is the third section of Domitian's palace. Probably used both as a garden and riding track, it may have been the Hippodromus Palatii referred to in the *Acts of the Martyrs* as the place where St Sebastian was killed. Installations of this kind, which included a huge central tribune, were a feature of the large private villas of this period.

THE DOMUS SEVERIANA. This modern name is incorrectly applied to Septimius Severus' enlargement of the Domus Augustana at the end of the 2nd century AD. All that is left of this building are the bare brick substructures that give the Palatine its most striking appearance. Baths were located in the space between this building and the exedra of the stadium. Their water was supplied by a branch of the Aqua Claudia that spanned the gap between the Coelian and the Palatine by means of massive arches (partially preserved). The part of the Palatine facing the Via Appia was adorned with the SEPTIZODIUM (see foot of facing page), a monumental nymphaeum designed, according to Septimius Severus' biographer, to impress travelers arriving from Africa.

THE ANTIQUARIUM OF THE PALATINE. Situated in the former Convent of the Sisters of the Visitation, this museum contains archeological remains from the Palatine Hill, including materials from the archaic huts ▲ 148 and paintings from Republican and Imperial buildings.

CHURCHES ON THE PALATINE AND THE TEMPLE OF HELIOGABALUS. The whole eastern sector of the Palatine consists of massive artificial terracing designed to support a single building, probably of the period of Domitian's adjacent palace. In the center is the beautiful CHURCH OF SAN SEBASTIANO. Since the 11th century it has belonged to the Benedictine Order, although its present appearance dates from the 17th century. South of this church are the remains of a temple that could be the one the Emperor Heliogabalus erected to the god El-Gabal, with the aim of persuading Rome to adopt the oriental custom of deifying living sovereigns. At the very end of the Via San Bonaventura stands the little church of the same name, founded in 1677.

S.P.Q.R: Senatus Populusque Romanus
This time-honored abbreviation stands for "The Senate and the Roman People". The Roman poet Giuseppe Belli ● *43* interpreted it as: *Solo i preti qui regnano* ("only priests rule here").

FROM THE FORUM
HOLITORIUM TO THE COLISEUM

THE FORUM HOLITORIUM AND FORUM BOARIUM

The plain between the Tiber and the group of hills closest to the river (the Capitol, the Palatine and the Aventine) was of vital importance from Rome's earliest days. Two of the main routes of communication for central Italy crossed in this spot: the Tiber, which was navigable from the sea, and the north-south route linking Etruria to Campania, which had an easy ford just downstream from Isola Tiberina ▲ *352*. Rome's first wooden bridge, the Pons Sublicius, was built here in the 7th century BC. The commercial port of the town, the Portus Tiberinus, occupied the area between the temple dedicated to Portunus (the guardian deity of the port) and a monumental square that became the fruit and vegetable market, the Forum Holitorium (where San Nicola in Carcere stands today). This forum extended from the slopes of the Capitol to the Tiber and was served by the Vicus Jugarius (probably the street of the yoke makers), which was one of the town's main streets. Another road

☆ Whole day

1. SANTA MARIA IN COSMEDIN
2. TEMPLE OF HERCULES VICTOR
3. TEMPLE OF PORTUNUS
4. ARCH OF JANUS
5. SAN GIORGIO IN VELABRO
6. AREA SACRA DI SANT'OMOBONO
7. SAN NICOLA IN CARCERE
8. THEATER OF MARCELLUS
9. SANTA MARIA IN CAMPITELLI
10. SANT'ANGELO IN PESCHERIA
11. PORTICO OF OCTAVIA
12. SANTA FRANCESCA IN TOR DE' SPECCHI
13. PALAZZO DI VENEZIA
14. BASILICA DI SAN MARCO
15. VICTOR EMMANUEL

from the Roman Forum was the Vicus Tuscus (its name no doubt came from the Etruscan merchants based there); this skirted the Palatine and led to the cattle market, the Forum Boarium, which is now the Piazza Bocca della Verità.

SANTA MARIA IN COSMEDIN. This church was founded in the 6th century on the ruins of the *statio annonae*, the food-distribution center of classical Rome. Enlarged by Pope Hadrian I in the 8th century, it was given to the Greek community who lived near the Tiber, in a district called the Ripa Grecae. From that time the church was known as Santa Maria in Cosmedin, after the name of a quarter in Constantinople. Beneath the portico is the famous BOCCA DELLA VERITÀ ● *47* ("the mouth of truth"), an ancient drain covering adorned with the face of the sea god Oceanus; if any liar was rash enough to place his hand inside its gaping mouth, the jaws were said to snap it off. Throughout its history this church was repeatedly restored and redecorated, especially in the 12th and 13th centuries. Noteworthy features include the portico, the elegant Romanesque campanile, the *schola cantorum* (choir), the rich Cosmatesque ● *76* pavement and decorations, and the Gothic *baldacchino* over the high altar. In the sacristy there is a fragment of 8th-century mosaic from the original St Peter's Basilica. The block of tufa from which the tiny crypt was hollowed out is thought to be the remains of an altar from the Forum Boarium erected in honor of Hercules (in view of his victory over the giant Cacus, who stole his cattle). At the end of the last century, the architect Giovanni Battista Giovenale gave the church its excessively medieval appearance.

THE TEMPLES OF PORTUNUS AND HERCULES VICTOR. The national registry office (*anagrafe*) of modern times is built on the site of the Portus Tiberinus, the ancient river port to the south of the Forum Holitorium. Next to it stands the rectangular Temple of Portunus (god of ports), better known as the Temple of Fortuna Virilis, founded in the 5th or 3rd century BC. Over the ages the present building, which dates from the 1st century BC, has undergone a series of restorations. Built of tufa and travertine, both temples were covered with stucco decorations. The circular temple farther to the south, close to the Tiber, is the oldest marble edifice to have survived in Rome. Although long known as the Temple of Vesta, it was in fact dedicated to Hercules Victor.

THE FORUM BOARIUM
The notorious Bocca della Verità (above left).

HERCULES OLIVARIUS
The Temple of Hercules Victor (above right) in the Piazza Bocca della Verità is also known as the Temple of Hercules Olivarius. The demigod was in fact the patron of the corporation of the *olearii* (oil merchants), and this temple was founded by a Roman merchant who had no doubt made his fortune in the oil trade. The architect was certainly Greek and may have been Hermodorus of Salamis, who worked in Rome in the second half of the 2nd century.

The house of the Crescenzi ● 72 (above).

TEMPLE OF APOLLO
The decoration of the pediment portrayed Amazons fighting in the presence of Athena. These Greek sculptures from the middle of the 5th century BC are now in the Capitoline Museums.

SAN GIORGIO IN VELABRO. Built in the 7th century in an area marked by an important Byzantine presence, this church has an 11th-century ciborium and a 12th-century portico and campanile. Restored several times over the centuries, it finally recovered its medieval appearance.

ARCO DEGLI ARGENTARII. According to the 204 AD inscription the monumental arch, or gate, next to the Church of San Giorgio in Velabro was dedicated to the Emperor Septimius Severus and his family by the guild of moneychangers (*argentarii*) and cattle dealers. On the inner walls a relief shows Caracalla making a libation on a portable altar. On the other side Septimius and his wife, Julia Domna, can be seen in the act of making a sacrifice.

THE ARCH OF JANUS. Close to the Arco degli Argentarii stands the Arco di Giano, said to have been built by Constantius II in the 4th century. As it straddled a busy road, it was given the name of Janus (one of the oldest Roman divinities), who had two faces and was the guardian of gates and thoroughfares. Close to the arch, a gate in the railings leads to a well-preserved section of the *cloaca maxima* ● 69. (Take Via di San Giovanni Decollato, where the 16th-century church of this name, with frescoes by Salviati, belonged to a confraternity that offered assistance to those who were sentenced to death. Then turn left into Vico Jugario.)

THE AREA SACRA DI SANT'OMOBONO. Near the small church of Sant'Omobono is a site that has provided exceptionally important historical evidence of the Etruscan presence here in archaic times. This sacred precinct includes two small temples, dedicated to Fortuna and Mater Matuta (Dawn), which according to an ancient tradition were founded by King Servius Tullius (579–534 BC). Archeological finds have fully confirmed this chronology and have also made it possible to date their destruction to the end of the 6th century BC. It seems that Etruscan temples were purposefully demolished at the time of the expulsion of the kings, prior to the establishment of the Republic in 509 BC. (Cross the Via del Teatro Marcello.)

SAN NICOLA IN CARCERE. This church owes its name to a prison (*carcere*) that existed in this spot in

156

the 8th century. The present church, erected on the site of a former shrine by Pope Honorius II in 1128 and flanked by a medieval bell tower, was radically rebuilt by Giacomo della Porta, who was also responsible for its façade (1599). The doorway on the right side is a rare example of 15th-century Gothic architecture in Rome. The columns separating the three naves all come from ancient temples. The *confessio* (the tomb of a confessor of the faith) is decorated with a cycle of frescoes depicting *The Baptism of Christ*. These paintings, which date from the beginning of the 13th century, are now in the Vatican Pinacoteca ▲ *215*. Three important Republican temples, dedicated to Janus, Spes (Hope) and Juno Sospita (the "helper"), occupied the site where the church now stands. It is built on a section of the central temple, vestiges of which are preserved in the crypt. Several columns from the other two temples are still visible, freestanding or embedded within the church walls.

THE CIRCUS FLAMINIUS AREA

Today nothing is left of the circus built in 221 BC by the "leader" of the people, Caius Flaminius Nepos, which extended along the Tiber to the south of the Campus Martius. Triumphal processions to the Capitol started from here. Consequently, especially at the end of the Republic, the neighboring district became the center of intense building activity (the construction of temples and porticos) by victorious generals.

THE THEATER OF MARCELLUS. This theater was begun by Caesar and completed by Augustus. The choice of site was determined by the proximity of the Temple of Apollo, in whose honor plays were performed. It was officially dedicated in 13 or 11 BC in the name of Marcellus, Augustus' nephew, son-in-law and heir designate, who died prematurely.

Reconstruction of the steps and tunnels of the Theater of Marcellus by Vaudoyer, who was awarded the Prix de Rome in 1783.

THE THEATER OF MARCELLUS
Like many ancient monuments, the theater was fortified in the Middle Ages and thus saved from destruction. In the 16th century the Savelli family commissioned the Sienese architect Baldassare Peruzzi to build the palace which now occupies the upper part; it was rebuilt by the Orsini in the 18th century.

The three columns of the Temple of Apollo Sosianus.

PORTICO OF OCTAVIA
The ruins visible today (the propylaea, part of the portico, five Corinthian columns and the inscription on the architrave) date from the restoration undertaken by Septimius Severus, after a fire in 191 AD during the reign of the Emperor Commodus.

It had previously been used for the Century Games of 17 BC, festivities traditionally held every hundred years to mark the beginning of a new era. This theater was the largest in Rome after that of Pompey ▲ *248*, with a capacity of about 15,000 spectators, and there is no doubt that it inspired the architecture of the Coliseum. One can still see part of the first and second (Doric and Ionic) tiers, while the top (Corinthian) tier has almost entirely disappeared. In the 16th century it was converted into a private residence. Practically nothing remains of the stage; it was demolished in the 4th century and served as a marble quarry, providing building material for the Pons Cestius ▲ *353*. In the 1930's the buildings that jostled against the theater were removed and it was restored.

THE TEMPLES OF APOLLO SOSIANUS AND BELLONA. The first of these temples was built on the site of a sacred grove, where a healing spirit was venerated after an epidemic of plague; it thus came to be dedicated, in 431 BC, to Apollo Medicus. It was the only important building to be erected during this time of crisis. In 34 BC it was completely rebuilt by a certain Caius Sosius. On the podium three magnificent columns remain, surmounted by a frieze of bucranes (ox skulls) and olive-leaf garlands. To the east of it the base of the TEMPLE OF BELLONA, the Latin goddess of war, has been identified. It was begun in 296 BC by Appius Claudius Caecus, who in 312 had commissioned the building of the Via Appia ▲ *318*. The Senate frequently met in these two temples, especially to decide whether or not to grant a Triumph to victorious generals. During the Empire such meetings took place in the Temple of Mars Ultor in Augustus' Forum ▲ *163*. (Take Via del Portico d'Ottavia, to the right of the Theater of Marcellus).

THE PORTICO OF OCTAVIA. Of the great porticos that lined the northern side of the Circus Flaminius, this is the only one that can still be seen. Inspired by Hellenistic architecture, these large squares flanked by colonnades were intended for State religious and political ceremonies. They also served as areas for walking. The Portico of Octavia stands on the site of that of Metellus

(146 BC), which included two temples. One was dedicated to Juno Regina; the other, the first Roman building to be totally made of marble, to Jupiter Stator. Under Augustus, between 33 and 23 BC, the portico was restored and officially dedicated to Octavia, the sister of the emperor Augustus, together with two libraries, Greek and Latin, which were installed in the complex. The Senate sometimes met in the Curia adjoining the temples. Thirty-four of the numerous statues that decorated these buildings were made of bronze, among them Alexander and his officers at the time of the Battle of the Granicus River (against the Persians in 334 BC) and Cornelia, the mother of the Gracchi, typifying the ideal Roman woman.

SANT'ANGELO IN PESCHERIA. In 770 Pope Stephen III founded this small church built into the ruins of the Portico of Octavia. The church owes its name to the fish market which was held in the portico during the Middle Ages. Inside the church, in the left nave, is a fresco of *The Virgin Enthroned between Angels* by Benozzo Gozzoli. (Take the Via della Tribuna di Campitelli).

SANTA MARIA IN CAMPITELLI. This church was built in 1663 to house the enamel icon known as the *Madonna del Portico* (12th century), a miraculous image of the Virgin much revered by the Romans, who attributed the end of a plague epidemic to her intervention. The architects Carlo Rainaldi and Vicenzo de' Rossi combined a building in the shape of a Greek cross with a square choir surmounted by a dome, producing a theatrical effect through their use of columns. (Take Via del Teatro Marcello, on the left).

SANTA FRANCESCA IN TOR DE' SPECCHI. The medieval tower called the Tor de' Specchi (Tower of Mirrors) because of the decoration of its windows, gave its name to the monastery founded by Santa Francesca Romana ▲ *169*, who lived there from 1436 to 1440. The chapel and refectory, which are decorated with a lovely sequence of 15th-century frescoes, can be visited, as well as the saint's cell. (Take Via d'Aracoeli on the left, then Via della Tribuna di Tor de' Specchi).

PIAZZA MARGANA. This lovely little piazza is enchanting, with its harmonious palazzi and houses from the 15th and 16th centuries, its irregular shape, and the charm of its uneven cobblestones. It still contains part of the fortified medieval tower of the Margani, the door of which is decorated with piers and a lintel made from fragments of a classical capitol. (On the right at the end of the piazza, two alleyways lead to Piazza Venezia).

PIAZZA VENEZIA

The layout and buildings of Piazza Venezia as they appear today are largely the product of the late 19th century and the Mussolini period: the Victor Emmanuel II Monument, the

A SYMBOLIC SITE
To build the Vittoriano, the remains of the *arx* ▲ *128* on the Capitol and a sizable part of medieval Rome had to be damaged or destroyed. On the right, just after the Museo del Risorgimento, some ancient and medieval ruins can still be seen. On the other side, the Tomb of Publicius Bibulus, from the Republican era, marks the end of the Servian Wall at the start of the Via Flaminia.

Assicurazioni Generali di Venezia building, the two avenues converging from the Imperial Forums and the Theater of Marcellus, and even the arrangement of Piazza Aracoeli. It is one of the city's principal junctions. The popular Via del Corso ▲ *308* begins here and, in a straight line, links Piazza Venezia with the Piazza del Popolo ▲ *306*.

THE VICTOR EMMANUEL II MONUMENT. This monument was built, between 1885 to 1911, to honor the memory of the first King of Italy, Victor Emmanuel II. It was the subject of ceaseless controversy, embracing town planning, art and politics. Criticized right from the start for its blinding "Nordic" whiteness, then threatened by Mussolini (who at first wanted to demolish it, then decided to use it for mass demonstrations), it was given a series of denigrating nicknames (such as "the typewriter", "the greatest public lavatory in Italy" and "the wedding cake") before finally being acquitted by a jury of architects, art historians, journalists and politicians. In commemoration of the king's death in 1878, Giuseppe Sacconi was accorded the dubious honor in 1885 of conceiving "an equestrian statue with, eventually, an architectural background". When the "Vittoriano" was inaugurated, unfinished, in 1911, a banquet for ten people was held in the belly of the horse of the equestrian statue. The *quadrigae* (two-wheeled chariots drawn by four horses) and the *Altare della Patria* (Altar of the Fatherland), which was eventually to house the tomb of the Unknown Soldier, were later additions. The finest artists of the day worked on the monument's decorations; and Sacconi, who died of exhaustion, was succeeded by a trio of architects composed of Gaetano Koch, Manfredo Manfredi and Pio Piacentini. The two allegorical groups of gilded

VICTOR EMMANUEL II (1829–78)
With the help of the French, he freed his country from Austrian domination, and with the help of Cavour, achieved the unification of Italy.

bronze at the foot of the stairway portray *Thought* and *Action*. Two great fountains frame it: *The Tyrrhenian Sea* and *The Adriatic*. Above the fountains, from left to right, are marble sculptures: *Strength, Concord, Sacrifice* and *Law*. On the first level the *Altare della Patria*, the work of the sculptor Angelo Zanelli, shows the *Triumphal Processions* of *Work* and *Love for the Fatherland*, which converge toward the statue of the goddess Rome. Finally, crowning it all, is the colossal equestrian statue of Victor Emmanuel, in bronze that was originally gilded, sculpted by Enrico Chiaradia. The portico is dominated by statues representing the regions of Italy. Adding the finishing touches to this powerful tribute to the united nation, two gigantic bronze *quadrigae*, driven by winged Victories symbolizing *Freedom* and *Italian Unity*, rise above the *propylaea* (porticos). Inside the monument are the MUSEO CENTRALE DEL RISORGIMENTO, devoted to the history of the country's unification, and the MUSEO DELLE BANDIERE (Flag Museum) devoted to Italian military history.

Part of a Garibaldi uniform in the Museo Centrale del Risorgimento.

PALAZZO DELLE ASSICURAZIONI GENERALI DI VENEZIA. Designed by Guido Cirilli to counterbalance Palazzo Venezia, this neo-Renaissance palace was built between 1906 and 1911 on the site of Palazzo Torlonia, which was demolished when the square was revamped. Its façade is decorated with a 16th-century winged lion, the symbol of the Serenissima (Venice).

PALAZZO DI VENEZIA. Pietro Barbo decided to build this palace when he became titular cardinal of San Marco in 1451; and when, in 1464, he became Pope Paul II he resolved to raise his residence to the dignity of a pontifical dwelling. After his death, work on it continued until the 16th century. Pius IV granted part of the palazzo to the Venetian ambassadors, who resided there from 1564 to 1797, and it was then that the building acquired its present name. In 1806, by order of Napoleon I, it became the headquarters of the French administration. The building inherited its powerful corner tower and crenelations from the medieval fortresses, but the mullioned windows in marble on the *piano nobile*, the great doorway on Piazza Venezia, the elegant courtyard and the decoration of the rooms all display the finesse of the Renaissance. A MUSEUM now occupies the apartments of Paul II and part of the PALAZZETTO VENEZIA (built by the same Pope at the foot of the tower, but moved to the rear of the palace in 1911 to improve the landscaping of the new square). Its collection

PALAZZO DI VENEZIA Mussolini's offices were in the palace from 1929 to 1943. He used to stand on the balcony overlooking the piazza in order to harangue the crowd below.

The courtyard of Palazzo di Venezia.

161

**THE
"RECONCILIATION"**
Priests filing past
Mussolini at the head
of a parade of Fascist
youth organizations
in the Imperial
Forums.

Julius Caesar.

includes tapestries, ceramics, weapons,
works in silver and gold, sculptures
and numerous paintings. The most
remarkable rooms in the palace are
the Sala Regia, where the ambassadors
met before being received in audience
by the Pope; the Sala del Concistorio,
where the cardinals used to meet; and
the Sala del Mappamondo, in which
Mussolini installed his study. On
Piazza San Marco is a figure of a
woman, known as Madama Lucrezia,
perhaps originally from the
neighboring Temple of Isis, that
became one of the famous talking
statues of Rome● 47.

BASILICA DI SAN MARCO. This church was founded in 336 by
Pope Mark, who dedicated it to the evangelist. In the 9th
century it was rebuilt by Gregory IV, and in the 12th century a
campanile was added. It underwent further modifications
when Pope Paul II included it in the new Palazzo di Venezia.
The outer portico with elegant arcades and the Loggia of the
Benediction, which date from this period, form one of the
city's most successful Renaissance façades. The interior,
designed as a traditional basilica with three naves, has
survived, as has part of the Cosmatesque paving ● 76. But the
beautiful coffered ceiling decorated with the coat of arms of
Paul II was added in the 15th century, and the stucco
decoration and paintings in the central nave date from the
18th century. These illustrate the story of St Abdon and St
Sennen, two Persian martyrs venerated in the Middle Ages
whose relics are preserved in the crypt, together with those of
the basilica's founder. The large mosaic with a gold
background in the apse dates from the 19th century and was
inspired by the one in the Church of Santi Cosma e Damiano
▲ 168.

THE IMPERIAL FORUMS

At the end of the Republic it was realized that the
Forum was not large enough to meet the needs of
the capital of an immense empire. Julius Caesar

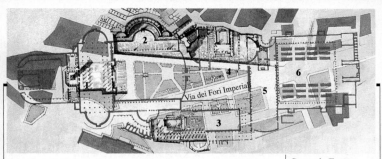

therefore initiated what was originally supposed to be a mere enlargement of the existing Forum ▲ *136* but subsequently became the development of the first of the Imperial Forums. Augustus, the Flavians and Trajan all added new monumental squares, thus creating a vast public complex stretching from the slopes of the Quirinal to the Velia. Into it the ideological, administrative, legal and commercial activities of the city overflowed and were eventually concentrated. The dissolution of the Roman Empire led to the abandonment of these squares, and during the Middle Ages they were gradually buried. Much of the area was only rediscovered in the 20th century, when on Mussolini's orders the medieval quarter was demolished to make room for the new Via dell'Impero (now the Via dei Fori Imperiali), linking the northern and southern parts of the city. The Fascist parades designed to exalt the rediscovered grandeur of the Empire took place on this broad avenue which leads from Piazza Venezia to the Coliseum.

CAESAR'S FORUM. In 54 BC Cicero wrote to his friend Atticus saying that he had agreed on Caesar's behalf to acquire the land required to build a new forum. To do this it was necessary to move the Curia and the Comitium ▲ *138*, to buy and then demolish the existing dwellings, and to spend the colossal sum of sixty million sesterces for the land alone. In 48 BC, on the battlefield of Pharsalus, Caesar vowed to build a temple to Venus (from whom he and the rest of the Julia family claimed descent through Aeneas) if she would grant him victory over Pompey. This is why he built the magnificent SHRINE TO VENUS GENITRIX (Venus the Mother), dedicated in 46 BC, as part of his Forum. Today all that remains is the podium and three columns. The ideological purpose of this act of piety is quite clear: following the example of the Hellenistic shrines dedicated to deified sovereigns, if Caesar's guardian goddess was to be exalted then so was the dictator himself. The temple was rebuilt several times, once under Trajan, being reinaugurated in May of 113 AD, on the same

CAESAR'S FORUM
This took the form of an elongated triangle (about 524 feet in length), surrounded by a double portico of columns under which there were shops (still visible today on the Clivus Argentarius). The forum was dominated by an equestrian statue of the dictator.

THE TEMPLE OF MARS ULTOR
From Augustus' Forum a majestic stairway flanked by fountains led up to the temple, which had a tufa podium faced with Carrara marble. The façade featured eight gigantic Corinthian columns; of the eight others that supported the sides, three are still standing. Statues of Venus, Mars and the Divine Julius stood in an apse at the end of the *cella*.

day as Trajan's Column.

AUGUSTUS' FORUM. The second of the Imperial Forums, with its TEMPLE OF MARS ULTOR (Mars the Avenger), was created by Augustus after a vow made before the Battle of Philippi (42 BC) to avenge Julius Caesar, who was his adoptive father. It was intended that the new square would provide more space, as the previous forums had been badly overcrowded, but it served above all to glorify the Emperor in his military and triumphal roles. To separate it from the popular neighborhood of ill repute known as the Suburra and to protect it against the frequent fires, Augustus had a monumental wall built in great blocks of *peperino* (a type of tufa) at the back of the square. Statues of historical personages decorated the lateral porticos, and at the end niches twice the size of the others held effigies of Aeneas, Romulus and their descendants. A statue of Augustus standing in a *quadriga* was placed at the center of the temple.

VESPASIAN'S FORUM AND TEMPLE OF PEACE. This complex was built by Vespasian between 71 and 75 AD to celebrate his victory over the Jews. The Temple of Peace contained the great marble plan of the town, the *Forma Urbis*, established under Septimius Severus, and items from the Temple of Jerusalem, including the seven-branched candelabra and silver trumpets shown on the Arch of Titus ▲ *146*.

AUGUSTUS
The Emperor is shown here as a pontiff (his head covered with a fold of his toga, in accordance with the custom of priests in the act of sacrificing). He assumed the title of *pontifex maximus* – a title inherited by the popes – which made him head of the Roman religion for life and gave his power a legitimate and sacred basis.

THE "FORMA URBIS"
This great marble town plan, vital for our topographical knowledge of ancient Rome, is kept in Palazzo Braschi ▲ *279*. Its area was over 2,500 square feet. Only a tenth of it has been found.

Two giant Corinthian columns (known as Colonnacce) in Nerva's Forum, guarded by Minerva.

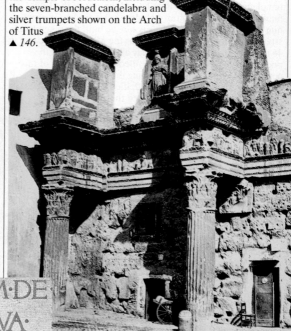

FORVM·DE
·NERVA·

Restored by Septimius Severus at the end of the 2nd century following a serious fire, the temple was damaged again in the 5th century – so badly that, according to the Byzantine historian Procopius, it had to be abandoned during the following century. Nevertheless, vestiges of two rooms are still visible. Of the first, only a brick wall remains, situated between the Basilica of Maxentius ▲ *145* and the entrance of the Church of Santi Cosma e Damiano. The *Forma Urbis* was found in fragments at the foot of this wall in 1552, and holes for the iron clamps that supported the marble slabs of the plan can still be seen. The best-preserved part of the complex, which is on the other side of the wall, within the church, undoubtedly formed part of one of the libraries of the Forum of Peace.

NERVA'S FORUM (THE FORUM TRANSITORIUM). Although construction of this long, narrow forum was begun and virtually completed by Domitian, it was inaugurated, after his death, by the Emperor Nerva in 97 AD. Because it linked the existing forums and the Temple of Peace, it came to be known as the Forum Transitorium ("the forum in between"). One end was dominated by a temple dedicated to Minerva; but Pope Paul V, who used marble from it to build the Fontana Paola in the 17th century ▲ *364*, was responsible for its almost total destruction. Two columns and the back wall of the lateral portico remain on the Via Cavour. A figure of Minerva appears on the attic, while the frieze, which illustrates feminine crafts, portrays the myth of Arachne, the young Lydian girl who was turned into a spider by Athena (the Greek counterpart of Minerva) for daring to compete with the goddess in the arts of weaving and embroidery.

TRAJAN'S FORUM. This is the last, the greatest and the best preserved of the Imperial Forums. Created by Trajan with booty plundered from the Dacians (a people who lived in what is now Rumania), it was built between 107 and 113 AD according to designs by Apollodorus of Damascus, the most famous architect of the age. He achieved some engineering miracles, leveling the high ridge that linked the Capitol to the Quirinal – as the inscription on the base of Trajan's Column records – and moving almost 30,000,000 cubic feet of soil to obtain space to build the imposing monuments. The entrance was from Augustus' Forum, through a triumphal arch; this led to a monumental square, in the center of which stood a gilded-bronze equestrian statue of the Emperor. As in Augustus' Forum, the porticos on each side opened out into semicircular exedras; the attic of the porticos was decorated with statues of Dacian prisoners, alternating with shields adorned by portraits. At the end of the square was the

This reconstruction of Trajan's Forum shows (from left to the right): the triumphal arch, the portico, Basilica Ulpia (in the center), Trajan's Column, the libraries and the temple.

BASILICA ULPIA
The medieval Torre delle Milizie and the remains of Trajan's Markets can be seen rising behind the ruins of the grandiose basilica that dominated Trajan's Forum.

A GREAT GENERAL
After his wars against the Dacians (one of a series of conquests), Trajan (98–117 AD) attacked the Parthians, a people of Iranian origin; forced to retreat, he died on the way back to Rome.

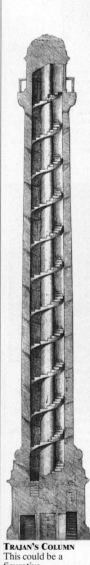

TRAJAN'S COLUMN
This could be a figurative transcription of Trajan's *Commentarii*, a narrative record of his wars against the Dacians (101–6 AD). The spiral of reliefs on the shaft (about 130 feet tall) resembles the form of a papyrus scroll.

BASILICA ULPIA (Trajan's family name), the largest basilica ever built in Rome, and beyond it stood a pair of libraries, Greek and Latin, on either side of the famous marble column. Finally, on the death and deification of the Emperor, a temple to Trajan and his wife, Plotina, was added. Through its many activities (the promulgation of laws, the distribution of money to the people, schools, etc.) this forum became one of the main political and administrative centers of the city. Moreover, it formed a complex of such monumental beauty that, according to the historian Ammianus Marcellinus, when the Emperor Constantius II visited Rome for the first time, in 357 AD, he was dazzled by "this monument unique under the heavens and admirable even in the eyes of the gods".

TRAJAN'S COLUMN. The libraries of Trajan's Forum were adorned with terraces from which the painted bas-reliefs of Trajan's Column could be seen perfectly. It consisted of seventeen drums of blue marble from Luni on a cubic base with bas-reliefs showing trophies of Dacian weapons. An inner staircase wound to the top, lit by forty-five loopholes almost invisible from outside. Above the entrance is an inscription framed by two Victories: it states that the column's

purpose was to indicate the "height of the hill, which was removed to make room for such large monuments". The column also served as a resting place for the Emperor, whose ashes, contained in a gold urn, were placed in the base. The bas-reliefs that relate the story of his victories over the Dacians unfold in a spiral 656 feet long. They are an exceptional historical record and a masterpiece of sculpture. From the crossing of the Danube (at the bottom) to the deportation of the Dacian population that ended the war (at the top), each successive stage of the conflict is depicted: the pitching of camps, speeches rallying the troops, battles, assaults, beheadings, and the native chieftains' submission to the Emperor. Erected in Trajan's honor, the monument portrays him no less than sixty times. Under Sixtus V, the Emperor's statue, which crowned the column, was replaced by a statue of St Peter made by Giacomo della Porta.

Santa Maria di Loreto. This church, to the left of the column, was built by Bramante and Antonio da Sangallo the Younger. Inside are frescoes by Pomarancio (second chapel on the right), François Duquesnoy's statue of *St Susanna* (1630) and two angels by Maderno. (To the right of the Church of the Santissimo Nome di Maria, built between 1736 and 1738, a steep flight of steps leads to Trajan's Markets).

From Trajan's Markets to the Coliseum

The Markets. Between Trajan's Forum and the lower slopes of the Quirinal, the architect Apollodorus of Damascus arranged a complex of utilitarian buildings which, after their discovery, were given the name of Trajan's Markets. The semicircular brick façade includes three superimposed rows of shops. The third level opens onto a rather well preserved ancient street, Via Biberatica (right), from which a flight of steps leads to a monumental hall (now the entrance to the markets) that served as the center of the complex. Occupying two floors, with small shops and perhaps also offices, it was covered by a huge vault, with six intersecting arches supported on massive travertine consoles. The complex was probably used both for storing the enormous quantities of foodstuffs managed by the State, especially for free distribution to the plebs, and also for retail purposes. All kinds of foodstuffs were sold, including wine, oil and saltwater fish kept in tanks.

Torre delle Milizie ● *73*. From the 11th to the 14th centuries the urban dwellings of

An apostle for an emperor
The bronze statue of St Peter was placed on top of Trajan's Column on December 4, 1587. Half a cannon from Castel Sant'Angelo, three doors (from Sant'Agnese, the Scala Santa and St Peter's) and part of a pilaster from the Pantheon were melted down to make the statue.

167

TORRE DE' CONTI
Called Turris Major or Turris Urbis, this was Rome's tallest tower. Like the Torre delle Milizie, it consists of three superimposed sections that become gradually narrower.

The campanile of Santa Francesca Romana.

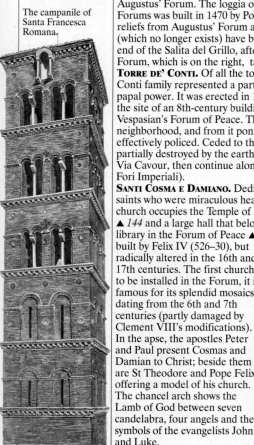

the aristocracy – both the feudal nobility and the city's elite – tended to take the form of fortified complexes with tall towers. "Roma turrita" boasted more than three hundred towers, many of which still exist, including those of the Arcioni, Capocci, Frangipani, Annibaldi, Margani and Orsini families (the latter near Campo de' Fiori), the Torre del Grillo and the Torre Millina. Built in the 12th to 13th centuries on the ruins of Trajan's Markets, then in the possession of the Arcioni, the Torre delle Milizie was shortened after an earthquake in the 14th century and crenelations were added. Subsequently it belonged to the Annibaldi and then the Caetani, great Roman families who vied for control of the town in the Middle Ages. (Take the Salita del Grillo, on the right.)

THE HOUSE OF THE KNIGHTS OF RHODES. At the end of the 12th century the Hospitaler Order of St John of Jerusalem installed its Roman priory in the northern hemicycle of Augustus' Forum. The loggia opening onto the Imperial Forums was built in 1470 by Pope Paul II. Sculptures and bas-reliefs from Augustus' Forum and the Church of San Basilio (which no longer exists) have been preserved here. (At the end of the Salita del Grillo, after the entrance to Augustus' Forum, which is on the right, take Via Tor de' Conti.)

TORRE DE' CONTI. Of all the towers of the nobles, that of the Conti family represented a particularly clear manifestation of papal power. It was erected in 1198 by Pope Innocent II on the site of an 8th-century building, itself built on the exedra of Vespasian's Forum of Peace. The tower stood guard over the neighborhood, and from it pontifical processions could be effectively policed. Ceded to the municipality in 1203, it was partially destroyed by the earthquake of 1349. (Turn right into Via Cavour, then continue along the Via dei Fori Imperiali).

SANTI COSMA E DAMIANO. Dedicated to two saints who were miraculous healers, this church occupies the Temple of Romulus ▲ 144 and a large hall that belonged to a library in the Forum of Peace ▲ 165. It was built by Felix IV (526–30), but radically altered in the 16th and 17th centuries. The first church to be installed in the Forum, it is famous for its splendid mosaics dating from the 6th and 7th centuries (partly damaged by Clement VIII's modifications). In the apse, the apostles Peter and Paul present Cosmas and Damian to Christ; beside them are St Theodore and Pope Felix, offering a model of his church. The chancel arch shows the Lamb of God between seven candelabra, four angels and the symbols of the evangelists John and Luke.

SANTA FRANCESCA ROMANA. Founded in the mid 10th century on part of the Temple of Venus and Rome ▲ *146*, this was at first called Santa Maria Nova, to distinguish it from Santa Maria Antiqua ▲ *142*, which had had to be abandoned because of flooding. The church acquired its present name in 1608 after the canonization of Francesca Buzzi dei Ponziani, who founded the Congregation of Oblates in 1421. The saint's remains are preserved in the crypt. The Romanesque campanile, decorated with ceramic cups and disks of porphyry, is one of the most beautiful in Rome. The apse is decorated with a 12th-century mosaic showing the Virgin and Child enthroned between four saints: Peter, Andrew, James and John. In the right branch of the transept are the paving stones on which St Peter is said to have knelt to pray to God to stop Simon Magus in full flight; according to tradition, the sorcerer then crashed to his death not far from the church.

THE ARCH OF CONSTANTINE. One of the largest triumphal arches to have survived, this was built to commemorate Constantine's Triumph, celebrated after his victory over Maxentius' troops at the Ponte Milvio ▲ *377* in 312 AD. This imposing edifice is unusual in that it consists of sculptures and decorations taken from other monuments. By this time Rome had probably relinquished her role as capital of the Empire to Constantinople; as a result sculptors, masons and other craftsmen who had relied on Imperial commissions found it hard to earn a living.

A MASTERPIECE OF FRESHNESS AND NATURALISM
This 6th-century mosaic, in the apse of Santi Cosma e Damiano, shows St Peter and St Paul presenting St Cosmas and St Damian to Christ. St Theodore (far right), and Pope Felix IV on the far left, offer Christ a model of the church.

MONUMENTAL MAPS
Mussolini had five huge stone maps hung near the Coliseum to demonstrate the extraordinary expansion of Rome since her origins. Only the four maps tracing Rome's development in antiquity now remain.

THE META SUDANS
A cone-like fountain (below) stood near the arch, dating from c. 80 AD. Although it was demolished in 1936 to make room for Fascist parades, its base was unearthed in the 1980's.

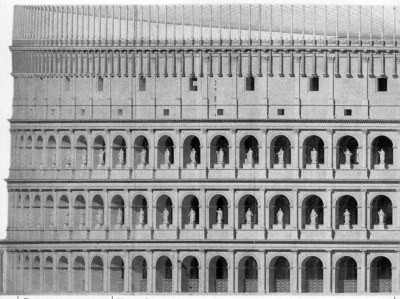

More than 3,500,000 cubic feet of travertine and 300 tons of iron were used for this façade. The first three stories have rows of arches framed by engaged columns superimposed in the classical sequence ● *94*: Doric, Ionic and Corinthian. The fourth story has no arches, but is adorned with Corinthian columns.

The interior of the Coliseum.

THE COLISEUM

THE FIRST STONE AMPHITHEATER. Gladiatorial combats were originally held in the Forum, where temporary step seating was erected and rented to spectators. It was only in the time of Augustus that these combats disappeared from the city center and moved toward the Campus Martius. In 29 BC Statilius Taurus built the first permanent amphitheater there, and when this burned down in 64 AD Nero replaced it with a wooden one. It was not until nearly ten years later that an amphitheater worthy of the Empire's capital was built, designed to gratify the people's appetite for entertainment. The most beautiful amphitheater of the Roman world, the Coliseum was erected on the site of the artificial lake with which Nero had embellished his villa, the Domus Aurea ▲ *174*. Begun in the early years of Vespasian's reign (from 72 AD), it was completed by his son, Titus. During its inauguration in 80 AD, which lasted for a hundred days, five thousand wild animals were slaughtered. The last time the Coliseum is known to have been used was in the reign of Theodoric, in 523 AD. Although it is not certain that Christians were martyred there, in the 19th century a Way of the Cross was set up around the arena in their honor, where the Pope still prays every year at Easter. The Coliseum's consecration to the Christian martyrs put an end to the pillaging of its marble and travertine, which had been going on since the Middle Ages.

ITS FUNCTIONAL ORGANIZATION. The elliptical amphitheater has a diameter of approximately 620 feet in its widest section and 490 feet in its narrowest. The façade is about 165 feet high. At the top, a row of consoles served to support the vast *velarium*, a linen awning which unfolded over the building to protect the spectators from the sun. This was the special task of a

detachment of the Imperial navy from the port of Misenum, stationed in a nearby barracks. The eighty arcades at ground level gave access to a complex system of stairways, the *vomitoria*, enabling as many as sixty or eighty thousand spectators to enter and leave without delay. Each spectator had a *tessera* (ticket) with a number corresponding to one of the numbers carved above each of the entrances. One of the four main entrances of the amphitheater led to the Imperial tribune; the other three were reserved for specific categories of spectators: magistrates, Vestals, guests of honor, etc. What remains of the exterior façade (about two fifths of the whole) is supported at each end by two huge walls built in the time of Pius VII.

THE LAYOUT OF THE AMPHITHEATER. The interior of the Coliseum, most of which has collapsed, can only give a vague impression of what it must have been like originally. The subterranean passages of the arena were once covered with a movable wooden floor that concealed the services indispensable for the games: machinery, cages for the wild animals, weapons, and so on. The thirty deep niches in the surrounding wall were probably equipped with a system of pulleys for raising animals and gladiators to the level of the arena. Huge swiveling panels of tufa, equipped with a system of rollers and hinges and moved by counterweights, made it possible to raise all kinds of scenery to the center of the arena, including artificial landscapes with hills and forests for the *venationes* (hunting contests). The arena's stepped seating, the *cavea*, was divided into five sectors; the places were allocated, and access depended on the specifically determined social class to which the spectators belonged. According to the historian Suetonius, the Emperor Augustus allocated the first row to the senators, special places to married plebeians, and others to adolescent boys still clad in the *toga praetexta*. He specified that women should occupy the upper rows. Between Via Labicana and Via San Giovanni in Laterano the remains are still visible of the LUDUS MAGNUS, the main barracks of the gladiators, which were linked directly to the subterranean passages of the Coliseum by a tunnel.

THE STATUE OF NERO
A bronze colossus of Nero, about 120 feet tall, stood beside the Coliseum. The name Colosseo, first used in the Middle Ages, came from the proximity of this colossal statue.

SUBTERRANEAN LIFE
The arena's underground passages are lit by the openings made for hoisting machinery.

The emperors continually strove to make themselves popular with the plebians. They resorted to the distribution of grain and money, the construction of public baths and, above all, the organization of games. Normally three kinds of building were used for the games: the theater, the circus and the amphitheater, where gladiators fought and wild beasts were hunted in exorbitantly costly shows designed to exalt the splendor of the reign.

In the 1st century, the helmets had visors.

EXOTIC ANIMALS
The great round-ups of animals for the *venationes* (hunts) impoverished the fauna of North Africa.

THE UMPIRE
Recognizable by his tunic and wooden rod, he directed the combats and kept watch over the proceedings.

ASTYANAX

ASTYANAX

PROTECTIVE ARMOR
The armor of a gladiator (arm guards and greaves) was designed to protect the parts of the body where the slightest wound might seriously handicap the fighter.

THE GREETING OF THE GLADIATORS
The games opened with a sumptuous procession. The gladiators entered the arena by the *Porta Triumphalis,* behind the magistrates and lictors. The pathetic sentence uttered as they stood before Claudius' Imperial tribune became traditional: "Hail Caesar! Those who are about to die greet you!"

A wind gauge was used to ensure that the wind was in the right direction when the strips of the *velarium* were raised.

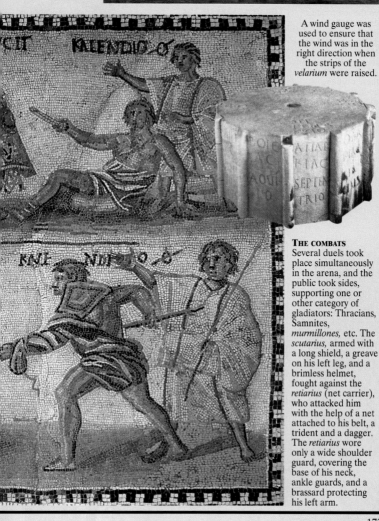

THE COMBATS
Several duels took place simultaneously in the arena, and the public took sides, supporting one or other category of gladiators: Thracians, Samnites, *murmillones,* etc. The *scutarius,* armed with a long shield, a greave on his left leg, and a brimless helmet, fought against the *retiarius* (net carrier), who attacked him with the help of a net attached to his belt, a trident and a dagger. The *retiarius* wore only a wide shoulder guard, covering the base of his neck, ankle guards, and a brassard protecting his left arm.

THE LAYOUT OF THE DOMUS AUREA
The modern entrance (special permission is needed for a visit) is reached along a large brick apse that was part of the Baths of Trajan. To the rear of the house is a vast courtyard surrounded by porticos on three sides – the fourth consisting of the famous cryptoporticus where the grotesques were found. The most important rooms are on the south side, divided into two apartments by a double central hall. Next to this are two rooms with an alcove; it is thought that these were the bedrooms (*cubicula*) of the Imperial couple.

THE DOMUS AUREA (THE GOLDEN HOUSE)

THE VILLA OF THE SUN. When the terrible fire of 64 AD destroyed his first palace, Nero replaced it with a much larger building, the Domus Aurea. The architects Severus and Celer were commissioned to build it, and its decoration was entrusted to a certain Fabullus (or Famulus). This complex, adorned with statues from many parts of Greece and Asia Minor, was surrounded by an enormous park. The astronomical orientation of the building confirms the ancient descriptions, all of which state that it symbolized the sun. Indeed everything about it was intended to recall the sun, with which Nero identified – as witness his colossal statue ▲ *171*, the great round hall which pivoted on itself following the revolving heavens, and the ubiquitous profusion of gold.

THE DISCOVERY OF THE "GROTESQUES". At the start of the 15th century laborers working on the hill found subterranean passages decorated with frescoes: these were part of Nero's palace, which had been covered over in the 2nd century by Trajan's baths. These tunnels came to be known as "grottoes", and their decoration of arabesques and mythological scenes as "grotesques". Renaissance artists were inspired by them, especially Raphael in his celebrated loggias in the Vatican ▲ *228*. The splendid rectangular nymphaeum to the east of the vast courtyard still retains part of these decorations: a mosaic medallion shows Polyphemus, the Cyclops, accepting a goblet of wine from Ulysses.

THE BATHS OF TRAJAN

Trajan's baths, partially built on the ruins of the Domus Aurea after the fire of 104 AD, were the work of Apollodorus of Damascus ▲ *165*. A demonstration of Imperial generosity to the plebs of the city, they were Rome's first great Imperial baths ● *68*. The remains of a nymphaeum and a library from the baths can still be seen in the Parco Oppio. On the other side of the Via delle Terme di Traiano stand the baths' monumental cisterns (the so-called "Seven Halls"), divided into nine huge intercommunicating chambers.

CIRCUS MAXIMUS AND THE AVENTINE

▲ CIRCUS MAXIMUS AND THE AVENTINE

As well as being the southernmost hill of Rome, the Aventine (Monte Aventino) was the closest to the Emporium, the Tiber's commercial port in antiquity. Because of this location the flat summit soon became a trading district, particularly popular with foreign merchants as it was outside the *pomerium*, the sacred boundary of the political and religious center of the city (with which it was not integrated until the reign of Claudius).

In the 6th century BC King Servius Tullius built a temple to Diana on the Aventine which became the official shrine of the Latins. Later, the history of the hill was to illustrate the continuing influence of these early episodes. During the first part of the 5th century a heterogeneous group of craftsmen, shopkeepers and small landowners – all excluded from the privileges of the patrician ruling class – moved to the Aventine, and the common people of Rome as a whole came to be known as the plebs. Under the pressure of mounting financial, military and political problems at the beginning of the Republic, the plebs threatened to secede and form an independent state by "retreating" to the Aventine, or alternatively to the Mons Sacer

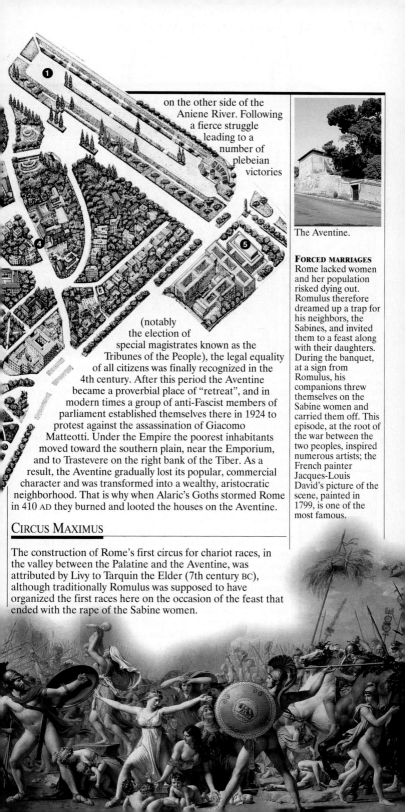

on the other side of the Aniene River. Following a fierce struggle leading to a number of plebeian victories

The Aventine.

(notably the election of special magistrates known as the Tribunes of the People), the legal equality of all citizens was finally recognized in the 4th century. After this period the Aventine became a proverbial place of "retreat", and in modern times a group of anti-Fascist members of parliament established themselves there in 1924 to protest against the assassination of Giacomo Matteotti. Under the Empire the poorest inhabitants moved toward the southern plain, near the Emporium, and to Trastevere on the right bank of the Tiber. As a result, the Aventine gradually lost its popular, commercial character and was transformed into a wealthy, aristocratic neighborhood. That is why when Alaric's Goths stormed Rome in 410 AD they burned and looted the houses on the Aventine.

CIRCUS MAXIMUS

The construction of Rome's first circus for chariot races, in the valley between the Palatine and the Aventine, was attributed by Livy to Tarquin the Elder (7th century BC), although traditionally Romulus was supposed to have organized the first races here on the occasion of the feast that ended with the rape of the Sabine women.

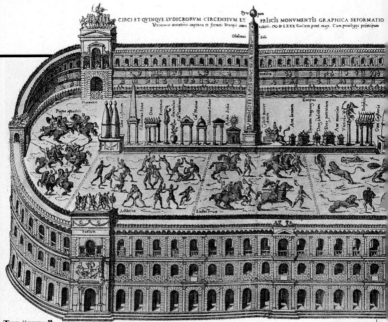

THE "SPINA"
On the *spina*, as well as two obelisks and the seven eggs and seven dolphins that served to mark the laps, there were various small buildings and shrines.

Subsequently stone steps with wooden seats were added. In 46 BC Julius Caesar had the circus enlarged substantially, but the most important event was the erection on the *spina* – the long, low central wall that linked the two turning posts – of the obelisk of Ramses II, brought from Heliolopolis by Augustus (in 1587 it was moved to Piazza del Popolo ▲ *306*). Much later Constantius II added a second obelisk, that of Tutmoses III, from Thebes (also removed by Sixtus V in 1587, to be re-erected in Piazza San Giovanni in Laterano ▲ *196*). The circus was nearly 2,000 feet long and was said to have a capacity of more than 300,000 spectators. Substantial remains are to be seen at the curved end on the Palatine side; they correspond to the middle of the *cavea* (steps) and date from the time of Hadrian (117–38 AD).

THE GAMES. Caesar organized a mock battle with a thousand infantry, six hundred horsemen and forty elephants. The *spina*, which the *quadrigae* (two-wheeled chariots drawn by four horses) had to circle counterclockwise seven times, was just over 1,100 feet long. The most important races took place during the Ludi Romani (Roman Games), from September 14 to 18. The four *factiones* (teams) of charioteers, Albata, Russata, Prasina and Veneta, with their white, red, green and blue colors, eventually developed the characteristics of full-blown political parties. The last races in the Circus Maximus were held in 549, during the reign of Totila.

AT THE FOOT OF THE AVENTINE. In line with the Circus Maximus, silhouetted against the sky are the buildings of the F.A.O. (Food and Agriculture Organization of the United Nations), inaugurated in 1951, and the obelisk of Axum (4th century AD) transported from the Ethiopian city to Rome in 1937. THE STATUE OF GIUSEPPE MAZZINI (1805–72) that adorns the Piazzale Romolo e Remo has had an eventful history. The Freemason sculptor Ettore Ferrari was commissioned to make it in 1890, but because of Mazzini's militant republicanism and controversial political image it was not inaugurated until 1949. (Return to the Tiber, turn left, and take the steep walled footpath called the Clivo di Rocca Savella.)

THE AVENTINE

In the morning, from the banks of the Tiber climb up the Clivo di Rocca Savella to discover the quiet, secret oasis of the Aventine. Public and monastic gardens afford a peaceful retreat where you can enjoy the beautiful view over the Circus Maximus and the Palatine. (Cross the Parco Savello and take Via di Santa Sabina to the right.)

SANTA SABINA. If tradition is to be believed, this church was built on the site of the house of Sabina, a noblewoman who was converted to Christianity by one of her slaves and died during Hadrian's persecutions. According to another source the saint's body was transferred here from Umbria, where Sabina is supposed to have suffered martyrdom under Vespasian. The church was founded by Peter of Illyria during the pontificate of Celestine I (422–32), on the foundations of two small temples and a 3rd–4th century house. The great biography of the popes, the *Liber Pontificalis*, testifies that the work was continued during the pontificate of Sixtus III (432–40). A portico and baptistery, today no longer standing, completed the basilica. Restorations were carried out in the 8th and 9th centuries; then in the following century Albericus, a Roman aristocrat of Frankish origins and rival of Pope John X, integrated the building within the fortifications he had built on the Aventine. It was here, in 1222, that St Dominic presented Pope Honorius III with the rule of the Order of Preachers (the church still belongs to the Dominicans). Several chapels were added later, slightly changing the original building. In 1914, a radical restoration eliminated the chapels, thus returning the apse area to its original state. The doors of carved cedar date from the 5th century, and are a superb and rare example of the iconographic themes of the age. Inside, above the entrance, a mosaic dating from the same period shows two women symbolizing the Church of the Gentiles (New Testament) and the Church of the Circumcision (Old Testament). These figures frame an inscription commemorating the church's construction by Peter of Illyria and Pope Celestine. Set into the paving of the central nave one can see, amongst others, the unusual mosaic-decorated tombstone of Muñoz

PARCO SAVELLO ★ (Giardino degli Aranci). Bordered by the crenelations and turrets of the fortress built by the Savelli family in the 13th century, this charming garden planted with orange trees, roses, pines and cypresses overlooks the Tiber and is one of the most pleasant spots from which to view Rome.

THE DOORS OF SANTA SABINA
Of the three original doors, only two remain. One of these 5th-century carved cedarwood doors, which is unusually well preserved, illustrates the parallel between Christ, Moses, and Elijah expressed by St Augustine.

Church of
Sant'Alessio.

Fresco in the Basilica
of San Clemente
▲ *193* depicting the
story of St Alexis
(right).

**THE ORDER OF THE
KNIGHTS OF MALTA**
This is a religious
order of the Roman
Catholic Church and
a Catholic order of
knighthood. It is
governed by an
elected Grand
Master; he bears the
titles of Eminence
and Highness, and is
recognized
internationally
as a Head of
State, due the
honors of a
sovereign.

de Zamora,
General Master
of the
Dominicans, who
died in 1300. Both
the bell tower and
the cloister of the
monastery date
from the 13th
century.
SANT'ALESSIO.
According to
tradition, the house of Eufimianus, the father of Alexis, stood
on this site. Converted to Christianity, Alexis fled on the eve
of his wedding and spent seventeen years as a pilgrim in the
East. After returning to Rome, he presented himself as a
slave in the house of his parents, who did not recognize him,
and died beneath the steps of his paternal home, having
entrusted the story of his life to Pope Clement so that he
could reveal it to his father. St Alexis' story was very popular
in the Middle Ages; in the 17th century it was set to music by
Stefano Landi with a libretto by
Cardinal Rospigliosi; and it
also appears in the frescoes of
San Clemente. Before the 10th
century a church dedicated to
St Boniface existed where
Sant'Alessio now stands. In

977 it was given to Archbishop Serge of Damascus, who
founded a Greek monastery on this spot. Both the Emperor
Otto III and Adalbertus, Bishop of Prague, stayed here
several times around the year 1000. In 1216 Pope Honorius
III rebuilt the church; its structure was further modified in
1750, except for the elegant 13th-century bell tower. In the
Romanesque crypt relics of St Thomas à Becket are
preserved together with the column to which,
according to tradition, St
Sebastian was bound.
**PIAZZA DEI CAVALIERI DI
MALTA ★, ● *50*.** The square
of the Knights of Malta and
the Order's church, Santa
Maria del Priorato, are the
only architectural works by
the famous engraver
Giambattista Piranesi
(1720–78) ● *I*. They were
built between 1764 and 1766
at the request of
Giambattista Rezzonico,
Grand Master of the Order
and nephew of Clement
XIII. The square is
decorated with trophies,
alluding to the Order's
military role. It is almost
impossible to get
permission to visit the
Priory, but you can peep

through the keyhole (though you may have to join a line of
tourists waiting to do so) and discover the vast dome of St
Peter's in this miniature frame. The church's façade can be
seen from Trastevere; it is punctuated by twin pilasters around
a giant oculus and has a neoclassical character. (Take Via di
Santa Sabina; turn right into Via Sant'Alberto Magno; then,
when you reach Largo Arrigo VII, take Via di Santa Prisca).
SANTA PRISCA. This is the oldest place of Christian worship on
the Aventine. The church was built on the site of a Roman
house, important remains of which can be seen on the lower
levels. Tradition identifies the house as belonging to St Prisca,
the daughter of Aquila and Priscilla, who offered hospitality
to St Peter. Baptized at thirteen, Prisca was condemned under
the Emperor Claudius to be devoured alive by lions;
miraculously saved, she was then decapitated. An early
church was built here during the 4th to 5th centuries and
restored at various times in the 8th and 9th centuries.
Damaged during the sack of Rome in 1084, it was successfully
repaired under the pontificate of Pascal II. But at the
beginning of the 15th century the building had to be radically
restored after being partially destroyed by a fire. The Baroque
façade (1660) by Carlo Lombardi is particularly noteworthy.
In the apse 17th-century frescoes illustrate the story of the
martyrdom of St Prisca, and her *Baptism by St Peter*, painted
around 1600 by Passignano, can be seen above the altar. A
flight of steps from the church's right nave leads to the
mithraeum.
MITHRAEUM OF SANTA PRISCA. Excavations of the church
begun in 1944 revealed, next to the crypt, a richly decorated
mithraeum (shrine for the worship of Mithras), which
occupies the rooms of an older house, perhaps that of
Licinius Sura, a friend of Trajan. From the marks on the
bricks, this building can be dated to about 95 AD. Beyond the
nymphaeum (small grotto) there is now a small museum
containing items found during the excavation. In the two
niches at the entrance were statues of the genii, or guardian
spirits, of fertility and sterility, Cautes and Cautopathes, of
which only the former has survived. The niche in the back wall
is unique in Rome: in addition to the usual figure of Mithras
killing the bull, there is also a recumbent Saturn whose body
is made of amphorae covered in stucco. Paintings covering the
walls above the seats where the faithful used to sit
portray two processions. The one on the right
illustrates the seven degrees of
initiation into the cult: *Corax*
(crow), *Nymphus* (spouse),
Miles (soldier), *Leo* (lion),
Perses (the Persian),
Heliodromus and Pater
(Father), while the one on the
left shows the *leones* (lions)
approaching Mithras and the Sun,
reclining ready for a banquet.
(Return to the Via di Santa
Prisca, cross Viale
Aventino, and from
Piazza Albania take Via
di San Saba. You are now
on the Little Aventine.)

When decorating the
stelae of the Piazza
dei Cavalieri di
Malta, Piranesi was
inspired by the
military iconography
of the Order and the
emblems of the
Rezzonico family (a
crenelated tower and
a two-headed eagle).
He took his designs
from antiquity.

**THE WORSHIP OF
MITHRAS**
In the 2nd century AD
worship of the
Persian god Mithras
took root in Italy and
in the ports and
garrison towns of the
Roman Empire,
where it competed
with Christianity
before sinking into
oblivion at the end of
the 4th century. A
religion of light,
offering its initiates
the guarantee of
salvation in the
afterlife, Mithraism
involved an elaborate
rite focusing on the
sacrifice of the bull,
which symbolized the
victory of
life over
evil.

After leaving Santa Sabina, descend the Via di Sant'Anselmo for a restful stroll in the shade of palm trees. The peaceful atmosphere of the Aventine is rediscovered here, in "that secret district, green, airy, filled with silence, where it always seems as if an eye is following you, invisible along the leafy streets…" (Julien Gracq). A pause in the cool, shady gardens of the

Church of Sant'Anselmo should not be missed.

THE PYRAMID
Measuring 100 feet around the base and 125 feet high, the Pyramid of Caius Cestius is built in masonry covered with marble tiles. It was inspired by the Egyptian models fashionable in Rome after the conquest of Egypt (30 BC).

THE LITTLE AVENTINE

At the time of the Roman Empire the Little Aventine, a low summit separated from the rest of the hill by a depression, was a district inhabited by aristocrats whose luxurious homes spread below. Although these were later destroyed to make room for the Baths of Caracalla ▲ *319*, excavations have brought to light some magnificent remains, notably of a large Imperial house, preserved today in the Hospice of Santa Margherita.

SAN SABA. The foundation of this church was undoubtedly due to Pope Gregory the Great and his mother, Silvia. According to 7th-century documents the religious community originally consisted of Eastern monks; these were succeeded by Monte Cassino Benedictines in the 10th century, monks from Cluny in the 12th century, and Cistercians in the 16th century. Shortly afterwards ordinary canons took the monks' place. Campaigns for the excavation and restoration of the church started at the end of the 19th century. In the sacristy frescoes of the 7th and 8th centuries include some admirable portraits of monks' faces. The church's Roman façade is preceded by a portico with pilasters supporting a lovely Renaissance loggia. (Take Via Annia Faustina on the left, then Via della Piramide Cestia.)

PORTA OSTIENSIS

PYRAMID OF CAIUS CESTIUS. Included in the Aurelian walls, the pyramid of Caius Cestius (possibly the Roman citizen of that name who was a praetor in 44 BC) has been known since the Middle Ages as the *Meta Remi*, the tomb of Remus. Like the *Meta Romuli*, just outside the Vatican (close to today's Via della Conciliazione), the Pyramid

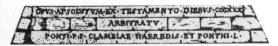

is a funeral monument, as is clear from the inscription on both sides: "Caius Cestius Epulon, son of Lucius, of the Pobilia tribe, praetor, tribune of the Plebs, septemvir (one of the seven attendants) at the sacred banquets." On the eastern side an inscription in smaller characters states that in accordance with the terms of his will the building was completed in less than 333 days. On the west side is a small door leading to the funeral chamber (not open to the public). The walls are painted with rich decorations of the third style, now mostly faded. Nearby, you can see the ancient road that started at one of the gates in the Aurelian Wall.

THE PROTESTANT CEMETERY. At the foot of the Pyramid of Cestius lies the Protestant (non-Catholic) Cemetery, the first granted by the popes to non-Catholic foreigners. In the shade of pines and cypress trees, colonies of cats have become the regular visitors of the illustrious dead, who include the poet Shelley, drowned in the Gulf of La Spezia in 1822, John Keats and his friend the painter Joseph Severn, Goethe's son Julius, and more recently Antonio Gramsci, one of the founders of the Italian Communist Party.

PORTA OSTIENSIS. Set within the Aurelian Wall ▲ *323* next to the Pyramid of Caius Cestius is the Porta di San Paolo, the ancient Porta Ostiensis from which the Via Ostia led to Rome's seaport. Together with the Porta Appia, it is the best preserved of the gates of ancient Rome. Originally it had two entrances framed by semicircular towers. At the time of Maxentius, in the 4th century AD, two crenelated walls were added, with a double gate which also had two arches of travertine marble; during the time of Honorius the two exterior arches were reduced to one. It was through the Porta Ostiensis that Totila's Goths entered Rome in 594 BC. Today it houses a museum where models of Ostia and the ports built by Claudius and Trajan are exhibited, along with casts of reliefs and inscriptions evoking the Via Ostia and its wayside monuments.

JOHN KEATS
The English poet John Keats (1795–1821) came to Rome hoping to recover from tuberculosis, a disease that had already carried off of his mother and his brother. But he died

three months later. The poet himself dictated the epitaph on his tomb: "Here lies one whose name was writ in water."

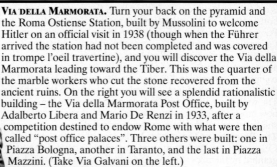

A slaughterhouse worker during the 19th century.

VIA DELLA MARMORATA. Turn your back on the pyramid and the Roma Ostiense Station, built by Mussolini to welcome Hitler on an official visit in 1938 (though when the Führer arrived the station had not been completed and was covered in trompe l'oeil travertine), and you will discover the Via della Marmorata leading toward the Tiber. This was the quarter of the marble workers who cut the stone recovered from the ancient ruins. On the right you will see a splendid rationalistic building – the Via della Marmorata Post Office, built by Adalberto Libera and Mario De Renzi in 1933, after a competition destined to endow Rome with what were then called "post office palaces". Three others were built: one in Piazza Bologna, another in Taranto, and the last in Piazza Mazzini. (Take Via Galvani on the left.)

THE SLAUGHTERHOUSE. The Mattatoio (slaughterhouse) was built by G. Ersoch between 1887 and 1892 to replace the old buildings on the Via Flaminia ▲ 238. The monumental gate is crowned by a slaughtered bull, a remarkable realist sculpture. The Mattatoio fell into disuse in the 1980s, and there are now plans to transform it into a cultural center or concert hall. In the surrounding neighborhood you can sample traditional Roman dishes featuring offal.

MONTE TESTACCIO

THE MOUNT OF SHARDS. The artificial hill in ancient times called *Mons Testaceus* is about 100 feet high; it has a circumference of just over half a mile, and a surface area of nearly 8 square miles. As its name indicates, it is in fact a heap of debris – the remains of the amphorae that contained products imported by Rome. These came mainly from the trading establishments on the Aventine and from the Emporium, the ancient commercial port on the nearby Tiber. The upper part of the "hill" consists almost entirely of amphorae that held oil from Spain, dating from 140 AD.

THE NEIGHBORHOOD. After the Unification of Italy it was decided to turn the Monte Testaccio area into a neighborhood of craftsmen and workmen. Building was begun in 1883, but was not finished until 1907 after the creation of the Institute for Popular Housing in 1903 put an end to a period of frenetic real-estate speculation. Today it is a lively neighborhood, with the colorful market of PIAZZA SANTA MARIA LIBERATRICE in its midst. The church of the same name was built in 1908, in Roman Byzantine style, replacing the Baroque church in the Forum demolished in 1899 for the restoration of Santa Maria Antiqua ▲ 142. (A little over a mile from the Porta Ostiensis is San Paolo fuori le Mura ▲ 382.)

THE AMPHORAE Because of their inscriptions (maker's mark, exporter's name, dates of inspection, etc.), some of the amphorae of Monte Testaccio have provided valuable evidence of the economy at the end of the Republic and under the Empire.

The Coelian Hill

The Coelian Hill
(Monte Celio),
a strip of high
ground which
stretches as far as the
Coliseum, was included within
the walls of Rome in the 7th century BC. At the end of the
Republic and during the Empire it became partly residential.
Its luxurious villas included those of Mamurra (Julius
Caesar's officer made notorious by Catullus' epigrams) and
those of the Lateranus and Symmachus families. Yet the area
also retained a popular character. After the great fire that
destroyed the city under Nero, apartment blocks (*insulae*)
were built on these slopes, particularly around the base of the
Temple of Claudius. Recent excavations have revealed their
remains. Another feature of this hill was the presence of
several barracks, including those of the 5th cohort of the
vigiles (city guards ▲ 356) near Santa Maria in Domnica, the
two barracks of the *equites singulares* (the Emperor's mounted
guards) and the Castra Peregrina
(around the Church of Santo Stefano
Rotondo), where soldiers from
outside Rome were posted for
special duties such as policing and
mail service. From the end of
antiquity the construction of
important religious buildings gave
this area a new profile. At its

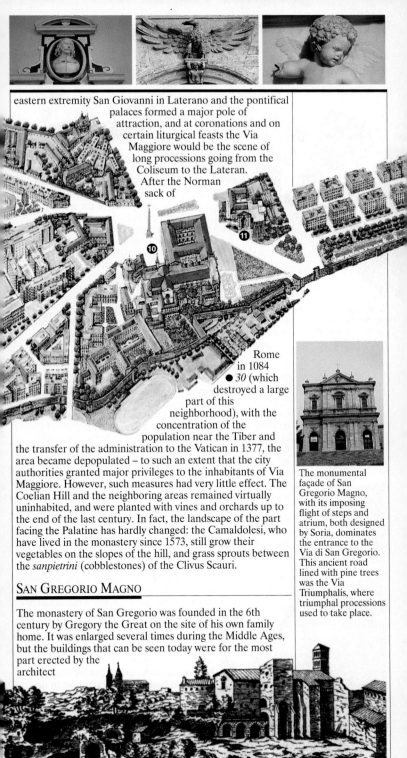

eastern extremity San Giovanni in Laterano and the pontifical palaces formed a major pole of attraction, and at coronations and on certain liturgical feasts the Via Maggiore would be the scene of long processions going from the Coliseum to the Lateran. After the Norman sack of Rome in 1084 ● *30* (which destroyed a large part of this neighborhood), with the concentration of the population near the Tiber and the transfer of the administration to the Vatican in 1377, the area became depopulated – to such an extent that the city authorities granted major privileges to the inhabitants of Via Maggiore. However, such measures had very little effect. The Coelian Hill and the neighboring areas remained virtually uninhabited, and were planted with vines and orchards up to the end of the last century. In fact, the landscape of the part facing the Palatine has hardly changed: the Camaldolesi, who have lived in the monastery since 1573, still grow their vegetables on the slopes of the hill, and grass sprouts between the *sanpietrini* (cobblestones) of the Clivus Scauri.

SAN GREGORIO MAGNO

The monastery of San Gregorio was founded in the 6th century by Gregory the Great on the site of his own family home. It was enlarged several times during the Middle Ages, but the buildings that can be seen today were for the most part erected by the architect

The monumental façade of San Gregorio Magno, with its imposing flight of steps and atrium, both designed by Soria, dominates the entrance to the Via di San Gregorio. This ancient road lined with pine trees was the Via Triumphalis, where triumphal processions used to take place.

187

Giambattista Soria (1629–33) under the direction of Cardinal Scipione Borghese. The church's interior was remodeled between 1725 and 1734 by Francesco Ferrari. At the top of the nave, to the left, the Salviati chapel contains a very early fresco portraying the Virgin Mary which, according to tradition, is supposed to have spoken to St Gregory. To the left of the church stand three small chapels that were rebuilt at the beginning of the 17th century. Santa Silvia (on the right) is dedicated to St Gregory's mother. Sant'Andrea (in the center) probably stands on the site of St Gregory's original oratory; it contains two notable frescoes, the one by Domenichino, the other by Guido Reni, both painted in 1608. In the third chapel, Santa Barbara, there is a table where, as legend has it, an angel sat among the poor to whom St Gregory was offering a meal.

1. CASTRENSE AMPHITHEATER
2. SANTA CROCE IN GERUSALEMME

CLIVUS SCAURI

The campanile and medieval buttresses of the Basilica of Santi Giovanni e Paolo.

The street that climbs from San Gregorio to San Giovanni is built over an ancient Roman street, and in some respects still looks like one. Along it the remains of several Imperial dwellings, which have survived at a relatively high level above ground, are linked by medieval arches. (At the end of the Clivus, after passing under the arches of the medieval buttresses, you will come to the Church of Santi Giovanni e Paolo.)

SANTI GIOVANNI E PAOLO. With its red-brick architecture, the high windowless walls of the monastery and the tall Romanesque campanile built on the remains of the Temple of Claudius, the Piazza dei Santi Giovanni e Paolo is as silent and desolate as those painted by de Chirico. Dedicated to St John and St Paul, two of Constantine's soldiers martyred under Julian the Apostate in 362, the basilica was built above

their house in the 5th century. It was damaged during the sack of Rome in 1084 by Emperor Henry IV ● *30*, then partly rebuilt between 1099 and 1118, when the campanile was erected. The narthex is of a slightly later period. Restoration work in the 1950's restored the exterior to its medieval appearance, but the interior retains its 18th-century decorations.

THE HOUSE OF ST JOHN AND ST PAUL. This can be reached by a small staircase to the right of the choir. It is a moving testimonial to how Christianity took root in heathen soil: mythological scenes appear alongside symbols of the new religion. At the end of the last century two large multistoried Imperial dwellings were unearthed beneath the church. Originally they were separated by a small courtyard, which was later

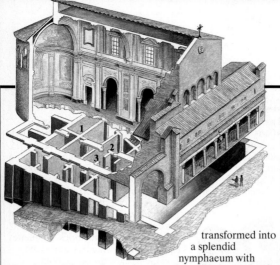

THE HOUSE OF THE SAINTS JOHN AND PAUL
This is painted with remarkable decorations on a white background showing youths supporting green bowers in which there are peacocks and other large birds. The vault is adorned with cupids and birds rampaging in the foliage. Later decorations, which probably date from the 4th century AD, are to be seen in rooms (2) and (3).

transformed into a splendid nymphaeum with fountains and decorations painted on the walls. A parade of cupids riding sea serpents can still be seen on the right. But the most remarkable element is a large fresco on one of the walls depicting Proserpina returning from Hades. From the court of the nymphaeum you reach the ground-floor rooms, which lead to the Clivus Scauri (1). On a well-preserved vault can be seen a fresco in twelve sections showing male figures carrying scrolls, and pairs of sheep. A praying figure painted on one of the lunettes gives evidence of the Christian character of the house at that time. At the top of a small staircase is the "confessio", a sort of alcove entirely decorated with frescoes from the second half of the 4th century, depicting scenes of martyrdom (arrests, decapitation, and general violence); these describe the passions of John and Paul and also those of Crispus, Crispinianus and Benedicta, who were all executed under Julian the Apostate and whose bodies were buried in this house.

THE TEMPLE OF CLAUDIUS. At the western tip of the Coelian Hill, overlooking the Palatine, stand the remains of a temple dedicated to the Emperor Claudius, who was deified by his wife Agrippina soon after his death in 54 AD. The temple was built on top of the ruins of a rectangular building. The western wall, which can be seen between the campanile and the monastery of Santi Giovanni e Paolo, belongs to the oldest part of the monument. To the east, the supporting walls that run along the Via Claudia down toward the Coliseum were built by Nero as a frame for the monumental gardens of the Domus Aurea ▲ *174*.

CLAUDIUS
The Emperor Claudius (41–54 AD) was often ridiculed, but he was in fact a scholar and a great administrator. As a soldier he pursued Augustus' policies and succeeded in conquering Britain. But this man who stammered and walked with a limp had the misfortune of marrying first Messalina, notorious for her debauchery, and then Agrippina, who had him assassinated to ensure her son Nero's succession to the throne.

SANTA MARIA IN DOMNICA

The aqueduct built by Nero (54–68 AD) started at Porta Maggiore and brought water to the Palatine Hill.

"The park [of the Villa Celimontana], almost unique in its variety and fantasy among Roman parks, follows the folds of the Coelian Hill, on the ridge of which it stands.**"**

Gabriel Fauré

"VIRGIN AND CHILD"
With its vivid colors and iconographic freedom, which combines the Hellenistic and Byzantine styles, this mosaic is one of the finest Carolingian works in Rome.

THE ARCH OF DOLABELLA AND THE AREA AROUND SANTA MARIA IN DOMNICA. From Piazza Santi Giovanni e Paolo, the Via San Paolo della Croce rises between high walls, along the side of the Villa Celimontana, toward a travertine arch supporting Nero's aqueduct. The attic bears an inscription (10 AD) giving the names of the consuls Publius Cornelius Dolabella and Caius Junius Silanus. This arch was no doubt originally the Porta Caelimontana, one of the gates in the Republican walls rebuilt by Augustus. It opens onto a very typical Roman scene. To the left is the isolated brick silhouette of a pilaster from Claudius' aqueduct; behind the trees in the background stands the round Church of Santo Stefano; and in the center is the NAVICELLA, a marble ship that was transformed into a fountain by Pope Leo X (1513–21). A portico built in the same period by Sansovino gives access to Santa Maria in Domnica.

SANTA MARIA IN DOMNICA. No mention of this church can be found earlier than the time of Pope Leo III (795–816), but its foundation, on the remains of the barracks of the 5th cohort of *vigiles* ▲ 356, probably goes back to the 7th century. The present building dates from the pontificate of Pascal I (817–24), as do the beautiful mosaics in the apse: the chancel arch portrays the Savior seated on the vault of heaven between two angels, while below this the apostles are shown being led by Peter and Paul, Moses and Elijah. At the back of the apse there is a hieratic Byzantine image of the *Virgin and Child* seated in the midst of a crowd of angels, while the Pope (distinguished by the square nimbus of the living) humbly touches her foot. To the left of the church, a monumental door opens onto the Villa Celimontana.

VILLA CELIMONTANA. On sunny days this villa's magnificent trees are an invitation to walk in their shade among the flowers and fountains. The park, which is now open to the public, has been in existence since the 15th century. It was then the garden of the Villa Mattei ▲ 369, which had been conceived as a pleasure palace and adorned with ancient sculptures collected by its owners. The *casino* was built between 1581 and 1586 by Giacomo del Duca, and an obelisk was erected in the garden. This had previously stood on the Capitol and was given in 1582 to Prince Mattei by the Senate of Rome in gratitude for his good works. Between the 16th and the 19th centuries the villa was open to the public one day a year: during the pilgrimage to the Seven

Pope Leo X had his name and his coat of arms carved on the Navicella fountain.

Churches ▲ *381*, rehabilitated by St Philip Neri in 1552, the faithful would come to the villa for rest and refreshment. In 1856 the estate was inherited by a Bavarian baron. It was confiscated by the Italian State in 1918 as an "enemy asset", and was then given to the city of Rome in 1925. Today the villa is the headquarters of the Italian Geographical Society.

SANTO STEFANO ROTONDO

The first circular church to be built in Rome. Founded by Pope Simplicius (468–83), it was modeled on the Holy Sepulcher in Jerusalem. The masonry and the capitals decorated with crosses show that it is not an ancient monument that was reused. Work continued through the 6th century under John I and Felix IV. Pope Innocent II (1130–43) added the entrance portico and the three internal transverse arches. On the walls erected to close the openings of the external arches Gregory XIII (1572–85) had frescoes painted portraying scenes of martyrdom; these have survived (see above). (From the Largo della Sanità Militare go into the piazza, then right along Via Celimontana as far as Via dei Santi Quattro Coronati.)

MARTYROLOGY
In Santo Stefano Rotondo there are thirty-two frescoes by Pomarancio showing the martyrdom of saints, and several by Antonio Tempesta (*The Life of St Stephen*, *The Massacre of the*

Innocents and *The Madonna of Seven Sorrows*).

A MONUMENTAL SANCTUARY
Originally Santo Stefano Rotondo had two concentric circular galleries, separated by two series of columns. When the sanctuary was restored in 1453 the outer gallery was destroyed because it was in danger of collapsing. The diameter of the building was thus considerably reduced. In 1658 excavations revealed the presence of a mithraeum (2nd to 3rd century AD) beneath the church, as well as remains of the Castra Peregrina barracks ▲ *186*.

THE CLOISTER
Behind its fortress-like exterior, the marvelous, secretive Church of the Santi Quattro Coronati conceals one of Rome's most poetic cloisters (early 13th century). In the time of Pascal II the basin for ablutions in the center adorned the atrium of the church.

SANTI QUATTRO CORONATI

This church was first mentioned in 595, but its foundation goes back to the 4th century. After being renovated by Leo IV (847–55) and then badly damaged when Rome was sacked in 1084 ● *30*, it was restored under Pascal II (1099–1118), though the side naves were eliminated and its length considerably reduced. The magnificent paving of the central nave also dates from this period. In 1623 Cardinal Millini had the mosaics of the apse destroyed and replaced by frescoes by Giovanni da San Giovanni. These illustrate the story of the "Quattro Coronati", the four soldiers Severus, Severian, Carpophorus and Victorinus, who were martyred under Diocletian for refusing to worship Aesculapius. In 1912 and 1957 excavations revealed some of the original structures, including the columns and the crypt of the Carolingian church. The monastery, which was known to have existed in the time of Leo IV, was transformed into an impregnable fortress in the 13th century. In fact, during the Middle Ages the complex was used as a bastion for the defense of the Lateran Palace ▲ *197* and as a refuge for the popes.

THE CHAPEL OF SAN SILVESTRO. The first courtyard leads to the Chapel of San Silvestro, which is preceded by a room adorned with a calendar painted in the 13th century. The chapel was decorated with a beautiful cycle of frescoes in 1246 portraying the legend of Constantine. Having become a leper, the Emperor dreams of Peter and Paul; he then sends messengers to Pope Sylvester I, in a retreat on Mount Soracte; the Pope

"THE TRIUMPH OF THE CROSS" ★ Glistening with gold and glowing colors, the apse of San Clemente displays a beautiful mosaic of the Roman school of the 12th century. The twelve doves within the cross symbolize the apostles.

obliges the Emperor to venerate images of the apostles and cures him of leprosy by baptizing him; finally the Emperor receives the Pope as sovereign of Rome. Beyond the naive and picturesque nature of their images, these frescoes are of great historical interest: they assert the supremacy of the papacy over civil authority, which at a certain period of the Middle Ages was a highly controversial issue. The second courtyard leads to the present church, where there are 14th-century frescoes on the walls of the lateral naves; the left nave leads to the early-13th-century cloister, which in turn leads to the 9th-century Chapel of Santa Barbara.

SAN CLEMENTE ★

THE BASILICA OF SAN CLEMENTE. This basilica dedicated to the third successor of St Peter, Pope Clement I (88–97), was founded before 385 on the site of existing Roman buildings. Councils were held in it in 417 and 499, and it was restored in the 8th and 9th centuries before being destroyed during the sack of 1084 ● *30*. Consequently Pascal II (1099–1118), who had been titular cardinal of San Clemente before becoming pope, commissioned the construction of a new basilica on the site of the old one. Much later Carlo Fontana made modifications to it between 1705 and 1709. The paleo-Christian basilica was only discovered in 1857.

THE UPPER CHURCH. Externally this has retained its medieval

Beneath the Crucifixion, two deer representing all those who aspire to baptism drink from a stream springing from the cross.

features, with a vestibule, a porch and an atrium. Inside, it is modeled on the lower church, but on a reduced scale. The 12th-century Schola Cantorum in the middle of the central nave is partly made of elements from the earlier church. The ciborium is 6th century, and the paschal candelabra 12th century. The apse is adorned with a splendid 12th-century mosaic, *The Triumph of the Cross*. To the right of the main entrance, the chapel dedicated to St Catherine is decorated with frescoes by Masolino da Panicale.

MASOLINO (C. 1430) ❝Catherine's eloquence here is pure and persuasive. The saint had not yet become, under Pinturicchio's brush, the disturbing princess on the walls of the Borgia Apartments.❞
Y. and E.-R. Labande, *Rome*

THE LOWER CHURCH. Through the sacristy one descends to what is virtually a picture gallery. The narthex has splendid 11th-century frescoes depicting the miracle of St Clement and the transfer of his body from the Vatican to San Clemente (above). In the nave there are frescoes of *The Ascension* (9th century) and *The Legend of St Alexis* ▲ *180*. Another 11th-century fresco cycle offers an amusing version of the pursuit of St Clement by the heathen Prefect of Rome, Sisinnius: his servants, blinded by God, bind a column, mistaking it for the Pope, and try to carry it off. The vivid expressions the Prefect uses to encourage his men, which are inscribed on the wall as in a cartoon strip, are the earliest known examples of the vernacular.

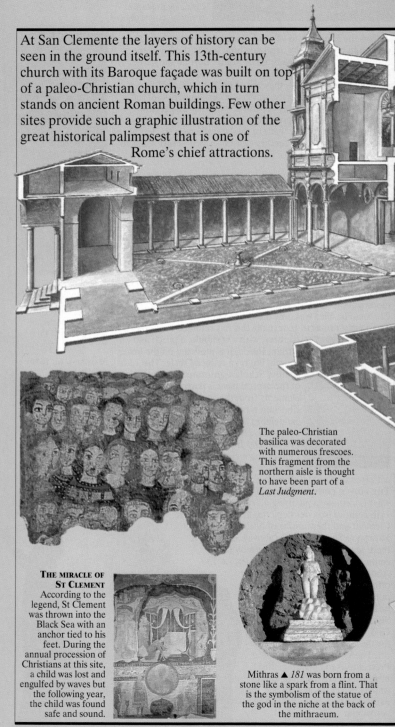

At San Clemente the layers of history can be seen in the ground itself. This 13th-century church with its Baroque façade was built on top of a paleo-Christian church, which in turn stands on ancient Roman buildings. Few other sites provide such a graphic illustration of the great historical palimpsest that is one of Rome's chief attractions.

The paleo-Christian basilica was decorated with numerous frescoes. This fragment from the northern aisle is thought to have been part of a *Last Judgment*.

THE MIRACLE OF ST CLEMENT
According to the legend, St Clement was thrown into the Black Sea with an anchor tied to his feet. During the annual procession of Christians at this site, a child was lost and engulfed by waves but the following year, the child was found safe and sound.

Mithras ▲ *181* was born from a stone like a spark from a flint. That is the symbolism of the statue of the god in the niche at the back of the mithraeum.

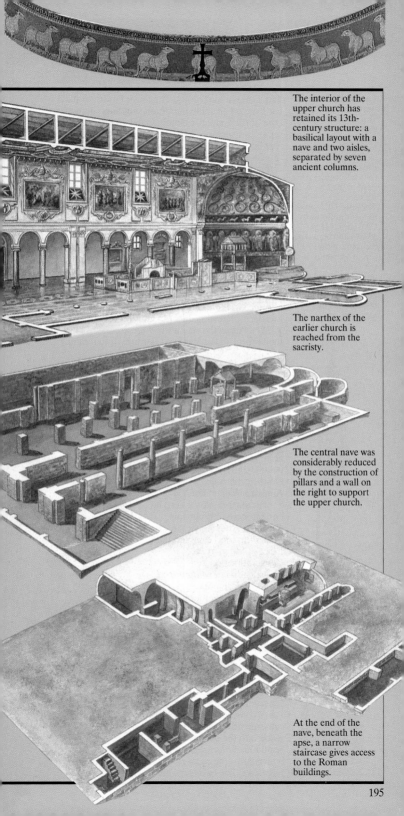

The interior of the upper church has retained its 13th-century structure: a basilical layout with a nave and two aisles, separated by seven ancient columns.

The narthex of the earlier church is reached from the sacristy.

The central nave was considerably reduced by the construction of pillars and a wall on the right to support the upper church.

At the end of the nave, beneath the apse, a narrow staircase gives access to the Roman buildings.

THE EARLIER BUILDINGS. The lower basilica is itself
constructed on some important buildings dating from the
time of the Emperor Domitian (81–96 AD). These were two
separate structures, separated by a very narrow corridor. The
first housed the Imperial mint, which had been transferred to
this spot during the Flavian period from its original site on the
Capitoline Hill. Its identification was made possible by the
discovery near San Clemente of a series of inscriptions
dedicated to several gods, including Apollo, Hercules and
Fortuna. The second edifice, located to the west of the church
and also built at the time of Domitian, was entirely made of
brick. Originally the central courtyard was covered by a vault
with skylights. The exact purpose of the building is still
unknown but it was certainly public, as the presence of the
mithraeum confirms.

THE MITHRAEUM. Its construction dates from the end of the
2nd or beginning of the 3rd century AD, a particularly
propitious time for the spread of oriental cults in the city. The
entrance to the room would have had doors, and the ceiling
was decorated with stars (an allusion to Mithraic cosmology
▲ *181*). Along the side walls there are the usual benches for
the faithful. (Take Via San Giovanni in Laterano.)

THE LATERAN

This is a very different part of Rome – a monumental Rome
with its huge basilica dominating the vast unattractive piazza.
The square was the meeting place of Rome's Communists in
the days when leaders such as Togliatti and Berlinguer drew
huge crowds. At one time the inhabitants of Rome used to
gather here on June 23, the eve of the Feast of St John, to sit
at long tables, eating *lumache*
(snails) and sipping white wine.
On the other side of the
Aurelian Wall, in the Via
Sannio market, clothes can be
bought incredibly cheaply.

ORIGINS. After his victory over
Maxentius in 312 AD and the
Edict of Milan in 313,
Constantine donated the
basilica as an *ex voto* offering
to the African pope
Melchiades, together with a
domus ecclesiae, which became
the Lateran Palace. This
remained the official residence
of the popes until their return
from Avignon in 1377. The
estate had been an Imperial
possession ever since Nero
confiscated it from the
Laterani family for their part in
Piso's conspiracy in 65 AD;
subsequently, in 197, it was
made into the barracks of
Septimius Severus' mounted
bodyguards, the *equites
singulares*. The basilica, which

was originally dedicated to the Savior, was inaugurated in
327. Recent excavations have revealed a few frescoes
from the Laterani residence, some remains from the
barracks and several walls from the original basilica.

THE EXTENSION OF THE PALACE. During the 5th
century the popes began to enlarge the *patriarchium*
(the core of the patriarchal palace) and erected
buildings to meet the requirements of a
centralized administration. However,
they never succeeded in making the
Lateran the real center of Rome.
Later, in order to receive
Charlemagne after crowning him
Emperor in St Peter's on Christmas day
800, Pope Leo III added a *triclinium*
(banqueting hall) sumptuously decorated with
mosaics. In the 11th and 12th centuries, with the
erection of dwellings for the prelates and Curia staff
around the basilica and palace, the Lateran assumed the
appearance of a small town. But the fires of 1308 and 1361,
combined with the absence of the popes throughout most of
the 14th century, led to such a degeneration of the palace that
when Gregory XI returned to Rome in 1377 he preferred to
take up residence in the Vatican – which had the advantage of
being easier to defend, due to the proximity of the Tiber and
Castel Sant'Angelo. After restorations commissioned by
Martin V (1417–31), Leo X (1513–21) and Paul IV (1555–9),
Sixtus V (1585–90) entrusted the architect Domenico Fontana
with the complete restructuring of the palace. The
patriarchium was demolished, and only the Chapel of San
Lorenzo in Palatio, the Scala Santa and the remains of Leo

**THE FEAST OF ST
JOHN**
The feast was last
celebrated in
traditional style in
Piazza San Giovanni
in Laterano in 1969.

197

THE NAVE
The theatrical appearance of the Lateran's central nave is due to the gigantic pilasters that frame an alternating series of vaulted arches and pillars, each containing a gray marble alcove flanked by green marble columns from the original basilica. In each alcove stands a colossal statue of one of the twelve apostles, dating from the early 18th century.

III's *triclinium* were spared. The Lateran Palace is the headquarters of the Vicariate of Rome, and it was here that the famous Lateran Treaty, or "Concordat", between the Holy See and Mussolini was signed on February 11, 1929.

THE LATERAN BASILICA. The basilica is still considered "*Omnium urbis et orbis ecclesiarum mater et caput*", the mother and head of all the churches of the city and the world. Not surprisingly, it bears traces of the endless rebuilding it has undergone. The entrance, as in all the major basilicas, consists of a portico with a balcony for pontifical blessings, traditionally given here on the Feast of the Ascension. In 1735 Alessandro Galilei built the façade surmounted – or crushed, as critics said at the time – by fifteen colossal statues. The statue of Constantine beneath the porch came from the Imperial baths on the Quirinal Hill. As in St Peter's, of the five doors, the one on the left, the Holy Door, is opened only in Holy Years ● *52*. The ancient panels of the central door came from the Curia in the Forum ▲ *138*. The appearance of the nave and the two aisles on either side, the same in number as in the original basilica, has changed hardly at all since Borromini redesigned the interior between 1646 and 1649. The central nave has a 16th-century carved-wood ceiling, while the lower aisles are adorned with stucco decorations.

The entire transept was painted with frescoes at the end of the 16th century under the direction of Cavaliere d'Arpino. In the transept crossing, a 14th-century Gothic tabernacle stands on the altar at which only the Pope celebrates Mass. Although it was modified in 1851 under Pius IX, it contains fragments of the altar on which the first popes of Rome, from St Peter to St Sylvester, officiated. In the choir and the apse, which were rebuilt and

THE LATERAN TREATY
▲ *202*
The "Treaty of Conciliation", that gave birth to the Vatican State rehabilitated Catholics in Italian political life after a hiatus of fifty-nine years. Being "extraterritorial", the Lateran is part of the Vatican State.

redecorated in 1884 under Leo XIII, remains of the older mosaic decorations by Jacopo Torriti (13th century) have also been incorporated. Through the left transept one can reach the splendid 13th-century cloister. The right transept provides access to the side of the piazza, which is dominated by the portico and loggia designed by Domenico Fontana in 1586, Sixtus V's urban replanning having made this side entrance facing the city into the basilica's main entrance. A statue of Henry IV of France by Nicolas Cordier (1608) stands under the portico. This ruler was particularly generous with gifts to the chapter; as a result, all subsequent French heads of state have been made honorary canons of the Lateran Basilica.

THE BAPTISTERY OF SAN GIOVANNI IN FONTE. Built under Constantine and restructured in the 5th century, the baptistery was remodeled under Urban VIII in 1637 and again by Borromini for Alexander VII. Its octagonal interior, accentuated by four symmetrical chapels, exalts the sacrament of baptism. The drum of the cupola displays scenes from the life of St John the Baptist by Andrea Sacchi, while frescoes by his pupils illustrate the conversion of Constantine. The

The cloister of the basilica is the work of the Vassalletto family.

The statues crowning the basilica's façade portray Christ, St John the Evangelist, St John the Baptist and the Fathers of the Church.

mosaics in the chapels dedicated to St John the Evangelist (5th century) and St Venanzio (7th century) afford proof of the building's age. The font (in the center) is a huge green basalt urn originally used for the total immersion of those being baptized; it is surrounded by eight porphyry columns and has a bronze cover made between 1677 and 1678.

THE SCALA SANTA AND SANCTA SANCTORUM. The steps of the Scala Santa are said to be the ones on which Christ stood in Pontius Pilate's palace during his trial, and St Helena is supposed to have brought them to Rome. Pilgrims climb these twenty-eight steps on their knees as an act of veneration. Sixtus V had them erected as a stairway to the private chapel of the popes, San Lorenzo in Palatio. This chapel, which was part of the medieval palace, owes its other name, the Sancta Sanctorum ("Holy of Holies"), to the precious relics it contains. The most famous of these is an *acheiropoieton*, an image of Christ "not made by human hands", which Innocent III (1198–1216) had covered with silver leaf. (Proceed along Viale Carlo Felice.)

THE CASTRENSE
AMPHITHEATER
The amphitheater
owes its survival to its
incoratation into
the Aurelian Wall,
although only one of

its three levels is well
preserved. The name
comes from the late
Latin *castrum*,
meaning "Imperial
palace".

CIRCUS VARIANUS
This circus derives its
name from the family
of the Emperor
Heliogabalus, the
Varii. It was recently
discovered at the
northern end of the
Sessorium, running
parallel to Claudius'
aqueduct and the
Aurelian Wall. On the
spina was placed the
obelisk that must
have adorned the
tomb of Hadrian's
favorite, Antinous, on
the Pincio. To the
north in the former
barracks of the
grenadiers are further
remains, most notably
the back wall of a vast
apse dating from the
time of Constantine.

Santa Croce in
Gerusalemme (right).

SANTA CROCE IN GERUSALEMME

The most important ancient remains in this area – the
Castrense Amphitheater, the Baths of Helena, the Circus
Varianus and the hall converted to create Santa Croce in
Gerusalemme – were all part of a single Imperial villa, the
Sessorium, begun by Septimius Severus
and completed by Heliogabalus in the
3rd century AD. The Baths of Helena
were covered over by the construction
work for the Via Felice instigated by
Sixtus V ● *61*.
**BASILICA OF SANTA CROCE IN
GERUSALEMME.** Tradition has it that
Santa Croce, one of the major basilicas,
was built by Constantine in 320 AD to
house the relics brought back from
Jerusalem by his mother, St Helena.
After frequent restorations in the Middle
Ages, it was almost completely rebuilt in
1743 by Domenico Gregorini. Behind its
convex façade there is an unusual oval
atrium with an elliptical ambulatory
(pictured on the left). The ancient
columns separating the nave from the
two aisles alternate with Baroque pillars.
The whole of the interior is adorned with
stucco decorations. The frescoes on the
main vault of the church and the walls of
the choir were painted by Corrado Giaquinto in 1745. The
choir vault still has its late-15th-century decorations. The mid-
18th-century *baldacchino* rests on the columns of the original
medieval ciborium. The underground chapel of St Helena,
below the nave, is adorned with a splendid 15th-century
mosaic designed by Melozzo da Forlì.
THE CHAPEL OF THE RELICS. Of all the churches in Rome,
Santa Croce has one of the richest collections of relics. A
special chapel was therefore built for them in 1930.
A staircase to the left of the choir leads to this chapel, where
one can see three pieces of the True Cross, one of its nails, a

fragment of the INRI
("Jesus of Nazareth,
King of the Jews")
inscription, two thorns
from Christ's crown of
thorns, a piece of the
sponge that was held
up to him, one of the
silver pieces paid to
Judas, St Thomas's
finger which touched
the wounds of Christ,
and the crossbar from
the Good Thief's
cross. The paving
stones are said to
have been laid on a
substantial amount of
earth from Golgotha.

THE VATICAN

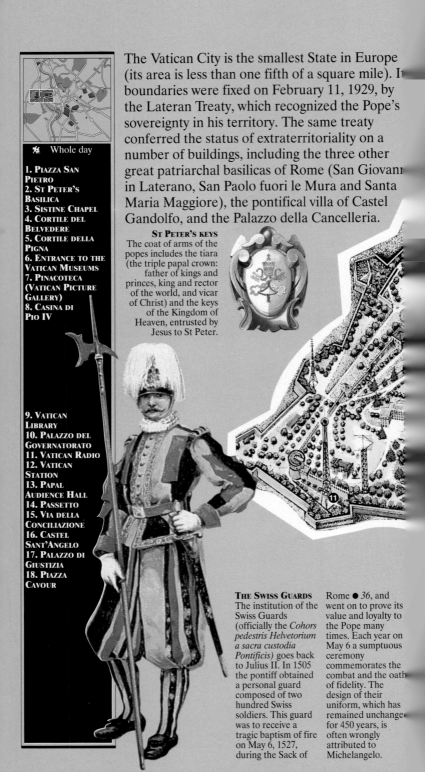

The Vatican City is the smallest State in Europe (its area is less than one fifth of a square mile). Its boundaries were fixed on February 11, 1929, by the Lateran Treaty, which recognized the Pope's sovereignty in his territory. The same treaty conferred the status of extraterritoriality on a number of buildings, including the three other great patriarchal basilicas of Rome (San Giovanni in Laterano, San Paolo fuori le Mura and Santa Maria Maggiore), the pontifical villa of Castel Gandolfo, and the Palazzo della Cancelleria.

ST PETER'S KEYS
The coat of arms of the popes includes the tiara (the triple papal crown: father of kings and princes, king and rector of the world, and vicar of Christ) and the keys of the Kingdom of Heaven, entrusted by Jesus to St Peter.

THE SWISS GUARDS
The institution of the Swiss Guards (officially the *Cohors pedestris Helvetorium a sacra custodia Pontificis*) goes back to Julius II. In 1505 the pontiff obtained a personal guard composed of two hundred Swiss soldiers. This guard was to receive a tragic baptism of fire on May 6, 1527, during the Sack of Rome ● *36*, and went on to prove its value and loyalty to the Pope many times. Each year on May 6 a sumptuous ceremony commemorates the combat and the oath of fidelity. The design of their uniform, which has remained unchanged for 450 years, is often wrongly attributed to Michelangelo.

The Vatican State has its own diplomats, citizens, police force, army and legal system; it mints its own money and has most forms of communication at its disposal, including a railway station, post offices, television, radio and newspapers. The daily Italian-language paper *L'Osservatore Romano*, founded in 1861, is printed in the Vatican City and contains a section that is the official mouthpiece of the Holy See; there are also weekly editions in several languages and a popular illustrated weekly edition, *L'Osservatore della Domenica*.

THE WALLS

After the Saracens sacked the Vatican in 846, Leo IV had the first fortifications built; these were subsequently extended many times. The bastions of the time of Nicholas V (1447–55) mark the present-day limits of the city.

THE PASSETTO

This is a fortified passageway linking the Vatican to the Castel Sant'Angelo.

Sixtus IV erected the Vatican's first purpose-built library, to house a collection of 2,527 volumes. Although more than 400 manuscripts were lost during the Sack of Rome in 1527, the increasing number of books led Sixtus V to organize a new library, still in use today.

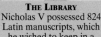

THE LIBRARY
Nicholas V possessed 824 Latin manuscripts, which he wished to keep in a library open to scholars.

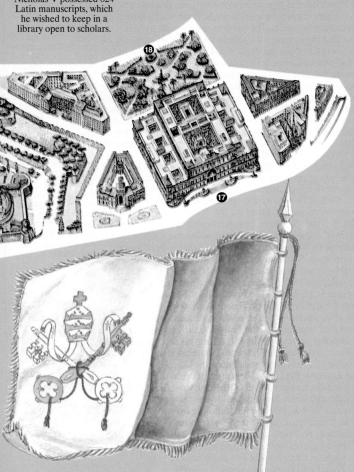

THE VATICAN FLAG
The Church's banner originally featured the figure of St Peter on a red background. Pope Innocent III replaced the figure with symbolic keys surmounted by a white cross; and Boniface VIII opted for a red silk standard spangled with gold stars. The flag remained unchanged until 1824, when Leo XII gave it the colors it has today, yellow and white; the keys have been crowned by the papal tiara ever since.

THE GREAT AGE OF BUILDING REACHED ITS CLIMAX WITH BERNINI'S MAGNIFICENT COLONNADES, WHICH MADE THE PIAZZA SAN PIETRO THE MOST THEATRICAL SQUARE IN THE WORLD.

The Ager Vaticanus (the plain between the Tiber and the Vatican Hill) was originally an unhealthy marshland area which, like other low-lying parts of the city, was often subject to terrible flooding by the river. For a long time it was sparsely populated, as the nucleus of the town was concentrated on the left bank of the Tiber.

AROUND ST PETER'S TOMB. In the days when the gardens of Domitian and Agrippina extended over this suburban area it was crossed by several roads, lined with a long procession of tombs. The gardens are thought to have included the circuses of Caligula and Nero, where many of the early Christian martyrs died. This was one of the most important buildings in the area, along with Trajan's *naumachia* and Hadrian's mausoleum ▲ *233*. Nevertheless, it appears to have been privately owned, like the Circus of Maxentius ▲ *328*, and to have formed part of Agrippina's villa. St Peter was buried in the vicinity of the circus, and it was the presence of the apostle's tomb that influenced the area's development. After his conversion to Christianity Constantine built a basilica over the tomb with an access route from the Pons Aelius (the ancient forerunner of the Ponte Sant'Angelo ▲ *239*), and houses soon sprang up along the road. A century later the first monasteries appeared around the shrine, and Pope Symmachus (498–514) constructed the embryo of an episcopal residence. From the 8th century the flood of pilgrims from Northern Europe coming to pray at the tombs of the apostles and martyrs led to the foundation of hospices to house them, such as the Scholae Francorum, Frisonorum, Saxonum and Langobardorum. The neighborhood experienced a fresh bout of growth under the influence of the Carolingians. At the request of Pépin le Bref, King of the Franks, Pope Stephen II turned the mausoleum of Theodosius into a chapel dedicated to St Petronilla, a Roman virgin venerated especially by the Franks; Charlemagne had an imperial palace built in 781, during his second visit to Rome; and Leo III (795–816) commissioned the building of a new papal residence.

THE LEONINE CITY. The Vatican neighborhood survived the ravages of the Goths and Vandals, even though it was located outside the Aurelian Wall ▲ *323*, and the imposing mass of the Castel Sant'Angelo ▲ *233* was its only protection. So when, in 846, the basilica and neighboring area were sacked by the Saracens the whole of Christendom was apprehensive and Pope Leo IV erected ramparts with the help of Lothair I. The newly enclosed quarter became known as the Leonine City, a name it retained throughout the Middle Ages – before becoming the Borgo in 1586, when it was integrated into the municipal administrative system. In the 12th century the popes embarked on a vast building project, but it was not until their return from Avignon in 1377 that they and the Curia left the Lateran ▲ *196* to definitively settle in the Vatican.

St Peter's tomb.

THE BORGO
At the end of the 15th century the ramparts were reinforced, and access to the basilica and palace was improved. A road named the Borgo Nuovo was created between the Borgo Santo Spirito and the Borgo Vecchio. At this stage the building of the basilica was started, and after the Sack of Rome in 1527 ● *36* the new fortifications of the area were begun. The major building period ended a century and a half later, when Bernini erected his magnificent colonnades.

Statue of St Peter.

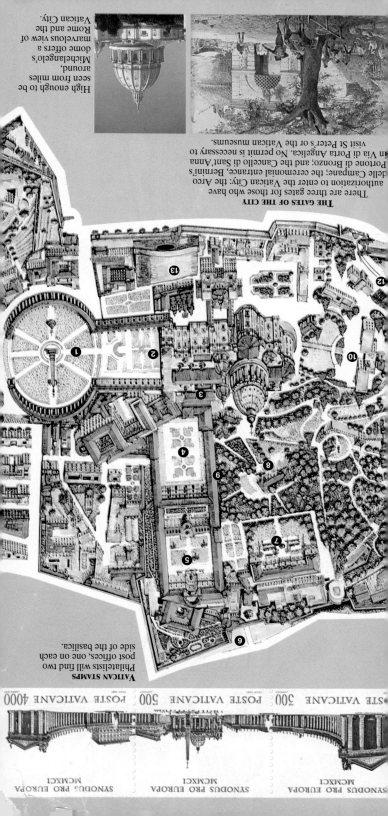

High enough to be seen from miles around, Michelangelo's dome offers a marvelous view of Rome and the Vatican City.

THE GATES OF THE CITY

There are three gates for those who have authorization to enter the Vatican City: the Arco delle Campane; the ceremonial entrance, Bernini's Portone di Bronzo; and the Cancello di Sant'Anna in Via di Porta Angelica. No permit is necessary to visit St Peter's or the Vatican museums.

VATICAN STAMPS

Philatelists will find two post offices, one on each side of the basilica.

POSTE VATICANE 4000   POSTE VATICANE 500   POSTE VATICANE 300

SYNODUS PRO EUROPA MCMXCI   SYNODUS PRO EUROPA MCMXCI   SYNODUS PRO EUROPA MCMXCI

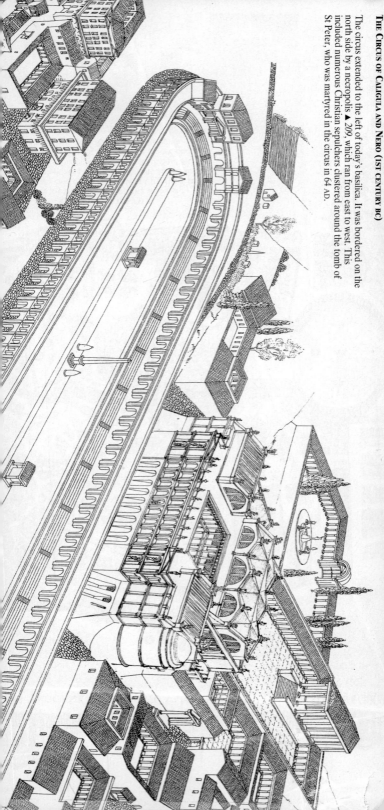

THE CIRCUS OF CALIGULA AND NERO (1ST CENTURY BC)

The circus extended to the left of today's basilica. It was bordered on the north side by a necropolis ▲ 209, which ran from east to west. This included numerous Christian sepulchers clustered around the tomb of St Peter, who was martyred in the circus in 64 A.D.

THE CHRISTIAN NECROPOLIS (2ND TO 3RD CENTURIES)

THE CHRISTIAN NECROPOLIS (2ND TO 3RD CENTURIES)

CONSTANTINE'S BASILICA (4TH OR 5TH CENTURY) Over St. Peter's burial place. Constantine built a vast basilica (about 400 x 200 feet) over St. Peter's burial place, with a central nave and four aisles preceded by a majestic atrium. The apostle's tomb was in the center of the choir and could be seen by the faithful.

CONSTANTINE'S BASILICA (4TH TO 8TH CENTURIES)
Constantine built a vast basilica (about 400 x 200 feet) over St Peter's
burial place, with a central nave and four aisles preceded by a majestic
atrium bordered with columns. The apostle's tomb was in the center of
the choir and could be seen by all the faithful.

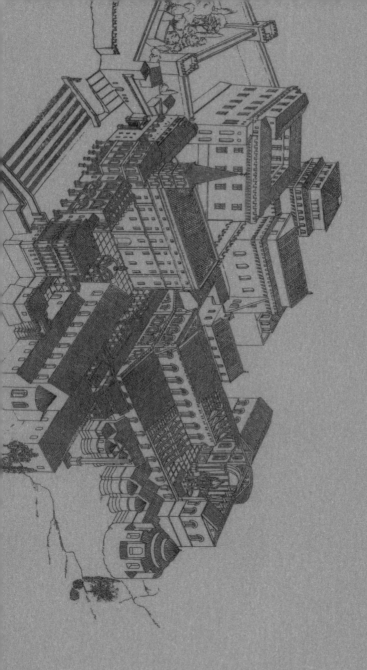

THE VATICAN IN THE MIDDLE AGES (4th to 15th CENTURIES)

THE VATICAN IN THE MIDDLE AGES (9TH TO 15TH CENTURIES)

THE REBUILT BASILICA (16TH TO 17TH CENTURIES)

THE REBUILT BASILICA (16TH TO 17TH CENTURIES)

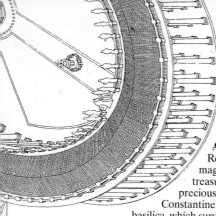

St Peter's Basilica

A NEW SHRINE. Resplendent with magnificent art treasures and precious metalwork, Constantine's ancient basilica, which survived for over a thousand years, threatened to collapse on the return of the popes from Avignon. Repairs and modifications proved insufficient, and Julius II (1503–13) invited Bramante to design a new church. The demolition and building work began in 1506, and was to last for a century and a half. Despite the multitude of architects who succeeded one another, often modifying the work of their predecessors, the new basilica turned out to be extraordinarily coherent as a whole.

RIVAL PLANS. Wanting, as he put it, "to perch the Pantheon on top of Constantine's basilica", Bramante planned a church in the form of a Greek cross crowned by a dome; and it is to Bramante that the four central piers and arches supporting the dome are due. After his death in 1514, his successors, Raphael, Giuliano da Sangallo, Baldassare Peruzzi and Antonio da Sangallo, put forward different plans in the shape of either a Greek or a Latin cross. Michelangelo, who took charge in 1546, opted for the Greek cross and conceived a new dome. Only the drum had been finished at the time of his death, but the dome was completed in accordance with the plans and model that he left. However, the Latin cross was the plan that prevailed. Partly so that the shrine would be able to hold a greater number of the faithful and partly for aesthetic reasons, Paul V (1605–21) asked Carlo Maderno to lengthen the nave by three bays, a modification which had at least one irksome result: the dome would no longer be

visible to the visitor standing at the entrance of the church.

A CONTROVERSIAL FAÇADE. Paul V also commissioned Maderno to build the façade. The work lasted from 1607 to 1614 and failed to meet with unanimous approval: it was too long in relation to its height and clearly revealed two stories surmounted by an attic, which seemed better suited to a palace than a church. Bernini returned to the idea of twin towers, which in Maderno's scheme were to have surmounted the exterior bays but had not yet been built. But opinion was so opposed to these towers that they were pulled down during the pontificate of Innocent X (1644–55). Valadier finally suggested incorporating the two great clocks visible today.

THE NECROPOLIS
There are two rows of brick mausoleums, one on each side of the funerary road. Those in the row to

the north date from the 2nd century AD, those to the south from the 3rd century. To the west, where the Christian tombs are concentrated, there is a small rectangular space: this is the site of the tomb identified as that of St Peter. To understand early Christianity it is essential to visit this initially pagan but later Christian necropolis, which was used from the 1st to the 4th centuries, up to the building of Constantine's basilica.

The central nave of Constantine's basilica (above).

THE OBELISK
When Domenico Fontana erected the obelisk from Nero's circus in front of the basilica, Sixtus V ordered that if

anyone engaged in the delicate operation spoke they would be condemned to death. Realizing the ropes were about to snap, a man yelled "Dampen the ropes!" – which was done at once, enabling the operation to be completed successfully. The Pope pardoned the man who had dared to break the silence and also rewarded him.

One of the proposed plans for the façade of St Peter's (center).

MICHELANGELO'S DOME
The dome of St Peter's dominates the city and could once be seen from many miles away. It rests on a drum pierced by windows surmounted by alternating curved and triangular pediments and separated by twin columns. Its dimensions are so vast that there is room for several people at a time inside the ball above the lantern.

PIAZZA SAN PIETRO ★. In 1626 Urban VIII commissioned Bernini to continue the work, especially the restructuring of the façade. Then, after falling from favor under Innocent X, he was brought back by Alexander VII (1655–67) to design the new square in front of the basilica. Maderno's façade needed to be given greater breadth; the irregular buildings surrounding the square had to be hidden; the obelisk set up in the square in 1586 had to be taken into account; and it was also necessary to enable a larger crowd to see the Pope during the "Urbi et Orbi" blessing ● 52. Bernini's solution was to design a *piazza* in the form of an ellipse, bordered by a quadruple colonnade forming a portico wide enough to let carriages pass. The foci of the ellipse are indicated by marble disks on each side of the two fountains: standing on either of these disks you can see only one row of columns, instead of four. Two wings link the colonnades to the basilica: the one on the right ends at the Scala Regia ● 83, the one on the left at the Arco delle Campane.

THE GREATEST CHURCH IN CHRISTENDOM

THE ENTRANCE PORTICO. Beneath Maderno's portico stand Bernini's *Constantine* (1669), at the back on the right, and *Charlemagne* by

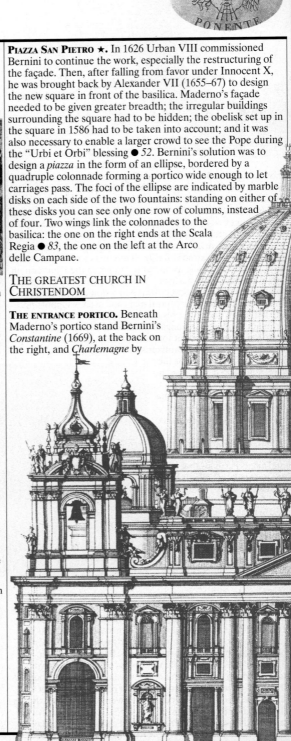

Cornacchini (1735) on the left. Thus the first of the Roman emperors to adopt Christianity and the first Holy Roman Emperor – the secular arms of spiritual power – seem to take the shrine under their symbolic protection. Access to the shrine is by five doors. The door on the extreme right, the Holy Door ● 52, is opened only at the beginning of a Holy Year, which occurs every 25 years. The central door dates from the 15th century; it was created by Antonio Averulino and is from Constantine's basilica. Another remnant from it can be seen if you turn your back to the doorway: the mosaic in the tympanum above the central entrance overlooking the piazza is a fragment of the *Navicella* mosaic, showing Christ walking on the water, made for Constantine's shrine.

THE NAVE. Although St Peter's Basilica is the largest Christian basilica, its immensity is not apparent at first sight due to its balanced proportions and the monumental size of all the works of art it contains. The statues of the principal founders of the monastic orders, enthroned in tall niches all along the main nave, are colossal; these were left to the initiative of each order and set up as they were completed (the oldest ones are closest to the choir). In addition, since the basilica was conceived to emphasize the eternal nature of the Church, fragile materials were eliminated.

THE DOOR OF DEATH
Of the basilica's five doors, the one on the left was made by the sculptor Giacomo Manzù (1963). Commissioned by John XXIII, with whom he had a close friendship, it depicts the descent from the Cross and the death of Mary. The background features the Pope welcoming bishops and cardinals to the second Vatican Council.

A stoup for holy water at the entrance of the nave.

THE SCALE OF THE BUILDING
Cherubs taller than any visitor, a *baldacchino* higher than the Palazzo Farnese – these give an idea of the vast scale of the building. In addition, to indicate the exceptional length of the nave (over 600 feet), the lengths of some of the largest Christian churches are inscribed in gilded bronze on the paving.

Bernini's gloria.

MICHELANGELO'S "PIETÀ"
Cardinal Jean Bilhère de Lagraulas commissioned Michelangelo to make this group during the sculptor's second stay in Rome. The contract stipulated it should be "the most beautiful work in marble that exists in Rome to this day". It is said that one night, irritated at hearing the statue attributed to another artist, Michelangelo crept into St Peter's to engrave his name on the Virgin's mantle. It is the only sculpture he signed. The marks of suffering such as the stigmata on Jesus' body are reduced to the barest essentials, and the virgin seems as young as her son. These effects are due to the sculptor's quest for ideal beauty.

From the end of the 17th century the pictures which decorated it (many of the originals are now kept in Santa Maria degli Angeli) were translated into mosaic. Also, a number of celebrated paintings from other churches in Rome were brought to the Vatican, including *The Transfiguration* by Raphael ▲ *228* and *The Last Communion of St Jerome* by Domenichino ▲ *231*, both now in the Pinacoteca.

BERNINI'S CONTRIBUTION. The basilica owes much of its character to Bernini. Under Urban VIII (1623–44) he constructed the transept crossing, and since Urban was a member of the Barberini family the three Barberini bees ▲ *292* appear almost everywhere. The pontifical altar stands in the transept crossing, above the site of St Peter's tomb, under a gigantic *baldacchino*, or canopy, with twisted columns (bronze ornaments were stripped from the Pantheon in order to make them ▲ *265*). He also sank niches into the pillars supporting the dome, where he placed statues of four saints, each corresponding to the most precious relics preserved in the basilica. Thirty years later Alexander VII commissioned him to create the apse. For it Bernini made the *Catedra Petri* (St Peter's Chair), a sort of huge

THE CUPOLA ▲ *262*
So that the
proportions might be
as harmonious inside
as outside, the
architect fitted one
dome into another.
The steps to the top
are built in the space
between them.

SAINTS AND RELICS
The four saints whose
statues Bernini set
into the pillars
supporting the dome
are those whose relics
are preserved in the
rooms just above.
Shown below are *St
Andrew*, with his X-
shaped cross, by
François Duquesnoy
and *St Longinus*, with
the lance that pierced
Christ's side, by
Bernini himself.

reliquary throne in bronze supported by statues of four
Doctors of the Church, enclosing the remains of a wooden
chair believed to be the original episcopal chair of St Peter.
Above it is an enormous gloria: a multitude of gilded bronze
angelic figures, clouds and rays frame a window in which the
dove of the Holy Spirit is surrounded by a shining halo.
Bernini also designed the tomb of Urban VIII – balanced, at
the back of the apse, by that of Paul III (1534–49) by
Guglielmo della Porta – and the grandiose monument of
Alexander VII (on the left after the transept). The latter
shows the Pope, in prayer, being called by Death, who holds a
golden hourglass (the door beneath the monument is
ingeniously incorporated in the composition). Both of these
tombs were to have a powerful influence on Bernini's
successors.

HOMAGE TO SCULPTURE. Works from the period before the
reconstruction of the church judged worthy to adorn it were
few. Among them are the tomb of Innocent VIII by
Pollaiuolo (second pillar on the left), which dates from 1498,
and the medieval statue of St Peter (by the right-hand pier in
front of the *baldacchino*) whose foot has been worn away by
the kisses of the faithful. Maria Clementina Sobieska – wife of
James Stuart (the Old Pretender), claimant to the throne of
England – has a monument sculpted by Filippo Bracci in
1739, between the first and second pillar on the left; just
beyond it is a memorial to the last Stuarts by Canova.
Opposite, between the second and third pillar on the right, is
the tomb of Gregory XIII (who introduced the Gregorian
calendar in 1582), which was rebuilt between 1715 and 1721.
Like several others, it dates from long after the pontiff's

Giuseppe Momo's
helicoidal staircase leading
to the Vatican Museums.

THE CASINA OF PIUS IV
This delightful pair of charmingly decorated buildings situated in the Vatican gardens was designed by the Mannerist architect Pirro Ligorio for Pope Pius IV (1559–65) to replace the Belvedere, the papal villa which had gradually evolved into a palace. Today these two buildings, which can easily be visited, are the headquarters of the Pontifical Science Academy. (Above, detail from the pediment of the Casina).

Fresco in the Vatican Library showing Domenico Fontana presenting the plans of the library to Sixtus V.

death – and is in fact closer in time to Canova's famous monument to Clement XIII in the arch beyond the right transept. It is also worth looking at the monument designed by Bernini – in 1630 at the request of Urban VIII – in honor of Countess Matilda of Tuscany, who defended Pope Gregory VII against the Emperor Henry IV in the 11th century and bequeathed her property to the Holy See. Nearby is the monument designed by Carlo Fontana between 1696 and 1702 to Queen Christina of Sweden, who like Maria Sobieska died in Rome exiled for converting to Catholicism. Finally, close to the entrance and protected by a plate-glass screen is the basilica's most precious statue: Michelangelo's *Pietà* ▲ *212*, sculpted for the Jubilee in 1500.

FROM THE GROTTOES TO THE DOME. If time allows, visit the Treasury, to inspect the Vatican's collection of religious and historical treasures, and descend to the grottoes where, as well as remains of Constantine's basilica, you can see the tombs of numerous popes for whom no one contributed the price of a monument. The ascent to the inside of the dome should not be missed – nor to the balcony surrounding the lantern, for the amazing panoramic view of Rome.

INSIDE THE VATICAN

THE MEDIEVAL CENTER. During the Middle Ages, until the return of the popes from Avignon, the Lateran Palace ▲ *197* was the official papal residence. However, near the basilica there were two other papal buildings: one to the south built by Pope Symmachus in the 5th century, and one to the north dating from the 9th century. Since these were in danger of falling into ruin, Eugene III (1145–53) constructed a new fortified residence, to the north of St Peter's, with a tower that is still standing in the Cortile dei Pappagalli. This became the core of the Vatican Palace: Nicholas III (1277–80) and his successors were to transform this fortress into a luxurious dwelling, gradually adding new wings.

FROM FORTRESS TO PALACE. The aggrandizement of the Vatican began in earnest under Nicholas V (1447–55). The Pope chose Fra Angelico to decorate his oratory in the Innocent III Tower; and Piero della Francesca to decorate his *stanze* (rooms) with frescoes, which were eventually replaced by Raphael's ▲ *222*. Later in the 15th century Sixtus IV (1471–84) commissioned Melozzo da Forli to paint frescoes for the newly-built library ▲ *226*, now on display in the Pinacoteca, and created the Sistine Chapel.

A MODEST VILLA. In 1484 Innocent VIII commissioned the architect Jacopo da Pietrasanta and the painter Antonio del Pollaiuolo to build the Palazzo del Belvedere, a simple villa where he could rest, in the vast gardens that extended to the north of the pontifical palace. Eventually the villa was linked to the palace by two long parallel wings, creating the Cortile del Belvedere.

Julius II (1503–13) wanted Bramante to build these, but he only completed the east wing. The west wing was built under Pius IV (1559–65) by Pirro Ligorio.

THE GREAT PROJECTS OF THE 16TH CENTURY. Under Paul III, Antonio da Sangallo restored the palace's oldest wing and remodeled the Pauline Chapel and the Sala Regia. Sixtus V commissioned Domenico Fontana to build the Biblioteca (library) wing (1587–90). This divided the Cortile del Belvedere, forming a new courtyard known as the Cortile della Pigna. In addition, he erected an imposing group of buildings to the east of the former medieval palace, thereby creating the Cortile San Damaso (1589).

THREE CENTURIES OF DECORATION.
Under the Renaissance popes the period of embellishment began. Alexander VI Borgia had his apartments decorated by Pinturrichio. Julius II commissioned Michelangelo to paint the ceiling of the Sistine Chapel ▲ *218* (1508–12), and Raphael to redecorate the *stanze* (rooms) ▲ *222*. Raphael only finished this work under Leo X, who commissioned him to decorate the Loggias ▲ *218* as well. Under Paul III, Michelangelo painted *The Last Judgment* in the Sistine Chapel, as well as two frescoes in the Pauline chapel. During the 16th and 17th centuries a whole range of other artists further exalted the glory of the popes, embellishing above all the Sala Regia and the Sala Ducale. In fact the decoration work continued until the 19th century.

THE MUSEUM ERA. From the late 16th century until 1870 the Palazzo del Quirinale ▲ *297* became the pontifical residence, so the Vatican underwent few modifications for 250 years. Apart from the Scala Regia ● *85*, a stairway added by Bernini in the 17th century, most of the changes were associated with the creation of the various museums and took place during the late 18th or early 19th century. Under Clement XIV and Pius VI the Palazzo del Belvedere was converted into a museum, the Museo Pio-Clementino. Pius VII (1800–23) built the Braccio Nuovo (New Wing) as an extension to the Chiaramonti sculpture gallery. He also had the *Aldobrandini Marriage* brought to the Vatican, an Augustan fresco based on a Greek fresco from the 4th century BC.

THE 20TH CENTURY. The restructuring work started again after the signing of the Lateran Treaty. Functional buildings were not the only ones to be erected. Pius XI commissioned Giuseppe Momo to construct a monumental staircase and Luca Beltrami to design the Pinacoteca where an outstanding collection of paintings and a number of important tapestries are on view.

EXPLORING THE VATICAN. Only parts of the Vatican are open to visitors, and fall into two categories, namely the rooms, galleries and chapels prized for their decoration (such as the Sistine Chapel) and the museums grouped around the Cortile del Belvedere.

Above, from left to right: the Palazzo del Governatorato, the Vatican station, and the Apostolic Palace.

The Vatican Gardens.

The corridor leading to the Sala Regia; and the hall's magnificent decorations.

Head of Augustus as a young man (his hairstyle was adapted to suit Baroque taste). This stands in the Cortile della Pigna, so called because of the large bronze pine cone there.

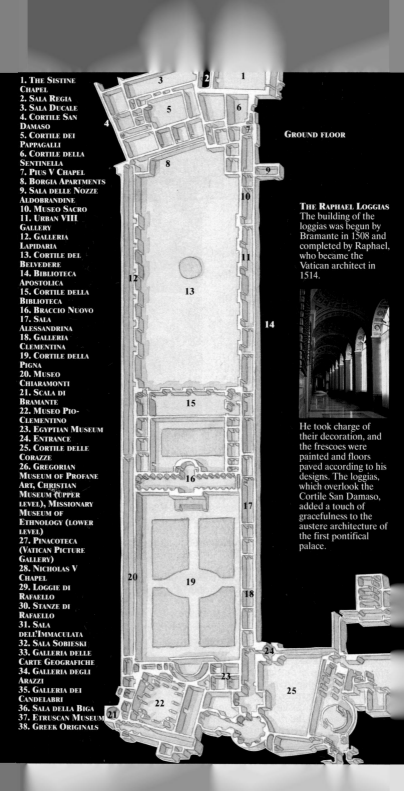

1. THE SISTINE CHAPEL
2. SALA REGIA
3. SALA DUCALE
4. CORTILE SAN DAMASO
5. CORTILE DEI PAPPAGALLI
6. CORTILE DELLA SENTINELLA
7. PIUS V CHAPEL
8. BORGIA APARTMENTS
9. SALA DELLE NOZZE ALDOBRANDINE
10. MUSEO SACRO
11. URBAN VIII GALLERY
12. GALLERIA LAPIDARIA
13. CORTILE DEL BELVEDERE
14. BIBLIOTECA APOSTOLICA
15. CORTILE DELLA BIBLIOTECA
16. BRACCIO NUOVO
17. SALA ALESSANDRINA
18. GALLERIA CLEMENTINA
19. CORTILE DELLA PIGNA
20. MUSEO CHIARAMONTI
21. SCALA DI BRAMANTE
22. MUSEO PIO-CLEMENTINO
23. EGYPTIAN MUSEUM
24. ENTRANCE
25. CORTILE DELLE CORAZZE
26. GREGORIAN MUSEUM OF PROFANE ART, CHRISTIAN MUSEUM (UPPER LEVEL), MISSIONARY MUSEUM OF ETHNOLOGY (LOWER LEVEL)
27. PINACOTECA (VATICAN PICTURE GALLERY)
28. NICHOLAS V CHAPEL
29. LOGGIE DI RAFAELLO
30. STANZE DI RAFAELLO
31. SALA DELL'IMMACULATA
32. SALA SOBIESKI
33. GALLERIA DELLE CARTE GEOGRAFICHE
34. GALLERIA DEGLI ARAZZI
35. GALLERIA DEI CANDELABRI
36. SALA DELLA BIGA
37. ETRUSCAN MUSEUM
38. GREEK ORIGINALS

GROUND FLOOR

THE RAPHAEL LOGGIAS
The building of the loggias was begun by Bramante in 1508 and completed by Raphael, who became the Vatican architect in 1514.

He took charge of their decoration, and the frescoes were painted and floors paved according to his designs. The loggias, which overlook the Cortile San Damaso, added a touch of gracefulness to the austere architecture of the first pontifical palace.

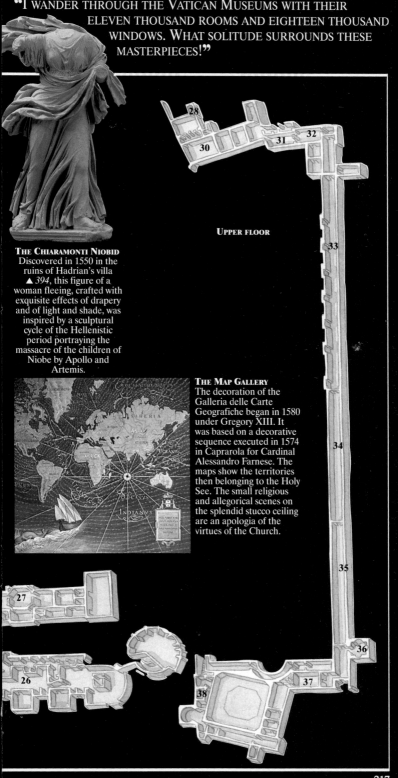

UPPER FLOOR

THE CHIARAMONTI NIOBID
Discovered in 1550 in the ruins of Hadrian's villa ▲ *394*, this figure of a woman fleeing, crafted with exquisite effects of drapery and of light and shade, was inspired by a sculptural cycle of the Hellenistic period portraying the massacre of the children of Niobe by Apollo and Artemis.

THE MAP GALLERY
The decoration of the Galleria delle Carte Geografiche began in 1580 under Gregory XIII. It was based on a decorative sequence executed in 1574 in Caprarola for Cardinal Alessandro Farnese. The maps show the territories then belonging to the Holy See. The small religious and allegorical scenes on the splendid stucco ceiling are an apologia of the virtues of the Church.

Julius II, who had brought Michelangelo to Rome to work on his tomb, commissioned him to paint frescoes on the ceiling of the Sistine Chapel, perhaps at Bramante's suggestion.

The scenes on the ceiling develop the theme of the Creation and the Fall of Man. In the center are the three events which made Christ's coming necessary: the Creation of Man, the Creation of Woman, and Original Sin. All around are signs of the forthcoming redemption, in the form of prophets and sibyls who either announced the coming of the Virgin and of Christ or prefigured his life – such as Jonah, who emerged after three days in the belly of the whale (Christ rose on the third day). The four pendentives are painted with scenes narrating the salvation of the Jewish people, which heralded that of humanity: Judith and Holofernes, David and Goliath, the Brazen Serpent, and the punishment of Haman at Esther's request. The lunettes portray the ancestors of Christ. Seated nudes with garlands and festoons surround the scenes of Genesis, supporting *trompe l'oeil* bronze medallions depicting scenes from the Old Testament.

Between 1508 and 1512 Michelangelo was to cover the entire ceiling (over 3,000 square feet) with more than three hundred figures. Before starting work, he had all the preparations made by his assistants erased and the scaffolding remade to ensure that he could paint the whole vault single-handedly, without leaving any gaps. He began by painting the frescoes near the door, progressing toward the altar – which explains the more formal style of *The Life of Noah*.

Recent restoration has revived the work's brilliance, which is typical of true fresco painting since the pigments are absorbed by the fresh mortar.

"He brought the blessing of light to the painting, which sufficed to illuminate a world plunged in darkness for centuries."

Vasari

Despite the indisputable grace of the *ignudi* (nudes), opinions differ as to the meaning Michelangelo intended to give them. As can be seen, he used the chapel's strong architectural framework to provide a structure that would unite the work as a whole.

"MOSES AND THE DAUGHTERS OF JETHRO" When the construction of the Sistine Chapel had been completed, Sixtus IV commissioned various Tuscan and Umbrian painters to decorate the walls with frescoes that would establish a parallel between the life of Moses and that of Jesus. Botticelli painted the events of Moses' early life.

The story runs from right to left. Moses kills an Egyptian (bottom right-hand corner) and takes refuge with the Midianites; he meets Jethro's daughters and puts to flight the shepherds who are preventing them from watering their flock; Jehovah appears to Moses (top left-hand corner) and he leaves Egypt with the Jews (bottom left). In Proust's *Un amour de Swann* Swann falls in love with Odette because of her resemblance to the figure of Zipporah, a daughter of Jethro (see detail, left): "He admired her large eyes, her delicate face which hinted at an imperfect skin, the marvelous strands of hair that clung to her tired cheeks."

"THE LAST JUDGMENT"
Michelangelo's *The Last Judgment* (1534–41) was the last of the chapel's decorations to be carried out. It was planned just after the Sack of Rome (1527) ● *36*. As well as reflecting the anxiety of the Romans, still recovering from the shock, it reveals the personal anguish of the defender of the Florentine Republic. The fresco aroused indignation. Aretino commented that it was more suitable for public baths or a brothel, and El Greco suggested replacing it with a work that was "more modest and more decent". The swathed draperies (*braghe*) were added by Daniele da Volterra in the 16th century, for the sake of decency.

221

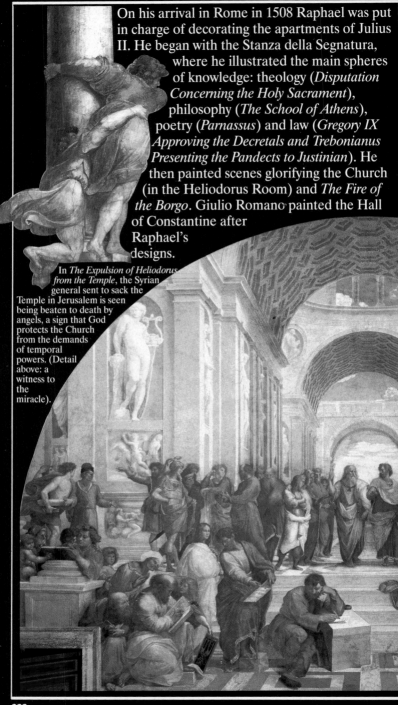

On his arrival in Rome in 1508 Raphael was put in charge of decorating the apartments of Julius II. He began with the Stanza della Segnatura, where he illustrated the main spheres of knowledge: theology (*Disputation Concerning the Holy Sacrament*), philosophy (*The School of Athens*), poetry (*Parnassus*) and law (*Gregory IX Approving the Decretals and Trebonianus Presenting the Pandects to Justinian*). He then painted scenes glorifying the Church (in the Heliodorus Room) and *The Fire of the Borgo*. Giulio Romano painted the Hall of Constantine after Raphael's designs.

In *The Expulsion of Heliodorus from the Temple*, the Syrian general sent to sack the Temple in Jerusalem is seen being beaten to death by angels, a sign that God protects the Church from the demands of temporal powers. (Detail above: a witness to the miracle).

"PARNASSUS" (DETAIL)

This fresco shows Apollo, in the company of nine Muses, inspiring the greatest ancient and modern poets (including Dante in profile, upper left). In the detail reproduced here Erato (the Muse of lyrical and erotic poetry) is sitting surrounded by Melpomene (Tragedy, holding the mask), Terpsichore (Dance) and Urania (Astronomy). Vasari said that these Muses "so incredibly beautiful and divinely expressive, exhale grace and life".

"THE SCHOOL OF ATHENS"

This work, painted between 1510 and 1511, is a synthetic representation of ancient wisdom, the precursor of Christianity. The main philosophers of antiquity are gathered in a vast building, reminiscent of Bramante's conception of St Peter's. Plato stands in the center, holding his *Timaeus* dialogue (which discusses the nature of divinity) and pointing to the heavens, while Aristotle, carrying the manuscript of his *Ethics* (concerned with human behavior), points to the earth. The statues of Apollo and Minerva represent Harmony and Wisdom. Raphael gave the various philosophers the faces of his contemporaries and included himself on the extreme right, together with his master, Perugino.

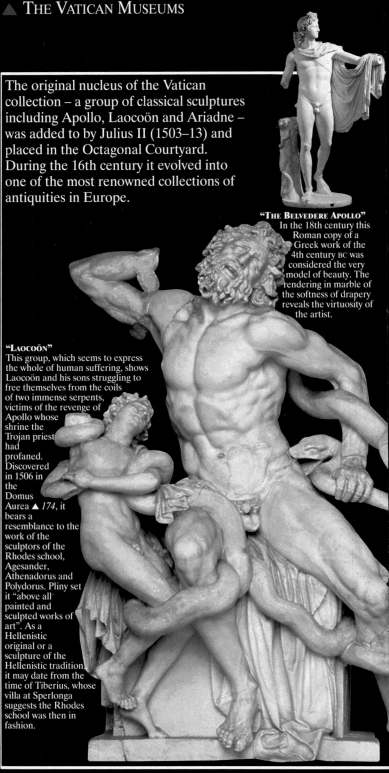

The original nucleus of the Vatican collection – a group of classical sculptures including Apollo, Laocoön and Ariadne – was added to by Julius II (1503–13) and placed in the Octagonal Courtyard. During the 16th century it evolved into one of the most renowned collections of antiquities in Europe.

"THE BELVEDERE APOLLO"
In the 18th century this Roman copy of a Greek work of the 4th century BC was considered the very model of beauty. The rendering in marble of the softness of drapery reveals the virtuosity of the artist.

"LAOCOÖN"
This group, which seems to express the whole of human suffering, shows Laocoön and his sons struggling to free themselves from the coils of two immense serpents, victims of the revenge of Apollo whose shrine the Trojan priest had profaned. Discovered in 1506 in the Domus Aurea ▲ 174, it bears a resemblance to the work of the sculptors of the Rhodes school, Agesander, Athenadorus and Polydorus. Pliny set it "above all painted and sculpted works of art". As a Hellenistic original or a sculpture of the Hellenistic tradition, it may date from the time of Tiberius, whose villa at Sperlonga suggests the Rhodes school was then in fashion.

"THE BELVEDERE TORSO"
"A marvelous oak deprived of its branches and foliage" was how the 18th-century art historian Joachim Winckelmann ● *41* described this powerfully modeled torso dating from the 1st century BC.

"AUGUSTUS OF PRIMA PORTA"
This sculpture of the deified emperor, discovered in Livia's villa at Prima Porta, is a masterpiece of Roman statuary. In the center of the cuirass, the King of the Parthians is returning the Roman standards captured from Crassus. Surrounded by divine and allegorical figures, the scene portrays the emperor as the custodian of a new order.

"THE SLEEPING ARIADNE"
This Roman copy of a masterpiece of Hellenistic sculpture shows Ariadne, abandoned by Theseus, asleep on a rock on Naxos. The subject lends itself to a sensuous pose and elaborate draperies, typical of the Hellenistic style.

"ANGEL MUSICIAN"
This was part of a fresco of *The Ascension* by Melozzo da Forlì (1438–95) that decorated the apse of the Basilica dei Santi Apostoli ▲ *300* until 1711. The halo was gilded and the sky painted with a color made from lapis lazuli.

"VIRGIN AND CHILD"
This tondo (round picture), a shape much used at the end of the 15th century, is the work of Pinturicchio (c. 1454–1513), a painter who received numerous commissions from Sixtus IV and Innocent VII, as well as Alexander VI for whom he decorated the Borgia Apartments. Consequently many of his works are to be found in Rome. Vasari judged this artist severely: "Bernadino embellished his paintings with gold so as to satisfy those with bad taste by lavishing greater brilliance and effect on them – the last word in vulgarity in painting." Nevertheless, in this picture there is an undeniable desire to infuse life into the two holy figures encircled by angels: the Virgin smiles and the infant Jesus is totally absorbed in his reading.

"SIXTUS IV APPOINTING PLATINA PREFECT OF THE VATICAN LIBRARY"
This fresco by Melozzo da Forlì originally decorated the Vatican Library. Sixtus IV's nephew, the future Julius II, stands before the Pope with the humanist Bartolomeo Sacchi, known as Platina.

"ST LAWRENCE ORDAINED DEACON BY ST SIXTUS"
This belongs to the cycle of frescoes Nicholas V asked Fra Angelico to paint for his chapel (c. 1450). The painter here combined contemporary Florentine discoveries in the rendering of three-dimensional space with the "subtlety" of gentle Gothic coloring.

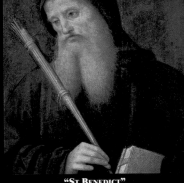

"St Benedict"
This portrayal of St Benedict by Perugino (1450–1523) originally formed part of a painting of *The Ascension* that he made for the Church of San Pietro in Perugia in 1495.

227

The loggias and rooms decorated by Raphael (1483–1520) in the Vatican are among his greatest works. In addition, three key pictures that mark his development as a painter are preserved in the Pinacoteca.

"THE MADONNA DI FOLIGNO"
This work was commissioned around 1512 by Sigismondo dei Conti as an *ex voto* offering. It portrays the Virgin and Child surrounded by St Francis, St John the Baptist and St Jerome, who is introducing the donor of the painting. It is one of the most important works painted by Raphael in the graceful style of his early days in Rome.

"THE TRANSFIGURATION"
The last picture Raphael painted was commissioned by Cardinal Giulio de Medici. The upper part (reproduced here) portrays the divine miracle. Christ rises in a supernatural light, with Moses and Elijah beside him, while three terror-stricken apostles avert their eyes. The lower part shows the other disciples unable to perform a miracle: in the absence of their master, they are seen to be incapable of healing a boy possessed by the devil. By revealing its strong luminous contrasts a recent restoration has retrieved the narrative power of this work, unanimously recognized as a masterpiece of universal art.

THE RAPHAEL LOGGIAS
(These can only be visited by special permission.) They were decorated by Raphael's pupils, following the designs of the master, then Superintendent of Antiquities.

Each of the thirteen bays contains four Old Testament scenes, while the walls and arches are embellished with grotesques inspired by the decorations of the Domus Aurea ▲ *174*, discovered in 1506.

The scenes reproduced here show *The Expulsion from Paradise*, *Isaac Blessing Jacob*, *The Parting of the Red Sea* and *The Building of the Ark*. These works, frequently reproduced in engravings, constitute what has been called "Raphael's Bible". European painting and decorative arts have drawn from it so often for Old Testament subjects that most representations are ultimately derived from it.

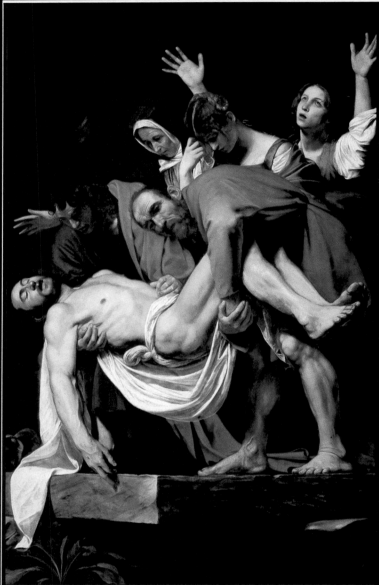

"DESCENT FROM THE CROSS"
Painted between 1602 and 1604 for the Oratorians, this picture originally hung in the Chiesa Nuova ▲ *281*. In 1797 it was requisitioned by the French, despite the discredit in which Caravaggio was held during the 18th century. Its dramatic force derives from the contrast between the pale body of Christ and the shadows enveloping the holy women and St John. The emphatic gesture of Mary Magdalene stresses the pain which Nicodemus' expression invites us to share. The dark background heightens the picture's relief. For the body of Christ, Caravaggio came nearer than usual to the classical ideal by choosing a rather beautiful body whose musculature he wished to emphasize.

THE "PIETÀ"

Pietro Berrettini (1596–1669), known as Pietro da Cortona, was the favorite painter of Pope Urban VIII, who in the 1640's commissioned him to decorate his oratory in the Vatican. The *Pietà* he painted there is much less dramatic than Caravaggio's. The delicate colors show his interest in Venetian painting, and the figures are elegant and graceful.

The Virgin between St Thomas and St Jerome (1625) dates from Guido Reni's mature period, when he sought to soften the contours and colors in his work. (Detail)

"THE LAST COMMUNION OF ST JEROME"

For the past two centuries this picture by Domenichino (1614) has been acknowledged as a masterpiece of expressive art. The saint is shown admitting his extreme weakness and witnessing his trust in the resurrection.

The Borgo before and after it was gutted.

Going down the Via della Conciliazione from St Peter's, on the right you come to Palazzo Cesi (1575), at No. 51, and then Palazzo Serristori (1555), the former Tuscan Embassy. On the same side, at No. 33, is the Palazzo dei Penitenzieri (15th century), built by Baccio Pontelli at the request of Cardinal della Rovere. Opposite is Palazzo Torlonia, followed by Santa Maria in Traspontina (1566–1637).

THE BORGO AND VIA DELLA CONCILIAZIONE

THE AVENUE OF RECONCILIATION. Formerly, after a long walk through narrow, twisting streets the visitor suddenly emerged at Piazza San Pietro. Its "great theater of colonnades", obelisk and fountains provided a violent contrast to the surrounding Borgo. Now, after the construction of the Via della Conciliazione – which provides advance preparation for the aesthetic shock from a distance – the effect of surprise, so typical of the Baroque, has vanished. As its name suggests, this broad straight avenue symbolizes the reconciliation of the Holy See and the Italian State, sanctioned by the Lateran Treaty ▲ *198*, *202*. Its construction caused a tremendous upheaval in the old quarters between Piazza San Pietro and Castel Sant'Angelo.

AN OLD IDEA. This was to become perhaps the most famous of the demolition operations that marked the urban developments of the Fascist period in Rome and in other cities, and it was strongly criticized. Yet the idea was not new. As long ago as the 15th century Nicholas V had asked Leone

Battista Alberti to rebuild the whole area. His plans included the demolition of a long row of houses that extended from the fortress to Piazza San Pietro, forming the *spina* ("backbone") of the Borgo. The idea was proposed again in the 16th century under Sixtus V and revived in the 18th and 19th centuries, but nothing came of it.

COUNTING THE COSTS. The operation, which was promoted by Mussolini himself, was entrusted to the architects Piacentini and Spaccarelli. On October 28,

1936, the Duce struck the first blow with a pickaxe, and buildings were torn down at breakneck speed. However, the reconstruction was not completed until 1950, and the toll was heavy. Although several buildings remained, a large number were destroyed (including the churches of San Giacomo a Scossacavalli, San Michele Arcangelo and Santa Maria delle Grazie) or reconstructed elsewhere. The Palazzo Alicorni was partially rebuilt inside the Palazzo del Governatore; the house of Leo X's surgeon, Giacomo di Bartolomeo da Brescia, was moved to No. 14 Via Rusticucci; and the 18th-century Church of the Annunziata was re-erected on the north bank of the Tiber.

CASTEL SANT'ANGELO

This building has had a checkered history. Originally a dynastic tomb, it was converted into a fortress, then became a noble dwelling and finally a papal residence; between times it served as a barracks, a prison and a museum.

HADRIAN'S MAUSOLEUM. Hadrian (117–38 AD) built a tomb in Domitian's gardens that was to become the dynastic sepulcher of the Antonines. Work started in 123 but was only completed in 139, after Hadrian's death. The Pons Aelius (the predecessor of the Ponte Sant'Angelo ▲ *239*), inaugurated in 134, linked the monument to the Campo Marzio.

THE SEPULCHRAL CHAMBER. The present entrance (which is about 10 feet above the level of the ancient one) leads via a short corridor to a square hall. The semicircular niche hollowed out in the back wall was probably intended to contain a statue of Hadrian. On the right is a spiral ramp leading to the *cella* (mortuary chamber), the heart of the monument. In this square room, which was originally faced with marble, the funerary urns of Emperor Hadrian and his wife, Sabina,

A view of the Borgo in the 19th century, painted by Roesler (left).

HADRIAN'S MAUSOLEUM
As far as is known, the mausoleum was made as follows. On a square base, a little less than 300 feet long, stood a gigantic rotunda faced with marble. On this was a mound of earth that served as a podium for an enormous bronze sculpture of a *quadriga* (four-horse chariot) driven by Emperor Hadrian. Numerous efforts were made in the 17th century to produce a satisfactory reconstruction of the building, and the French architect Vaudremer (1829–1914) also had a go at tackling the problem. While at the Villa Medici ▲ *315*, in 1857 he presented a comprehensive project for restoring the mausoleum, including plans, section and façade (detail below).

THE PASSETTO
(above)
This originally
formed part of Leo
IV's ramparts.
Nicholas III
(1277–80) converted
it into a fortified
passageway linking
Castel Sant'Angelo to
the Vatican. It was
further modified by
Alexander VI.

Fireworks
at the Castel
Sant'Angelo.

**THE PRISON OF
CASTEL SANT'ANGELO**
Until 1870 the lower
part of the castle was
a prison. The
dungeons, which had
a terrifying
reputation, held
captive such
personalities as the
Cenci ▲ 254, the
philosopher
Giordano Bruno
▲ 249, Count
Cagliostro ● 47, and
the goldsmith and
sculptor Benvenuto
Cellini – despite his
heroic participation
in the defense of the
castle in 1527 ● 36, if
his boastful memoirs
can be believed.

were kept, together with those of the Antonine emperors and
Septimius Severus (193–211).

FROM A MAUSOLEUM TO A FORTRESS. Around 270 the ancient
sepulcher became an advanced bastion of the Aurelian Wall
▲ 323; it was then strengthened by the Emperor Honorius in
403 AD. In 537 the building resisted the siege of the
Ostrogoths under Witigis, but shortly afterward fell into the
hands of Totila who, concentrating on new fortifications,
made it into a citadel. As a powerful fortress, the building
served as a prison from the 10th century and also as a refuge:
Gregory VII fled there in the 11th century when Rome was
taken by the Emperor Henry IV; the demagogue Cola
di Rienzo ● XV sought shelter there in the 14th
century; and much later, in 1527, this was
where Clement VII withstood the six-
month siege of the troops of Charles V
● 36. Moreover, since Castel
Sant'Angelo was Rome's most important
fortified area, anyone who held it had
virtually the whole town at his mercy.
Consequently, its history reflected the city's
turbulent internal conflicts. Between the 10th and
11th centuries it passed into the hands of the most powerful
noble families before suffering a massive attack by the Roman
people, who made up their minds to demolish it in 1379.

FORTIFICATIONS AND MODIFICATIONS. Under Nicholas III the
castle became papal property. Most of the alterations to the
building carried out between the pontificates of Nicholas V
(1447–55) and Urban VII (1623–44) had a military purpose.
Access to the subterranean galleries was blocked, two
towers were built at the entrance and four bastions at the
corners, a moat was dug, pentagonal ramparts
were erected with five small forts (today no longer
standing) and, finally, the Corridoio or Passetto, the
fortified passageway linking St Peter's to the castle,
was strengthened.

SUMPTUOUS APARTMENTS. From the time of
Nicholas V the popes had
apartments inside the
castle. The most
sumptuous were Pope
Paul III's, which faced
the Tiber, and the most
remarkable his SALA
PAOLINA, or Council
Hall, with its

A cross-section of Hadrian's mausoleum.

Between 608 and 615 Hadrian's funerary

parallel frescoes showing the lives of St Paul and Alexander the Great (Paul III's own name being Alessandro Farnese). Perino del Vaga was put in charge of painting these frescoes, as well as those of the Camera del Perseo and the Camera di Amore e Psiche. The Pope's apartments communicate, via a little vestibule (attributed to Antonio da Sangallo the Younger) followed by a few steps, with Julius II's lovely loggia and colonnade, built by Bramante, facing Ponte Sant'Angelo. It balances Paul III's loggia (1543) – overlooking the garden and the Passetto – which can be reached by the circular external corridor.

BENEATH THE ARCHANGEL MICHAEL. The castle's central stairway will take you to the upper terrace, dominated by Verschaffelt's colossal bronze angel (cast by Giardoni in 1753). This replaced a marble angel by Raffaello da Montelupo (1544), now in another part of the castle (in the Cortile del Angelo). These two statues recall a miracle that happened under Pope Gregory the Great. The legend claims that in 590 the Archangel Michael appeared on the summit of the building brandishing his sword before all the people in procession, who were praying for a plague to end. At the end of the visit you can take a well-earned rest at the little bar on the top floor while enjoying the magnificent view over the Campo Marzio, St Peter's and the Janiculum.

chamber was converted into a shrine dedicated to St Michael. In 852 the Sepulchrum Hadriani became the Castellum Sancti Angeli.

PRATI

A PIEDMONTESE NEIGHBORHOOD. The Prati quarter, behind the Vatican, is in many ways a typically Piedmontese neighborhood. It was planned in 1870, with a view to housing

the innumerable employees of the newly formed Italian State who came from Turin. Its construction gave rise to a flurry of property speculation, the agricultural land being bought for a song by a consortium of bankers who resold it, making huge profits. Rows of apartment buildings line the roads, which are laid out to an octagonal plan. Although Prati is adjacent to the Vatican, the new quarter seems to ignore it, since the dome of St Peter's cannot be seen from its

streets (one wonders if this was by chance, in view of the papacy's resistance to the unitarian forces ● *33*). All the apartment blocks are built to the same design: large courtyards planted with palm trees, huge apartments with dark corridors. Ettore Scola's film *The Family* (1987) gives a good impression of these interiors.

PALAZZO DI GIUSTIZIA (PALACE OF JUSTICE). This stands at the end of the neighborhood facing the Renaissance town. Erected by Guglielmo Calderini between 1889 and 1911, the vast neo-Baroque building cost 40 million lire, instead of the estimated 8 million; it was discovered that it was built on unstable marshy ground, and the affair became a scandal. The outside is adorned with statues of Italian lawmakers and surmounted by a bronze *quadriga*, the work of Ettore Ximenes. Frescoes by Cesare Maccari decorate the interior.

NEIGHBORING BUILDINGS. THE CASA DEI MUTILATI, on the left, is a fine example of the architecture of the Mussolini period, built in 1928 by Marcello Piacentini. Its decoration is based entirely on the theme of war, glorifying condottieri and other soldiers. Within, the Aula Magna and chapel are decorated with mosaics and frescoes (*The Sentinel, The Combatant, The Departure, The Assault* and *The Return of the Soldier*). On the other side of the Palazzo della Giustizia is the neo-Gothic Church of the Sacred Heart (1890) – as well as the astonishing Museum of Souls in Purgatory, containing a collection of objects that are supposed to bear the imprints of the hands of the deceased.

FROM PONTE SANT'ANGELO
TO THE GHETTO

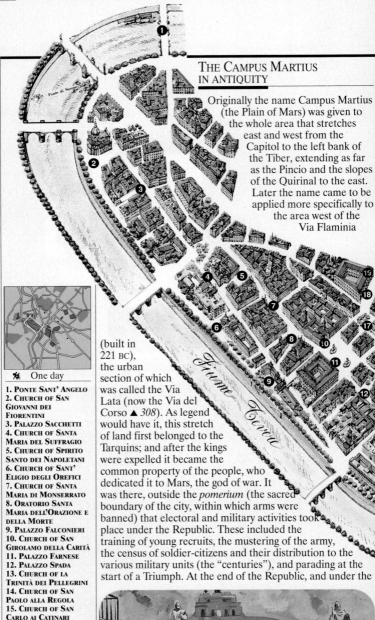

THE CAMPUS MARTIUS
IN ANTIQUITY

Originally the name Campus Martius (the Plain of Mars) was given to the whole area that stretches east and west from the Capitol to the left bank of the Tiber, extending as far as the Pincio and the slopes of the Quirinal to the east. Later the name came to be applied more specifically to the area west of the Via Flaminia

(built in 221 BC), the urban section of which was called the Via Lata (now the Via del Corso ▲ 308). As legend would have it, this stretch of land first belonged to the Tarquins; and after the kings were expelled it became the common property of the people, who dedicated it to Mars, the god of war. It was there, outside the *pomerium* (the sacred boundary of the city, within which arms were banned) that electoral and military activities took place under the Republic. These included the training of young recruits, the mustering of the army, the census of soldier-citizens and their distribution to the various military units (the "centuries"), and parading at the start of a Triumph. At the end of the Republic, and under the

Empire, with the withdrawal of the plebs from political life the Campus Martius was opened up to popular entertainment and leisure activities (theaters, amphitheaters, and public baths). It also became a venue for Imperial celebrations.

THE PHASES OF ITS DEVELOPMENT. Today the urban layout of antiquity is recognizable, even if certain buildings have not survived. The group of ruins known as the Area Sacra del Largo Argentina provides a complete range of temples from the end of the 4th to the beginning of the 1st century BC. In the 2nd century BC most of the building developments took place around the Circus Flaminius. Later Pompey built a major complex on the central part of the Campus Martius, including a huge portico and a theater; and Augustus erected an altar to peace (the Ara Pacis Augustae) and his own mausoleum. After the great fire that devastated the area in 80 AD a new intensive phase of construction began, including the Odeon ▲ 276 and stadium (now Piazza Navona ▲ 276) built by Domitian. The remains of vast public buildings of this period have been discovered beneath the Palazzo Farnese, among them remarkable mosaics of *desultores* (acrobats on horseback). In the following century Hadrian and the Antonines completed the urbanization of the area. In 273

THE OCTOBER HORSE
On October 15 the ancient Romans used to hold a chariot race at the end of which the right-hand horse of the winning chariot was sacrificed near the altar of Mars. This ritual marked the close of the military year, which had begun the previous March with ceremonies such as the ritual dance of the Salians (the war priests), purification of the horses, and the sacrifice of a pig, a sheep, and a bull known as the *suovetaurilia*.

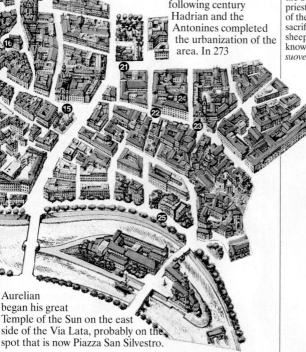

Aurelian began his great Temple of the Sun on the east side of the Via Lata, probably on the spot that is now Piazza San Silvestro.

PONTE SANT'ANGELO

Linking Castel Sant'Angelo to the Campus Martius, this bridge was for a long time the only one to the north of the Ponte Sisto ▲ 363. It had been built in the 2nd century to create an impressive approach to Hadrian's mausoleum ▲ 233. As this was the preferred route of processions to St

"The Via Crucis"
In September 1667, Clement IX, then Pope for two months, began payments to his old friend Bernini for "eight statues of white marble". The drama of the Passion was chosen as the theme: each angel was to bear an instrument of the martyrdom of Christ, such as the nails and cross. Later the number was increased to ten.

Peter's, two chapels were added at the end of the bridge and used as firing posts for crossbow snipers during the siege of the fortress in 1527. Three years later Clement VII had them destroyed, replacing them with statues of St Paul and St Peter by Paulo Romano and Lorenzetto Lotti respectively. Between 1667 and 1669 Clement IX added ten statues of angels, made by pupils of Bernini after drawings by the master. The approach to the bridge on the Campus Martius side was radically modified when, at the end of the 19th century, the Lungotevere embankments were built and the Corso Vittorio Emanuele was put through. Two streets lead from the bridge which once served as main routes within the Campo Marzio (as the area is now called): the Via del Banco di Santo Spirito and Via Paola, which crosses the Via Giulia in front of San Giovanni dei Fiorentini.

Via Giulia

Julius II's street. At the beginning of the 16th century Pope Julius II replaced the maze of streets that led from the Capitol to the Vatican with a long straight thoroughfare to which he gave his name. It long served as Rome's main street, apart for a brief interval around 1655 when Innocent X had the state prison moved to No. 52. Its entire length is dotted with palazzi and churches, making it one of Rome's most attractive streets to walk along.

A neighborhood of contrasts. For centuries this aristocratic street has been adjacent to a colorful and noisy neighborhood bustling with tradesmen and travelers. The Via del Pellegrino was created by Sixtus IV to funnel pilgrims toward St Peter's, and the followers of St Philip Neri could be seen wending their way along Via di Monserrato to make their devotions at the Seven Churches ▲ 381. The area was also a meeting place for visitors from out of town. The Spaniards had their national church in Via di Monserrato; from 1362 the English had a hospice there (which became the Venerable English College) at No. 45; and the Bolognese, the Sienese, and the Neapolitans had churches in the Via Giulia. All these visitors could stay in the countless inns, ranging from

IN THE 19TH CENTURY EMILE ZOLA WROTE EVOCATIVELY OF THIS "FINE OLD QUARTER FALLEN INTO THE SILENCE, INTO THE EMPTINESS OF ABANDONMENT, INVADED BY A KIND OF SOFTNESS AND CLERICAL DISCRETION".

noble *alberghi* to humble *locande*, in and around Campo de' Fiori, where they could visit the print shops and booksellers long-established in the area. It was an area for crafts of all kinds – among them *baullari* (trunk makers), *capellari* (hatters), *giubbonari* (tailors) and *chiavari* (locksmiths) – and many of these traditions still survive. Trunks are still sold in Via dei Baullari; and Via dei Giubbonari has as many clothes shops as houses. In Campo de' Fiori the daily market still plays an important role, even if many different languages are to be heard there. A small bookshop that stays open till midnight helps to keep culture alive in the Campo.

SAN GIOVANNI DEI FIORENTINI. The Via Giulia was once the main center of the Tuscan colony in Rome, which is why this church came to be dedicated to John the Baptist, the patron saint of Florence, and was commissioned by a Medici, Leo X. Out of the schemes presented in tender for this contract, which included designs by Michelangelo, Peruzzi, and Raphael, the Pope chose Jacopo Sansovino's. However, his original plans were greatly modified by his successors, among them Antonio Sangallo the Younger (1520), Giacomo della Porta (from 1583 to 1602) and Carlo Maderno, who started work on the project in 1608 and completed it in 1620. The church, which has three naves, is in the form of a Latin cross and is surmounted by a cupola. Its façade, by Alessandro Galilei, was not built until

SAN GIOVANNI DEI FIORENTINI
Originally Michelangelo was invited to design the dome, but again it was Carlo Maderno who actually built it (1614).

Palazzo Sacchetti seen from the Tiber.

KING DAVID'S GLORY
The Mannerist Francesco Salviati (1510–63) was one the most able decorative painters of his generation. His frescoes in Palazzo Sacchetti brilliantly illustrate the epic vein characteristic of the major compositions of the 16th century. The detail reproduced here is from one of the frescoes portraying episodes in the life of David, the shepherd, musician, poet and King of Israel, whose life as a warrior, wanderer and lover inspired many artists.

1734. At the request of Prince Falconieri, Borromini designed the high altar. Among the important figures buried here are the two architects Maderno (1556–1629) and Borromini (1599–1667). Of the many paintings in the church, the works in the St Jerome chapel (third on the right) are of particular interest, as is the large canvas by Salvator Rosa depicting *The Martyrdom of St Cosmas and St Damian* (1669), which hangs in the right transept. (Walk up the Via Giulia to the Palazzo Sacchetti, which is No. 66.)

PALAZZO SACCHETTI. Cardinal Ricci di Montepulciano had this palace built by Nanni di Baccio Bigio on the site of the house where the architect Antonio Sangallo the Younger (1483–1546) had lived. In the 17th century the palazzo was bought by the Sacchetti, a Florentine family that had been living in Rome since the previous century. This is one of the street's most remarkable buildings, with its long façade adorned with decorated windows and a balcony over the main door. Between 1553 and 1554 Francesco Salviati decorated the hall of the piano nobile, known as the Map Room or Cardinal's Audience Hall.

ALONG THE VIA GIULIA. A little further along on the right stands Santa Maria del Suffragio, built in 1669 by Carlo Rainaldi (1611–91). In the next street on the right (Via del Gonfalone) you will find the Oratorio di SANTA LUCIA DEL GONFALONE, used today as a concert hall for chamber music. It is decorated with an ensemble of frescoes on the theme of the Passion by a variety of late-16th-century artists.

SPIRITO SANTO DEI NAPOLETANI. Continuing along the Via Giulia, you will pass the national church of the Neapolitans. Rebuilt by Carlo Fontana between 1701 and 1709, it was radically transformed

in the mid 19th century by Antonio Cipolla, who designed the façade. The last sovereigns of the Two Sicilies, King Francesco II and Queen Maria Sofia, are buried here. (Continue to the right and take Via Sant'Eligio degli Orefici).

SANT'ELIGIO DEGLI OREFICI. This building was erected by Raphael in 1509 for the goldsmiths' guild, St Eligius being the patron saint of goldsmiths and blacksmiths. The façade and the frescoes and painting behind the high altar date from the 17th century. (Return to the Spirito Santo dei Napoletani and take the street facing the church; this leads to a small piazza.)

PALAZZO RICCI. The piazza is dominated by the façade of Palazzo Ricci. Traces of the grisaille frescoes painted in the middle of the 16th century by Polidoro da Caravaggio and Maturino da Firenze can still be seen on the façade. (Turn right into Via di Monserrato.)

SANTA MARIA DI MONSERRATO. This church, begun by Antonio Sangallo the Younger in 1518, has been the national church of Spaniards in Rome since 1875. Its façade, built by Francesco da Volterra, is adorned with a relief showing the Virgin and Child sawing a mountain, an allusion to the Catalan shrine of Monserrat. The painting of *San Diego* in the first chapel on the right is attributed to Annibale Caracci; the chapel also contains the mortal remains of Pope Alexander VI and of King Alfonso XIII of Spain, who died in exile in 1941. On the altar of the third chapel on the left stands a beautiful statue of St James by Jacopo Sansovino. (Cross the delightful Piazza di Santa Caterina della Rota.)

SAN GIROLAMO DELLA CARITÀ. Once famous for Domenichino's painting of *The Last Communion of St Jerome* above the high altar – removed by the French in 1797 and now in the picture gallery of the Vatican (a copy has replaced it) – this church was redesigned by Domenico Castelli in the mid 17th century. Two chapels are of particular interest. The first on the right, the SPADA CHAPEL, was long attributed to Borromini but was designed by Virgilio Spada, perhaps under the master's guidance. Medallions portraying previous members of the Spada family adorn the walls of yellow-and-brown marble. The balustrade is formed by two kneeling angels with removable wings holding a marble drape. The other is the elegant ANTAMORO CHAPEL, to the left of the high altar, which is the only work in Rome of the architect Filippo Juvara (1678–1736). (Return to the Via Giulia.)

"FINESTRE INGINOCCHIATE"
A particularly fine feature of the Palazzo Sacchetti is its "kneeling" ground-floor windows: the frame of each window is supported on consoles.

The façade of Santa Maria di Monserrato.

The *Last Communion of St Jerome* by Domenichino, now in the Vatican picture gallery.

Fontana del Mascherone.

PALAZZO FARNESE
A pair of large twin fountains enliven the piazza. The water runs into Egyptian granite basins brought here from the Baths of Caracalla, surmounted by what are often taken to be *fleur-de-lys*. The flowers are in fact irises, the emblem of the Farnese family.

FAMOUS FRESCOES
After studying Michelangelo's frescoes in the Sistine Chapel, Annibale Carracci (1560–1609), youngest and most brilliant artist of the Carracci family, painted the vaulted ceiling of the great gallery of Palazzo Farnese. Within a framework of *trompe l'oeil* architectural effects, these Baroque frescoes brought mythology to life in joyfully exuberant style.

PALAZZO FALCONIERI. Orazio Falconieri, who had bought two adjacent palazzi, asked Borromini to unite them. The façade on the Via Giulia is composed around two doorways framed in rustic bossage; at the back an ample loggia overlooks the Tiber. At each end of the façade there are two tall pilasters supporting falcons' heads on female busts, the vivid emblem of the originally Tuscan Falconieri family.

SANTA MARIA DELL'ORAZIONE E DELLA MORTE. This oratory belonging to the confraternity of the "buona morte", which ensured Christian funerals to the poor of Rome, was rebuilt according to plans by Ferdinando Fuga between 1733 and 1738. Its curved façade with pilasters and columns alternating on two levels is clearly influenced by Borromini and the high cupola is a fine achievement. The small skulls used as a decorative motif throughout, particularly over the main door, recall the purpose of this pious confraternity. The building supports a bridge over the Via Giulia to the gardens of Palazzo Farnese. Another bridge was originally to span the Tiber and connect the Palazzo with the Farnesina ▲ *360*; however, Michelangelo's plans for linking the two palaces were never carried out. Farther down the street is the FONTANA DEL MASCHERONE, built of ancient marble remains, which takes its name from the mask that decorates it. (Take the Via del Mascherone opposite the fountain.)

PALAZZO FARNESE

PIAZZA FARNESE. Somewhat severe in appearance today, the piazza (formerly also known as Piazza del Duca) was at one time animated by frequent celebrations and spectacles, including bullfights. Due to the influence of Renato Nicolini, a member of the municipal council who organized the *estate romana* ("Roman summer") for a few years in the 1980's, it briefly recovered some of its past glory.

THE CONSTRUCTION OF THE PALACE. The Palazzo Farnese is the largest of Rome's patrician palaces. Originally planned by Antonio Sangallo the Younger in 1510 for Cardinal Alessandro Farnese, the project was vastly amplified in 1534

when the latter became Pope, taking the name of Paul III. In 1546, following Sangallo's death, Michelangelo was entrusted with its continuation. He was responsible for the design of the second floor, the cornice and the two upper orders of columns in the courtyard. After Michelangelo's death in 1564, Giacomo della Porta completed the building, erecting the façade and the splendid loggia that overlooks the Via Giulia. In the 18th century the palace was inherited by the Bourbons of Naples. Today it houses the French Embassy and the magnificent library of the Ecole française de Rome, a research institute for archeologists and historians ▲ *VII*. The Roman nickname for the palace is *il dado* ("the dice").

ARCHITECTURE. Some of the materials used for the building were from ancient ruins: the travertine marble that frames the windows is said to have come from the Coliseum. The façade on Piazza Farnese is quite austere. Composed of thirteen bays, it is devoid of decoration save for the window frames and the bossage of the main entrance, which is surmounted by a loggia. The courtyard, which used to contain the Farnese collection of ancient statuary, is particularly elegant. The three orders of classical columns (Doric, Ionic and Corinthian) are superimposed in a rhythmic succession of windows and open arches. The façade on the garden side of the building echoes this use of the three orders. Inside the palace the most outstanding features are the Salotto Dipinto decorated with frescoes by Francesco Salviati and Federico Zuccaro; the Sala delle Guardie, which is dominated

The imposing main entrance of Palazzo Farnese.

The *Triumph of Bacchus and Ariadne*, the central fresco by Annibale Carracci in the gallery of Palazzo Farnese.

PALAZZO SPADA
The façade of Palazzo Spada has niches enclosing eight stucco statues of the great men of ancient Rome, among them Marcellus and Caesar (shown above). The walls of the courtyard are decorated with mythological figures such as Venus, Mars, and Pluto.

BORROMINI'S PERSPECTIVE ★
The impression of depth in this corridor, less than 30 feet long, is mainly achieved by the use of diminishing columns placed ever closer together. The perspective effect, which contracts and extends the space deceptively, gives the illusion of a depth of over 120 feet. The actual height of the seemingly tall statue at the end of the corridor, including the pedestal, is less than that of an average person.

The fountain in front of the Monte di Pietà.

by a copy of the statue of Ercole Farnese ▲ *320* (the original is in Naples); and above all the Galleria, with its superb frescoes depicting the loves of the gods and goddesses painted by Annibale Carracci, with the help of his brother Agostino, between 1597 and 1604. (Take Via dei Venti.)

THE AREA AROUND PALAZZO SPADA ● 87

Cross the minute Piazza della Quercia, where an evergreen oak lends a note of rusticity, and you will come to the front of Palazzo Spada. Its façade, in full splendor after restoration work, is festooned with statues, medallions, garlands, and other decorative moldings by Giulio Mazzoni, providing a startling contrast to Palazzo Farnese.

PALAZZO SPADA. Built for Cardinal Girolamo Capo di Ferro between 1549 and 1559, but modified for the Spada family in the 17th century, this palace has been the seat of the Council of State since 1927. On the left as one enters the courtyard one can view the astonishing *trompe l'oeil* perspective devised by Borromini. The Galleria Spada, one of the most important collections of 17th century paintings in Rome, can also be visited. It contains works by Guercino, Honthorst, Reni and Valentin, among others. A remarkable statue of Pompey stands in the Sala Grande. (Turn right as you come out of the palace.)

LA TRINITÀ DEI PELLEGRINI. The celebration of the jubilee every fifty years attracted crowds of pilgrims to Rome and hostels were created in almost every part of the city. This church was built near one of the hostels between 1603 and 1616. The rendered brick façade, designed by Francesco de Sanctis, was added in 1723. Above the high altar there is Guido Reni's *Holy Trinity* (1624) painted to look like a relief.
SAN PAOLO ALLA REGOLA. According to tradition this church was built on the site of the house where St Paul stayed while in Rome. Its plan, in the shape of a Greek cross, and façade were designed in the 18th century by Giacomo Cioli and Giuseppe Sardi. (Continue through Piazza San Paolo alla Regola and Piazza San Salvatore to the Monte di Pietà.)
MONTE DI PIETÀ. This institution was founded by Pope Paul III to provide Romans with pawnbroking facilities. The financial system of the Pontifical States being largely based upon the fiduciary issue of currency, the Monte di Pietà acquired economic importance in modern times. The present building, erected in the 17th and 18th centuries, was completed by Nicola Salvi (1697–1751), the architect of the Fontana di Trevi ▲ 298. The chapel was decorated in a remarkable Baroque style during the first half of the 18th century. (Take Via dei Specchi, then the first turning on the left.)

AROUND CAMPO DE' FIORI

SAN CARLO AI CATINARI. This church belonging to the Barnabites (who took their name from San Barnaba, their original church, in Milan) was built between 1611 and 1646 according to plans by Rosato Rosati. The façade is the work of Giambattista Soria. The interior is rich in ancient marbles and is surmounted by a fine dome with stucco decorations. On the pendentives paintings by Domenichino illustrate the four cardinal virtues; and above the high altar, which is

adorned with ancient columns, hangs Pietro da Cortona's *St Charles Borromeo during the Plague of Milan*, painted in 1667.
VIA DEI GIUBBONARI. This bustling street is famous for the variety of its shops, and the little restaurant in the Largo dei Librari which serves *filetti di baccalà* (cod in batter), with white wine from the Castelli. (Take the second turning on the right, Via dei Chiavari. The houses in the first street to the left Via di Grotta Pinta stand on the site of Pompey's theater ▲ 248.)

CHARLES BORROMEO
Born in 1538 in Arona, he was raised to the rank of cardinal in 1560 and named archbishop of Milan by his uncle Pius IV. He died in 1584 and was canonized in 1610. The Church of San Carlo ai Catinari was dedicated to him in 1611, and Guido Reni painted this portrait of him in 1636.

THE "CATINARI"
The church received its name because of the presence of makers of wooden bowls (*catini*) in the neighborhood. Today there are still a number of craftsmen in the surrounding streets who ply the traditional trades of the area.

This painting of *The Annunciation* in San Carlo ai Catinari, with its remarkable luminosity and chiaroscuro effects, is one of Giovanni Lanfranco's finest works. The face of the Virgin is illuminated by the light of the Holy Spirit.

The inner curve of the theater is faithfully echoed by the shape of the buildings of Via di Grotta Pinta. This is one of the most remarkable examples of urban continuity in Rome. Parts of the theater's walls still stand in the basements of a number of these buildings and also inside the Pancrazio restaurant, which can be reached on foot through the Passaggio del Biscione. These walls are among the earliest examples of opus *reticulatum*.

POMPEY'S THEATER AND PORTICOS. In 61 BC work began on Rome's first permanent theater. Until then there had only been wooden stages because it was feared that lasting constructions would encourage people to attend entertainments ▲ *172* too often. Heartened by the particularly sumptuous Triumph he received upon his return

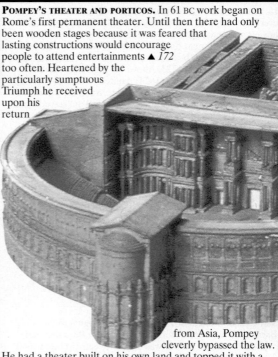

from Asia, Pompey cleverly bypassed the law. He had a theater built on his own land and topped it with a temple dedicated to Venus Victrix (the goddess of victory), so he could claim that the hemisphere of seats was an immense flight of steps leading to the temple! The complex, designed to enhance the creator's image, conferred on him the status of a Hellenistic monarch. The theater, which could hold 17,000 spectators, was inaugurated in 55 BC with literary and musical events, and with hunts lasting several days. One hundred lions, twenty elephants and a number of lynxes were massacred during the festivities. Behind the stage a portico of massive dimensions had been erected. It was adorned with numerous statues of women, and at the end of it was a large exedra which became the Curia (meeting place) of the Senate; this was where Julius Caesar was assassinated. Inside the Curia, diametrically opposite the temple of Venus Victrix, there was a statue of Pompey holding a globe in his hand. Today, remains of the Curia can be seen in the Area Sacra del Largo Argentina ▲ *250*.

The Campo de' Fiori market.

CAMPO DE' FIORI. This piazza owes its name to the fields full of flowers which were here before the erection of buildings in the 15th century. It soon became the site of inns, bookshops and the colorful market still held here

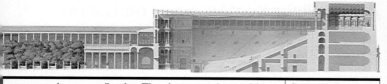

every morning except Sunday. The piazza was also used for executions, and it is was in the Campo de' Fiori that the philosopher Giordano Bruno was burnt at the stake for heresy by the Inquisition on February 17, 1600. (At the far end of the Campo, turn right into Piazza della Cancelleria.)

PALAZZO DELLA CANCELLERIA. Built at the end of the 15th and beginning of the 16th century for Cardinal Raffaele Riario, this palace was traditionally attributed to Bramante (1444–1515); however, it now seems probable that he only contributed to the design of the magnificent courtyard. Leo X confiscated the palace from Cardinal Riario for hatching a plot against him, which is how it became the residence of prelates and served as the *cancelleria* (chancellery) for the drafting of pontifical acts. Today it still enjoys the extraterritorial privileges granted to the Vatican under the Lateran Agreement ● *33*, ▲ *198*. The long, elegant travertine façade is given rhythm by a series of pilasters (the main doorway was designed by Vignola). Under Paul III, in 1546 Vasari decorated the Sala Grande with frescoes showing scenes relating to the Pope's life. It came to be known as the "hall of the hundred days", referring to the time it took Vasari to complete the work. "It shows!" is reputed to have been Michelangelo's comment on it. The granite columns of the courtyard came from the original church of San Lorenzo in Damaso, which stood here; excavations beneath the paving have revealed the remains of this 4th-century basilica.

SAN LORENZO IN DAMASO. On the right of the façade of the Palazzo della Cancelleria there is a door, also designed by Vignola, which is the entrance of the present church of San Lorenzo in Damaso. Retaining the form of a basilica, with three naves, this church was rebuilt as part of the palace at Cardinal Riario's request. Its decoration was modified several times in the course of the 17th and the 19th centuries. (Turn right into the Corso Vittorio Emanuele.)

THE BARRACCO MUSEUM. The small Renaissance palazzo known as the Farnesina ai Baullari, built in 1523 by Sangallo the Younger but with a late-19th-century façade by Enrico Gui, houses a museum of ancient sculpture bequeathed by Senator Giovanni Barracco to the city of Rome in 1902. This collection has Egyptian, Assyrian, Etruscan and Roman sculptures, and is one of the few in Rome that includes Greek

GIORDANO BRUNO
The unveiling of his statue in 1889 gave rise to confrontations between Republicans and supporters of the Pope.

LILIES AND IRISES
French lilies feature on the façade of the Barracco Museum because the building was constructed in the 16th century for Thomas Le Roy, a Breton prelate and emissary of Francis I. The similarity between *fleur-de-lys* and blue irises, part of the Farnese arms gave rise to the name *Piccola Farnesina* by which this building is known.

Head of a priest, or possibly of Caesar, Barracco Museum.

"THE CHURCH OF TOSCA"
In one of the chapels of Sant'Andrea della Valle is where Puccini set the first act of *Tosca*; the action takes place in this area, from the Palazzo Farnese to Castel Sant'Angelo, where the tragic story ends. In July 1992 a live television production of the opera was made using the locations indicated by Puccini, each scene being performed at the time of day specified in the libretto.

THE DOME OF SANT'ANDREA
Maderno and other great artists of the 17th century contributed to the decoration of the church. Borromini designed the capitals and the lantern; Lanfranco and Domenichino painted the interior.

originals. Part of the garden of a Roman house dating from 60 AD can be visited in the foundations of the palace. (Continue along the Corso Vittorio Emanuele.)

SANT'ANDREA DELLA VALLE ★. As fine an achievement as the Gesù ▲ *257*, this church has the highest dome in Rome after St Peter's ▲ *210, 213*. Both the dome and the façade were designed by Carlo Maderno, although the façade was completed by Rainaldi and Fontana between 1662 and 1664. It is the church of the mother house of the Theatine Order, founded in 1540 by St Gaetano di Thiene. Construction began in 1591, the design being the outcome of a compromise between the plans of the architect chosen by the Order, Fr Francesco Grimaldi, and those of Giacomo della Porta, who was a protégé of the project's main financial backer, Cardinal Gesualdo. The relative nudity of the nave contrasts with the lavish decorations of the transepts and the apse. The church's frescoes are representative of two different trends. In the cupola Lanfranco painted a trompe l'oeil fresco of the *Assumption of the Virgin Mary* (1625–8), covering the inside of the dome completely. Domenichino, in his frescoes of the Evangelists in the four pendentives and his *Scenes from the Life of St Andrew* in the coffers of the vault over the choir, demonstrates a preference for line and idealized form. The three frescoes in the choir by Mattia Preti depicting *The Martyrdom of St Andrew* were painted in 1650. Among the tombs the ones of the Piccolomini popes, Pius II and Pius III, on either side of the nave are the most notable; these were moved here from St Peter's in 1614.

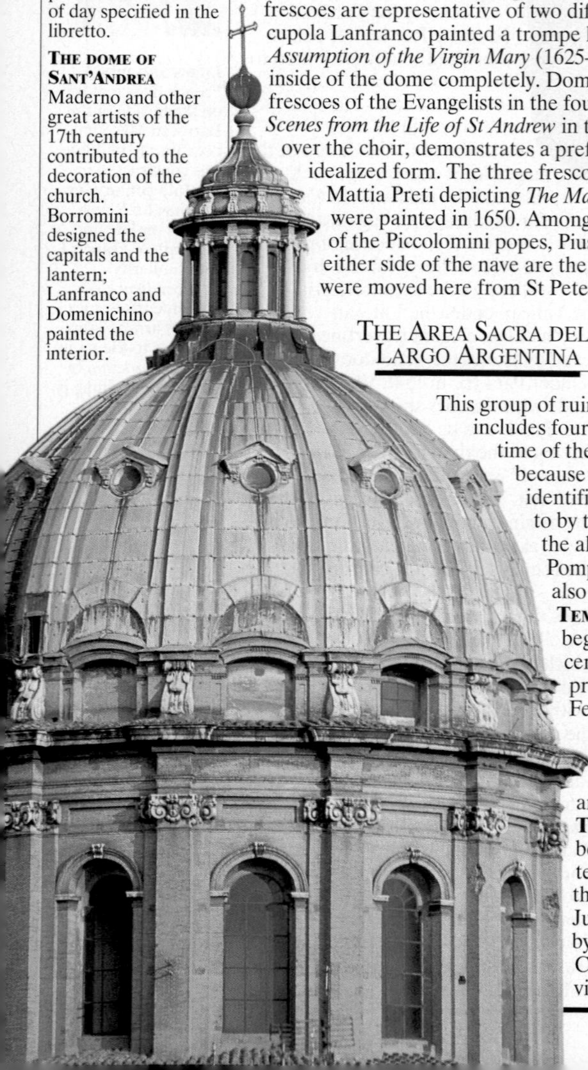

THE AREA SACRA DEL LARGO ARGENTINA

This group of ruins, below street level, includes four temples from the time of the Republic that, because of uncertain identification, are referred to by the first four letters of the alphabet. Remains of Pompey's Curia ▲ *248* can also be seen here.

TEMPLE C. Built at the beginning of the 3rd century BC, this was probably dedicated to Feronia, the goddess of springs and forests. Her cult was introduced in Rome around 290 BC.

TEMPLE A. This is believed to be the temple dedicated to the water nymph Juturna ▲ *142* erected by Caius Lutatius Catulus after his victory over Carthage

Largo Argentina.

in 241 AD. A church of St Nicholas was built on this site in the Middle Ages, of which two apses with traces of frescoes have survived. East of the temple there are the remains of Pompey's Hecatostylon, an immense portico with a hundred columns.

TEMPLE D. This temple was probably the one erected by Marcus Aemilius Lepidus following his naval victory over King Antiochus in 179 BC.

TEMPLE B. Fragments of a colossal female statue made of Greek marble were discovered beside this circular temple. These fragments can now be seen in the Museo del Palazzo dei Conservatori (Braccio Nuovo) ▲ *132* and are almost certainly the remains of the statue of the deity worshiped in the temple. The building is thought to be the *aedes Fortunae huiusque dei* ("temple of today's good fortune") erected in 102 BC by Catulus, colleague of the Roman commander Marius, after their victory at Vercelia over the Cimbri, one of the Teutonic tribes that were threatening northern Italy.

PORTICUS MINUCIA FRUMENTARIA. To the east of Largo Argentina in ancient times there was an enclosed space within a building called the Villa Publica. This was where the census of the Roman population, as well as other administrative activities, took place. Claudius demolished the buildings here and replaced them with a large square surrounded by porticos known as the Porticus Minucia Frumentaria, used for the distribution of free wheat to the people of Rome. In the center stood a temple of the Republican period, probably the Temple of the Nymphs. Two of its columns with Corinthian capitals can be seen in the Via delle Botteghe Oscure, where they were discovered during excavations in 1938.

TEATRO ARGENTINA. In 1816 this public theater which replaced the former private theater of a ducal family, the Sforza-Cesarini, presented the premiere of Rossini's *The Barber of Seville*. All the great Italian opera composers subsequently had their works produced on this stage. (Between Largo Argentina and the Tiber is the area that was once the Ghetto.)

"THE ROARING LION"
This relief on the house of Caius Manilius, in the Via del Portico d'Ottavia, shows a lion (the symbol of Rome) seizing a deer.

THE GHETTO

THE JEWS OF ROME. Jews are known to have settled in Rome as early as the 1st century BC, and there was such a strong Jewish presence in Trastevere during the Empire that this quarter was described as "the fortress of Roman Judaism". Later, Jews also settled in other parts of the city, such as the Campus Martius, the Suburra and the Aventine; and the Pons Fabricius ▲ *175* came to be known as the Pons Iudaeorum (the bridge of the Jews). Nevertheless, the main synagogues remained in Trastevere, and under the city's bylaws of 1363 the Jewish population had to bury their dead near the church of San Francesco a Ripa ▲ *354*. Due to the concentration of Jewish inhabitants in this area, by 1309 it had already come to be called the Contrada Iudaeorum (the Jewish quarter). At this time Jews were not excluded from mingling with the Christian community; however, they were forced to indicate their religious background by their clothing, and their ability to practice their religion in public depended on the varying goodwill of the different popes. With the exodus of Jews from Spain and Portugal in 1492 and 1498, the community expanded further: Pope Alexander VI (1492–1503) welcomed nine thousand of them in Rome against payment in gold.

THE CREATION OF THE GHETTO. When Pope Paul IV (1555–9), who had previously been the Grand Inquisitor of the Kingdom of Naples, issued the bull *Cum nimis absurdium* proclaiming the creation of the

Ghetto, the Jewish community – which had gradually moved to the left bank of the Tiber during the 14th century – was confined within the boundaries of the Sant'Angelo district. Several thousand people were thus forced to live in an area of barely 2.5 acres. From Piazza Giudea (today an anonymous part of the Piazza delle Cinque Scole that was previously called Via del Progresso) the boundary ran parallel to Via del Portico d'Ottavia and then veered right toward the Tiber at the Via della Pescheria. Sixtus V enlarged the Ghetto to include the banks of the river, where the poorest families settled. In this area when the Tiber was in spate water reached the third floor of the houses, and the Jewish community was forced to pay 100 scudi per stonemason to construct an embankment. At sunset the gates of the Ghetto in Piazza Pescheria and Piazza Giudea were closed.

UNFETTERING THE GHETTO. After a final enlargement in 1823 under Leo XII, the walls were at last demolished in 1848; and in 1883 the Ghetto was officially abolished by law. Today the Ghetto area lacks any architectural unity. The history of its tormented past is evident from the number of neglected houses and derelict sites left by reckless demolition. But it has not lost its character, and it is fascinating to explore Via del Portico d'Ottavia, where Roman inscriptions set in the walls of medieval houses vie with the signs of kosher food shops and those of *trattorie* offering delicious *carciofi alla Giudea* (deep-fried artichokes that look like golden sunflowers).

VIA DELLE BOTTEGHE OSCURE AND THE MATTEI PALACES. The Via delle Botteghe Oscure owes its name ("the street of dark workshops") to the existence in the Middle Ages of workshops with special ovens used to reduce ancient marble to lime for the production of building materials. Taking Via Paganica, which crosses it, you will come to the Mattei *insediamento,* a cluster of buildings owned by the Mattei family. To the left are the PALAZZO CAETANI, built in 1564 for Alessandro Mattei, and PALAZZO MATTEI-PAGANICA built in 1541 for Ludovico Mattei. The remains of the theater of Balbus, the smallest of the theaters of the Campus Martius, were found in the cellars of the latter. The theater was built in 32 BC on the proceeds of the booty seized from the Garamantes (an African people); behind the stage the remains of a large portico, the Crypta Balbi, have also been found.

PIAZZA MATTEI. A little further on, the centerpiece of Piazza Mattei is the

THE ROUND-UP OF 1943
On October 16, 1943, the Ghetto was the victim of a huge round-up of Jews. The German officer in charge forced the residents to pay a ransom of 110 pounds of gold per person. Although this sum was collected, the Nazis surrounded the Ghetto and deported all the Jews who were there. *La Storia* by Elsa Morante and Carlo Lizzani's film *L'oro di Napoli* are both based on this tragic event.

A kosher shop in the Ghetto.

Alessandro Mattei.

delightful FONTANA DELLE TARTARUGHE (Tortoise Fountain) built between 1541 and 1584 by Taddeo Landi, possibly to a design by Giacomo della Porta. It faces the PALAZZO COSTAGUTI (No. 10), which is famous for its frescoes by some of the greatest artists, including Guercino and the Zuccari. The third Mattei palace, on the left in Via dei Funari, is the PALAZZO MATTEI di Giove, built by Carlo Maderno in 1611, which is distinguished by its monumental size and the wealth of its decoration. The remains of one of the finest collections of ancient marble statuary can be seen in the two courtyards. This building now houses the Italian Center for American Studies and the Library of Modern History. The entrance is on Via Caetani (to the left). This was the street where on May 9, 1978, halfway between what was then the headquarters of the Italian Communist Party (in Via delle Botteghe Oscure) and the headquarters of the Christian Democrats (in Piazza del Gesù), the body of the Christian Democrat leader Aldo Moro was found after his assassination by the Red Brigades.

The Fontana delle Tartarughe (Tortoise Fountain), one of the most famous and elegant in Rome.

SANTA CATERINA AI FUNARI. This church was founded in the 12th century and rebuilt between 1560 and 1564; the façade, by Guidetto Guidetti, is a fine example of Renaissance architecture. The name of the church refers to the rope makers (*funari*) that formerly worked in the neighborhood. (Return to Piazza Mattei and, skirting Palazzo Costaguti, walk downhill toward the Tiber.)

PALAZZO CENCI. The knoll on which the palace was built is formed by the ruins of the Circus Flaminius. The edifice has four wings, and its main façade and the family chapel (San Tommaso dei Cenci, founded in the 12th century) face onto a small square. This chapel was rebuilt and embellished in 1575 by Francesco Cenci in order to hold the future sepulcher of his children Beatrice and Giacomo. (Take Via Catalana.)

THE CENCI
At the end of the 16th century Francesco Cenci, the head of this powerful Roman family, tried to abuse his daughter Beatrice. With her stepmother and her brothers, she murdered him on September 9, 1598. They were executed the following year in front of the Ponte Sant'Angelo.

THE SYNAGOGUE. After the walls of the Ghetto were torn down a new synagogue was built, by the architects Costa and Armanni, and inaugurated in 1904. It is a massive building in travertine marble, with an aluminium dome in Assyrian-Babylonian style that is clearly visible from the Aventine. Next door to it is the Jewish Museum.

THE CAMPO MARZIO
FROM THE GESÙ
TO PALAZZO MADAMA

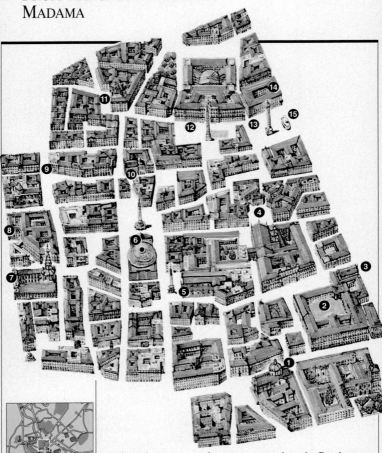

Given the presence of monuments such as the Pantheon, Baroque churches like the Gesù and Sant'Ignazio, and buildings such as the Palazzo di Montecitorio and the Palazzo Chigi, you might expect this neighborhood to be fossilized by its very grandeur. Admittedly it is no longer the popular area it once was, and it's a long time since farm laborers in search of work assembled around the Fontana della Rotonda. But its narrow, winding streets are full of surprises: the enormous marble foot of a Roman colossus; the Bernini elephant and, scattered throughout the district, hidden courtyards and little piazzas like the ones in provincial towns.

THE CAMPO MARZIO IN THE MIDDLE AGES

CHURCHES. In the early Middle Ages the Campo Marzio area was not at all densely inhabited. Only three titular churches had been built there: San Marco, San Lorenzo in Damaso and San Lorenzo in Lucina. The wars against the Goths in the first half of the 6th century and then the Lombard sieges had catastrophically reduced the population and radically changed its distribution within the Aurelian Wall. Settlements began to appear in the Forum and the Campo Marzio in this period. In 609 Boniface IV, with the assent of the Emperor Phocas, turned the Pantheon into the Church of Santa Maria dei

Martiri. Churches then multiplied in the area bounded by the Tiber, the Quirinal and the Capitoline.

SETTLEMENT. While settlements remained scarce in the 10th and 11th centuries, they subsequently developed along the banks of the Tiber and in the vicinity of several dynamic churches and monasteries. In the northern part of the Campo Marzio property-development projects were started in the 12th and 13th centuries under the auspices of the monasteries of San Silvestro in Capite, Santa Maria in Campo Marzio and San Ciriaco in Via Lata. The result of these real-estate operations was the creation of new neighborhoods with a regular urban landscape and a modest and homogeneous social fabric. They contrasted with the older urban areas at the center of the Campo Marzio, where the towers and palaces of the nobles stood out prominently, dominating the humbler houses of their retainers.

THE CHURCH OF THE GESÙ ● *78, 81*

COUNTER-REFORMATION ARCHITECTURE. From 1540 the Jesuits had only had a small church, which they were eager to rebuild in a way that would symbolize the spread of the most dynamic Order of the Counter-Reformation. Cardinal Alessandro Farnese, who decided to fund the project, imposed his choice of architect, Vignola, and work began in 1568. After Vignola's death in 1573, Giacomo della Porta designed the façade, which is adorned with pilasters; its broad volutes disguise the difference of width between the two levels. The ribbed cupola, designed by Vignola and completed by della Porta, is a relatively low one – at least by the standards of that time. When completed in 1582, the church was a sober building: the ceiling of the only nave was bare, and the pilasters were not of rich marble but of travertine. In the side chapels, late Mannerist painters such as Pomarancio, Federico Zuccaro and Francesco Bassano left their mark.

ST IGNATIUS OF LOYOLA
(1491–1556)
This Spanish nobleman and soldier who experienced a conversion at the age of thirty made a pilgrimage to Jerusalem then dedicated himself to the spiritual life. In 1534 he found his first disciples in Paris. They all made vows of chastity and poverty, and pledged themselves to going wherever the Pope needed them. In 1540 Paul III gave official approval to their association, the Society of Jesus. They then established their first "religious humanist" missions in the East Indies, Brazil, the Congo and Ethiopia at the request of the Spanish and Portuguese Crowns. Ignatius urged his colleagues to found colleges for the study of languages and local history.

ORDER AND PRAYER
The architecture of the Gesù is designed to favor personal prayer in a large congregation. The altar is visible from all points in the church so that the whole congregation can follow the Mass. The separation between choir and nave clearly emphasizes the distinction between clergy and laity.

▲ THE CAMPO MARZIO
FROM THE GESÙ TO PALAZZO MADAMA

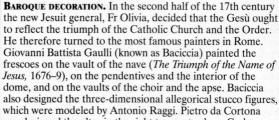

THE ALTAR OF ST IGNATIUS
The statue of St Ignatius of Loyola by Pierre Legros was melted down by Pius VI to help pay for the Napoleonic wars. It was remade in Canova's workshop in 1814, soon after order was reestablished.

THE PERFECT ILLUSION
In this *trompe l'oeil* corridor Fr Pozzo used ingenious tricks of perspective to create fantastic spacial effects that are as pleasing as they are astonishing.

BAROQUE DECORATION. In the second half of the 17th century the new Jesuit general, Fr Olivia, decided that the Gesù ought to reflect the triumph of the Catholic Church and the Order. He therefore turned to the most famous painters in Rome. Giovanni Battista Gaulli (known as Baciccia) painted the frescoes on the vault of the nave (*The Triumph of the Name of Jesus*, 1676–9), on the pendentives and the interior of the dome, and on the vaults of the choir and the apse. Baciccia also designed the three-dimensional allegorical stucco figures, which were modeled by Antonio Raggi. Pietro da Cortona designed the altar in the right transept, where Carlo Maratta's painting of *The Death of St Francis Xavier* (1679) was hung.

THE TRIUMPH OF ST IGNATIUS. Artists who were members of the Society were also called upon; and one of the most remarkable of them, Fr Andrea Pozzo, designed the monumental altar dedicated to St Ignatius of Loyola in the left transept of the church. This altar is the richest in Rome. It shows the apparition of the Trinity to St Ignatius, with the Eternal Father and Christ enthroned on a gigantic block of lapis lazuli. The saint's monumental figure, covered with silver, gilded bronze and lapis lazuli, was executed by Pierre Legros. On either side of the tomb, two allegorical groups represent the Jesuits' mission: the struggle against heresy (*Faith's Triumph over Heresy,* by Legros, on the right) and evangelization (*The Triumph of the Christian Religion over Idolatry,* by Giovanni Théodon, on the left). In addition to a history of the Order's foundation, there is an extraordinary corridor in *trompe l'oeil* by Fr Pozzo as well as frescoes by Jacques Courtois, nicknamed "il Borgognone" (the Burgundian), which should not be missed. On the square in front of the church is the PALAZZO CENCI-BOLOGNETTI (1737), the headquarters of the Christian Democrats. (Take the Via del Plebiscito, then turn left into Via della Gatta.)

THE COLLEGIO ROMANO. Its building began in 1582, and it remained the first great Jesuit college until 1870. Fr Athanasius Kircher, one of the Order's most famous scholars, lived here from 1635 to 1680 and amassed a collection of curiosities. In 1875, when Rome became the capital of Italy, the Biblioteca Vittorio Emanuele II (the national library) was first housed in this building, since many of the books came from the Jesuits' collection; a hundred years later it was transferred to Castro Pretorio ▲ *335*, near the Città Universitaria and Stazione Termini.

PALAZZO DORIA-PAMPHILI

THE PALACE. Opposite the Collegio Romano is the vast Doria-Pamphili palace, built in several stages by its various owners. It was acquired by the family of Pope Julius II in the 16th century and then purchased by Cardinal Pietro

258

The *Flight into Egypt*, one of the four lunettes Annibale Carracci painted for Palazzo Aldobrandini.

Salome with the Head of John the Baptist is one of Titian's early works, but its richness of color and his treatment of light reveal the artist's mastery. Claude Lorrain's *Landscape with Dancers* (bottom) is also an undisputed masterpiece: it demonstrates his virtuosity in rendering the interplay of light and shade, with its subtle passage from the limpid blue of the sky to the deep shadows of the woods.

Aldobrandini, the nephew of Pope Clement VIII. In 1647 it was inherited by the nephew of Innocent X, Camillo Pamphili, who enlarged the important Aldobrandini and Pamphili art collections. Between 1731 and 1735 Gabriele Valvassori built the façade facing the Corso and completed the upper loggia overlooking the courtyard to house the galleries. Then in about 1740 Paolo Ameli added the façade on the Via del Plebiscito. The branch of the Doria-Pamphili family that inherited the palace in 1760 still owns it today.

THE PICTURE GALLERY. Some of the most important pieces in the collection were part of the Aldobrandini bequest, such as the celebrated *Aldobrandini Lunettes*. These historical landscapes with biblical scenes, painted by Annibale Carracci and Albani, were originally in the palace chapel, as were Titian's *Salome with the Head of John the Baptist* and Parmigianino's *The Nativity*. The works acquired by the Pamphili in the 17th century include Velázquez's portrait of Pope Innocent X, Caravaggio's *Mary Magdalene* and *Rest on the Flight into Egypt*, the magnificent paintings of the Bologna school, and much of the rich collection of landscapes (especially those by Claude Lorrain). The Doria-Pamphili enriched the collection with pictures by Bronzino, primitives and tapestries. (The gallery and private apartments are open to the public three times a week; the gallery's entrance is in Piazza del Collegio Romano.)

One of the plaques on the walls of Santa Maria sopra Minerva recording the flood levels of the Tiber.

Michelangelo's *Christ Bearing the Cross* (1514) in Santa Maria sopra Minerva has the classical beauty of an Apollo reclining nonchalantly against the cross. The prudish bronze drape was a later addition.

SANTA MARIA IN VIA LATA

Returning from the Piazza del Collegio Romano to the Corso, on the left is the picturesque FONTANELLA DEL FACCHINO – a small fountain featuring a water carrier in 16th-century costume, who became one of Rome's "talking statues" ● *46* thanks to a supposed resemblance to Martin Luther. Facing the fountain is the church of Santa Maria in Via Lata. This ancient church was rebuilt several times before its appearance was transformed in the 17th century. Bernini designed the high altar and the choir between 1636 and 1643; Cosimo Fanzago redecorated the nave with marble inlays; and Pietro da Cortona created its graceful façade between 1658 and 1663. The two superimposed colonnades standing out against the vestibule create contrasting effects of light and shadow, and distinguish it from the numerous façades with integrated columns. This was the parish church of the Bonaparte family, many of whose members are buried here. On a lower level vestiges of the paleo-Christian church and early frescoes can be seen, the most beautiful of which is *The Seven Sleepers of Ephesus,* dating from the 7th century.

AROUND THE PIAZZA DELLA MINERVA

VIA PIE DI MARMO. This narrow street owes its name to the gigantic marble foot of a Roman statue firmly planted on the corner of Via Santo Stefano del Cacco. It probably came from the ancient Temple of Isis and Serapis (today the Church of Santo Stefano del Cacco, built in the Middle Ages and restored in the 18th century). The small obelisks to be seen in the area also came from the Temple of Isis: one stands in the Piazza della Rotonda, another in Piazza della Minerva.

THE CHURCH OF SANTA MARIA SOPRA MINERVA. On its façade there are marks dating from the 16th and 17th centuries indicating the level of the various floods of the Tiber: the water rose to 65 feet in this neighborhood, which is one of the lowest areas in Rome. Founded in the 8th century on the site of an ancient temple of Minerva, the church belongs to the Dominicans. It was rebuilt around 1280 and is the only church in Rome with pointed Gothic arches. In the mid 19th century, in order to restore its Gothic character, the vault was painted and the pillars were faced with imitation marble. St Catherine, the fiery Sienese who did not hesitate to admonish the Pope at the time of the great debates of the Avignon schism, died in Rome. Her relics are preserved in the sarcophagus under the high altar. Her reputation was so widespread that many popes wished to be buried beside her and she eventually became the patron saint of Italy. Filippino Lippi was summoned from Florence at the end of the 15th century to decorate the Carafa chapel (in the right transept). Michelangelo's *Christ Bearing the Cross* (1519–21) stands in front of the left pillar in the choir. Finally, the Dominican painter Fra Angelico from the monastery of San Marco in Florence, who died in 1455, has a movingly simple tombstone placed in a dark

passageway on the left of the choir. (Leave the church by the corridor to the left of the choir and take Via Beato Angelico; then turn left and proceed along Via di Sant'Ignazio to Piazza di Sant'Ignazio, which is off it, at the end, on the right.)

SANT'IGNAZIO

THE PIAZZA. This piazza is like a stage set placed at the foot of the towering façade of the Church of Sant'Ignazio. The conception of the piazza, designed by Filippo Raguzzini in 1727–8, is one of the most successful and most original in Rome. The symmetrical streets opening into it are concealed by the façades of the houses, creating the effect of "wings" as on a theater stage. In one of these streets, the Via dei Burrò, the French set up their administrative headquarters during the Napoleonic occupation – its name is a corruption of "bureaux".

THE CHURCH ● 84. The façade of Sant'Ignazio is on two levels like that of the Gesù, to achieve similar effects; it has generally been attributed to Algardi but may have been the work of Orazio Grassi, the church's architect. Due to lack of funds to build a cupola as initially intended, Fr Andrea Pozzo, a master in the theories of perspective, painted an altar in *trompe l'oeil* (1684–5). He went on to paint the frescoes in the choir and those covering the entire vault of the nave, completing them in 1694; *The Triumph of St Ignatius* and *The Order's Expansion in the Four Parts of the World* are represented as an optical illusion, the walls of the church extended by false columns as if opening onto the sky. A disk of yellow marble set in the middle of the floor of the nave marks the spot on which to stand in order to get the full benefit of the perspective and *trompe l'oeil* effects. The right transept is adorned with a sumptuous altar dedicated to Luigi Gonzaga, again designed by Fr Pozzo, with a high relief sculpted by Pierre Legros; in the left transept Filippo Valle built the altar of the

SANT'IGNAZIO
"Go forth and give light to the world." The ceiling illustrates St Ignatius' words. "The Father's light, through the Son, descends upon Ignatius and thus illuminates all the known continents."

The famous *trompe l'oeil* cupola in Sant'Ignazio.

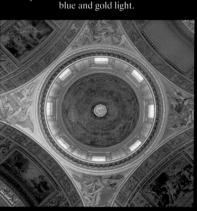

ST PETER'S ▲ *210*
The elliptical sixteen-ribbed dome is flooded with blue and gold light.

SAN LUIGI DEI FRANCESI ▲ *270*
A rim of shadow beneath the lantern sets off the sinuous forms of the sculptures.

SANT'ANDREA DELLA VALLE ▲ *250*
The sixteen windows in the drum and the lantern illuminate Carlo Maderno's cupola.

SANT'IVO ▲ *272*
An exercise in architectural virtuosity, revealed in the dome's purity and fluidity of form.

SAN BERNARDO ALLE TERME ▲ *295*
The only illumination is a shaft of light provided by the single central oculus.

SANTA MARIA DEL POPOLO ▲ *306*
An explosion of *trompe l'oeil* framed by a plain, rigorous octagon.

262

The Renaissance model of a cupola – as conceived by Brunelleschi, then Bramante, Antonio di Sangallo the Younger and finally Michelangelo – was a spherical dome with convergent ribbing resting on a drum and surmounted by a lantern. This eventually gave way to the variations of the Mannerist architects, who replaced the sphere with an ellipse, got rid of the lantern, and used frescoes for effect.

SAN ROCCO
The amazing use of color in the pendentives contrasts with the dark cupola.

SANTA MARIA MAGGIORE ▲ *342*
(The Pauline Chapel)
Cigoli's fresco fills the whole cupola.

SANTA MARIA IN CAMPITELLI ▲ *159*
An exercise in sobriety, with its monochrome uniformity and even lighting.

SANT' AMBROGIO E CARLO AL CORSO ▲ *309*
An option for color in a monochromatic symphony of warm tones.

SAN CARLO AI CATINARI ▲ *247*
Diminishing coffers and pictorial foreshortenings enhance the cupola's depth.

SANTA MARIA DELLA VITTORIA ▲ *294*
The architecture is little more than support for an orgy of Baroque painting and stucco decoration.

·M·AGRIPPA·L·F·COS·TERTIVM·FECIT·

It was the Emperor Hadrian who had the following inscription placed on the architrave: *M(arcus) Agrippa L(ucii) f(ilius) c(on)s(ul) tertium fecit* ("Marcus Agrippa, son of Lucius, third time consul, made [this temple]"). Beneath it another inscription, in smaller lettering, provides evidence of restoration work in 202 AD under Septimus Severus and Caracalla.

Annunciation in 1750. (On leaving the church, turn left into Via del Seminario, which will take you to Piazza della Rotonda.)

THE PANTHEON ★ ● 70

PIAZZA DELLA ROTONDA. The square in which the Pantheon is set was created under Clement XI (1700–21) and involved the demolition of several buildings. At the same time Giacomo della Porta's fountain (1578) was drastically modified: it was given a pedestal decorated with dolphins and the Pope's coat of arms, and an obelisk was added which, like the one in Piazza della Minerva, came from the neighboring Temple of Isis.

AGRIPPA'S TEMPLE. The plan of the Pantheon combines the pronaos (porch) of a temple with a rotunda of the kind found in Roman baths ● 68. A brilliant composite of geometrical forms and contrasting features, its architecture was intended to reflect the terrestrial and cosmic order. This is the best preserved building of ancient Rome – thanks to the Byzantine Emperor Phocas' donation of it to Pope Boniface IV and its transformation into a church, which received the name of Santa Maria dei Martiri (St Mary of the Martyrs) in 609 AD. It was originally built in 27 to 25 BC by Agrippa, who wanted to dedicate it to Augustus, his father-in-law and friend. When Augustus declined the honor, it was dedicated to the major deities venerated by the families of Claudius and Julius Caesar (Mars, Venus and the divine Julius himself) instead. The building was then rectangular and faced south. What we see today dates from the early years of Hadrian's reign, between 118 and 125 AD. The pediment was adorned with a crowned eagle, as witness the sockets. The great portico is supported by eight monolithic granite columns with white marble capitals and bases. It is

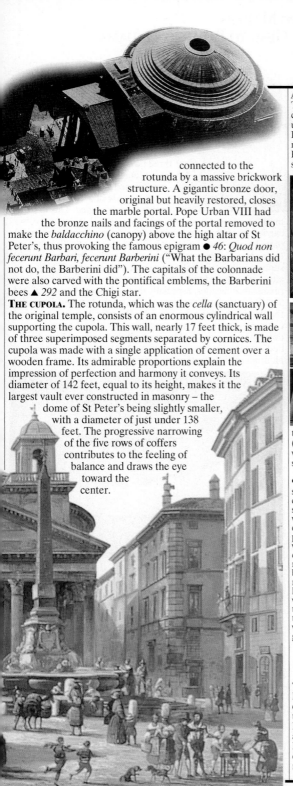

connected to the rotunda by a massive brickwork structure. A gigantic bronze door, original but heavily restored, closes the marble portal. Pope Urban VIII had the bronze nails and facings of the portal removed to make the *baldacchino* (canopy) above the high altar of St Peter's, thus provoking the famous epigram ● *46*: *Quod non fecerunt Barbari, fecerunt Barberini* ("What the Barbarians did not do, the Barberini did"). The capitals of the colonnade were also carved with the pontifical emblems, the Barberini bees ▲ *292* and the Chigi star.

THE CUPOLA. The rotunda, which was the *cella* (sanctuary) of the original temple, consists of an enormous cylindrical wall supporting the cupola. This wall, nearly 17 feet thick, is made of three superimposed segments separated by cornices. The cupola was made with a single application of cement over a wooden frame. Its admirable proportions explain the impression of perfection and harmony it conveys. Its diameter of 142 feet, equal to its height, makes it the largest vault ever constructed in masonry – the dome of St Peter's being slightly smaller, with a diameter of just under 138 feet. The progressive narrowing of the five rows of coffers contributes to the feeling of balance and draws the eye toward the center.

A CELESTIAL VAULT
The image of "a celestial vault" was used by the historian Dion Cassius with reference to the Pantheon. The only source of light in the

temple is the oculus (30 feet in diameter), which is open to the sky.

"This open and secret temple was conceived as a sundial. The hours were to circle the center of its carefully polished pavement, where the disk of the day was supposed to rest like a golden buckler; there the rain would make a limpid pool from which prayer could transpire like smoke toward the void where we place the gods."

Marguerite Yourcenar,
Memoirs of Hadrian

This was how Pasquino ● *46* characterized the twin bell turrets that Bernini added to the antependium of the Pantheon in the 17th century. They were removed in 1883.

265

THE PORTICO OF THE ARGONAUTS
Along the left side of the Pantheon is the back wall of the portico that separated Agrippa's temple from the Saepta, a large square used for electoral meetings under the Republic (under the Empire it became a center for entertainment). A reconstruction of the portico is shown above.

THE NICHES
These were originally decorated with statues of the gods and are now chapels. Beneath the third aedicule on the left is the tomb of Raphael (1483–1520), inscribed with the famous epitaph composed by Cardinal Bembo: *Ille hic est Raffaello Sanzio, timuit quo sospite vinci rerum magna parens et moriente mori.* (Alexander Pope, who borrowed the couplet for another epitaph, translated it as "Living, great nature feared he might outvie Her works; and dying, fears herself to die.") Other artists buried here include Giovanni da Udine, Perino del Vaga, Annibale Carracci, Taddeo Zuccaro and Baldassare Peruzzi, as well as two kings of Italy, Vittorio Emanuele II and Umberto I.

THE NICHES. Opposite the door is the main niche, over which there is an arch. Its two fine columns are made of *pavonazzetto*, a beautiful violet-veined marble from Synnada in Asia Minor. The other niches – three on either side, alternating from rectangular to circular in shape – are fronted with monolithic columns made of a Tunisian marble known as *giallo antico*. This use of marbles, which was so important in classical architecture, is carried through in the paving of the floor, where geometrical patterns alternate, and also in the shrines (*aedicoli*) between the niches. Columns of red porphyry, *giallo antico* and granite support either triangular or rounded tympanums. Their alternation is said to have served as a model for many renaissance façades, especially that of Palazzo Farnese ▲ *244*.

THE BASILICA OF NEPTUNE AND BATHS OF AGRIPPA. Behind the Pantheon, along the Via della Palombella, there are columns, a brick wall and a marble frieze which includes dolphins and tridents. These are all that is left of a basilica dedicated to Neptune, erected by Agrippa and rebuilt by Hadrian. A little further on, near the Corso Vittorio

Emanuele, is the site of Rome's most ancient baths, inaugurated in 19 BC with an artificial lake, the Stagnum Agrippae. Both were fed by the Aqua Virgo.

THE TEMPLE OF MATIDIA. Hadrian is surely the only man in the world to have deified his mother-in-law and to have dedicated a temple to her. Situated close to the present-day Piazza Capranica, it can be reached by the Via degli Orfani. A truncated column from it can be seen in the alley called the Vicolo della Spada d'Orlando. (Take Via dei Pastini to the Piazza di Pietra.)

The Temple of Hadrian.

THE TEMPLE OF HADRIAN. After Hadrian's death his son, Antoninus Pius, erected a temple in his honor, which was dedicated in 145 AD. Eleven white-marble columns, now imprisoned within the northern wall of the Borsa (STOCK-EXCHANGE BUILDING) on the Piazza di Pietra, testify to the grandeur of the temple. Reliefs from it portraying allegorical figures, alternating with trophies, are preserved in the courtyard of the Palazzo dei Conservatori and in the National Museum of Naples. (Walk through to the Piazza Colonnay, which is nearby.)

PIAZZA COLONNA

The urbanization of this section of the Campo Marzio began under the Antonines in the 2nd century.

THE COLUMN OF MARCUS AURELIUS. In the center of the square rises the column of Marcus Aurelius. Just over 83 feet tall, it was made between 180 AD (the year of the emperor's death) and 196 AD. The lower part of the column commemorates his victories over the Germanic tribes on the Danube frontier, and the upper part his success against the Sarmatians (in the area between the Volga and the Vistula rivers). Its base, originally nearly 30 feet taller, was decorated with festoons and reliefs showing victories and scenes of barbarians being forced to submit: these were destroyed in 1589 by Sixtus V. The column itself has twenty complete rings of reliefs, rather fewer than its model, Trajan's column ▲ *166*. With its simplification and violent contrasts, it heralds the eminently dramatic 3rd-century style. The facial expressions, for example, are quite remarkable – especially those of the terror-stricken or desperately beseeching barbarians, the soldiers and the emperor-philosopher, who is most

The Bocconi ● *90* department store (now Rinascente) opened in Piazza Colonna in 1886. With its metal and glass structure the building was influenced by the stores that had sprung up in other European capitals, such as La Belle Jardinière and Le Printemps in Paris.

THE COLUMN OF MARCUS AURELIUS Inside the column a spiral staircase with 190 steps leads to the top, where the Emperor's statue originally stood. In 1589, at Sixtus V's request, Domenico Fontana replaced it with a statue of St Paul.

LEGIONARIES CROSSING A RIVER (THE EMPEROR IS TALKING TO TWO OFFICERS).

AUXILIARY TROOPS PROTECTING THE ARMY ON THE MARCH.

BATTLE SCENE, WITH LEGIONARIES MASSACRING BARBARIANS.

Drawings of the reliefs made by Giovanni Guerra when the column was restored in 1589.

THE COLUMN OF ANTONINUS PIUS
The reliefs on the base depict the apotheosis of the Emperor and his wife Faustina, being carried to heaven by a winged *genius*. On the two smaller sides there are equestrian parades.

frequently sculpted face on, no doubt to make him appear more majestic. Ranuccio Bianchi Bandinelli, a specialist in Roman art, emphasizes the artistic originality of the image of Marcus Aurelius: "Among the scenes of death and destruction, the face of the emperor in person emerges … deeply marked by anguish, exhaustion and age. He must have been about 54 years old: this is certainly not the face of a triumphant conqueror exalted by his victories but that of a man who was 'a total stranger to the habits of the rich' (*The Meditations of Marcus Aurelius*, I, 3), a genuine, suffering lay saint." (The fountain to the right of the column is by Giacomo della Porta. Palazzo Chigi faces it on one side of the square; opposite, on the other side of the Corso, is the Galleria Colonna.)

PALAZZO CHIGI. Carlo Maderno and Felice della Greca both had a hand in the construction of this stark palazzo of the Counter-Reformation period. Building began in 1562 but it was not completed until 1630. The Baroque courtyard is decorated with stucco motifs and a fountain bearing the Chigi arms. The palazzo, acquired by the State in 1917, was the headquarters of the Ministry of Foreign

Affairs before it became the seat of the Presidenza del Consiglio dei Ministri (Prime Minister's office).

GALLERIA COLONNA. When the Palazzo Piombino was demolished by the Municipality of Rome in 1889 there were lengthy discussions about what should be done with the site. In the end it was decided to build a large covered gallery which could also house the headquarters of the Banca Italiana di Sconto. The gallery was inaugurated in 1922. Nearby, on Largo Chigi, the Bocconi department store (now Rinascente), completed in 1886, was one of the first buildings in Rome to use modern materials (metal and glass) while retaining a Neo-Renaissance style. Its architect, Giulio De Angelis, was one of the principal exponents of the Roman eclectic trend. (Cross the Corso and the Piazza Colonna again to get to Piazza di Montecitorio.)

The pictures above show Palazzo di Montecitorio (left and center) and Piazza Colonna with Palazzo Chigi (right).

MONTECITORIO

PIAZZA DI MONTECITORIO. Under the Antonines the site occupied by the Palazzo di Montecitorio (which houses the Italian Chamber of Deputies) was used for the emperors' cremation ceremonies; the remains of the *ustrina* (logs) found here can be seen in the National Roman Museum. In 1703 the base of Antoninus Pius' column, now in the Cortile della

PALAZZO DI MONTECITORIO Its two façades contrast in every way. Whereas Bernini's is

Pigna at the Vatican, was also discovered here. Other fragments of the huge granite column were used for restoring and stabilizing the obelisk of Psammetichus II (6th century BC), which was erected in the middle of the piazza in 1792. Transported from Heliopolis to Rome in 10 BC, the obelisk was originally set up in the Campus Martius by Augustus to serve as the *gnomon* (pointer) of an enormous sundial. It was unearthed in 1748 between the Piazza del Parlamento and San Lorenzo in Lucina. **PALAZZO DI MONTECITORIO.** This building has two very different aspects: the original façade by Bernini and a 20th-century Art Nouveau façade (on the Piazza del Parlamento) by Ernesto Basile. The lovely, harmonious Baroque façade was begun in 1650 under Pope Innocent X, who

wanted to build a palace for the Ludovisi. After being held up until 1694 the project was completed by Carlo Fontana, and Innocent XII decided to install the Tribunals (the Curia Innocenziana) there. When the Piedmontese entered Rome in 1870, they were faced with the problem of finding a suitable

fluid and grandiose, the façade added by Ernesto Basile has a rather cold and stolid appearance.

The colorful market held in Piazza delle Coppelle presents an irresistible invitation to stop and browse.

The Church of Santa Maria in Campo Marzio.

site for the new parliament. In the end it was decided to use the great courtyard to accommodate the Chamber of Deputies, enclosing it with a glass roof. However, it soon became necessary to enlarge the building. Basile's design for the extension is a fine example of the style known as *floreale* (floral) in Italy because of decorative motifs inspired by exuberant vegetation. Flanking the entrance on the Piazza del Parlamento are two statues by Domenico Trentacoste (1911). The semicircular Chamber, entirely paneled in oak, is decorated with a huge fresco by Giulio Aristide Sartorio portraying Italian civilization, the virtues of the Italian people and the most significant episodes of the nation's history. There is also a bas-relief by Davide Calandra celebrating the glory of the House of Savoy. (To reach the Church of Santa Maria in Campo Marzio, take Via Ufficio del Vicario, where you will find the *gelateria* Giolitti, which sells some of the best ice cream in Rome.)

SANTA MARIA IN CAMPO MARZIO. This church has existed since the 7th century, but it was rebuilt between 1670 and 1685 by Giovanni Antonio de Rossi. From the street nothing but the walls of the convent can be seen, recently repainted their original color, a very pale blue. Restorers have been returning to the pale colors which were used for painting façades in Rome before the 19th century. The church's portico opens onto a pretty courtyard, and its graceful cupola has a flattened, oval shape. (From here you can make a detour through the picturesque Piazza delle Coppelle, and stop at the fashionable Hemingway bar; then follow Via delle Coppelle and turn right into Via della Maddalena.)

SANTA MARIA MADDALENA. This 15th-century church was rebuilt in the 17th century by Carlo Fontana. But the façade, a combination of Baroque and Rococco surmounted by a circular pediment, was added in 1735 by Giuseppe Sardi, who was greatly influenced by Borromini. The interior has the same sense of movement combined with sumptuous decorations: the organ loft is astonishing – with its gilded woodcarvings, statues and cherubs – and the sacristy is one of the most beautiful in Rome. (Continue to Piazza della Rotonda and turn right into Via Giustiniani, which leads to San Luigi dei Francesi.)

SAN LUIGI DEI FRANCESI

THE SANTA CECILIA CHAPEL. In the Church of San Luigi dei Francesi Domenichino painted a cycle of frescoes based on the saint's legendary life. The *Glory of Cecilia* is shown here.

This is a particularly French neighborhood. Next to San Luigi dei Francesi, which is the French national church, are the

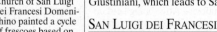

One of the
salamanders (the
emblem of Francis I)
that adorn the façade
of San Luigi dei
Francesi.

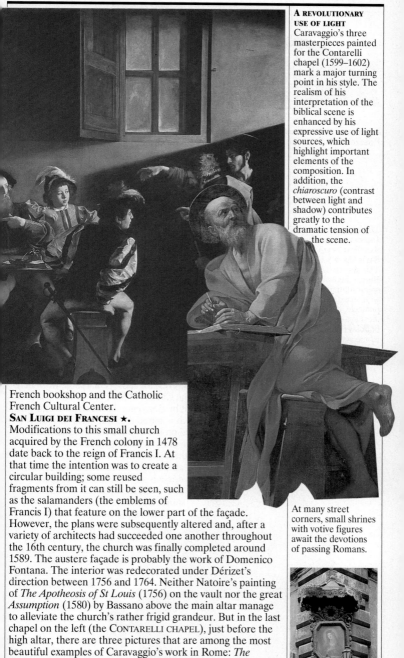

**A REVOLUTIONARY
USE OF LIGHT**
Caravaggio's three
masterpieces painted
for the Contarelli
chapel (1599–1602)
mark a major turning
point in his style. The
realism of his
interpretation of the
biblical scene is
enhanced by his
expressive use of light
sources, which
highlight important
elements of the
composition. In
addition, the
chiaroscuro (contrast
between light and
shadow) contributes
greatly to the
dramatic tension of
the scene.

French bookshop and the Catholic
French Cultural Center.
SAN LUIGI DEI FRANCESI ★.
Modifications to this small church
acquired by the French colony in 1478
date back to the reign of Francis I. At
that time the intention was to create a
circular building; some reused
fragments from it can still be seen, such
as the salamanders (the emblems of
Francis I) that feature on the lower part of the façade.
However, the plans were subsequently altered and, after a
variety of architects had succeeded one another throughout
the 16th century, the church was finally completed around
1589. The austere façade is probably the work of Domenico
Fontana. The interior was redecorated under Dérizet's
direction between 1756 and 1764. Neither Natoire's painting
of *The Apotheosis of St Louis* (1756) on the vault nor the great
Assumption (1580) by Bassano above the main altar manage
to alleviate the church's rather frigid grandeur. But in the last
chapel on the left (the CONTARELLI CHAPEL), just before the
high altar, there are three pictures that are among the most
beautiful examples of Caravaggio's work in Rome: *The
Calling of St Matthew* (on the left), the *Martyrdom of St
Matthew* (on the right) and *St Matthew and the Angel* (over the
altar). Also outstanding are the frescoes of the *Life of Santa*

At many street
corners, small shrines
with votive figures
await the devotions
of passing Romans.

271

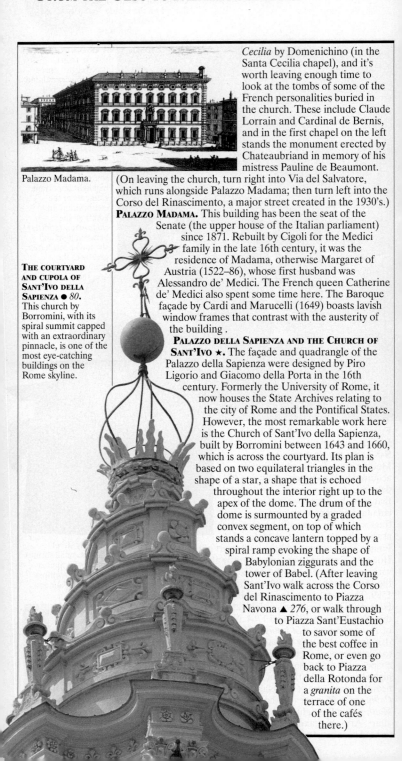

Palazzo Madama.

Cecilia by Domenichino (in the Santa Cecilia chapel), and it's worth leaving enough time to look at the tombs of some of the French personalities buried in the church. These include Claude Lorrain and Cardinal de Bernis, and in the first chapel on the left stands the monument erected by Chateaubriand in memory of his mistress Pauline de Beaumont. (On leaving the church, turn right into Via del Salvatore, which runs alongside Palazzo Madama; then turn left into the Corso del Rinascimento, a major street created in the 1930's.)

PALAZZO MADAMA. This building has been the seat of the Senate (the upper house of the Italian parliament) since 1871. Rebuilt by Cigoli for the Medici family in the late 16th century, it was the residence of Madama, otherwise Margaret of Austria (1522–86), whose first husband was Alessandro de' Medici. The French queen Catherine de' Medici also spent some time here. The Baroque façade by Cardi and Marucelli (1649) boasts lavish window frames that contrast with the austerity of the building .

THE COURTYARD AND CUPOLA OF SANT'IVO DELLA SAPIENZA ● *80.* This church by Borromini, with its spiral summit capped with an extraordinary pinnacle, is one of the most eye-catching buildings on the Rome skyline.

PALAZZO DELLA SAPIENZA AND THE CHURCH OF SANT'IVO ★. The façade and quadrangle of the Palazzo della Sapienza were designed by Piro Ligorio and Giacomo della Porta in the 16th century. Formerly the University of Rome, it now houses the State Archives relating to the city of Rome and the Pontifical States. However, the most remarkable work here is the Church of Sant'Ivo della Sapienza, built by Borromini between 1643 and 1660, which is across the courtyard. Its plan is based on two equilateral triangles in the shape of a star, a shape that is echoed throughout the interior right up to the apex of the dome. The drum of the dome is surmounted by a graded convex segment, on top of which stands a concave lantern topped by a spiral ramp evoking the shape of Babylonian ziggurats and the tower of Babel. (After leaving Sant'Ivo walk across the Corso del Rinascimento to Piazza Navona ▲ *276*, or walk through to Piazza Sant'Eustachio to savor some of the best coffee in Rome, or even go back to Piazza della Rotonda for a *granita* on the terrace of one of the cafés there.)

AROUND
PIAZZA NAVONA

Via dei Coronari

"We came to stay at the Bear, where we remained the following day too; on the second day of December we rented rooms in a Spaniard's house, opposite Santa Lucia della Tinta [Via di Monte Brianzo]. We were quite comfortably accommodated with three fine rooms, a hall, a pantry, a stable and a kitchen, all for twenty Ecus a month: for which our host also cooked and provided fire wood for the stove. Lodgings are generally furnished a little better than in Paris, and the more costly lodgings are upholstered with gilded leather. ... M. de Montaigne was peeved to find so many French people in town that he hardly found anyone in the streets who failed to greet him in his own tongue."

Montaigne,
Journal de voyage

Map of Rome, showing the city as it was in 1637.

THE CAMPO MARZIO DURING THE RENAISSANCE

Between the pontificates of Martin V (1417–31) and Paul III (1534–49) the Campo Marzio underwent major transformations and acquired more or less the appearance it has today. During the Renaissance this area became the true heart of Rome, with about four fifths of the city's entire population settled in it (an estimated forty thousand inhabitants in 1527).

POPES AS TOWN PLANNERS. In this period the occasional isolated attempts to improve the appearance of the city that had characterized the first half of the 15th century, as exemplified by Eugenius IV's restoration of the Pantheon ▲ *264*, were replaced by a policy of town planning based on two priorities: to ensure adequate conditions for the movement of traffic through the city, especially in the direction of the Vatican, and to improve the network of streets. At first these measures mostly affected the streets leading to Ponte Sant'Angelo ▲ *239*: for example, the old Via Recta (now Via dei Coronari) was widened by Sixtus IV (1471–84) and began to be lined with majestic palazzi decorated with grisaille frescoes. Then in the early 16th century Julius II (1503–13) had the Via Giulia built ▲ *240* to link the Ponte Sisto (recently constructed by Sixtus IV) to San Giovanni dei Fiorentini ▲ *241*. Palazzi and churches, such as Palazzo Sacchetti and San Biaggio della Pagnotta, began to appear along this long, straight thoroughfare. However, urban restructuring was not limited to the area leading to St Peter's, which was then under construction: Pope Paul II (1464–71), who built what was later to be known as Palazzo Venezia ▲ *161*, widened and straightened the Via del Corso ▲ *308*. In order to facilitate entry into the city, Leo X (1513–21), whose work was continued by Clement VII and Paul III, had the Piazza del Popolo enlarged ▲ *306*, new streets built, and older ones modernized (including Via Leonina and eventually Via di Ripetta, Via del Babuino and Via Flaminia ▲ *308*). The network of side streets was affected by less ambitious but no less important measures. Since the medieval streets were cluttered with porticos, external stairways and all sorts of other architectural protuberances that hindered traffic, efforts to eliminate such obstructions began during the pontificate of Sixtus IV. With the paving of the city's streets and squares, gradually the medieval town disappeared.

A NEW COMMERCIAL CENTER. Other measures focused on converting the Campo Marzio into the commercial center of

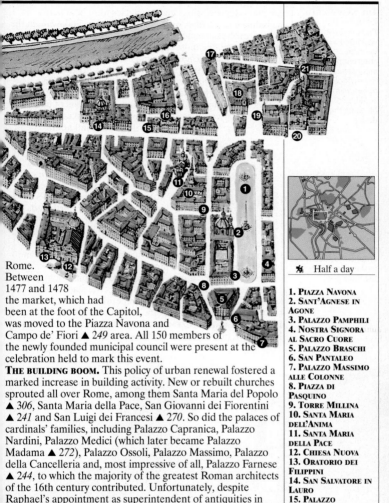

Rome.
Between
1477 and 1478
the market, which had
been at the foot of the Capitol,
was moved to the Piazza Navona and
Campo de' Fiori ▲ *249* area. All 150 members of
the newly founded municipal council were present at the
celebration held to mark this event.

THE BUILDING BOOM. This policy of urban renewal fostered a
marked increase in building activity. New or rebuilt churches
sprouted all over Rome, among them Santa Maria del Popolo
▲ *306*, Santa Maria della Pace, San Giovanni dei Fiorentini
▲ *241* and San Luigi dei Francesi ▲ *270*. So did the palaces of
cardinals' families, including Palazzo Capranica, Palazzo
Nardini, Palazzo Medici (which later became Palazzo
Madama ▲ *272*), Palazzo Ossoli, Palazzo Massimo, Palazzo
della Cancelleria and, most impressive of all, Palazzo Farnese
▲ *244*, to which the majority of the greatest Roman architects
of the 16th century contributed. Unfortunately, despite
Raphael's appointment as superintendent of antiquities in
1515, these ambitious undertakings involved the almost
systematic destruction of the monuments of ancient Rome.

PIAZZA NAVONA ★

A BAROQUE MASTERPIECE. This piazza, which displays the
genius of such masters of the Baroque as Bernini and
Borromini, is one of the finest in papal Rome. Its harmony
and colors, combined with its elegance and popularity, give it
a special charm that is enhanced by the surprising contrast of
architecturally sober houses alternating with a number of
monumental buildings.

THE HEART OF THE CITY. Of all Rome's piazzas, this *isola
pedonale* (pedestrian precinct) is the one where the liveliness
of Roman life is most tangible. It has long been a meeting
place for the inhabitants of Rome. In the past, in addition to

🐾 Half a day

1. PIAZZA NAVONA
2. SANT'AGNESE IN AGONE
3. PALAZZO PAMPHILI
4. NOSTRA SIGNORA AL SACRO CUORE
5. PALAZZO BRASCHI
6. SAN PANTALEO
7. PALAZZO MASSIMO ALLE COLONNE
8. PIAZZA DI PASQUINO
9. TORRE MILLINA
10. SANTA MARIA DELL'ANIMA
11. SANTA MARIA DELLA PACE
12. CHIESA NUOVA
13. ORATORIO DEI FILIPPINI
14. SAN SALVATORE IN LAURO
15. PALAZZO LANCELLOTTI
16. PALAZZO CESI
17. MUSEO NAPOLEONICO
18. PALAZZO ALTEMPS
19. SANT'APOLLINARE
20. SANT'AGOSTINO
21. SANT'ANTONIO DEI PORTOGHESI

275

CIRCVS

THE "NAUMACHIAE"
Until the 19th century
Piazza Navona
remained a center for
nautical
entertainments: the
naumachiae. Since
the surface of the
piazza was concave it
could be flooded by
blocking the
drains

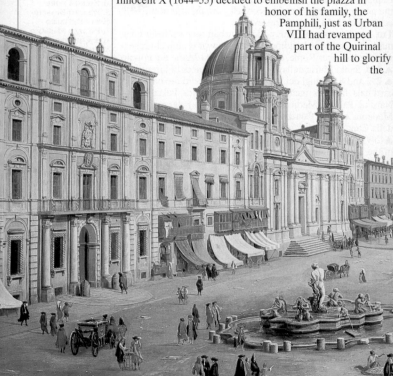

from
the
fountains, allowing
carriages to move
around the rim. Some
of them even entered
the huge pool.

the market, processions and spectacles were held here – including *naumachiae*, or mock naval battles. Today life in the piazza revolves around the open-air cafés and the seasonal fairs. Of these, the most popular is the one held in December and early January where toys and crib figures are sold. Its theme is the Feast of Epiphany as well as Christmas, so *la Befana* (the Epiphany witch, who is roughly the Italian equivalent of Father Christmas) features prominently. In the summer the piazza provides a continuous festival of painters, caricaturists, fortune-tellers and buskers, who entertain visitors until the small hours.

DOMITIAN'S STADIUM. Piazza Navona is a perfect example of urban continuity in Rome ● *60*. It covers exactly the area occupied by the track of Rome's first stadium (built by Domitian between 81 and 96 AD) and retains the stadium's oblong shape with a rounded north end. The buildings surrounding the piazza are built on top of the *cavea*, the stepped stone seating, designed to accommodate thirty thousand spectators. Beside the stadium – which was devoted to athletic events – Domitian built an odeon, or auditorium for musical competitions. These contests took place during the Certamen Capitolinum, the games instituted by Domitian in 86 AD . The stadium was known as the Circus Agonalis (competition arena), which became corrupted to "n'Agona" and eventually "Navona".

PONTIFICAL AGGRANDIZEMENT. Soon after being elected Pope, Innocent X (1644–55) decided to embellish the piazza in honor of his family, the Pamphili, just as Urban VIII had revamped part of the Quirinal hill to glorify the

Barberini family ▲ 290. With this in mind, he had his family's palace and the church of Sant'Agnese in Agone rebuilt, ordered the restoration of the two fountains that Gregory XIII (1572–85) had installed at either end of the piazza, and commissioned the colossal Fontana dei Quattro Fiumi in the center.

THE ENCHANTMENT OF WATER ★. The three fountains, fed by the Aqua Virgo aqueduct ▲ 298, are the main decorative elements of the piazza. The most remarkable of these, the FONTANA DEI QUATTRO FIUMI (1651), is an expression of Bernini's most consummate artistry. Innocent X wanted a monument that would form a centerpiece for this elongated space but not disrupt its unity. An obelisk from the circus of Maxentius ▲ 328 was erected over a rocky grotto, from which a lion and a sea monster are to be seen emerging. The hieroglyphics

give an official version of Domitian's coming to power in 81 AD . The fountain is all the more impressive because the obelisk appears to be resting on an open cavity; in this Bernini achieved a remarkable tour de force that gives it a sense of weightlessness. The large figures reclining precariously on the rocks above the glistening water represent the main rivers of the four continents: the Danube, the River Plate, the Ganges and the Nile (with a veiled head to indicate that its source was still unknown at that time). All around the monument, and also on the tip of the obelisk, the Pope had his family crest sculpted: a dove holding an olive branch. The other two fountains, the basins of which were made in the 16th century to designs by Giacomo della Porta, only took on their present appearance in the 19th century. Their light-colored stone illuminates the piazza. At the southern end, the figure of an Ethiopian hunting a dolphin that dominates the Fontana del Moro is a copy of a statue designed by Bernini. The surrounding

AN IRONIC GESTURE? The figure of the River Plate has its hand raised with the palm toward the Church of Sant' Agnese in what Romans say is a gesture of fear – lest the Baroque façade by Bernini's rival, Borromini, should collapse on top of it.

The Church of Nostra
Signora del Sacro Cuore.

A cross-section
of Sant'
Agnese in
Agone.

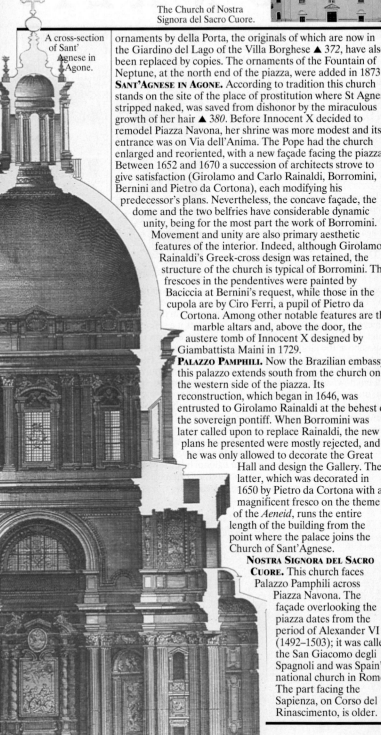

ornaments by della Porta, the originals of which are now in
the Giardino del Lago of the Villa Borghese ▲ 372, have also
been replaced by copies. The ornaments of the Fountain of
Neptune, at the north end of the piazza, were added in 1873.
SANT'AGNESE IN AGONE. According to tradition this church
stands on the site of the place of prostitution where St Agnes,
stripped naked, was saved from dishonor by the miraculous
growth of her hair ▲ 380. Before Innocent X decided to
remodel Piazza Navona, her shrine was more modest and its
entrance was on Via dell'Anima. The Pope had the church
enlarged and reoriented, with a new façade facing the piazza.
Between 1652 and 1670 a succession of architects strove to
give satisfaction (Girolamo and Carlo Rainaldi, Borromini,
Bernini and Pietro da Cortona), each modifying his
predecessor's plans. Nevertheless, the concave façade, the
dome and the two belfries have considerable dynamic
unity, being for the most part the work of Borromini.
Movement and unity are also primary aesthetic
features of the interior. Indeed, although Girolamo
Rainaldi's Greek-cross design was retained, the
structure of the church is typical of Borromini. The
frescoes in the pendentives were painted by
Baciccia at Bernini's request, while those in the
cupola are by Ciro Ferri, a pupil of Pietro da
Cortona. Among other notable features are the
marble altars and, above the door, the
austere tomb of Innocent X designed by
Giambattista Maini in 1729.
PALAZZO PAMPHILI. Now the Brazilian embassy,
this palazzo extends south from the church on
the western side of the piazza. Its
reconstruction, which began in 1646, was
entrusted to Girolamo Rainaldi at the behest of
the sovereign pontiff. When Borromini was
later called upon to replace Rainaldi, the new
plans he presented were mostly rejected, and
he was only allowed to decorate the Great
Hall and design the Gallery. The
latter, which was decorated in
1650 by Pietro da Cortona with a
magnificent fresco on the theme
of the *Aeneid*, runs the entire
length of the building from the
point where the palace joins the
Church of Sant'Agnese.
**NOSTRA SIGNORA DEL SACRO
CUORE.** This church faces
Palazzo Pamphili across
Piazza Navona. The
façade overlooking the
piazza dates from the
period of Alexander VI
(1492–1503); it was called
the San Giacomo degli
Spagnoli and was Spain's
national church in Rome.
The part facing the
Sapienza, on Corso del
Rinascimento, is older.

The church was restored several times, notably by Antonio Sangallo the Younger in the 16th century. It has been redecorated in its original colors – as have several neighboring buildings, which have fine *trompe l'oeil* windows.

PALAZZO BRASCHI. The building on the southwest corner of Piazza Navona was the last of the palaces built in Rome for the family of a pope. Begun in 1792 by Cosimo Morelli for the nephews of Pius VI, in 1871 it was sold to the State and for a while served as the Ministry of the Interior. In 1930 the Fascist Federation of Rome took it over, then in 1949 it was given to the city and became the MUSEO DI ROMA. Sculptures, paintings, drawings, prints and other items illustrate the history of Rome from the Middle Ages. The collection includes works by Canova and a charming series of views of Rome by Ippolito Caffi.

Palazzo Pamphili (above left).

A *tartufo* (chocolate ice cream) from the Tre Scalini is a must (above right).

Pope Innocent X (left).

THE MIRACLE OF MARCH 16
On the second floor of the Palazzo Massimo the room where St Philip Neri resuscitated Paolo, the son of Fabrizio

Massimo, on March 16, 1584, is now a chapel. On the anniversary of the miracle the palazzo is open to the public, and continuous Masses are celebrated in the chapel.

AROUND SAN PANTALEO

SAN PANTALEO. Founded in the 12th century and dedicated to the patron saint of doctors, this church (in the Piazza di San Pantaleo, just beyond Palazzo Braschi) was rebuilt in the 17th century by Giovanni Antonio de Rossi. Behind the splendid façade by Valadier (1806) it has a surprisingly rich interior. The particularly fine high altar is by Carlo Mureno (1713–64).

PALAZZO MASSIMO ALLE COLONNE. To the south of Piazza Navona the Via della Posta Vecchia leads to the back of the Palazzo Massimo complex. A column from Domitian's odeon was placed here as a monument, in front of one of the few grisaille frescoes to have survived on a domestic building. These frescoes, attributed to the school of Daniele da Volterra, earned this building the name "Palazzo Istoriato" (the illustrated palace). The main façade of the Palazzo Massimo, on the Corso Vittorio Emanuele, is a masterpiece of Mannerist architecture. Designed by Baldassare Peruzzi, it echoes the curve of the *cavea* (stone seats) of Domitian's odeon, on which it stands. Peruzzi rebuilt the palace for the Massimi (one of the oldest Roman families) between 1532 and 1536, following the sack of Rome in 1527 ● 36.

PIAZZA DI PASQUINO. To the west of the southern end of Piazza Navona is an ancient copy of a Hellenistic statue from Pergamon, part of a group representing Menelaus carrying the body of Patroclus. Known as Pasquino ● 46, "he" presides over a small piazza, once known as the Piazza dei Librari because of the publishers, printers and booksellers established there. The first guide to Rome in a foreign language (German) was published here by a certain Maurizio Bona. (Take Via Santa Maria dell'Anima.)

TORRE MILLINA. At the top of this tower, built in the Middle Ages, one can see the birds that were the emblem of the Guelfs, the political faction which supported the Pope; their rivals, the Ghibellines, supported the Emperor. The rivalry between the two factions, which was particularly ardent in Florence, soon spread to other medieval cities.

"PASQUINO"
This statue, which Bernini greatly admired, has long been one of the most loquacious of Rome's talking statues ● 46.

The façade of Santa Maria della Pace.

SANTA MARIA DELL'ANIMA. (The entrance is in Piazza della Pace.) The national church of the Germans; also of the Flemish and the Dutch in the 16th century, when it was rebuilt (1500–23). The high Renaissance façade, attributed to Giuliano da Sangallo, is adorned with carved doors which are the work of Andrea Sansovino. Inside, its three naves inspired by German church architecture are unusual in Rome. The church contains many funerary monuments dating from the 16th to the 19th century. The imposing tomb by Peruzzi in the choir is that of Hadrian VI (1522–3), the last non-Italian pope before John Paul II. Over the high altar

there is a remarkable painting of *The Holy Family with Saints* by Giulio Romano. On the other side of Via dell'Anima is SAN NICOLA, the national church of Lorraine, decorated with frescoes by Corrado Giaquinto (1731).

SANTA MARIA DELLA PACE

THE SIBYLS
The four Sibyls (of Cumae, Persia, Phrygia and Tibur) show the influence of Michelangelo's Sistine Chapel ▲ 218. This composition flows with an extraordinary variety of rhythms, like a festoon along the curve of the arch.

THE CHURCH OF SANTA MARIA DELLA PACE ★. The elegant façade dominates the Piazza della Pace, a delightful setting for it designed by Pietro da Cortona during the pontificate of Alexander VII (1655–67). The first major reconstruction of this sanctuary was undertaken (possibly by Baccio Pontelli) at the behest of Sixtus IV. The work began in 1482 – the Pope chose the name "della Pace" to celebrate the peace he hoped to restore in Italy – and was finished under Julius II (1503–13). In the 17th century, under Alexander VII, the church was rebuilt again by Pietro da Cortona, who created its present façade. While a series of Corinthian columns give rhythm to the upper part, beneath it a circular portico supported by Doric columns projects into the piazza. Inside, a

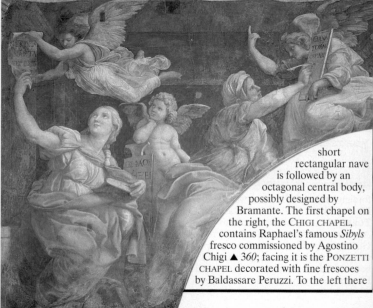

short rectangular nave is followed by an octagonal central body, possibly designed by Bramante. The first chapel on the right, the CHIGI CHAPEL, contains Raphael's famous *Sibyls* fresco commissioned by Agostino Chigi ▲ 360; facing it is the PONZETTI CHAPEL decorated with fine frescoes by Baldassare Peruzzi. To the left there

is a short rectangular nave followed by an octagonal central body, possibly designed by Bramante. The first chapel on the right, the CHIGI CHAPEL, contains Raphael's famous *Sibyls* fresco commissioned by Agostino Chigi ▲ *360*; facing it is the PONZETTI CHAPEL decorated with fine frescoes by Baldassare Peruzzi. To the left there is a passage leading to the sacristy and then to the CLOISTER (1500–4). It was Bramante's first work in Rome; he determined the proportions so as to ensure remarkable effects of light and shade. (Take Via della Pace to the junction with Via Tor Millina – where there are two cafés that are among the liveliest in Rome in the evening – then continue into Via del Parione and turn right at the end.)

VIA DEL GOVERNO VECCHIO. No.39 is the PALAZZO DEL GOVERNO VECCHIO (Old Government Palace), built between 1473 and 1477, which became the official residence of the Governor of Rome in 1624. It acquired its present name when the government was moved to Palazzo Madama by Pope Benedict XIV (1740–58). The building is now in disrepair and looks rather shabby but this street is full of charm, with numerous antique and junk shops and an excellent wine bar. (Turn left into the Via della Chiesa Nuova.)

CHIESA NUOVA ★

PIAZZA DELLA CHIESA NUOVA. Until the Corso Vittorio Emanuele was built, this small piazza was the only open space in front of the church. The fountain (called the FONTANA DELLA TERRINA because of its curious shape, resembling a covered soup tureen) was originally in the center of the Campo de' Fiori ▲ *249*, on the spot where the statue of Giordano Bruno now stands. The two adjacent façades overlooking the piazza belong to Santa Maria in Vallicella – known as the Chiesa Nuova (the New Church) – and the Oratorio dei Filippini (the Oratory of St Philip Neri).

The cloister of Santa Maria dell'Anima (above left); Piazza della Pace (center); and the Fontana della Terrina.

THE ORATORIAN CONFEDERATION
This was founded by the Florentine saint Philip Neri in 1561. Gaining great popularity in Rome, it soon became the figurehead of the Counter-Reformation and was officially

approved by Gregory XIII in 1575. Its priests gathered together to meditate and listen to sacred music. They created a new musical genre: the oratorio.

Gregory XIII gave the church of Santa Maria in Vallicella to St Philip Neri's Oratorian Confederation, who commissioned its rebuilding in 1575. The reconstruction was entrusted first to Matteo da Città di Castello and then to Martino Longhi the Elder. Originally conceived as a single-naved church, it

A detail from the church of San

Salvatore in Lauro.

THE LIBRARY OF THE ORATORIO
Inside the Oratorio a majestic staircase designed by Borromini leads to the magnificent Biblioteca Vallicelliana, also the work of Borromini. Together with the Biblioteca Angelica (to the right of Sant'Agostino) it was one of the first libraries in Rome to be open to the public.

was widened and aisles were added. The façade by Fausto Rughesi was completed in 1605.

THE INTERIOR. At the time of the Counter-Reformation the interior was very plain, but it was subsequently given rich Baroque decorations. Federico Barocci provided *The Visitation* (in the fourth chapel on the left) and *The Presentation in the Temple* (in the left transept); and Caravaggio supplied a *Descent from the Cross*, which was later moved to the Vatican and replaced by a copy (second chapel on the right). The choir has three masterpieces by the young Rubens; the one in the center is composed around an ancient image of the Virgin with miraculous properties. The splendid frescoes in the apse, the cupola and the nave were all painted by Pietro da Cortona between 1650 and 1665; the one in the nave "supported" by *putti* (cherubs) portrays a miracle that is supposed to have taken place during the construction of the church when, in response to St Philip Neri's prayers, the Virgin stopped some scaffolding from collapsing.

THE ORATORIO DEI FILIPPINI. In 1637 the Oratorians invited architects to tender plans for the construction of an oratory specifically for choral services. Borromini was selected, work went ahead fast and the building was consecrated three years later. The façade contrasts with the more conventional one of the Chiesa Nuova and is built in brick, in accordance with the wishes of the Oratorians. It is full of movement thanks to Borromini's use of curves: although its entire surface is slightly concave, the central bay is convex on the first floor, with a concave niche on the floor above. The pediment is also curvilinear, and the windows are ornate. Because the façade is unrelated to what is behind it, the central door is not the main entrance. (Take Via dei Filippini, alongside the oratory.)

AROUND THE CHIESA NUOVA. Borromini gave a finishing touch to his work by erecting a graceful clock tower (1647–9) in what came to be known as the Piazza del Orologio, at the back of the oratory.

(Continue into Via degli Orsini, then turn left into Via di Panico.)

The turret of Borromini's clock tower in Piazza del Orologio is surmounted by a metal structure supporting a star that has 24 points.

The nearby PALAZZO TAVERNA DI MONTEGIORDANO was built in the 15th century on the ruins of the Orsini fortress, which dominated the whole area as far as the Tiber. The courtyard is an amazing mixture of styles – ranging from Renaissance decorations and a late-17th-century fountain to "medieval" façades rebuilt in the 19th century.

VIA DEI CORONARI ★

Antique shops are now scattered on either side of this long, straight street where vendors of *corone* (rosaries) once vied for the custom of pilgrims approaching St Peter's.

SAN SALVATORE IN LAURO. After being destroyed by fire in 1591, this medieval church was rebuilt to plans by Ottaviano Mascherino. Its neoclassical façade designed by Guglielmetti in 1862 is adorned with a relief by Rinaldo Rinaldi, *The Flight of the Sacred House of Nazareth to Loreto*. The nave, in the form of a Latin cross with travertine Corinthian columns standing clear of the walls, recalls Palladio's Venetian churches. In the third chapel on the right there is a remarkably fine *Adoration of the Magi*, one of Pietro da Cortona's first altar paintings (c. 1628). The transept and the choir were added by Ludovico Rusconi Sassi in the 18th century. The ancient monastery beside the church has an elegant Renaissance cloister. The back wall of the refectory is decorated with a large fresco portraying *The Wedding at Cana* by Francesco Salviati. (Return to Via dei Coronari and discover the charming little Piazzetta di San Simeone, with a fountain by Giacomo della Porta erected in 1589. Then turn left into Via Lancellotti.)

PALAZZO LANCELLOTTI. This palazzo was begun by Francesco da Volterra and finished by Carlo Maderno. The *portone*, framed with columns and dominated by a balcony, was designed by Domenichino, who for the first and only time in his life tried his hand at architecture. Its sumptuous courtyard is full of stuccos and marbles. The main rooms are decorated with frescoes by Agostino Tassi and Guercino. (Proceed along Via della Maschera d'Oro.)

AROUND PIAZZA TOR DI SANGUIGNA

Via dei Coronari.

IRRITATING LODGINGS Chateaubriand was not very favorably impressed by his stay in Palazzo Lancellotti in 1803, judging by a letter in which he described his new lodgings: "Such a huge number of fleas hopped onto my legs that my white trousers went all black. I really thought I was back in my New Road kennels."

PALAZZO CESI. This 16th-century palazzo (No. 21 Via della Maschera d'Oro), which now houses the Military Supreme Court, has its entrance at No. 2 Via degli Acquasparta. In 1603, when it was the home of Prince Federico Cesi, the Accademia dei

THE "TORRE DELLA SCIMMIA"
A monkey is said to have carried off an infant but due to the Virgin's intervention deposited the child on the spot where an effigy of the Madonna now stands. Nathaniel Hawthorne used this story in *The Marble Faun* (1860).

"ISAIAH"
According to Vasari, Raphael was influenced by Michelangelo, whose work on the ceiling of the Sistine Chapel had been shown to him, secretly, by Bramante. The prophets on the other pillars were painted by Gagliardi in 1856.

Lincei ▲ *362* held their first meetings here and Galileo stayed for a while as the prince's guest. Although its grisaille fresco decorations have disappeared, those of the Palazzo Milesi are quite well preserved. (Go down Via Arco di Parma toward Via Tordinona. Now tucked away behind a high wall, this was once a lively street where one of Rome's most famous theaters was situated from 1670 until 1889; Verdi's operas *Il Trovatore* and *Un Ballo in Maschera* had their premieres at the theater in 1853 and 1859. Return to Via degli Acquasparta to reach the Museo Napoleonico, in Piazza di Ponte Umberto I.)

THE MUSEO NAPOLEONICO. This 16th-century palazzo was bought in 1820 by the Primoli family. In 1909 Count Giuseppe Primoli, the son of Pietro Primoli and Charlotte Bonaparte, had it restored by Raffaele Ojetti, who adapted the building due to the upheavals caused by the construction of the Ponte Umberto I and the creation of Via Zanardelli. The rebuilt palazzo was designed to house a museum devoted to the history of the First and Second Napoleonic Empires. It also includes the Primoli Foundation for the promotion of Franco-Italian cultural relations, as well as an important library of French works and Pietro Primoli's admirable collection of turn-of-the-century photographs. (Take Via dei Soldati.)

PALAZZO ALTEMPS. Begun in the late 15th century, this palazzo was restructured in 1578 by Martino Longhi the Elder, who designed the graceful belvedere in the form of a turret and the courtyard with its elegant arcades. The Altemps' love of letters led them to assemble a fine collection of ancient Roman inscriptions, some of which still remain in the courtyard. Their rich library is now part of the Vatican collections.

VIA DELL'ORSO. During the Middle Ages and the Renaissance this area was renowned for its inns. The only one left today is the HOSTARIA DELL'ORSO, which counted Rabelais, Montaigne and Goethe among its guests.

SANT'ANTONIO DEI PORTOGHESI. Its recently restored façade, with the neighboring Palazzo Scapucci and the Torre della Scimmia, form a picturesque group. The national church of the Portuguese dates from the 15th century, though rebuilt two centuries later. The two superimposed orders of columns of the façade (1631), designed by Martino Longhi the Younger, are linked by male mythical figures rather than the usual simple volutes. Its interior is resplendent with gold, stucco decorations and marbles. The first chapel on the right contains the funerary monument of Alessandro de Souza, sculpted by Canova between 1806 and 1808. Facing the church is the AUGUSTINIAN MONASTERY. (Cross Via dell'Orso and take Via dei Pianellari.)

THE "MADONNA OF THE PILGRIMS" ★
In Caravaggio's masterpiece painted between 1603 and 1605 (also known as *The Madonna of Loreto*) the sculptural beauty of the Virgin is heightened by the tenderness of her silent dialogue with her humble admirers. The contrast between Mary, who is portrayed as a Roman patrician, and the poverty of the two praying peasants is particularly striking.

THE MADONNA DEL PARTO ★
This splendid statue, which stands against the inner wall of the façade of Sant'Agostino, is by Jacopo Sansovino (1521). In 1982 *The Virgin and Child with St Anne* (1512) by his mentor Andrea Sansovino, from whom he took his name, was returned to its original position, in the niche of the third pillar on the right. This sculpture was particularly admired by Vasari: "The older woman's expression betrays great natural gaiety, the Virgin's beauty is divine, and the charming child Jesus is of unmatched perfection."

SANT'AGOSTINO ★. This church, dedicated to St Augustine of Hippo, was completed in 1483; the architects were Giacomo da Pietrasanta and Sebastiano Fiorentino. Its monumental character is reinforced by the broad flight of steps preceding the dignified façade. The interior is divided into three naves by pillars; these once had niches, which were filled in by Luigi Vanvitelli when the church was restored in 1760. To the left, above the third pillar, is one of Raphael's most famous frescoes, *The Prophet Isaiah* (1512); the first chapel contains one of Caravaggio's masterpieces, *Madonna of the Pilgrims*. The whole transept on the same side, dedicated by the Pamphili family to St Thomas of Villanova, was decorated by Giovanni Maria Baratta between 1660 and 1669. The first chapel to the left of the high altar is decorated with frescoes by Lanfranco; the second, which contains the tomb of St Augustine's mother, St Monica, is attributed to Isaia da Pisa (15th century). In the center a fine Byzantine Madonna is set into the high altar by Torriani, which is surmounted by two angels (1628) based on designs by Bernini. Finally, the right transept contains a splendid reredos by Guercino.

SANT'APOLLINARE. This group of buildings was given to the Jesuits by Gregory XIII in 1574. In it they installed the German College, or seminary. The church was rebuilt between 1742 and 1748 by Ferdinando Fuga. He designed it to include two places of worship: a square narthex (vestibule) for the general public and a nave for the members of the college. The 15th-century Madonna presiding over the ample narthex was discovered in the 17th century. The ceiling of the nave depicts the glorification of St Apollinaris; the rich marble altar, copied from a painting by Graziani (1748), is dedicated to the saint. In the third chapel on the right there is a fine statue of St Francis Xavier by Pierre Legros.

The façade of Sant'Apollinare.

"Here and there one sees a fine orange ocher that has retained a warm glow, a serene density, beneath its slowly acquired patina."
Valéry Larbaud, *Aux couleurs de Rome*

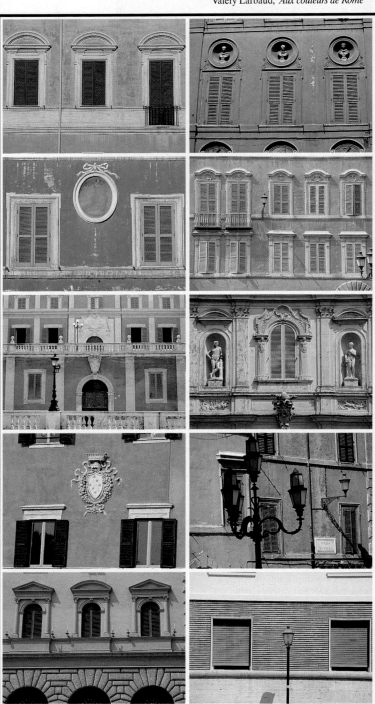

THE QUIRINAL

The shape of Rome's highest hill has changed drastically since ancient times, when it had steeper slopes and deeper valleys. Nevertheless, its network of streets – long parallel thoroughfares following the lie of the land – has survived relatively intact. **The hill of Quirinus.** Tradition has it that its first inhabitants were the Sabines, under King Titus Tatius, who were subsequently absorbed into Romulus' Latin city ● 26. Since the earliest times many shrines were built here: the one of Semo Sanctus Dius Fidius (originally a Sabine cult), the very ancient temple of Quirinus, and in Imperial times the shrine dedicated by the Emperor Domitian to his family, situated on the spot where he was born. But the most grandiose of all these buildings was the temple of Serapis

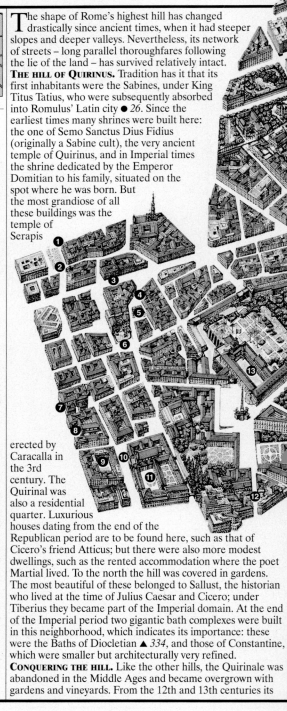

erected by Caracalla in the 3rd century. The Quirinal was also a residential quarter. Luxurious houses dating from the end of the Republican period are to be found here, such as that of Cicero's friend Atticus; but there were also more modest dwellings, such as the rented accommodation where the poet Martial lived. To the north the hill was covered in gardens. The most beautiful of these belonged to Sallust, the historian who lived at the time of Julius Caesar and Cicero; under Tiberius they became part of the Imperial domain. At the end of the Imperial period two gigantic bath complexes were built in this neighborhood, which indicates its importance: these were the Baths of Diocletian ▲ 334, and those of Constantine, which were smaller but architecturally very refined. **Conquering the hill.** Like the other hills, the Quirinale was abandoned in the Middle Ages and became overgrown with gardens and vineyards. From the 12th and 13th centuries its

slopes began to be inhabited again, starting with the area around Trajan's Forum on one side and the Rio de' Trevi on the other. In the middle of the 16th century its summit was still a relatively remote spot with country villas and cottages. It was at this time, in 1560, that Pius IV had the spacious Via Pia constructed (later renamed Via del Quirinale and then Via XX Settembre); and in 1585 Sixtus V had the Via Felice (now Via Sistina-Via delle Quattro Fontane-Via de'Pretis) put through to link the Pincio and Santa Maria Maggiore. In order to encourage building along the two roads, the Quattro Fontane crossroads was created at their intersection and one of the branches of the Aqua Felice ▲ 295, the aqueduct built by Claudius, was rehabilitated to supply water primarily to this area. In the meantime, the building of the Palazzo del Quirinale as the summer residence of the popes began. In the 17th century the Barberini established themselves to the northwest of the Quattro Fontane crossroads, while the southeastern slopes remained in the hands of the Jesuits. After the unification of Italy, in 1871 the summer palace of the popes became a royal residence; and later, after the proclamation of the Republic, in 1947 it became the presidential palace. From the end of the 19th century various ministries were established in the vicinity.

QUIRINUS
Like Mars and Jupiter this ancient Sabine deity had warlike attributes, such as the lance, and was for this reason often mistaken for Mars or Romulus.

THE DIOSCURI
Castor and Pollux, the Dioscuri ("the sons of Zeus") ▲ 142, were the offspring of Zeus and Leda, the wife of Tyndareus. They are also the brothers of Clytemnestra (wife of Agamemnon) and of the beautiful Helen of Troy. Their gigantic statues originate from the Baths of Constantine, which were located near the current Piazza del Quirinale, whose fountain they now decorate.

Horse-drawn
carriages parked in
the Piazza Barberini
in 1933.

**"THE TRIUMPH OF
DIVINE PROVIDENCE"**
The ceiling of the
principal salon of the
Palazzo Barberini is
thought to have the
largest fresco ever
painted for a non-
ecclesiastical
building. The three
bees, the crest of the
Barberini, are
magnified to gigantic
proportions.

THE BARBERINI DISTRICT

PIAZZA BARBERINI. Today large modern buildings provide the
background to this piazza, which is at the junction of the Via
del Tritone and the Via Vittorio Veneto, two of the main
avenues created in 1871 after the unification of Italy. In fact
the character of the area has totally changed since the 17th
century. It is hard to imagine just how rural and picturesque a
place it was then, and remained until the following century.
Artists frequented its *osterie*, and many of them lived and
worked in the area. Their presence lives on in the names of
some of the streets: Via degli Artisti, Via dei Modelli, etc. As
for the piazza itself, it was in 1625 that it lost the name of
Piazza Grimani to become Piazza Barberini when this great
Roman family purchased a villa with grounds stretching from
the square to Via Pia. The family of Urban VIII contributed
relatively little to the street furniture of the area, apart from
the Fontana del Tritone (sculpted for the sovereign pontiff by
Bernini between 1642 and 1643) and nearby, at the foot of the
Via Veneto, the Fontana delle Api (the Bee Fountain) also by
Bernini. (Continue up the Via Veneto.)
SANTA MARIA DELLA CONCEZIONE. (The Capuchin Church.)
The Barberini were, however, rather ostentatious in the way
they put their mark on this church, which they wished to have
under their protection. When Antonio Barberini, a Capuchin
friar and Urban VIII's younger brother, became cardinal, he
decided to rebuild the church of his Order; the Pope granted
him a subsidy. From then on, many of the great figures of the

time, including the Emperor Ferdinand II, sought to sponsor the decoration of the side chapels – so much so that the Capuchins had to make repeated appeals for their church not to be too richly decorated. While the Pope seized this opportunity to refuse all help, it did not prevent him and his brother from calling upon some of the greatest painters of the time for the altar paintings. The crypt is definitely worth a visit: it is decorated, in extremely Baroque taste, with the bones of some four thousand Capuchin friars. (Cross Piazza Barberini and take the Via delle Quattro Fontane.)

PALAZZO BARBERINI. The overall plan was entrusted to the architect Carlo Maderno, who had to incorporate a palace that stood on the land bought by the Barberini in 1625. Casting aside the traditional scheme for Roman palaces (built around a square courtyard), he finally adopted that of the villa (a central edifice flanked by two wings). The work, which began in 1627, was continued after Maderno's death in 1629 by Bernini, who retained his predecessor's principal assistant, Francesco Borromini. Bernini designed the façade on the garden side of the building, including the main entrance, and the square staircase in the left wing, which leads to the gallery. Borromini was responsible for the oval staircase in the right wing, as well as the *trompe l'oeil* windows on the second floor. Inside, most of the rooms of the *piano nobile* have painted ceilings – notably by Andrea Camassei and Andrea Sacchi, including his *Divine Wisdom*, painted between 1629 and 1633. However, the most remarkable of all is the ceiling in the principal salon, painted between 1633 and 1639 by Pietro da Cortona. Its allegorical theme was provided by Francesco Bracciolini, a protégé of Urban VIII and his brother's secretary. In the center Divine Providence triumphs over Time and assigns the Barberini emblem to Immortality, while the lateral scenes portray the virtues of Urban VIII and the achievements of his pontificate. Nowhere else in Rome does a painting so shamelessly exalt a pope and his family.

"ST MICHAEL TRAMPLING ON THE DEVIL"
Great painters of the Bologna school such as Guido Reni, whose famous *St Michael Trampling on the Devil* (first chapel on the right) is pictured here, Lanfranco (second chapel on the right) and Domenichino (third chapel) made their contribution to the Capuchin church, as did painters of the younger generation like Pietro da Cortona (first chapel on the right) and Andrea Sacchi (fifth chapel on the right).

THE CRYPT OF THE CAPUCHIN CHURCH
It took no fewer than three hundred journeys with full cartloads to gather the bones that adorn the crypt of Santa Maria della Concezione.

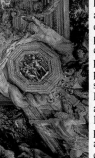

The Barberini family emblem.

Since it became the property of the State in 1949, the Palazzo Barberini has housed the Galleria Nazionale di Arte Antica, created at the end of the 19th century. This museum, which is one of the most important in Rome, takes up practically the whole of the palace's piano nobile. In these rooms one finds works by many of the great Italian and foreign painters of the 13th to the 18th century. The floor above, which was redecorated between 1750 and 1770, offers a fine setting for the collection of 18th-century paintings.

To the very rare items remaining from the Barberini collection have been added works from other private collections and State acquisitions and legacies. Thus the museum is able to show paintings by such Italian masters as Filippo Lippi, Lorenzo Lotto, Andrea del Sarto, Perugino, Bronzino and Caravaggio together with works by foreign artists like Quentin Metsys, Holbein and Nicholas Poussin.

"LA FORNARINA"
This painting, long considered to be the most precious work in the Barberini collection, was purchased by the State when the collection was dispersed. It is commonly thought to be a portrait of La Fornarina, the mistress with whom Raphael was said by Vasari to have indulged in the pleasures of love to such an extent that it caused his death. However, the attribution to Raphael is now disputed.

Reaching Rome around 1591, Caravaggio (1573–1610) worked under the patronage of Cardinal del Monte. He left Rome in 1606.

"MADONNA AND CHILD"
This work by Filippo Lippi is an elaborate exercise in perspective. It dates from 1471, a period when Lippi was under Flemish influence.

"JUDITH BEHEADING HOLOFERNES"
This painting by Caravaggio belongs to the period of his transition from naturalism (when his compositions were simple and his tones lighter) to his later manner, characterized by violent contrasts and chiaroscuro.

293

QUATTRO FONTANE
The crossroads seen from two different viewpoints. The statues of the 16th-century fountains represent the Nile and the Tiber (on the north side) and Juno and Diana (on the south side). From here one can see the Porta Pia as well as the obelisk in Piazza

della Trinità dei Monti ▲ *314* and those on the Quirinal and the Esquiline.

"THE ECSTASY OF ST TERESA OF AVILA"
● *82* (center)
"Bernini, who in St Peter's seemed to me ridiculous, has in this work found a modern form of sculpture, entirely based on expression. To achieve it, he has allowed daylight to suffuse this pale, delicate face with a luminosity that is like an inner flame – so that, through the transfigured, palpitating marble, we see the soul flooded with joy and rapture, shining like a lamp."

Hyppolite Taine,
Voyage en Italie

AROUND QUATTRO FONTANE

QUATTRO FONTANE. This crossroads – designed toward the end of the 16th century at the intersection of the new streets put through under Pius IV and Sixtus V (then called Via Pia and Via Felice) – was constructed with shorn-off corners so as to open up the view. In each of the corners a fountain with a statue was built, to be supplied with water from the recently rehabilitated Aqua Felice aqueduct ▲ *295*. (Follow the Via XX Settembre as far as Piazza San Bernardo.)

SANTA SUSANNA. In 1589 a shrine dating from the 4th century was turned into a parish church to cater to the newly developed area on the top of the Quirinal hill. It was refurbished for this purpose by Carlo Maderno, who added the choir, the main altar, the confessio, the sculpted wood ceilings and the original façade. This church represents an important step in the development of a new architectural language that was to mark the 17th century: while the walls remain rectilinear, the portal is given relief by being framed in closely grouped columns. Today Santa Susanna is the parish church of American Catholics in Rome.

SANTA MARIA DELLA VITTORIA. This church is also the work of Carlo Maderno, except for the façade built a few years later by Giambattista Soria, who designed it to complement that of Santa Susanna. The originally very sober interior was enriched during the 17th and 18th centuries with frescoes, stuccos, jasper and marble. It contains some important works, such as the *Holy Trinity* (third chapel on the left), and three paintings by Domenichino (second chapel on the right). But the most striking is the CORNARO CHAPEL, designed and executed by Bernini in 1646. Architecture,

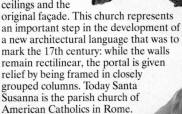

painting and sculpture play equal parts in enhancing the dramatic effect and illustrate the master's fundamental principle: the fusion of the arts. The central theme is St Teresa's vision: "God let me see an angel in bodily form on my left … He was not tall, but he was very beautiful; his glowing face showed that he belonged to the order of the heavenly hierarchy in which the angels seem to be incandescent … In his left hand he held a gold javelin, the iron point of which gave off a flame. He suddenly pierced my heart to its deepest fibers … Then he left me encumbered with the love of God. The pain was so vivid that it made me groan, but the sweetness that came with it was so great that I would not have wanted the pain removed…." The members of the Cornaro family are portrayed on the side walls on either side of the altar. The curved antependium conceals a window

that Bernini made to bathe the ecstatic scene in diffused light.
THE AQUA FELICE. The fountain facing the church was built by Domenico Fontana at the request of Sixtus V. The Pope had inherited Gregory XIII's project and persevered in having the Claudian aqueduct restored to bring water from the Alban hills to the highest parts of the city. Thanks to these works (1585–9), also entrusted to Domenico Fontana, an extra five million gallons of water were made available to the inhabitants of Rome. The monumental fountain in front of Santa Maria della Vittoria was its point of arrival; the water was then distributed to the other fountains on the Quirinal and toward the Campidoglio. Both the aqueduct and the fountain were called Felice, the Christian name of the Pope.

SAN BERNARDO ALLE TERME. This church was built between 1598 and 1600 on the site of one of the rotundas dispersed along the outer walls of the Baths of Diocletian. Its cupola, inspired by the Pantheon's ● *70*, ▲ *265*, was covered with plaster moldings during the last century.

SAN CARLO ALLE QUATTRO FONTANE. This church and its neighbor, Sant'Andrea al Quirinale, magnificently illustrate the two main schools of Roman baroque. In 1634 Borromini received what was probably his first commission from the Spanish discalced Trinitarians, who wanted a monastery, a cloister and a church. By means of ingenious planning, the architect resolved the problems posed by the confined area and the irregular shape of the land. He erected a building said to be small enough to fit inside one of the pillars supporting

THE AQUA FELICE FOUNTAIN
This fountain has three large niches separated by columns. The sculptural ensemble develops the theme of the Israelites in

the wilderness, led by Moses (whose gigantic figure by Prospero da Brescia stands in the center niche) and Joshua.

THE CUPOLA OF SAN BERNARDO ALLE TERME ▲ *262*
The coffers of this cupola, which has a diameter of 50 feet, diminish in size toward the center, where there is a large circular window.

SAN CARLO ALLE QUATTRO FONTANE
The lines of the central bay are inverted in the two registers of the façade. From being convex in the lower register, above the curving cornice, they become concave like the lateral bays. The façade is crowned by a large oval medallion supported by two angels, which breaks the horizontal line of the entablature.

THE CUPOLA OF SAN CARLO ALLE QUATTRO FONTANE ● 81
The coffering takes the form of alternating crosses, octagons and hexagons. Yet this busy pattern retains geometric purity and achieves a certain beehive effect.

Piazza del Quirinale painted by Vanvitelli in the 18th century.

the dome of St Peter's. The façade, which was completed in 1685, long after the architect's death, relies on the interplay of concave and convex lines to give a monumental character to the structure as a whole. The interior, which is oval in shape and decorated with white stuccos, is composed of three distinct superimposed zones. At the base, powerful columns punctuate the undulations of the walls, which are a succession of curves and countercurves; above this there is a link zone, surmounted finally by an elliptical dome ● 81 resting on a strong ring whose deep coffers, by diminishing in size toward the summit, accentuate the illusion of height. Light penetrates abundantly through the ample lantern and through skylights in some of the coffers. As a result, the dome seems to be floating weightlessly above the heavy shapes of the area in which visitors can move about.

SANT'ANDREA AL QUIRINALE ● 79. In 1658 Bernini was asked to build a church for the novices of the Society of Jesus. He too, being faced with a restricted area, chose an elliptical shape and placed the main altar and the entrance on the shortest diameter. On the front of the building two quarter circles of wall prolong and enhance the narrow façade (pictured above, on the right). Inside the building the eye surveys an uninterrupted series of gigantic pilasters until it comes to rest on the recess of the altar, which is a concave echo of the portal's projection. The dark multicolored marbles of the church contrast with the white-and-gilt moldings of the cupola ● 81. The light, which penetrates through the windows placed between the ribs of the dome and through the lantern, illuminates the central space evenly but leaves the side chapels in shadow. It is said that this great rival of Borromini considered this to be his most successful work and, as he grew old, found pleasure in coming to sit and contemplate it. Through the sacristy one reaches the upper floor of the convent where St Stanislas Kotska lived (a Pole who came to Rome as a Jesuit novice and had a vision of the Virgin Mary). A statue of the saint on his deathbed by Pierre Legros (1703) provides a remarkable example of Baroque illusionism in its use of colored marbles.

Piazza del Quirinale seen from the air.

THE QUIRINAL

PIAZZA DEL QUIRINALE. The construction of this piazza took place over several centuries. In the 16th century Sixtus V had the two statues of the Dioscuri and their horses erected in the center – which is why the square is also known as Piazza Montecavallo – moving them from the 4th-century Baths of Constantine. In the early 17th century the square was leveled under the supervision of Carlo Maderno. Then in 1783 Pius VI added the obelisk, brought from the Mausoleum of Augustus ▲ *143*; and in 1813 the fountain was completed with the addition of the basin, which came from near the temple of the Dioscuri in the Forum, where for centuries it had been used as a drinking trough for cattle. With its multiple

components of different origins, the fountain illustrates an essential feature of Roman art: the reuse of ancient materials or architectural elements in new constructions. As a finishing touch, in 1886 the balustrade that encloses the piazza on the west side was added, from which there is a magnificent view over the city, stretched out at the bottom of the hill with St Peter's in the distance.

PALAZZO DEL QUIRINALE. Originally the summer residence of the popes, then a pontifical palace, this building served as a royal palace between 1870 and 1944, and when the Republic was proclaimed it became the official residence of the President. Construction began in the late 16th century under Gregory XIII and was completed under Clement XII (1730–40); there were few Roman architects of the Counter-Reformation and Baroque period who did not make some contribution to it, and Bernini built the Loggia of the Benedictions over the main entrance. The palace was gradually surrounded by all sorts of annexes, among them the PALAZZO DELLA CONSULTA, which flanks the north side of the piazza. This edifice, built between 1732 and 1734 by Ferdinando Fuga, now houses Italy's constitutional court. (Take Via 24 Maggio.)

VIA 24 MAGGIO. Immediately on the left is the side entrance of the PALAZZO

The Corazzieri (presidential guards) in the hall of honor of the Palazzo del Quirinale

Pictured on the left is the elegant helicoidal staircase designed by Ottaviano Mascherino for Gregory XIII. With its pairs of polished-marble columns, it is one of the finest architectural elements in the Palazzo del Quirinale.

ROSPIGLIOSI-PALLAVICINI, built between 1611 and 1616 for Cardinal Scipione Borghese. Its gardens boast the Casino dell'Aurora, which has a famous fresco by Guido Reni (1615). On the other side of the street an imposing balustrade marks the entrance to the gardens of the Palazzo Colonna ▲ 299. Michelangelo is reputed to have frequented them in order to meet his great friend the poetess Vittoria Colonna, whose last breath he witnessed. One can still see there a few remains of Caracalla's temple of Serapis.

SAN SILVESTRO. This richly decorated church of the late 16th century is concealed behind a 19th century façade.(Return toward the Piazza del Quirinale and go down the Via della Dataria, designed by Paul V as the official access to the papal residence, then take the second street on the right, Via San Vicenzo.)

FONTANA DI TREVI

THE WISHING FOUNTAIN. At the bottom of the street, backed by the façade of the Palazzo Poli, looms the most stunning of the fountains of Rome: the central figure, the Ocean (by Pietro Bracci) is shown dominating sea horses guided by Tritons, while in the niches on either side are the figures of Abundance (on the left) and Health (on the right), both by Filippo della Valle. Bernini had initially been commissioned by Urban VIII to construct a monumental fountain , but the project had been abandoned after the Pope's death. It was Nicola Salvi, almost a century later, who was to build this ensemble on the site of one of Rome's earliest fountains designed to receive the water of the Aqua Virgo. The bliss of returning to the Eternal City is guaranteed to all foreigners who, with their back turned, throw a coin over their shoulder into the fountain. (Before leaving the square be sure to look at the church of Santi Vincenzo ed Anastasio. Cardinal Mazarin commissioned Martino Longhi the Younger to design the ornate Baroque façade, which was built between 1641 and 1650.)

RIO DE' TREVI. Strolling through the streets of the neighborhood around the fountain, you will discover one of the most picturesque parts of Rome. This area, once densely populated, remained one of the liveliest sections of the city throughout the Middle Ages and the Renaissance. In the 16th century its narrow streets abounded in craftsmen's workshops which attracted many foreigners, and some craftsmen even chose to live here. Later, demolition works did not affect its inherent charm. Whether you take the Via della Panetteria or the Via del Lavatore, which has an open market every morning, you will find that this is still a lively neighborhood. (Take the Via della Stamperia to the right of the fountain.)

ACCADEMIA DI SAN LUCA. In 1934 this academy, founded in 1577, moved into the ancient building once known as Palazzo Vaini, which was renamed the Palazzo Carpegna in the 17th century when it was modified by Borromini. The original

Anita Ekberg bathing in the Fontana di Trevi in Fellini's film *La Dolce Vita* (1960).

The aqueduct built by Agrippa in 19 BC to supply water for his baths was given the name Aqua Virgo, as the location of the spring feeding it was supposed to have been revealed to some Roman soldiers by a virgin. This bas-relief on the Fontana di Trevi illustrates the legend.

Aurora by Guido Reni, of which the 18th-century French President de Brosses said: "Nothing is better conceived, so graceful, so light, nor better drawn; it is an 'incanto' (a delight)."

purpose of this institution, which brought together famous painters, was to provide an apprenticeship and theoretical training for young painters so as to control the production and distribution of art in keeping with the strict rules of the Counter-Reformation. In the 17th century it was truly dictatorial: no artist could have a studio in Rome without its authorization. Its picture gallery, containing collections made up of gifts from its members and from various popes, includes works by Raphael, Titian, Bronzino, Poussin and Panini.

ISTITUTO DELLA CALCOGRAFIA (6 Via della Stamperia). This museum of engravings has one of the most important collections of its kind in the world – comprising more than 23,000 items, including 16th-century plates, works by Rossini and Raimondi, and a complete set of Piranesi's engravings ▲ *I.* (Retracing your steps, walk back along the Via San Vincenzo. Then take its continuation, the Via dei Lucchesi, until you reach Piazza della Pilotta – from the Spanish *pelota*, a ball, but today it is the realm of study rather than ball games. Here you will find two great Jesuit institutions: the BIBLICUM, with its remarkable orientalist library, and the GREGORIANA, the largest Catholic university in Rome. (Take Via della Pilotta.)

PALAZZO COLONNA AND ITS GALLERY.
You will emerge behind the Palazzo Colonna, which is linked to its terraced gardens by four bridges over the road. (The entrance is in Piazza dei Santi

ACCADEMIA DI SAN LUCA. The name of the academy originates in the Christian tradition that attributes the talent of painting to St Luke.

St Luke Painting the Virgin Mary by Raphael.

The Fontana di Trevi.

Its sumptuous decoration was designed by Antonio del Grande in the mid 17th century and completed under the supervision of Girolamo Fontana after del Grande's death.

Peasant Eating Beans by Annibale Carracci (1560–1609), one of the paintings in the Galleria Colonna.

The Basilica of Santi Apostoli.

Apostoli, on the far side of the palace from Via della Pilotta.) Originally built between 1417 and 1431 by Pope Martin V, a member of the Colonna family, the building was restructured several times before the 18th century. Worthy of note is the Salone della Colonna Bellica after the red column it contains, the emblem of the family; its ceiling is decorated with a fresco to the glory of Marcantonio Colonna, the commander of the papal fleet at the battle of Lepanto (1571). The picture gallery contains a magnificent collection, largely put together by Lorenzo Onofrio Colonna under the guidance of the painter Carlo Maratta. In the 19th century it was developed further with the acquisition of paintings by primitives and Renaissance masters. Both the palace and the gallery still belong to this ancient Roman family. (Return to Piazza dei Santi Apostoli.)

BASILICA DEI SANTI APOSTOLI. To avoid the risk of it falling into ruins, despite restoration work carried out in the Renaissance, the original 6th-century basilica was almost completely rebuilt between 1701 and 1714 by Carlo Fontana and his son Francesco. It was then given a neoclassical façade designed by Valadier in 1827. The portico at the front dates from the 15th century. This work by Baccio Pontelli (1450–92) was enclosed with railings in the 17th century by Carlo Rainaldi, who also added the balustrade and the statues of the apostles. The interior is decorated with gilt plasterwork, stuccos and frescoes in the taste of 18th-century Rome. On the vault Christ is portrayed receiving the saints of the

Franciscan Order (Baciccia, 1707). At the very end of the left nave stands the tomb of Clement XIV, the first monument Canova sculpted in Rome (1789).

PALAZZO ODESCALCHI (facing the Basilica dei Santi Apostoli). The façade, designed by Bernini in 1664 for Alexander VII's nephew Flavio Chigi, served as a model for a number of Baroque palaces. Bernini broke with the Roman tradition of building palace façades without vertical articulation: while the ground floor serves as a foundation, on the upper stories gigantic pilasters divide the seven bays of the central body of the building, which is framed by two wings set further back. The balance of this façade was destroyed when in 1745, at the request of the new owner, Prince Odescalchi, Nicola Salvi enlarged the palace, doubling the width of the central body and building a second door for the sake of symmetry. A small detour can be made to discover, further on, up a narrow alleyway, the Chapel of the Madonna del Archetto, built by Virginio Vespignani. In the same street is one of Rome's few well-known *birrerie* (beer cellars); a popular meeting place for young people. (Return to the Via dei Santi Apostoli and proceed to the Corso.)

SAN MARCELLO AL CORSO. Although founded in the 4th century, this church was rebuilt after a fire in 1519. It was designed by Jacopo Sansovino and has a Baroque façade by Carlo Fontana (1682–83). Parts of the interior, including the coffered ceiling, go back to the 16th century. The tombs of Cardinal Giovanni Michiel and Bishop Antonio Orso, to the left of the entrance, are the work of Andrea and Jacopo Sansovino. The third, fourth and fifth chapels on the left are decorated with frescoes by Francesco Salviati, Perino del Vaga and Federico Zuccaro respectively. The fourth chapel on the right contains a 15th-century crucifix which used to be carried in penitential processions. (On leaving the church, take the first street on the right, Via dell'Umiltà.)

GALLERIA SCIARRA. A fine example of Roman eclecticism, this gallery, which links Via Minghetti and Via dell' Umiltà, was built in 1883 by Giulio de Angelis. (Go through the gallery.)

PIAZZA SAN SILVESTRO

Three churches are in or close to this piazza, which has changed considerably over the past two centuries.

SANTA MARIA IN VIA. The first, which stands on the corner of Via del Tritone, belongs to the Servite Order. It was rebuilt by Francesco da Volterra in the late 16th century on the site of a medieval shrine. The upper section of the façade is attributed to Carlo Rainaldi (1681). Inside, the third chapel on the right has an *Annunciation* by Cavaliere d'Arpino.

SAN CARLO DE' BORGOGNONI. This church, rebuilt by Antoine Derizet between 1728 and 1731, had been the church of the Burgundians of the Franche-Comté.

GALLERIA SCIARRA
This modern (late 19th century) structure has very pretty Pompeian-style decorations painted by Giuseppe Cellini. Among other inscriptions, on the right is this verse from Virgil's fourth *Eclogue*: *Incipe, parve puer, risu cognoscere matrem* ("Little boy, learn to greet your mother with a smile").

The Via della Pilotta, which leads to the gardens of Palazzo Colonna.

THE MIRACLE OF SANTA MARIA IN VIA
A miracle is said to be at the origin of this church's foundation. An image of the Virgin painted on a tile fell into a well, which overflowed, so that the image emerged from the well. Many faithful still come here to drink the well's water and venerate the "Madonna del Pozzo" (the Madonna of the Well).

SAN SILVESTRO IN CAPITE
This church was constructed on the ruins of the Temple of the Sun built by Aurelian. The name "in Capite" refers to the head of St John the Baptist, which has been preserved here as a relic for centuries.

SAN SILVESTRO IN CAPITE. Both the atrium in front of the church and the bell tower date from the 13th century, but the main part of the building was begun in the 16th century by Francesco da Volterra and finished by Carlo Maderno. The façade was erected by Domenico de Rossi who, with his brother Mattia, redecorated the interior at the end of the 17th century. Don't omit to look at the fresco in the nave by Giacinto Brandi (1623–91), as well as the Pomarancio frescoes in the transept crossing (1605). In 1890 Pope Leo XIII gave San Silvestro in Capite to the English Catholics in Rome as their parish church. The former convent buildings next to it now house Rome's central post office.

FROM THE VIA VENETO TO THE PORTA PINCIANA

The Via Vittorio Veneto has been used as a set for numerous films, and especially in the 1960's show-business personalities used to frequent the terraces of its famous bars, cafés and luxury hotels. Going up the Via Veneto, you enter the Ludovisi neighborhood, named after the beautiful villa that once stood here; its grounds were sold and divided into building lots in the 1880's. Leaving to your right the former Ministry of Corporations (now the Ministry of Industry and Trade) – built in 1932, during the Fascist period, by Marcello Piacentini and Giuseppe Vaccaro – you will pass in front of the Banca Nazionale del Lavoro, also built by Piacentini, and will then come to the Palazzo Piombino, which is now the American Embassy. It is also known as the Palazzo Margherita, because it became the residence of Queen Margherita after the assassination of Umberto I in 1900. This building was erected between 1886 and 1890, its architect,

Paparazzo, the photographer in Fellini's *La Dolce Vita* (played by Walter Santesso), in a night of follies on the Via Veneto.

Gaetano Koch was inspired by the Palazzo Farnese. If you walk back down the Via Veneto then take Via Bissolati, you will come to Largo Santa Susanna and the Geological Museum built by Raffaele Canevari in 1873. The façade shows the influence of the iron-and-glass construction of the Industrial Revolution.

Il Tridente

✗ Half a day

1. CHURCH OF SANTA
MARIA DEL POPOLO
2. CHURCH OF SANTA
MARIA DI MONTESANTO
3. CHURCH OF SANTA
MARIA DEI MIRACOLI

4. CHURCH OF
SAN GIACOMO
5. CHURCH OF GESÙ
E MARIA
6. CHURCH OF SANTI
AMBROGIO E CARLO
AL CORSO
7. MAUSOLEUM OF
AUGUSTUS
8. ARA PACIS AUGUSTAE
9. PALAZZO BORGHESE
10. PALAZZO RUSPOLI
11. CHURCH OF SAN
LORENZO IN LUCINA
12. PIAZZA DI SPAGNA
13. PALAZZO DI
PROPAGANDA FIDE
14. CHURCH OF
SANT'ANDREA DELLE
FRATTE
15. CHURCH OF LA
TRINITÀ DEI MONTI
16. VILLA MEDICI
17. THE PINCIO

THE MODERNIZATION OF CAMPO MARZIO

The cosmopolitan atmosphere of modern Rome is evident
throughout most of this quarter, which is pleasant for
strolling, a shopper's paradise and full of luxury hotels. Yet
until the middle of the 20th century, it was still the scene of
such typically Roman events as the races of barb horses down
the Via del Corso and the Easter Monday fireworks on the
Pincio. Begun in 1851 and continued until just after the end of
World War II, these firework displays marked the anniversary
of the signing of the Statuto Albertini ▲ *100*. In fact, after the
French occupation the neighborhood underwent radical
changes for a period of 150 years. The Piazza del Popolo
(1809–14) and the gardens of the Pincio (1818) were the first
to be transformed. Then, as the area around Piazza di Spagna
was attracting an increasing number of tourists, more hotels

were built there. Old houses were either replaced by new buildings, or restructured. By the time of Pius IX (1846–78) many of the ancient buildings in the area had been converted (including Palazzo Lepri in Via Condotti and Palazzo Nunez in Via Borgognona), and new ones such as the Hotel Inghilterra (1842) had gone up. In the mid 19th century, Antonio Sarti built the Academy of Fine Arts on the site of the Palazzo Camerale in Via di Ripetta. The area had always been on the route of pilgrims and other visitors coming into Rome along the Via Flaminia. The construction of Stazione Termini ▲ *338* in the 1860's prompted the humbler hoteliers (*locandieri*) to move to the Esquiline; the Campo Marzio became the preserve of the more affluent. In addition, the government established there the headquarters of institutions such as the Ministry of Public Works and the new Parliament in Piazza Montecitorio ▲ *269*; and in 1878 Malvezzi adapted a former convent in Piazza San Silvestro to house the Postal Ministry. The imposing architecture of the Galleria Colonna ▲ *300* and the Rinascente ▲ *267* department store add to the impression of architectural modernity. The Ponte Cavour was built to link the Campo Marzio with the new residential area of Prati ▲ *236* on the opposite bank – demolishing in the process the Porto di Ripetta that occupied the site where the Marine Ministry now stands. Another bridge, the Ponte Margherita, was also built. Other main streets, such as Via Tomacelli and Largo Goldoni, were widened. Finally, in 1934, the revamping of the Mausoleum of Augustus totally transformed the area around it; to perpetuate the ethos of Imperial Rome, the Fascist regime decided to glorify the memory of Augustus.

"What a strange thing the natural history of Rome is, in its modern growth!... The dream of Rome the Capital [that has existed] since 1860. And everything has been sacrificed to this necessary but fatal patriotic idea. The struggle against nature, the town that people wanted to restore in spite of the physical obstacles. The lead weight of Antiquity.... And the surge of enthusiasm in the pride of its conception. Intoxication, followed by total collapse when the truth became apparent: an enormous town built for a population that does not exist, the capital of dreams wrecked by the real town with its lack of communications, its deadly belt of sterile land, its dead river. Pride has dreamed of things that reality cannot achieve. What an astonishing and interesting case, what a page in the natural history of a town!"
Zola, *Rome*

The churches of Santa Maria dei Miracoli and Santa Maria di Montesanto guarding the entrance to the Via del Corso.

Bust of Giuseppe
Valadier (1762–1839).

A ROYAL ARRIVAL
In 1655 Rome gave a
triumphal welcome to
Queen Christina of
Sweden, whose
conversion to
Catholicism was,
according to Pope
Alexander VII, the
"Church's revenge for
the humiliation of
Westpl,alia". Her
entry into the city was
celebrated with
extraordinary
splendor, including
illuminations and the
enhancement of the
Porta del Popolo. The
Queen rode her horse
down the Corso
before proceeding to
St Peter's.

PIAZZA DEL POPOLO

PORTA DEL POPOLO. This triumphal arch offers a theatrical
entrance to the city; one of the gateways in the Aurelian Wall,
it corresponds to the ancient Porta Flaminia. The inscription
engraved on the attic (upper section) is Rome's welcoming
greeting to visitors: *Felici faustoque ingressui MDCLV* ("For a
happy and blessed entrance, 1655"). It was inscribed for the
visit of Queen Christina of Sweden ▲ *362*, and Bernini was
commissioned to design a new inner façade to give the queen
an appropriate welcome. At the center of the piazza stands
the Egyptian obelisk of Ramses II, which Sixtus V got
Domenico Fontana to move from the Circus Maximus ▲ *177*
in 1589. The fountains and lions were added by Valadier in
1823, during the pontificate of Leo XII.

VALADIER'S DESIGN. To cope with the influx of pilgrims and
other travelers, Giuseppe Valadier was commissioned by the
Prefect of Tournon, who represented France during the
Napoleonic occupation, to review the layout of the piazza.
This work, which was the first of its kind in Rome not to rely
on convicts for labor, was executed between 1816 and 1824.
The architect's plans had to take into account the existing
buildings, such as the churches of Santa Maria del Popolo,
Santa Maria di Montesanto and Santa Maria dei Miracoli,
and also, of course, the obelisk, the Porta Flaminia and the
Via del Corso. He built the Pincio ramp as a solution to the
problem of the difference of level between the piazza and the
hill. To appreciate the character of the piazza, visit one of the
two famous rival cafés in the square, *Rosati* and *Canova*.

SANTA MARIA DEL POPOLO ★. Silhouetted against the pines of
the Pincio, the church nestles under the Aurelian Wall
(nicknamed the *Muro Torto*, or "twisting wall", because of its
tortuous outline). The Renaissance façade of the church rises
above a flight of steps. After its reconstruction by Baccio
Pontelli and Andrea Bregno
under Sixtus IV in the 15th
century, the church was
embellished by Rome's
leading

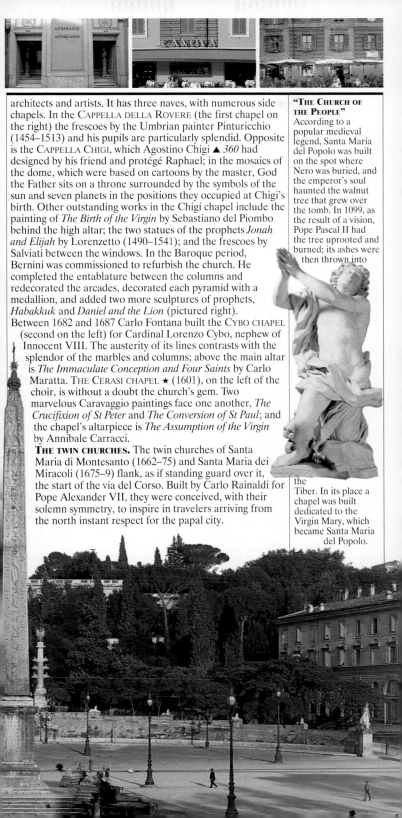

architects and artists. It has three naves, with numerous side chapels. In the CAPPELLA DELLA ROVERE (the first chapel on the right) the frescoes by the Umbrian painter Pinturicchio (1454–1513) and his pupils are particularly splendid. Opposite is the CAPPELLA CHIGI, which Agostino Chigi ▲ *360* had designed by his friend and protégé Raphael; in the mosaics of the dome, which were based on cartoons by the master, God the Father sits on a throne surrounded by the symbols of the sun and seven planets in the positions they occupied at Chigi's birth. Other outstanding works in the Chigi chapel include the painting of *The Birth of the Virgin* by Sebastiano del Piombo behind the high altar; the two statues of the prophets *Jonah and Elijah* by Lorenzetto (1490–1541); and the frescoes by Salviati between the windows. In the Baroque period, Bernini was commissioned to refurbish the church. He completed the entablature between the columns and redecorated the arcades, decorated each pyramid with a medallion, and added two more sculptures of prophets, *Habakkuk* and *Daniel and the Lion* (pictured right).

Between 1682 and 1687 Carlo Fontana built the CYBO CHAPEL (second on the left) for Cardinal Lorenzo Cybo, nephew of Innocent VIII. The austerity of its lines contrasts with the splendor of the marbles and columns; above the main altar is *The Immaculate Conception and Four Saints* by Carlo Maratta. THE CERASI CHAPEL ★ (1601), on the left of the choir, is without a doubt the church's gem. Two marvelous Caravaggio paintings face one another, *The Crucifixion of St Peter* and *The Conversion of St Paul*; and the chapel's altarpiece is *The Assumption of the Virgin* by Annibale Carracci.

THE TWIN CHURCHES. The twin churches of Santa Maria di Montesanto (1662–75) and Santa Maria dei Miracoli (1675–9) flank, as if standing guard over it, the start of the via del Corso. Built by Carlo Rainaldi for Pope Alexander VII, they were conceived, with their solemn symmetry, to inspire in travelers arriving from the north instant respect for the papal city.

"THE CHURCH OF THE PEOPLE"
According to a popular medieval legend, Santa Maria del Popolo was built on the spot where Nero was buried, and the emperor's soul haunted the walnut tree that grew over the tomb. In 1099, as the result of a vision, Pope Pascal II had the tree uprooted and burned; its ashes were then thrown into the Tiber. In its place a chapel was built dedicated to the Virgin Mary, which became Santa Maria del Popolo.

▲ IL TRIDENTE

The Silenus.

FAMOUS CAFÉS
Many of the famous cafés that enlivened the neighborhood have now vanished. Among them, the Caffè degli Inglesi, decorated by Piranesi; the Caffè del Buon Gusto, whose owner, imitating the English habit, introduced "sandwiches" into Italy; the Caffè delle Nocchie, run by three very plain spinsters; and the famous Caffè Argano, near Piazza Colonna, which was a meeting place for the artistic and literary world.

A horse race during Carnival.

THE MAIN STREETS. The neighborhood is called "Il Tridente" because of the three streets that fan out, like the prongs of a trident, from Piazza del Popolo. The left-hand prong is the Via del Babuino; along it a variety of antique shops runs all the way to Piazza di Spagna. The street owes its name to an unprepossessing statue of Silenus which now adorns a fountain near the Church of Sant'Atanasio dei Greci: Romans found the sculpture so ugly that they likened it to a *babuino* (baboon). Parallel to Via del Babuino runs Via Margutta, which has a street fair in June and October where painters exhibit their work. The right-hand prong of the trident is the VIA DI RIPETTA, which used to lead to the old port of Rome (the Porto di Ripetta, which no longer exists today, although many prints and pictures of it have survived). The trident's central prong is the VIA DEL CORSO.

VIA DEL CORSO

THE STREET OF ALEXANDER VII. According to Stendhal, "Via del Corso is perhaps the most beautiful street in the Universe". However, it gets very crowded, particularly at the end of the afternoon. Absolutely straight, and rather narrow in comparison with the wide streets built in the 19th century and the time of Mussolini, it is now lined with clothes shops. It follows the course of the ancient Via Flaminia, then continues for more than a mile between two rows of palazzi and churches before ending at Piazza Venezia. Pope Alexander VII (1655–67) realigned it by demolishing all the buildings in its way and obliged the owners of the remaining palazzi to build new façades. It was nicknamed the "Corso" because of the numerous races (*corse*) that took place there during the Carnival period: human races (for children, old men and Jews), animal races (for donkeys and buffaloes)

and, above all, races for barb horses, which attracted the biggest crowds. Spectators lined the windows of the palazzi (which were decked out with flags) in order to watch the extravagant processions, parades and masquerades. Writers on the Grand Tour, including Goethe and Dickens ● *113*, were greatly impressed by the festivities. During the 18th and 19th centuries elegant ladies liked to be seen driving along the Via del Corso in their carriages. Today its first section is a pedestrian precinct. It would be interesting to see inside the palazzi, but they are closed to visitors. Among them are such fascinating buildings as Palazzo Rondini, with its courtyard full of antiquities; Palazzo Fiano, which housed a small puppet theater in the 19th century; and (toward Piazza Venezia) Palazzo Mancini – the seat of the French Academy from 1725 to 1803 – and Palazzo Bonaparte, which was the residence of Letizia, mother of Napoleon I. Sadly the many cafés, which from the 18th century onward made this area a center of literary and artistic life, have passed into history and the bar of the Hotel Plaza, an immense haven of peace that still retains its *fin-de-siècle* decor, is now completely deserted.

THE CHURCHES OF SAN GIACOMO AND GESU E MARIA. SAN GIACOMO is located just after the long façade of PALAZZO SAN SEVERINO. The first church in Rome to have an elliptical design, it was built at the end of the 15th century by Francesco da Volterra and Carlo Maderno. Facing it, near the Goethe Museum (No.20), is the CHURCH OF GESU E MARIA (1633); the lovely façade (1670–5), one of the few in Rome to be based on the Palladian model, was designed by Carlo Rainaldi. The lavish interior is decorated with multicolored marble and Sicilian jasper. A ceiling painted by Giacinto Brandi makes it a real Baroque theater.

THE CHURCH OF SANTI AMBROGIO E CARLO AL CORSO. The "national" church of the Lombards (right) was initially dedicated to St Ambrose, the patron saint of Milan. However, it was rebuilt in honor of St Charles Borromeo ▲ *247* (who had been Archbishop of Milan) following his canonization in 1610. Its medieval plan, designed by Onorio and

Martino Longhi, is particularly unusual in Rome because of the ambulatory which circles the choir. In 1668 Pietro da Cortona added its elegant dome, one of the largest in the city after that of St Peter's ▲ *210*. (Take Via Canova, on the right, to the Piazza Augusto Imperatore.)

THE MAUSOLEUM OF AUGUSTUS

THE EGYPTIAN FASHION. On his return from Alexandria in 29 AD after defeating Mark Antony and conquering Egypt, Octavian (who became the Emperor Augustus) had a grandiose tomb built in the Campus Martius. It was obviously inspired by the Mausoleum of Alexander in Alexandria, and was conceived as a dynastic monument. Excavations between 1936 and 1938 cleared a space in the midst of the cypresses,

RES · GESTAE · DIVI · AVGVSTI

The Mausoleum of Augustus.

THE "RES GESTAE"
This summary of Augustus' achievements is engraved on bronze tablets hung on two pilasters on either side of the entrance to the Mausoleum. One of the ancient copies of this has been found engraved on the entrance walls of the Temple of Rome and Augustus in Ankara. A modern copy can be seen on the façade of the pavilion protecting the Ara Pacis.

Detail of the procession (on the north side of the Altar of Peace).

and a circular building with a diameter of about 285 feet was discovered, consisting of a series of concentric walls. The two obelisks that stood before the south-facing door of the building now adorn the Piazza del Quirinale and the Piazza dell'Esquilino.

THE MAUSOLEUM'S INTERIOR.
A passage rings the circular burial chamber, which has several niches. These originally held the tombs. In the center, the tomb of Augustus lay exactly beneath the bronze statue of the Emperor that crowned the building. The first to be buried there was Augustus' nephew Marcellus ▲ *157*, who died in 23 BC. His inscription and that of his mother Octavia are engraved on the same block of marble. In the Middle Ages the mausoleum fell into disuse and the Colonna family transformed it into a fortress; in 1780 it was an arena for bull races; and in the 19th century it served as a concert hall known as the Augusteo.

THE ARA PACIS AUGUSTAE

THE ALTAR OF PEACE. This monument (originally further south, in the vicinity of the Via Flaminia) was dedicated in 9 BC, on January 30, to celebrate the peace established by Augustus after his victories in Gaul and Spain. Fragments of it were unearthed as far back as the 16th century. In the late 1930's it was restored to celebrate the 2,000th anniversary of Augustus' inauguration as Emperor and was encased in a monstrous cement-and-glass cage to protect it from the weather. The monument is a four-sided marble enclosure, on a podium, with steps leading up to it (the two openings in the walls would originally have had huge doors). The altar itself is at the top of three steps inside the enclosure.

A MASTERPIECE OF ROMAN SCULPTURE ★. The marble walls enclosing the altar are very richly sculpted. The lower part is identical on all four sides, with an intricate tracery of acanthus leaves branching out from a single stem at the center of each panel. The upper part is more varied, the panels beside the doorways being ornamented with reliefs representing mythological and allegorical scenes. One of them (unfortunately badly damaged) is of the Lupercalium, the grotto where the she-wolf is supposed to have suckled Romulus and Remus ● *26*. The other relief on the same side shows Aeneas preparing to sacrifice the sow with thirty piglets which, in his prophetic dream, indicated the place where the city of Rome would be built. On the opposite side, Earth is represented in the form of a buxom woman with her two children (pictured opposite on the right). Two

half-naked female figures symbolize the other elements: Water riding on a sea monster, and Air on a swan. Most of the right-hand panel is missing, but it is thought to have featured a figure personifying the triumph of Rome. On the other sides are historical scenes. The relief on that nearest to the Via di Ripetta side is the best preserved. It shows portraits of the most important members of the Imperial family filing past in strict hierarchical order: Augustus, Agrippa, Livia (the wife of Augustus), Tiberius, Drusus the Elder and Caius Caesar can all be recognized. The reliefs convey the political message as well as the artistic skills of the new regime; legend, history and religion combine to honor the name of Augustus and glorify the peace established by the power of Rome. (Continue along Via di Ripetta, until just after Via dell'Arancio.)

FROM PIAZZA BORGHESE TO LARGO GOLDONI

PALAZZO BORGHESE. This palace was acquired in 1604 by Cardinal Camillo Borghese, the future Pope Paul V, who offered it to his brothers in 1605, the year of his election. Intended as a symbol of the power and glory of the pontifical family in the very heart of Rome, it was begun in 1560 by Martino Longhi and Flaminio Ponzio, and Ponzio designed the beautiful courtyard. Around 1670 the palace was extensively remodeled by Carlo Rainaldi, who rebuilt the façade facing the piazza and redesigned the gardens. Its irregular shape has earned it the nickname of the *cembalo* ("the harpsichord"). If you are interested in second-hand books and engravings, visit the stalls in Largo della Fontanella di Borghese. (Take the Via della Fontanella di Borghese to return to the Corso.)

Stalls selling engravings in the Largo della Fontanella di Borghese.

THE PALAZZO BORGHESE
This palace has one of the most successful and best preserved of Rome's Baroque gardens; its inner courtyard, a truly peaceful haven, is rich with statues, garlands, *putti* (cherubs) and fountains.

Caffé Greco
A.D. 1760
Roma, via Condotti 86

THE CAFFÈ GRECO (No. 85 Via Condotti) The oldest (1760) and for a long time the most prestigious of Rome's cafés is traditionally the haunt of the beau monde and has always been a very cosmopolitan spot. Illustrious clients have included Stendhal, Goethe, D'Annunzio, Berlioz, Modigliani and Toscanini.

PALAZZO RUSPOLI. This building overlooking Largo Goldoni originally belonged to a rich Florentine family, the Rucellai. Around 1556 they commissioned Bartolommeo Ammannati, architect of the courtyard of the Palazzo Pitti in Florence, to build a residence for them in Rome; they then invited another Florentine, Jacopo Zucchi, to decorate it with a cycle of allegorical frescoes. The ground floor is now occupied by the Memmo Foundation, which organizes interesting exhibitions there (the entrance is at No. 418A Via del Corso). (Take the Via di Leoncino to reach Piazza San Lorenzo in Lucina.)

SAN LORENZO IN LUCINA. According to tradition this church was founded during the pontificate of Sixtus III (432–40) on the site of the house of Lucina, a rich Roman matron who bought the remains of martyrs so she could give them a decent burial. Pope Pascal II had it rebuilt at the beginning of the 12th century, and the portico and bell tower have survived from that period. In 1650, the whole building was restored and side chapels added. Of these, the lovely FONSECA CHAPEL (the fourth on the right) by Bernini is particularly striking. The church also contains the tomb of the French painter Nicolas Poussin (1594–1665), which Chateaubriand had made in 1830. In the fifth chapel on the left are the canvases of Simon Vouet's Caravaggio period. Guido Reni's luminous yet somber Crucifixion adorns the high altar. (Walk back to the Corso and take Via Condotti, which is opposite Palazzo Ruspoli.)

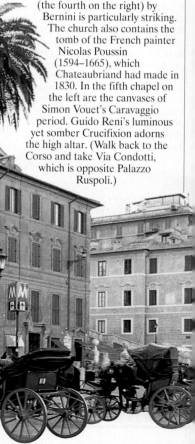

Palazzo di
Propaganda Fide.

COLLEGIVM
VRBANVM
DE PROPAGANDA
FIDE

PIAZZA DI SPAGNA

ONE OF THE DELIGHTS OF ROME. People never cease to be
seduced and surprised by Piazza di Spagna. Today this area,
partly owned by the Spanish (the embassy) and the French
(Trinità dei Monti), is swarming with luxury boutiques. It
consists of two irregular triangular piazzas that interconnect.
The Piazza di Spagna owes its name to the first permanent
embassy to be established in Rome, the PALAZZO DI
SPAGNA. Built by Antonio del Grande in 1674
between Via Borgognona and Via Frattina, it is still
the headquarters of the Spanish Embassy to the
Holy See. It was a favorite refuge for artists in
the 17th century (Claude Lorrain, Poussin and
Van Laer all stayed there). For a brief rest one
might prefer BABINGTON'S TEA-ROOMS with
their utterly Victorian charm to Rome's first
McDonald's, which has opened on the square
much to the disgust of the Romans. At the foot
of the Spanish Steps is the CASINA ROSSA (No.26
Piazza di Spagna), the house where the poet Keats
died in 1821 ▲ *183*. It houses a small museum
dedicated to him, as well as to Shelley and Byron.

**FEAST OF THE
IMMACULATE
CONCEPTION**
Every year on
December
8 the

COLLEGIO DI PROPAGANDA FIDE. On the right of the piazza is
the headquarters of the congregation founded by Gregory
XIV in 1627 for the training of young missionaries, which was
gradually to become the center of Catholic missionary
activity. Since it is Vatican property, it enjoys the privilege of
extraterritoriality. Bernini started to remodel the building and
designed the façade on the piazza, then after 1646 his great
rival Borromini took over and built the small internal church,
the ORATORIO DEI RE MAGI. In front of the college is the
COLUMN OF THE DOGMA OF THE IMMACULATE CONCEPTION,
the last great Roman monument to be commissioned before
the Unity of Italy ● *33*. Designed by Luigi Poletti, it consists
of an ancient column with a statue of the Virgin Mary erected
during the pontificate of Pius IX, after the proclamation of
the Dogma in 1854. Ever since, on December 8, the
anniversary of this event, the Pope blesses the crowd that has
flocked there to celebrate the Feast of the Immaculate
Conception. (Continue to Via di Capo le Case.)

Pope visits Piazza di
Spagna and hands
firemen a garland of
flowers with which
they crown the statue
of the Virgin at the
top of the column.
The faithful then
heap masses of
flowers around the
base.

The Casina Rossa
and the Church of
San Lorenzo in

SANT'ANDREA DELLE FRATTE. This church once stood amid
rural surroundings, hence the name "*delle Fratte*"
(of the thickets). If the chronicles can be trusted,
a building dedicated to St Andrew
already existed here around 1370.
When it became a parish church in
the 16th century the shrine was
entrusted to the Minims, who set
about rebuilding it in 1604.
However, once the nave had been
completed, in 1622 the work was
interrupted due to lack of funds, and
only continued thirty years later
under Borromini's direction. The
elegant bell tower (each level of
which is stylistically different) has a
special charm, as does the undulating shape of
the dome. (Return to Piazza di Spagna.)

TRINITÀ DEI MONTI

FONTANA DELLA BARCACCIA (FOUNTAIN OF THE BOAT). At the foot of the steps is an unusual fountain resembling a half-submerged boat, which – like the Navicella on Monte Celio ▲ *190* – was probably based on one of the fountains of antiquity. Urban VIII decided to have it made in 1627 and

channeled the Aqua Virgo ▲ *298* to it. It is not known whether it was designed by Bernini or by his father, Pietro.

A MAJESTIC FLIGHT OF STEPS. The transformation of Piazza di Spagna was completed in the 18th century with the building of a *scalinata* (flight of steps), creating a succession of terraces up to the Church of Trinità dei Monti. The project was financed by King Louis XV of France. His predecessor, Louis XIV, had wanted to build a flight of steps dominated by his own equestrian statue, but the pontiffs opposed this idea. As a result, the project was not begun until 1723 (during the pontificate of Innocent XIII) when the architect Francesco de Sanctis obtained permission to build the steps. The Spanish Steps are at their most charming in the spring, when they are covered with flowering azaleas. Today they are a meeting place for young

people, street vendors, caricaturists and, above all, tourists.

(a reminder of the diplomatic wrangling between the Holy See and France that preceded their construction). In 1660 Mazarin offered to have the steps built at his own expense, though his proposal did not get anywhere, and even commissioned the priest Elpidio Benedetti to produce a design. A dilettante architect and an eccentric if ever there was one, Benedetti had built for himself a villa on the Janiculum in the shape of a galleon (hence its name the Villa del Vascello), which was eventually destroyed in 1849 during the fighting between Garibaldi and the French troops. From time to time the Italians still reassert their claim to the steps.

TRINITÀ DEI MONTI. This church was founded by the French in 1502 at the request of Louis XII and was entrusted to the Minims. A double flight of steps by Domenico Fontana (1587) leads up to Carlo Maderno's soaring façade with twin bell towers. Inside, the SECOND CHAPEL ON THE LEFT contains one of the most famous frescoes in Rome, the *Descent from the Cross* (1541) by Daniele da Volterra, thought to have been executed according to a preparatory sketch by Michelangelo. THE CONVENT next door belongs to the Dames du Sacré-Coeur (Sisters of the Sacred Heart). The PIAZZA TRINITÀ DEI MONTI, at the center of which stands an obelisk found in the gardens of Sallust ▲ *288*, marks the end of the street formerly called the Via Felice; this extends all the way to Santa Maria Maggiore ▲ *342*, after crossing the Quirinal, the Viminal and the Esquiline. At this same end of the piazza is the Via Gregoriana; here stands the curious 16th-century PALAZZO ZUCCARO, built for the Mannerist painter, Federico Zuccaro, member of the Accademia di San Luca ▲ *299*. Its door and windows are framed by the gaping mouths of monsters. Here David painted *The Oath of the Horatii* (1784). Today it is the headquarters of the German Institute for Art History and the Hertziana Library. (Walk back through the piazza and take the Viale della Trinità dei Monti, which climbs toward the Pincio. (Follow the wall alongside the Convent of

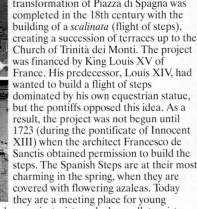

the Dames du Sacré-Coeur and the gardens of the Villa
Medici until you come to the villa itself.)

THE VILLA MEDICI

A RENAISSANCE VILLA. In 1564, at the request of Cardinal
Giovanni Ricci di Montepulciano, Annibale Lippi totally
transformed a building on the site of the gardens of Lucullus
(the military commander famous for his hedonism and
extravagance), which extended over this
area in the 1st century BC. It then
passed into the hands of the Medici
family. Like many Roman villas built in
the 16th and 17th centuries, it has a
severe, unadorned, almost military
façade facing the city, while the façade that overlooks the
garden incorporates a loggia and is much less austere and
more ornate. Integrated in the wall facing the garden are bas-
reliefs, some of which came from the Ara Pacis Augustae ▲
310 – reflecting the enthusiasm of the great Roman and
Florentine families of the end of the 16th century for
collecting antiquities.

AN ITALIAN-STYLE GARDEN. Although it has been
drastically rearranged, the villa's park still retains some
of the features typical of Renaissance Italian gardens:
hedged walks, arbors, alcoves, secret gardens, and
fountains, all decorated with statues. At the back,
looking onto the Muro Torto ▲ *306*, is the *studiolo*
(study) of Ferdinando di Medici, totally restored
in the 1980's; some 16th-century Mannerist
frescoes were discovered here, as well as a
magnificent aviary. Between the Villa Medici
and the Trinità dei Monti, recent excavations
have revealed the site of a gigantic curved
nymphaeum built by Valerius Asiaticus, who
owned a villa here during the reign of
Claudius.

THE FRENCH ACADEMY. The Académie de
France à Rome was founded in 1666 by Louis
XIV to enable young artists to be imbued
with classical art, and was moved to the
Villa Medici in 1804 by a decree
of Napoleon. (Continue
along the Viale della
Trinità dei Monti.)

From left to right: Via
Gregoriana and views
of the Villa Medici.

BERLIOZ IN ROME
In 1830 Berlioz won
the Grand Prix de
Rome, which entitled
him to a period of
residence at the Villa

H. Berlioz

Medici. In his
memoirs - probably
with a touch of
romantic
exaggeration - he
recounts how,
climbing the Spanish
Steps to reach the
Villa Medici, he
had to whip out
his knife to fend
off pickpockets
who wanted to
rob him of his
purse.

Monument to Enrico Toti.

MONUMENT TO THE CAIROLI BROTHERS
Close to the point where the Viale della Trinità dei Monti meets Viale Gabriele D'Annunzio stands this memorial, built by Ercole Rosa in 1883, to Enrico and Giovanni Cairoli, victims of the fighting in the Villa Glori in 1867 at the time of Garibaldi's ill-fated march on Rome ● *33*.

THE PINCIO ★

The Pincio Gardens, which overlook Piazza del Popolo, are a magical place to wander in. In the 4th century the land belonged to the Pinci family. The promenade, designed by Giuseppe Valadier and opened to the public in 1828, affords one of the loveliest views of Rome. With its broad walks shaded by parasol pines, palm trees and oaks, it was an immediate success both with Romans and with artists and foreigners who lived in the Eternal City. The avenues and walks of the Pincio conformed to the contemporary taste for a disciplined and urbanized "nature" and for "belvederes" (places from which to admire the view); they were also ideally suited to the fashionable practice of "promenading". On foot or in carriages, Roman high society met there regularly, and travelers, diarists and writers – such as Stendhal, Gide and D'Annunzio – celebrated the Pincio's charms.

THE CASINA VALADIER. This enchanting small villa stands in the Viale Mickiewicz. You can sample a *granita di caffè* here while admiring the view. It was planned as a restaurant in 1813, and looks like a garden pavilion built in the finest 18th-century taste. Nevertheless, it fell into disfavor for a time before becoming fashionable in 1922.

THE COMMEMORATIVE MONUMENTS. An array of busts adorns the walks of the Pincio, placed there to honor great Italians from the days of ancient Rome. In addition to statues of men such as Metastasio, Canova and Titian, there is a memorial commemorating the Battle of Legnano (the victory, in 1176, of the first Lombard League against the Holy Roman Empire ▲ *100*); dedicated to the municipalities of Italy, it was erected in 1911. A little further on are monuments to Raphael (1838) and Enrico Toti (1922), a *bersagliere* (light-infantryman) who after losing a leg participated in the fighting in 1916, supporting himself with his crutch. At the center of the avenue named the Viale dell'Obelisco stands the obelisk erected by the Emperor Hadrian to commemorate his favorite, Antinous, which was moved here in 1822.

Via Appia antica

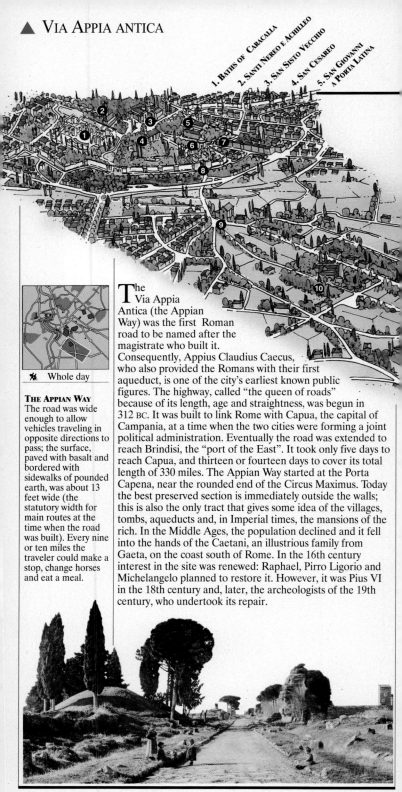

▲ Via Appia antica

✹ Whole day

THE APPIAN WAY
The road was wide enough to allow vehicles traveling in opposite directions to pass; the surface, paved with basalt and bordered with sidewalks of pounded earth, was about 13 feet wide (the statutory width for main routes at the time when the road was built). Every nine or ten miles the traveler could make a stop, change horses and eat a meal.

The Via Appia Antica (the Appian Way) was the first Roman road to be named after the magistrate who built it. Consequently, Appius Claudius Caecus, who also provided the Romans with their first aqueduct, is one of the city's earliest known public figures. The highway, called "the queen of roads" because of its length, age and straightness, was begun in 312 BC. It was built to link Rome with Capua, the capital of Campania, at a time when the two cities were forming a joint political administration. Eventually the road was extended to reach Brindisi, the "port of the East". It took only five days to reach Capua, and thirteen or fourteen days to cover its total length of 330 miles. The Appian Way started at the Porta Capena, near the rounded end of the Circus Maximus. Today the best preserved section is immediately outside the walls; this is also the only tract that gives some idea of the villages, tombs, aqueducts and, in Imperial times, the mansions of the rich. In the Middle Ages, the population declined and it fell into the hands of the Caetani, an illustrious family from Gaeta, on the coast south of Rome. In the 16th century interest in the site was renewed: Raphael, Pirro Ligorio and Michelangelo planned to restore it. However, it was Pius VI in the 18th century and, later, the archeologists of the 19th century, who undertook its repair.

ROADSIDE TOMBS. Since the earliest times the common custom was to bury the dead outside the *pomerium*, the sacred walls of the city. The first few miles of Roman roads were therefore usually flanked by necropolises, distinguished by social status and diversity of funeral rites. Indeed burial and cremation were practiced concurrently, one or the other prevailing according to the fashion. Under the Republic cremation was prevalent so they constructed columbariums (buildings housing thousands of funerary urns) and altars with the ashes of the deceased. Conversely, in the Imperial times

The Via Appia.

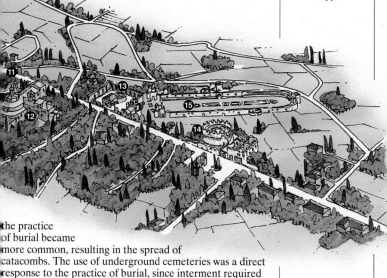

the practice of burial became more common, resulting in the spread of catacombs. The use of underground cemeteries was a direct response to the practice of burial, since interment required more space than cremation. From the 4th century the catacombs became almost exclusively Christian, following the conversion of the Roman people.

THE BATHS OF CARACALLA

ROMAN BATHS. From the end of the Republic the Romans frequented public baths, not just for reasons of hygiene and exercise but also for entertainment. The activities offered by the baths and their increasingly important social role led the emperors to build ever larger establishments, accommodating more bathers (the Baths of Caracalla had a capacity of nearly 1,600). Progressively, areas for sport were introduced, auditoriums for music, lecture theaters, libraries, gardens, fountains, and porticos to protect walkers from rain and from the sun. At the same time, the architecture and decoration of these buildings became more sophisticated, richer in mosaics, stucco decorations, colonnades, paintings and sculptures. Eventually premises of a monumental size became indispensable because of the large service staff that was necessary (cloakroom attendants, masseurs, those responsible for depilation, doctors, etc.) and the hordes of entertainers that the bathers came to expect (ranging from itinerant

THE BATHS OF CARACALLA
On either side of the portico there was a huge *exedra* enclosing a *palestra* (gymnasium). At the rear a sort of half stadium concealed the enormous water tanks, each with a capacity of about 20 million gallons.

319

CARACALLA (188–217)
Given access to
power in 198 AD by
his father Septimius
Severus, Caracalla
became Emperor in
211. He continued his
father's initiatives,
and his edict of 212
granting Roman
citizenship to all
inhabitants of the
Empire marked the
fruition of the policy
of "Romanization".
He also pursued an
ambitious foreign
policy, and was
assassinated during a
campaign against
Parthia.

The *Ercole Farnese*
▲ *245*. This statue
of Hercules was
found in the
Baths of
Caracalla.

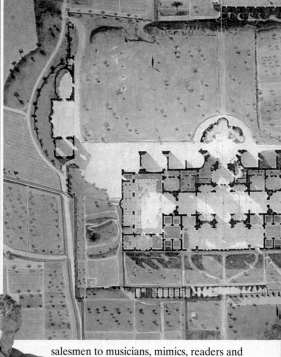

salesmen to musicians, mimics, readers and
orators). Thus, unlike the Greek gymnasiums,
which were limited to the education and
physical development of young men, the
Roman baths were places for social
encounters and leisure activities, where
sport and culture combined in forming, as
the poet Juvenal put it, *mens sana in
corpore sano* ("a healthy mind in a healthy
body"). The baths were open to everyone
until sunset; and it was only from the time of
Hadrian (117–38 AD) that the sexes were
segregated. Today the Baths of Caracalla are
still used for cultural purposes: in summer
there are open-air performances of opera
and ballet.

THE BATHER'S RITUAL. The Baths of
Caracalla (Terme di Caracalla), also known
as the Thermae Antoninianae, are the most
magnificent and best preserved of all the
Imperial baths. Built between 212 and 216
AD, they form an almost perfect square
covering 27 acres and are surrounded by a
wall erected later by Heliogabalus ▲ *151*
and Alexander Severus. The
arrangement of the central block, which
was reserved for sports, is traditional.
Access was through the four gates on

the northeast façade. Each of the vestibules led to a square room, probably the dressing rooms (*apodyteria*), then to one of the two gymnasiums (*palestrae*). Indeed this is where the bather's ritual program began, with intense gymnastic exercises intended to warm up the muscles and induce heavy breathing. After that the body was scraped and oiled, then in the following rooms submitted to contrasting treatments of hot and cold: first dry sweating in the *laconium*, then a hot bath (immersion or aspersion) in the *caldarium*, a great circular room with a diameter of about 110 feet, covered by a vast dome; from here the bather passed into the temperate hall, the *tepidarium*, to accustom the body before plunging into the cold waters of the *frigidarium* (probably only partly roofed), which contained cold baths and a swimming pool (*natatio*). Between the last two rooms was the basilica, a large covered hall that served as a general relaxation room. Other rooms, between this central hall and the dressing rooms, were for massage and medical consultations; there were terraces that served as solariums; and there were also latrines. Finally, the service quarters necessary for the operation of the baths were housed in the basement, which consisted of a vast network of underground rooms and passages. In one of these passages (near the great northwest exedra), a *mithraeum* has been discovered ▲ *181* that is the largest known in Rome. (At the exit of the baths, turn right.)

THE MOSAIC OF THE ATHLETES
The floors of the palestra were covered with magnificent polychrome mosaics. The one depicting athletes, found in 1824, is now in the Vatican Museums.

SANTI NEREO E ACHILLEO. According to tradition, when St Peter was escaping from the Mamertine prison ▲ *131* it was on this spot that the bandage (*fasciola*) wrapped around the sores caused by his chains dropped from his leg. A church, called the Titulus Fasciolae, is known to have existed here as early as 337. It was first enlarged around 800, during the pontificate of Leo III, and the very beautiful mosaic on the chancel arch has survived from that time. During the 15th century the church was almost entirely rebuilt; it was then redecorated by Cardinal Baronius, who commissioned the frescoes in 1597.

SAN SISTO VECCHIO. This very ancient foundation was restored by Pope Innocent III (1198–1216), who gave it to St Dominic so he could found the first monastery for his order in Rome. Both the church and the monastic buildings were restructured by Filippo Raguzzini between 1724 and 1730, under the patronage of Benedict XIII. Remains of the medieval church are visible in the cloister; the Romanesque bell tower dates from the restoration of Innocent III.

THE HOUSE OF CARDINAL BESSARIONE
Next to the Church of San Cesareo ▲ *322* is a lovely 15th-century building where the great humanist scholar Cardinal Bessarione is said to have gathered together the best intellects of his time. Inside, some of the original frescoes have survived, as well as the Renaissance furniture.

The rich decorations of the Columbarium of Pomponius Hylas. Part of this room was hollowed out of the rock.

THE TOMB OF THE SCIPIOS
Almost nothing is left of the original northwest-facing façade, nor of the foundations carved into the rock and covered by frescoes.

THE SARCOPHAGUS OF SCIPIO BARBATUS
The inscription on the coffin praises the merits of the conqueror of the Samnites and Etruscans: "Lucius Cornelius Scipio Barbatus, son of Cnaeus, a brave and wise man; he was a consul in your country and an aedile (magistrate responsible for buildings and public works). He took Taurasia and Cisauna in Samnium and subdued Lucania, from which he took hostages." (The original sarcophagus and the funerary inscriptions found here are now in the Vatican Museums.)

PARK OF THE SCIPIOS

SAN CESAREO. This church was erected in the 15th century on top of a ruined building (possibly baths) dating from the 2nd century AD. Just below the paved floor of the church, a black-and-white mosaic with marine motifs has survived from this earlier building. Inside, the splendid mosaics of *The Eternal Father* in the apse and *The Annunciation* on the chancel arch were executed to designs by Cavaliere d'Arpino, who painted the frescoes on the upper part of the walls of the nave.

THE TOMB OF THE SCIPIOS. In 1780, in the basement of a private property, several rooms containing sarcophagi were discovered, of which the oldest dated from the beginning of the 3rd century BC. This was the sepulcher of a great Roman family, the Scipios, most famous for having defeated Hannibal in 202 BC. This celebrated discovery taught archeologists that the Romans were already familiar with burial rites at the time of the Republic. The actual entrance to the tomb is on the Via di Porta San Sebastiano. Hollowed out of a natural mound of tufa, it is made up of six intersecting galleries. At the back of the central gallery is a copy of the oldest tomb of all, that of Lucius Cornelius Scipio Barbatus, consul in 298 BC; and to the left of the central passage you can see the remains of the original sarcophagus of Lucius' son, who was consul in 259 BC.

THE COLUMBARIUM OF POMPONIUS HYLAS. On request the caretaker will take visitors to see a small, extremely well-preserved underground columbarium dating from the early years of the Empire. Situated just across the park wedged between the Via di Porta San Sebastiano and the Via di Porta Latina, it is reached by a flight of steps that has survived from

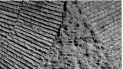

the same period. Opposite the last few steps there is a niche decorated with a mosaic inscription showing two names: *Cn[aeus] Pomponius Hyla and Pomponia Vitalis* (left). The rectangular room, part of which is hollowed out of the rock, is beautifully decorated with stuccos and paintings almost entirely from the time of Nero. During the 19th century three other columbariums were discovered close by, in the Vigna Codini (now privately owned).

ORATORIO SAN GIOVANNI IN OLEO. This small octagonal chapel erected in 1509 by the French prelate Benoît Adam stands on the spot where, according to tradition, St John emerged unharmed from the cauldron of boiling oil into which he had been flung; after this episode the Evangelist was exiled to Patmos. Benoît Adam had his coat of arms engraved above the door, with his motto: "Au plaisir de Dieu". The chapel was restored in 1658 by Borromini, then again in 1716 under Clement XI.

SAN GIOVANNI A PORTA LATINA. This church was founded by Pope Gelasius I (492–6) and built according to an oriental design. In the 11th century it housed a community of priests who practiced poverty and obedience. Animated by intense zeal, they were at the root of the Gregorian reform ● *30* led by Popes Gregory VI and Gregory VII. In recent times the church has recovered its medieval appearance. A portico with five arches supported by graceful marble-and-granite columns precedes the façade, which is flanked by an elegant six-story campanile. The central nave is decorated with an important cycle of 12th-century frescoes depicting scenes from the Old and New Testaments.

THE AURELIAN WALL

PORTA LATINA. The Emperor Aurelian (270–5) undertook to give Rome new walls as a protection against barbarian invasions. All of the masons' guilds in Rome were called to work on them. Building began in 271 and was completed by the time of Aurelian's death. The ramparts, nearly 12 miles long, about 13 feet wide and fortified every 100 feet with a square tower, originally constituted a fairly modest defense system. They were therefore improved several times, especially between 401 and 402, so as to withstand attacks from the Goths. The height of the wall was raised; the exposed walkway for the sentries was replaced by a covered gallery with windows, above which a second passageway was built, fortified with crenelations; and the towers, also reinforced, virtually became independent fortresses.

THE AURELIAN WALL
From the Porta San Sebastiano, which houses a museum devoted to the history of the Aurelian Wall, you can follow part of the sentries' beat. The construction of the wall followed a strategic line that encompassed the seven hills of Rome and incorporated many monumental buildings, including the Castrense Amphitheater ▲ *290*, the Castro Pretorio ▲ *335* and the Pyramid of Caius Cestius ▲ *182*. Thus one tenth of the ramparts consisted of pre-existing buildings.

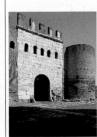

PORTA LATINA
The Porta Latina was doubly secure. As well as its two internal gates, there was a portcullis on the outside that could be lowered to instantly block access. In the upper part five arched windows lit the room used for operating the portcullis; these were probably blocked during the war against the Goths.

▲ Via Appia antica

PORTA SAN SEBASTIANO
An interesting figure is engraved on the left gatepost. It represents the Archangel Gabriel and is accompanied by an inscription in curious medieval Latin commemorating the Roman victory over Robert d'Anjou, King of Naples, on

September 29, 1327.

One of the milestones on the first section of the Appian Way.

AN UNUSUAL RESTAURANT
You can eat in a columbarium! Since the end of the 19th century there has been a restaurant in the Columbarium of the Freedmen of Augustus (on the left, after the junction with the Via Appia Pignatelli).

The section between the Porta Appia and the Porta Latina is one of the best preserved parts of the wall. The façade of the Porta Latina, faced in travertine, more or less retains its original appearance but the size of the gate was reduced when it was restored in the 5th century, and the tower on the left is medieval. (Take the Via di Porta San Sebastiano.)

PORTA SAN SEBASTIANO. Just after the ARCH OF DRUSUS – originally part of the aqueduct feeding the baths of Caracalla – you will come to the Porta San Sebastiano (in ancient times called the Porta Appia), which marks the beginning of the first stretch of the Appian Way outside the city walls. The most monumental of the gates in the Aurelian Wall, it was rebuilt five times. Originally the road was spanned by twin arches between two round towers. During its final reconstruction the towers were enlarged and reinforced, and the intermediate section was raised one story. Like the Porta Latina, it could be secured with double doors and a portcullis.

CLIVUS MARTIS. About 350 feet from the gate, on the right is a column marking the position of the first milestone of the Via Appia (the original milestone is in the Piazza del Campidoglio ▲ 129). A little farther on, to the left, is a TEMPLE TO MARS – hence the name Clivus Martis ("Ascent of Mars") given to this section of the Via Appia. Remains of several tombs from different ages are visible just before the railway bridge. The road then dips and crosses the Almone, the stream where in ancient times every year on March 27 the statue of the goddess Cybele ▲ 415 was ritually washed, after being carried in procession to this spot. On the right-hand side, just before the crossroads with the Via Ardeatina, an ancient hostelry conceals a large tomb generally identified as that of Titus Flavius Abascantus, Domitian's powerful freed slave, who had it built for his wife, Priscilla. Opposite this tomb, the small church known as DOMINE QUO VADIS ("Lord, whither goest thou?") indicates the spot where Jesus is said to have appeared to St Peter as he was fleeing the persecutions of Nero's reign. To the apostle's question, Jesus replied, "To Rome, to be crucified a second time," which Peter understood as an indication that he should return to Rome to suffer martyrdom.

Visitors to the church are shown a replica of the stone that was miraculously impressed with Christ's footprints (the original is in the Church of San Sebastiano ▲ 327).

THE CATACOMBS

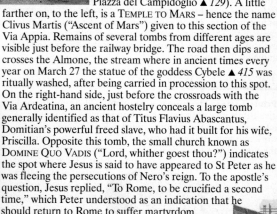

UNDERGROUND CEMETERIES. The vast labyrinth of the catacombs was formed from simple hypogeums (vaults) which were eventually linked by passages. At first these underground cemeteries were private, but later they were managed by funeral associations as the practice of burial in the Roman world gradually became more widespread among pagans, Jews and Christians. People were buried in the catacombs until the 6th century AD, but very soon these cemeteries also became places of

324

De Rossi discovered twenty-six catacombs (today sixty-seven are known). He published the results of his research in a work entitled *Roma sotteranea*, which is still used for reference.

"QUO VADIS?"
In 1951 the American film director Mervin LeRoy made a film of the novel by the Polish author Henryk Sienkiewicz (1896).

worship. Contrary to notions propagated by such novels as *Fabiola* or *Quo Vadis?*, Christians did not hide in them to flee persecution; nor did they gather there for Sunday worship. From the 3rd century the deceased were commemorated in the catacombs, though these celebrations usually took place within the walls of the cemetery rather than in the galleries. Once Christianity became an authorized religion in 312, and the State religion in 392, hordes of pilgrims crowded round the saints' tombs. Alterations were made to the catacombs: flights of steps and altars were built, tombs were decorated, and the relics of foreign saints were transferred there. This is why long after they had lost their funerary function they continued to be frequented by pilgrims. Gradually, however, the catacombs were abandoned. Then after the 8th century their existence was forgotten until they were rediscovered thanks to Antonio Bosio (1575–1629) and above all to Gian Battista De Rossi (1822–94). (Access to the Catacombs of San Callisto is from Via Appia No. 102 or No. 110.)

THE CATACOMBS OF SAN CALLISTO. These catacombs were explored and excavated by De Rossi in 1849. They are

QUO VADIS
UN FILM M.G.M.
DISTRIBUÉ PAR CINEMA INTERNATIONAL CORPORATION

Chi-Rho monogram (the first two letters of Christ's name in Greek). A symbolic praying figure (far right).

The good shepherd, one of the numerous Christian symbols that can be seen on the walls of the catacombs.

the largest of the Christian burial complexes and were widely used from the 3rd century; at the same time it also became customary for the popes to be buried there. Calixtus, to whom they owe their name, administered these catacombs while he was a deacon and enlarged them after he became Pope in 217. In places they were developed on four levels, and their galleries extend for more than 6 miles. Like many Christian catacombs, they are the result of the 4th-century unification of several earlier nucleuses. The oldest part, the Crypt of Lucina, beside the Via Appia, probably dates from the end of the 2nd century AD. This section is itself composed of two parts, certainly linked at the time of the burial of Pope Cornelius in 253. ZONE I, through which the catacombs are reached, was constructed later. Visitors first enter a *cella trichora* (room with three apses), which originally housed the bodies of Pope Zephyrinus (who died in 217) and the martyr Tarsicius. This *cella* became an underground basilica in honor of Sixtus II, who was martyred with four deacons in the cemetery during Valerian's persecutions in 258. Steps then lead to a vestibule with walls covered in graffiti, which opens on to the CRYPT OF THE POPES, discovered in 1854, where four niches for the sarcophagi may be seen and six *loculi* ("niches for bodies") on each side. It is thought that at least fourteen popes were buried in San Callisto, and it is certain from the inscriptions that five of them reposed in this crypt: namely Pontian (230–5), Anterus (235–6), Fabian (236–50), Lucius I (253–4) and Eutychian (275–83). De Rossi believed that the crypt known as the CRYPT OF ST CECILIA contained her tomb, but this opinion is now rejected. The learned archeologist thought he recognized the figures of Cecilia, Pope Urban and Christ in the Byzantine frescoes, which were in fact too badly damaged to allow identification. The niche which according to this tradition was destined to contain St Cecilia's sarcophagus now contains a copy of her effigy by Stefano Maderno (the original is in the Church of Santa Cecilia in Trastevere ▲ 353). Other sections of the catacombs that can be visited include the five *cubicula* ("funeral chambers") known as the Crypt of the Sacraments, which are adorned with 3rd-century frescoes, and the Crypt of Pope Eusebius, who died in 310.

The Catacombs of San Callisto.

IΧΘΥC

The fish, a symbol of Christ.

The catechumen struggling with the serpent.

THE BASILICA AND CATACOMBS OF SAN SEBASTIANO

This complex is located just after the crossroads between the Via Appia and the Via delle Sette Chiese. The latter acquired its name from the custom revived in the 16th century of making a pilgrimage to the seven most important churches of Rome ▲ 381, including San Sebastiano.

THE BASILICA. This basilica-cemetery built in the time of

Constantine was originally dedicated to the apostles Peter and Paul. Its shape resembled that of a circus, with three naves separated by masonry pillars surmounted by brick arches. In the 17th century Cardinal Scipio Borghese had it rebuilt, and the edifice was reduced to a single nave. Above the tomb of St Sebastian, whose veneration had overshadowed that of the two apostles after the 9th century, a new chapel was built (the first on the left) in which a statue of the martyr was placed, based on a model by Bernini. The altar now in the Chapel of Relics (the first on the right) once stood in the center of the basilica, above the Triclia (see below) where the apostles were venerated. It also contains some venerable relics, including the famous stone supposed to bear the impression of Christ's footprints ▲ 324. From the apse, where the ambulatory has been transformed into a museum, one reaches the PLATONIA, a richly decorated tomb at the back of the basilica that contains the relics of St Quirinus, Bishop of Pannonia.

THE CATACOMBS. Throughout the period of late antiquity this cemetery was simply referred to by the expression *ad catacumbas*, from the Greek *kata kymbas* ("near the caves", which may possibly have referred to the neighboring stone quarries). Subsequently the name was used for all necropolises of this type. Here the sepulchers of pagans and Christians lie side by side, as they do in almost all the catacombs. The first of the four levels of galleries has been virtually destroyed. The CRYPT OF SAN SEBASTIANO, the first site visited, no longer contains the martyr's remains, as they were removed in the 9th century. Next to be seen are the three pagan hypogeums, which were columbariums ▲ 319 before becoming burial places. Magnificently preserved, they have stucco decorations and frescoes combining pagan motifs (such as the Gorgon's head) with Christian ones (the miracle of the demoniac of Gerasa), some of them as early as the 1st or 2nd century AD. The inscription reveals that Marcus Claudius Hermes was the owner of the tomb on

The frescoes in the Catacombs of Priscilla (on the Via Salaria) and Commodilla (on the Via Ostiense).

The first and last letters of the word "martyr".

The Catacombs of San Sebastiano.

SANT'URBANO ALLA CAFFARELLA
Several of the buildings of the Triopius of Herodes Atticus have survived destruction. These include a temple which in the 9th century became the Church of Sant'Urbano alla Caffarella (below); and the Nymphaeum of Egeria, a sort of water castle, richly decorated and adorned with a fountain, that has

never ceased to intrigue travelers and artists.

The Circus of Maxentius.

the right. One then passes into the MEMORIA APOSTOLORUM, an irregular room remarkable for its red-painted walls covered with about a hundred graffiti, dating from the 3rd and 4th centuries, in honor of the apostles Peter and Paul. This room, known as the Triclia, was formerly an open space where funeral banquets were celebrated in honor of the apostles. No convincing archeological argument has yet made it possible to choose between two interpretations that have puzzled generations of scholars. Were the bodies of the two apostles buried *ad catacumbas* just after their martyrdom, then transferred from the catacombs at a much later date? Or were they merely temporarily buried here at the time of Valerian's persecution in 258? Either way, the Constantinian basilica was built around the Memoria Apostolorum, which was painstakingly preserved as a place of veneration.

THE VILLA AND CIRCUS OF MAXENTIUS

Between the second and third milestones of the Via Appia, on the left, is a complex built by the Emperor Maxentius, whose brief reign lasted from 306 to 312 AD. It included three main buildings: a palatial villa, a circus and a mausoleum.
THE CIRCUS OF MAXENTIUS. This building is the most intact part of the complex, and the two great towers at the western end attract instant attention. Some 1,700 feet long, it had a capacity of at least 10,000 spectators. A long corridor linking the Imperial palace with the circus and the mausoleum gave the Emperor direct access to his box, located above the finishing post. On the south side was a box for the magistrate who oversaw the games. The chariot teams started from twelve *carceres* (stalls) at the western end of the circus. The archway that served as the main entrance was at the center of these stalls, which were flanked by the two towers. On the east side stood another great arch (the triumphal entrance), where in 1825 fragments of a dedication to Maxentius' son Romulus were found, making it possible to identify the monument. As in other circuses, the *spina* ▲ *177–9* around which the chariots raced was surmounted by a variety of ornamental features,

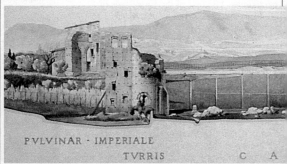

PVLVINAR · IMPERIALE
TVRRIS   C   A

including fountains and, in the middle, an obelisk. This was Domitian's obelisk, perhaps taken from the Campus Martius; in 1650 Pope Innocent X had it moved to Piazza Navona ▲ 276 to crown Bernini's Fontana dei Quattro Fiumi.

MAUSOLEUM OF ROMULUS. Maxentius' son Romulus, who died in 309, was certainly buried here, but this was probably a dynastic tomb intended for the whole family. The mausoleum itself, which stands in the middle of a grandiose quadriportico (four-sided portico) facing the Via Appia, is a circular building, about 100 feet in diameter, with a projecting pronaos (porch) similar to that of the Pantheon ▲ 264. Surrounding it are numerous monumental tombs of the 4th century. Originally there were two floors, of which only the lower one remains, partly buried and half hidden by a modern farmhouse; niches for sarcophagi were hollowed out in the wall. The upper floor has almost entirely disappeared, but it was probably devoted to the funerary cult of Maxentius' son and would have been covered by a vast dome.

THE TRIOPIUS OF HERODES ATTICUS AND VILLA OF MAXENTIUS. Herodes Atticus was a very rich Greek from Athens. A gifted public speaker, he became the tutor of the children of the Emperor Antoninus Pius (138–61) and married Annia Regilla, a Roman aristocrat who owned a villa on the Appian Way. When his young wife died suddenly, her family accused Herodes of murdering her. After his acquittal he dedicated his land to the

gods of the underworld and to the funerary cult of his wife. A temple was also built here in honor of the goddess Demeter and Antoninus Pius' wife Faustina. The whole heritage was renamed "Triopius", from the name of the Thessalonian Triopas whose cult in Cnides, in Asia, was associated with that of Demeter. Later, Maxentius' villa was built on this site; hardly anything remains of it, but the few ruins that have survived, particularly those of the great reception hall, give an idea of the sumptuousness of the villa.

AN IMAGINATIVE RECONSTRUCTION
In reconstructing the decoration of the Circus of Maxentius (above), Alfred Recoura, who was awarded the Prix de Rome in 1894, aimed to give an idea of its former splendor. Hence the abundance of marble and ornaments, with *quadrigae* surmounting the twin towers (decorated with bas-reliefs), sculptures of magistrates set in niches in the façade, and a statue of the Emperor in gilded bronze in the center. On the left is the Imperial box, which was connected to the villa by a corridor.

The Circus of Maxentius.

·TRIVMPHALIS   TRIBVNAL · IVDICVM
TA · PRIMA   PORTA · LIBITINENSIS
C   E   R   E   S   TVRRIS

At the entrance remains of tombs on the Via Appia excavated in 1836 are set into the walls.

EASTERN INFLUENCES
The form of the Tomb of Cecilia Metella is similar to that of the Mausoleum of Augustus ▲ *309* and other tombs from the same period found in Italy. These buildings provide evidence of the evolution of funerary architecture both in Rome and elsewhere in Italy, and indicate the progressive diffusion of new ideological models influenced by Asian and Hellenistic traditions.

THE TOMB OF CECILIA METELLA ● 72

After the Maxentius complex, the Via Appia rises steeply toward a massive tomb (on the left). This is the best known and best preserved of the mausoleums beside the road. Its dedication states that it was the tomb of Cecilia Metella, the daughter of Quintus Metellus Creticus (consul in 69 BC) and wife of Crassus (probably the son of the fabulously wealthy contemporary of Caesar and Pompey). The building consists of a circular tower, about 95 feet in diameter and 36 feet high, set on a square cement base that has been stripped of its facing. It leans against the ruins of a fortress built in the 12th century by the Caetani, who used it as a dungeon. The marble frieze is decorated with a relief featuring garlands of flowers, weapons and *bucranes* (ox skulls); because of the *bucranes* the locality became known as Capo di Bove. Inside the castle (to the right of the entrance) there is a display of fragments of inscriptions and decorations from tombs on the Via Appia. From here a narrow corridor leads to the funeral chamber, the upper part of which consisted of an enormous cone faced with bricks.

ROMANTIC RUINS. Opposite the mausoleum, on the other side of the road, stands the small church of SAN NICOLA DA BARI built by the Caetani family. This section of the Appian Way has been considerably damaged, and the villas and numerous tombs with which it was lined are now barely identifiable ruins. But if you are traveling by car, go as far as the fifth milestone; near it (on the right) are three tumulus-shaped tombs. In the 19th century it was believed that these were the TOMBS OF THE HORATII AND THE CURIATII who died in the famous duel which ended the war between Rome and Alba Longa. A little further on (on the left) you will come to the picturesque ruins of the VILLA DEI QUINTILII (2nd century AD), part of a huge estate that belonged to one of the great aristocratic families of ancient Rome. The four Quintilii brothers came to an untimely end: under the pretext that they were plotting against him, the Emperor Commodus (180–92) had them assassinated and confiscated their villa, which he wanted for himself.

FROM THE BATHS OF DIOCLETIAN TO SAN PIETRO IN VINCOLI

▲ From the baths of Diocletian to San Pietro in Vincoli

The northern part of Rome underwent a fresh bout of town planning activity in the mid 15th century and again at the time of Sixtus V (1585–90) who concentrated on the reorganization and repopulation of the upper part of the town. Here he

moved the cattle market that had traditionally been held on the grounds of the Abbey of Farfà and installed workshops for silk production in his own villa (the Villa Peretti, now vanished), planning to divert water there from the Aniene River. A network of streets was woven around Santa Maria Maggiore, the starting point for pilgrimages to the basilicas outside the walls ▲ 380 and to San Giovanni in Laterano ▲ 198. The district retained its new features until the 1850's, when Rome's main station was built. **FUNCTIONAL TOWN PLANNING.** In modernizing Rome, Pius IX (1846–78) respected the grand design of Sixtus V's plans. The first of the new arterial roads was Via Nazionale, built in 1867 in accordance with the directions of Msgr de Merode, who had acquired part of the area included in the project. After 1870 and the arrival of the Piedmontese ● 33, who wanted to make "modern Rome" the capital of a united Italy, the government had to decide on the location of the future ministries, and the Ministry of Finance was built along Via XX Settembre. The 1871 general urban plan also provided for the construction of dwellings in the Esquiline, Castro Pretorio and Viminale areas. This was an incentive for particularly aggressive property speculation around Piazza Vittorio Emanuele, Santa Maria Maggiore and Porta San Lorenzo. The whole district between the station and the Piazza Vittorio

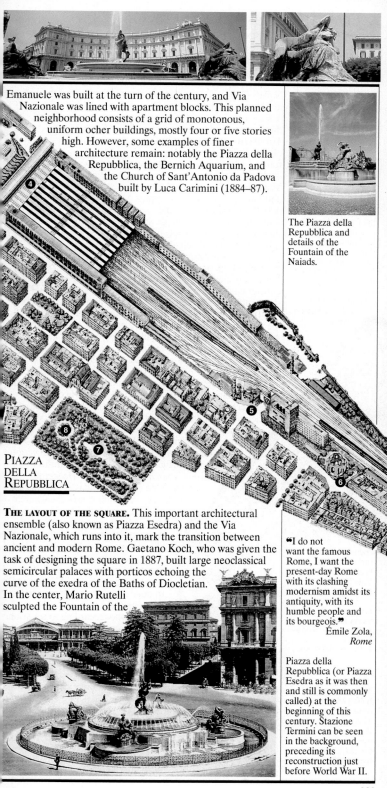

Emanuele was built at the turn of the century, and Via Nazionale was lined with apartment blocks. This planned neighborhood consists of a grid of monotonous, uniform ocher buildings, mostly four or five stories high. However, some examples of finer architecture remain: notably the Piazza della Repubblica, the Bernich Aquarium, and the Church of Sant'Antonio da Padova built by Luca Carimini (1884–87).

The Piazza della Repubblica and details of the Fountain of the Naiads.

PIAZZA DELLA REPUBBLICA

THE LAYOUT OF THE SQUARE. This important architectural ensemble (also known as Piazza Esedra) and the Via Nazionale, which runs into it, mark the transition between ancient and modern Rome. Gaetano Koch, who was given the task of designing the square in 1887, built large neoclassical semicircular palaces with porticos echoing the curve of the exedra of the Baths of Diocletian. In the center, Mario Rutelli sculpted the Fountain of the

❝I do not want the famous Rome, I want the present-day Rome with its clashing modernism amidst its antiquity, with its humble people and its bourgeois.❞
Émile Zola, *Rome*

Piazza della Repubblica (or Piazza Esedra as it was then and still is commonly called) at the beginning of this century. Stazione Termini can be seen in the background, preceding its reconstruction just before World War II.

ST BRUNO
(c. 1030–1101)
This statue of the
saint who founded
the Carthusian order
is in the passage
leading to the
transept of the
Church of Santa
Maria degli Angeli. It
is the work of the
sculptor Jean-
Antoine Houdon
(1741–1828), who
was a

"pensionnaire"
(art scholar) at the
French Academy's
Villa Medici ▲ *315*,
from 1764 to 1768.

**1. CHURCH OF
SANTA BIBIANA
2. TEMPLE OF MINERVA
MEDICA
3. PORTA MAGGIORE**

**THE SUNDIAL OF
SANTA MARIA DEGLI
ANGELI**
This sundial in the
floor of the transept
was used to regulate
the clocks of Rome
from 1702 to 1846.

Naiads (1901), which created a furor, the nudity of the
lovely bathers outraging local sensibilities. Finally
passions cooled, and the central group alone was altered:
the marine deity Glaucus now grasps a dolphin.

THE BATHS OF DIOCLETIAN
(Terme di Diocleziano). On his
return from Africa in the autumn
of 298 AD, the Emperor
Maximian undertook the
building of a sumptuous complex
of baths, designed to enable
some three thousand people at a
time to engage in a variety of
sports and cultural activities. The
baths were only completed after
the abdication, on May 1, 305, of
Maximian and his co-emperor
Diocletian. Surrounded by a wall,
the complex covered an area measuring about 1,250 x 1,200
feet (the central building alone measured approximately 800
feet x 600 feet). It was constructed according to the usual plan
● *68*, ▲ *319*: a large central hall, a *caldarium-tepidarium-
natatio* complex along the minor axis, and gymnasiums on
either side of the major axis. These central structures are the
best preserved, but important vestiges of the outer walls are
still standing; some sections of the baths now form part of the
National Roman Museum. The façade of the Facoltà di
Magistero stands on the site of the northwestern façade of
the ancient buildings. On the west corner, toward Via
Cernaia, the great octagonal hall (transformed in 1928
into a planetarium and then a cinema) has since 1991
housed a display of ancient sculptures from various
baths in the city, including such magnificent
bronzes as *The Boxer* and *The Hellenistic
Prince*. One of the rotundas at the corners
of the external walls is now the Church
of San Bernardo alle Terme ▲ *295*.

**SANTA MARIA DEGLI ANGELI E DEI
MARTIRI.** Responding to the vow of
a Sicilian priest who had a vision of a
cloud of angels flying round the
Baths of Diocletian, in 1561 Pope
Pius IV commissioned Michelangelo
to build a church here dedicated to
the angels and to the Christian
martyrs who, according to tradition,
had been forced to build the baths.

One of the well-preserved apses of the *caldarium* forms the
church's entrance (as seen in the picture at the foot of the
facing page). Through it one enters a small circular room with
two great square exedras, flanked by the tombs of the painters

Salvator Rosa (1615–73) and Carlo Maratta (1625–1713); this is the former *tepidarium.* One finally reaches the main body of the church, which occupies what was the central hall of the baths. Despite the modifications introduced by Michelangelo and then by Vanvitelli in 1749, the church retains the vast proportions of the ancient building. Its vaults, as well as the eight immense columns of red granite, also belong to the original building. Gigantic paintings – many of which come from St Peter's ▲ *212*, where they were replaced with mosaics – decorate the walls of the transept and the choir. The most remarkable of these are the *Fall of Simon the Magician* by Pompeo Batoni (18th century), the *Martyrdom of St Sebastian* by Domenichino, and the *Baptism of Jesus* by Carlo Maratta. (Turn left on leaving the church. The entrance of the National Roman Museum is in Piazza dei Cinquecento.)

NATIONAL ROMAN MUSEUM (Museo delle Terme). Inaugurated at the end of the last century, this museum ▲ *336* is spread over part of the baths and the Carthusian convent that was built at the same time as Santa Maria degli Angeli. (From the museum, take the Via Gaeta.)

CASTRO PRETORIO (Praetorian barracks). Between 21 and 23 AD the Emperor Tiberius built a huge barracks complex on the northwest boundary of the town for the Praetorian cohorts (the permanent guard for the emperor, originally created by Augustus), who until that time had been billeted in different parts of Rome. The Praetorian guard used the area between the barracks and the Servian Wall for training. As well as containing the guards' dwellings, the barracks included various functional buildings: the commander's headquarters, the treasury, the armory, a hospital and granaries (*horrea*), etc. The perfectly preserved wall of the building is visible to the northeast of Stazione Termini, between Viale Castro Pretorio and Viale del Policlinico. The main national library, the Biblioteca Vittorio Emanuele II, built between 1965 and 1975, now occupies part of the site. (Walk back toward the station, taking the Via San Martino della Battaglia and Via Solferino.)

As the inscription at the entrance of the National Roman Museum indicates, it was necessary to demolish numerous buildings in order to make room for the Baths of Diocletian. It took an army of workmen eight years to build the gigantic baths complex – including, according to medieval tradition, 40,000 Christians.

NATIONAL ROMAN MUSEUM
It is pleasant to walk in the Great Cloister and the old garden of the Baths, which include archeological remains, sarcophagi and ancient inscriptions.

This museum (also known as Museo delle Terme) was established in 1889 in the Carthusian convent to house the archeological finds of the period particularly the stuccos and paintings discovered in the gardens of the Farnesina. It was enriched by numerous acquisitions and became one of the most important museums in the world as regards the art of antiquity. Today some of its treasures, including the famous collection gathered in the 17th century by Cardinal Ludovisi, are housed in the Palazzo Altemps and in the former Collegio Massimo (in Piazza dei Cinquecento).

"THE MAIDEN OF ANZIO"

This young girl is standing, with her head slightly bowed, holding a tray. Her tunic, which is slipping off one shoulder, is gathered at the waist. The vivacity, the freshness and the grace expressed in the motion of the body and the position of her head, freed from classical conventions, date this as a 3rd century BC work.

THE PORTONACCIO SARCOPHAGUS

In the center a Roman general, whose expression is clearly depicted, spurs his horse against the enemy; all around him Roman soldiers with helmets and breastplates are triumphing over barbarians, shown in pathetic attitudes. This theme of the fray, rendered here with splendid relief work, was frequently used in the iconographic repertoire of the Roman sarcophagus workshops in the 2nd century AD.

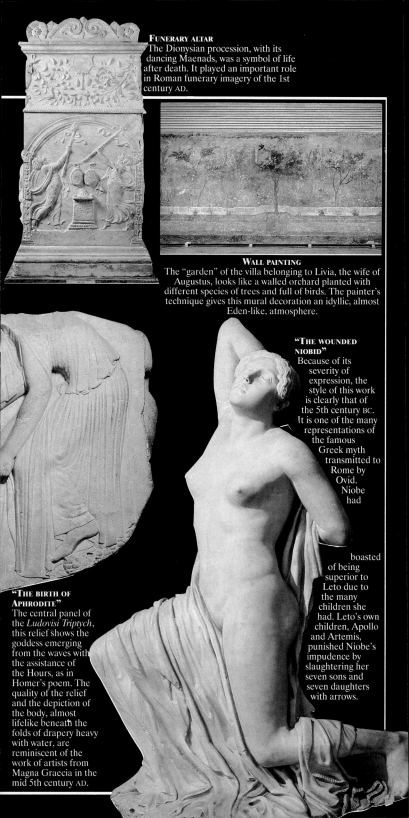

FUNERARY ALTAR
The Dionysian procession, with its dancing Maenads, was a symbol of life after death. It played an important role in Roman funerary imagery of the 1st century AD.

WALL PAINTING
The "garden" of the villa belonging to Livia, the wife of Augustus, looks like a walled orchard planted with different species of trees and full of birds. The painter's technique gives this mural decoration an idyllic, almost Eden-like, atmosphere.

"THE WOUNDED NIOBID"
Because of its severity of expression, the style of this work is clearly that of the 5th century BC. It is one of the many representations of the famous Greek myth transmitted to Rome by Ovid. Niobe had boasted of being superior to Leto due to the many children she had. Leto's own children, Apollo and Artemis, punished Niobe's impudence by slaughtering her seven sons and seven daughters with arrows.

"THE BIRTH OF APHRODITE"
The central panel of the *Ludovisi Triptych*, this relief shows the goddess emerging from the waves with the assistance of the Hours, as in Homer's poem. The quality of the relief and the depiction of the body, almost lifelike beneath the folds of drapery heavy with water, are reminiscent of the work of artists from Magna Graecia in the mid 5th century AD.

Stazione Termini

Piazza dei Cinquecento. This square served in the 19th century as a parade ground for the troops stationed in the Praetorian barracks. At the beginning of the Via delle Terme stands an obelisk (far left) dedicated to the 548 Italian soldiers killed in an ambush in 1887 during the attempted conquest of Eritrea.

The history of the station. Pius IX developed the railways in the Pontifical States. About 1857 the idea was conceived of bringing together the arrivals and departures, which until then had been divided. The site for the new station was chosen in 1860, but not until 1867 was the scheme for it, proposed by the architect Salvatore Bianchi, accepted: a building flanked by two wings, with alternating Tuscan, Ionic and Corinthian columns concealing a metal structure. The right wing was for arrivals, the left for departures. Following the creation of the Ferrovie dello Stato (State Railways), from 1905 proposals were put forward for the general restructuring of Stazione Termini. The Universal Exhibition of 1942 ▲ *386* contributed a new impetus, and in 1938 the old station was partially replaced with buildings designed by Angiolo Mazzoni del Grande. In 1967 the refurbishment was completed with the impressive structure housing the main hall, ticket offices and restaurant. Thus the present station combines the architecture of the Fascist period and that of the 1960's. (Follow the via Giovanni Giolitti, then take Via Cattaneo as far as Piazza Fanti.)

The Bernich Aquarium (below right).

Rome's station
The name Stazione Termini was chosen for the station because of the baths (*terme*) nearby.

VIA GIOVANNI GIOLITTI

The station in 1866.

THE BERNICH AQUARIUM. Between the station and Piazza Vittorio Emanuele II, one can now visit a very pretty but long neglected building put up between 1885 and 1887. Designed as the municipal aquarium, it combines travertine marble and cast iron in an extremely original setting entirely focused on the marine environment. It is now used for a variety of cultural activities, including exhibitions and concerts. (Follow Via Rattazi in order to return to Via Giovanni Giolitti.)

SANTA BIBIANA. Now practically nestling against the railway track, this small 5th-century basilica was originally located in the heart of the country. In 1624 the bodies of St Bibiana, her parents and her sister were exhumed from under the main altar; consequently Urban VIII decided to rebuild the church. Bernini designed the façade as well as the main altar, which he crowned with his first great religious sculpture. The saint's left hand holds carefully worked folds of drapery which give life and movement to the statue. Above the colonnade in the nave, frescoes representing Bibiana's life were painted by Agostino Ciampelli (on the right) and Pietro da Cortona (on the left). This was Cortona's first major work, and henceforth Urban VIII involved these two painters in all the important artistic enterprises of his pontificate.

TEMPLE OF MINERVA MEDICA. This large decagonal hall, which once had a circular dome, was originally part of the Gardens of Licinius. It dates from the 4th century AD and was named after a statue of Minerva found close by, now preserved in the Vatican.

TEMPLE OF MINERVA MEDICA
The bold architecture of the temple inspired many Renaissance buildings. Today, bordered by railway tracks and ugly

apartment blocks, it has lost much of the charm that Stendhal found in it.

PORTA MAGGIORE

CLAUDIUS' AQUEDUCT. The Porta Maggiore, a magnificent archway in travertine marble, was formed from arches belonging to two aqueducts, the Aqua Claudia and the Anio Novus, begun by Caligula in 38 AD and completed by Claudius fourteen years later. It only became a true gateway when it was included in the Aurelian Wall ▲ *323*. In the 5th century Honorius added an external bastion, the demolition of which in 1838 led to the discovery of the tomb of Eurysaces. On the upper part of the structure one can read the inscriptions, repeated on both sides, of Claudius and also of Vespasian and Titus, who restored the arch in 71 and 81 AD respectively.

THE TOMB OF EURYSACES. This tomb was built around 30 BC

PORTA MAGGIORE
The tall attic (upper section) with three superimposed bands corresponds to the conduits of the two aqueducts. The monument was built using the so-called "unfinished" technique typical of the time of Claudius, which merely hinted at many of the architectural elements.

for Marcus Vergilius Eurysaces, a baker who supplied bread to the army, and his wife Atistia, as the inscriptions recall. Its location between the Via Labicana and the Via Prenestina determined its curious trapezoidal design. The cylindrical architectural elements are evocative of the receptacles in which dough was kneaded, and the relief shows the various phases of breadmaking (above). All the decorative motifs of the tomb are designed to exalt the profession of this freed slave who lined his pockets during the civil wars.

THE UNDERGROUND BASILICA OF PORTA MAGGIORE. This intriguing building (closed to the public) was discovered by chance in April 1917. Its function is not known for certain: it may have been a tomb, a funeral basilica, a nymphaeum, or a neo-Pythagorean temple. It comprises a large hall (about 40 x 30 feet), preceded by a square vestibule divided into three naves; the central one ends in an apse. All the walls are covered with stucco decorations, but the vault and the apse are the most interesting elements; the former consists of three sections featuring mythological and realistic scenes, masks and other decorative elements that are arranged in an evident attempt at symmetry. In the apse one can see Sappho who, pushed by a cupid, is flinging herself into the sea from the cliff of Leucas; under the gaze of Apollo, she is welcomed by a triton and Leucothea, who is raising her veil. The decoration is rich in mysterious metaphysical and symbolical meanings which are not yet fully understood. (Take the Via di Porta Maggiore, then Via Principe Eugenio.)

The tomb of Eurysaces.

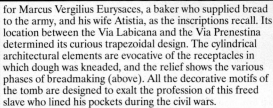

The stucco decorations of the vault of the underground basilica.

PIAZZA VITTORIO EMANUELE II

AN ANIMATED CENTER. In building the Esquiline neighborhood, the first large urban project in Italy's new capital ● *33*, the vast square dedicated to King Victor Emmanuel II formed the focal point for the streets leading from San Giovanni in Laterano, Santa Croce in Gerusalemme and Porta Maggiore. Its porticos, completed in 1882 and 1887, reflect the influence of Piedmontese architecture, as Turin

THE ARCH OF GALLIENUS
(Take Via Merulana, then Via San Vito.) Completely rebuilt by Augustus, this is one of the gateways in the oldest of the city walls; it was originally called the Porta Esquilina. The inscription of Marcus Aurelius Victor to the Emperor Gallienus and his wife Salonina, engraved on the cornice bordering the attic, is a later addition.

Piazza Vittorio Emanuele II in the last century.

was the first capital of the new kingdom; and at its center is one of Rome's most picturesque markets. In the gardens there is a fountain by Mario Rutelli, a mass of tritons, dolphins and octopuses originally designed to adorn the Fountain of the Naiads in Piazza della Repubblica ▲ *334*. This marine cluster has earned the fountain the nickname of *fritto misto* ("fish fry")!

THE TROPHIES OF MARIUS. The monumental brick structure in the northwest corner of the gardens was, in Renaissance times, named "I Trofei di Mario" due to the two 1st-century marble reliefs that adorned it before they were moved to the balustrade of the Capitol ▲ *334*. It is in fact the remains of a massive fountain dating from the time of Alexander Severus (3rd century AD), which crowned the water tower of the Aqua Julia. Nearby stands the intriguing Porta Magica, inscribed with an alchemist's formula for making gold. (Turn left into Via Leopardi.)

THE AUDITORIUM OF MAECENAS. This was certainly part of the house of Maecenas, Augustus' famous minister who was a patron of many writers and poets. An apsidal hall, partly underground and completely structured in *opus reticulatum*, it may have been designed for public readings of literary works by authors such as Horace or Virgil, who both lived in the neighborhood. There are six deep rectangular niches on either side of the hall, with sumptuous bucolic decorations. The exedra has seven narrow steps, above which there are five niches decorated with garden scenes; under them runs a frieze with a black background showing hunting scenes, which are a continuation of the decorations in the main part of the hall. (Take Via Merulana.)

TROPHIES OF MARIUS There is no doubt that the fountain resembled the proposed restoration shown on the left; a monumental façade with a central niche flanked by two open arches. These held the two trophies portraying the weapons of the "barbarians" (the Chatti and the Dacians) conquered by Domitian in 89 AD.

TROPHEE·VULGAIREMENT·APPELE·DE·MARIVS·TROVVE·SVR·LES·RVINES·DV·CHATEAV·DE·L'EAV·IVLES

PIAZZA DELL'ESQUILINO AND PIAZZA SANTA MARIA MAGGIORE
The Basilica of Santa Maria Maggiore is framed by two squares on which the popes left their mark. To match the obelisk in the Piazza dell'Esquilino, Paul V had the fluted marble column from the Basilica of Maxentius ▲ 145 erected in the Piazza Santa Maria Maggiore. Carlo Maderno set it on a pedestal and crowned it with a statue of the Virgin.

BASILICA OF SANTA MARIA MAGGIORE ★

CHURCH OF MANY NAMES. The Virgin Mary herself is supposed to have shown Pope Liberius (352–66) where this church was to be built by causing snow to fall on the top of the Esquiline on August 5, 356. The church is therefore also known as the Liberian Basilica, but it was built by St Sixtus III (432–40) immediately after the maternity of Mary had been defined at the Council of Ephesus (431). Dedicated to the Virgin Mary, the fourth patriarchal basilica was subsequently given the name of Santa Maria ad Praesepe ("St Mary of the Crib") because of a shrine dedicated to the holy crib situated under the altar of the Sixtus V chapel.

THE FAÇADE. On the Piazza di Santa Maria Maggiore the basilica has a baroque façade enhanced by a loggia, designed by Ferdinando Fuga for Pope Benedict XIV in the mid 18th century. Returning from Avignon in 1377, Gregory XI had the CAMPANILE (bell tower) built; approximately 245 feet high, it is still the tallest in Rome. Under the 12th-century PORTICO, restored by Gregory XIII for the Holy Year of 1575, there is a bronze statue of Philip IV of Spain, the benefactor of the basilica. To the left of the portico a flight of stairs leads to the loggia, where one can admire the fine mosaics with which Filippo Rusuti adorned the original façade at the end of the 13th century. From here the Pope used to bestow his benediction "Urbi et Orbi" upon the crowds.

PAPAL MODIFICATIONS. Despite the numerous alterations introduced by various popes over the centuries, the general appearance of the basilica's interior is still quite similar to what it originally was. Forty Ionic columns, of which 36 are marble monoliths, divide the inner space into three naves of majestic proportions. In the 9th century Pascal I undertook the restoration of the choir and Benedict III rehabilitated the baptistery. The beautiful paving that Eugene III had made by the Cosmati (1145–53) was, however, radically rearranged when Ferdinando Fuga was commissioned to restore the basilica in the 18th century. But the most important modifications were carried out under Nicholas IV (1288–92), who had a transept and a new apse designed. Rodrigo Borgia, the future Pope Alexander VI (1492–1503), commissioned Giuliano da Sangallo to make the splendid coffered ceiling with the Borgia arms. The fact that its ornamental roses are some 3 feet in diameter gives an idea of the building's dimensions. This ceiling is said to have been gilded with the first gold brought from the New World.

THE MOSAICS ★. Thirty-six panels of 5th-century mosaics along the central nave above the architrave illustrate scenes from the Old Testament; they are among the earliest Christian mosaics in Rome. Those on the chancel arch, which date from the same period and display Byzantine influence, show scenes of the birth and childhood of Jesus above representations of the towns of Jerusalem and Bethlehem (below). They proclaim the glory of the Virgin, who is dressed as an Oriental empress. The mosaics in the apse, which complete the series in the nave in a blaze of color, are by Jacopo Torriti (1295), a pupil of Cavallini. They consist in part of 5th-century elements (the foliage and the Jordan, for example) and consecrate the triumph of Mary: between the windows episodes of her life unfold, and in the arched vault above the apse is Torriti's masterpiece *The Coronation of the Virgin* (above).

THE CHAPELS. Two domed chapels stand on either side of the confessio. On the right is the richly ornamented SISTINE CHAPEL, which Sixtus V commissioned Domenico Fontana to build in 1586. It was adorned with marbles from the Septizodium ▲ 150 and decorated with frescoes. Fontana also designed the monumental tombs of Sixtus V and Pius V, each decorated with five bas-reliefs. When Paul V asked Flaminio Ponzio to build the PAULINE CHAPEL to the same design, Ponzio also used the form of the Greek cross and for

"THE CORONATION OF THE VIRGIN"
In Torriti's masterpiece, Christ and the Virgin are seated on a precious throne; the Son is crowning his Mother. To the right, in the midst of a procession of angels and saints are St Francis and St Anthony, the Franciscan saints, as well as the Order's former general, Pope Nicholas IV, kneeling beside Cardinal Jacopo Colonna. In the episode of the *Dormition*, the artist and his assistant are shown kneeling at the feet of Our Lady.

THE PAULINE CHAPEL
Between 1611 and 1615 most painters in Rome worked on the decorations of this chapel. One finds the older generation – Cipoli (*The Virgin Mary and the Apostles*, in the dome) and Cavaliere d'Arpino (*Prophets and Sibyls*, in the pendentives of the dome and *Apparition of the Virgin and St John*, above the altar) – as well as younger artists such as Lanfranco and Guido Reni, who painted the figures of saints above the tombs.

FROM THE BATHS OF DIOCLETIAN TO SAN PIETRO

THE APSE OF SANTA PUDENZIANA ★
The mosaic in the apse portrays Christ teaching the apostles in a circle around him. In the foreground are Peter and Paul; behind them, holding up crowns, are two women personifying the Church of the Circumcision and the Church of the Gentiles. A portico closes off the scene, beyond which the roofs of a town, no doubt Jerusalem, are visible. In the sky, on each side of a cross encrusted with precious stones, are the four evangelists in their symbolic forms of the eagle, the bull,

the tombs of Paul V and Clement VIII imitated Fontana's arrangement.

PIAZZA DELL'ESQUILINO. Sixtus V transformed this square and re-erected there one of the obelisks that had stood outside the entrance to the Mausoleum of Augustus ▲ 309. When the twin cupolas of the chapels of Santa Maria Maggiore were completed, it became apparent that they needed to be integrated with the basilica as a whole. Eventually Clement X (1670–76) entrusted the building of the apsidal end to Carlo Rainaldi, and the basilica now appears in its full glory at the top of his magnificent tiers of steps leading from the Piazza dell'Esquilino. (Turn left into Via Urbana.)

SANTA PUDENZIANA AND SANTA PRASSEDE

A HOLY FAMILY. According to tradition, St Peter was given hospitality by a senator named Pudens who had two daughters, Pudentiana and Praxedes, and two sons, Novatus and Timothy. The latter was probably St Paul's companion. After the death of her parents and husband, Pudentiana is said to have turned her house in Vicus Patricius (now the Via Urbana) into a church. A few years later, after the death of Pudentiana and Praxedes, Pope Pius I (1402–55) is reputed to have built two churches, one in Vicus Patricius dedicated to St Pudentiana and the other dedicated to St Praxedes.

SANTA PUDENZIANA. Excavations below the church have revealed a Roman house over which baths were built in the 2nd century. Although the church itself dates back to the 4th century, a variety of modifications radically altered the

the lion and the angel.

Santa Pudenziana: the bell tower, the doorway, and a detail of the façade.

appearance of this paleo-Christian building. The bell tower was added at the end of the 12th century, and the lovely doorway in the 16th century (using much older materials); then in 1589 Francesco da Volterra was entrusted with a major refurbishment of the church and the building of an elliptical dome. Santa Pudenziana is best known for the mosaic in the apse (although it suffered some damage during the restoration work of the 16th and early 17th centuries); dating from the end of the 4th or beginning of the 5th century, it is one of the earliest Christian mosaics in Rome. The CAETANI CHAPEL in the left nave – perhaps the first place of worship in Pudens' home – is one of the richest in Rome, embellished with marble and stucco decorations. (Return to Piazza Santa Maria Maggiore and Via di Santa Prassede.)

SANTA PRASSEDE
Mosaic of the
Heavenly City on the
chancel arch (above).

The mosaics in the
apse (left).

SANTA PRASSEDE
Mosaic of the
Heavenly City on the
chancel arch (above).

The mosaics in the
apse (left).

THE CHAPEL OF ST ZENO
The door is flanked
by two columns – the
one of granite, the
other of black
porphyry – and
surmounted by
mosaics showing the
Virgin and Child
between St Praxedes
and St Pudentiana.
On the vault of the
chapel, four angels
are bearing the
Savior's image. The
walls are decorated
with figures of saints
in the heavenly
paradise (Praxedes,
Pudentiana and
Agnes are on the left;
Andrew, James and
John on the right).

SANTA PRASSEDE ★. There is no archeological evidence of a
church here before 489, and the earliest restorations date
from the pontificate of Pope Hadrian I (772–95). The present
building dates from the time of St Pascal I (817–24), who
rebuilt the church completely, changing its orientation and
adding a monastery. The splendor of its Carolingian mosaics
have earned it renown, especially those in the choir and in the
Chapel of St Zeno. The mosaics in the apse, similar to those
in the Church of Santi Cosma e Damiano ▲ *168*, show the
Savior surrounded by six people: to the right, St Peter, St
Pudentiana and St Zeno, or perhaps St Cyriaca; to the
left, St Paul, St Praxedes and Pope Pascal I
holding a model of the church. Two palm
trees (the two Testaments) frame the
composition; a phoenix, the symbol of
the Resurrection, perches on the one
on the left. Above, twelve sheep
representing the Apostles converge
toward the mystical Lamb. On the
chancel arch, the elect proceed
toward the heavenly Jerusalem,
where Christ is flanked by two
angels. Part of the mosaic had to
be sacrificed in order to sink
niches into the piers of the arch:
St Charles Borromeo intended
them to house the martyrs' relics.
The CHAPEL OF ST ZENO ★ opens
off the right-hand nave. It was
built by Pascal I in honor of his
mother Theodora, who was buried
there. The chapel, in the form of a
square, is entirely covered with
mosaics; a matching chapel
dedicated to St John the Baptist
was planned for the opposite

▲ FROM THE BATHS OF DIOCLETIAN TO SAN PIETRO IN VINCOLI

nave. (Take Via di San Martino ai Monti.)

BASILICA OF SAN MARTINO AI MONTI. Pope Silvester I (314–35) had established an oratory in the house of a priest called Equitius, and a later pope, St Symmachus (498–514), built a basilica there dedicated to St Martin of Tours. From 1635 to 1663 it was radically transformed by Pietro da Cortona. Gaspard Dughet, Poussin's brother-in-law, subsequently painted the lateral naves with frescoes in which the countryside of the Roman Campagna features prominently. Behind the basilica, in the Piazza di San Martino ai Monti, are two crenelated medieval towers, much restored, that belonged to the families Graziani (on the left) and Capocci; both towers were built with bricks from the Baths of Trajan ▲ *174*. (Take Via delle Sette Sale, in front of the church on the right.)

PIAZZA SAN PIETRO IN VINCOLI.
This watercolor by Roesler shows the medieval tower of the Margini, which was converted into a bell tower for the national church of the Calabrians, San Francesco di Paola.

A "TRAGEDY"
The construction of the tomb of Julius II took nearly forty years; Michelangelo described it as a "tragedy".

The Salita Borgia, which leads to the Basilica of San Pietro in Vincoli, is lined with medieval houses.

BASILICA OF SAN PIETRO IN VINCOLI

ST PETER'S CHAINS. The basilica owes its name (St Peter in Chains) to the precious relic it guards: the links of the chains used to fetter St Peter during his imprisonment in Jerusalem and in Rome. According to tradition, when the two chains were brought together, they were miraculously united. Preserved in the confessio, they are the object of veneration of pilgrims.

ADDITIONS OVER THE CENTURIES. The original basilica, dedicated to the Apostles and built over a 3rd-century house, first saw the light during the 4th century; it was rebuilt and consecrated under Sixtus III in 439. Cardinal Giuliano della Rovere, the future Julius II, completely transformed the church between 1471 and 1503, and it was further modified in the 18th century. Entered via a portico with five arches, the church is built to the plan of a basilica. The interior is divided by twenty ancient marble columns, and on the ceiling there is a beautiful fresco painted by the Genoese artist Giovanni Battista Parodi in 1706. Of particular note, among the church's numerous works of art are the paleo-Christian sarcophagus in the crypt, paintings by Guercino and Domenichino, a Byzantine mosaic showing a bearded St Sebastian, and the tomb of Nicholas of Cusa (a philosopher and the church's titular cardinal from 1448 until his death in 1464).

THE TOMB OF JULIUS II. Located at the end of the right nave, this work by Michelangelo, although very

different from its grandiose initial conception, eclipses all the other riches of the church. In 1505, intent on commissioning a splendid mausoleum, Pope Julius II summoned the sculptor from Florence. The monument, intended for St Peter's, would have included more than forty statues. Interrupted by a quarrel between the artist and the Pope, then by the decoration of the Sistine Chapel in the Vatican, the substantially reduced project was continued in 1513 after the Pope's death. It was at this moment that Michelangelo sculpted the two slaves now in the Louvre and the famous *Moses*, the only work on the tomb for which he alone was responsible. Work was again suspended in 1516, since the new pontiff, Leo X, preferred to make Michelangelo work for his family, the Medici. It was not until between 1542 and 1545 that the monument was finally completed. The master entrusted the main part of the work to his pupils, especially Raffaello da Montelupo. However, he himself was largely responsible for the two female figures next to *Moses* representing Jacob's wives, *Rachel* (on the left) and *Leah* (on the right), which evoke the Contemplative Life and the Active Life respectively. The statue of the Pope and those of the sibyl and the prophet and the Virgin and Child were successfully executed in accordance with his designs. (From Via Cavour, go up the Via dei Serpenti, which leads into Piazza Madonna dei Monti. The church there dates from 1580 and is one of the masterpieces of Giacomo della Porta.)

TOWARD THE VIA NAZIONALE

VIA PANISPERNA. This street, at right angles to the Via dei Serpenti, was created by Sixtus V (1585–90) to link Santa Maria Maggiore with the center of Rome. Situated in the ancient Suburra neighborhood, its construction resulted in the modernization of the surrounding area. In front of the Church of SAN LORENZO IN PANISPERNA – known to have existed in the 9th century and rebuilt during the 17th to 18th centuries – stands the residence of the Portuguese ambassador, the PALAZZO CIMARRA. Work on it began in 1736, and it became famous for the banquets held there. In this same street, the

AN ANCIENT DISTRICT
It is well worth taking a stroll through the Monti district, one of the few quarters (*rioni*) that has succeeded in keeping its lively character relatively unchanged. In particular, explore Via Baccina, Via dei Serpenti and Via degli Zingari, the streets trodden by the beggar pilgrim Benoît Labre (1748–83) during the last six years of his life. "A spectacle that edifies some and shocks others", wrote Cardinal de Bernis. The holy man is buried in the Madonna dei Monti church.

THE DISAPPEARANCE OF ETTORE MAJORANA
Ettore Majorana was one of the most brilliant physicians of his time. Probably tormented by the disastrous potential

of his discoveries, in 1938 he announced that he intended to commit suicide and vanished without trace. The famous author Leonardo Sciascia wrote an account of his disappearance, *La Scomparsa di Majorana*, that reads like a thriller.

347

SAN PAOLO ENTRO LE MURA
The alternating bands of red brick and travertine marble, together with the elegant bell tower, are proof of the desire to give this Episcopalian church "an Italian character".

"EST, EST, EST". In the Middle Ages a German prelate traveled through Italy preceded by a servant who had been told to sample the local wines. "Est," the servant said when the wine was good. When he arrived in Monte-fiascone, near Lake Bolsena, the white wine was so delicious that in his enthusiasm he exclaimed "Est, est, est!" The wine took its name from this anecdote, as did the popular pizzeria in the Via Genova.

scientists Enrico Fermi and Ettore Majorana from the science faculty of Rome perfected the fission of uranium in the 1930's. (Return to the Via dei Serpenti.)

VIA NAZIONALE. Begun under Pius IX, this became the main thoroughfare of Piedmontese Rome. On the left is the great neo-Renaissance palace of the BANK OF ITALY, built between 1888 and 1889 by Gaetano Koch. Opposite one can see the cast-iron and reinforced-cement structure of the former MAGAZZINI ROVATTI (now the Renault building) erected around 1900, notable for the innovative treatment of the

windows and display areas. Together with the PICCOLO ELISEO, these buildings are the most outstanding examples of Liberty (Art Nouveau) architecture in Rome. On the same side of the street, after the Umberto I Tunnel, is the vast PALAZZO DELLE ESPOSIZIONI built by Pio Piacentini between 1878 and 1882. This building excited considerable controversy at the time of its construction: its windowless façade, massive size and style, considered "not at all Italian", were all furiously criticized. Inside, large open areas separated by columns give it a neoclassical character. Recently restored, the building is intended to provide the "cultural space" that has been lacking in Rome. Along with temporary exhibitions, it has a cinematheque and, on the top floor, in pleasant surroundings, a cheap and welcoming cafeteria. On the corner of Via Napoli stands the American Episcopalian Church of SAN PAOLO ENTRO LE MURA (St Paul's within the Walls). Built in 1873, it was the first non-Catholic place of worship to be erected in Rome after the fall of the Papal State. The work of George Edmund Street, a gifted Victorian architect, is also the only example in

Italy of the English Arts and Crafts style. The mosaics in the apse and the choir, made in Murano, are by the pre-Raphaelite painter Sir Edward Burne-Jones, and the ceramics decorating the internal walls by William Morris. The HOTEL QUIRINALE, built in 1874, is linked by an underground passage to the Opera (above). Verdi stayed here for the Rome premiere of his opera Falstaff in 1893. The apartments close to the Piazza della Repubblica are the oldest in the Via Nazionale, dating from the time of the real-estate operation undertaken by Msgr de Merode. Built in a flaky, poor-quality white stone, they surprised Pius IX: when he visited the building site, he asked if the apartments were made of ricotta.

TRASTEVERE

▲ TRASTEVERE

From early times Trastevere (which means "across the Tiber") was primarily a working-class quarter. In the 2nd and 3rd centuries it was the main center for communities belonging to

🎒 Whole day

oriental religions ● *252*. The early presence of Christians in this area led to the foundation of three titular churches in the 4th century: Santa Maria in Trastevere, San Crisogono and Santa Cecilia. After the period of decline following the great invasions and repeated sacking of the city ● *30*, the population was concentrated around these buildings.

EXPANSION. From the 10th and 11th centuries, like the rest of the city, the neighborhood experienced rapid expansion, marked by the development of the new river port known as Ripagrande or the Ripa Romea. Then in the middle of the 13th century Trastevere was integrated into the administrative system of the city of Rome, which brought the number of Rome's districts or *rioni* up to thirteen. A few noble families

(including the Stefaneschi, Papareschi and Alberteschi) lived in the area, but of their homes only those belonging to the Anguillara and the Mattei have survived from that period (both heavily restored). When the papacy returned from Avignon, for a little while Trastevere became the seat of the Studium Urbis university. At that time, there were only two points of communication with the left bank of the Tiber: the Isola Tiberina (Tiber island) and from 1475 the Ponte Sisto, which was intended to give pilgrims access to St Peter's.

ACCESS ROUTES. Until the 14th century no great town planning initiatives affected this district, its population being concentrated close to the Tiber.

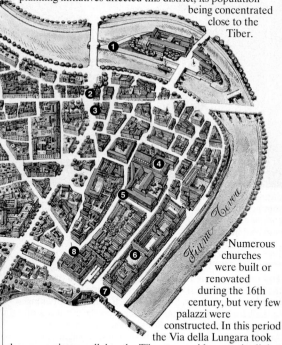

Numerous churches were built or renovated during the 16th century, but very few palazzi were constructed. In this period the Via della Lungara took shape, running parallel to the Tiber to provide an easier link with the Borgo (the *rione* of St Peter's ▲ *232*). But it was not until the 19th century that the main avenues were built: the Viale di Trastevere running through the middle of the district, and the Lungotevere skirting the river.

A LIVELY QUARTER. Trastevere remained a predominantly working-class area until the 1960's, when it increasingly came to be seen as a neighborhood of restaurants and nightlife. But in the morning it retrieves some of its traditional character, and the *vicoli* (small streets) around Santa Maria in Trastevere offer a glimpse of the daily life of the past. The true spirit of the district is revealed in the month of July

"Everywhere, along the alleyways of the Trastevere, in the ditches of the Giancolo, in the massive shadow of the Teatro marcello, which welds its enormous, smoke-blackened ruins to the low houses of a piazza bright with lemons and tomatoes – everywhere a younger generation swarms, adolescent sons and brothers of these spirited soldiers. Often we feel like envying their exuberant poverty, and their number gives pause. Impossible not to see them, for the family custom, even among the well-to-do, is to make a place for the child in a restaurant, at reunions, and on the afternoon strolls."

Colette,
Earthly Paradise

THE TRASTEVERINI
With their own dialect, the people of Trastevere had always considered themselves the descendants of the ancient Romans. The quarter was frequently a source of uprisings; consequently the popes distrusted the Trasteverini. In 1849 this was the area that continued to defend the short-lived Republic of Rome to the very end.

SAN BARTOLOMEO
Only the Romanesque campanile of the old church remains. A well with beautiful medieval statues stands beside the presbytery. The church was completely rebuilt in 1624 by Martino Longhi the Younger but still retains the columns of the pagan temple.

PONTE ROTTO
At the southern tip of the island is the Ponte Rotto (the "broken bridge"). This is all that remains of the Pons Aemilius (2nd century BC), which was rebuilt several times before it finally collapsed in the 15th century. The point of the island is formed by a ship's prow sculpted in travertine in reference to the story of Aesculapius – part of a marble wall that once encircled the island to make it look even more like a ship.

The Tiber.

during the *Festa de' Noantri* ("our own feast") ● *44*. On summer nights in the back streets behind Via Garibaldi it is common to see people bringing chairs out into the street for a convivial improvised meal with neighbors.

ISOLA TIBERINA

THE ORIGIN OF THE ISLAND. According to legend the island in the Tiber was formed when the people flung the wheat harvest of the Campus Martius (which at that time belonged to the Etruscan kings) into the river after the expulsion of Tarquinius Superbus from Rome in the 4th century BC. Another legend has it that in order to end a plague some Romans went to Epidaurus in Greece to fetch Aesculapius, the god of medicine, and brought back a sacred serpent symbolizing the god. The serpent swam ashore to the island, the shape of which is said to be identical to that of the ship. In 293 BC a temple to Aesculapius was built here; its ruins lie beneath the Church of San Bartolomeo, erected in the 10th century by the German Emperor Otto III. Until the 19th century this was the church of the millers' corporation, who used to celebrate their feast on the island on December 8.
A SPARSELY POPULATED ISLAND. The Isola Tiberina was barely inhabited until the Middle Ages, when the Pierleoni and Caetani families settled there. A tower that formed part of

their fortifications remains standing at the head of the Ponte Fabricio. In the 17th century, especially during the plague of 1656, it was used as a place of quarantine for plague victims in order to limit epidemics in the city. The island's medical vocation has remained; even today the Fatebenefratelli hospital covers almost all of it. The Baroque interior of the little church of San Giovanni Calibita should not be missed.

BRIDGES OVER THE TIBER. Two bridges span the Tiber from the island. The one, the Ponte Fabricio, links the island with the Campo Marzio; on it is an inscription giving the name of its builder (Lucius Fabricius, son of Caius) four times over and the date 62 BC. The two four-headed busts of Janus framing the entrance on the Campo Marzio side have earned it the popular nickname of Ponte dei Quattro Capi ("Bridge of the Four Heads"). The other bridge, the Ponte Cestio, built in the 1st century BC as a link with Trastevere, was partly demolished in 1888 and rebuilt in 1892.

The Ponte Rotto (above left) and the Church of Santa Cecilia.

RIPAGRANDE

THE PORT OF RIPAGRANDE. Sadly this was destroyed when the Lungotevere embankments were built at the end of the 19th century. The river now flows between high walls (*muraglioni*) and it is not possible to imagine how colorful and busy it once was. Barges arriving from Ostia used to be hauled from the right bank of the Tiber by men or buffaloes, which explains the presence near Porta Portese of an area called the *bufalara*. The port was also known as the Ripa Romea (the "bank for pilgrims going to Rome") because pilgrims bound for St Peter's used to alight there.

Medieval buildings in the vicinity of Santa Cecilia.

PIAZZA IN PISCINULA. The piazza's appearance today dates from the end of the last century when the palazzo facing Palazzo Mattei was demolished. Some rather questionable restorations have attempted to recreate a medieval Roman piazza. There are theories that Palazzo Mattei dates back to the time of Gregory IX (1227–41), or even to the time of Innocent II (1130–43) and the Papareschi family; but as it now stands it doesn't go back further than the 14th or 15th century. SAN BENEDETTO IN PISCINULA is the smallest Romanesque basilica in the city and boasts a fine bell tower, a 13th-century fresco of *St Benedict* in the porch and a splendid Cosmatesque ● *76* paving in the nave. In the area around the square there are many fine medieval features to be seen, such as the beautiful porches of some of the houses (in Via dell'Atleta, for instance) or the little church of Santa Maria in Capella, which you come to after taking Via Anicia and passing SAN GIOVANNI DEI GENOVESI, which has a 15th-century cloister attributed to Baccio Pontelli.

THE MARTYRDOM OF SANTA CECILIA
On her wedding night Cecilia, a devout Christian, revealed to her husband Valerian that her purity was protected by an angel and that he would be able to see it if he converted. Valerian agreed to be baptized on the Via Appia, and was able to see the angel. Their faith was discovered and they were both martyred. When their remains were unearthed in 1600, Stefano Maderno was commissioned to make a statue of the saint in the exact position her body was found in.

The church of the Madonna dell'Orto.

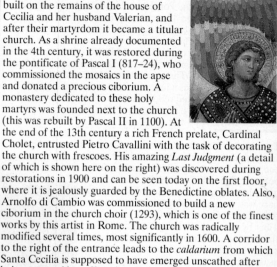

BASILICA OF SANTA CECILIA. Set aside from the bustle of Piazza dei Mercanti (where the restaurant Da meo Patacca aims to provide tourists with the atmosphere of a traditional tavern) and protected by a quadrangle planted with a rose garden, Santa Cecilia offers a haven of silence. It is believed to have been built on the remains of the house of Cecilia and her husband Valerian, and after their martyrdom it became a titular church. As a shrine already documented in the 4th century, it was restored during the pontificate of Pascal I (817–24), who commissioned the mosaics in the apse and donated a precious ciborium. A monastery dedicated to these holy martyrs was founded next to the church (this was rebuilt by Pascal II in 1100). At the end of the 13th century a rich French prelate, Cardinal Cholet, entrusted Pietro Cavallini with the task of decorating the church with frescoes. His amazing *Last Judgment* (a detail of which is shown here on the right) was discovered during restorations in 1900 and can be seen today on the first floor, where it is jealously guarded by the Benedictine oblates. Also, Arnolfo di Cambio was commissioned to build a new ciborium in the church choir (1293), which is one of the finest works by this artist in Rome. The church was radically modified several times, most significantly in 1600. A corridor to the right of the entrance leads to the *caldarium* from which Santa Cecilia is supposed to have emerged unscathed after being tortured by suffocation. Beneath the church, as well as the crypt containing Cecilia's and Valerian's sarcophagi, one can see important remains of Roman buildings from different periods of antiquity, including pavements, baths, columns and inscriptions. (Take Via di San Michele, on the right, then turn into Via della Madonna dell'Orto.)

MADONNA DELL'ORTO. This church was founded in 1492 by the corporation of market gardeners. Its façade, built between 1566 and 1579, was probably designed by Vignola. But its most remarkable features are inside, where an exuberant profusion of garlands, wreaths, flowers and fruit constitutes a sumptuous display of Baroque decoration. These stuccos, dating from the 18th century, were donated by the local guilds (*università*), which included the gardeners (*ortolani*), the millers (*molinari*) and the fruit, poultry and pasta vendors (*fruttaroli*, *pollari* and *vermicellari*). The high altar by Giacomo della Porta has a superb image of the Virgin Mary. (Take Via Anicia, on the right.)

"THE BLESSED LODOVICA ALBERTONI"
As in Santa Maria della Vittoria ▲ 294, in the Church of the Madonna dell'Orto Bernini paid careful attention to lighting effects. An indirect light heightens the movement of the copiously draped agonizing figure. Her body rests on a mattress of multicolored marble fringed with gilded bronze. Above the statue a painting by Baciccia (*The Virgin and Child with St Anne*, 1675) reveals the nature of the blessed visionary's apparition.

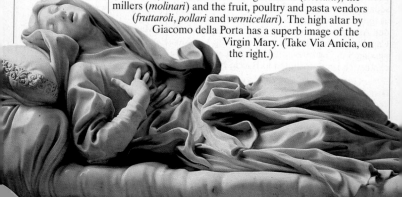

SAN FRANCESCO A RIPA. This church is built on the site of the San Biagio Hospice, where St Francis is supposed to have stayed, and it still belongs to the Franciscan Order. Remodeled by Mattia de' Rossi around 1682, it contains many sepulchers dating from the 17th and 18th centuries. In the first chapel on the left there is a splendid *Birth of the Virgin* by Simon Vouet, painted between 1618 and 1620 and clearly influenced by Caravaggio. Three chapels farther on, you will find *The Blessed Lodovica Albertoni*, one of Bernini's last and greatest sculptures. The funerary monuments here bring to mind an item mentioned by Stendhal in his *Chroniques*

PORTA PORTESE
Rome's famous flea market has been used as a location for many films. In *Bicycle Thieves* (Vittorio de Sica, 1948) the hero takes his son to Porta Portese in the hope of finding his stolen bicycle. In *Mamma Roma* (Pier Paolo Pasolini, 1960) the son of the prostitute Mamma Roma (played by Anna Magnani ● *43*) goes there to try to sell a record he has just stolen from his mother.

italiennes: a Roman princess was reported to have had a midnight Requiem Mass celebrated here for the lover she was about to have killed. Skirting the church and taking Via Ascianghi, you will come to the PIAZZA DI PORTA PORTESE (in ancient times the arsenal of Rome stood near here). On Sunday mornings the city's famous flea market takes place in this piazza and in the neighboring streets. From the corner the SAN MICHELE complex, which has a façade more than 1,000 feet long, stretches back along the Tiber embankment. This gigantic building was erected at the end of the 17th century as a home for the poor, then became an institution for juvenile delinquents. Its restoration, which began in 1972, is almost complete and it now houses a variety of departments belonging to the Ministero per i Beni Culturali e Ambientali (the ministry responsible for Italy's cultural and environmental heritage). One crosses two magnificent courtyards, the first of which has been disfigured by a modern staircase, in order to reach the now seemingly permanent "temporary" exhibition of the most famous paintings from the Galleria Borghese's collection ▲ *372*, which for years had remained inaccessible while awaiting the hypothetical reopening of the gallery. (Return to Viale Trastevere and take Viale Glorioso and Via Dandolo to No. 47.)

THE SYRIAN TEMPLE ON THE JANICULUM. From the end of the Republic the commercial area on the Tiber attracted many traders and freed slaves of oriental origin. It is therefore not surprising that on both sides of the river traces have been found of religions originating in Anatolia (the cult of Cybele), Egypt and Syria. These include inscriptions confirming that a close

The long façade of San Michele.

AN INTRIGUING ROOM
In the Syrian temple on the Janiculum there is an octagonal room with an apse at the end of it. In a cavity beneath the triangular altar a bronze statuette was found, portraying a human figure entwined in a serpent's coils – probably the Egyptian deity Osiris.

355

link existed between slave traders and the goddess of Syria. The temple in Trastevere, discovered in 1906, proves the continuity from the 1st century AD of a Syrian cult, probably dedicated to Hadad (Heliopolis' equivalent of Jupiter), Atargatis (the Syrian goddess most widely worshiped in Rome) and Simios (the equivalent of Mercury). The sanctuary is made up of three parts: a rectangular central courtyard; a room to the east containing a triangular altar; and a basilica, on the western side, preceded by a sort of atrium. (Go back down Via Dandolo to Piazza San Cosimato.)

PIAZZA DI SAN COSIMATO. The Benedictine monastery facing the piazza passed into the hands of the Franciscans in the 13th century and is now a hospital. It has two cloisters, one Romanesque and the other dating from the 15th century. (Return to the Viale di Trastevere.)

VIALE DI TRASTEVERE. This wide avenue, originally named Viale del Re, was built between 1880 and 1890 to link Ponte Garibaldi to Stazione Trastevere. Few buildings along it are modern, save for the TOBACCO FACTORY (1863) designed by Antonio Sarti.

THE EXCUBITORIUM. On the corner of Via di Monte Fiore and Via della VIIª Coorte is the entrance of the Excubitorium, a building dating from Imperial times that was the guardhouse of the seventh cohort of the *vigiles* (city guards). This private house, which was turned into a barracks toward the end of the 2nd century AD, provides a valuable insight into the activities of the *vigiles*. These units were formed under Augustus in 6 BC and served as a police force for the city as well as a fire brigade.

SAN CRISOGONO. The present building was erected in the 12th century on top of a paleo-Christian church, but on a much greater scale, with three wide naves separated by 22 ancient columns. The campanile (bell tower) dates from 1125; the mosaics attributed to Pietro Cavallini and the Cosmatesque paving ● 76 are 13th century. The rest of the building was restored by Giambattista Soria in 1620. Bernini designed the CHAPEL OF THE BLESSED SACRAMENT. From the sacristy you can go down to the church beneath, the Titulus Chrysogonus, built in the 5th century to house the tomb of the holy martyr beheaded in the time of Diocletian. This sanctuary with a single nave was restored and decorated with frescoes during the pontificate of Gregory III (731–41). The *Scenes from the Life of St Benedict* were added in the 10th century. (Walk across Piazza Sonnino.)

THE ANGUILLARA PALAZZO AND TOWER. The name of the Anguillara family, already famous in the 11th and 12th centuries, came

from their feudal domain near Lake Bracciano. In the 13th century their dwelling in Trastevere resembled an urban fortress. Then in 1464 modifications transformed it into a residential palace, leaving nothing but the tower – the only one today of the many that were erected in Trastevere in the Middle Ages. The Anguillara family died out in the 18th century, and the building was restored in 1887. Today it houses the Casa di Dante, dedicated to the author of the *Divina Commedia*. On the piazza facing the river is a statue of the poet Giuseppe Gioacchino Belli ● *43* by Michele Tripisciano, erected in 1913. (Turn left into Via della Lungaretta; Piazza Santa Maria in Trastevere is at the western end.)

Residents of Trastevere.

BASILICA OF SANTA MARIA IN TRASTEVERE ★

PIAZZA SANTA MARIA IN TRASTEVERE. This is the heart of Trastevere, one of Rome's most picturesque neighborhoods with its lively, tortuous little streets. The piazza's elegant FOUNTAIN, restored by Carlo Fontana in 1692, faces PALAZZO SAN CALLISTO, which was built by Paul V in 1613. The palace is attached to the Church of San Callisto, erected in the Middle Ages on the site of St Calixtus' martyrdom and rebuilt in the 17th century.

THE FOUNDATION OF THE CHURCH. According to tradition, in 38 BC a fountain of foul-smelling oil (probably petroleum) sprang spontaneously from this spot. The site of the *fons olei* is indicated beneath the choir of the basilica. The Jewish population took the miracle as a sign of the coming of the Messiah, but the first

THE FAÇADE OF SANTA MARIA IN TRASTEVERE
Above the windows there is a 12th to 14th century mosaic frieze of Byzantine influence. It depicts bearers of gifts kneeling respectfully at the feet of the Virgin and Child, who are flanked on either side by ten female figures. Carlo Fontana added the portico surmounted by statues of popes in 1702.

Christian shrine commemorating it was not established until the 3rd century. The existence of the shrine led to friction between the Christians and the local innkeepers. The Emperor Alexander Severus was asked to intervene and is said to have sided with the former, preferring the building to be occupied by an unconventional sect rather than by drunkards. The official biography of the popes, the *Liber pontificalis*, gives a different version, stating that Calixtus (who was Pope from 217 to 222) invited the faithful to a Mass in a domestic church (*titulus*) which was later converted into a basilica. Between 772 and 795 Hadrian I added the lateral naves. Then Gregory IV (827–44) made extensive changes. As well as having the choir raised, the altar covered with a ciborium, and a crypt made to accommodate the relics of Saints Calixtus, Calepodius and Cornelius, he had a chapel to the Holy Crib built (in imitation of Santa Maria Maggiore ▲ *342*) and added a monastery to serve the basilica.

INNOCENT II's BASILICA. In the 12th century Innocent II (who belonged to one of the great Trastevere families, the Papareschi) further modified the building, adding the transept and decorating the apse with splendid mosaics. Most of the materials came from the baths of Caracalla ▲ *319*. The new

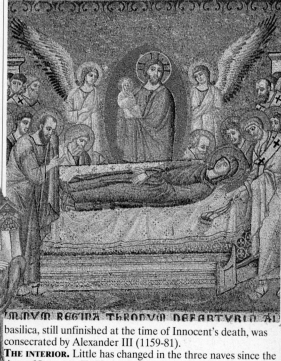

basilica, still unfinished at the time of Innocent's death, was consecrated by Alexander III (1159-81).

THE INTERIOR. Little has changed in the three naves since the time of Innocent II. The ceiling was designed by Domenichino, who also painted *The Assumption of the Virgin* in the center. The handsome Cosmatesque paving ● *76* was restored in 1870. To the left of the apse, the ALTEMPS CHAPEL (1584) was probably the first Counter-Reformation chapel to

Achille Pinelli

be dedicated to an ancient cult of the Virgin.

MOSAICS OF THE CHOIR ★. These mosaics show traces of Byzantine influence, but belong to the Roman tradition. Those on the chancel arch portray the prophets Isaiah and Jeremiah, the symbols of the four evangelists, the seven candelabra of the Apocalypse, and the cross with the Alpha and the Omega. In the apse one sees Christ and the Virgin enthroned (above); to the left are St Calixtus, St Lawrence and Pope Innocent II donating the church to the Virgin; to the right are the saints Peter, Cornelius, Julius and Calepodius; below, two rows of sheep are shown emerging from Jerusalem and Bethlehem and converging toward the Lamb of God. These 12th-century mosaics mark a renewal in the devotion to the Virgin, and the theme of the coronation of the Virgin was to recur a century later in Jacopo Torriti's masterpiece in Santa Maria Maggiore ▲ *342*. Lower down is one of the finest works of Pietro Cavallini: six episodes from the life of St Mary (1291). The artist makes an astonishing use of color, treating the mosaic as if it were a fresco. (Follow Via della Paglia, on the left as you come out of the basilica, until you reach Piazza Sant'Egidio, where you will find the 17th-century Church of Sant'Egidio and the Museo del Folklore e dei Poeti Romaneschi. Then take Via della Scala.)

SANTA MARIA DELLA SCALA. This church, which belongs to the Discalced Carmelites, was built by Francesco da Volterra. Although the Superiors of the Order refused *The Death of the Virgin* painted for them by Caravaggio, many of his pupils' works found their place in this church. They include *The Decapitation of St John the Baptist* by Honthorst in the first chapel on the right, and *The Death of the Virgin* by Saraceni in the second chapel on the left. The monastery's pharmacy has retained its 17th-century furnishings and decoration. (Continue into Via della Lungara.)

VIA DELLA LUNGARA

PORTA SETTIMIANA. This triumphal arch was built by Septimius Severus as an entrance to one of his villas; but in the 6th century it was incorporated, as a gateway, into the Aurelian Wall. Its present appearance dates from the modifications to the city made by Alexander VI (1498).

VIA DELLA LUNGARA. This long, straight road was constructed during the pontificate of Pope Julius II. Before the building of the Tiber embankments it was the only road linking

MUSEO DEL FOLKLORE
This small museum is dedicated to the life, customs and traditions of Rome in the 18th and 19th centuries. It is in five sections: the Carnival, aspects of daily life, the watercolors of Ettore Roesler Franz, the Artists' Festival in Cervara and firework displays. As well as engravings of the Piè di Marmo, the Bocca della Verità and Pasquino, there is a reconstruction of the poet Trilussa's study, containing paintings, photographs, documents and other possessions, and manuscripts of some of his poems. (This museum is fascinating, but by no means a substitute for visiting the Museo delle Arte e Tradizioni Popolari in EUR ▲ *387*.)

ACHILLE PINELLI (1809–41)
The son of the painter Bartolomeo Pinelli (1781–1835), Achille began painting at an early age. His best-known works are two hundred watercolors of the churches of Rome, including the one of Santa Maria della Scala, above. They are now in the Museo di Roma.

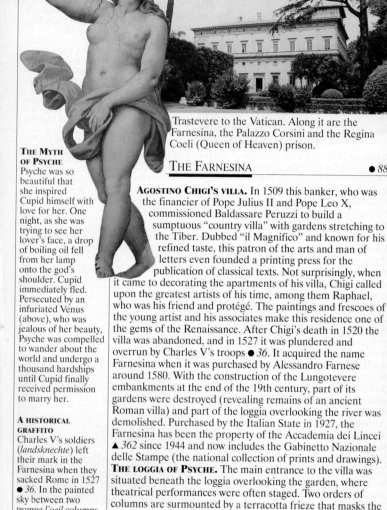

Trastevere to the Vatican. Along it are the Farnesina, the Palazzo Corsini and the Regina Coeli (Queen of Heaven) prison.

THE MYTH OF PSYCHE
Psyche was so beautiful that she inspired Cupid himself with love for her. One night, as she was trying to see her lover's face, a drop of boiling oil fell from her lamp onto the god's shoulder. Cupid immediately fled. Persecuted by an infuriated Venus (above), who was jealous of her beauty, Psyche was compelled to wander about the world and undergo a thousand hardships until Cupid finally received permission to marry her.

A HISTORICAL GRAFFITO
Charles V's soldiers (*landsknechte*) left their mark in the Farnesina when they sacked Rome in 1527 ● 36. In the painted sky between two *trompe l'oeil* columns they scratched the fateful date.

AGOSTINO CHIGI'S VILLA. In 1509 this banker, who was the financier of Pope Julius II and Pope Leo X, commissioned Baldassare Peruzzi to build a sumptuous "country villa" with gardens stretching to the Tiber. Dubbed "il Magnifico" and known for his refined taste, this patron of the arts and man of letters even founded a printing press for the publication of classical texts. Not surprisingly, when it came to decorating the apartments of his villa, Chigi called upon the greatest artists of his time, among them Raphael, who was his friend and protégé. The paintings and frescoes of the young artist and his associates make this residence one of the gems of the Renaissance. After Chigi's death in 1520 the villa was abandoned, and in 1527 it was plundered and overrun by Charles V's troops ● 36. It acquired the name Farnesina when it was purchased by Alessandro Farnese around 1580. With the construction of the Lungotevere embankments at the end of the 19th century, part of its gardens were destroyed (revealing remains of an ancient Roman villa) and part of the loggia overlooking the river was demolished. Purchased by the Italian State in 1927, the Farnesina has been the property of the Accademia dei Lincei ▲ 362 since 1944 and now includes the Gabinetto Nazionale delle Stampe (the national collection of prints and drawings).
THE LOGGIA OF PSYCHE. The main entrance to the villa was situated beneath the loggia overlooking the garden, where theatrical performances were often staged. Two orders of columns are surmounted by a terracotta frieze that masks the third-floor windows. The loggia, is decorated with frescoes depicting Cupid and Psyche; these were painted by pupils of Raphael, following cartoons by the master. Giovanni da Udine is the author of the pergola composed of garlands of fruit and flowers that supports the two *trompe l'oeil* tapestries on the ceiling; these show the council of the gods welcoming Psyche on Mount Olympus and the wedding feast of Cupid and Psyche. Painted *putti* above the arches of the loggia and the false windows bear the attributes of the gods, while the lunettes recount the main episodes of Psyche's story.
THE LOGGIA OF GALATEA. To the right of the loggia of Psyche is the Galatea Room, named after Raphael's fresco *The Triumph of Galatea*; the artist is reputed to have used no models for it apart from ideal beauty as he conceived it.

When Ettore Roesler Franz painted this watercolor in 1880, the Farnesina's loggia overlooking the Tiber still existed. It was demolished between 1884 and 1886 during the construction of the Lungotevere embankments.

Peruzzi painted the ceiling with mythological frescoes showing the constellations of the zodiac in their position at the time of Agostino Chigi's birth. The lunettes are decorated with frescoes based on Ovid's *Metamorphoses* by Sebastiano del

Piombo, who also painted the fresco on the wall of Polyphemus, the Cyclops, pining for the nymph Galatea.

THE SALA DELLE PROSPETTIVE. Also known as the "room of the columns", this vast room on the *piano nobile* is famous for its imposing *trompe l'oeil* frescoes by Peruzzi. The artist's intention was to create the illusion of an open loggia offering views over the Roman countryside and the city's monuments. It is recognized as one of the masterpieces of the early 16th century. Peruzzi's virtuosity makes this a pictorial *tour de force* of the Roman Baroque style. The floor pattern extends into the illusory loggia, and the painted scenery is organized around the focal point of the doorway through which you enter the room.

THE SALA DI ALESSANDRO. For his bedroom Chigi commissioned Giovanni Antonio dei Bazzi, known as Il Sodoma, to adorn the main wall with a fresco depicting the marriage of Alexander the Great to Roxana. Painted around 1513, this is based on an ancient model by Aetion that no longer existed but of which the Greek writer Lucian had provided a description. The wall on

A TROMPE L'OEIL ROOM
The originality of Baldassare Peruzzi's work in the Sala delle Prospettive lies neither in the decorative elements, such as the landscapes and columns, nor in the taste for *trompe l'oeil* perspectives (which was very widespread at the time), but in his ingenious use of traditional motifs to achieve the perfect optical illusion of making the walls of the room "disappear".

"THE TRIUMPH OF GALATEA"
Standing on an ethereal chariot drawn by dolphins, Galatea is no longer the cold figure of the Hellenistic and Roman traditions, but has entered the limpid world of the Muses of Parnassus. In this fresco the formal vitality of the figures is derived from the clarity of Raphael's classicism.

THE ACCADEMIA DEI LINCEI. Founded in 1603 by Federico Cesi and of which Galileo was an eminent member, this society brought together scholars who wished to "read the great book of the true and universal world, to visit its different parts, and to learn to observe and experiment". They . chose as their symbol the lynx (*lince*), known for the sharpness of its eyesight.

"VENUS AND ADONIS" By casting a pale light over the whole scene Giuseppe Ribera abandoned the chiaroscuro that was such a prominent feature of his earlier work.

"REBECCA AT THE WELL" In this composition Carlo Maratta (1625-1713) strove to capture Raphael's manner of painting draped figures and Annibale Carracci's gift for portraying facial character.

the right portrays the family of Darius submitting to Alexander. Finally, to the left of the entrance is a fresco of inferior quality showing Alexander taming Bucephalus.

PALAZZO CORSINI

Facing the Farnesina across Via della Lungara, Palazzo Corsini replaced the Palazzo Riario, the residence of Queen Christina of Sweden from 1662 until her death in 1689. It was built between 1736 and 1758 by Ferdinando Fuga for Cardinal Neri Corsini, a nephew of Clement XII. The original conception was much more ambitious than what was built. The long façade is articulated around a central body with three portals leading into three galleries. The middle entrance

was designed to allow vehicles to reach the courtyard and gardens, while the other two lead to two staircases that meet on the *piano nobile*. This building is now the headquarters of the Accademia dei Lincei. **GALLERIA NAZIONALE D'ARTE ANTICA.** The main floor now houses part of the collection of the Galleria Nazionale d'Arte Antica, the remainder being in Palazzo Barberini ▲ *291*.

The Orto Botanico contains a rich variety of Mediterranean trees and plants.

Among the most outstanding works are Caravaggio's *St John the Baptist*; *Salome Bearing the Head of John the Baptist*, attributed to Guido Reni; paintings by the Bologna school and the school of Caravaggio; and a number of Neapolitan Baroque works, including Salvator Rosa's *Prometheus*.

THE ORTO BOTANICO. The botanical garden belonging to the University of Rome was originally the park of Palazzo Corsini. It covers an area of nearly 30 acres and boasts a splendid staircase with a waterfall. (Go back along Via della Lungara and turn left into Via Santa Dorotea.)

PONTE SISTO

THE HOME OF LA FORNARINA. The house at No. 20 Via Santa Dorotea (now the Romolo restaurant) is supposed to have been the bakery owned by the father of Raphael's mistress, La Fornarina, traditionally identified as the subject of the famous portrait in Palazzo Barberini ▲ *292*. It is said that in order to accelerate work on the Farnesina, Agostino Chigi allowed the painter to have her live with him on the premises. (Walk to the end of Via Santa Dorotea.)

PIAZZA TRILUSSA. This piazza bears the name of the Trastevere poet Carlo Alberto Salustri (1871–1950), known as Trilussa. When alterations were made to the piazza during the construction of the Tiber embankments at the end of the 19th century, the fountain commissioned by Paul V from Giovanni Fontana and Giovanni Vasanzio in 1613 was moved here from the end of the Via Giulia. This fountain was designed to distribute the water supplied by the Aqua Paola aqueduct ▲ *364*.

PONTE SISTO. This bridge, which links Trastevere to the left bank of the Tiber, was built in 1475 under Sixtus IV to replace an ancient Roman bridge which had been destroyed ▲ *364*. Widened in the 19th century, it is now closed to motor vehicles. The middle of the bridge affords splendid views: of the dome of St Peter's; of the Aventine hill and the Aqua Paola, dominated by the Janiculum. (Go back along Via Santa Dorotea, past the Church of SANTA DOROTEA E SAN GIOVANNI DELLA MALVA, which is in the shape of a Greek cross; built in 1475, it was remodeled in the 18th century. Then take Via Garibaldi.)

THE JANICULUM

The name Gianicolo, or Janiculum, is derived from the cult of the god Janus. The hill still bears traces of the fierce fighting that took place here between French troops and the supporters of the Republic of Rome in 1849 ● *33*. The Via

The Ponte Sisto fountain.

VIEW OF ROME FROM THE JANICULUM
From left to right Sant'Andrea della Valle, the Gesù, Santa Maria Maggiore, San Carlo ai Catinari and the monument to Victor Emmanuel.

The Fontana Paola.

THE TEMPIETTO
Bramante's small circular temple (right) is believed to have been the first Renaissance monument inspired by the architecture of ancient Rome. Modeled on the Sibyl's shrine in Tivoli ▲ 392, it was based on early Renaissance research.

Garibaldi used to be called Via delle Fornaci because of the brick factories beside it. It leads to the most beautiful panoramic view of the city, which according to one French 18th-century diarist, de Brosses, was in itself sufficient to justify "the journey to Italy".

BOSCO PARRASIO. To the right of Via Garibaldi there is a path leading to what was once the seat of the Arcadia academy, founded in 1690. With its aim of "exterminating bad taste" and of refining poetry, Arcadia exerted a profound influence on Italian literature. In 1926 it became the Italian Academy of Literature.

SANTA MARIA DEI SETTE DOLORI. Built between 1646 and 1667 according to a design by Borromini, this church is characterized externally by simple brickwork in an interplay of curves and countercurves. Inside, the 19th-century decoration detracts from the rhythm and balance of Borromini's architecture. (Continue up Via Garibaldi.)

SAN PIETRO IN MONTORIO. This church provides a splendid point from which to view the city, which until the end of the 19th century was clearly divided in two distinct parts: ancient Rome on the right and modern Rome on the left. The church's austere façade was built at the end of the 15th century with funds provided by the Spanish sovereigns Ferdinand of Aragon and Isabella of Castile. Attached to the church is a convent which is now largely occupied by the Spanish Academy. The church contains many 16th-century works of art, including Sebastiano del Piombo's famous fresco *The Flagellation*, based on a drawing by Michelangelo. Bernini worked on the RAIMONDI CHAPEL and the fourth chapel on the left has lunettes painted by David de Haan as well as a *Descent from the Cross* by Dirk van Baburen. In the middle of a cloister to the right of the church, on the spot where St Peter is supposed to have been crucified, stands one of the most elegant buildings of the Renaissance, Bramante's TEMPIETTO (1502).

THE FONTANA PAOLA. This fountain was built by Flaminio Ponzio and Giovanni Fontana to receive the waters of Trajan's ancient aqueduct, rehabilitated by Paul V to supply water to Trastevere, the Via Giulia area and the Vatican. Its three arches, modeled on the Aqua Felice fountain ▲ 295, stand in front of a charming garden. (The street to the left after the fountain leads to the PORTA SAN PANCRAZIO, rebuilt in 1854.)

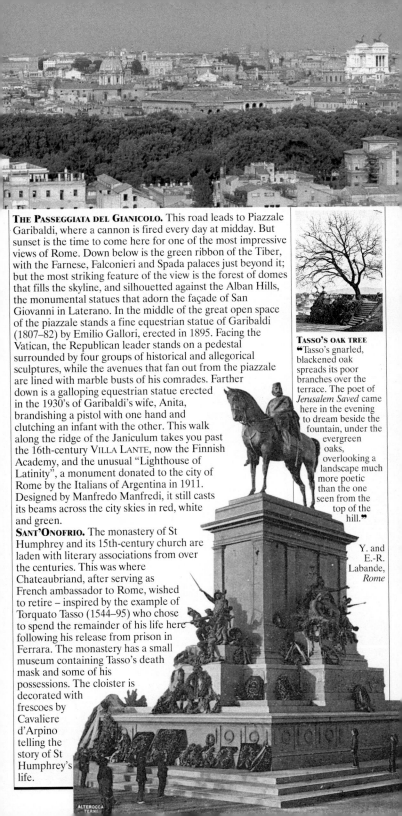

THE PASSEGGIATA DEL GIANICOLO. This road leads to Piazzale Garibaldi, where a cannon is fired every day at midday. But sunset is the time to come here for one of the most impressive views of Rome. Down below is the green ribbon of the Tiber, with the Farnese, Falconieri and Spada palaces just beyond it; but the most striking feature of the view is the forest of domes that fills the skyline, and silhouetted against the Alban Hills, the monumental statues that adorn the façade of San Giovanni in Laterano. In the middle of the great open space of the piazzale stands a fine equestrian statue of Garibaldi (1807–82) by Emilio Gallori, erected in 1895. Facing the Vatican, the Republican leader stands on a pedestal surrounded by four groups of historical and allegorical sculptures, while the avenues that fan out from the piazzale are lined with marble busts of his comrades. Farther down is a galloping equestrian statue erected in the 1930's of Garibaldi's wife, Anita, brandishing a pistol with one hand and clutching an infant with the other. This walk along the ridge of the Janiculum takes you past the 16th-century VILLA LANTE, now the Finnish Academy, and the unusual "Lighthouse of Latinity", a monument donated to the city of Rome by the Italians of Argentina in 1911. Designed by Manfredo Manfredi, it still casts its beams across the city skies in red, white and green.

SANT'ONOFRIO. The monastery of St Humphrey and its 15th-century church are laden with literary associations from over the centuries. This was where Chateaubriand, after serving as French ambassador to Rome, wished to retire – inspired by the example of Torquato Tasso (1544–95) who chose to spend the remainder of his life here following his release from prison in Ferrara. The monastery has a small museum containing Tasso's death mask and some of his possessions. The cloister is decorated with frescoes by Cavaliere d'Arpino telling the story of St Humphrey's life.

TASSO'S OAK TREE
"Tasso's gnarled, blackened oak spreads its poor branches over the terrace. The poet of *Jerusalem Saved* came here in the evening to dream beside the fountain, under the evergreen oaks, overlooking a landscape much more poetic than the one seen from the top of the hill."

Y. and E.-R. Labande, *Rome*

As monuments in piazzas or discreet ornaments in courtyards and on street corners, fountains abound in every part of Rome.

FROM VILLA GIULIA
TO THE FORO ITALICO

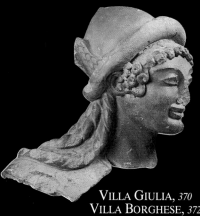

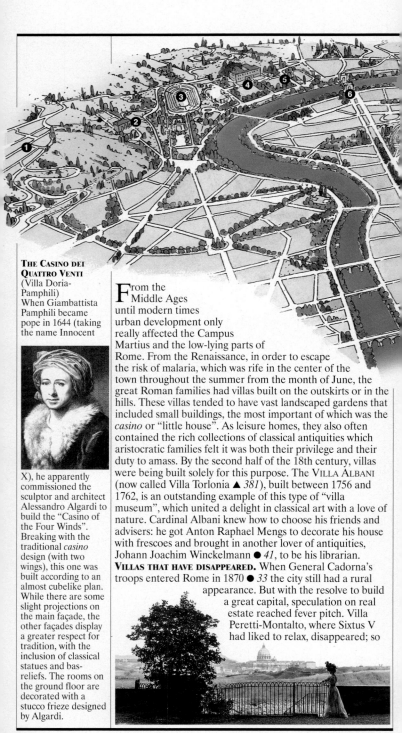

THE CASINO DEI QUATTRO VENTI
(Villa Doria-Pamphili)
When Giambattista Pamphili became pope in 1644 (taking the name Innocent

X), he apparently commissioned the sculptor and architect Alessandro Algardi to build the "Casino of the Four Winds". Breaking with the traditional *casino* design (with two wings), this one was built according to an almost cubelike plan. While there are some slight projections on the main façade, the other façades display a greater respect for tradition, with the inclusion of classical statues and bas-reliefs. The rooms on the ground floor are decorated with a stucco frieze designed by Algardi.

From the Middle Ages until modern times urban development only really affected the Campus Martius and the low-lying parts of Rome. From the Renaissance, in order to escape the risk of malaria, which was rife in the center of the town throughout the summer from the month of June, the great Roman families had villas built on the outskirts or in the hills. These villas tended to have vast landscaped gardens that included small buildings, the most important of which was the *casino* or "little house". As leisure homes, they also often contained the rich collections of classical antiquities which aristocratic families felt it was both their privilege and their duty to amass. By the second half of the 18th century, villas were being built solely for this purpose. The VILLA ALBANI (now called Villa Torlonia ▲ *381*), built between 1756 and 1762, is an outstanding example of this type of "villa museum", which united a delight in classical art with a love of nature. Cardinal Albani knew how to choose his friends and advisers: he got Anton Raphael Mengs to decorate his house with frescoes and brought in another lover of antiquities, Johann Joachim Winckelmann ● *41*, to be his librarian.
VILLAS THAT HAVE DISAPPEARED. When General Cadorna's troops entered Rome in 1870 ● *33* the city still had a rural appearance. But with the resolve to build a great capital, speculation on real estate reached fever pitch. Villa Peretti-Montalto, where Sixtus V had liked to relax, disappeared; so

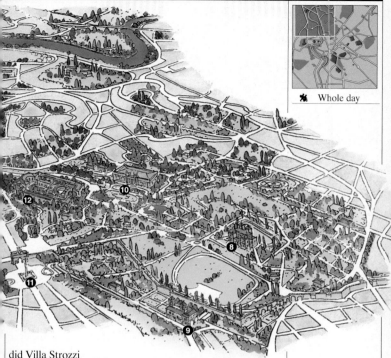

✷ Whole day

did Villa Strozzi
on the Viminal Hill and
the huge Villa Ludovisi in the northern part of the town
(about 2½ acres of its grounds remain around the Casino
dell'Aurora).

ARCHEOLOGICAL SITES. Other villas were integrated into
groups of ancient buildings. THE FARNESE AND BARBERINI
VILLAS on the Palatine Hill, built in the 16th and 17th
centuries respectively, now form part of the archeological site
there, their gardens having been destroyed or radically
modified by the late-19th-century excavations.

PUBLIC PARKS. The grounds of several villas have become
public parks. Thus VILLA MATTEI, built between 1583 and
1586, was completely transformed in the 19th century and its
park relandscaped *all'inglese* to become the Celimontana park
▲ *190*. The VILLA DORIA-PAMPHILI, behind the Janiculum,
has one of the most varied and largest parks in Rome (nearly
455 acres). The undulating terrain lent itself to cascades,
grottoes, a lake, and numerous fountains. It also has two
casini, a small one overlooking Via Aurelia, which was used as
a residence by the family, and a larger one designed originally
for receptions and to house art collections.

ACADEMIES AND MUSEUMS. Several villas have been reused
without being greatly altered – such as the VILLA MEDICI
▲ *315*, which now houses the French Academy. With its
façade overlooking the gardens at the back, decorated with
bas-reliefs from antiquity, it served as a model for most villas
built at a later date. Several villas in the Pincio area, including
VILLA GIULIA and VILLA BORGHESE, have become museums.

THE VILLAS OF ROME
Many of the villas
were opened to the
public, and their
entrances often
display Latin
inscriptions
welcoming visitors.
One of the most
ancient of these is to
be seen at the Villa
Giulia: "In this villa
which is the most
beautiful, if not in the
world, at least in this
city, and which was
built for honest
pleasures, let all
people walk or rest as
they please.... Let
them stroll at their
leisure, but spoil
nothing.... May the
guests be entertained
by the play of fish and
delight in the songs of
birds, but let them
refrain from
disturbing them."

369

In 1551 Pope Julius III asked Vignola and Ammannati to build him a summer villa. The two architects erected a delightful group of Mannerist buildings in the midst of pleasant gardens, which used to stretch as far as the Tiber, enabling the Pope to reach his villa by boat. A portico leads to the famous nymphaeum resembling a three-tiered theater. On the upper levels there are niches with statues, which include figures such as the Arno and the Tiber, while below the Aqua Virgo fountain is decorated with marble caryatids. In 1889 Villa Giulia became Rome's Etruscan Museum.

URNS AND VASES (5TH TO 4TH CENTURY BC)
Greek terracotta ceramics were highly appreciated and imitated in Etruria, where these two red-figure vases were found. The larger one, showing figures of Amazons, is from Attica; the smaller one, showing Aurora's chariot, was made in Etruria.

THE FICORONI "CISTA"
(4th century BC)
An inscription gives the name of the maker of this famous bronze *cista* (casket) as Novius Plautius. The handle on the lid portrays Dionysus between two satyrs; the fine engravings illustrate an episode from the legend of the Argonauts.

APOLLO
(c. 500 BC)
This polychrome terracotta statue stood on the roof of the temple of Minerva at Veii, together with several others illustrating Apollo's contest with Hercules for possession of the stag with gold antlers. The god's smiling expression owes much to Ionian influence but, as was common in Etruscan art, the model was reinterpreted. The stylization of the tunic, which has no equivalent in Greek art, was perfectly suited to this type of decoration, designed to be seen against the sky from a distance.

CORNER ORNAMENT
(c. 650 BC)
This bronze composition, with human figures, centaurs, and monstrous creatures with human bodies in their mouths, is thought to have adorned a funerary couch.

LID OF A "CISTA"
(4th century BC)
The skillfully crafted figures forming the handle portray two warriors bearing the body of one of their fallen companions.

"THE SARCOPHAGUS OF THE BRIDE AND BRIDEGROOM"
(c. 510 BC). This couple are shown reclining in the classical banqueting attitude. The woman is probably pouring perfume into her spouse's hand. The harmonious composition and graceful gestures of the reclining figures are powerful expressions of the affectionate ties that united Etruscan men and women.

This is one of Rome's largest villas, extending over the Pincio, behind the ramparts of the city. It was created by Cardinal Scipione Borghese, Paul V's nephew, and was sold to the Italian State in 1901. The park, which had already been transformed by the creation of the Giardino del Lago, was subsequently opened to the public. The Casino Borghese, built by Giovanni Vasanzio around 1615, is now a museum containing the remarkable collections created by Cardinal Borghese. In May equestrian events are held in the park, which is dotted with fountains, gazebos, and fake ruins.

THE CASINO BORGHESE
The casino was redecorated in 1782 by Prince Marcantonio Borghese, who was forced to sell its finest classical statues to his brother-in-law, Napoleon Bonaparte, in 1807. These are now in the Louvre.

"PAULINE BORGHESE"
This famous work by Canova portrays Pauline Bonaparte as Venus. Napoleon's sister had married Prince Marcantonio Borghese.

SCIPIONE BORGHESE
The cardinal's passion for works of art made him ruthless in seeking to enlarge his collection. He even imprisoned Cavaliere d'Arpino in 1607 so he could confiscate his collection of paintings, which consisted of about 105 canvases; and he had Domenichino arrested to force him to sell his painting of *Diana the Huntress*, originally commissioned by Cardinal Aldobrandini.

The beauty of its lines lends this sculpture such propriety that the art historian Mario Praz described Canova as an "erotic frigidaire". The work was originally covered with a layer of slightly tinted wax, which made it even more striking by torchlight. Defying the morals of the time, Pauline is said to have posed in the nude for Canova – yet she was indignant when her husband, after their separation, showed the statue to guests.

The park is adorned with statues that form a veritable bestiary.

"THE RAPE OF PROSERPINA"

In this work intended to be viewed from all sides, Bernini contrasts the two bodies twisting in opposite directions. Pluto's muscular figure is described by Michelangelo's sculptures, but Proserpina's flesh demonstrates the artist's concern with rendering nature rather than seeking to portray "Ideal Beauty".

"APOLLO AND DAPHNE"

This sculpture by Bernini portrays the moment, as described by Ovid, when Daphne turned into a bay tree in order to escape from Apollo's embrace. A masterly use of the marble heightens the contrast between the nymph's lithe body and the bark beginning to cover her and her hair changing into branches. On the pedestal, as well as Ovid's verses, there is an inscription by the future Urban VIII attempting to moralize about the scene, which many had found too libertine.

"SACRED AND PROFANE LOVE"

This early work by Titian was painted in 1514 for N. Aurelio, a collector linked to the humanist movement in Venice. It expresses the abstract theme of the "two Venuses": one being the symbol of universal and eternal beauty, while the other symbolizes the progenitive force. But it is the quality of the artist's painting that is striking, rather than the complexity of the theme.

"THE MADONNA OF THE SERPENT"

Painted by Caravaggio in 1605 for the Chapel of Sant'Anna dei Palafrenieri in the Vatican, this picture found its way into the Borghese collection either because it was deemed too irreverent by the Corporation of Palafrenieri, who commissioned it, or because the cardinal exerted the necessary pressure. Under the eye of St Anne (the patron of the Corporation), the Virgin Mary and Jesus are shown crushing the serpent under foot. This was a way of affirming, in opposition to Protestant denials, that Mary actually participated in the salvation of humanity. The very natural appearance of Christ and the portrayal of Mary as a woman of the common people make the fusion of the human and the divine almost tangible. The novelty of such a representation might well have shocked certain people in those days.

The nudity of sacred Love, or the celestial Venus, symbolizes innocence and scorn for earthly goods. The lamp in her left hand evokes the love of God.

"THE DEPOSITION"

This was one of the last works Raphael painted before he left for Rome. It was commissioned by Atlanta Baglioni of Perugia in memory of her son, who had been murdered a few years previously. Raphael borrowed the composition from a sarcophagus of the classical period and made every effort to convey pathos by a careful study of expressions of grief in the figures portrayed.

"DANAË"

This is one of four erotic paintings Federico II di Gonzaga ordered from Correggio in 1530 as a gift for Charles V. Correggio's graceful style earned him a reputation equal to that of Raphael and Titian. Until the 19th century it was essential for great collections to include an example of his work.

"Universal exhibitions transfigure the exchange value of merchandise. They inaugurate a world of fantasy to which humanity lends itself for its entertainment. The entertainment industry helps in this process by elevating humanity itself to the level of merchandise."
Walter Benjamin

GALLERIA NAZIONALE D'ARTE MODERNA

THE EXHIBITION OF 1911. To commemorate the fiftieth anniversary of the Unification of Italy, a huge exhibition was organized in the northern part of the city. It included an ethnographic and regional section, set up on the right bank of the Tiber, and an exhibition of fine arts in the Valle Giulia (on the site of the Villa Cartoni, on the left bank). In addition, major archeological discoveries were displayed in the Baths of Diocletian; and celebrations in the honor of Garibaldi, the "Father of the Nation", were held in the Vittoriano ▲ *160*, which was inaugurated at the same time. The two main centers of the exhibition were linked by a new bridge, the Ponte Risorgimento, built in reinforced concrete by the French architect François Hennebique. The numerous foreign pavilions brought together an amazing profusion of architectural styles. The BRITISH PAVILION, designed by Lutyens in neoclassical style, was built to last and is now the British Academy of Rome. One of the most interesting pavilions was the Austrian one, devised by Josef Hoffmann, which has a room decorated by Gustav Klimt. This lush green valley has been chosen as the site for many academies and research institutes, including the Belgian, Danish, Dutch, Swedish, Rumanian, and Egyptian academies.

GALLERIA NAZIONALE D'ARTE MODERNA. Another building that remained, the Palazzo delle Belle Arti designed by Cesare Bazzani, became Rome's museum of modern art. The same architect was responsible for landscaping the Valle Giulia, with its avenues, shady piazzas, and fountains approached by flights of steps. The gallery contains the most important collections of 19th- and 20th-century Italian

paintings and sculptures. These include works of the neoclassical school, the romantics, historical painters, and of course the Macchiaioli, the Futurists, "metaphysical" painters such as Giorgio de Chirico, and artists of the Novecento such as Ardengo Soffici. The regional schools of Italy are also well represented.

Monte Mario

To the north of the Prati area ▲ *236* is the Piazzale Maresciallo Giardino (which can be reached by car or bus). From here one can go up to the astronomical and meteorological observatory of Monte Mario and the Astronomy and Copernican Museum (1870). Monte Mario (height 600 feet) owes its name to Marius, the Roman general and statesman (186–57 BC). In the Middle Ages it was known as Mons Gaudii ("Mount of Joy"). Pilgrims arriving by what is now the Via Trionfale caught their first glimpse of the city and of St Peter's Basilica, the object of their journey, from the crest of this hill. Today it offers a fine view over the most modern parts of Rome, as well as the northern section of the ancient city.

PONTE MILVIO. Further north the Ponte Milvio spans the Tiber, guarding the point where the Via Cassia, Via Flaminia, Via Clodia, and Via Veientana converged. Constantine's victory over Maxentius here in 312 AD ● *29* marked the triumph of Christianity.

The Foro Italico

At the foot of Monte Mario, in the midst of pine trees, extends the imposing complex of the Foro Italico, originally called the Foro Mussolini. The construction of this huge sports center began during the Fascist period under the direction of the architect Enrico del Debbio and ended when the finishing touches were given to the Olympic Stadium in 1953. The regime required stadiums both for its gigantic political rallies and to provide worthy settings for its "ceremonies" devoted to youth and to sport. It aimed to cultivate a "strong and healthy" youth that would be "more virile", thus ensuring the "physical improvement of the race". In the center of the buildings stands an enormous monolithic marble obelisk dedicated to Mussolini ● *93*.

Ponte Milvio.

THE CULT OF PHYSICAL EDUCATION The Foro Mussolini was inaugurated on November 4, 1932, on the last day of the celebrations marking the tenth anniversary of the March on Rome. The occasion was also used to solemnly celebrate the large number of medals won by Italian athletes at the Los Angeles Olympics – the trophies being perceived as shining evidence of the physical superiority of Fascist youth.

Statues of athletes in the Stadio dei Marmi.

AN OLD RIVALRY
Rome has two long-established soccer teams which have always been rivals, namely Roma (founded in 1927) and Lazio (1900). The yellow-and-red of the Roma team and the blue-and-white of Lazio meet twice a year for "local Derby" matches.

SUMPTUOUS DECORATIONS
Giulio Romano, Baldassare Peruzzi, Giovanni da Udine, and the Florentine sculptor Baccio Bandinelli were jointly commissioned to decorate Villa Madama. It took the artists four years to complete their work.

STADIO DEI MARMI. The "Marble Stadium" is the highlight of the Foro Mussolini. Designed for twenty thousand spectators, its elegant space is surrounded by sixty statues of athletes modeled on those of antiquity, provided by the provinces of Italy. Two wrestlers, in bronze, adorn the tribune of honor. In front of the obelisk a vast forum, paved with mosaics illustrating the Fascists' punitive missions and the March on Rome, stretches as far as the splendid Fountain of the Sphere, inaugurated in 1934.

THE ACADEMY OF PHYSICAL EDUCATION. This academy was founded in 1928 to enable the regime to train instructors and to develop a national taste for sports. The establishment built by del Debbio has the appearance of a school or barracks; it consists of two symmetrical buildings linked by a loggia adorned with statues of athletes. The use of Pompeian red with white ornamentation is a reference to the Roman Empire and the "gymnasiums" of antiquity. It is now the headquarters of the Italian Olympic Committee (CONI).

STADIO OLIMPICO. Built with the 1960 Rome Olympics in mind, this stadium capable of holding 100,000 spectators was inaugurated in 1953. It was enlarged in 1990 for the soccer World Cup, and on most Sunday afternoons it is overrun by the supercharged *tifosi* (supporters) of Roma or Lazio.

PALAZZO DELLE TERME. The group of buildings on the right, known as the Palazzo delle Terme (1937), houses an indoor swimming pool decorated with mosaics and marble. Part of this complex was turned into a youth hostel. Behind the Foro Italico is the MINISTRY OF FOREIGN AFFAIRS (Affari Esteri). Originally conceived in 1937 as the Lictor's palace, it was only completed and inaugurated in 1956. (Return to the Piazzale Maresciallo Giardino and take Via di Villa Madama.)

VILLA MADAMA. Impressed by Agostino Chigi's residence ▲ *360* and eager to have an even more sumptuous abode built for himself, Cardinal Giulio de' Medici (who later became Pope Clement VII) chose Raphael for this task in 1516. The latter drew up the plans but left the actual construction to Antonio Sangallo the Younger. Like Palazzo Madama ▲ *272*, this villa owes its name to "Madama", alias Margaret of Austria (1522–86), who married first Alessandro de' Medici and then Ottavio Farnese. The villa now belongs to the Italian State and is used for official receptions.

ROME OUTSIDE THE WALLS

THE HOLY MARTYR
It is said that when Agnes was stripped of her clothes in a brothel, her hair grew miraculously, covering her nakedness; at the same time, an angel brought her a dazzling white garment from heaven. Condemned to being burned alive at the stake, she prayed so fervently that the flames spared her. In order to kill her, the torturer had to plunge a dagger into her throat.

SANT'AGNESE AND SANTA COSTANZA

THE MARTYRDOM OF ST AGNES. Tradition claims that Agnes, who belonged to an aristocratic family, suffered martyrdom in the year 250 when she was barely twelve years old. Her parents buried her in one of their properties on the Via Nomentana, where several catacombs already existed. Their daughter appeared to them surrounded by other young martyrs, with a lamb beside her. This is why every year on the Feast of St Agnes, two live lambs are blessed on the altar of the church of Sant'Agnese fuori le Mura and offered as a tithe to the Lateran Basilica: their wool is used to weave the palliums presented by the Pope to the archbishops of the Catholic Church. St Agnes' burial place became a center for pilgrimages, and Constantia, a daughter of the Emperor Constantine, subsequently bought the surrounding land and built a basilica above the catacomb.

BASILICA DI SANT'AGNESE. Rebuilt by Pope Honorius I (625–38) and restored by Hadrian I (772–95), the basilica was extensively modified during the 16th century: the choir was renovated, chapels added, and the new altar crowned with a *ciborium*. The basilica underwent further restoration in the 19th century. The apse was decorated with a splendid 7th-century mosaic, one of the finest examples of Byzantine art in Rome. In the center is the saint, draped like a Byzantine empress, at her feet the instruments of her martyrdom, the fire and the sword; at her side Pope Symmachus and Pope Honorius are shown presenting the church to her. The entrance to the catacombs is in the left nave. Don't miss seeing the mausoleum of Constantia (now the Church of Santa Costanza), which is reached via a path through the garden.

SANTA COSTANZA. Built in the 4th century to receive the sepulcher of Constantia and Helen (who was also a daughter of Constantine), the mausoleum was transformed

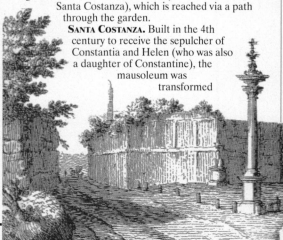

into a baptistery, and, in 1254, it became a church. However, to make matters even more confusing, the church was dedicated to Santa Costanza, a nun, instead of to Constantia. The mausoleum's interior is built with perfect classical proportions according to a concentric design. Twelve pairs of columns support the drum dome, which has twelve openings. An aisle circles this central space, above which is a vault covered with 4th-century mosaics – some of the oldest in Rome to have survived *in situ*. The exquisite floral and geometrical motifs, characteristic of the art of the declining Empire, are splendidly well preserved. (Return by either the 36, 37 or 60 bus to the junction of Via Nomentana and Viale Regina Margherita. Then take a 19 or 30 tram for San Lorenzo fuori le Mura; get off at Piazzale del Verano.) If you have time, while visiting the basilicas outside the walls, you can make a detour in order to explore a part of Rome that is less well known. Turning off the Via Nomentana at the junction with Viale Regina Margherita, you can see the PERONI BREWERY (a rare example of industrial architecture in Rome), the rich Art Nouveau decorations of the VILLINO XIMENES (Piazza Galeno), or the park of the 19th-century VILLA TORLONIA (open to the public since 1978). Another interesting neighborhood is the area around San Lorenzo fuori le Mura: the streets trodden by little Useppe and his mother in Elsa Morante's *La Storia* are still just the same.

SAN LORENZO FUORI LE MURA

LAWRENCE THE DEACON. The ban on burying the dead within the city led Romans to bury their deceased on the fringes of the town, along the main roads ▲ 319. Via Tiburtina, like others, was lined with tombs and catacombs. St Lawrence, who was burnt to death on a grid in 258, was buried there and pilgrims soon flocked to the spot.

THE BASILICA. In 330, in order to cope with the increasing flow of pilgrims, Constantine built a basilica over the martyr's tomb; this church (known as the Minor Basilica) was totally rebuilt by Pelagius II in the 6th century. A century earlier, St Sixtus III had erected a second edifice, the basilica dedicated to the Virgin (known as the Major Basilica), which has also been attributed to Pope Hadrian I. Either Honorius III (1216–27) or Hadrian I was responsible for enlarging Pelagius'

Above, from left to right: the Church of Santa Costanza, Villa Torlonia, and the Peroni brewery.

THE PILGRIMAGE TO THE SEVEN CHURCHES
This is a very ancient pilgrimage, and numerous engravings illustrate the itinerary leading from St Peter's to Santa Maria Maggiore by way of San Paolo fuori le Mura, San Sebastiano on the Via Appia ▲ 326, San Giovanni in Laterano ▲ 198, Santa Croce in Gerusalemme ▲ 200 and San Lorenzo fuori le Mura. The pilgrimage was reinstated in the 16th century by St Philip Neri, who on Shrove Tuesday led an enormous crowd on this pious walk. As the pilgrimage proceeded, people sang, prayed and ate in a festive atmosphere – a spiritual "carnival" that contrasted with the approaching constraints of Lent.

San Lorenzo fuori le Mura.

THE SARCOPHAGUS OF THE GRAPE HARVEST (5th–6th century) The name is due to the decorations of vine branches and

edifice and combining the two churches by demolishing their respective apses. In the same period Pietro Vassalletto added the portico, where amazing frescoes illustrate the life of St Lawrence and St Stephen. Between 1864 and 1870 Virginio Vespignani restored the basilica and did away with the Baroque additions. San Lorenzo was severely damaged by bombing in July 1943, in common with the rest of the area, but was restored soon after the war. The front section of the church corresponds to the former basilica dedicated to the Virgin and is divided into three naves, while the raised chancel is formed by the 6th-century building. The paved floor – where the imagination of the Cosmati is evident in the sense of color and the variety of the geometrical motifs – spreads its carpet of white marble, porphyry and serpentine in the central nave. A 6th-century mosaic on the CHANCEL ARCH, which distinctly divides the two churches, portrays Christ in the act of blessing; on the left Pope Pelagius II advances, offering the church to the Lord, who is enthroned on a blue globe. The CIBORIUM (1148), the oldest to have been made by the Roman marble workers, dominates the altar, its simplicity contrasting with the rich colors of the EPISCOPAL THRONE (1254). Access to the 12th-century cloister is through the sacristy. At the side of the basilica stands a beautiful bell tower (also 12th century); behind it stretches the vast Campo Verano cemetery, which has a monumental entrance (1874–8) designed by Vespignani.

grapes.
THE CLOISTER OF SAN PAULO ★ ● 76 This elegant 13th-century construction, partly the work of the Vassalletto family, is enchanting due to the sheer variety of the columns (some studded with gems, some smooth, some twisted), which are encrusted with multicolored marble and mosaics. The frieze, which consists of stylized heads of lions, wolves and monsters, is reminiscent of ancient Etruscan sculpture.

THE CITTÀ UNIVERSITARIA. Marcello Piacentini was the architect of the campus of the University of Rome built between 1932 and 1935 to replace the Palazzo della Sapienza, which had long been overcrowded. The university library, the Biblioteca Alessandrina, was founded by Pope Alexander VII (1655-67) and inaugurated in 1670. (Turning south, beyond the city walls you will find two of the seven churches of the traditional Rome pilgrimage: San Sebastiano, on the Via Appia ▲ *326*, and San Paolo fuori le Mura on the Via Ostiense.)

SAN PAOLO FUORI LE MURA ● *74*

THE FIRST BASILICA. Rome's largest church until the rebuilding of St Peter's in the 16th century, it was built on the site of a small chapel, about a mile from the Aurelian Wall, on the spot where St Paul was supposed to have been buried after his martyrdom in 67 AD . Construction began under Constantine, but the building was enlarged and only completed in 395 under Honorius. During the 13th to 15th centuries it was decorated with mosaics, frescoes and paintings by some of the leading artists of the time.
THE GREAT RESTORATION. On the night of July 15 to 16, 1823, a terrible fire devastated the basilica. Only part of the façade, the chancel arch, the transept and the cloister were saved. After much agonizing the architects called in by Leo XII

(Luigi Poletti in particular) decided to rebuild the basilica, relying on pictures and documentation to make the new church as similar as possible to the old one. An appeal was made to the public to finance the work; and, as well as money, gifts in kind were received, such as the alabaster columns sent by the Viceroy of Egypt and the blocks of malachite sent by Tsar Nicholas II. The restoration lasted for more than a century, and was completed with the building of a huge quadriportico (covered atrium) by Guglielmo Calderini that has a hundred columns (1928). Although the church is grandiose and majestic, its atmosphere is cold.

THE TREASURES INSIDE. The fire spared some of the church's treasures, including fragments of frescoes by Pietro Cavallini (kept in the basilica's museum), the Gothic *ciborium* by Arnolfo da Cambio, the marble candelabra by Nicolò di Angelo and Pietro Vassalletto (in the choir), the original Byzantine door, and the apse mosaic made by Venetian artists commissioned by Honorius III. This shows the Pope prostrate in adoration at the feet of the Redeemer; the pontiff's diminutive size emphasizes his humility. In the Chapel of the Blessed Sacrament (1725) is a 13th-century mosaic representing the Mother of God that was also rescued from the flames; in front of this mosaic St Ignatius founded the Company of Jesus in ✠ 1541.

Perchè l'Italia Fascista
diffonda nel mondo
più rapida la luce
della civiltà di Roma

Roma - Stabilimenti
Cinematografici

CINECITTÀ

THE FIRST STONE
On the morning of January 29,
1936, Benito Mussolini laid the
foundation stone of the
Cinecittà studios and thus
launched the megalomaniac
project of creating an Italian
Hollywood.

Hidden behind high walls, the long
studio buildings of Cinecittà extend
between the fifth and sixth mile of the
Via Tuscolana. Originally designed to
produce propaganda for the Fascist
regime, these studios have been used for
shooting countless films and have
enabled many of the great Italian film
directors to make their debut. Nowadays,
abandoned by the film industry, they are
mostly used for making television series
and advertisements – and the props from
the great productions are being sold off.

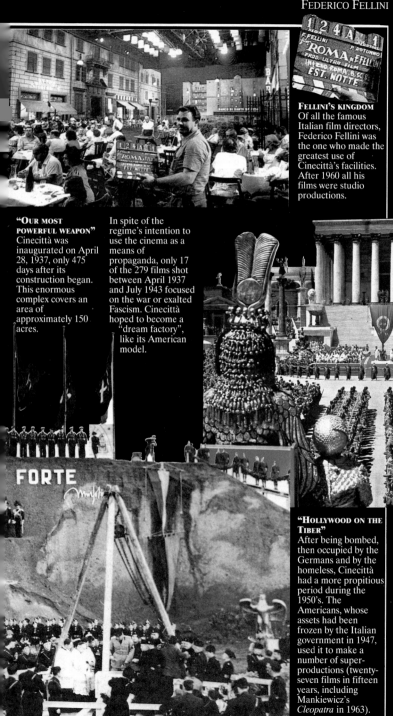

> MORE THAN MOST OTHER DOORS OR THRESHOLDS, THE GATES OF CINECITTÀ ARE SYMBOLIC FOR ME: THEY MARKED A TURNING POINT IN MY LIFE."

FEDERICO FELLINI

FELLINI'S KINGDOM
Of all the famous Italian film directors, Federico Fellini was the one who made the greatest use of Cinecittà's facilities. After 1960 all his films were studio productions.

"OUR MOST POWERFUL WEAPON"
Cinecittà was inaugurated on April 28, 1937, only 475 days after its construction began. This enormous complex covers an area of approximately 150 acres.

In spite of the regime's intention to use the cinema as a means of propaganda, only 17 of the 279 films shot between April 1937 and July 1943 focused on the war or exalted Fascism. Cinecittà hoped to become a "dream factory", like its American model.

"HOLLYWOOD ON THE TIBER"
After being bombed, then occupied by the Germans and by the homeless, Cinecittà had a more propitious period during the 1950's. The Americans, whose assets had been frozen by the Italian government in 1947, used it to make a number of super-productions (twenty-seven films in fifteen years, including Mankiewicz's *Cleopatra* in 1963).

385

Benito
Mussolini
(1883–
1945).

**THE GRANDEUR OF
ANTIQUITY**
EUR is a tangible
manifestation of
Mussolini's vision of
the *"Urbs Magna"*, an
Imperial Rome
linking the city of
Augustus with the
megalopolis of il
Duce's dreams.

"The Square
Coliseum".

EUR

The vast wasteland along the Via Cristoforo isolating the
suburb of EUR from Rome is bounded by Via
Laurentina, Via Ostiense and Via del Mare. The layout of
EUR imitates that of a Roman town: the main roads of
the Via Imperiale (today the Via Cristoforo Colombo)
and the Viale Europa cross at right angles.
THE THIRD ROME. Mussolini planned to celebrate the
twentieth anniversary, in 1942, of his March on Rome
with a universal exhibition "open to all the sciences, arts,
and all possible forms of work and activity". A group of
administrative buildings were to be built between Rome
and the sea; the area was initially called E 42 and then
EUR (Esposizione Universale di Roma), and was supposed
to have been the nucleus of a modern urban center – "the
Third Rome" – a visible symbol and apotheosis of Imperial
power. The overall plan was prepared in 1938 by the Roman
architect Marcello Piacentini, who had already created several
of the monumental works most typical of the Fascist period.
Piacentini surrounded himself with a group of architects,
varying philosophies, including Giuseppe Pagano, Luigi
Piccinato, Ettore Rossi and Luigi Vietti. Originally, on little
more than 6 acres, there was to be a Palazzo del Turismo, a
Palazzo degli Italiani all'Estero (for Italians domiciled
abroad), a museum of ancient art, a museum of modern art, a
Palazzo del Cinema and a Palazzo delle Esposizioni, including
exhibition halls devoted to telecommunications and the
economics of cooperatives, etc. But the war put an end to the
work and the buildings were badly damaged first by German
and then by Allied occupation.
THE NEW ADMINISTRATIVE CENTER. When the project
continued in 1951, provision was made for additional
buildings and the decentralization of
administrative offices (some political,
others the headquarters of
big companies,
such as

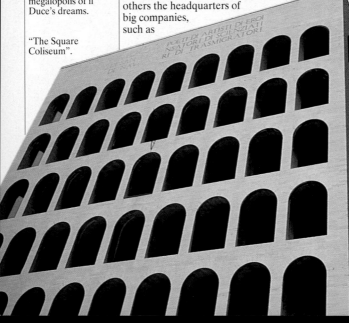

ENI and Alitalia) and more museums. Consequently the status of EUR changed: conceived as a monumental center, it became an administrative one. At the same time a residential district was developed, making EUR – now linked to Rome by the Metro – into a satellite town with shady avenues and vast panoramas.

PIAZZALE DELLE NAZIONI UNITÀ. This esplanade is flanked by two semicircular buildings with porticos designed by Giovanni Muzio, Mario Paniconi and Giulio Pediconi.

THE PALAZZO DELLA CIVILTÀ DEL LAVORO. Without a doubt this building (pictured below, left), begun by Giovanni Guerrini, Ernesto Bruno La Padula and Mario Romano in 1938, is the most beautiful in EUR. It has been nicknamed the "Square Coliseum" by the Romans, and its massive white walls punctuated by six floors of rhythmic arcades dominate the Tiber. The statues in each arcade on the ground floor represent the arts and human activities; four sculptured groups decorate the monumental stairway. At the opposite end of the Viale della Civiltà del Lavoro stands the PALAZZO DEI CONGRESSI, designed by the rationalist architect Adalberto Libera (1938). Its cube-shaped central section projects from behind a vast portico. Both the technical installations and the general concept of the building are remarkably well thought out.

PIAZZA MARCONI. Originally called Piazza Imperiale, this square was renamed because of the obelisk (1939–59) in memory of Guglielmo Marconi, inventor of the radio, in the center, which was intended as the focal point of EUR and of Mussolini's Universal Exhibition. Among the buildings that surround the square is the GRATTACIELO ITALIA, a skyscraper that includes offices and a hotel. To the right stands the PALAZZO DELLE SCIENZE, which now houses the Museo Preistorico ed Etnografico Luigi Pigorini and the Museo dell'Alto Medievo; to the left the MUSEO DELLE ARTI E TRADIZIONI POPULARI, which displays examples of popular crafts collected at the beginning of the century for the great ethnographic exhibition held in 1911 ▲ *92*. Some interesting prehistoric and ethnographic exhibits collected in the 17th century by the Jesuit Athanase Kircher and added to by Luigi Pigorini are on view in the MUSEO PIGORINI, which was founded by Pigorini in 1875. The MUSEO DELL'ALTO MEDIEVO (early Middle Ages), inaugurated in 1967, houses the 4th to 10th century collections formerly in the National Roman Museum ▲ *335*.

The buildings of EUR are not unlike the ones that two decades earlier had haunted the canvases of the metaphysical painter Giorgio De Chirico (1888–1978) – such as *The Melancholy of the Politician*, painted in 1913 (above).

ORDER AND GRANDEUR
Fascist architects aimed to impress the "new man" with the values of Mussolini's

regime. A sense of grandeur, order and symmetry was a fundamental part of the image that the regime wished to give of itself.

▲ ROME OUTSIDE THE WALLS

THE MODEL OF ROME
Measuring more than
650 feet in length,
this gigantic model of
Rome at the time of
Constantine (306–37
AD) is said to be the
largest architectural
model in existence.
Produced by Italo
Gismondi between
1933–37, it is now one
of the major exhibits
of EUR's Museo
della Civiltà Romana.

The Ferris Wheel at
Rome's Luna Park,
near the Abbazia
delle Tre Fontane.

MUSEO DELLA CIVILTÀ ROMANA (Museum of Roman
Civilization). The archeological material from the great
prewar exhibitions – the 1911 exhibition ▲ 376 and the one
devoted to Rome under Augustus in 1937 to 1938 – was
reassembled in the vast rooms of this museum opened in
1955. Plaster casts of statues and monuments, reconstructions
of buildings, reproductions, charts and models (including an
enormous model of Rome at the time of Constantine)
illustrate what life in ancient Rome was like and trace the
history and influence of Roman civilization.

VIALE EUROPA On the right at the end of this avenue stands
the massive BASILICA DI SANTI PIETRO E PAOLO (1938). On the
left is the ARCHIVIO DELLO STATO building, initially intended
to house a museum devoted to the armed forces; the original
documents of all the laws and decrees of the Italian State
since it came into being are kept in the archives here.

VIALE AMERICA Parallel to this avenue is an artificial lake
almost three quarters of a mile long, which was supposed to
have been spanned by a great arch. The Passeggiata Giappone
by the water is bordered by thousands of cherry trees donated
by the people of Japan. Also interrupting the Via Cristoforo
Colombo is the spectacular PALAZZO DELLO SPORT, built by
Marcello Piacentini and Pier Luigi Nervi for the 1960
Olympic Games ● 33, 93.

ABBAZIA DELLE TRE FONTANE This fresh green oasis is
located just off Via Laurentina, the eastern boundary of
EUR. St Paul is supposed to have been martyred here,
and it is said that after he was beheaded his head
bounced three times, causing three fountains
to gush from the ground. Three churches
were therefore built on this spot:
Santi Vincenzo ed Anastasio,
Santa Maria Scala Coeli, and
San Paolo alle Tre Fontane.
Since 1868 the area has
belonged to the Trappists,
who drained the marshy
land and planted
eucalyptus trees in
order to rid the
neighborhood of
malaria. These
trees now serve
another purpose:
the monks make a
eucalyptus liqueur,
which you can buy
at the abbey's
shop.

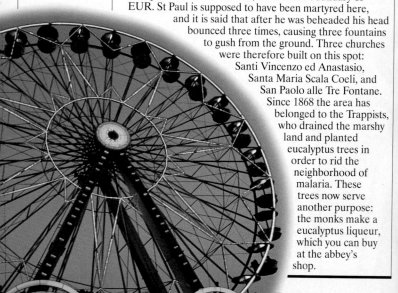

TIVOLI AND PALESTRINA

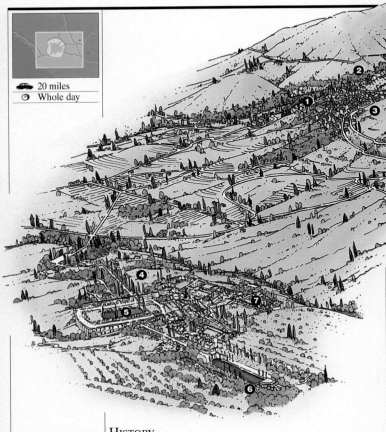

MEDIEVAL HOUSES
A number of these
can still be seen along
Via Campitelli, and a
fine group stands in
Via del Colle. Both
the Via del Duomo
and the streets
leading into it have
fully retained their
medieval appearance.

HISTORY

THE ANCIENT TIBUR. Tivoli (Latin name: Tibur) occupies a
strategic position, being located at the point where the
Aniene (the ancient Anio) flows down from the Abruzzi to
the valley. It thus controlled the only viable route to Latium
from these mountains, which were originally inhabited by the
Volsci, Sabine and Samnite tribes. The town's origins are
uncertain. According to one legend it was a colony of Alba
Longa, while another legend links it with Tiburnus, one of the
sons of the Greek hero Amphiaraos. All that is known of its
early history is its hostile encounters with Rome: initially in
361 BC, when Tibur seems to have been an ally of the Gauls,
and finally during the Latin War, which ended with the total
submission of Latium in 338 BC. From that time on, Tivoli's
history was identical with Rome's. From the 2nd century AD
the Roman aristocracy fell under the spell of the natural
beauty of the place, which had become a part of the Roman
campania, and luxurious villas began to appear amid "the
thick bowers of Tibur", as the poet Horace eulogized them.
FROM THE MIDDLE AGES TO TODAY. Having become a
prosperous episcopal town and an autonomous commune,
Tivoli was often prey to Rome's expansionist policies. It was

not until 1816, however, that it completely lost its autonomy (until 1870), becoming a small town like so many others in the Papal States.

VIA TIBURTINA

Whereas today's Via Tiburtina winds its way to Tivoli through olive groves, the old road, after Ponte Lucano, used to lead straight to the town. It passed close to a large domed circular hall, the Tempio della Tosse (Temple of the Tosse), which was turned into a church in the Middle Ages. Then it ran alongside the sanctuary of Hercules Victor, the god of war, assimilated with Mars, and also the god of commerce. The temple, which contained an oracle, was at the end of an enormous square surrounded by a portico reached by two great stairways on either side; between these rose the steps of a theater. This combination of temple and theater was typical of sanctuaries in central and southern Italy, such as Praeneste ▲ *398*, Pietrabondante and the Teatro Pompeo in Rome ▲ *248*.

A WALK IN THE TOWN

Starting with Piazza Trento, one can discover numerous medieval houses in the streets of this little town, which is dominated by the Rocca Pia fortress built by Pius II (1458–64).

SANTA MARIA MAGGIORE. This church, founded in the 5th century but rebuilt in the 13th century, has a Romanesque façade and a Gothic portal. Its atrium has a fine 13th-century fresco of *The Virgin and Child*. (Proceed to Piazza del Duomo, part of which is built on the site of the ancient forum.)

THE DUOMO. The cathedral dedicated to St Lawrence was rebuilt in 1650. However, its Romanesque campanile dates from the 12th century. Inside, one should see the famous 13th-century sculpture of *The Deposition* in the fourth chapel on the right; and the *Triptych of the Saviour* (12th–14th century) in the third chapel on the left, opened on request.

VILLA GREGORIANA. This was created by Pope Gregory XVI at the beginning of the 19th century. The park extends along both banks of the Aniene, which the pontiff had partly channeled. Go to the belvedere halfway up the great waterfall and you will appreciate the force with which the river roars down this 350-foot cataract.

TEMPLE OF THE SIBYL. Two temples (reached through the La Sibilla restaurant) stand on the edge of the Aniene falls. The rectangular one, the older of the two (2nd century BC), is dedicated to Tiburnus, the legendary founder of the town. The round temple, built in the Corinthian style, is that of the sibyl Albunea. Surrounded by columns and built of great slabs of travertine, it stands on a podium, the steps of which have disappeared. (Go along Via del Colle as far as the CHURCH OF SAN SILVESTRO, which is Romanesque and has very

A CURIOUS AEDICULE Between the portal and the great rose window of Santa Maria Maggiore there is a small Gothic aedicule.

THE TEMPLE OF HERCULES VICTOR The cult of Hercules Victor, which had a major following in Latium, certainly started in Tibur, reaching Rome by the end of Republican times. The opulence of this temple was so well known that Octavian, the future Augustus, attempted to gain possession of it in 41 BC. Subsequently, the Emperor's cult was linked to this deity.

IPPOLITO D'ESTE
A favorite retreat of the ancient Romans, Tivoli was bound to appeal to this cardinal who was a patron of the arts, friend of the humanists and avid reader of classical texts. The richest of all the Italian cardinals, after his hopes of becoming pope were dashed he lavished his wealth on the Villa d'Este.

"The green, blue or almost black waters of these vast pools add their tranquil tones to the insistent, impassioned song of the cascades. On all sides, water jets and

cypresses compete, thrusting skyward in bold rivalry."
Gabriel Fauré

fine 13th-century frescoes. A little further on is the old entrance of the Villa d'Este. The perspective of the gardens was originally designed to be seen from this spot. Finally, return to Piazza Trento.)

VILLA D'ESTE ● 88

In 1550 Cardinal Ippolito d'Este was appointed Governor of Tivoli. He wasted no time in taking possession of the Governor's palace, located in a former Benedictine monastery which he asked Pirro Ligorio to remodel to his taste. The Villa d'Este's fame, however, is due more to its gardens than to the building itself. Each alley, path or avenue reveals a new mossy fountain in a carefully landscaped vista: there are supposed to be five hundred fountains altogether. This most famous of Italian-style gardens, which has been widely imitated, reverberates with the sound of so many fountains that it inspired the Romantic composer Franz Liszt to write a piano suite called *Fountains of the Villa d'Este*.

THE LAYOUT OF THE GARDENS. To clear space for the gardens a whole area of the town had to be demolished, many inhabitants being forced to sell or face expropriation. Due to the steepness of the terrain, enormous earth-moving works were undertaken in order to create alternating terraces and slopes. In addition, the site had an irregular shape. The overall layout, designed to be seen from the original entrance at the foot of the hill, had to achieve two main purposes: to create the illusion that the villa was centrally placed (it is in fact slightly off-center) and to set it back by visually increasing the depth of the property. The means chosen to achieve this were unusual for the time. A central alley prolonging the loggia, known as the Avenue of Perspectives, was made to intersect with five paths linking the monumental fountains;

these were mostly positioned toward the sides to give the effect of an enclosure in relation to the surrounding landscape.

DECAY AND RENEWED SPLENDOR. When the cardinal died, the gardens were unfinished despite the speed with which the project had been implemented, and the work was continued by his descendants. This was followed by a period of decay, when the Habsburgs inherited the property. The furniture and the collections in the villa were sold and, since the upkeep of the gardens proved too costly, they were left to grow wild, forming the unkempt thickets painted by Fragonard and Hubert Robert in the 18th century. After being confiscated by the Italian State during the First World War, the villa was completely restored and opened to the public in the 1920s.

A SOBER AND MAJESTIC BUILDING. The *cortile*, surrounded by a portico and adorned with a fountain, took the place of the former cloister of the Benedictine monastery. Passing through it, you come to the Appartamento Vecchio. This apartment is at ground level on the courtyard side but one floor up on the façade

overlooking the gardens. The villa has a central living room which opens onto a terrace offering a magnificent view. All the rooms are decorated with 16th-century frescoes and hung with Flemish paintings as well as copies of famous pictures. You then descend to the Appartamento Nobile, with ceilings painted by Federico Zuccaro and Girolamo Muziano exalting the glory of the d'Este family and the mythological origins of Tivoli. Its middle room opens onto a loggia (the only decorative feature of an otherwise austere façade), which leads to the gardens.

A TOUR OF THE GARDENS. From the first avenue at the foot of the building you come to the Cardinal's Walk, in the center of which there is a loggia echoing that of the palace above. Immediately below this, facing the Avenue of Perspectives, is the Fontana del Bicchierone designed by Bernini. On the third level down you enter the Avenue of a Hundred Fountains (below), at the south end of which stands the Rometta Fountain, created according to a design by Ligorio (1567) and representing ancient Rome in its Tiber setting. Below, the disturbing Fountain of the Dragons, at the center of the avenue that bears its name, emphasizes the perspective with its powerful jet of water. From the level of the fish ponds you can see the gigantic Fontana dell'Organo Idraulico (Water-Organ Fountain) designed by Claude Vernard, which unfortunately no longer plays music. Going still lower, you reach the Rotunda of the Cypresses, the final landmark of the perspective from the loggia. To find the other fountains, all of which have resounding names, explore the smaller paths and alleys; you will also discover the innumerable "grottoes" scattered all over the gardens, like the Grotto of Diana near the villa.

THE AVENUE OF A HUNDRED FOUNTAINS
Water jets gush high in the air between the eagles of the Este family and the *fleurs-de-lys* of France. This alley symbolically links the Rometta Fountain (designed to resemble the Tiber) and the huge Fontana dell'Ovata created by Ligorio.

VILLA ADRIANA

This enormous estate created by the Emperor Hadrian (117–138 AD) extends over the slopes of the Tiburtine Hills. Its size (nearly 300 acres), the variety of its architecture and the sheer beauty of the place make it one of Italy's most extraordinary archeological sites.

FROM PLUNDER TO ARCHEOLOGY
The Villa Adriana's fate was the same as that of many other Roman monuments: it was laid waste by the barbarians and became a marble quarry until the 16th century. Then the architect Pirro Ligorio undertook its excavation and drew a map of it. Since then, archeologists have tried their best to reconstruct it and to identify its buildings, most of which were richly decorated.

TRAVEL SOUVENIRS. Hadrian built two of Rome's greatest monuments, his mausoleum ▲ *233* and the Pantheon ▲ *264*, but his masterpiece was the Villa Adriana. Thanks to a 6th-century biographer we know that Hadrian, a cultured man and a great traveler, wanted his villa to mirror the famous sites of the Empire – bringing together, as it were, his travel souvenirs. Each part of the estate was thus named after the thing or place it was supposed to represent: the Lyceum, the Academy, the Prytaneum, the Stoa Poikile, Canopus, the Vale of Tempe, etc. "And to make sure nothing was omitted, he even included Hades (Hell)."

THE LARGEST ROMAN VILLA. This gigantic complex, which was built during the first ten years of Hadrian's reign and was actually designed by the Emperor himself, consisted of a series of pavilions skillfully placed in a natural setting. As well as the Imperial abode, it included accommodation for the Emperor's retinue and for guests, special housing for slaves and bodyguards, three bath complexes, libraries, a stadium and an esplanade with a swimming pool, all of which were adorned with fountains, ponds and lakes to reflect the harmony of earth and sky. Underground, more than one and a half miles of service tunnels were excavated, some of them wide enough for horse-drawn carriages to pass through. The most important of these converged in the south to form "Hades" – a long trapezium, more than 15 feet wide, formed by four of the tunnels, which may have been nothing more sinister than a "chariot park"!

THE TERRACE OF TEMPE. A model of the villa is on view in a modern structure near the entrance. From there, go due east as far as the terrace overlooking a valley that Hadrian called Tempe after the famous valley in Thessaly, in Greece. Further on, to the right one finds the *hospitalia*. These sleeping quarters with mosaic floors were probably reserved for the Praetorian guards responsible for guarding the entrance to the Imperial palace, which consisted of three courtyards with peristyles.

THE LIBRARY COURTYARD. This was the site of two libraries (Greek and Latin) located on the north side. A set of

Model of Villa Adriana.

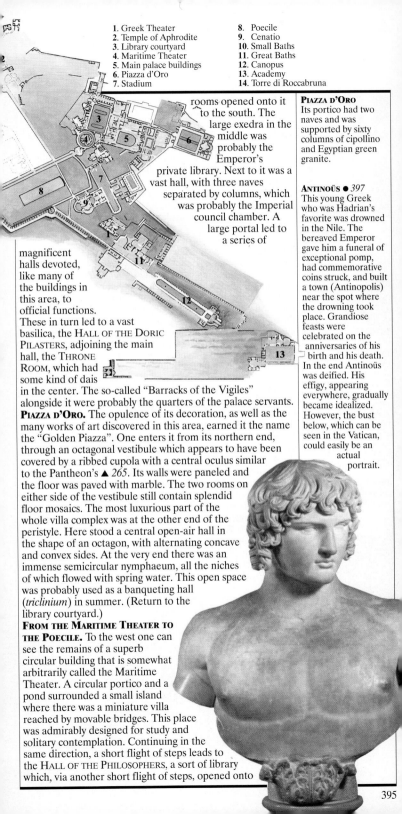

rooms opened onto it to the south. The large exedra in the middle was probably the Emperor's private library. Next to it was a vast hall, with three naves separated by columns, which was probably the Imperial council chamber. A large portal led to a series of magnificent halls devoted, like many of the buildings in this area, to official functions. These in turn led to a vast basilica, the HALL OF THE DORIC PILASTERS, adjoining the main hall, the THRONE ROOM, which had some kind of dais in the center. The so-called "Barracks of the Vigiles" alongside it were probably the quarters of the palace servants.

PIAZZA D'ORO. The opulence of its decoration, as well as the many works of art discovered in this area, earned it the name the "Golden Piazza". One enters it from its northern end, through an octagonal vestibule which appears to have been covered by a ribbed cupola with a central oculus similar to the Pantheon's ▲ 265. Its walls were paneled and the floor was paved with marble. The two rooms on either side of the vestibule still contain splendid floor mosaics. The most luxurious part of the whole villa complex was at the other end of the peristyle. Here stood a central open-air hall in the shape of an octagon, with alternating concave and convex sides. At the very end there was an immense semicircular nymphaeum, all the niches of which flowed with spring water. This open space was probably used as a banqueting hall (*triclinium*) in summer. (Return to the library courtyard.)

FROM THE MARITIME THEATER TO THE POECILE. To the west one can see the remains of a superb circular building that is somewhat arbitrarily called the Maritime Theater. A circular portico and a pond surrounded a small island where there was a miniature villa reached by movable bridges. This place was admirably designed for study and solitary contemplation. Continuing in the same direction, a short flight of steps leads to the HALL OF THE PHILOSOPHERS, a sort of library which, via another short flight of steps, opened onto

PIAZZA D'ORO
Its portico had two naves and was supported by sixty columns of cipollino and Egyptian green granite.

ANTINOÜS ● 397
This young Greek who was Hadrian's favorite was drowned in the Nile. The bereaved Emperor gave him a funeral of exceptional pomp, had commemorative coins struck, and built a town (Antinopolis) near the spot where the drowning took place. Grandiose feasts were celebrated on the anniversaries of his birth and his death. In the end Antinoüs was deified. His effigy, appearing everywhere, gradually became idealized. However, the bust below, which can be seen in the Vatican, could easily be an actual portrait.

the Poecile. This double portico, flanked by a vast rectangular space and measuring more than 750 feet in length, owes its name to the Athenian Stoa Poikile (multicolored portico) on which it was modeled. Its two rows of columns, on either side of a high central wall, were originally covered by a gabled roof. Thanks to the building's clever orientation one could walk along its cool north-facing side in summer and keep to the warm, sheltered south-facing side in the winter. As an inscription discovered in the 18th century testifies, it was prescribed for health-giving walks (*ambulatio*). The square itself has an ornamental garden and a large rectangular pool in the center. Its western end rests on an astonishing substructure consisting of the "Cento Camerelle" (one hundred cells), which probably housed the villa's staff. Going south, one reaches a space with three exedras paved in marble. This was a huge dining hall (*cenatio*) used for official banquets. Since it was north-facing, it seems likely that it was designed only for summer use; the Emperor would in any case have done his winter entertaining on the Palatine ▲ *146*. To the east there is a *pinacoteca* (picture gallery) and then a nymphaeum (long thought to have been a stadium), which linked the dining hall to a spacious area where there is a swimming pool and a cryptoporticus. Continuing to the south, one reaches the Small Baths and the Great Baths, which are separated by a courtyard. The fact that they are so close together would seem to indicate that the one complex was for women and the other for men; moreover, their proximity to the "Cento Camerelle" suggests that they were reserved for the villa's staff.

CANOPUS. South of the baths there is a valley with a long pond surrounded by a splendid colonnade. At the bottom end stands a nymphaeum that is recognizably a temple of Serapis (*Serapeum*). It consists of a semicircular exedra with a ribbed cupola, extended by a long vaulted corridor. This ensemble, which is decorated with fountains and statues, was for a long time believed to be an evocation of the Egyptian town of Canopus, linked to Alexandria by a canal from the Nile and famous for its Temple of Serapis. A more recent interpretation gives it another meaning: the pond is not the canal but the Mediterranean, which explains the presence of Greece (symbolized by copies of the caryatids from the Erechtheion in Athens) and of Asia (represented by copies of two *Amazons* by Phidias that

adorned the Temple of Artemis in Ephesus and a copy of Praxiteles' renowned *Venus of Cnidus*). The architectural complex at the bottom of the lake is seen as symbolizing Egypt; at least that is what one may deduce from the three sculptured groups that decorated it, the layout of which is reconstructed in the Vatican's Egyptian Museum. Its composition consisted of Osiris-Apis in the center, Isis-Demeter at the back and, on the walls, several repetitions of Antinoüs ▲ *395*, Hadrian's young favorite who, after his premature death in Egypt in 130 AD, was deified by the Emperor. (Allow time to visit the small museum beside Canopus to see the items discovered during the excavations of the 1950's.)

TORRE DI ROCCABRUNA AND THE ACADEMY. On the hill overlooking the valley of Canopus from the southwest, one can see a number of places of long-standing fame. The first is the Torre di Roccabruna, an octagonal building with two floors covered by a dome, probably erected as a sort of panoramic observatory. One then reaches the Academy, a vast square surrounded by a portico. The best-preserved buildings in this area are the TEMPLE OF APOLLO, a large circular hall surmounted by a cupola, and to the south the ODEON, a small theater of which the stage front remains. The finest works of art discovered in the Villa Adriana came from the Academy, including the *Mosaic of the Doves* ▲ *135*. Returning to the entrance of the archeological site, one can walk down a pleasant avenue lined with cypresses to reach the Greek theater and the nymphaeum, which are at the northern end of the villa.

THE CARYATIDS OF CANOPUS
In the middle the columns are replaced by six caryatids, four of which are copies of those supporting the roof of the Erechtheion, one of the temples of the Acropolis in Athens; the other two are Sileni. The original statues are now in the museum.

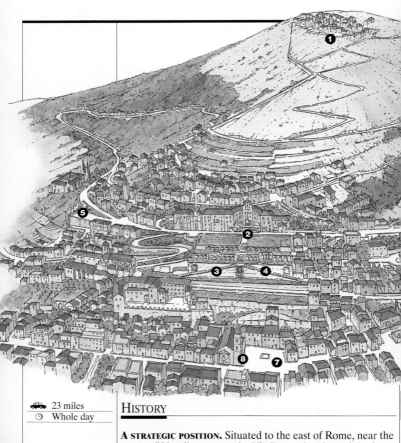

🚗 23 miles	
🕐 Whole day	

The exedra on the right of the Terrace of the Hemicycles.

HISTORY

A STRATEGIC POSITION. Situated to the east of Rome, near the twenty-fifth milestone on the Via Prenestina, in ancient times Palestrina was called Praeneste. Built on the slopes of Mount Ginestro, the southernmost bastion of the Praenestine Hills, the town overlooks the gorge separating them from the Alban Hills and also dominated the Via Labicana and Via Latina, which lay at the bottom of the valley. This geographical location explains the importance the town acquired from the 7th century BC. Legends abound as to its origins. Some link its foundation to Praenestos, the son of King Latinos; others to Teleganos, the putative son of Ulysses and Circe, or to Caeculus, the son of the god Vulcan.

REBELLION AND SUBMISSION. The earliest references by historians to Praeneste concern its fraught relations with Rome: conquered in 380 BC, it rebelled several times, formed an alliance with the Gauls in 358, and took part in the last Latin War. At the end of the 2nd century BC the town seems to have enjoyed great prosperity – presumably due to its trade with the East – and grandiose constructions, including the shrine to Fortuna, transformed its appearance. In the following century Praeneste sided with Marius, thus earning the hatred of Sulla, who massacred the Praenestines in reprisal. At the beginning of the Empire the town's importance diminished. However, the oracle that had ensured its posterity retained its influence until the 4th century AD.

A COLONNA FIEFDOM. In the Middle Ages a new town was born on the site of the sanctuary. As a fiefdom of the Colonna's, the town was destroyed several times. Finally, in 1630, this great family sold it to Carlo Barberini, Urban VIII's brother.

THE TEMPLE OF FORTUNA

NUMERIUS' DREAM. In a passage recounting the myth of the town's foundation and the sanctuary's vocation, Cicero speaks of a certain Numerius Sufficius who was told in his dreams to go and break a stone in a precise spot. Since the dreams recurred, he decided to obey. The split stone revealed *sortes* ("lots"), oak tablets inscribed with prophetic words. The author added that the spot where the lots were discovered was not far from the place where mothers venerated the statue of the goddess Fortuna and her two children, Jupiter and Juno. At the same time, near the Temple of Fortuna honey flowed from an olive tree and convinced the priests to proclaim that the Praeneste *sortes* were destined for celebrity. Cicero thus clearly distinguished between two very ancient places of worship: the statue of Fortuna associated with the oracle and the temple where the miracle of the olive tree occurred. These affirmations are in fact confirmed by the layout of the site, which consists of a series of superimposed terraces linked by sloping ramps and flights of steps that converge at the top.

FORTUNA AND THE "SORTES". The main access was provided by two oblique ramps. Where these two met, in the center, a flight of steps led to the TERRAZZA DEGLI EMICICLI (Terrace of the Hemicycles), named after the two porticoed exedras on either side of the steps. The better preserved of the two is the one on the right, which is covered by a coffered vault. The oracle was located directly in front, as can be seen from the base, which probably supported the statue of Fortuna – the statue near which, according to Cicero, the lots were found.

THE UPPER TEMPLE. The steps then lead up to the TERRAZZA DEI FORNICI A SEMICOLONNE (Terrace of the Niches with Two Columns) and up another flight to the TERRAZZA DELLA CORTINA (Terrace of the Curtain), which with its colonnade and porticoes constituted the upper sanctuary. The terrace was open on the valley side, but on the three other sides was closed by a portico with a double row of Corinthian columns. In its center was the

A PROSPEROUS TOWN
Items from Praeneste's remarkable princely tombs – such as the bowl shown above – are exhibited as part of the Bernardini, Barberini and Castellani collections in the Villa Giulia ▲ 370 and on the Capitol ▲ 132. They provide ample evidence of the town's prosperity in the 7th century BC.

"THE WELL OF THE SORTES"
Near the base of the statue of Fortuna there is a well covered by a circular aedicule, with columns set on a high podium. This was the shrine of the oracle into which, according to Cicero, a child would descend to choose one of the oracular tablets (*sortes*). The text inscribed on it would then be read out to the faithful waiting in the neighboring exedra.

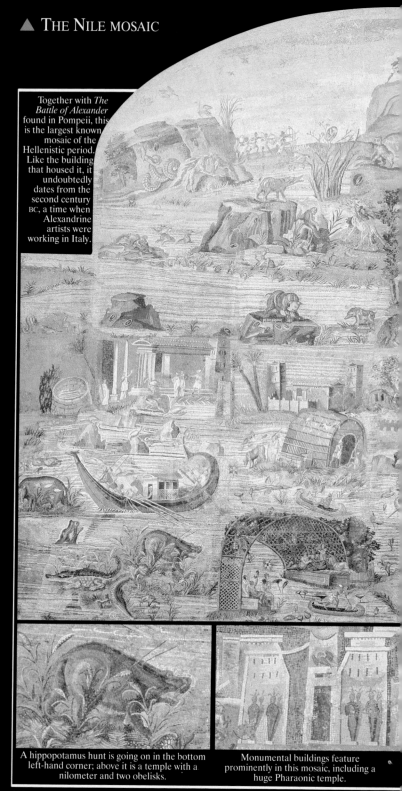

▲ THE NILE MOSAIC

Together with *The Battle of Alexander* found in Pompeii, this is the largest known mosaic of the Hellenistic period. Like the building that housed it, it undoubtedly dates from the second century BC, a time when Alexandrine artists were working in Italy.

A hippopotamus hunt is going on in the bottom left-hand corner; above it is a temple with a nilometer and two obelisks.

Monumental buildings feature prominently in this mosaic, including a huge Pharaonic temple.

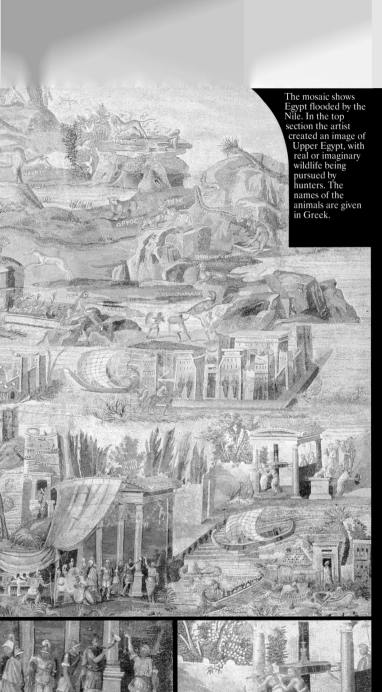

The mosaic shows Egypt flooded by the Nile. In the top section the artist created an image of Upper Egypt, with real or imaginary wildlife being pursued by hunters. The names of the animals are given in Greek.

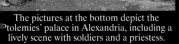

The pictures at the bottom depict the Ptolemies' palace in Alexandria, including a lively scene with soldiers and a priestess.

On the right a warship and a sailing ship symbolize the military and commercial ports. The scene above depicts a religious ceremony.

A statue of the famous composer Giovanni Pier Luigi da Palestrina (1525–94) stands in the main piazza (top). The Church of Sant'Agapito (bottom).

THE ROAD TO CASTEL SAN PIETRO
The tireless historian and traveler Gregorovius (1821–91) tells how on a hot day in August he walked up the rocky path to Castel San Pietro, the small village on the site of the citadel of Praeneste. It was along this same path that Gina Lollobrigida rode her donkey in the film *Pane, Amore e Fantasia*. You don't have to follow in Gregorovius' footsteps, but a car ride to this spot, and beyond to Guadagnolo, the highest village in Lazio, offers panoramic views over mountain landscapes and the finest natural scenery in the region.

cavea (semicircular stepped stone seating) of a theater, beneath which ran the portico. A round temple crowned the sanctuary.

THE MUSEUM. Palestrina's Palazzo Colonna-Barberini was converted into a museum in 1953. Some of its treasures are quite remarkable. Room III contains a large 2nd-century Hellenistic marble head, which probably came from the statue of Fortuna, since it was found near the Well of the Sortes ▲ *399*. Also in this room is a fine example of Hellenistic sculpture from Rhodes, a tall female figure in black marble (possibly Isis since black was the color of this goddess). Rooms VIII and IX contain objects such as bronze *cistae* and mirrors, ceramics, and toilet articles made of wood and ivory that were traditionally placed inside sarcophagi and tufa urns with the remains of the deceased. These objects come from the Praeneste necropolis. Finally, in Room XIV there is the famous *Nile Mosaic* ▲ *400,* which originally covered the apse of the great hall in the forum. (One can also visit the citadel of Praeneste, now a small village, Castel San Pietro.)

AROUND THE ANCIENT FORUM

FROM PAGAN TEMPLE TO CATHEDRAL. Piazza Regina Margherita, in the middle of the modern town, corresponds to the forum of the ancient Praeneste. The cathedral (above left), built on the site of a temple dating from the 4th century BC, is dedicated to the town's patron, St Agapitus, who was martyred in the amphitheater during Aurelian's persecutions in the 3rd century AD.

THE NILE MOSAIC ▲ *400.* Also in the main piazza there is an ancient basilica (on the right). It is flanked on one side by a natural grotto known as the Antro delle Sorti (Cave of the Sortes), decorated and paved with a fine fish-motif mosaic, and on the other by a vast hall with an apse. This has been identified as a shrine to Isis (*Iseum*) because of the mosaic portraying the Nile and the black marble statue, both now in the museum (see above), as well as two obelisks found outside. In the lower part, reached through a low-vaulted door, there is a small barrel-vaulted room that served as the town's treasury (*aerarium*).

Ostia

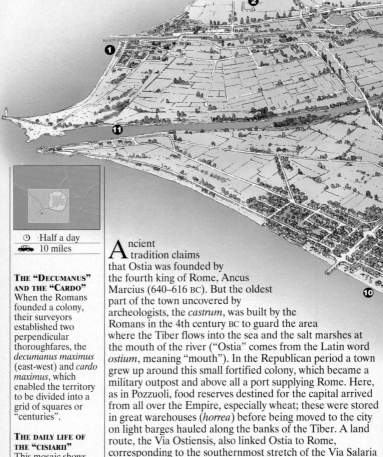

⊙	Half a day
🚗	10 miles

THE "DECUMANUS" AND THE "CARDO"
When the Romans founded a colony, their surveyors established two perpendicular thoroughfares, the *decumanus maximus* (east-west) and *cardo maximus*, which enabled the territory to be divided into a grid of squares or "centuries".

THE DAILY LIFE OF THE "CISIARII"
This mosaic shows details of the carters' life, including a journey, a halt, the animals being harnessed, and even the names of the mules: Pudes, Podagrosus, Barosus …

Ancient tradition claims that Ostia was founded by the fourth king of Rome, Ancus Marcius (640–616 BC). But the oldest part of the town uncovered by archeologists, the *castrum*, was built by the Romans in the 4th century BC to guard the area where the Tiber flows into the sea and the salt marshes at the mouth of the river ("Ostia" comes from the Latin word *ostium*, meaning "mouth"). In the Republican period a town grew up around this small fortified colony, which became a military outpost and above all a port supplying Rome. Here, as in Pozzuoli, food reserves destined for the capital arrived from all over the Empire, especially wheat; these were stored in great warehouses (*horrea*) before being moved to the city on light barges hauled along the banks of the Tiber. A land route, the Via Ostiensis, also linked Ostia to Rome, corresponding to the southernmost stretch of the Via Salaria (the ancient salt route). In the 1st century BC Ostia was the victim of several disasters – including being sacked by Marius' troops in 87 – and was radically modified. Sulla fortified it with great ramparts, and Augustus embarked on a major public works program, which included the forum and the theater. From the reign of Claudius the creation of a new port (later enlarged by Trajan) reduced Ostia's role; the old Roman colony nevertheless remained one of the centers of Rome's supply network, henceforth managed by a special official, the procurator of the *annona*. Between the reigns of Domitian and Hadrian, Ostia acquired the features that are recognizable today: large public buildings, warehouses, and residential quarters characterized by tall brick apartment blocks (*insulae* ● 69) several stories high. The town had been virtually deserted when, between the 4th and 5th

404

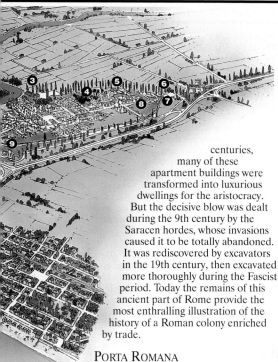

THE PORTS OF CLAUDIUS AND TRAJAN
Aware of the need to increase Ostia's storage capacity, when he came to power the Emperor Claudius decided to build another harbor to the north of the mouth of the Tiber. Work began in 42 AD and was completed, in the reign of Nero, in 54. However, at the end of the 1st century this basin proved inadequate and began to silt up. Trajan therefore built a new port, while allowing the old one to continue operating. Warehouses (*horrea*) along the wharfs provided storage facilities for newly arrived merchandise.

centuries, many of these apartment buildings were transformed into luxurious dwellings for the aristocracy. But the decisive blow was dealt during the 9th century by the Saracen hordes, whose invasions caused it to be totally abandoned. It was rediscovered by excavators in the 19th century, then excavated more thoroughly during the Fascist period. Today the remains of this ancient part of Rome provide the most enthralling illustration of the history of a Roman colony enriched by trade.

PORTA ROMANA

In accordance with the Roman tradition ▲ *319*, the Via Ostiensis was lined with tombs, the oldest of which date from the 2nd century BC. It ended at the Porta Romana, the main entrance to Ostia for those arriving from Rome. Set back a little in relation to the walls and flanked by two square towers, this monumental gate has retained traces of its elegant marble decorations due to the restoration works carried out during the reign of the Emperor Domitian. This is where the colony's main road, the *decumanus maximus* (see left), begins. It runs absolutely straight for nearly half a mile and forms the urban tract of the Via Ostiensis; the *cardo maximus* crosses it at right angles.

PIAZZALE DELLA VITTORIA. On the left of the Porta Romana, this vast square of the Imperial age owes its modern name to the winged statue of Minerva Victoria, which was probably part of the gate's ornamentation at the time of Domitian's building work. One of the two inscriptions adorning the gate identifies the man responsible for this restoration as "*P. Clodius Pulcher consul*".

TERME DEI CISIARII. In Republican times a sort of bazaar extended along the right side of the road, which under Hadrian was partially transformed into the Terme dei Cisiarii ("the Baths of the Carters"). The *frigidarium* has retained its superb mosaic (opposite), which mainly portrays scenes from the carters' daily life (even the names of their mules are given). There is no doubt that these baths belonged to a school for this profession.

Minerva as the goddess of victory.

405

An inscription in the Caserma dei Vigili.

THE MITHRAEUM OF THE SEVEN SPHERES
Initiates had to pass through seven stages, symbolized by semicircles representing the seven spheres of the planets: on the left, Diana (the Moon), Mercury and Jupiter; on the right, Mars, Venus, Saturn and finally Mithras (the Sun).

THE THEATER
As well as being influenced by Greek drama, Roman theater drew on an Italic tradition in which humor was an important element: hence the success of farces, mimes and the comedies of Plautus and Terence. The masks worn by actors inspired the decorative motifs commonly used in Roman theaters.

HADRIAN'S QUARTER

This quarter, which extends to the right from the crossing with the Via dei Vigili, dates entirely from the time of Hadrian. The street was bordered by a magnificent portico sheltering numerous shops.

THE BATHS OF NEPTUNE ★. Ostia had a number of public baths, most of which were richly decorated with mosaics, marble and statues. The name of the Baths of Neptune, whose monumental size can be admired from a terrace overlooking the *decumanus* ▲ *404*, derives from a black-and-white mosaic showing the sea god surging forth on his *quadriga* of sea horses, surrounded by a multitude of Tritons, Nereids and dolphins. In the neighboring hall another mosaic shows Neptune's wife, Amphitrite. The bathing rooms occupy the eastern side of the complex, while opposite a gymnasium bordered by a lovely colonnade served for warming-up exercises ▲ *321*. The cistern was located beneath it.

THE CASERMA DEI VIGILI. Continuing on the left, you will see the entrance to the barracks of the *vigiles* ▲ *356*. A detachment of these soldiers, who acted as night police and firemen, was stationed at Ostia from the time of Claudius. The barracks give onto a large central courtyard surrounded by a covered arcade; this originally had two floors onto which the living quarters opened. At the back is a sanctuary, the *Caesareum*, for the cult of the Emperor. (Return to the *decumanus*.)

THE THEATER AND PIAZZALE DELLE CORPORAZIONI ★

THE THEATER. Like baths, theaters were a salient feature of the scenery of Roman towns. The theater of Ostia, with the adjacent square, forms one of the town's most important architectural groups. It was built by Agrippa and partially restored at the end of the 2nd century by the Emperor Commodus. Its present appearance (mainly tiers of steps and a portico) dates to its radical restoration in 1927. It had a capacity of about three thousand (four thousand after Commodus' restoration). The stage (*orchestra*) has alternating rectangular and curved niches; above are decorative

elements in marble, found during the excavations. On the *decumanus* side the steps (*cavea*) were flanked by two circular fountains; one was turned into a Christian chapel dedicated to St Cyriacus, Bishop of Ostia, at the end of the 4th century. Today plays are performed in the theater in summer.

PIAZZALE DELLE CORPORAZIONI. Unique of its kind, this group of buildings famous for their splendid mosaics has provided important documentation on the commercial life of Ostia. It includes a huge portico (some 350 x 250 feet), in the center of which is a temple probably dedicated to Vulcan. The sides of the square are divided into sixty rooms, which were clearly the offices of the corporations of shipowners and merchants who had settled in Ostia. The black-and-white mosaics in each of these offices, which date from the time of the Severians (early 3rd century AD), depict scenes featuring navigation and trade. In effect they provide a trade map of the Roman world. *Navi[cularii] Narbonenses*, one can read on the mosaic in the office of "the shipbuilders of Narbonne"; in another, *Navicul[arii] et Negotiantes Karalitani* ("the shipbuilders and merchants of Cagliari", in Sardinia); and so on.

THE HOUSE OF APULEIUS. Southwest of the Piazzale delle Corporazioni stands the entrance to a beautiful house (*domus*) dating from the 2nd century AD. Its structure testifies to the evolution of private Roman architecture: the *atrium* is no longer a simple room open to the sky, and the presence of columns heralds the peristyles of later houses ● 69. This building is especially remarkable for its rich decoration of mosaics and marble.

THE MITHRAEUM OF THE SEVEN SPHERES. This is one of the best preserved of the seventeen sanctuaries of the Persian god Mithras discovered in Ostia. The mithraeum has a typical arrangement and decoration. The doorway is off the road, so that the interior was not visible from outside; within, the benches along the sides were reserved for initiates; and at the far end, on a throne, is the image of Mithras slaughtering the bull. Also of interest are the two *genii* bearing torches (Cautes and Cautopathes), and along the corridor the seven semicircles symbolizing the seven degrees of initiation.

One of the numerous representations
of Ostia's lighthouse (below).

The Romans gave pride of place to mosaics,
which they arranged on walls, floors and
ceilings, exploring all the possibilities of
this art form, from purely decorative
motifs and polychrome geometrical
pavings to the most complex figurative
images. The mosaics in Ostia (especially the
2nd-century ones in the Piazzale delle
Corporazioni ▲ *406*) are notable for their figurative designs in
black and white, with the outlines of men and animals
silhouetted on the ground like Chinese shadows.

**OIL FROM
MAURETANIA**
Quantities of
foodstuffs arrived at
Ostia from all the
Mediterranean
ports. The amphora
between two palm
trees, symbolizing
the oil trade, bears
the initials M.C.
("Caesar's
Mauretania"),
indicating its place
of origin.

MARINE THEME

Known to be earlier than the others, this mosaic with a Nereid sitting on a sea horse is reminiscent of the mosaics in the Baths of Neptune ▲ *406*. It captures movement with the same artistry, and the same lightness of form.

THE IVORY TRADE

The inscription reads: *sta[tio] Sabratensium*. This refers to the authority in Sabratha, in Libya, that was in charge of the ivory trade. It may also have been responsible for supplying elephants for the Roman arenas.

AFRICAN GAME RESERVE

The boar is part of a mosaic which also shows a deer and an elephant, all animals used for games in the amphitheaters of Rome: hunts (*venationes*), combats between gladiators and animals, and combats between animals.

CUPID WITH A WHIP

In the center a Cupid is riding a dolphin. The two medallions above possibly symbolize Africa. Everything is full of movement: the sea is suggested by parallel lines, and the dolphins' bodies have white lines to emphasize their undulations.

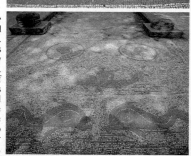

"INSULAE" ● *69*
Most of what is known about *insulae* (apartment buildings) is due to the excavations in Ostia. They could have as many as seven or eight floors, but Augustus limited their height to approximately 65 feet. Unlike the *domus* (house), which was built around an *atrium* (inner courtyard), the *insula* faced the street, as shown above.

FOUR REPUBLICAN TEMPLES. To the south of the mithraeum four small temples stood on the same podium, built at the beginning of the 1st century BC by an influential citizen, Publius Lucilius Gamala. They were dedicated to Venus, Fortuna, Ceres and Spes (Hope), goddesses associated with good fortune and therefore patrons of shipping and trade.

AROUND THE "CASTRUM". Great quantities of wheat destined for the capital arrived at the port of Ostia. The grain was temporarily stored in the *horrea* (the remains of a gigantic example can be seen behind the four temples). Ostia also supplied Rome with flour for bread; this is why mills are often found close to the warehouses, like the one situated a little further on, in Via dei Molini. Between the *decumanus* and the Via dei Molini, you come to the gate of the *castrum* (the original heart of the town ▲ *404*), built with great blocks of tufa. Excavations on this spot have revealed the level of the road in Republican times. A well-preserved section of the wall of the *castrum* is also visible. (Take Via di Diana.)

VIA DI DIANA ★

CASA DI DIANA. This *insula* with several floors and a projecting balcony was built in the 2nd century AD. It had apartments for rent, but the arrangement of some of the rooms, where light and air are lacking, make it likely that it was also an inn, especially since Ostia was an important port for travelers. On the opposite side of the street one can recognize a *THERMOPOLIUM* (refreshment bar) by its broad marble counter and shelves for the display of dishes; its situation within a stone's throw from the forum must have brought it a roaring trade in ancient times. During the summer clients could eat or drink in a small inner courtyard with a delightful fountain.

CASEGGIATO DEI DIPINTI. This group made up of three apartment

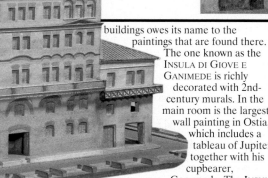

buildings owes its name to the paintings that are found there. The one known as the INSULA DI GIOVE E GANIMEDE is richly decorated with 2nd-century murals. In the main room is the largest wall painting in Ostia, which includes a tableau of Jupiter together with his cupbearer, Ganymede. The INSULA DEI DIPINTI is also decorated with frescoes and has an attractive garden area. A beautiful view of the whole site can be enjoyed from the terrace on the upper floor, opposite the *thermopolium*.

THE MUSEUM. At the end of Via di Diana is a small museum containing works of art found in Ostia. The large marble statue of the eastern god Mithras ▲ 406 slaying the bull (in Room III, devoted to oriental cults) and the fine 4th-century marble-inlay wall decoration depicting lions attacking deer are particularly remarkable. Room XII is devoted to paintings from the necropolis of the Isola Sacra ▲ 416. (Take Via del Capitolium to rejoin the *cardo maximus* ▲ 404.)

This sign and the type of construction made it possible to date the refreshment bar to the 4th century AD.

VIA DEI MOLINI
One large mill still has its millstones of volcanic rock (below left). In front of it are six shops, which may have sold bread.

CASA DI DIANA
In the courtyard is an image of Diana, the divinity who was the patron of the house that today bears her name. The two rooms on the northeastern side were converted into a mithraeum ▲ 181 at the end of the 2nd century.

AROUND THE FORUM

THE CIVIC CENTER OF OSTIA. It was not until the reign of the Emperor Hadrian that the colony of Ostia was endowed with a monumental square worthy of its commercial and political status. To the north, an imposing brick building with a podium faced in marble replaced the ancient religious buildings. This was the most important temple of the town, the CAPITOLIUM, a place of worship dedicated to the principal gods of the Roman religion. Its façade, which had six columns and was approached by a fine flight of steps, has been entirely stripped of its decorations; but from 19th-century drawings one can get an idea of the geometrical motifs of the marble pavement of the *cella*. Inside, statues adorned the wall niches, and at the back were three rooms where the cult statues were kept.

Like all of Rome's forums, Ostia's had a Curia, where the council of *decuriones* sat. However, this monument (to the north of the *decumanus*) looks more like a temple, and its identification is still uncertain. Finally, to the south (on the other side of the *decumanus*) is the BASILICA that housed the law courts. This consists of a large hall with a nave bordered by a colonnade; on its southern side the remains of the podium which was used by the judges can still be seen.

THE FORUM
The buildings must be imagined with their decorations (all removed) made from various marbles, including white Carrara marble and antique yellow from North Africa.

The Temple of Hercules.

THE LATRINES
Beyond the east portico of the forum you enter the Via della Forica (Street of the Latrine). On the left, after a series of shops, two public latrines, for men and for women, have been identified, with the stone seats ranged around the sides and a small basin between the entrances.

Below (from left to right): the latrines; the Temple of Rome and Augustus; a detail of the polychrome pavement in the House of Cupid and Psyche; and the Casa degli Aurighi.

THE TEMPLE OF ROME AND AUGUSTUS. In honor of his adoptive father, Tiberius had one of the most elegant buildings of the colony erected on the south side of the forum, opposite the Capitolium. Today the remains of this temple have lost their marble facing, and fragments of its decorations have been left where they were found. The winged statue of *Victory* now fixed against the wall probably stood on the temple rooftop. (Leaving to the south the monumental baths of the forum built in the 2nd century AD and restored in the 4th century, return to the *decumanus* ▲ *404.*)

CASA DEL LARARIO. The *insula* of the shrine of the Lares is an interesting example of a market with shops opening onto it. This shopping center owes its name to the presence of a small shrine consecrated by the shopkeepers to their gods, the Lares. Opposite is the TEMPIO ROTONDO (Round Temple), which was probably dedicated to the cult of the Imperial family. It was originally covered with a dome and had a large rectangular courtyard in front of it. (Go through the western gate of the *castrum.*)

HORREA EPAGATHIANA AND EPAPHRODISIANA. As the marble slab above the entrance indicates, these warehouses of the 2nd century AD belonged to two rich freed slaves named Epagathos and Epaphroditos. The presence of a double door suggests that they contained precious merchandise. Sixteen rooms open onto an inner courtyard surrounded by a portico; the largest one was no doubt used as an office. (Take Via della Foce, toward the *foce* or ancient mouth of the Tiber.)

VIA DELLA FOCE

THE REPUBLICAN SANCTUARY. This sacred area included three temples: the Temple of Aesculapius, the god of medicine, on the north side of the precinct; the one known as the "Temple with the Circular Altar"; and the largest, the Temple of Hercules (about 100 BC), set on a raised podium with an impressive flight of steps leading up to it. Hercules was honored here as a god of war whose oracle had to be

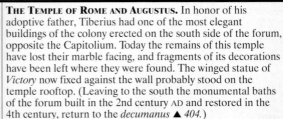

consulted by the captains of the military fleet before each expedition. Indeed, a votive relief showing a *haruspex* consulting the oracle was discovered near the building. The idealized statue of Cartilius Poplicola ("friend of the people"), the most important politician in Ostia's history, is another votive monument. (Take Via del Tempio di Ercole.)

THE HOUSE OF CUPID AND PSYCHE. A family of important officials or wealthy merchants lived in this richly decorated house dating from the 4th century AD. Like many others, it was built on an earlier construction consisting of shops. The large hall at the back has magnificent marble decorations and a marble pavement with geometrical motifs. One of the rooms opening onto the passage is adorned with a copy of a sculpture of *Cupid and Psyche* (center);

the original is in the museum ▲ *411*. Going back down Via della Foce, you come to the Baths of Buticosus, an interesting example of private baths (*balnea*) of the 2nd century AD. As well as being smaller, they differed from the public baths in that they had no *palestra*. However, their fresco and mosaic decorations (pictures of gardens and marine scenes) are no less refined. (Retrace your steps and take the Via del Serapide).

THE SERAPEUM ★. Many foreign cults that were not officially recognized by the Roman religion were practiced in the outskirts of this port town, such as the cult of the Egyptian god Serapis, who was identified with Jupiter. The entire decoration consists of motifs associated with Egypt, and the mosaic in the courtyard features scenes of life on the Nile. (Return to the Via della Foce.)

THE BATHS OF THE SEVEN SAGES

The whole block between Via della Foce and Cardo degli Aurighi is a magnificent architectural group, built under Hadrian and Antoninus Pius. It includes two apartment buildings, the Insula del Serapide and the Insula degli Aurighi, separated in the center by the Baths of the Seven Sages, which were reserved for the residents' use. The floor of the main room of the baths, a large circular hall (*frigidarium*) originally covered with a dome, is decorated with mosaics featuring hunting scenes and foliage. A small adjacent room has frescoes showing seven Greek sages with their names written in Greek: Solon, Thales, Chilon, Periander, Bias, Cleobulus and Pittacus. Each is described with a piquant Latin epigram: for example, *Ut bene cacaret ventrem palpavit Solon* ("To defecate well, Solon rubbed his stomach"). This reveals a whole tradition of humor, of the type that was representative of Roman culture, and was particularly lively in the theater. (Rejoin the *decumanus* and proceed toward the west.)

Four views of the Baths of the Seven Sages, and the Serapeum (above).

THE LARES
These were the gods of the places frequented by man, such as homes, fields, shops and neighborhoods.

THE IMPERIAL CULT
When an Emperor died his deification was entrusted to a *flamen*, a priest appointed for life from among the city's eminent personalities.

413

▲ Ostia

THE MITHRAEUM ▲ 181 OF FELICISSIMUS
A fragment of mosaic that includes the dedication from the man who had the shrine built.

THE SYNAGOGUE
The earliest part of the building dates from the 1st century BC, which could mean that the development of the Jewish community in Ostia was linked to the increase of trade after Claudius built the port.

AROUND THE INSULA DELLE VOLTE DIPINTE

On the right-hand side of the *decumanus* is a CHRISTIAN BASILICA, the largest Christian building to have survived in Ostia. Built partly over some preexisting baths, it is an elongated building with two naves preceded by a kind of vestibule. A little further on is the TEMPIO DEI FABRI NAVALES, where the naval smiths worshiped. The imposing "SCHOLA DEL TRAIANO", facing the temple, was in fact the official seat of their corporation, the importance of which is obvious in a town that relied on the sea. (At the crossroads take Cardo degli Aurighi, then Via delle Volte Dipinte.) Built in Hadrian's reign, the residential complex known as the INSULA DELLE VOLTE DIPINTE includes a sequence of rooms opening onto a long corridor; its name refers to some remarkable 2nd-century frescoes that have been preserved there. Close by, the Case a Giardino offered their residents the amenity of a large garden adorned with six fountains. Two groups of buildings should be imagined in the middle of the garden, each consisting of four almost identical houses with a covered passage between them. The absence of shops suggests the refined character of these dwellings, and this is confirmed by a mosaic on one of the fountains that features Nile scenes with crocodiles and Pygmies. (Take the *decumanus* as far as the Porta Marina.)

PORTA MARINA

A large suburb developed outside this "Marine Gate", which formed part of the Republican walls. On the right stands the DOMUS FULMINATA ("the house struck by lightning"), with an inscription stating: *F[ulgur] d[ium] c[onditum]* ("A divine thunderbolt fell here"). As in the House of Apuleius ▲ 407, the *atrium* has made way for a peristyle – an inner courtyard surrounded by columns, which assumed the central function of the building. A little farther on, in the first street on the left, is the Tomb of CARTILIUS POPLICOLA ▲ 412, in the shape of an altar; the upper part is decorated with a naval battle scene. You can then continue to the SYNAGOGUE, which dates from the 1st century AD. Discovered in 1961, this is the oldest

THE TOMB OF CARTILIUS POPLICOLA
The frieze of the tomb (right) shows a naval battle, no doubt an episode in the war against Sextus Pompeius (c. 39 BC). The prow of the trireme on the right is decorated with a head of Minerva; on the left are armed infantrymen accompanied by an unusually tall person.

synagogue found in the ancient Roman West.

Returning to the *decumanus*, just after the junction with Via del Pomerio, you will come to the MEAT MARKET (*macellum*), with shops arranged around an inner courtyard. Access is through a portico and an entrance with columns, where there are two shops that probably sold fish. (Go back to the *cardo maximus* ▲ *404*.)

CAMPO DELLA MAGNA MATER

Between the *cardo maximus* ▲ *404* and the Porta Laurentina, Hadrian created a sacred precinct dedicated to Cybele, the Phrygian goddess of fertility ▲ *148*. In Ostia this is one of the

most widely attested oriental cults. The goddess was worshiped together with two other divinities: Attis, her male companion, and Bellona, goddess of war. These two divinities had a smaller shrine on the south side of the precinct, at the end of the long portico that borders it. Eunuch priests called Galli celebrated the cult in the month of March. (Return to the *cardo,* then take the Semita dei Cippi, an important commercial route, and Via della Fortuna Annonaria.) Here stands one of the richest houses in Ostia. Built on the site of a former *insula*, with its large courtyard framed by a portico, it is typical of the aristocratic dwellings of the 4th century AD. In the Via degli Augustali there is a 2nd-century *fullonica* (laundry and dyers' workshop). Returning to the *decumanus,* you will come to a temple that probably belonged to a corporation of shipwrights and carpenters. From here on, the right-hand side of the *decumanus* is occupied by the HORREA OF HORTENSIUS, a string of warehouses dating from the end of the Republic that opens onto a large courtyard surrounded by columns.

The *Horrea* of Hortensius.

CYBELE AND ATTIS
During the Feast of the Hilaria the faithful mutilated themselves, imitating the act of Attis, to become Galli, the eunuch priests of the goddess Cybele.

DYERS' WORKSHOP
Four large basins were used for washing the wool, which was then trampled (above), squeezed, dyed and mangled. Wool from Puglia, Istria and Padua was dyed in Ostia before going on to Rome.

415

THE OSTIA AREA

CASTELLO DI GIULIO
Completed by the future Pope Julius II, the castle served to defend the Tiber.

THE ROMAN SUMMER
Even if he was describing a bygone era, in his *Racconti romani* (published in 1954) Alberto Moravia captures the flavor of these picturesque outings *fuori porta* ("outside the city gates"), either

to the Castelli or to the beaches. *Domenica d'agosto*, a film from the time of neo-Realism, gives a vivid impression of what the summer crowds in Ostia are like.

THE "ISOLA SACRA"
This necropolis, traversed by a wide road connecting Portus to Ostia, sprang up at the end of the 1st century AD. The inscriptions and reliefs decorating the tombs give an idea of the social background of the dead, including shopkeepers, craftsmen, tradesmen and some professions.

THE MEDIEVAL VILLAGE. During Imperial times a necropolis sprang up outside Ostia, and it was there that St Aurea, martyred during the reign of Claudius II (268–70), was buried. This led to the development of a suburb that, in the Middle Ages, became the last refuge of the population of Ostia. The castle (above) guarded access to the Tiber, which formerly flowed past this spot. Although the keep was erected by Martin V (1417–31), the rest of the castle was built by Cardinal Giuliano della Rovere (the future Pope Julius II) between 1483 and 1486. The CHURCH OF SANTA AUREA, which stands within the fortified medieval village, over the martyr's tomb, was totally rebuilt in the 15th century. The body of St Augustine's mother, St Monica, who died in Ostia in 387, was interred here before being moved to the Church of Sant'Agostino ▲ *284* in Rome.

THE MODERN TOWN. Ostia Antica gives no hint of the modern town. With its sad grid of apartment buildings, the town survives mainly because of its beaches, to which the Roman crowds flock from May to September. Although the seashore has been badly spoiled by the number of bathing establishments (most of which are *abusivi* – that is, built without the necessary permit from the municipal administration), and despite a frequently polluted sea, Romans still love these beaches with their black volcanic sand. Among the villages on the sea front, Fregene – further to the north and certainly rather more attractive – has taken root in

a landscape that was transformed during the Fascist period when the Maccarese marshes were drained. The very flat land, crisscrossed by canals edged with reeds, is regularly punctuated by farms and small red houses; it is a far cry from Ostia's surroundings, with their lovely pine woods. Fiumicino (between Ostia and Fregene) is a well-known name because of its vicinity to the huge Leonardo da Vinci airport, built between 1950 and 1957 but totally altered and modernized in the early 1990's. Today a metro line links it to the center of Rome.

PRACTICAL
INFORMATION

Traveling to Rome is perfectly simple. There are few formalities and visitors from many countries do not need to obtain special travel documents. According to popular opinion, the best time to visit is the early fall, because you avoid the hordes of tourists while still enjoying the summer climate.

FORMALITIES

ITALIAN CONSULATES

UK
4 Upper Tachbrook St, London SW1
Tel: 071 828 1604

US
690 Park Avenue, New York, NY 10021
Tel: 212 737 9100

ITALIAN STATE TOURIST OFFICES

UK
1 Princes St, London W1
Tel: 071 408 1254

US
630 Fifth Avenue, New York, NY 10111
Tel: 212 245 4822/ 245 4861

You will need a valid passport and, in some cases, a visa. An identity card is all that is required for EC nationals.

HEALTH

Vaccinations are not required. If you are an EC national do not forget an E111 form, available from your doctor or a post office; it enables you to be admitted to hospital for emergency care. If you are not an EC national it is in your interest to take out a special health insurance policy before traveling.

BIBLIOGRAPHY

Rome has always had a strong appeal for artists and writers. The following have all written books which might help you to plan your visit or entertain you during your stay:
Robert Browning, Anthony Burgess, Byron, Charles Dickens, Gibbon, Goethe, Robert Graves, Gregorovius, Augustus Hare, Henry James, Keats, Cecil Roberts, Shelley, Thackeray, Mark Twain, Vasari, Marguerite Yourcenar... not to mention a host of Italian authors, from Virgil to Pier Paolo Pasolini ▲ 105, ◆ 478.

Ponte Sant'Angelo in the fall.

WHEN TO GO

Holy Week should be avoided because of the vast number of pilgrims in Rome for the Easter celebrations. August is not recommended for those who do not like the idea of visiting a deserted town; Romans traditionally flee the city during the heat of the summer. But solitude does have its charm. If you want to visit Rome during the winter months, remember to pack warm clothing. The temperature rarely drops below zero, but do not overestimate the mildness of the climate.

ROME'S CHARM

Autumn in Rome: the town returns to life after its summer sleep, the temperature is still ideal for walking and the October light intensifies the red and ocher of the walls. Sunsets in this season are at their most romantic.

Piazza San Pietro in the snow.

DRESS TIPS

In Rome you will only be allowed to enter the churches if dressed decently: avoid shorts, sleeveless T-shirts, and low necklines.

SPRING		March to May

In Rome, the tourist season starts in March. It soon becomes possible to enjoy open-air festivities organized in the city and take part in the Easter celebrations.

MARCH
46°–64°

MARCH 19	**FEAST OF ST JOSEPH**, Trionfale area
GOOD FRIDAY	**STATIONS OF THE CROSS, LED BY THE POPE** in and around the Coliseum, 9 pm
EASTER SUNDAY	**THE POPE'S BLESSING**, Piazza San Pietro, 12.00 noon
EASTER MONDAY, National holiday	
APRIL 21	**ANNIVERSARY OF THE FOUNDATION OF ROME**, Piazza del Campidoglio
APRIL 25, National Holiday	**ANNIVERSARY OF THE LIBERATION**
MAY 1, National Holiday	**LABOR DAY**
LAST WEEK IN MAY	**TENNIS INTERNATIONALS**, Foro Italico

APRIL
48°–68°

MAY
58°–78°

★ The papal blessing "Urbi et Orbi" on Easter Sunday.

SUMMER		June to August

Summer heat, evening entertainments. The inhabitants gradually desert the town (sales are in July, shops close in August). Meanwhile tourists, thirsting for magnificence and cool water by day, appreciate Rome in the refreshing evening air.

JUNE
66°–84°

JUNE, JULY–AUGUST	**OPEN-AIR CONCERTS AND OPERAS**, Basilica of Maxentius, Villa Ada, Baths of Caracalla, Ostia Antica.
JUNE 23–24	**FEAST OF ST JOHN**, Piazza di porta San Giovanni
JUNE 29	**FEAST OF ST PETER AND ST PAUL**, the Vatican, St Peter's Basilica
JULY	**ROMA JAZZ FESTIVAL**, Foro Italico and EUR
JULY	**ROMAEUROPA, CONCERTS, DANCE AND THEATER**, Villa Medici
15–30 JULY	**FESTA DI NOANTRI, TRADITIONAL FEAST** in Trastevere (fireworks on last night)
AUGUST 15, National Holiday	**FERRAGOSTO AND ASSUMPTION**

JULY
70°–90°

AUGUST
70°–88°

★ Open-air opera at the Baths of Caracalla.

FALL		September to November

Events tend to be more spread out but the town is still lively. Tourists and locals alike flock to the streets, right up until rainy November, the only month of the year when a trip to Rome is not recommended.

SEPTEMBER
66°–80°

SEPTEMBER	**OPEN-AIR ART EXHIBITION**, via Margutta
SEPTEMBER–MAY	**SCUDETTO, FOOTBALL CHAMPIONSHIP**, every Sunday afternoon, Stadio Olimpico
NOVEMBER 1 National holiday	

OCTOBER
56°–68°

NOVEMBER
46°–58°

★ The city should be seen from the Janiculum, in the sunshine.

WINTER		December to February

Traveler's wisdom is that hot countries should be visited only in summer, but Rome is an exception because of Christmas celebrations.

DECEMBER
44°–54°

DECEMBER 8 National Holiday	**FEAST OF THE IMMACULATE CONCEPTION**, Piazza di Spagna
DECEMBER 24	**MIDNIGHT MASSES** in most churches
DECEMBER 25, National holiday	
DECEMBER 26, National holiday	
JANUARY 1, National holiday	
JANUARY 5	**FEAST OF THE EPIPHANY, LAST DAY OF PIAZZA NAVONA FAIR**
JANUARY 6, National holiday	

JANUARY
42°–52°

FEBRUARY
44°–56°

★ Christmas Mass at Basilica San Pietro.

☀ sunny and warm　　☁ variable to overcast　　🌧 rainy　　❄ cold, snow possible

The minimum and maximum temperatures for each month are given in degrees Fahrenheit.

TOTAL EXPENDITURE
FOR A TYPICAL FOUR-DAY VISIT
- Couple only, charter flight and average accommodation: £950/$640
- Couple with two children, package tour: £1200/$800 to £2300/$1500
- Couple only, regular flight and high-class accommodation: £1750/$1200 to £2700/$1800

◆ Traveling to Rome

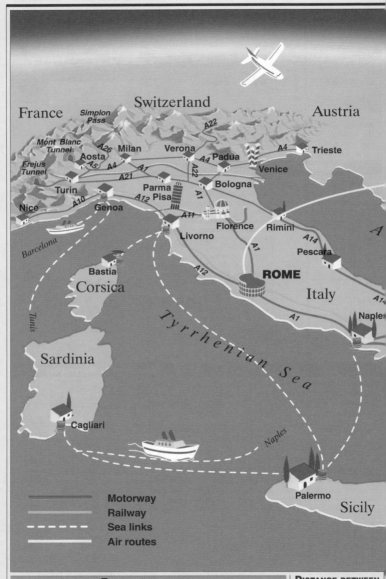

THE PRICE OF THE TRIP	
Route	**Price**
First-class flight from London	£524 Return
Regular flight from London (off peak)	£234 Return
Regular flight from London (peak)	£285 Return
Flight from New York (excursion)	$850 Return
Flight from Los Angeles (excursion)	$1048 Return
Flight from Houston (excursion)	$1018 Return
First-class train journey from London	£275 Return
Second-class train journey from London	£189 Return
Coach from London	£129 Return

DISTANCE BETWEEN ROME AND OTHER BIG INTERNATIONAL CITIES (IN MILES)

London	1056
Paris	870
Berlin	963
Madrid	1243
Amsterdam	1025
New York	4225
Tokyo	5779

BY PLANE
LEONARDO DA VINCI AIRPORT is located at Fiumicino (the Romans often call it by this second name), which is about 17 miles from Rome.

You can fly to Rome from most major US airports.

From the **UK BRITISH AIRWAYS** has four daily flights from Heathrow Airport, London, and one flight on Saturdays from Manchester. (Tel: 081 897 4000). **ALITALIA** has four daily flights from Heathrow Airport. (071 602 7111).

719 and 718 all go to Piazza Venezia, as does 95 from Ostiense, until evening.
Caution: Line A metro stops running after 11.30 pm every day, and Line B at 9.30 pm in the week and 11.30 pm at the weekend.

BY TRAIN
From the UK trains depart daily from London Victoria train station for Rome, traveling via Paris. The train arrives at the Stazione Termini in Rome, where there are bus and metro connections and taxis.

Aeroporti di Roma

GETTING FROM THE AIRPORT TO THE CITY CENTER
By taxi the 4-5min. trip will cost 60,000 to 70,000 lire.
By train you can go direct to Termini Station (Fiumicino–Termini non-stop trains leave every 25 mins. from 7 am to 8.50 pm); it is a 30-min. journey).
Alternatively you can take the Tiburtina Line metro to Tuscolano, Ostiense, Trastevere, Magliana, Muratella, Ponte Galeria and Tiburtina (trains run every half hour from 6 am to 10 pm).
There is no metro at Trastevere Station but buses nos. 710,

BY BUS
From the UK every Saturday, from Victoria Coach Station, London.

BY CAR
In Italy there are motorway toll stations; the charges can be paid in cash, or with a Viacard, an electronic payment card that may be purchased for the values of 50,000 or 90,000 lire.
On arriving in Rome take the *raccordo annulare* (ring road) and follow signs to the *centro* (center). It is strongly recommended that you leave your car in a car park at this point.

TRAVEL DISCOUNTS
◆ Airline fares from the UK are cheaper in winter than summer. The best deals can usually be obtained by traveling midweek (Monday to Thursday) and staying over the Saturday night before returning. Fares are much higher over Easter or Christmas
◆ Train or coach fares do not increase but places may get booked up over holiday periods.

Platform, exit

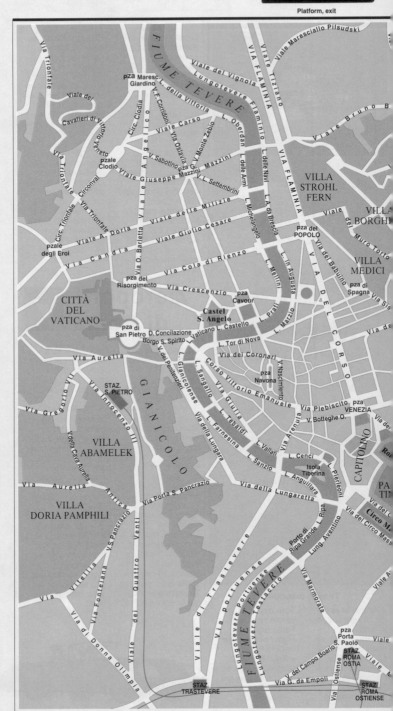

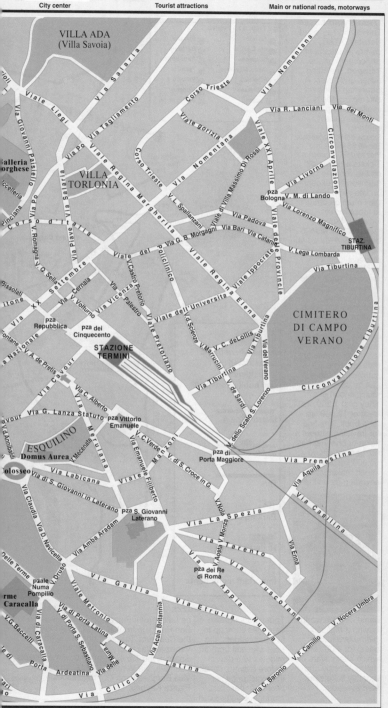

 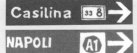
VILLA ADA
(Villa Savoia)

VILLA
TORLONIA

Viale Liegi

Via Salaria

Viale Tagliamento

Via Po

Corso Trieste

Corso Trieste

Viale gorizia

Via Nomentana

Via R. Lanciani   Via dei Monti

Via Giovanni Paisiello

alleria
orghese

ccelleria

Viale Regina Margherita

Via Salaria

Via Plave

Circonvalazione

Via Livorno

pza
Bologna V. M. di Lando

Via Lorenzo Magnifico

STAZ.
TIBURTINA

Pinciana

Corso d'Italia

V.L. Spallanzani

Via di Villa Massimo Di Rossi

Viale XXI Aprile

Via Padova

Via Bari Via Catanie

Viale delle Provincie

V. Lega Lombarda

V.G. Romagna V.G. Sella

Via Po

Via G.B. Morgagni

Viale del Policlinico

Via Regina Elena

Via Tiburtina

issolati

tone XX Settembre

Via Cernaia

Via Vicenza

Via Castro Pretorio

Palestro

Viale dell'Università

Viale Ippocrate

CIMITERO
DI CAMPO
VERANO

Via V. Volturno

Viale Pretoriano

Viale delle Scienze

V.C. deLollis

Via Tiburtina

Via del Verano

Circonvallazione Tiburtina

Via XX

pza
Repubblica

pza dei
Cinquecento

V.Metrucini

fontane

V.A. de Pretis

a Nazionale

STAZIONE
TERMINI

Via Tiburtina

V. de Sardi

dello Scalo S. Lorenzo

Circonvallazione Tiburtina

Via Cavour

Via C. Alberto

avour Via G. Lanza Statuto

pza Vittorio
Emanuele

ESQUILINO
Domus Aurea

V.d'Ambaldi

V.C.Verdi

Merulana

Via Emanuele Filberto

Mai...zoni

V. di S. Croce in G

pza di
Porta Maggiore

Via Prenestina

Colosseo

Via di S. Giovanni in Laterano

Via Labicana

Mecenate

Viale

Via Aquila

Via Claudia

Via D. Navicella

Via Amba Aradam

pza S. Giovanni
Laterano

V.Nola

Via La Spezia

Via Casilina

lelle Terme

V. Druso

pzale
Numa
Pompilio

Viale Metronio

Via di Porta Latina

V. el Porta S. Sebastiano

Via Galilia

Via Acaia Britannia

Via Aosta Via Monza

Via Taranto

pza dei Re
di Roma

Via Appia

Via Enna

Via Tuscolana

V.F. Camillo

rme
Caracalla

V.G. Baccelli

Via di Caracalla

Via Etruria

Via Nuova

V. Nocera Umbria

i di

Porta

Ardeatina

Via delle

Via Clicia

Latina

V. C. Baronio

◆ LOCAL TRANSPORT

ATAC 3099

TRAMS AND BUSES

The Public Transport Network, ATAC, covers all means of city-center surface transport, including buses and trams. A clear map of the different routes is available from the two information centers:
Piazza del Risorgimento Tel: 46 95 44 44 and Piazza dei Cinquecento. Tickets are not sold on the vehicles themselves (except on late-night buses); they must be bought at tobacconists, kiosks or bus stations. It is wise to buy several ahead of time (the tickets are also available in books of eleven) as these outlets tend to close early in the evening; ticket machines don't give change and tend not to work in Rome, anyway. The tickets last 90 minutes from the moment they are date and time stamped, but they can be used for multiple journeys. They cost 1,200 lire each or 12,000 lire for a book. The fine for traveling without a ticket or one that has not been stamped is 50,000 lire. If you intend making several trips on the

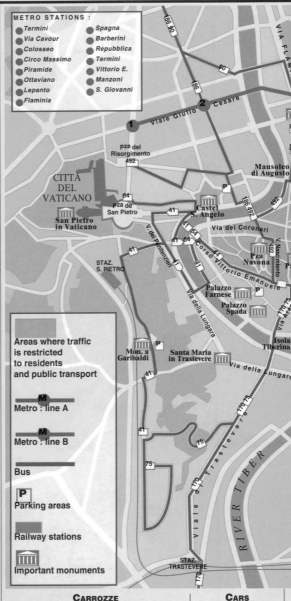

METRO STATIONS :
- Termini
- Via Cavour
- Colosseo
- Circo Massimo
- Piramide
- Ottaviano
- Lepanto
- Flaminia
- Spagna
- Barberini
- Repubblica
- Termini
- Vittorio E.
- Manzoni
- S. Giovanni

Areas where traffic is restricted to residents and public transport

M Metro : line A

M Metro : line B

Bus

P Parking areas

Railway stations

🏛 Important monuments

same day it is worth buying a *biglietto giornaliero* (a day pass) for 4,000 lire, which also covers the metro. Weekly and monthly tickets are also available.

CARROZZE

These horse-drawn carriages carry up to five passengers; the rides can last from 30 minutes to a day. Before leaving, check the exact price per person or per carriage. Buggies can be taken from: Piazza San Pietro, in front of the Coliseum, Piazza Venezia, Piazza di Spagna, the Trevi Fountain, Via Veneto, Villa Borghese and Piazza Navona.

CARS

It is not advisable to use a car in Rome due to the heavy traffic, the small number of car parks and strict parking regulations.

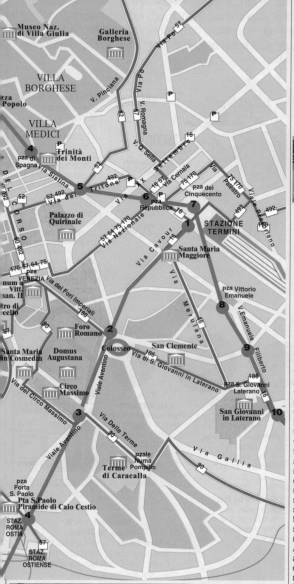

Map labels:
- Museo Naz. di Villa Giulia
- Galleria Borghese
- Via Poli 57
- VILLA BORGHESE
- V. Pinciana
- V. d Poli 57
- V. Romagna
- pza Popolo
- VILLA MEDICI
- Trinità dei Monti
- 4
- pza di Spagna Via Sistina
- Via del
- V. G. Sella Settembre
- 16
- 52
- 492
- Via Tritone
- 5
- Via del
- 16 57
- Via Cernaia
- 75 170 Via Palestro
- Viale Plave Tiano
- 492
- Palazzo di Quirinale
- 6
- pza Repubblica
- pza dei Cinquecento
- 7
- 1
- STAZIONE TERMINI
- Via Nazionale
- Via Cavour
- Santa Maria Maggiore
- 57 64 75
- pza VENEZIA Via dei Fori Imperiali
- num Vitt man. II
- tro di cello
- Via Merulana
- pza Vittorio Emanuele
- 8
- V. Emanuele
- Foro Romano
- 2
- Santa Maria in Cosmedin
- Domus Augustana
- Colosseo
- San Clemente
- Via di S. Giovanni in Laterano
- 186
- 9
- Filiberto
- Circo Massimo
- Viale Aventino
- pza S. Giovanni Laterano
- 186
- San Giovanni in Laterano
- 10
- Via del Circo Massimo
- 3
- Via Delle Terme
- 90
- Via Gallia
- 90
- Viale Aventino
- pzale Numa Pompilio
- Terme di Caracalla
- pza Porta S.Paolo
- Pta S.Paolo
- Piramide di Caio Cestio
- 4
- STAZ. ROMA OSTIA
- 57
- STAZ. ROMA OSTIENSE

METRO

The two lines (A & B) intersect at Stazione Termini. Line A runs from Ottaviano, near the Vatican, to Anagnina; Line B runs from Rebibbia to Laurentina. Stations are clearly signposted by a large white M on a red background. Tickets are only valid for one

journey and cost 1,000 lire. They are sold in the metro stations and in some kiosks, but day passes are available, as for the buses. Line A is open every day from 5.30 am to 11.30 pm; Line B is open from 5.30 am to 9.30 pm during the week and until 11.30 pm on Saturdays and Sundays.

TAXIS

Taxis are not an economical way to travel around Rome, but can be useful if you are heavily laden. The official taxis are yellow or white (in a few years they will all be white) and easily recognizable. They can be found at a taxi rank or hailed in the street. There are also several radio-taxi firms, but you pay a supplement for making a reservation. Additional charges also apply at night, during weekends and national holidays, and for extra luggage.

The historical center is concentrated in an area small enough to be covered on foot: this is the fastest and the most pleasant way to get from one place to another. For longer distances take the bus; just one ticket can get you to any point of interest within the city. To cross the whole town, the fastest and cheapest means is by metro. The cost is 1,000 lire per journey.

RENTING A BICYCLE
BICIROMA
Piazza del Popolo
Piazza di Spagna
Piazza San Lorenzo in Lucina
COLLALTI
Via del Pellegrino
Tel: 66 80 10 84
LOCATION (PHONE RENTAL)
Tel: 68 80 33 94

TAXI COMPANIES
COSMOS RADIO TAXI
TEL: 88177
SOCIETÀ LA CAPITALE
TEL: 4994
SOCIETÀ COOPERATIVA
AUTORADIOTAXI ROMA
TEL: 3570

Rome is an expensive city. Although there are a few inexpensive options, the costs of accommodation, food, refreshments and sightseeing mount up. Therefore don't give yourself too little leeway. Also, book your hotel before visiting; this is vital during the most popular months.

MONEY-WISE

The unit of Italian currency is the lire (LIT).
◆1,000, 2,000, 5,000, 10,000, 50,000 and 100,000 lire notes are available, as well as coins worth 50, 100, 200 and 500 lire.
◆ Although new 100 and 50 lire coins have recently been minted, the old ones are still valid.
◆ *Gettoni* (telephone tokens), worth 200 lire, are also accepted as current coinage.

500 LIT   *200 LIT*   *100 LIT*   *50 LIT*

Gettone (telephone token) 200 LIT

EMERGENCIES
In case of loss or theft
EMERGENCY HELP FOR TOURISTS
Tel: 42 23 71
POLICE Tel: 112.

TIPS AND SERVICE
In restaurants service is always included, but a tip is usually left too. The same is true for bars, cafés, taxis and hotel personnel, but only leave a tip if you are satisfied.

RECEIPTS

Make sure you ask for a *scontrino* (receipt) whenever you pay for something: this is obligatory by law. The police could ask for your receipt and you will be fined if you fail to produce it.

CREDIT CARDS

Credit cards and travelers' checks are accepted by most hotels, restaurants and shops. However, *trattorie*, food stores and petrol stations will not usually take them. Cash may be withdrawn from cash dispensers using credit cards.

CHANGING MONEY

Banks are open Monday to Friday between 8.30 am and 1.30 pm and in the afternoon between 2.45 pm and 3.45 pm; most offer exchange facilities. Note, however, that bank queues in Rome are often rather long. Alternatively automatic money dispensers may be used; these can be found throughout the city, at the airport and in stations. The machines give instructions in four languages and are easy to use. Hotels and bureaux de change will also change foreign currency but at a slightly lower rate. Rates: $1 = about

1,600 lire; £1 = about 2,400 lire.

BOOKING YOUR STAY IN ROME
◆ Most Roman hotels are full in May and June and at the start of the fall; Easter and Christmas are also busy periods. It is not advisable to arrive in Rome without a hotel booking. Reservations can, of course, be made by phone from abroad or, for high-class hotels, through a travel agent.
◆ If you do arrive in Rome without a booking during the less busy months, go to the tourist information center where reservations can be made on your behalf.

ACCOMMODATION

HOTELS

Hotels are rated from one to five stars, according to the European standard. Their actual standard of comfort generally lives up to their rating. There is also a wide price range. These prices are higher on average than elsewhere in Europe for the same standard of quality. They are calculated per room and not per person.

◆ A double room with a bath will cost in high season:
Hotel* : 70,000 to 100,000 lire
Hotel** : 100,000 to 150,000 lire
Hotel*** : 150,000 to 250,000 lire
Hotel****: 250,000 to 350,000 lire
Hotel*****: over 350,000 lire
Breakfast is not usually included in the price of a room.
◆ In most cases the room must be vacated by 2 pm.

"PENSIONI"

Over the last ten years pensioni, usually converted apartments, have become rare, but they can still be found and offer tourists more modest and cheaper accommodation. Other types of accommodation include residential hotels, convents, monasteries, youth-hostels and camp sites.

◆ For information on youth hostels, contact the Associazione Italiana Alberghi per la Gioventù.
◆ For information on accommodation in religious institutions and convents, and for help for pilgrims, consult "Peregrinatio ad Petri Sedem", Tel: 6988 58 00 during office hours, or contact the Italian Tourist office.
◆ Most camp sites are far from the city center and are rather expensive. The nearest (4 miles) is the Flaminio:
Via Flaminia Nuova 821, Tel: 333 26 04.

EATING OUT

An Italian meal may start with *antipasti* (starters), followed by a *primo* (different kinds of pasta or soup), then a *secondo* (meat or fish). To finish, you might choose between *formaggio* (cheese), *frutta* (fruit) and *dolci* (desserts). In the *trattorie*, simpler and less expensive than the *ristoranti*, a dish of pasta will often be enough for a full meal. If you are made to pay for the *pane e coperto* (bread and cover charge) do not be surprised; this is the custom. Also check whether the *contorno* (vegetables and other extras) is included in the price of the *secondo*. It rarely is and the cost of the meal could be rather different from your estimate as a result. Restaurants are generally open from 12 noon until 3 pm and from 8 pm to 11 pm. However, some places stay open until 12 pm, 1 am or even 2 am. Many Roman restaurants take their annual holidays in August and close on Sundays. There are exceptions, however, for which you will no doubt be thankful.

MARKETS

A visit to the markets is essential to discover a more intimate side of the city and its inhabitants. In fact, these markets play such an important role in Rome that food stores are relatively rare in the center.

FOR FOOD, you can choose between the markets in Piazza Vittorio Emanuele II (the cheapest), Piazza San Cosimato in Trastevere, Via Trionfale and Campo de' Fiori, which is the best known and the most picturesque.

FOR CLOTHES, go to Via Sannio or Piazza Testaccio.

FOR BOOKS, prints and engravings, there are stands on Piazza Borghese.

FOR CUT FLOWERS or plants, try Via Trionfale on Tuesday mornings after 10.00 am.

The popular FLEA MARKET is at Porta Portese on Sunday mornings.

THE ART OF DRINKING COFFEE

If the Italian *espresso* is not strong enough for you, order a *caffè ristretto* (concentrated); if it feels too explosive inside you, try a *caffè lungo*. An *espresso* with a drop of milk is called a *caffè macchiato*, while a *capuccino* is a frothy, creamy drink made with extra strong coffee and milk that has been steamed into a froth. The *latte macchiato*, the opposite of a *caffè macchiato*, is made by pouring a drop of coffee into a glass of milk, while *caffè latte* resembles the French "café au lait". Coffee can be drunk hot or cold. Last but not least try the *caffè freddo* (iced coffee), one of Italy's specialties, and the *caffè corretto*: coffee topped up with *grappa* (a wine-based spirit).

TELEPHONES

Calls can be made from telephone booths or from public telephone centers (*centri telefoni*). Here you pay after making the call, which is more convenient.

"CENTRI TELEFONI"
Unfortunately the public telephone centers are closed during the cheap-rate periods, except for the one in the Palazzo delle Poste at Piazza San Silvestro, which is open 24 hours a day.

PHONE BOOTHS
Calls can be made using 100, 200, or 500 lire coins, telephone tokens, or

phonecards. However, increasing numbers only accept phonecards, costing 5,000 or 10,000 lire (on sale in post offices, bars and some tobacconists).

PHONING WITHIN ITALY
◆ LOCAL CALLS
Simply dial the desired number.

◆ NON-LOCAL CALLS
Add the dialling code for the town you are calling before the number (Florence 055, Venice 041, Bologna 051, Genoa 010, Milan 02, Naples 081, Turin 011).

CALLING ABROAD
Dial 00 (international code), followed by the code of the country you are calling (44: UK, 1: US), then dial the number preceded by the code for the town you are calling. For Britain remember to drop the zero before the town or area code. If you have a US telephone credit card, international calls can be debited to your home phone bill by dialing 172 10 11 for an AT&T card, 172 00 22 for an MCI card and 172 18 77 for a Sprint card. For collect (reverse charge) or card calls to the UK, dial 172 00 44. English-speaking operators will answer and provide assistance.

INFORMATION SERVICES
◆ IN ITALY
National: dial 1800 or 12.
International dial: 176.
◆ FROM ABROAD
For international directory enquiries in the UK, dial 153. In the US, dial the operator and ask for directory assistance.

MAIL

Postal rates: a letter to Europe costs 850 lire, a postcard 800 lire. An airmail letter to the US costs 1,250. The Italian

post is not renowned for its efficiency, particularly during August.

◆ Stamps are sold in post offices and tobacconists. Italian letter boxes are red.
◆ The Vatican post uses the same tariffs

as the Italian post but is usually quicker. Its stamps can be found at the post offices near the entrance to the Vatican Museums and on Piazza San Pietro. The letter boxes are blue.

TIME

Remember that there is a time difference even between some European countries — for example, it is one hour later in Italy than in England. Museum opening times vary according to season and according to other rather eccentric and unorthodox (Roman) criteria.

Consequently, all information is only approximate, but bear in mind that museums are generally open only in the morning. It is sensible to check opening times once in Rome and allow a little extra time for the visits that you do not want to miss at any cost. Although these days more and more shops are open from 10.30 am to 7.30 pm, particularly in the center, trade traditionally takes place between 9 am and 1 pm, and 5.30 pm and 7.30 pm in winter. In the summer season, the hours change to 9.30 am to 2 pm and 4 pm to 8 pm, but the city tends to operate in slow motion after 2 pm, particularly in the heat. Caution: food stores are closed Thursday afternoon in winter and Saturday afternoon in summer, and other shops tend to close on Monday mornings.

> **EMERGENCY NUMBERS**
> S.O.S.: **113**
> Fire brigade: **115**
> First aid and help for tourists: **42 23 71**
> Lost property **581 60 40** (bus)
> **73 89 48** (metro)
> Breakdown service for motorists **116**

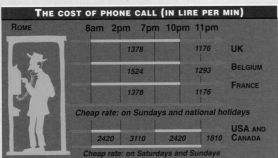

THE COST OF PHONE CALL (IN LIRE PER MIN)					
ROME	8am	2pm	7pm	10pm 11pm	
			1378	1176	**UK**
			1524	1293	**BELGIUM**
			1378	1176	**FRANCE**
Cheap rate: on Sundays and national holidays					
	2420	3110	2420	1810	**USA AND CANADA**
Cheap rate: on Saturdays and Sundays					

THE PRESS AND THE MEDIA

The main Roman daily newspapers are *Il Messaggero* and *La Repubblica* (whose Thursday supplement, *Trovaroma*, provides complete information on cultural activities and entertainments in the city for the week to come). The kiosks also sell a selection of foreign papers.
◆ The public television sector consists of three RAI channels. The most popular of the many privately owned channels (of which there are about 50) are probably the three owned by Silvio Berlusconi, nicknamed Sua Emittenza, the Italian media magnate. If you stay in a high-class hotel, you will probably also receive foreign channels via satellite.

ENTRANCE TO MUSEUMS

Entrance cards to Rome museums are available and valid for two, four or seven days. The cards give you access to most of the city's museums. They can be purchased at the tourist information centers, in the museums themselves, or by mail from **ASSOCIAZIONE NAZIONALE MUSEIDON**, Via A. Silvani 23, 00139 Roma. They cost between 15,000 and 50,000 lire according to the number of days you choose.

WHAT THINGS COST

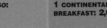

1 *ESPRESSO*: 1,200 L

1 CONTINENTAL BREAKFAST: 2,000 L

1 *TIRAMISU*: 2,000 L

SALTIMBOCCA ALLA ROMANA FOR ONE: 12,000 L

1 GLASS OF *AMARETTO* OR *SARONNO*: 1,500 L

1 POST CARD WITH A STAMP FOR EUROPE 1,800 L; FOR THE US 1,850 UP TO 5 WORDS OR 2,250 L

1 ENTRANCE TICKET TO A MUSEUM: 5,000 TO 10,000 L

1 DOUBLE ROOM: 120,000 L

SALES

Italian luxury products, especially haute couture, designer clothes and fine leather goods, are extremely expensive. The sales periods, from mid-June to early September and from the end of December to the beginning of February, are the best times to buy quality goods, often reduced to half price.

SECURITY

Without becoming too alarmed, bear in mind the high risk of theft in Rome. Simple common-sense precautions should be sufficient to ensure a peaceful holiday. Do not walk around carrying too much cash; most hotels have personal safes for their clients. Do not leave any valuables in a parked car. When using public transport keep your eyes open. Keep a photocopy of your passport and other important documents.

EQUIVALENT MEN'S SIZES	
US/UK	ITALY
COLLAR	
14	36
14½	37
15	38
15½	39
16	41
16½	42
17	43
TROUSERS	
34	44
36	46
38	48
40	50
42	54
44	56
SHOES	
6½/6	40
7½/7	41
8½/8	42
9½/9	43
10½/10	44
11½/11	45

EQUIVALENT WOMEN'S SIZES	
US/UK	ITALY
DRESSES AND SKIRTS	
6/8	40
8/10	42
10/12	44
12/14	46
14/16	48
16/18	50
JACKETS	
6/8	40
8/10	42
10/12	44
12/14	46
14/16	48
16/18	50
WOMEN'S SHOES	
5¼/4	36
6½/5	37
7½/6	38
8½/7	39
9½/8	39½
10½/9	40½

◆ ROMAN FOOD

Café in Via Garibaldi.

"Trattoria" by the Tiber.

Rome could not be called an ascetic town. The pleasure derived from food has never been spurned or seen as a vice; on the contrary, food is celebrated and kept in high regard. Eating in Rome is first and foremost about enjoying abundant food in a friendly atmosphere. Meals are simple but varied, and above all rely on the quality of their ingredients.

ROMAN CUISINE

Although one eats well in Rome, one is neither in Tuscany nor Emilia-Romagna. Enormous ribs of beef are not show-pieces on the menu, nor does one stagger to a halt before charcuterie displays that are reminiscent of a cornucopia. Rome's cuisine has more of a southern character that is deeply rooted in local country traditions, but open to influences from elsewhere. It seems, however, that the latest password is *molto fine* (very fine); but be careful, by following Romans into fashionable restaurants and hunting for refinements everywhere at any price (the bills are often exorbitant) you risk missing the best places that give Rome its true charm for visitors.

DISHES TO LOOK OUT FOR

CARCIOFI ALLA GIUDEA

This dish consists of small and very tender artichokes, cooked in water with lemon juice, then deep-fried in olive oil. The leaves must be golden and crisp.

CODA ALLA VACCINARA

Workers in the slaughterhouse (*vaccinari*) were partly paid with the heads and tails of the animals killed; nothing could be wasted! The dish they created is so delicious that it might well have reconciled the enemy factions of Trastevere and Testaccio.
THE INGREDIENTS: oxtail, onions, garlic, cloves, salt and pepper, white wine, peeled tomatoes, olive oil.
FOR THE SAUCE: celery, pine kernels, raisins and bitter chocolate.

MEAL TIMES

When do people eat in Rome? As in most other parts of Italy, rather late. Lunch is at about 1 pm or 1.30 pm, and one doesn't go to a restaurant for dinner much before 9 pm or 9.30 pm. If you really want to get into the swing of things, bear in mind that Romans love to linger at the dinner table until late. Having chosen the time, the last question is where to eat? The choice depends on how rich you feel and on how much time you have. If you want a full meal, you can choose between the *ristorante* or the *trattoria*, which has more of a family atmosphere and serves traditional cooking. If you do not have much time on your hands and would prefer a quick snack, then go to a wine bar or to a *birreria* (although these are becoming rare). As for the *pizzerie*, remember that in Italy beer is usually drunk with pizza. Also do not forget the very simple *vino e cucina*, now very scarce, and the *tavola calda*. This is more modest with lower prices than the *trattoria* and is sometimes just as good, though you often cannot sit down and have to eat at the bar. Other choices are the *spaghetteria*, which only serves pasta; or the *panineria*, where you will find a wide range of sandwiches, hot or cold. If you prefer a picnic, you will find the Roman version of everything you need in one of the innumerable places that sell slices of pizza to take away (*pizza al taglio*), or in one of the *rosticcerie* that provide roast chicken and *supplì* (rice croquettes), or in bars that sell *tramezzini*, white bread sandwiches.

The Caffè Greco in Via Condotti.

Ice cream and drinks van.

WHAT TO ORDER?

◆ OFFAL

Dishes based on offal, such as *coda alla vaccinara*, *coratella* (fried lamb offal), *trippa alla romana* (tripe in a tomato and mint sauce served with Parmesan cheese) and a *gran misto di cervello, ricotta, carciofi e zucchine* (brains with ricotta, artichokes and zucchini), are typically Roman. To find them, try the old slaughterhouse area, where these are a specialty. A few good addresses include Turriddu al Mattatoio and Checchino or even the Trattoria Agustarella.

◆ MEAT AND PASTA DISHES

There are many other Roman specialties that can be found almost anywhere in the city. Try for example *abbacchio alla cacciatora* (lamb baked in milk, with a mushroom and tomato sauce), *brode spado* (lamb cooked with lemon) or *saltimbocca alla romana* (escalopes of veal, served with Parma ham and flavored with sage). Do not overlook the different kinds of pasta topped with delicious sauces: *pasta alla matriciana* (cubes of smoked and unsmoked bacon, onions and tomatoes), *al cacio e pepe* (cheese made from sheep's milk and olive oil) and *all'aglio e olio* (olive oil and garlic). Some simple places are excellent, like the very ancient Fiaschetteria Beltrame; while other more expensive addresses are worth remembering because of the beauty of their location, such as Sora Lella on Isola Tiberina.

◆ FISH

Romans also like their fish. It is not necessary to go as far as the sea (although there are some good restaurants in Fiumicino's docks) to find excellent fish restaurants. Some are very famous, like La Rosetta or Alberto Ciarla. But be warned, refinement and prestige are expensive.

◆ JEWISH COOKING

Those who want to treat themselves to succulent *filletti di baccala alla giudea* (Jewish-style fillets of cod deep-fried in batter) have only to visit the Ghetto and eat at places as famous as Giggetto or Piperno. Or, if you feel like an evening stroll in the Santa Barbara area, try the Filettaro restaurant.

CAFÉS AND TEA ROOMS

The numerous Roman cafés open early in the morning and close late at night. You will have no difficulty in finding bars, to quench your thirst, have a snack, meet the locals, share the Romans' daily life...

Caffè Greco, Rosati and Doney are well known for their elegance, and the Zodiaco for its view. Depending on the time of day, one might have a *capuccino*, a coffee (La Tazza d'Oro or Sant'Eustachio bar are supposed to make the best), an iced tea, an aperitif, or an ice cream. It is true that everyone has their favorite place to buy the famous Roman ice creams, but there are two that should not to be missed: Giolitti and Tre Scalini.

You prefer pastries? Don't feel guilty. Go to one of the many tea rooms like Babington's.

WINE BARS

The best are really wine shops where you can sample what you intend to purchase or just have a drink. A few in the center are real family institutions. Bear in mind the laid-back Cul de Sac (where the food is just an excuse for tasting one of their 11,000 wines), Costantini (where a light meal and pastries may be eaten in the evening) and Anacleto (for a quick bite at lunchtime and a walk round the Ghetto).

Posters of famous films in which Rome is an unforgettable location...

What is there to do in the evening? While staying in the Italian capital, it would be a crime not to enjoy the local culture. There are many options to choose from, including opera, ballet, concerts, theater and cinema earlier in the evening, and later on, you can relax in one of the bars or "pubs", or visit a cabaret or a nightclub.

THEATER

If you are in Rome in the theater season, between October and May, and would like to see some of the plays from the traditional repertoire (Goldoni, Pirandello, Eduardo De Filippo and so on) find out what is on at the Argentina, the Quirino and the Valle. Or, if you prefer a contemporary or an avant-garde play, try the programs at the Tordinona, the Politecnico or the Ateneo. If you like puppets, then the Teatro Mongiovino and the Nuova Opera dei Burattini should interest you; and the Teatro dei Pupi Siciliani dei Fratelli Pasqualino will give you the joy of discovering, or rediscovering, Sicilian or Neapolitan puppets. If you are mad about Greek tragedy and Roman comedy, then do not miss the performances at Ostia Antica. Those with more eccentric tastes should try the Amfiteatro della Quercia del Tasso.

CINEMA

Big productions are unfailingly dubbed into Italian – which will undoubtedly sadden a number of cinema lovers, as well as all those who are not fluent in Italian. Luckily some cine-clubs and cultural centers show films with their original soundtracks, such as the Alcazar on Mondays, while the Pasquino shows only English-language films. Other cine-clubs include: the Azzuro Scipioni, which is open all summer; the Nuovo Sacher, which shows films in the open air in summer; and the Dei Piccoli, which specializes in children's films. Some cine-clubs require you to become a member.

CONCERTS AND CHAMBER MUSIC

Rome hosts a wide range of musical events. The Accademia Filarmonica di Roma performs at the Teatro Olimpico and the RAI orchestra appears in the auditorium of the Foro Italico, while the Accademia di Santa Cecilia performs at both its concert hall in the Via della Conciliazione and the Sala Accademica in the Via dei Greci. Quality concerts are also given in the Auditorio del Gonfalone and in the Aula Borromini of the Oratorio di San Filippo Neri – two superb concert halls where the pleasures of sight and sound are combined. Between October and May, the Teatro Eliseo gives chamber-music concerts and throughout the year concerts of sacred music are held in churches; concerts also take place fairly regularly in the basilicas, particularly in St John the Lateran and from time to time in the minor shrines. Check the posters on church doors and all over the city, because the newspapers do not announce all musical events. Finally, musical evenings are frequently organized in summer in the ancient ruins, in the courtyards of palazzi and in cloisters. Some fall within the category of festivals ◆ *419*, but many are regular events.

◆ *419*

WHERE TO FIND THE INFORMATION?
All the daily papers have an entertainment column, but the fullest program for Rome and its suburbs appears every Thursday in *Trovaroma*, a supplement of *La Repubblica*. Alternatively consult the weekly magazine *Città Aperta* (there is an English section for tourists) or the monthly bulletin published free by the Ente Provinciale per il Turismo (Italian local tourist office, at Via Parigi no. 5).

A night at the opera in the Baths of Caracalla.

The Teatro Eliseo.

OPERA

In winter (November to June) operas are performed at the Teatro dell'Opera and in summer (July to August) at the Baths of Caracalla. These performances cannot be compared to those at the Scala in Milan, the Fenice in Venice or San Carlo in Naples, but the beauty of the settings makes up for any shortcomings.

BALLET

The winter program of the Teatro dell'Opera and the summer program of the Baths of Caracalla both include ballet; ballet can also be seen at the Teatro Brancaccio and the Teatro Olimpico. However, lovers of classical and contemporary dance risk being somewhat disappointed.

WHEN TO GET TICKETS

In general Italians do not book in advance. Tickets for classical-music concerts tend to be sold on the day at the ticket office, while theater tickets can either be bought on the day or in advance. Telephone bookings are not accepted at the theater ticket office.
EXCEPTIONS: The dance performances at the Teatro dell'Opera, and particularly the opera evenings, when seats are booked months ahead (this can be done by mail) and tickets are sold up to two days before the performances.
To book tickets for both seasons, go to the Teatro dell'Opera (note that the office is shut on Mondays). Alternatively you can take a chance and turn up on the day of the performance at the Baths of Caracalla.

WHERE TO MAKE RESERVATIONS

If you want to book a concert ticket in advance you can do so by ringing the Pronto Spettacolo (Tel: 39 38 72 97). For theater tickets, if you do not want to go to the theater itself, book through an agency (Gesman 92, Via Angelo Emo No. 65, Tel: 63 18 03, Fax: 39 37 83 31, or Box Office Italia, Viale Giuglio Cesare No. 88, Tel: 372 02 15 or 16), but you will pay about 10 percent more than the normal ticket price.

SOCIAL OUTINGS

If Italians do not go out as a family, they tend to go out in groups of friends, which accounts for the number of private clubs. You will only be allowed in if one of you is a member with a club membership card. Also, although some pubs and bars stay open until very late, most places close at about 3 am or 4 am, unlike those in other European capitals.

LIVE ROCK, JAZZ AND LATIN-AMERICAN MUSIC

The best jazzmen usually play at the Paladium, the Castello and the Alpheus (the latter also holds rock and Latin-American concerts in its three halls). Two addresses where you can be sure to find Latin-American music are: El Charango (South American specialties are served and there is dancing) and Yes Brazil (where you need to book in advance). For both the syncopated Latin-American rhythms and some powerful rock try the Caffè Latino, the Caffè Caruso in Testaccio and Melvyn's in Trastevere. Finally a few places where rock can be found, and which are remarkable for their bizarre locations: the Villaggio Globale al Mattatoio, held in an old slaughterhouse in Testaccio; il Castello, already mentioned above, is organized in an old cinema; and Forte Prenestino (in a former prison).

BARS, DISCOS

Politicians and businessmen go to the Tartarughino bar, while artists prefer the Picasso, the Zelig and the Cornacchio. For dancing, elegant Rome goes to the Gilda, the younger set haunts the Veleno, the New Life and the Alien (but trends change quickly). The gay world goes to the Alibi, while night owls haunt Le Stelle, and the less select Blue Zone; both are open until dawn.

CABARETS

There are several cabaret-restaurants in Trastevere, such as Ciceruacchio and Da Meo Patacca, where one can dine to the sound of Roman and Neapolitan songs. This type of evening entertainment tends to be more popular with tourists than local residents.

◆ Shopping

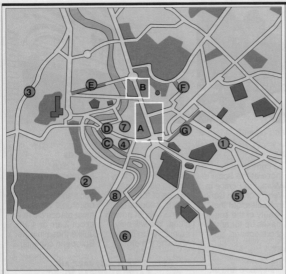

There are relatively few large stores and supermarkets in the Eternal City because Romans prefer to use the small shops and markets. What should you buy to take home? As for all trips to Italy, clothes, shoes and other leather articles. It will be up to you to choose between the luxury products and the less expensive versions.

LUXURY

Rome offers a large choice of goods at the top of the range, and the advantage that most of the shops are concentrated in a small area stretching from Piazza di Spagna to Via del Corso (**A**). There are famous names, Roman and others (Valentino, Laura Bagiotti) in haute couture and luxury ready-to-wear clothing, quality shoes (made by Ferragamo, Fratelli, Rossetti), equally famous fur and leather specialists (Fendi, Gucci), great tailors (Battistoni, Cucci) and renowned jewelers (of which Bulgari is perhaps the most famous in the world). Even if one doesn't buy anything, window shopping can be fun.

GOOD DEALS

For food shopping go to the markets in Piazza Vittorio Emanuele II (**1**), Piazza San Cosimato (**2**), Via Trionfale (**3**) and Campo de'Fiori (**4**). For clothes go to Via Sannio (**5**), where dozens of stalls sell both new and secondhand articles. To find a pair of shoes (even a good make) at unbeatable prices, try Piazza Testaccio market (**6**).

Avoid shopping in Via del Corso, Via Nazionale (**G**) or Via Vittorio Veneto (**F**); instead go to Via Cola di Rienzo (**E**), where almost anything can be found at a slightly lower price. Remember that asking for a *sconto* (discount) before you pay is perfectly normal, almost a national tradition, and sometimes it works!

ART AND ANTIQUES

Rome offers a wide range of antique and designer furniture, linen and decorative objects, and old and modern paintings. Italian design items are on show and for sale in the museum shop at the Palazzo delle Esposizioni (at the top of the steps next to the tunnel in Via Milano). Most of the antique shops and art galleries are located in two main areas: Via Giulia and the parallel Via Monserrato (**C**), and il Tridente, between Via di Ripetta and Via Margutta (**B**). Some smaller antique shops can be found in the Via dei Coronari (**D**), offering high quality, though highly-priced, objects.

SPECIALIST AREAS

◆ Via del Pellegrino: booksellers, art books at half price
◆ Via del Governo Vecchio: second-hand clothes
◆ Via dei Cappellari: restorers and furniture makers
◆ Piazza Borghese (**7**): market selling books, old prints and engravings
◆ Via Trionfale (**3**): flower market
◆ Porta Portese (**8**): flea market (get there very early on Sunday morning to find bargains).

THE LAST WORD

◆ *Bisea*, Via del Gesù No. 93: the largest fabric collection
◆ *Cesari*, Via Barberini: impressive linen and lingerie
◆ *Rizzoli*, Largo Chigi: Rome's largest bookshop
◆ *C. Tupini*, Piazza San Lorenzo in Lucina No. 98: the most expensive glassware shop in Rome.

Water clock in the Pincio Gardens.

Villa Sciarra.

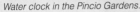

Like all large European towns, Rome has plenty to offer for those on a tight budget. Visit a church for a musical interlude, discover the parks, see a film at a reduced rate, or look around one of the museums that do not charge entrance fees. Also, don't forget that on the outskirts of Rome the hotels and restaurants are less expensive.

CHURCHES

Many Roman churches house spectacular works of art, which the public can visit at almost any time, like the beautiful Caravaggios inside San Luigi dei Francesi ▲ *270*, Sant'Agostino ▲ *284* and Santa Maria del Popolo ▲ *306*. The churches are free, or almost; sometimes an offering is required for the doors of a chapel to be opened, and lighting is often coin-operated (100 or 500 lire).

MUSEUMS

In Rome, the military museums are free, as are the scientific ones. Without spending a lira, one can also visit:
◆ Museo dell'Alto Medievo ▲ *387*
◆ Gabinetto Nazionale dei Disegni e delle Stampe ▲ *360*

◆ Casino Aurora in the Palazzo Pallavicini (can be visited on the first of every month, simply by requesting Princess Pallavicini's permission).
◆ Do not forget that on the last Sunday of every month the Vatican Museums are also free.

MUSIC

Concerts organized in churches are not usually free. However, you will be able to listen free of charge to:
◆ The Gregorian chant, every Sunday morning and on important religious feast days, at Sant'Apollinare ▲ *285*.
◆ The Cappella Giulia choir at Mass (10.30 am) and at Vespers (5 pm) at St Peter's ▲ *209*.
◆ In a quite different style, brass bands perform on the Pincio on Sunday mornings from April to the end of July.

CINEMA

Wednesday is cut-price day for Roman cinemas; some, such as the Tibur, also give student reductions. If you are in Rome during a festival, you will be able to see several films in one evening for a modest amount ◆ *419*.

PARKS AND VILLAS

"One can … have a villa for each day of the week. … There are more than the senses can handle, with their views, their sounds, their smells and the memories they bring back," wrote Henry James. Many have been turned into parks and public gardens: Villas Doria-Pamphili and Sciarra, in the west; Villas Ada, Torlonia and Borghese in the north; Villa Celimontana in the south. As there were fewer villas in the south of Rome, public gardens have been created: Porta Capenna (and its

"archeological walk"), the Giardini delle Rose (wonderful in May), degli Aranci and Savello (with a beautiful view over the Tiber and Rome).

> The public gardens open at 7 am or 9 am and close at 5 pm.

FOUNTAINS

The sparkling, fresh water that trickles out of the fountains in Rome is drinkable, and is freely available for anyone to quench their thirst or to fill their water bottles.

THE OUTSKIRTS OF ROME

If you are traveling by car, eat in the picturesque villages around Rome: they are usually much cheaper than in the city. If you would like to stay in the outskirts, try the rural hostels or houses for rent; information about this is provided by Agri-Turismo, Corso Vittorio Emanuele, 101, (Tel: 685 23 42).

DATES TO REMEMBER
Sung Masses:
JANUARY 25: San Paolo fuori le Mura
JUNE 24: San Giovanni in Laterano
JUNE 29: St Peter's
(Sistine Chapel choir)
DECEMBER 31: the *Te Deum* at the Gesù.

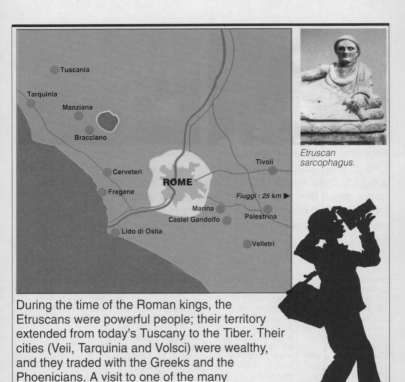

Etruscan
sarcophagus.

During the time of the Roman kings, the
Etruscans were powerful people; their territory
extended from today's Tuscany to the Tiber. Their
cities (Veii, Tarquinia and Volsci) were wealthy,
and they traded with the Greeks and the
Phoenicians. A visit to one of the many
archeological sites of this fine civilization will
complete your sightseeing of ancient Roman sites.

PUBLIC TRANSPORT OUTSIDE ROME		
DESTINATION		**LEAVES FROM**
◆ Ostia	by metro and fast train	Termini Station, Piazza dei Cinquecento
◆ Ostia Antica	by train	Roma–Lido Station, Porta San Paolo, inf Tel: 577 83 90
◆ Tivoli ◆ Palestrina	by coach by coach	Via Gaeta (near Piazza dei Cinquecento) Piazza dei Cinquecento (opposite the Termini main entrance)
◆ Bracciano ◆ Cerveteri	by train	Termini Station Piazza dei Cinquecento inf Tel: 47 75
◆ Bracciano ◆ Cerveteri ◆ Tarquinia ◆ Tuscania	by coach	Via Lepanto (corner of Viale Giulio Cesare)
◆ All destinations in the Castelli Romani	by coach	Last stop of the metro Anagnina (Line A) Piazza Cinecittà et via Tito Labieno
◆ All destinations on the south coast	by metro	Metro EUR Fermi (Line B)

Coaches are run by the coach company A.CO.TRA.L.,
Via di Portonaccio, no. 25, Tel: 575 31.
For the Castelli Romani area, organized tours are also available.
Ask for details in a local travel agent.

The lid of an Etruscan sarcophagus.

Fresco from the Tomb of the Augurs.

THE GREAT ARCHEOLOGICAL SITES

CERVETERI
On a hill near the sea there once stood a town that the Greeks called Agylla; it was Caere, one of the most prosperous towns in ancient Etruria. During the 7th and 6th centuries BC the town reached the peak of its maritime power, with three ports (Alsium, Punicum and Pygri). Later in the 6th century it became a satellite of Rome, as one of Rome's first allies. Its necropolis is one of the largest in the Mediterranean and is just over one mile to the northwest of Cerveteri (follow the signs and you will find the site without difficulty). The Etruscans, who believed in life after death, made many preparations for the afterlife. Funerary urns and tombs reproduced the home with all its furnishings so that the dead person would be in familiar surroundings. Therefore, the styles of the tombs built between the 7th and 3rd centuries BC reflect the evolution of Etruscan dwellings from their origins to the Hellenistic period. The Tomba della Campana (built in first half of the 7th century BC) is a very interesting model of an archaic house, with a straw-covered roof; the Tomba degli Scudi e delle Sedie is a faithful reproduction of a 6th-century house; and the Tomba dei Rilievi (end of the 4th century) is an example of a Hellenistic tomb.

TARQUINIA
According to tradition, Tarquinius Priscus, the first Etruscan king, was born in this town. The ancient town was built on a hill slightly to the west of today's town, the Pian di Civiltà, where the remains of a large temple (the Ara della Regina) can be seen. The focus of interest, however, is the group of hypogeums (underground vaults) concentrated on a hill to the southeast of the modern town; these painted tombs form the largest collection of paintings of the pre-Roman classical world. Only some of the main hypogeums may be visited; they are open alternately. Before leaving the town have a look at the Cosmatesque decorations in the Church of Santa Maria di Castello and the Palazzo Comunale.

ETRUSCAN CITIES

VEII
Due to its southerly position, this large city was the first to fall into the hands of the Romans. Although its name is enchanting enough to encourage a visit to the site, the excavations are closed. Even if they were open, a trip to the site might be disappointing since the treasures have been removed to enrich the collection at the Villa Giulia Museum ▲ *370.*

TUSCANIA
An ancient Etruscan city, which became a Roman free town and a bishopric in the Middle Ages, Tuscania was at its peak in the 11th and 13th centuries. There are two Romanesque churches outside the town, San Pietro and Santa Maria Maggiore, which have remarkable façades.

BRACCIANO
Visit the imposing castle built by the Orsini in the 15th century, for its decorations (Zuccari frescoes) and the wonderful view from the battlements. To relax, take a stroll around the lake ◆ *440.*

OPENING TIMES
EXCAVATIONS AT CERVETERI AND TARQUINIA: 9 am to one hour before sunset.
NATIONAL CERITE MUSEUM, CERVETERI (Ruspoli Palace, 16th century): same as the excavations.
NATIONAL MUSEUM, TARQUINIA: (Vitelleschi Palace, 16th century) 9 am–2 pm; 4 pm–7 pm in summer; closed Mon.
VEII: weekdays, 10 am–2 pm in winter, 10 am–4 pm in summer; Sundays and feast days from 9 am to one hour before sunset.
BRACCIANO CASTLE: Thurs.–Sun. and feast days, 9 am–12 noon and 3 pm–7 pm in summer; 10 am–6 pm in winter.

◆ EXCURSIONS TO CASTELLI ROMANI

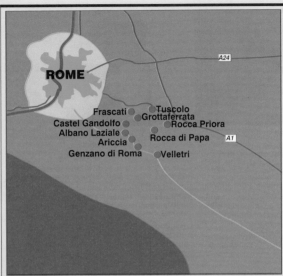

ROME

Frascati
Castel Gandolfo
Albano Laziale
Ariccia
Genzano di Roma
Tuscolo
Grottaferrata
Rocca Priora
Rocca di Papa
Velletri

OPENING TIMES
FRASCATI
◆ Villa Aldobrandini, every day, 9 am–1 pm (park only) apply to, Villa Aldobrandini, Tel: 94 22 560
◆ Villa Falconieri, apply to the European Education Center, Tel: 94 21 019
◆ The tourist information center (Piazza Marconi no. 1, Tel: 94 20 331), organizes guided tours of some villas.
GROTTAFERRATA
◆ Abbey and churches: 9 am–12.30 pm and 4–7 pm, Sun. and national holidays 8–10 am and 3–6 pm.
◆ Museum: 8.30 am–12 noon and 4.30–6 pm. Sun. 8.30–10 am and 4– 6 pm. Closed Mon. and religious feast days.

The Castelli Romani area was a holiday resort for rich Romans in antiquity, and has continued to be since the Renaissance. The area derived its name from the thirteen villages perched on the Alban hills that turned into strongholds (*castelli*) during the Middle Ages. One can easily spend a day or two discovering the beautiful patrician villas and the countryside, remembering to taste the region's famous white wine.

GROTTAFERRATA

The abbey was founded in 1004 by monks from Calabria who remained faithful to the Greek rite. It is well worth a visit, as is the lovely museum next door. The abbey itself was built on a Roman villa; the first school of Greek paleography was founded here, and its library contains some ancient Greek books. Enjoy the spellbinding charm of the Romanesque steeple, the mosaics above the Byzantine portal and the chancel arch, the Cosmatesque paving and the frescoes by Domenichino that decorate the St Nilus chapel of the Church of Santa Maria. You can also explore the Ad Decimum catacombs in the Villa Senni. If you are interested in local customs, try to visit Grottaferrata at the end of March and the beginning of April to witness the meat products' fair. This four-hundred-year-old celebration is an institution, famous throughout the region for its hams and salamis.

TUSCOLO

Wealthy Romans were fond of this spot: Sulla, Cicero, Tiberius and Nero all had villas here. Although little is left of the amphitheater and the forum, a wool-processing workshop, a mithraeum, baths, shops, a sanctuary dedicated to the Bona Dea and a temple belonging to the carpenters' guild make this an interesting site. The citadel on the crest of the hill is all that is left of the medieval town.

The Villa Aldobrandini at Frascati.

Lake Albano.

FRASCATI

It is hard to tell whether Frascati's fame is due more to its white wine, its views or its 16th- and 17th-century villas; the popularity of this town is part of its charm. After visiting the cathedral and fountain in the Piazza San Pietro, the Church of the Gesù (façade by Pietro da Cortona), the Bishop's Palace and the Church of San Rocco, you may well be tired. Make the most of the beautiful gardens of Piazza Marconi, now open to the public, and of the old Villa Torlonia, before touring the main villas. Villa Aldobrandini (or Belvedere) dominates Frascati and from its glorious gardens, with gushing fountains and waterfalls, one can see the sea. Take a quick look at the Church of San Francesco before discovering the following villas: Falconieri, Lancelotti, Mondragora and finally La Ruffinella (or Tuscolano).

CASTEL GANDOLFO

Castel Gandolfo is a charming hill town perched on the edge of the steep crater surrounding Lake Albano. The papal palace cannot be visited. Urban VIII (1628) commissioned Maderno to build this palace, which stands at the top of the central square; Bernini left his mark with the fountain and the Church San Tommaso da Villanova. From a terrace, behind the church, there is a spectacular view of Lake Albano (above).

ACROSS THE COUNTRYSIDE

Starting with the route from Frascati to Tuscolo, many roads in this area have a "panoramic" rating, and their scenic viewpoints contribute to the pleasure of the trip. Particularly spectacular are Rocca Priora and Monte Cavo (Mount Albanus of the ancients) is one of the highest points of the region at over 3,100 feet. A toll road leads up the mountain. The large stone slabs on the side are those of the ancient sacred way which led to the temple of Jupiter at the summit. A monastery replaced the temple, but today this has given way to a restaurant. Another road descends into the greenery, leading to the splendid Via dei Laghi; the route will eventually take you to Velletri. Or take a short cut through Nemi, a lovely village perched high above the water, then follow the little road that encircles the lake. It was once called the "Mirror of Diana" because it reflected the image of a famous temple dedicated to the goddess.

IF YOU HAVE A LITTLE EXTRA TIME

Pass by Rocca di Papa, which derived its name from the citadel (*rocca*) built by the popes; you will be enchanted by its setting and its medieval neighborhoods. Have a look at the Cesarini di Genzano Palace and do not forget Ariccia; it deserves a slightly longer stop, if only to pay homage to Bernini, who renovated the Chigi Palace, built the Church of Santa Maria dell'Assunta and designed the square on which it stands. At Albano Laziale you'll find a twofold link with antiquity; its name comes from Domitian's Villa Albana, and it is the site of architectural remains: the ruins of a villa (incorrectly identified as that of Domitian) in the public gardens and Porta Pretoria. Before reaching Albano Laziale from Ariccia, you will cross an aqueduct; at the foot of it, tucked away, is a tomb said to be that of the Horatii and the Curiatii. If you are tempted by a romantic lakeside walk at Castel Gandolfo, a road travels round the northwestern edge of the volcanic Lake Albano, in the direction of Marino.

Lake Nemi.

Ski resort, Terminillo.

Do you feel an irresistible need for fresh air and tranquility? Follow the example of the Romans who, fleeing from their city, have always sought refuge in the heights of the Alban hills or, more recently, at the seaside or in the mountains, all of which are close.

ON THE LAKES

Romantics will appreciate the lakes of the Castelli Romani: Nemi (or the Mirror of Diana), and Lake Albano, enclosed in the depths of a forest-covered valley. Fishermen will prefer Lake Bracciano (also of volcanic origin), where they will find eels, carp, perch and pike. Boat tours are organized on this lake in summer (leaving from Bracciano, stopping at Anguillara and Trevignano). A variety of water sports are also possible (consult Bracciano's nautical center).

AT THE SEASIDE

For a simple picnic on the beach, go to Ostia. If you hope to swim, go a little further north to Fregene, which is popular with the Romans.

IN THE MOUNTAINS

If you like walking, try a medium altitude course: go to Fiuggi, the large spa (at 1,968 feet) and the Ernici hills. For winter skiing the closest resort is Terminillo.

"ROMAN WEEKENDS"

The *gite fuori porta* (excursions outside the walls) or *scampagnate* (excursions to the Campagna) have always been a chance for Romans to *mangiare al sacco* (have a picnic). At Easter, *porchetta*
◆ *439* (even in a *panino*: sandwich) is a must.

TRADITIONAL FEASTS

If you are interested in folklore, find out about the Sagre. These major popular festivals, commemorating historical events, are linked to extremely old traditions (*palio* and other competitions between different neighborhoods) and provide an opportunity to taste some ancient traditional recipes. Several parts of Lazio participate in these great festivities in the fall, mainly in October.

FOOTBALL

If you have nothing to do on a Sunday afternoon, go and watch a football (soccer) match at 3 pm at the Stadio Olimpico. The main sport in Italy, *calcio* (football) divides Rome into Roma (red and yellow) and Lazio (blue) supporters. Information:
◆ Associazione sportiva Lazio, Via col di Lana, 8
◆ Associazione sportiva Roma, Via Circo Massimo, 7

CHILDREN IN ROME

Rome is not an ideal place to spend a holiday with young children. Other than visiting the zoo, the botanical gardens, and Luna Park at EUR, you might try the following:

AT CHRISTMAS BETWEEN DECEMBER 20 AND JANUARY 10

◆ Visit the traditional *presepi* (cribs) in Via Giulia, or in Santa Maria in Aracoeli, San Giacomo al Corso, Santa Maria in Via, San Lorenzo in Lucina, San Marcello or Sant'Ignazio, and in most other churches.
◆ Go to the Advent-Epiphany toy fair in Piazza Navona.

ALL YEAR ROUND

◆ Go to a puppet show at the Ringhiera or the Teatro dei Puppi Siciliani dei Fratelli Pasqualino. There are open-air shows with hand puppets (Pulcinella) on the Janiculum.
◆ Go to the cinema: Cinema dei Piccoli specializes in cartoons and films for children.

> ### ADDRESSES
> THE CRIB MUSEUM, Via Tor dei Conti, 31, Tel: 67 87 135.
> THE ZOO, Viale Giardino Zoologico, 20, Tel: 87 20 31.

ROME À LA CARTE

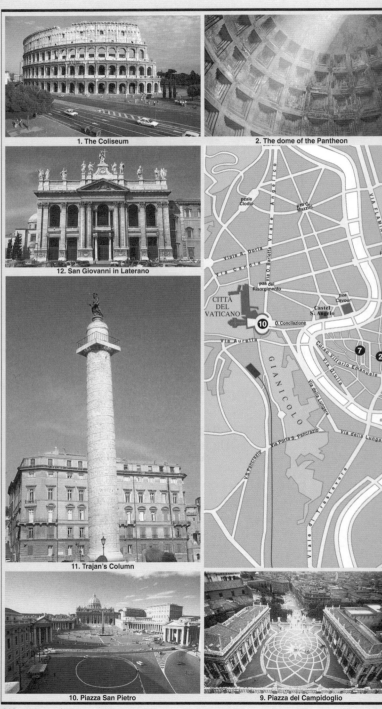

1. The Coliseum

2. The dome of the Pantheon

12. San Giovanni in Laterano

11. Trajan's Column

10. Piazza San Pietro

9. Piazza del Campidoglio

3. Roman Forum

4. Arch of Constantine

5. Villa Adriana

6. Fontana di Trevi

8. Trinità dei Monti

7. Piazza Navona

ARCHEOLOGICAL SITES		
The excavations are usually open from 9am to one hour before sunset.		
ANCIENT MONUMENTS		
• Ara Pacis Augustae		
• Circus of Maxentius	Via Appia Antica	9am–2pm; Sun. 9am–1pm Closed Mon. Permission required 67 10 38 19
• Coliseum	Piazza del Colosseo	9am–3pm
• Augustus' Forum and other Imperial Forums	Via dei Fori Imperiali	
• Roman Forum	Via dei Fori Imperiali	9am–3pm Closed Tues.
• Mausoleum of Augustus	Piazza Augusto Imperatore	Permission required: Tel: 67 10 38 19
• Pantheon	Piazza della Rotonda	9am–2pm. Closed Mon.
• Baths of Caracalla	Via delle Terme di Caracalla	9am–3pm. Closed Tues.
• Tomb of the Scipios	Via di Porta San Sebastiano, 9	9am–1.30pm; Summer 4–7pm, Tues., Thurs., Sat. Closed Mon.
• Tomb of Cecilia Metella	Via Appia Antica	9am–3pm
ARCHEOLOGICAL MUSEUMS		
• Museo Preistorico ed Etnografico Pigorini	Piazza Marconi, 14 Tel: 591 91 32	9am–1.30pm; Sun. 9am–12.30pm
• Museo Nazionale dell'Arte Orientale,	Palazzo Brancaccio, Via Merulana 248,	9am–2.pm, Tues. 9am–1pm, 3.30–7pm; Sun. 9am–1pm
• Forense–Palatino Antiquarium	Piazza Santa Maria Nuova, 53 Tel: 67 90 333	Summer 9am–6pm; Winter 9am–3pm. Closed Tues.
• Musei Capitolini	Piazza del Campidoglio Tel: 67 82 862	9.am–1.30pm; Sun. 9am–12.30pm
• Museo Barracco	Piazza dei Baullari Tel: 65 40 848	9am–1pm; Wed., Thurs. 5–8pm. Closed Mon.
Museo Etrusco di Villa Giulia,	Piazza di Villa Giulia, 9 Tel: 32 01 951	9am–1.30pm; Sun. and Wed.: 9am–12.30pm. Closed Mon.
• Museo Nazionale Romano (or Museo delle Terme)	Via de Nicola, 79 Tel: 48 80 530	9am–1.30pm; Sun. 9am–12.30pm. Closed Mon.
Only a small part of its ancient collection can be seen here. The rest has been moved to the Planetarium, to the former Collegio Massimo and to the Palazzo Altemps: the last two are not open to the public yet .		
HISTORY, FOLKLORE AND TRADITIONS		
• Museo della Civiltà Romana	Piazza G. Agnelli Tel: 59 26 041	9am–1:pm; Wed., Thurs. 3–5.30pm. Closed Mon.
• Museo delle Mura	Porta di San Sebastiano Tel: 75 75 284	Summer 9.am–12 noon; Sun. 9am–1pm; winter 10am–5pm. Closed Mon.
• Museo di Roma	Palazzo Braschi Piazza San Pantaleo,10	Currently closed to the public, except for temporary exhibitions
• Museo dell'Alto Medioevo	Piazza Marconi, 3 Tel: 59 25 806	9am–2pm; Sun. 9am–1pm
• Museo del Folklore	Piazza Sant'Egidio, 1b Tel 58 16 563	9am–1pm; Thurs. 9am–1pm, 5–7.30pm. Closed Mon.
• Museo Nazionale delle Arti e delle Tradizioni Popolari	Piazza Marconi, 8 Tel: 59 26 148	9am–1.30pm; Sun. 9am–12 noon
• Museo Napoleonico	Piazza di Ponte Umberto I Tel: 65 40 286	9am–1.30pm; 5–8pm; Sun. 9am–1pm
• Museo Nazionale di Castel Sant'Angelo	Lungotevere Castello Tel: 65 44 572	9am–6.30pm; Mon. 2–6pm; Sun. 9am–1pm
PAINTING AND SCULPTURE		
• Pinacoteca dei Musei Capitolini	(see Musei Capitolini – Archeological museums)	
• Galleria Nazionale d'Arte Antica di Palazzo Barberini	Via delle Quattro Fontane, 13 Tel: 48 14 591	9am–2pm; Sun. 9am–1pm
• Galleria Nazionale d'Arte Antica di Palazzo Corsini	Via della Lungara, 10 Tel 65 42 323	9am–2pm; Sun. 9am–1.pm
• Galleria Borghese (Villa Borghese)	Via Raimondi Tel: 85 48 577	9am–7pm; Sun. 9am–1pm
• Galleria Doria-Pamphili	Piazza del Collegio Romano, 1a	Wed., Fri., Sat., Sun. 10am–1pm
• Galleria Colonna	Via della Pilotta 17 Tel: 67 94 362	Sat. 9am–1pm
• Galleria dell'Accademia di San Luca	Largo Accademia di San Luca, 77 Tel: 67 89 243	Mon., Wed., Fri. 10am–1pm
• Galleria Spada	Piazza Capo di Ferro, 13 Tel: 68 61 158	9am–2pm, National holidays 9am–1pm

• Museo di Palazzo Venezia	Piazza Venezia	9–2pm; Sun. 9am–1pm. Closed Mon.
• Farnesina	Via della Lungara, 230	9am–1.pm on working days
• Galleria Nazionale d'Arte Moderna	Via delle Belle Arti, 13 Tel: 32 24 151	9am–pm; National holidays 9am–1pm
• Galleria Municipale d'Arte Moderna	Palazzo Braschi Piazza San Pantaleo, 1	Sat. 9am–2pm
GRAPHIC AND APPLIED ARTS		
• Gabinetto Nazionale dei Disegni e delle Stampe	Via della Lungara, 230 Tel: 65 40 565	9am–1pm. Closed Sun.
• Calcografia Nazionale	Via della Stamperia, 6 Tel: 67 94 916	9am–1pm; Tues. 9am–1pm and 3pm–5.30pm; closed Sun. and national holidays
• Museo dei Calchi e dei Gessi	Città Universitaria Istituto di Archeologia Tel: 44 53 270	
• Museo delle Cere	Piazza Venezia, 67 Tel: 67 96 482	9am–7.30pm
• Museo Numismatico della Zecca Italiana	Via XX Settembre, 97 Tel: 47 611	9–11am Closed Sat.
MUSIC, CINEMA AND THEATER		
• Museo degli Strumenti Musicali	Piazza Santa Croce in Gerusalemme 9 Tel: 70 11 796	9am–1pm Closed national holidays
• Museo del Fonografo	Via Caetani, 32, Tel: 68 68 364	9am–1pm
• Cineteca Nazionale	Via Tuscolana, 152 Tel: 72 29 41	9am–3pm Closed Sat. and Sun.
• Raccolta Teatrale del Burcardo	Via del Sudario, 44 Tel: 65 40 755	9am–1pm; Closed in August
• Museo del Teatro Argentina	Largo del Teatro Argentina Tel: 68 77 390	10.am–1.pm; Closed Sun. and Mon.
NATURAL SCIENCES		
• Orto Botanico (botanical gardens)	Largo Cristina di Svezia, 24 Tel: 68 64 193	9am–6pm; Closed Sun.
• Museo Civico di Zoologia	Via Aldrovandi, 18 Tel: 87 35 96	Summer 8.30am–7pm Winter 8.30am–4.30pm
RELIGION		
• Museo d'Arte Ebraica	Lungotevere dei Cenci Tel: 68 75 051	9.30am–2pm; 3.pm–4.30pm; Fri. 9.30am–2pm; closed Sat.
• Museo del Presepio Tipologico	Via Tor dei Conti, 31a Tel: 67 96 146	Wed. and Sat. 5–8pm
• Museo delle Anime dei Defunti	Lungotevere Prati, 12 Chiesa di Santa Croce del Suffragio, Tel: 65 40 517	7.30am–11am; 5–6.30pm
LITERARY MUSEUMS		
• Keats–Shelley Memorial House	Piazza di Spagna, 26 Tel: 67 84 235	9am–12.30pm; 2.30–5pm Closed Sat. and Sun.
• Museo di Goethe	Via del Corso, 18 Tel: 36 13 356	10am–1pm; 4–7pm Closed Sun. afternoon and Mon.
• Museo del Tasso	permission required: Tel: 68 61 571	
CHURCHES		
Except for the main basilicas (St Peter's, Santa Maria Maggiore...) churches close in the afternoon, but they are usually open 7–9am/12 noon–1pm and 3.30–4pm/5–7pm.		
THE VATICAN		
• Museums, palazzi, chapels,	Vatican City	9am–2pm; 9am–5pm July to September and during the Easter period; closed on religious feast days and Sun. except for the last Sun. of each month when entrance is free.
OUTSIDE ROME		
• Museo delle Navi Romane	Aeroporto Fiumicino Via A. Guidoni, 35–37 Tel: 60 11 089	9am–12.30pm; Wed. and Thurs. 2–5pm
• Museo Archeologico Ostiense	Ostia Tel: 56 50 022	9am–4pm
• Museo Colonna-Barberini	Palestrina	Summer 10am–1pm; 3–7pm pm; winter 10am–4.30pm
• Villa d'Este	Tivoli	9am to one hour before sunset
• Villa Gregoriana	Tivoli	9am to one hour before sunset

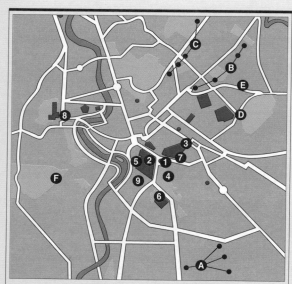

OPENING TIMES

◆ Auditorium of Maecenas, Largo Leopardi: 9am–1.30pm; Sun. 9am–1pm; closed Mon.
◆ The nine-chamber reservoir of Trajan's baths (Sette sale), Via delle Terme di Traiano: 9am–1.30pm; Sun. 9am–1pm; Tues., Thurs. and Sat. 4–7pm; closed Mon. and from April 1st–September 30th
◆ Baths of Caracalla: 9am–two hours before sunset; Sun. and Mon. 9am–1pm
◆ Coliseum: 9am to two hours before sunset; Wed. and national holidays 9am–1pm
◆ For places whose name is followed by *permission must be obtained from the Soprintendenza Archeologica di Roma (Piazza delle Finanze 1) or from the Xª Ripartizione del Comune.
◆ For the Vatican Necropolis and the parts of the grottoes that cannot be visited, ask the Ufficio Scavi, Piazza San Pietro.

After the sumptuous settings above ground, exploring Rome's buried sites reveals a more secret facet of the town. In fact, such sites lead to the discovery of two cities: a Rome, dating back to antiquity and the early Christian era, that was gradually buried over the years, and an underground city that was built centuries ago. This adventure requires some preparation, since special permission is often needed.

DWELLINGS

Are you interested in Roman dwellings? If so, visit the most famous Imperial residence: the Domus Aurea (1) ▲ 174 first. Then discover the House of Livia (2) ▲ 148 and the lovely House of the Griffins ▲ 150, hidden like an *Iseum*, below the Domus Flavia (to visit, ask the curator of the Antiquarium). Also take a look at the cryptoporticus (2) which runs along the Domus Tiberiana. This tour of patrician Rome could finish with the semi-underground Auditorium of Maecenas (3) ▲ 341. To see a more modest side of Rome, go to the Basilica of Santi Giovanni e Paolo* (4) ▲ 188. As well as a medieval oratory, you will discover the remains of five ancient buildings in its underground passages (entrance at the end of the nave), and you will also see a good example of an *insula*.

TEMPLES

Centers of pagan worship were often covered by Christian constructions. Thus in the crypt of San Nicola in Carcere (5) ▲ 156, the remains of three temples can be seen.

COLOMBARIUMS

Are they a part of buried Rome or of underground Rome? Perhaps they belong to both since these communal sepulchers, where the urns of the dead were placed, were often built underground. You can see two by going to Piazzale Numa Pompili: the Columbarium of Pomponius Hylas (6) ▲ 322, inside the park of the Scipios (to visit ask the curator), and at no. 13 Savelli* (6), which was formerly known as Vigna Codina.

FROM SAN CLEMENTE TO SAN PIETRO

Finish with a visit to San Clemente (7) ▲ 193. Consisting of three levels (Romanesque basilica, paleo-Christian basilica and Roman buildings), it is the best example of architectural stratification in Rome. Beneath St Peter's Basilica (8) ▲ 209 lie grottoes* and necropoli*.

MITHRA

House of Livia (on the Palatine).

Catacombs of San Callisto.

EARTH AND WATER

Tufa, the volcanic rock on top of which most of Lazio rests, facilitated the creation of a vast network of passages, used for channeling water, very early in antiquity. Visit the *cloaca maxima** (5) ▲ 156, (at Via del Velabro 3); it was ancient Rome's extensive sewage system. Water was supplied via aqueducts and reservoirs. The most impressive is the so-called seven-chamber (actually nine-chamber) reservoir (3) ▲ 174, that supplied Trajan's baths. Also remember the cryptoporticus that borders the Domus Tiberiana, already mentioned. Complete the tour by exploring the underground passages of the Baths of Caracalla (6) ▲ 319 and the ancient corridors beneath the Coliseum (1) ▲ 170, most of which are now in the open air.

MITHRAEUMS

In Rome there are a number of pagan sanctuaries dedicated to Mithras; some of these can be seen while visiting several of the more famous monuments. The largest is hidden beneath the Baths of Caracalla; another lies in the depths of San Clemente. There are two on the northernmost side of the Circus Maximus* (5) ▲ 177 and beneath the church of Santa Prisca* (9) ▲ 181 (entrance is via the church).

HYPOGEUMS

To get an idea of what these family burial caves were like (hypogeum in Greek means "underground"), visit the catacombs; while touring those of Domitilla it is possible to see the hypogeum of the Flavii. The hypogeum of the Acilii can be seen at the catacombs of Priscilla, while those of San Sebastiano contain the three hypogeums referred to as *ad catacumbas*.

CATACOMBS

The catacombs are underground passages used in the Christian era as cemeteries. They are concentrated into three areas (two in the north and one in the south of Rome); several others are spread along the important routes leading from the ancient city. Two belonging to this last category can be easily visited: the catacombs of San Pancrazio and Ottavilla (ask the Carmelites of the Church of San Pancrazio for permission), and those of Cyriaca (entrance is via the cloister of San Lorenzo Fuori le Mura). To visit the catacombs of Pretestato (A), Via Appia Pignatella; of Nicomedes (B), Via Villini 32; the Cimitero Maggiore, Via Asmara; of San Felicità (C), Via Semeto 2; of San Panfilo, Via Paisello; of Giordani, Via Taro; the anonymous ones on Via Anapo; and those of Sant'Ippolito (E), Viale delle Provincie, obtain permission from the Pontificia Commissione Archeologica Sacra (Via Napoleone III). To see the Jewish catacombs of Villa Randanini (A) and of Villa Torlonia and Via Salaria (B), contact the Soprintendenza Archeologica (Piazza delle Finanze 1).

CATACOMB ADDRESSES

IN THE SOUTH:
◆ San Callisto (A), Via Appia Antica, 102: winter 8.30am–12 noon; 2.30–5pm; summer 2.30–5pm; closed Wed. (enter from the car park at the crossroads with Via Ardeatina).
◆ San Sebastiano (A), Via Appia Antica, 136: same opening times; closed Thurs. ◆ Domitilla (A), Via Ardeatina, 280: same opening times; closed Tues.
IN THE NORTH:
◆ Priscilla (C), Via Salaria, 430: 8.30am–12 noon; 2.30–5pm; closed Mon.
◆ Sant'Agnese Fuori le Mura (B), Via Nomentana, 349: 9am–12am; 4–6pm; closed Tues. afternoon and in the morning on feast days (enter through the narthex of the church).
OTHERS:
◆ Cyriaca (D): 3–5pm; closed Tues. and Fri.
◆ San Pancrazio and Ottavilla (F), Via Aurelia Antica.s

447

◆ WALL MOSAICS

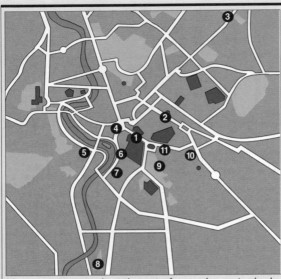

How can one neglect the art of mosaic, so typical of the classical civilizations and of the paleo-Christian and Byzantine worlds? Although the Romans borrowed the techniques for floor mosaics from the Greeks, it was undoubtedly in Rome in the 1st century AD that wall mosaics first appeared and were developed. As fate would have it, Rome was to bequeath this artistic form of expression to the Eastern Empire, before submitting to the influence of Byzantium.

THE FASHION FOR WALL MOSAICS
The technique of wall mosaic, which became popular between the 1st and 4th centuries, was developed by the wide application of mosaic to the decoration of paleo-Christian churches. This new art form, inherited from classical antiquity, kept many realistic traits, though it had no formal icono-graphy. From the 9th century, Byzantium laid down rules to eliminate the remaining traces of realism and replaced them with a more hieratic art. Roman mosaics were also affected and it was only in the Carolingian period that they recovered their freedom. During the 11th and 13th centuries, Roman mosaics flourished, culminating with the work of Cavallini (13th century) who made mosaic closer than it had ever been to pictorial art.

THE OLDEST MOSAICS
These are the mosaics of Santa Costanza (3) (4th century) ▲ 380, of Santa Pudenziana (2) (4th–5th century) ▲ 344, and of Santa Sabina (7) (5th century) ▲ 179. Later came those in the baptistery of San Giovanni in Fonte (10), in the Lateran (5th–7th century) ▲ 196, and of Santi Cosma e Damiano (1) (6th–7th century) ▲ 168.

FROM BYZANTIUM TO THE CAROLINGIANS
The best expressions of Byzantine art are probably those of Sant'Agnese fuori le Mura (3), from the 7th century ▲ 380, and the fragment in Santa Maria in Cosmedin (6) ▲ 155. Fine examples of 9th-century Carolingian mosaics are found in Santa Prassede (2) ▲ 344 and in Santa Maria in Domnica (9) ▲ 190.

THE 12TH AND 13TH CENTURIES
Both the Byzantine and Roman traditions were influential in the creation of the mosaics in Santa Maria in Trastevere (5) ▲ 357 and San Clemente (11) ▲ 193 in the 12th century. There are examples from the 13th century in San Paolo Fuori le Mura (8) ▲ 382 and the Lateran Basilica. Also important are those made by Cavallini and his school in Santa Maria Maggiore (2) ▲ 342, Santa Maria in Aracoeli (4) ▲ 130, Santa Maria in Trastevere, San Paolo Fuori le Mura, San Giorgio in Velabro (6) ▲ 156, and San Crisogono (5) ▲ 356.

FLOOR MOSAICS
Observe the beautiful Cosmatesque paving ● 76 (12th–13th century) of Santa Maria Maggiore, Santa Maria in Trastevere and Santa Maria in Cosmedin.

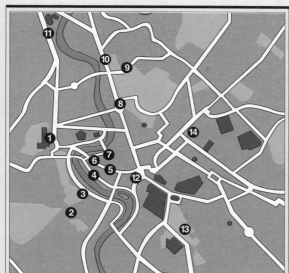

The art of the Renaissance has not left the deepest mark on the Eternal City; in fact, Rome did little more than accept an art form that was developed elsewhere. However, during this period between the return of the popes (after their Avignon exile) and the sack of Rome in 1527, the city attracted many famous artists. This is enough to justify us paying them a small tribute.

With a few exceptions, the Renaissance works of art are found mainly in the Ansa del Tevere (the bend in the Tiber), or just across the river in the Vatican area.

◆ **A RIVERSIDE CITY** Renaissance Rome centered on the river. A vast number of noble palaces were built between the Tiber and the Via del Corso.

◆ **A PAPAL CITY** The Popes' whims were also responsible for many urban transformations. Seeking to assert their spiritual and temporal power, the sovereign pontiffs continued embellishing the Vatican Palace and rebuilding the basilica. To do this they commissioned the best-known artists, almost all of whom were either Tuscan or Umbrian.

VISITS
◆ San Pietro in Montorio: no fixed opening times
◆ Villa Madama and Palazzo Farnese: visits on request
◆ Palazzo Massimo: can only be visited in mornings in March; non-stop masses are held in the chapel.

IN ROME
MICHELANGELO
12. Piazza del Campidoglio ▲ 129.
14. Santa Maria degli Angeli ▲ 334.
12. San Pietro in Vincoli, *Moses* ▲ 346.
RAPHAEL
6. Santa Maria della Pace ▲ 280.
7. Sant'Agostino ▲ 285.
8. Santa Maria del Popolo ▲ 306.

3. The Farnesina ▲ 360.
11. Villa Madama ▲ 378.
PINTURICCHIO
12. Santa Maria in Aracoeli ▲ 130.
8. Santa Maria del Popolo ▲ 306.
BRAMANTE
2. San Pietro in Montorio, *Tempietto* ▲ 364.
6. Santa Maria della Pace, cloister ▲ 281.
VIGNOLA
10. Sant'Andrea in Via Flaminia.
9. Villa Giulia ▲ 370.
PERUZZI
5. Palazzo Massimo alle Colonne, courtyard ▲ 279.
ANDREA SANSOVINO
13. Santa Maria in Domnica ▲ 190.
ANTONIO DA SANGALLO
4. Palazzo Farnese (with Michelangelo) ▲ 244.

ALSO WORTH SEEING
12. Palazzo di Venezia ▲ 161.
5. Palazzo della Cancelleria ▲ 249.

THE VATICAN (1)
BOTTICELLI, GHIRLANDAIO, MICHELANGELO, PERUGINO, PIERO DI COSIMO,

PINTURICCHIO, LUCA SIGNORELLI: Sistine Chapel ▲ 218.
FRA ANGELICO: Chapel of Nicolas V ▲ 226.
MICHELANGELO: St Peter's, the *Pietà*, and the dome ▲ 212.
RAPHAEL: Stanze ▲ 222, Loggias ▲ 228, the Grisaille Chamber.
PINTURICCHIO: Borgia Apartments ▲ 215.
BRAMANTE: Belvedere courtyard and staircase, loggias ▲ 214, St Peter's ▲ 208.

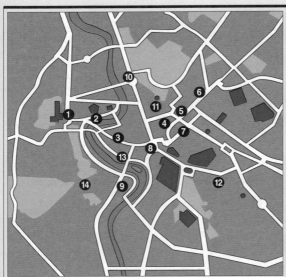

Church of San Carlo.

Statue by Bernini on the Ponte Sant'Angelo.

It is not a bad idea to start with the greatest representatives of Baroque art: Bernini and Borromini. You could devote a whole day to each artist, but you might find it more interesting to discover them together and so be able to compare them better. Their respective masterpieces, Sant'Andrea al Quirinale and San Carlo alle Quatro Fontane, are so close that it is easy to see both in one visit.

VISITS
Santa Maria dei Sette Dolori: permission may be obtained from the religious order. To visit the Capella dei Re Magi: Tel: 67 96 941 or ask the porter.

BERNINI

Gian Lorenzo Bernini, architect and sculptor, was born in Naples. He was successful from his youth, and his skill never questioned. He contributed to St Peter's Basilica and also built the square. In the Vatican he designed the Sala Ducale and the Scala Regia; other works of his are scattered all over the city. His most beautiful achievement, apart from Sant' Andrea al Quirinale, is the Cornaro Chapel in Santa Maria della Vittoria, a true synthesis of all art forms. His most surprising work is probably the statue of the elephant carrying an obelisk in Piazza della Minerva.

BERNINI'S MAIN WORKS
1. The Vatican ▲ 210.
ARCHITECTURE
3. Palazzo di Montecitorio ▲ 269.
8. Palazzo Odescalchi ▲ 301.
7. Sant'Andrea al Quirinale ▲ 296.
SCULPTURE
4. Sant'Andrea delle Fratte ▲ 313.
5. Piazza Barberini, Fontana del Tritone ▲ 290.
3. Piazza Navona ▲ 275.
2. Ponte Sant'Angelo ▲ 239.
9. San Francesco a Ripa ▲ 354.
6. Santa Maria della Vittoria ▲ 294.
3. Piazza della Minerva ▲ 260.
10. Santa Maria del Popolo ▲ 306.

BORROMINI
Francesco Borromini (his real name was Giovanni Domenico Castelli) was the son of a Milanese architect. He arrived in Rome in 1621 and became Carlo Maderno's assistant. Though he produced fewer works than his rival, they show his mastery of pure architecture in its broadest sense and his ability to convey both movement and precision.

BORROMINI'S MAIN WORKS
7. San Carlo alle Quatro Fontane ▲ 295.
13. Palazzo Spada ▲ 246.
3. Oratorio dei Filippini ▲ 282.
13. Palazzo Falconieri ▲ 244.
14. Church of Santa Maria dei Sette Dolori ▲ 364.
3. Sant'Ivo della Sapienza ▲ 272.
12. San Giovanni in Fonte ▲ 198.
3. Sant'Agnese in Agone ▲ 278.
11. Collegio di Propaganda Fide and Oratorio dei Re Magi ▲ 313.
4. Sant'Andrea delle Fratte ▲ 313.

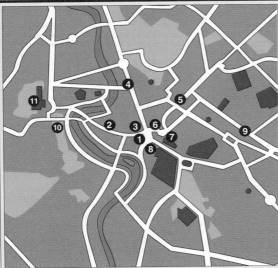

Sant'Andrea della Valle.

The vault of the Gesù.

Baroque art tends toward a synthesis of the arts. Massive painted scenes spread over vaults and ceilings, while a proliferation of sculpted figures on cornices and pendentives seem almost to leap out toward the viewer. In the 17th century, alongside these incredible theatrical effects, Caravaggio added a touch of realism to sacred art.

CARAVAGGIO

SEE:

◆ CHURCHES

4. Santa Maria del Popolo ▲ *306*, for *The Crucifixion of St Peter*

2. San Luigi dei Francesi ▲ *271*, for *The Martyrdom of St Matthew*

2. Sant'Agostino ▲ *285*

◆ MUSEUMS AND VILLAS

5. Casino dell'Aurora ▲ *298*

10. Galleria Nazionale d'Arte Antica ▲ *362*

5. Villa Borghese ▲ *374*

5. Palazzo Barberini ▲ *291*

11. The Vatican ▲ *215*

1. Capitoline Museums ▲ *132*

FRESCOES

If sculpture is an extension of painting, frescoes put the finishing touches to architecture, with trompe l'oeil effects, creating breathtaking perspectives.

1. The Gesù vault ▲ *258* by Giovanni Battista Gauli, known as Bacciccia (1676-9).

1. Palazzo Altieri, vault of the great drawing-room by Carlo Maratta (1674–7).

2. Palazzo Pamphili ▲ *278*, piano nobile (reception rooms) decorated by Pietro da Cortona and other artists.

2. Collegio Innocenziano, library vault by Francesco Cozza.

3. Sant'Ignazio ▲ *261*, vault by Jesuit Brother Andrea Pozzo ▲ *258*.

6. Palazzo Colonna ▲ *300*, vault of the Sala Bellica (Giuseppe Bartolomeo Chiari), of the Sala dei Grande (Filippo Gherardi, Giovanni Coli, Giovanni Paolo Schor), of the Sala dei Paesaggi (Sebastiano Ricci).

7. Santi Domenico e Sisto, vault by Canuti and Henri Haffner (1674–5).

2. Sant'Andrea della Valle ▲ *250*, cupola decorated by Lanfranco.

VISITS

◆ Collegio Innocenziario, Via di Santa Maria dell'Anima 30

◆ Palazzo Altieri, Piazza del Gesù 49, ask at the Associazione Bancaria Italia: it is their headquarters.

◆ Santi Domenico e Sisto: ask at the porter's lodge of the Pontificio Ateneo Angelicum, next to the church on the right.

PIETRO DA CORTONA

DECORATOR

5. Palazzo Barberini ▲ *291*.

4. Santi Ambrogio e Carlo al Corso ▲ *309*.

9. Santa Bibiana ▲ *339*.

2. Santa Maria in Vallicella (or Chiesa Nuova) ▲ *281*.

ARCHITECT

4. Santi Ambrogio e Carlo al Corso ▲ *309*.

2. Santa Maria della Pace ▲ *280*.

3. Santa Maria in Via Lata ▲ *260*.

8. Santi Luca e Martina ▲ *131*.

◆ USEFUL WORDS AND PHRASES

◆ BASICS ◆

Yes: *sì*
No: *no*
Today: *oggi*
Tomorrow: *domani*
Yesterday: *ieri*
I do not understand: *non capisco*
What time is it? *Che ora è? / Che ore sono?*

◆ POLITE PHRASES ◆

Please: *per favore / per cortesia*
Thank you: *grazie*
Thank you very much: *grazie mille*
Excuse me (asking permission to pass): *permesso*
Excuse me (catching someone's attention, formal): *mi scusi*
Excuse me (catching someone's attention, informal): *scusami*
Goodbye (informal): *ciao*
(formal): *arriverderci, arrivederla*
Good morning: *buongiorno*
Good evening: *buona sera*
Good night: *buona notte*

◆ DAYS ◆

The day: *il giorno*
The night: *la notte*
The morning: *la mattina*
The afternoon: *il pomeriggio*
The evening: *la sera*
Monday: *lunedì*
Tuesday: *martedì*
Wednesday: *mercoledì*
Thursday: *giovedì*
Friday: *venerdì*
Saturday: *sabato*
Sunday: *domenica*

◆ THE MONTHS ◆

January: *gennaio*
February: *febbraio*
March: *marzo*
April: *aprile*
May: *maggio*
June: *giugno*
July: *luglio*
August: *agosto*
September: *settembre*
October: *ottobre*
November: *novembre*
December: *dicembre*

◆ NUMBERS ◆

One: *uno*
Two: *due*
Three: *tre*
Four: *quattro*
Five: *cinque*
Six: *sei*
Seven: *sette*
Eight: *otto*
Nine: *nove*
Ten: *dieci*
Eleven: *undici*
Twelve: *dodici*
Thirteen: *tredici*
Fourteen: *quattordici*
Fifteen: *quindici*
Sixteen: *sedici*
Seventeen: *diciasette*
Eighteen: *diciotto*
Nineteen: *diciannove*
Twenty: *venti*
Twenty-one: *ventuno*
Twenty-two: *ventidue*
Thirty: *trenta*
Forty: *quaranta*
Fifty: *cinquanta*
Sixty: *sessanta*
Seventy: *settanta*
Eighty: *ottanta*
Ninety: *novanta*
One hundred: *cento*
One thousand: *mille*

◆ TRAVEL ◆

Luggage: *i bagagli*
The customs: *la dogana*
Travel documents (passport, ID): *i documenti (il passaporto, la carta d'identità)*
The train: *il treno*
The station: *la stazione*
The platform: *il binario*
The plane: *l'aereo*
The airport: *l'aeroporto*
The porter: *il facchino*
The bus/coach: *l'autobus*
The stop: *la fermata*
The car: *una macchina*
A hired car: *una macchina a noleggio*
the taxi: *il tassi*

◆ ON THE ROAD ◆

The road: *la strada*
The motorway: *l'autostrada*
Petrol or gas: *la benzina*
Oil: *l'olio*
The fault (motor): *il guasto*
The tyre: *la gomma*
To inflate /to put air in: *rigonfiare*
The exit: *l'uscita*

◆ FINDING YOUR WAY ◆

Where is ...? *Dove si trova...?*
Is it far/close? *È lontano/vicino?*
On the right: *a destra*
On the left: *a sinistra*
Straight ahead: *dritto*

◆ MOVING AROUND IN TOWN ◆

The street: *la via*
The high street: *il corso*
The side street: *il vicolo*
The square: *la piazza*
The city ring road: *il raccordo anulare*

◆ VISITING ◆

Opening times/timetable: *l'orario*
Open: *aperto*
Closed: *chiuso*
Working days: *i giorni feriali*
Sundays and national holidays: *i giorni festivi*
The ticket: *il biglietto*
The church: *la chiesa*
The palace: *il palazzo*
The excavations: *gli scavi*
The museum: *il museo*
The gallery: *la galleria*

◆ FOOD AND DRINK ◆

A coffee: *un caffè*
A coffee with frothy milk: *un cappuccino*
An ice cream: *un gelato*
A cake: *un dolce*
A pastry: *un pasticcino*
To have lunch: *pranzare*
To dine: *cenare*
Place setting: *il coperto*
A glass: *un bicchiere*
The plate/dish: *il piatto*
Plain tap water: *l'acqua naturale*
Mineral water (usually fizzy): *l'acqua minerale*
Wine: *il vino*
Bottle: *la bottiglia*
Wine by the carafe: *il vino sfuso*
Beer: *la birra*
Starter: *l'antipasto*
Meat: *la carne*
Fish: *il pesce*
Vegetables: *la verdura/il contorno*
Cheese: *il formaggio*
Fruit: *la frutta*
The bill: *il conto*

◆ AT THE HOTEL ◆

I would like a room for tonight: *Vorrei una camera per questa notte*
I would like to book a room for the...: *vorrei prenotare una camera per il...*
For one person: *per una persona*
For two people: *per due persone*
With a double bed: *con letto matrimoniale*
With two beds: *camera doppia*
With bathroom: *con bagno*
With shower: *con la doccia*
To order breakfast: *ordinare la prima colazione*

◆ AT THE POST OFFICE ◆

The mail, post office: *la posta*
Postage stamp: *il francobollo*
The letter: *la lettera*
The postcard: *la cartolina*
The telegram: *il telegramma*

◆ HEALTH ◆

The chemist or pharmacy: *la farmacia*
The hospital: *l'ospedale*
Could you please call a doctor? *Mi chiami un medico per favore?*

◆ SHOPPING ◆

The market: *il mercato*
A bakery: *un panificio*
A confectioner's: *una pasticceria*
A butcher's shop: *una macelleria*
A grocer's shop: *una drogheria/una salumeria*
A tobacconist: *un tabaccaio*
A bookshop: *una libreria*

◆ CLOTHING ◆

A pair of trousers: *pantaloni/calzoni*
A shirt: *una camicia*
A skirt: *una gonna*
A dress: *un vestito*
A jacket: *una giacca*
A coat: *un cappotto*
A jerkin: *un giubbotto*
A sweater: *un maglione*
It is too large/small: *È troppo grande/piccolo*
The size: *la taglia*

◆ ACCESSORIES ◆

Boots: *gli stivali*
Earrings: *degli orecchini*
A belt: *una cintura*
Shoes: *le scarpe*
A necklace: *una collana*
A tie: *una cravatta*
A handbag: *una borsa*
A travel bag: *una valigia, un borsone*

◆ USEFUL EXPRESSIONS ◆

Where can I make a phone call? *Dove posso telefonare?*
How much does this cost? *Quanto costa?/Quanto viene?*
That is too expensive: *È troppo caro*
Where can I change some money? *Dove posso cambiare dei soldi?*
Where can I find...? *Dove posso trovare...?*
When does this shop open? *A che ora apre questo negozio?*
When does it shut? *A che ora chiude?*

Useful addresses

≭ EXTENSIVE VIEW
🅒 CENTRAL LOCATION
🖙 ISOLATED
🕮 LUXURY RESTAURANT
◑ TYPICAL RESTAURANT
○ BUDGET RESTAURANT
🏛 LUXURY HOTEL
🛏 TYPICAL HOTEL
⌂ BUDGET HOTEL
🅿 CAR PARK
🚗 SUPERVISED CAR PARK
▭ TELEVISION
◿ QUIET
⌇ SWIMMING POOL
▭ CREDIT CARDS ACCEPTED
🕇 REDUCTIONS FOR CHILDREN
⌘ PETS NOT ALLOWED
♫ MUSIC
🎤 LIVE MUSIC
☎ ROOM WITH TELEPHONE
♣ PARK OR GARDEN
⊤ MEALS SERVED OUTSIDE

◆ CHOOSING A HOTEL

◆ < 150,000 LIT ◆◆ 150,000 LIT to 300 000 LIT ◆◆◆ > 300,000 LIT	PRICE	VIEW	QUIET	GARDEN/TERRACE	BAR	CAR PARK	RESTAURANT	NO. OF ROOMS
CAPITOL-FORUM-COLISEUM								
Casa Kolbe**	◆		●	●			●	63
Edera***	◆◆	●		●		●		55
Forum****	◆◆◆	●	●	●	●	●	●	76
THE VATICAN								
Ara Pacis**	◆◆				●			37
Atlante Star****	◆◆◆	●	●			●	●	62
Cicerone****	◆◆◆					●	●	237
Columbus***	◆◆					●	●	105
Forti's Guest House*	◆		●					22
Santa Anna***	◆◆		●					20
Visconti Palace Hôtel****	◆◆◆		●			●		247
CAMPO MARZIO								
Abruzzi**	◆							25
Campo de' Fiori**	◆	●	●					27
Cardinal****	◆◆		●					66
Cesari***	◆◆		●					51
Della Lunetta**	◆							31
Holiday Inn Crowne *****	◆◆◆		●	●			●	134
Navona*	◆							21
Pomezia**	◆				●			22
Ponte Sisto***	◆◆		●	●		●	●	129
Portoghesi***	◆◆		●			●		27
Raphael****	◆◆◆		●					70
Del Senato***	◆◆							51
Sole**	◆		●			●		54
Del Sole al Pantheon****	◆◆◆							26
Tiziano***	◆◆					●	●	52
THE QUIRINAL								
Aberdeen***	◆◆		●					27
Accademia***	◆◆		●					
Adria**	◆							18
Ambasciatori Palace****	◆◆◆						●	100
Bel Soggiorno**	◆	●	●	●			●	17
Brasile***	◆◆					●		55
Britannia***	◆◆		●			●		32
Delle Nazioni****	◆◆◆		●			●		74
Dolomiti*	◆		●				●	17
Elide**	◆					●		12
Eliseo****	◆◆◆							56
Fontana***	◆◆	●		●				27
Galileo***	◆◆		●	●	●	●		38
Golden Residence***	◆◆		●			●		13
Imperiale****	◆◆◆						●	95
Katty*	◆		●					9
King***	◆◆	●	●			●		72
Londra e Cargill****	◆◆		●			●	●	105
Majestic*****	◆◆◆					●	●	98
Marcella***	◆◆		●					75
Medici***	◆◆			●				69
Oxford***	◆◆		●				●	57
Pullman Boston****	◆◆		●			●	●	124
Ranieri***	◆◆						●	40
Sant'Andrea**	◆							24

	PRICE	VIEW	QUIET	GARDEN/TERRACE	BAR	CAR PARK	RESTAURANT	NO. OF ROOMS
SICILIA*	♦							60
SISTINA*	♦♦		●	●				28
SIVIGLIA*	♦♦				●	●		41
TEA*	♦		●	●	●			40
TIZI*	♦		●					18
TRITONE*	♦♦			●	●			43
VICTORIA ROMA**	♦♦	●	●	●		●	●	110
IL TRIDENTE								
CONDOTTI*	♦♦		●					16
D'INGHILTERRA**	♦♦♦			●			●	100
EDEN***	♦♦♦			●				112
FORTE**	♦		●					16
GREGORIANA*	♦♦		●					19
HASSLER***	♦♦♦	●	●	●	●	●	●	100
INTERNAZIONALE*	♦♦		●			●		42
LOCARNO*	♦♦		●	●		●		38
MARGUTTA**	♦		●					21
SCALINATA DI SPAGNA*	♦♦	●		●				15
SUISSE**	♦		●					13
TRINITÀ DEI MONTI*	♦♦							23
AROUND THE BATHS OF DIOCLETIAN								
ALEX**	♦						●	23
ART DECO**	♦♦♦			●			●	49
CANOVA*	♦♦			●		●	●	15
DANIELA*	♦♦		●	●		●		48
DIANA*	♦♦		●					185
DINA**	♦							60
FATIMA*	♦			●		●		7
GENOVA**	♦♦♦					●		91
GIAMAICA*	♦	●	●					9
IGEA**	♦							42
MARECHIARO**	♦							21
MASSIMO D'AZEGLIO**	♦♦♦			●		●	●	210
NAPOLEON**	♦♦		●			●	●	80
NEW-YORK**	♦		●			●		42
PERUGIA*	♦		●					11
QUIRINALE**	♦♦♦			●		●	●	186
VIMINALE*	♦♦	●	●	●	●			46
TRASTEVERE								
ESTY*	♦							8
VILLA BORGHESE–VILLA GIULIA								
ALDROVANDI PALACE HOTEL***	♦♦♦		●	●		●	●	139
LORD BYRON***	♦♦♦			●		●		40
TIVOLI–PALESTRINA								
ALBERGO AURORA* (TIVOLI)	♦	●	●				●	20
ALBERGO STELLA* (PALESTRINA)	♦		●				●	
OSTIA								
ALBERGO BELLAVISTA**	♦	●	●			●	●	
OUTSKIRTS OF ROME								
ALBERGO CASTELVECCHIO* (CASTELGONDOLFO)	♦♦					●	●	
ALBERGO EL PASO* (CERVETERI)	♦		●			●	●	
ALBERGO TARCONTE* (TARQUINIA)	♦						●	

◆ CHOOSING A RESTAURANT

◆ < 50,000 LIT
◆◆ 50,000 LIT to 100,000 LIT
◆◆◆ > 100,000 LIT

	PRICE	VIEW	EATING OUTSIDE	SETTING	ROMAN SPECIALTIES	ITALIAN SPECIALTIES	FISH SPECIALTIES	PIZZERIA
CAPITOL-FORUM-COLISEUM								
ANGELINO A TOR MARGANA	◆◆		●		●			
CICILARDONE	◆◆			●				
NERONE	◆		●		●			
TABERNA ULPIA	◆	●	●	●				
VECCHIA ROMA	◆◆		●	●		●		
THE AVENTINE								
AGUSTARELLA	◆				●			
CHECCHINO DAL 1887	◆◆		●		●			
REMO	◆							
LA SCOPETTARO	◆		●		●			
TURRIDDU AL MATTATOIO	◆				●			●
THE CELIO (COELIAN HILL)								
ALFREDO A VIA GABI	◆		●		●			
ANNAVOTA	◆◆					●		
CHARLY'S SAUCIÈRE	◆◆							
LA TAVERNA DEL QUARANTA	◆							
THE VATICAN								
L'ABRUZZESE	◆							
MIMI	◆◆		●			●	●	
OSTERIA DELL'ANGELO	◆		●			●		
SAN LUIGI	◆◆◆							
CAMPO MARZIO								
L'ANTIQUARIO DI GIORGIO NISTI	◆◆		●				●	
IL BACARO	◆		●					
DA BAFFETTO	◆							
LA CAMPANA	◆◆							●
CAMPONESCHI	◆◆◆				●	●		
LA CARBONARA	◆◆	●	●		●			
IL DRAPPO	◆◆		●			●		
L'EAU VIVE	◆◆◆			●				
GIGGETTO	◆◆		●					
GRAPPOLO D'ORO	◆◆		●					
HOSTARIA DELL'ORSO	◆◆◆			●				
LA MONTECARLO	◆		●					
AL MORO	◆◆							
ORSO OTTANTA	◆◆				●			
PANCRAZIO	◆◆		●					●
PAPÀ GIOVANNI	◆◆				●			
PASSETTO	◆◆◆		●	●				
PATRIZIA E ROBERTO DEL PIANETA TERRA	◆◆◆							
AL POMPIERE	◆◆				●		●	
LA ROSETTA	◆◆◆						●	
TRE SCALINI	◆◆		●	●	●			
THE QUIRINAL								
COLLINE EMILIANE	◆◆					●		
CORIOLANO	◆◆◆				●			
GEORGE'S	◆◆◆		●					
SANS SOUCI	◆◆◆							

	PRICE	VIEW	EATING OUTSIDE	SETTING	ROMAN SPECIALTIES	ITALIAN SPECIALTIES	FISH SPECIALTIES	PIZZERIA
IL TRIDENTE								
DA MARIO	◆					●		
DAL BOLOGNESE	◆◆	●	●			●		
FIASCHETTERIA BELTRAME	◆							
IL RE DEGLI AMICI	◆◆		●					
VIA APPIA ANTICA								
CECILIA METELLA	◆◆	●	●					
SORA ROSA	◆◆		●	●	●			
AROUND THE BATHS OF DIOCLETIAN								
COLONDRA	◆◆					●		
IL DITO E LA LUNA	◆					●	●	
TANA DEL GRILLO	◆◆					●		
TRATTORIA MONTI	◆◆					●		
TRASTEVERE								
ALBERTO CIARLA	◆◆◆						●	
CICERUACCHIO	◆◆		●		●			
DA GILDO	◆		●					
GINO IN TRASTEVERE	◆◆				●		●	●
IVO	◆							
MEO PATACCA	◆◆		●					●
PANATTONI	◆		●					
PARIS	◆◆		●		●			●
PIPERNO	◆◆		●	●	●			
ROMOLO	◆◆◆		●	●				
SORA LELLA	◆◆			●	●			
VILLA BORGHESE–VILLA GIULIA								
LE BISTROQUET	◆◆					●		
AI PIANI	◆◆				●		●	
PRIMO PIANO	◆◆		●		●			
LA PISCINE	◆◆◆		●			●		●
OUTSIDE THE WALLS								
AL CEPPO	◆◆							
(GIGGETTO) ER PESCATORE	◆◆					●	●	
LE MASCHERE	◆							
SEVERINO	◆◆				●			●
TIVOLI–PALESTRINA								
SIBILLA (TIVOLI)	◆◆	●	●	●	●			
OSTIA								
RISTORANTE OTELLO	◆	●	●		●			
OUTSKIRTS OF ROME								
ANTONELLO OLONNA	◆◆◆			●	●			
BRICIOLA DI ADRIANA (GROTTAFERRATA)	◆		●					
CACCIONI (FRASCATI)	◆◆		●					
D'ARTAGNAN (GROTTAFERRATA)	◆◆		●		●	●		
LA GROTTA (GENZANO)	◆◆				●			
L'ORATORIO (FRASCATI)	◆				●			
RICHELIEU	◆◆	●	●	●	●			
TAVERNA MAMI LIUS (FRASCATI)	◆		●		●			
TAVERNA DELLO SPUNTINO (GROTTAFERRATA)	◆◆				●			

GENERAL INFORMATION

EMERGENCIES

POLICE:
(CARABINIERI)
Tel: 112
(POLIZIA)
Tel: 113

FIRE BRIGADE:
(POMPIERI)
Tel: 115

ASSISTANCE FOR MOTORISTS:
Tel: 116

HOSPITAL FATEBENEFRATELLI
Piazza San Bartolomeo
Tel: 689 37 90

INTERNATIONAL PHARMACY
Piazza Barberini 49
Tel: 482 54 56 or
487 11 95
Open 24 hours.
OR
Stazione Termini,
Piazza dei Cinquecento,
49/51,
Tel: 488 00 19
Open 24 hours

USEFUL ADDRESSES

POST OFFICE
Via Monterone 11
Open 8.30 am–7.40 pm
Mon. to Fri.; 8.30–11.50
am Sat. and on the last
day of the month;
closed on Sun.

ENTE PROVINCIALE TURISMO (EPT)
Via Parigi 5
Tel: 488 37 48
Open 8.15 am–7.15pm
Mon.–Sat.
For Rome and the
Rome area there is an
office in Termini Station.

ITALIAN NATIONAL TOURISM CENTER (ENIT)
Via Marghera 2
Tel: 497 11/497 12 22

Fax: 446 33 79
Open 9 am–1 pm; and
also 3–6 pm on Mon.,
Wed. and Fri.; closed
Sat. and Sun.
For the whole of Italy.

EMBASSIES AND CONSULATES

AUSTRALIA
Via Alessandria, 215
Tel: 832 721

CANADA
Via Zara, 30
Tel: 440 30 28

UK
Via XX Settembre, 80a
(Porta Pia)
Tel: 482 54 41

IRELAND
Largo Nazareno, 3
Tel: 678 25 41

NEW ZEALAND
Via Zara, 28
Tel: 440 29 28

SOUTH AFRICA
Via Tanaro, 14/16
Tel: 855 44 85
844 32 41, 844 08 48

US
Via Veneto, 119a
Tel: 46 74 1

ACCOMMODATION

CAMPING FLAMINIO
Via Flaminia Nuova 821
Tel: 333 26 04
Open all year round,
600 places. The closest
to the center (4 miles).
Take Metro Line A to
Piazzale Flaminio, then
the 225 tram.

SEVEN HILLS CAMPING
Via Cassia 1216
Tel: 30 31 08 26
Open March to October.
In the northwest of
Rome.

CAPITOL CAMPING CLUB
Via Castel Fusano 195,
Tel: 566 27 20
Open all year round.
Take the metro to Ostia
Lido centro, then bus
no. 5 in the Casal
Palocco direction. It is
located in a pine forest,
just over one mile from
the sea.

HAPPY CAMPING
Via Prato della Corte
1915

Tel 33 62 64 01
Open March to October.

AGRI–TURISMO
Corso Vittorio Emanuele
101
Tel: 685 23 42
For all information on
rural accommodation
around Rome.

OSTELLO DEL FORO ITALICO
Viale delle Olimpiadi 61
Tel: 323 62 67/62 79
Fax: 324 26 13
Youth hostel.

For complete list of
simple but inexpensive
accommodation
available in religious
institutions and
convents contact:
VICARIATO DI ROMA,
Piazza S. Giovanni in
Laterano, 6a, 00184
or:
ROME TOURIST BOARD
Via Parigi, 11, 00185

For group bookings try:
Peregrinatio Ad Petri
Sedem, Piazza Pio XII,
10a (near St Peter's)
Tel: 686 50 90

LEISURE ACTIVITIES

CHILDREN
ARCI RAGAZZI,
Via G.B. Vico 22
Tel: 446 59 62
Association for
children's entertainment
and leisure activities.

ENTERTAINMENT RESERVATIONS
Box Office, Via Giulio
Cesare 88
Tel: 361 26 82
For theater
reservations.

GESMAN
Via Angelo Emo 65
Tel: 63 18 03 or
39 37 83 31
Open 9 am–1 pm,
2–6 pm; closed Sat.
afternoon and Sun.
Theater reservations.

ORBIS
Piazza Esquilino 37
Tel: 482 74 03
Booking agency.

PRONTO SPETTACOLO
Tel: 39 38 72 97
Open 10 am–5 pm
Telephone bookings
for theaters, concerts
and sporting events.

TRANSPORT

AIRLINES
Alitalia, Via della
Magliana 886
Tel: 656 31

SCOOTER RENTAL
SCOOT-A-LONG,
Via Cavour 302
Tel: 678 02 06
SCOOTER FOR RENT,
Via della Purificazione
84
Tel: 488 54 85

BICYCLE RENTAL
BICIROMA,
Piazza di Spagna,
Piazza di San Lorenzo,
Piazza del Popolo
COLLALTI,
Via del Pellegrino 80/82
Tel: 68 80 10 84
Open 8.30 am–1 pm;
3–8 pm, closed on Mon.
Bicycle rental, sale and
repairs.

CAR RENTAL
AVIS,
Fiumicino airport,
Tel: 65 01 15 79 or
65 01 15 31
Ciampino airport
Tel: 79 34 01 95
EUROPCAR,
Fiumicino airport
Tel: 65 01 08 79
Fax: 65 95 45 57, or at
Via Lombardia 7
Tel: 487 12 74 or
481 71 62
HERTZ,
Fiumicino airport
Tel: 65 01 14 48 or
65 95 41 43
Fax: 65 29 119
Stazione Termini
Tel: 474 03 89
Maggiore, Stazione
Termini
Tel: 488 00 49, or at
Via Po 8a
Tel: 854 86 98 or
884 01 37

HORSE-DRAWN CARRIAGES OR BUGGIES
Piazza Navona,
Villa Borghese,
Via Veneto,
Piazza di Spagna,
Piazza Venezia,
Piazza San Pietro

TAXIS
COSMOS RADIO TAXI,
Via Monte Urano 76
Tel: 881 93 00
SOCIETÀ COOPERATIVA
AUTORADIO TAXI,
Via Valle Aurelia 257
Tel: 35 70

PUBLIC TRANSPORT
A.T.A.C.
INFORMATION BUREAU,
Piazza dei Cinquecento,
Via Volturno 65
Tel: 46 95 44 44
ACOTRAL.,
Via Ostiense 131/l
Tel: 57 00 51 or
591 55 51
Via di Portonaccio 25
Tel: 43 85 79 64

CAPITOL–FORUM–COLISEUM

CULTURE

TEATRO ELISEO
Via Nazionale 183
Tel: 488 21 14
*Classic Italian theater
is performed in this
outstanding Art
Nouveau building.*

RESTAURANTS

ANGELINO A TOR MARGANA
Piazza Margana 37
Tel: 678 33 28
Closed Sun.
*Local specialties and
tables outside in
summer.*
40,000–100,000 lire
🚗 🕇

CICILARDONE
Via Merulana 77
Tel: 73 38 06
Closed Sun. evenings
and Mon. Closed July
15–August.
Elegant restaurant.
50,000 lire

NERONE
Via delle Terme di Tito
96
Tel: 474 52 07
Open Mon. to Sat.
Closed August.
*Local cooking. Booking
essential.*
35,000–40,000 lire
🕇

TABERNA ULPIA
Foro Traiano 1b/2
Tel: 678 99 80
Closed Sun
*Massive restaurant with
a capacity of 300,
classified as a historical
monument. Wonderful
view of Trajan's Forum.*
🚗 ⩗ 🕇

VECCHIA ROMA
Piazza Campitelli 18
Tel: 686 46 04
Closed Wed. and for 3
weeks in August.
*Typical restaurant in an
18th-century setting.
Seafood specialties.
Booking recommended.*
35,000–100,000 lire
🚗 ◖ 🕇

HOTELS

CASA KOLBE**
Via San Teodoro 42
Tel: 679 49 74
Fax: 69 94 15 5
*Hotel with restaurant.
Groups accepted.
63 rooms.*
60,000–90,000 lire.
⌂ 🚗 ☎ ⩓

EDERA***
Via A. Poliziano 75
Tel: 70 45 38 88
Fax: 70 45 37 69
55 rooms.
160,000 –250,000 lire
🚗 ⩗ ▢ ☎ 🕇
🚗

FORUM****
Via Tor de' Conti 25
Tel: 679 24
Fax: 678 64 79
*Hotel with restaurant
(international cooking).
Accepts groups. Terrace
with panoramic view.
76 rooms.*
400,000+ lire
⌂ ⌂ 🚻 ▢ ☎ ⩗
⊕ 🚗 ⩓

AVENTINE

RESTAURANTS

AGUSTARELLA
Via G. Branca 100
Tel: 574 65 85
Open 12.30 am–3 pm;
7.45–11 pm; closed
Sun. and from 10
August–10 September.
*Trattoria. Roman
Specialties.*
35,000 lire

CHECCHINO DAL 1887
Via di Monte Testaccio
30
Tel: 574 63 18
Closed Sun. evening
and Mon. Closed in
August and at
Christmas.
*A typical restaurant in
the slaughterhouse
area. Ideal for tasting
dishes based on offal.*
80,000 lire
🚗 🕇

REMO
Piazza S. Maria
Liberatrice 44
Tel: 574 62 70
Open Mon.
Closed in August.
*Pizzeria. Young
clientele.*
20,000 lire

LA SCOPETTARO
Lungotevere Testaccio 7
Tel: 574 24 08
Closed Tues.
*4 rooms. Roman
cooking. Offal
specialties.*
35,000 lire
🚗 🕇

TURRIDDU AL MATTATOIO
Via Galvani 64

Tel: 575 04 47
Closed Wed. and Sun.
evening, and last week
of August.
*A good address. Roman
cooking.*
30,000 lire

NIGHTLIFE

ALIBI 2000
Via di Monte Testaccio
39
Tel: 574 34 48
Gay discotheque.
♫

CAFFÈ CARUSO
Via di Monte
Testaccio 96
Tel: 574 40 20
Closed August–
September.
*3 rooms: cinema, art
gallery, and cabaret/
discotheque. Rock, jazz,
rhythm 'n blues and
Latin disco.*
♫

CAFFÈ LATINO
Via di Monte Testaccio
36
Tel: 574 50 19
Closed Mon. and from
July to September.
*3 rooms: disco, bar,
concerts, theater,
cabaret. There is a
Tevere Jazz festival on
the banks of the Tiber.*
♫

L'HISTOIRE
Via di Monte Testaccio
44
Closed Mon.
*Fashionable nightclub.
Free entrance. One
drink compulsory.*
♫

LA SPAGO
Via di Monte
Testaccio 35
Closed Mon.
Discotheque.
♫

VILLAGGIO GLOBALE IL MATTATOIO
Lungotevere Testaccio
Tel: 57 30 03 29
Closed Mon. and in
August.
*This cultural association
has exhibitions and
debates in the afternoon
and becomes a
discotheque every
evening, sometimes
with groups playing live
African and South
American music.*
♫

Located between the Coliseum and the Church of Santi Giovanni e Paolo. Booking recommended. 25,000–35,000 lire

CELIO

CULTURE

TEATRO BRANCACCIO
Via Merulana 244
Tel: 482 78 59

RESTAURANTS

ALFREDO A VIA GABI
Via Gabi 36
Tel: 77 20 67 92
Closed Tues and in August.
Local specialties.
35,000–45,000 lire

ANNAVOTA
Piazza San Giovanni in Laterano 20
Tel: 77 20 50 07
Closed Wed and in August.
Traditional cooking.
40,000–55,000 lire

CHARLY'S SAUCIERE
Via San Giovanni in Laterano 270
Tel: 70 49 56 66
Open for lunch from Tues. to Fri. and every evening.
Closed Sun. and for two weeks in August.
French specialties.
60,000 lire

LA TAVERNA DEL QUARANTA
Via Claudia 24
Tel: 700 05 50
Closed Sun. except in summer.

SHOPPING

DEPARTMENT STORES
Coin, Piazzale Appio 7
Five stories of clothing and household goods.

VATICAN

CULTURE

AUDITORIUM OF L'ACCADEMIA DI SANTA CECILIA
Via della Conciliazione 4
Tel: 654 10 44. For bookings: 68 80 10 44

TEATRO DEI PUPPI SICILIANI DEI FRATELLI PASQUALINO
Via Gregorio VII 292
Tel: 53 65 75

RESTAURANTS

L'ABRUZZESE
Via dei Gracchi 27
Tel: 314 914
Closed Mon. and in May.
Trattoria. No credit cards.
25,000 lire

MIMI
Via G.G. Belli 59/61
Tel: 321 09 92
Closed Sun. and in August.
Neapolitan cooking. Fish specialties.
30,000–60,000 lire

OSTERIA DELL'ANGELO
Via G. Bettolo, 24
Tel: 372 94 70
Closed Sun. and Sat. at lunchtime. Closed in August and for 10 days over Christmas.
Traditional Italian cooking. Tables outside in summer.
30,000 lire

SAN LUIGI
Via Mocenigo, 10
Tel: 39 72 07 04
Closed Sun.
Italian and international cooking.
60,000–100,000 lire

HOTELS

ARA PACIS**
Via Vittorio Colonna, 11
Tel: 320 44 46/44 47
Fax: 321 13 25
37 rooms.
110,000–160,000 lire

ATLANTE STAR****
Via Vitelleschi, 34
Tel: 687 32 33
Fax: 687 23 00
Hotel restaurant with a breathtaking view of St Peter's. 62 rooms.
200,000–350,000 lire

CICERONE****
Via Cicerone, 55/c
Tel: 35 76
Fax: 68 80 13 83
237 rooms. Hotel with restaurant.
260,000–360,000 lire

COLUMBUS***
Via della Conciliazione 33
Tel: 686 54 3
Fax: 686 48 74
105 rooms. Hotel with restaurant and garden.
170,000–245,000 lire

FORTI'S GUEST HOUSE*
Via Fornovo, 7
Tel: 320 07 38
Fax: 321 22 22
Closed in August for 20 days. *22 rooms.*
70,000–100,000 lire

SANTA ANNA***
Borgo Pio, 133–134
Tel: 68 80 16 02
Fax: 68 30 87 17
20 rooms.
160,000–230,000 lire

VISCONTI PALACE HOTEL****
Via Federico Cesi 37
Tel: 36 84
Fax: 320 05 51
247 rooms.
260,000–360,000 lire

SHOPPING

STANDA
Via Cola di Rienzo 173
Department store, supermarket.

LIBRERIA MONDADORI
Piazza Cola di Rienzo 81/83
Bookshop.

NIGHTLIFE

IL CASTELLO
Via Porta Castello 44
Tel: 686 83 28

FOOD AND DRINK

COSTANTINI
Piazza Cavour 16
Tel: 321 32 10
Closed Mon. mornings,

Sat. mornings and in August.
Wine merchant offering over 5,000 vintages from all over the world. These can be tasted on the spot along with a wide range of cheeses.

CAMPO MARZIO

CULTURE

AUDITORIUM DEL GONFALONE
Via del Gonfalone 32a
Tel: 687 59 52
Tickets on sale in the Vicolo della Scimia 1b.

TEATRO ARGENTINA
Largo Torre Argentina 56
Tel: 654 46 01 or 68 80 46 01

TEATRO TORDINONA
Via degli Acquasparta 16
Tel: 68 80 58 90

40,000–65,000 lire

IL DRAPPO
Vicolo del Malpasso 9
Tel: 687 73 65
Open for lunch and
evenings until midnight.
Closed Sun and in
August.

PANTHEON

HOTELS
1 ABRUZZI**
4 CESARI***
6 HOLIDAY INN
  CROWNE *****
7 NAVONA*
13 DEL SENATO***
15 DEL SOLE
  AL PANTHEON****

NIGHTLIFE
17 PICASSO
19 ZELIG

FOOD AND DRINK
21 GIOLITTI
22 SANT'EUSTACHIO
23 TAZZA D'ORO

TEATRO VALLE
Via Teatro Valle 23a
Tel: 68 80 37 94

RESTAURANTS

**L'ANTIQUARIO DI
GIORGIO NISTI**
Piazzetta S. Simeone
26/27
Tel: 687 96 94
Closed Sun, end August
and Christmas.
Fish specialties.
60,000 lire

IL BACARO
Via degli Spagnoli 27
Tel: 686 41 10
Open evenings only.
Closed Sun and for two
weeks in August.
Light food.
40,000 lire.

DA BAFFETTO
Via del Governo
Vecchio 114
Tel: 656 16 17
Popular pizzeria.
20,000 lire

CAMPANA
Vicolo della Campana,
18
Tel: 687 52 73
Closed Mon. and in
August.
Local clientele.
40,000 lire

CAMPONESCHI
Piazza Farnese 50a
Tel: 687 49 27
Open evenings until
1 am. Closed Sun.
*Refined Italian and
Roman cuisine. Ideal
for supper after a show.*
80,000–120,000 lire

LA CARBONARA
Campo de' Fiori 23
Tel: 686 47 83
Closed Tues and for two
weeks in August.
*Roman specialties.
Booking recommended.*

LA

Sardinian dishes. A
good place to know
about. Meals served
outside in summer.
65,000 lire

L'EAU VIVE
Via Monterone 85
Tel: 654 10 95
Closed Sun and for 15
days in August.
*Located in a 16th-
century palace
managed by a French
secular order. It is
frequented by prelates
and senators. Booking
recommended.*

GIGGETTO
Via del Portico d'Ottavia
21a
Tel: 686 11 05
Closed Mon.
*Roman Jewish cooking.
One of the most famous
places in the Ghetto.*
50,000 lire

GRAPPOLO D'ORO
Piazza della Cancelleria 80/81
Tel: 689 70 80
Closed Sun. and for 3 weeks in August.
Trattoria.
40,000 lire

HOSTARIA DELL'ORSO
Via dei Soldati 25
Tel: 686 42 50 or 686 42 21
Open evenings only.
Closed Sun. and in the summer.
An excellent restaurant set in a 13th-century palace. Very expensive. Piano-bar and nightclub, on three floors.
120,000 lire.

LA MONTECARLO
Vicolo Savelli, 12
Tel: 687 22 00
Closed 1–15 August.
16,000 lire

AL MORO
Vicolo delle Bollette, 13
Tel: 678 34 95 or 684 07 3
Closed Sun. and in August.
Excellent cooking.
60,000 lire

ORSO OTTANTA
Via dell'Orso, 33
Tel: 686 49 04 or 686 17 10
Closed Mon and in August.
Pizzeria and Roman cooking. Booking recommended.
65,000 lire

PANCRAZIO
Piazza del Biscione, 9
Tel: 686 12 46
Closed Wed. and for 3 weeks in August.
40,000–50,000 lire.

PAPÀ GIOVANNI
Via dei Sediari
Tel: 686 53 08

Closed Sun. and in August.
Light Roman cuisine.
80,000–90,000 lire

PASSETTO
Via Zanardelli, 14
Tel: 687 99 37
Closed Sun.
Roman cooking in a centuries old setting.
60,000–120,000 lire

PATRIZIA E ROBERTO DEL PIANETA TERRA
Via dell'Arco del Monte, 95
Tel: 686 98 93 or 654 16 63
Closed Mon. and 7 August–2 September.
Excellent cooking. Booking strongly recommended.
130,000 lire

AL POMPIERE
Via Santa Maria dei Calderaria
Tel: 686 83 77
Closed Sun. and in August.
Roman specialties (fried vegetables, fried fish...). A welcoming restaurant
50,000–70,000 lire

LA ROSETTA
Via della Rosetta 8/9
Tel: 686 10 02
Closed Sat. evening and Sun. and for 15 days in August.
Fish-based Mediterranean cooking.
60,000–120,000 lire

TRE SCALINI
Piazza Navona 35
Closed Wed. and at the beginning of December.
A historical restaurant founded in 1815. Roman specialties.
50,000–60,000 lire

HOTELS

ABRUZZI**
Piazza della Rotonda
Tel: 670 20 21
25 rooms.
70,000–90,000 lire

CAMPO DE' FIORI**
Via del Biscione, 6
Tel: 68 80 68 65
Fax: 687 60 03
27 rooms. 6th floor terrace with panoramic view.
77,000–150,000 lire

CARDINAL****
Via Bresciani 35
Tel: 683 38 06
Fax: 687 63 76
66 rooms.
160,000–260,000 lire

CESARI***
Via di Pietra 89a
Tel: 679 23 86
Fax: 679 08 82
51 rooms.
110,000–160,000 lire

DELLA LUNETTA**
Piazza del Paradiso 68
Tel: 686 10 80
Fax: 689 20 28
31 rooms.
65,000–110,000 lire

HOLIDAY INN CROWNE PLAZA*****
Piazza della Minerva, 69
Tel: 69 94 18 88
Fax: 676 41 65
134 rooms. Hotel with restaurant
375,000–535,000 lire

NAVONA*
Via dei Sediari, 8
Tel: 686 42 03
Fax: 68 80 38 02
21 rooms. This hotel has a restaurant for

groups.
65,000–105,000 lire

POMEZIA**
Via dei Chiavari, 12
Tel: 686 13 7
22 rooms.
85,000–110,000 lire

PONTE SISTO***
Via dei Pettinari, 64
Tel: 686 88
Fax: 6830 80 22
129 rooms. Hotel with restaurant.
145,000–190,000 lire
🏠 🔲 ☎ 🚗 ⛪

PORTOGHESI***
Via dei Portoghesi, 1
Tel: 686 42 31
Fax: 687 69 76
27 rooms.
110,000–240,000 lire
🏠 ⬜ 🔲 ☎ 🚗

SOLE**
Via del Biscione 76
Tel: 68 80 68 73
54 rooms. One of Rome's oldest hotels. A good address! Small conference rooms available.
65,000–110,000 lire
🏠 🅿

DEL SOLE AL PANTHEON****
Piazza della Rotonda 63
Tel: 678 04 41
Fax: 684 06 89
26 rooms.
320,000–400,000 lire
⬜ 🔲 ☎

TIZIANO***
Corso Vittorio
Emanuele II 110
Tel: and Fax: 686 50 19
52 rooms. Hotel with restaurant.

VIA GIULIA

HOTELS	
2 CAMPO DE' FIORI**	**9** POMEZIA**
3 CARDINAL****	**10** PONTE SISTO***
5 DELLA LUNETTA**	**14** SOLE**
	16 TIZIANO***

RAPHAEL****
Largo Febo 2
Tel: 68 28 31
Fax: 687 89 93
70 rooms.
220,000–385,000 lire
🏠 ⬜ 🔲 ☎

DEL SENATO***
Piazza della Rotonda 73
Tel: 678 43 43
Fax: 69 94 02 97
51 rooms.
154,000–204,000 lire
⬜ 🔲 ☎

150,000 lire
⬜ 🔲 ☎ 🚗

SHOPPING

DEPARTMENT STORE:
LA RINASCENTE
Via del Corso 189
6 floors, clothes, perfumes, toys...

BOOKSHOPS

RINASCITÀ
Via delle Botteghe
Oscure
Tel: 679 74 60
*This large bookshop
also has a concert
booking service.*

NIGHTLIFE

PICASSO
Piazza della Pigna 23
Tel: 678 82 11
Closed Sun. and in
August.
*Latin American and jazz
concerts.*

TARTARUGHINO
Via della Scrofa 1/3
Tel: 686 41 31
Open from 9 pm.
Closed Sun. and from
mid-June to mid-
September.
*Restaurant and piano-
bar, popular with
politicians and
businessmen.*

ZELIG
Via Monterone 74
Tel: 687 92 09
Closed Mon. and in
August.
*Jazz, Blues and Latin
American music.*

FOOD AND DRINK

CUL DE SAC 1
Piazza Pasquino
Tel: 68 80 10 94
Closed Mon.
*The cellar of this wine
bar contains more than
1,200 Italian wines.
Snacks are also
available.*
22,000 lire

GIOLITTI
Via degli Uffici del
Vicario 40
Closed Mon.
*One of Rome's most
famous ice cream bars.*

SANT'EUSTACHIO
Piazza Sant'Eustachio
82
Tel: 686 13 09
Open 8.30 am–1 am.
Closed Mon. and for 3
weeks in August.
*Coffee lovers can find
one of the best Italian
coffees here, to drink on
the premises or to take
home.*

TAZZA D'ORO
Via degli Orfani 82, 84
Tel: 678 97 92
Open 7 am–10 pm.
Closed Sun. and for 15
days in August.
Typical setting.

TRE SCALINI
Piazza Navona 28
Tel: 686 12 34
Closed Wed.
*Famous for its delicious
chocolate tartufi (truffle
icecreams).*

THE QUIRINAL

CULTURE

BRITISH COUNCIL
Via delle Quattro
Fontane
Tel: 482 66 41

ISTITUTO DELLA
CALCOGRAFIA
Via della Stamperia 6

Open 9 am–1 pm and
4–7 pm, Tues. and
Thurs.

TEATRO QUIRINO
Via delle Vergini 1
Tel: 679 45 85
*Tickets from Via
Minghetti 1.*

TEATRO SISTINA
Via Sistina 129
Tel: 482 68 41

RESTAURANTS

COLLINE EMILIANE
Via degli Avignonesi 2
Tel: 481 75 38
Closed Fri. and in
August.
*Emilian cooking.
45,000–60,000 lire*

CORIOLANO
Via Ancona 14
Tel: 841 95 01
Closed Sun.and for 15
days in August.
*Specialties from Rome
and Piedmont. Booking
recommended.
70,000–100,000 lire*
🔲

GEORGE'S
Via Marche 7
Tel: 48 45 75 or
474 52 04
Closed Sun. and in
August.
*Piano-bar in the
evenings.
80,000–100,000 lire*
🔲 ⴲ ♫

PIAZZA NAVONA

HOTELS
11 PORTOGHESI***
12 RAPHAEL****

NIGHTLIFE
18 TARTARUGHINO

FOOD AND DRINK
20 CUL DE SAC 1
24 TRE SCALINI

SANS SOUCI
Via Sicilia 20
Tel: 445 61 94
Open from 8 pm–1 am.
Closed Mon. and in
August.
International cuisine.
120,000–150,000 lire
⌷

TULLIO
Via San Nicola da
Tolentino 26
Tel: 487 41 25
Closed Sun. and in
August.
Tuscan and Roman
cuisine.
70,000 lire
⌷

HOTELS

ABERDEEN***
Via Firenze 48
Tel: 482 39 20
Fax: 482 10 92
27 rooms.
100,000–210,000 lire
⌂ ⌷ ☐ ☎

ACCADEMIA***
Piazza del Accademia
di San Luca 75
Tel: 679 22 66
Fax: 678 58 97
180,000–220,000 lire
⌂ ⌷ ☐ ☎

ADRIA**
Via XX Settembre 58a
Tel: 474 52 09
18 rooms.
50,000–100,000 lire

AMBASCIATORI
PALACE****
Via Vittorio Veneto 62
Tel: 474 93
Fax: 474 36 01
100 rooms. Hotel with
restaurant.
330,000–460,000 lire
⌷ ☐ ☎

BEL SOGGIORNO**
Via Torino 117
Tel: 488 17 01
Fax: 481 57 55
17 rooms. Hotel with
restaurant, breakfast
served on the terrace.
75,000–95,000 lire
⌂ ⌷ ☎ ☒

BRASILE***
Via Palestro 13
Tel: 481 94 33
Fax: 482 94 78
55 rooms.
80,000–100,000 lire
⌷ ☐ ☎ ☒

BRITANIA***
Via Napoli 64
Tel: 488 31 53

Fax: 488 23 43
32 rooms.
170,000–250,000 lire
⌂ ⌷ ☐ ☎ ☒

DELLE NAZIONI****
Via Poli 7
Tel: 679 24 41
Fax: 678 24 00
74 rooms.
210,000–355,000 lire
⌂ ⌷ ☐ ☎ ☒

DOLOMITI*
Via San Marino della
Battaglia 11
Tel: 491 058
Fax: 445 46 65
Hotel with restaurant.
17 rooms.
40,000–75,000 lire
⌂ ⌷

ELIDE**
Via Firenze 50
Tel: 488 39 77
Fax: 48 90 43 18
12 rooms.
80,000–110,000 lire
⌷ ☎ ☒

ELISEO****
Via di Porta Pinciana 30
Tel: 487 04 56
Fax: 481 96 29
54 rooms.
270,000–420,000 lire
⌷ ☐ ☎

FONTANA***
Piazza di Trevi 9
Tel: 678 61 13
Fax: 679 00 24
27 rooms.
Terrace with a view on
the Trevi fountain.
110,000–190,000 lire
⌷ ☐ ☎ ☒

GALILEO***
Via Palestro 33
Tel: 444 12 07
Fax: 444 12 08
Breakfast served on the
terrace. 38 rooms.
143,000 lire
⌂ ⌷ ☐ ☎ ☒

GOLDEN
RESIDENCE***
Via Marche 84
Tel: 482 16 59 or
482 18 93
Fax: 482 16 60
13 rooms.
140,000–165,000 lire
⌂ ⌷ ☐ ☎ ☒

IMPERIALE****
Via Vittorio Veneto 24
Tel: 482 63 51
Fax: 482 63 52
95 rooms. Hotel with
restaurant.
220,000–380,000 lire
⌷ ☐ ☎

KATTY*
Via Palestro 35
Tel: 444 12 16
9 rooms. Popular with
students, this hotel
offers some interesting
discounts during the low
season.
50,000–80,000 lire
⌂

KING***
Via Sistina 131
Tel: 488 08 78
Fax: 487 18 13
72 rooms. Breakfast is
served on the terrace in
summer. Panoramic
view.
140,000–225,000 lire
⌂ ⌷ ☐ ☎ ☒
☒ ♞

LONDRA E
CARGILL****
Piazza Sallustio 18
Tel: 473 871
Fax: 474 66 74
105 rooms. Hotel with
restaurant.
190,000–240,000 lire
⌂ ⌷ ☐ ☎ ☒

MAJESTIC*****
Via Veneto 50
Tel: 48 68 41
Fax: 488 09 84

98 rooms. Hotel with
restaurant.
350,000–540,000 lire
⌷ ☐ ☎ ☒

MARCELLA***
Via Flavia 106
Tel: 474 62 06
Fax: 481 58 32
75 rooms.
170,000–300,000 lire
⌂ ⌷ ☐ ☎

MEDICI***
Via Flavia 96
Tel: 482 73 19
Fax: 474 07 67

69 rooms.
160,000–200,000 lire
⌷ ☐ ☎

OXFORD***
Via Boncompagni 89
Tel: 482 89 52
Fax: 481 53 49
57 rooms. Hotel with
restaurant.
160,000–220,000 lire
⌂ ⌷ ☐ ☎

PULLMAN
BOSTON****
Via Lombardia 47
Tel: 47 80 21
Fax: 482 10 19
129 rooms. Hotel with
restaurant.
235,000–325,000 lire
⌂ ⌷ ☐ ☎ ☒

RANIERI***
Via XX Settembre 43
Tel: 481 44 67
Fax: 481 88 34
40 rooms. Hotel with
restaurant.
100,000–180,000 lire
⌷ ☐ ☎

SANT'ANDREA**
Via XX Settembre 89
Tel: 481 47 75
Fax: 481 47 75
24 rooms.
55,000–90,000 lire
⌷

SICILIA***
Via Sicilia 24
Tel: 482 19 13
Fax: 482 19 43
60 rooms.
80,000–150,000 lire
⌷ ☎

SISTINA***
Via Sistina 136
Tel: 48 90 03 16
Fax: 481 88 67
28 rooms.
In summer, breakfast
served on the terrace.
180,000–280,000 lire
⌂ ⌷ ☐

SIVIGLIA***
Via Gaeta 12
Tel: 444 11 97

Fax: 444 11 95
41 rooms.
120,000–160,000 lire

TEA***
Via Sardegna 149

Tel: 488 59 64
Fax: 482 70 58
*Bar. 40 rooms. Pleasant
terrace.*
110,000–144,000 lire

TIZI*
Via Collina 48
Tel: 482 01 28
Fax: 474 32 66
18 rooms. Group meals

snacks. Wine cellar
contains 600 varieties
of wine.
30,000 lire

NIGHTLIFE

BLUE ZONE
Via Campania 37a
Tel: 482 18 90

Open until dawn.
Discotheque.

NEW LIFE
Via XX Settembre 90
Tel: 474 09 97
Discotheque.

VELENO CLUB
Via Sardegna 27
Tel: 482 18 38
Closed Mon. and from
July to August.
*Discotheque and piano-
bar.*

IL TRIDENTE

CULTURE

VILLA MEDICI
Viale Trinità dei Monti,
1a
Tel: 676 11
Open 10 am–1 pm;
3–7 pm.
Closed Mon.

**GALLERIA INCONTRO
D'ARTE**
Via del Vantaggio, 17a
Tel: 361 22 67
Open 10.30 am–1 pm;
4.30–8 pm.
Closed Mon. and Tues.
morning and in summer
from mid-July.

RESTAURANTS

DA MARIO
Via della Vite, 56
Tel: 678 38 18
Closed Sun. and in
August.
*Excellent and
inexpensive. Tuscan
cooking. Booking
recommended.
40,000 lire*
▭

DAL BOLOGNESE
Piazza del Popolo, 1/2
Tel: 361 14 26
Closed Mon.
in winter and Sat. and
Sun. in summer.
*Bolognese cuisine.
70,000 lire*
⚜ ⌖

**FIASCHETTERIA
BELTRAME**
Via della Croce, 39.
Closed for 2 weeks in
August.
*Family atmosphere.
Traditional cooking.*

IL RE DEGLI AMICI
Via della Croce 33b
Tel: 678 25 55 or
679 53 80
Open Sun.
45,000–50,000 lire
▭ ⌖

HOTELS

CONDOTTI*
Via Mario de' Fiori 37
Tel: 679 46 61
Fax: 679 04 5
*16 rooms.
190,000–240,000 lire*
🏠 ▭ 🖥 ☎

D'INGHILTERRA**
Via Bocca di Leone, 14
Tel: 67 21 61
Fax: 69 92 22 43
*Hotel with restaurant.
100 rooms.
310,000–410,000 lire*
🏛 ▭ 🖥 ☎

EDEN***
Via Ludovisi, 49
Tel: 474 35 51

*available.
35,000–60,000 lire*
🏠

TRITONE*
Via del Tritone 210
Tel: 66 78 94 44
Fax: 678 58 97
*Bar. 43 rooms. Roof-top
terrace.
180,000–220,000 lire*
▭ 🖥 ☎

VICTORIA ROMA**
Via Campania 41
Tel: 47 39 31
Fax: 487 18 90
*110 rooms. Hotel with
restaurant. Breakfast
served on the terrace,
with a panoramic view
of Villa Borghese.
180,000–300,000 lire*
🏠 ▭ 🖥 ☎ 🚗

SHOPPING

**UPIM DEPARTMENT
STORES**
Via del Tritone 172
Main Roman branch.

RIZZOLI BOOKSHOP
Largo Chigi 15
*The largest bookshop in
Rome.*

FOOD AND DRINK

DONEY
Via Vittorio Veneto 145
Tel: 482 17 90
Closed Mon.
*Tea room, also serves
drinks, light meals and
ice creams.*

TRIMANI WINE BAR
Via Cernaia 37b
Tel: 446 96 30
Fax: 446 83 51
Closed Sun. and for two
weeks in August.
*A wine bar since 1821.
On the spot tasting of
some 30 vintages with*

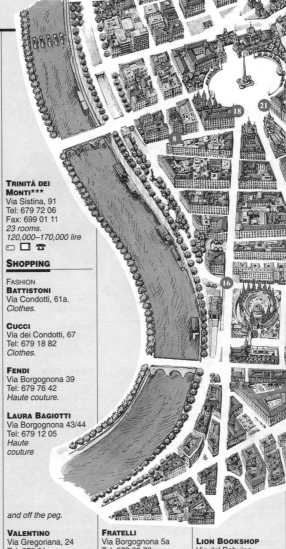

Fax: 482 15 84
*112 rooms. Roof
terrace.*
315,000–550,000 lire
🏛 🏠 ▭ ☎

FORTE**
Via Margutta 61
Tel: 320 76 25
16 rooms.
75,000–115,000 lire
🏠 ▭

GREGORIANA***
Via Gregoriana, 18
Tel: 679 42 69
Fax: 678 42 58
19 rooms.
165,000–250,000 lire
🏠 ▭ ☎

HASSLER*****
Piazza Trinità dei Monti,
6
Tel: 678 26 51
Fax: 678 99 91
*100 rooms. Hotel with
luxury restaurant on the
6th floor. Piano-bar in
the evenings.*
380,000–750,000 lire
🏛 🏠 🈁 ▭ ▭ ☎
🔆 ♪ 🍴 🎾

INTERNAZIONALE***
Via Sistina 79
Tel: 678 46 86 or
679 30 47
Fax: 678 47 64
42 rooms.
180,000–250,000 lire
🏠 ▭ ▭ ☎ 🚗

LOCARNO***
Via della Penna, 22
Tel: 361 08 41
Fax: 321 52 49
38 rooms.
140,000–210,000 lire
🏠 ▭ ▭ ☎ 🚗

MARGUTTA**
Via Laurina, 34
Tel: 679 84 40 or
322 36 74
21 rooms.
120,000–130,000 lire
🏠 ▭ ☎

**SCALINATA DI
SPAGNA*****
Piazza Trinità dei Monti,
17
Tel: 679 30 06
Fax: 69 94 05 98
15 rooms.
250,000–300,000 lire
▭ ▭ ☎ 🔆

SUISSE**
Via Gregoriana, 54
Tel: 678 36 49
Fax: 678 12 58
13 rooms.
80,000–140,000 lire
🏠 ▭ ☎

**TRINITÀ DEI
MONTI*****
Via Sistina, 91
Tel: 679 72 06
Fax: 699 01 11
23 rooms.
120,000–170,000 lire
▭ ▭ ☎

SHOPPING

FASHION
BATTISTONI
Via Condotti, 61a.
Clothes.

CUCCI
Via dei Condotti, 67
Tel: 679 18 82
Clothes.

FENDI
Via Borgognona 39
Tel: 679 76 42
Haute couture.

LAURA BAGIOTTI
Via Borgognona 43/44
Tel: 679 12 05
*Haute
couture*

and off the peg.

VALENTINO
Via Gregoriana, 24
Tel: 673 91
Haute couture.

OTHER ADDRESSES
BULGARI
Via dei Condotti, 10
Tel: 679 38 76
Jeweler.

CROFF
Via Tomacelli 137
*Household objects and
small pieces of furniture
at reasonable prices.*

FERRAGAMO
Via Condotti 73/74
Tel: 679 15 65
Shoe shop.

FRATELLI
Via Borgognona 5a
Tel: 678 26 76
Shoe shop.

GUCCI
Via dei Condotti 8
Tel: 678 93 40.
Fur and leather.

BOOKSHOPS

FELTRINELLI
Via del Babuino 39/41

REMAINDER'S
Piazza San Silvestro 28

**ANGLO-AMERICAN
BOOKSHOP**
Via Frattina

LION BOOKSHOP
Via del Babuino

FOOD AND DRINK

ACHILLE
Via dei Prefetti, 15
Tel: 687 34 46
*Closed Sun., Mon.
mornings and in 2nd
half of August.*
*Wine bar with a great
selection of wines,
spirits and champagnes.
Snacks available. On
the spot sales and
wines, spirits and
pastries to take away.*
2,000–15,000 lire
▭

Closed Sun. and for 2
weeks in August.
*This elegant café,
founded in 1760, was a
meeting place for artists
during the 18th century.*
🖃

ANTICA ENOTECA DI VIA DELLA CROCE
Via della Croce, 76
Tel: 679 08 96
Closed Sun. and during
the 1st week of August.
*The oldest wine bar in
Rome (1842).
A splendid setting and a
good selection of wines.
A variety of snacks are
also served.
20,000–30,000 lire*
🖃

BABINGTON'S TEA ROOMS
Piazza di Spagna, 23
Tel: 678 60 27
Open from 9 am–8 pm.
Closed Tues. and Sun.
in summer.
*Tea rooms founded by
two English ladies in*

1893. Meals are also
served at any time
throughout the day.
Expensive.
🖃

BUCCONE
Via di Ripetta, 19
Tel: 361 21 54
Open from 9 am–
1.30 pm and 4–8 pm.
Closed Sun. and for
three weeks in August.
*Very old wine bar.
3,000–9,000 lire*

CAFFÈ GRECO
Via Condotti, 86
Tel: 679 17 00.
Open from 8 am–9 pm.

CANOVA
Piazza del Popolo, 16
Tel: 361 22 31 or
361 22 27
Open 7.30 am–1 am.
*Bar, restaurant and
luxury shop. One of
Rome's best known
cafés.*
🖃 ☂

LA CAPRICIOSA
Largo Lombardi (off the
Corso)
Tel: 687 86 36
Closed Tues.
*Large, reliable,
traditional Italian
restaurant with
courteous service.
Tables outside, pizza in
the evening.
25–35,000 lire*

469

CASINA VALADIER
Viale del Belvedere
(Pincio)
Tel: 679 20 83.
Open from 9 am–2 am
(dinner not served after
11.15 pm).
Closed Mon.
Bar and restaurant.
60,000–90,000 lire

EUROPEO
Piazza S. Lorenzo in
Lucina, 33
Tel: 687 63 04 or
687 63 00
Closed Wed. and
August.
Ice cream bar and café.
10,000 lire

HOSTARIA AL 31
Via delle Carrozze, 31
Tel: 678 61 27
Closed Sun.
*Small, friendly and
Sardinian.*
25–35,000 lire

ROSATI
Piazza del Popolo 5
Tel: 322 58 59 or
322 73 78.
Closed Tues.
*Very elegant café and
ice cream bar.*
10,000 lire

VANNI
Via Col di Lana 10
Tel: 322 36 42
Closed Mon.
Via Frattina 94
Tel: 679 18 35
Open 7–11 pm.
Closed Mon.
*Bar, ice cream bar and
restaurant.*

NIGHTLIFE

GILDA
Via Mario de Fiori 97
Tel: 678 48 38 or
679 73 96
Closed Mon. and in
summer.
*A discotheque popular
with the Rome jet set.
Meals are served.*
50,000–100,000 lire

VIA APPIA ANTICA

CULTURE

BATHS OF CARACALLA
Via delle Terme di
Caracalla 52
Tel: 575 83 02
*Opera and ballet in
summer, usually ends in
early August.*

RESTAURANTS

CECILIA METELLA
Via Appia Antica,
125/129
Tel: 513 67 43
Closed Mon. and for 2
weeks in August.
*A good view and
tables outside in
summer.*
50,000–70,000 lire.

SORA ROSA
Via Tor Carbone, 74
Tel: 718 84 53
Closed Mon.
*Picturesque restaurant
with a family
atmosphere. Booking is
recommended in
summer.*
40,000–55,000 lire

BATHS OF DIOCLETIAN

CULTURE

TEATRO NAZIONALE
Via del Viminale, 51
Tel: 487 06 10

TEATRO DELL'OPERA
Via Firenze 62
Tel: 481 70 03
*Tickets on sale at
Piazza Beniamino
Gigli, 1.*

RESTAURANTS

COLONDRA
Via Torino, 34
Tel: 487 39 20 or
482 69 70
Open 12.30–3 pm;
7.30–11 pm.
Closed Sun. and in the
last 2 weeks in August.
*Traditional Italian
cooking.*
42,000 lire

IL DITO E LA LUNA
Via dei Sabelli, 47/51
Tel: 494 07 26
Open evenings only.
Closed Sun. and in
August.
*Sicilian cuisine,
especially fish dishes.*
40,000 lire

TANA DEL GRILLO
Via V Alfieri, 4
Tel: 70 45 35 17
Closed Mon.
*Ferrara cuisine.
Friendly.*
50,000 lire

TRATTORIA MONTI
Via San Vito, 13a
Tel: 446 65 73
Closed Tues and from
end of August to early
September.
*A trattoria famous for
offering dishes from the
region of the Marches.*
40,000 lire

HOTELS

ALEX**
Via Giovanni Giolitti,
425–427
Tel: 70 45 15 21
Fax: 700 00 87
*23 rooms. Hotel with
restaurant.*
120,000 lire

ART DECO****
Via Palestro, 19
Tel: 445 75 88
Fax: 444 14 83
*49 rooms. Hotel with
restaurant.*
230,000–360,000 lire

CANOVA***
Via Urbana, 10a
Tel: 487 33 14
Fax: 481 91 23
*15 rooms. Hotel with
restaurant (Neapolitan
cooking).*
120,000–190,000 lire

DANIELA***
Via Luigi Luzzatti 31
Tel: 702 78 17
Fax: 702 79 22
48 rooms.
100,000–200,000 lire

DIANA***
Via Principe Amedeo, 4
Tel: 482 75 41
Fax: 48 69 98
185 rooms.
130,000–185,000 lire

DINA**
Via Principe Amedeo,
62
Tel: 474 06 94 or
481 88 85
Fax: 48 61 03
60 rooms.
110,000 lire

FATIMA*
Viale Castro Pretorio, 25
Tel: 445 42 01
7 rooms.
45,000–75,000 lire

GENOVA***
Via Cavour, 33
Tel: 476 951
Fax: 482 75 80
91 rooms.
230,000–350,000 lire

GIAMAICA*
Via Magenta, 13
Tel: 490121
Fax: 445 19 63
*9 rooms. Group meals
served.*
36,000–50,000 lire

IGEA**
Via Principe Amedeo,
97
Tel: and Fax: 446 69 11
42 rooms.
75,000–100,000 lire

MARECHIARO**
Via Gioberti, 30
Tel: 446 53 95 or
446 53 67
Fax: 443 53 85
21 rooms.
65,000–110,000 lire

MASSIMO
D'AZEGLIO****
Via Cavour, 18
Tel: 488 06 46
Fax: 482 73 86
*210 rooms. Hotel with
restaurant and terrace
for summer.*
230,000–315,000 lire

NAPOLEON**
Piazza Vittorio
Emanuele, 105
Tel: 44 70 04 20
Fax: 446 72 82
*80 rooms. Hotel with
restaurant for dinner
only. Very peaceful
atmosphere.*
170,000–275,000 lire
🏠 ⬜ 📺 ☎

NEW-YORK**
Via Magenta, 13
Tel: 49 17 93
Fax: 494 17 14
*42 rooms. Comfortable
and welcoming.*
35,000–120,000 lire
🏠 ⬜ 📺 ☎ 🚗

PERUGIA*
Via del Colosseo, 9
Tel: 679 72 00
Fax: 678 46 35
*11 rooms. Good value
for money.*
30,000–80,000 lire
🏠 ⬜ ☎

QUIRINALE**
Via Nazionale, 7
Tel: 47 07
Fax: 482 00 99
*186 rooms and a
garden. Hotel with
restaurant.*
265,000–350,000 lire
🏛 ⬜ ☎ 🚗 ♻

VIMINALE*
Via Cesare Balbo, 31
Tel: 488 19 10
Fax: 474 47 28
*46 rooms. Attractive
terrace with a
panoramic view.*
105,000–250,000 lire
🏠 ⬜ 📺 ☎ ♻

SHOPPING

**UPIM DEPARTMENT
STORES**
Piazza Santa Maria
Maggiore or Via
Nazionale, 211

BOOKSHOP

**ECONOMY BOOK AND
VIDEO CENTER**
Via Torino, 136

FOOD AND DRINK

CHIARRA
Via Torino, 133
Tel: 48 56 59
Open 7 am–2 am.
Closed Sun. and for one
week in August.
*Wine bar with a very
large selection of Italian
wines.*
🍷

TRASTEVERE

CULTURE

**ACCADEMIA
AMERICANA**
Via Angelo Masina
Tel: 584 61
Open 9 am–5 pm.
Closed Sat., Sun.
and for 2 weeks in
August.

L'ALCAZAR
Via Cardinale Merry del
Val 14
Tel: 588 00 99
*Subtitled original
versions shown on Mon.*

**ANFITEATRO QUERCIA
DEL TASSO**
Via Passeggiata del
Gianicolo
Tel: 575 08 27
*Open-air performances
in summer. In winter this
theater company moves
to the Teatro Anfitrione,
Via San Saba, 24.
Comedies.*

NUOVO SACHER
Largo Ascianghi, 1
Tel: 581 81 16
*This is Nanni Moretti's
Cinema.Open air
showings in summer.
Subtitled original
versions shown Mon.
and Tues.*

RESTAURANTS

ALBERTO CIARLA
Piazza S.
Cosimato, 4
Tel: 581 86 68.
Open Mon.
Closed for 2 weeks in
January and August.
*A sophisticated
restaurant. Fish
specialties.*
100,000 lire
🍽

CICERUACCHIO
Via del Porto, 1
Tel: 580 60 46Open
5–11 pm.
Closed Mon.
and in August.
*Roman and
international cuisine.
Same style as the*

restaurant Da Meo
Patacca.
45,000 lire
🍽 🍴

DA GILDO
Via della Scala, 31a
Tel: 580 07 33
Closed Wed.
Open evenings only
from May to October.
Pizzeria and trattoria.
25,000–40,000 lire
🍽 🍴

GINO IN TRASTEVERE
Via della Lungaretta, 85
Closed Sun. and August
10–31.
*Credit cards not
accepted. High prices
but equally high quality
cooking. Fish
specialties.*
50,000 lire

IVO
Via S. Francesco a
Ripa, 158
Tel: 581 70 82
Closed Tues.
*One of Rome's most
famous pizzerias.*
15,000–20,000 lire
🍴

DA MEO PATACCA
Piazza dei Mercanti, 30
Tel: 581 61 98
Open in the evenings
only. Closed in
Christmas period.
*Very touristy. Meals are
accompanied by local
music.*
55,000 lire
🍽 🍴 🎵

PANATTONI
Viale Trastevere, 53
Tel: 580 09 19
Closed Wed. and 8–28
August.
*Pizzeria. Very lively in
the evenings.*
12,000 lire
🍴

PARIS
Piazza S. Callisto, 7a
Tel: 581 53 78
Closed Sun. evening,
Mon. and in August.
Roman cooking.
50,000–80,000 lire
🍽 🍴

PIPERNO
Via Monte de' Cenci, 9
Tel: 654 06 29 or
68 80 27 72
Closed Sun. evenings
and Mon., in August and
over Christmas and
Easter.
Roman and Jewish

*cuisine. An elegant
restaurant. Booking is
recommended.*
70,000 lire
🍴

ROMOLO
Via Porta Settimiana, 8
Tel: 581 82 84
Closed Mon. and for two
weeks in August.
*A restaurant with a
wealth of historical and
romantic memories.
In summer, dinner is
served in a courtyard
within the Aurelian
walls. It is said that La
Fornarina, Raphael's
mistress, lived here for
a while.*

**SABATINI A SANTA
MARIA**
Piazza S. Maria in
Trastevere, 18
Tel: 581 20 26
Closed Wed.
*Good food, fashionable,
cozy in winter. Splendid
terrace on the piazza.
Book, especially in
summer.*
50,000–100,000 lire

SORA LELLA
Via Ponte Quattro Capi,
16
Tel: 686 16 01
Closed Sun.
*A good address on Isola
Tiberina. Traditional
cooking. Booking is
recommended.*
70,000 lire
🍽

HOTELS

ESTY*
Viale Trastevere, 108
Tel: 588 12 01
8 rooms.
40,000–80,000 lire

SHOPPING

**STANDA DEPARTMENT
STORE AND
SUPERMARKET**
Viale Trastevere, 62–64
*In line with the
reasonable prices of this
neighborhood.*

BOOKSHOPS

**THE CORNER
BOOKSHOP**
Via del Moro, 48
Tel: 583 69 42

**OPEN DOOR
BOOKSHOP**
Via della Lungaretta, 25
Tel: 589 64 78

New, secondhand and English videos.

NIGHTLIFE

EL CHARANGO
Via di Sant'Onofrio, 28
Tel: 687 99 08
Closed Mon. and July to mid-September.
Dancing to live Latin American music.
♫

IL MELVYN'S
Via del Politeana, 8a
Tel: 580 30 77
♫

YES BRAZIL
Via San Francesco a Ripa, 103
Tel: 581 62 67
Open from 8 pm
Closed Sun.
Brazilian music.
♫

CULTURE

AUDITORIUM OF THE FORO ITALICO
Piazza Lavio de Bosis, 28
Tel: 36 86 56 25

TEATRO OLIMPICO
Piazza Gentile da Fabriano, 17
Tel: 323 98 91

RESTAURANTS

LE BISTROQUET
Via G. Sacconi, 55
Tel: 322 02 18
Open evenings only
Closed Sun. and in August
Refined cuisine.
75,000 lire
▭

AI PIANI
Via Denza, 35
Tel: 807 97 04
Open 12.30 am–4713.30 pm and in the evening to 2 am. Closed Mon. and in August.
Roman cuisine, fish

specialties.
60,000 lire
▭

LA PISCINE
Via Mangili, 6
Tel: 321 61 26
Closed Sun. evening.
French chef. Italian and French specialties.
Booking recommended.
50,000–100,000
▭ ⟐ ⊤

PRIMO
Piano Via Cassia, 999b
Tel: 30 31 07 11
Stays open late.
Closed Mon.
Traditional cuisine; pizzas.
50,000–60,000 lire
▭ ⊤

HOTELS

ALDROVANDI PALACE HOTEL ★★★★★
Via Aldrovandi, 15
Tel: 322 39 93
Fax: 322 14 35
139 rooms (including 16 suites). There are three restaurants in this hotel.
🏛 🏠 ▭ ☐ ☎ 🚗 ⛲

LORD BYRON ★★★★★
Via Giuseppe de Notaris, 5
Tel: 322 04 04
Fax: 322 04 05
40 rooms.
250,000–420,000 lire
🏛 ▭ ☐ ☎ 🚗 ⛲

CAFES

ROCCHI
Via A. Scarlatti, 7/9
Tel: 855 10 22
An excellent wine bar.

ZODIACO
Viale Parco dei Mellini, 90
Tel: 349 66 40
Sometimes stays open to 4 am. Closed Tues. morning.
Café, bar, ice creams. It is one of the only cafés in Rome with a view over the whole city.
▭ ⚊ ⊤

NIGHTLIFE

LE STELLE
Via C. Beccaria, 22
Tel: 361 12 40
Closed Mon.
Fashionable 471 discotheque. Cuban music and salsa.
♫

CULTURE

L'AZZURO SCIPIONI
Via degli Scipioni, 82
Tel: 39 73 71 61
Dei Piccoli Viale della Pinta, 15
Tel: 855 34 85
Cinema specializing in cartoons and films for children.

TEATRO ATENEO
Viale delle Scienze, 3
Tel: 49 91 46 89
In the university campus.

TEATRO I MONGIOVINO
Via G. Genocchi, 15
Tel: 513 94 05 or 860 17 33

TEATRO DI VILLA LAZZARONI
Via Appia Nuova, 522b
Tel: 784 04 53 or 78 77 91
Performances for children. Acting courses, concerts and debates.

RESTAURANTS

AL CEPPO
Via Panama, 2
Tel 841 96 96
Closed Mon. and August 10–30.
50,000–80,000 lire
▭

(GIGGETTO) ER PESCATORE
Via Antonio Sant'Elia, 13
Tel: 807 99 29
Closed Sun.
Specializes in fish and seafood prepared Roman style.
80,000 lire
▭

LE MASCHERE
Via Umbri 8/14
Tel: 445 38 05
Closed Mon. and in May.
Pizzeria.
20,000 lire

SEVERINO
Piazza Zama, 5c
Tel: 700 08 72
Closed Mon. and in August.
Good traditional cooking. You are given a souvenir plate if you choose the "saltimbocca alla romana".
60,000 lire
▭

SHOPPING

SHOPPING CENTER:
CINECITTÀ DUE CENTRO COMMERCIALE
Via Tuscolano
The oldest of the large shopping centers in Rome.

NIGHTLIFE

ALIEN
Via Velletri 13/19
Tel: 841 22 12
Discotheque.

ALPHEUS
Via del Commercio, 36/38
Tel 57 47 78 26
The best jazzmen.
♫

FORTE PRENESTINO
Via F. Delpino Palladium
Piazza B. Romano, 8
Tel: 511 02 03
Open from 9.30 pm.
Closed in August.
Live groups (jazz, rock and Italian music).
♫

HOTELS

ALBERGO AURORA ★★★
Via A. Manzoni, 19
Tivoli
Tel: 0774/52 91 76
Fax: 0774/35 40 92
20 rooms. Restaurant in the hotel (Roman cuisine). You are given a good view of the surrounding area.
98,000–140,000 lire
🏠 ▭ ☐ ☎ ◑ ⚊

ALBERGO STELLA***
Piazzale della
Liberazione, 3
Palestrina
Tel: 953 86 37
Fax: 957 33 60
Restaurant in hotel.
50,000–80,000 lire
⌂ ⊡ ▢ ☎

RESTAURANTS

SIBILLA
Via della Sibilla, 50
Tivoli
Tel: 0774/20281
Closed Mon.
This has been an inn
since 1730. There are
two ancient temples in
the garden. Roman
specialties.
60,000 lire
⊡ ☗

OSTIA

RESTAURANTS

RISTORANTE OTELLO
Via delle Tartane, 57
Ostia
Tel: 562 33 94
Closed Mon.
Regional cuisine.
15,000–30,000 lire
⊡ ⋇ ☗

HOTELS

HOTEL ALBERGO
BELLAVISTA**
Piazzale Magellano, 16
Ostia
Tel: 562 43 93
Fax: 562 16 67
Restaurant in the hotel.
70,000–95,000 lire
⌂ ⊡ ⋇ 🚗

SURROUNDING AREA

RESTAURANTS

ANTONELLO OLONNA
Via Roma, 89 (24 miles
out of Rome on Via
Casilina Labico)
Tel: 951 00 32
Closed Sun. and Mon.
Prices are high but the
cooking is excellent and
the surroundings
superb; the restaurant
even contains a library.
Regional cuisine.
Reservations essential.
80,000–90,000 lire
⊡

BRICIOLA DI ADRIANA
Via Gabriele
d'Annunzio, 12
Grottaferrata
Tel: 945 93 38
Closed Mon. and Sun.
evening and for 2 weeks
in August.
Traditional cuisine.
40,000 lire
☗

CACCIONI
Via A. Diaz, 13
Frascati
Tel 942 03 78
Closed Mon., 10 days in
January and 10 days in
August.
An excellent address.
60,000 lire
⊡ ☗

D'ARTAGNAN
Via Tuscolana, 17 miles
out of Rome)
Grottaferrata
Tel: 940 62 91

Closed Sun. evening
and Mon.
Roman and local
specialties.
40, 000–80,000 lire
⊡ ☗

LA GROTTA
Via Italo Belardi, 31
Genzano
Tel: 936 42 24
Closed Wed. and a few
days in early Jan.
Traditional Roman
cuisine.
30,000–70,000 lire
⊡

L'ORATORIO
Via Don Bosco, 41
Frascati
Tel 941 73 66
Closed Wed. and two
weeks in August.
Traditional and
international cuisine.
35,000 lire
⊡ ☗

RICHELIEU MONTE
PORZIO CATONE
Via Frascati Colonna
(3 miles out of Rome)
Tel: 948 52 93
Closed Sun. and Mon.
evening.
A lovely place in the
residential area of the
Castelli. Wide choice of
wines and Roman
specialties on the menu.
Unforgettable view of
Rome and the valley.
50,000 lire
⊡ ⋇ ☗

TAVERNA MAMI LIUS
Viale Bolilla, 1
Frascati
Tel: 942 15 59
Closed Wed., Sun.
evening and for 2 weeks
in August.
Traditional Roman
cuisine. Home-made
products. Booking
recommended
40,000 lire
⊡ ☗

TAVERNA DELLO
SPUNTINO
Via Cicerone, 22
Grottaferrata
Tel: 945 93 66
Closed Wed. and in
August.
Regional cuisine.
50,000–80,000 lire

HOTELS

ALBERGO
CASTELVECCHIO***
Via Pio Undicesimo, 23
Castelgandolfo
Tel: 936 03 08
Fax: 936 05 79
Two restaurants
110,000–160,000 lire
⊡ ⊸ ◑ 🚗

ALBERGO EL PASO***
Via Settevene Palo, 293
Cerveteri
Tel: and Fax: 994 35 82
Restaurant in the hotel
(Roman cuisine).
60,000–105,000 lire
⌂ ⊡ ℗

ALBERGO
TARCONTE***
Via Tuscia, 19
Tarquinia
Tel: 0766/85 61 41
Fax: 0766/85 65 85
Restaurant in the hotel.
75,000–1100 lire

FOOD

CATTLE PRODUCTS
FAIR
Grottaferrata
25 March–5 April
This fair has been going
on for 400 years. It is a
great opportunity to buy
salamis, hams etc.

APPENDICES

◆ BIBLIOGRAPHY

ESSENTIAL
◆ READING ◆

◆ GREGOROVIUS (F.): *History of the City of Rome in the Middle Ages*, English tr., London, 1906; reprinted New York, 1967
◆ MASSON (G.): *Companion Guide to Rome*, London, 1965
◆ NASH (E.): *Pictorial Dictionary of Ancient Rome*, London, 1966
◆ *Michelin Guide to Rome*, London (many editions)
◆ SHOWERMAN (G.): *Monuments and Men of Ancient Rome*, New York, 1935
◆ STORTI (A.): *Rome, A Practical Guide*, Venice, 1980
◆ VARRIANO (J.): *Rome, A Literary Companion*, London, 1991

◆ GENERAL ◆

◆ ARMELLINI (M.), CECCHILLI (C.): *Le Chiese di Roma dal secolo IV al XIX*, 2 vol., Rome, 1942
◆ *Attraverso l'Italia, Roma*, Touring Club Italiano, Milan, 1986
◆ BENTLEY (J.): *Rome: Architecture, History, Art*, London, 1991
◆ CIPRIANI (G.B.): *Architecture of Rome*, originally from Rome 1835–7, reprinted New York, 1986
◆ *Civiltà del Lazio primitivo* (exhibition catalogue), Rome, 1976
◆ DE TOMMASSO (F.): *Le Cupole di Roma*, Rome, 1991
◆ D'ONOFRIO (C.): *Castel Sant'Angelo*, Rome, 1972
◆ *Fontana di Trevi*, Fratelli Palombi Editori, Rome, 1992
◆ GALASSI PALUZZI (C.): *Chiese romane*, Ente provinciale per il turismo di Roma
◆ *Guida al Quirinale*, Fratelli Palombi Editori, Rome, 1985
◆ HAUSER (E.D.): *Italy, a Cultural Guide*, New York, 1981
◆ Hutton (E.): *Rome*, London, 1950
◆ LANCIANI (R.): *New Tales of Old Rome*, London, 1901
◆ LANCIANI (R.): *Wandering through Ancient Roman Churches*, New York, 1924
◆ *Lazio*, Touring Club Italiano, Milan, 1967

◆ MENEN (A.): *Rome Revealed*, London, 1960
◆ MORETTI (U.): *Artists in Rome, Tales of the Babuino*, (tr. W. Weaner), London and New York, 1958
◆ PARTNER (P.): *The Lands of St. Peter*, London, 1972
◆ PEREIRA (A.): *Rome*, London, 1990
◆ PIETRANGELI (C.), PERICOLI (C.): *Guide rionali di Roma*, Fratelli Palombi Editori, Rome 1971–80
◆ POTTER, (O.M.): *The Colour of Rome*, London and Philadelphia, 1909
◆ RAVAGLIOLI (A.): *La Storia in piazza. Breve profilo della storia urbanistica della citta de Roma*, Edizioni di "Roma Centro Storico", 1987
◆ RAVAGLIOLI (A.): *Tutta Roma*, Rome, 1983
◆ *ROMA*, Touring Club Italiano, Milan, 3 1992
◆ SHARP (M.): *A Guide to the Churches of Rome*, Philadelphia, 1966
◆ VENTRIGLIA (U.): *La Geologia della citta di Roma*, Rome, 1971
◆ WILLEY (D. AND M. C.): *Welcome to Rome*, Glasgow, 1981

GENERAL
◆ HISTORY ◆

◆ DURUY (V.): *History of Rome and the Roman Peoples*, Boston, 1890
◆ GIBBON (E.): *The Decline and Fall of the Roman Empire* (many editions)
◆ HIBBERT (C.): *Rome – the Biography of a City*, London, 1985
◆ MOMMSEN (T.): *The History of Rome* (many editions)
◆ NIEBUHR (B.C.): *The History of Rome*, London, 1855-60

ANCIENT
◆ ROME ◆

◆ ASBY (TH.): *The Roman Campagna in Classical Times*, E. Benn, London, 1927
◆ BAKER (G.B.): *Twelve Centuries of Rome, 753 BC–AD 476*, London, 1936
◆ BALSDON (J.P.V.D.): *Julius Caesar and Rome*, Harmondsworth, 1967
◆ BARROW (R.H.): *The Romans*, Harmondsworth, 1949
◆ BARTON (I.M.) (ED.): *Roman Public*

Buildings, Exeter, 1989
◆ BERTOLOTTI, IOPPOLO, SARTORIO: *La Residenza Imperiale di Massenzio*, Itinerari d'Arte di Cultura, Rome, 1989
◆ BIRLEY (A.): *Marcus Aurelius*, London, 1966
◆ BORTOLOTTI (L.): *Roma fuori le mura*, Laterza, Rome-Bari, 1988
◆ CAPRINO (C.), COLINI (A.M.), GATTI (G.), PALLOTTINO (M.), ROMANELLI (P.): *La Colonna di Marco Aurelio*, Rome, 1955
◆ CARCOPINO (J.): *Daily Life in Ancient Rome*, Harmondsworth, 1941
◆ CARY (M.): *History of Rome down to the Reign of Constantine*, London and New York, 1935
◆ CASTAGNOLI (F.): *Il Campo Marzio nell'antichita*, Mem. Acc. Lincei, 7,1, 1946, p.93
◆ CASTAGNOLI (F.): *Il Circo di Nerone in Vaticano*, Rendic Pont. Acc. 32, 1959–60, pp. 97 sqq.
◆ CASTAGNOLI (F.): *Topografia e urbanistica di Roma antica*, Società Editrice Internazionale, Turin, 1969
◆ CASTAGNOLI (F.), CECCHELLI (C.), GIOVANNONI (G.), ZOCCA (M.): *Topografia e urbanistica di Roma*, Bologna, 1958 (Storia di Roma, 22)
◆ COARELLI (F.): *Il Campo Marzio occidentale, storia e topografia*, in *Mélanges de l'Ecole française de Rome*, 89, 1977, pp.807 sqq.
◆ COARELLI (F.): *L'"Ara di Domizio Enobarbo" e la Cultura artistica in Roma nell'il secolo a. C.*, in *Dialoghi di Archeologia*, 2, 1968, pp.302 sqq.
◆ COARELLI (P.): *Public Building in Rome between the Second Punic War and Sulla*, in *Papers of the British School at Rome*, 45, 1977, pp. 1 sqq.
◆ COARELLI (F.): *Il Complesso pompeiano del Campo Marzio e la sua decorazione scultorea*, Rendic. Pont. Acc. 44, 1971–72, pp. 99 sqq
◆ COARELLI (F.): *Il Foro romano*, 2 vol., Quasar, 1985
◆ COARELLI (F.): *Il Sepolcro degli Scipioni a Roma*, Itinerari d'Arte e di

Cultura, Rome, 1989
◆ COARELLI (F.): *Italia centrale*,Laterza, Rome-Bari, 1985
◆ COARELLI (F.): *L'Identificazione dell'Area Sacra dell'Argentina*, in *Palatino*, 12, 4, 1968, pp. 365 sqq.
◆ COARELLI (F.): *Roma sepolta*, Curcio, Rome, 1984
◆ COLINI (A.M.): *Il Campidoglio nell'antichita*, in *Capitolium*, 40, 4, 1965, pp. 175 sqq.
◆ COLINI (A.M.), COZZA (L.): *Ludus Magnus*, Rome, 1962
◆ DE ROSSI (G.B.): *La Roma sotterranea cristiana*, 3 vol., Rome, 1864–77
◆ DILL (S.): *Roman Society from Nerito Marcus Aurelius*, London, 1925
◆ DIXON (S.): *The Roman Family*, London and Baltimore, 1992
◆ D'ONOFRIO (C.):*Gli Obelischi di Roma*, Rome, 1965
◆ FRANK (T.): *Roman Buildings of the Republic*, Rome, 1924
◆ GIULIANI (C.F.): *Domus Flavia: una nuova lettura*, in *Römische Mitteilungen*, 84, 1977, pp.91 sqq.
◆ GARDNER (J.F.) AND WIEDEMANN (T.): *The Roman Household, A Sourcebook*, London, 1991
◆ GRANT (M.): *The World of Rome*, London, 1960
◆ GRANT (M.): *The Roman Emperors, 31 BC–476 AD*, London
◆ GREENIDGE (A.H.J.): *Roman Public Life*, New York, 1901
◆ GREENIDGE (A.H.J.) AND CLAY (A.M.): *Sources for Roman History*, Oxford, 1903
◆ GUARDUCCI (M.): *L'Isola Tiberina e la sua tradizione ospitaliera*, Rendic. Acc. Lincei, 26, 3–4,1971, pp.26 sqq.
◆ GUIDOLBALDI (F.): *Complesso archeologico di San Clemente. Risultati degli scavi piu recenti e nesame dei resti architettonici*, Rome, 1978
◆ GUZZO (P.G.): *Antico e archeologia. Scienza e politica delle diverse antichità*, Nuova Alfa Editoriale, Bologna, 1993
◆ HANFMAN (C.M.P.): *Roman Art, A Modern*

Survey of the Art of Imperial Rome, New York, 1975
◆ IVERSEN (E.): *Obelisks in Exile,* 1, Copenhagen, 1968
◆ JORDAN (H.): *Forma Urbis Romae,* Berlin, 1874
◆ *La Colonna Traiana,* Ed. Carte segrete, Rome, 1988
◆ *L'Area Sacra di S. Omobono,* coll. La Parola del Passato, No. 32, 1977, pp. 9 sqq.
◆ LANCIANI (R.): *L'Antica Roma,* Rome, 1970
◆ LANCIANI (R.): *The Destruction of Ancient Rome,* New York, 1899
◆ LANCIANI (R.): *Storia degli scavi di Roma,* I-IV, Rome 1902–4 (reprinted. 1989–92)
◆ LEWIS (N.) AND REINHOLD (M.): *Roman Civilization. 1. The Republic,* New York, 1952
◆ LEWIS (N.) AND REINHOLD (M.): *Roman Civilization. 2. The Empire,* New York, 1955
◆ LIDDEL (H.G.): *A History of Rome, from the Earliest Times to the Establishment of the Empire,* 1889
◆ LUGLI (G.): *La Tecnica edilizia romana,* Rome, 1957
◆ MEIGGS (R.): *Roman Ostia 2,* Oxford, 1973
◆ MOATTI (C.): *The Search for Ancient Rome,* London and New York, 1993
◆ NASH (E.): *Pictorial Dictionary of Ancient Rome,* London, 1982
◆ PARKER (J.H.): *The Archaelogy of Rome,* Oxford and London, 1974
◆ PAVOLINI (C.): *Ostia, Laterza,* Rome-Bari, 1988
◆ PLATNER (S.B.), ASBY (TH.): *A Topographical Dictionary of Ancient Rome,* Oxford University Press, 1929
◆ QUENNEL (P.): *The Colosseum,* New York, 1971
◆ QUILICI (L.): *Via Appia da Porta Capena al Colli Albani,* Fratelli Palombi Editori, Rome, 1989
◆ RODRIGUEZ ALMEIDA (E.): *Aggiornamento topografico dei colli Oppio, Cispio e Viminale secondo la Forma Urbis Marmorea,* Rendic. Pont. Acc, 48, 1975–6, pp.263 sqq. *Roma Antiqua 2.*

Grandi edifici pubblici, Ed. Carte segrete, Rome, 1992
◆ SAVAGE (S.M.): *The Cults of Ancient Trastevere,* in *Memoirs of the American Academy in Rome,* 17, 1940, pp.26 sqq.
◆ SEAR (F.): *Roman Architecture,* London, 1982
◆ SYME (R.): *The Roman Revolution,* Oxford, 1939
◆ TODD (M.): *The Walls of Rome,* London 1978
◆ UCELLI (G.): *Le Navi dei Nemi,* Libreria dello Stato, Rome, 1950
◆ WARD-PERKINS (J.B.): *Roman Architecture,* London, 1979
◆ WILKINSON, (L.P.): *The Roman Experience,* London, 1975
◆ ZANKER (P.): *Forum Augustinum,* Tübingen, 1968

MEDIEVAL ROME ◆

◆ BARBERINI (M.G.): *I Santi Quattro Coronati a Roma, Itinerari d'Arte e di Cultura,* Rome, 1989
◆ BERTOLINI (O.): *Roma di fronte a Bisanzio e i Longobardi,* Bologna, 1941 (Storia di Roma, 9)
◆ BOYLE (L.): *Piccola guide di San Clemente,* Rome, 1976
◆ BRENTANO (R.): *Rome before Avignon, a Social History of 13th century Rome,* London, 1991
◆ BREZZI (P.): *Roma e l'Imperio Medioevale,* 774-1252, Bologna, 1947, in *Storia di Roma,* 10
◆ CARDILLI (L.) (ED): *Edicole sacre romane* Fratelli Palombi Editori, Rome, 1990
◆ DUPRE-THESELDER (E.): *Roma dal Comune di Popolo alla Signoria Pontificio (1252–1377),* Bologna, 1952, in *Storia di Roma,* 11
◆ *Fragmenta picta, affreschi e mosaici staccati del Medioevo romano,* Rome, 1989
◆ HERMANIN (F.): *L'Arte in Roma dal secolo VII al XIV,* Bologna, 1945 (Storia di Roma, 27)
◆ FROTHINGHAM (A.L.): *The Monuments of Christian Rome,* New York, 1908
◆ GOLZIO (V.), ZANDER (G.): *Le Chiese di Roma dal XI al XVI secolo,* Bologna, 1963 (Roma cristiana, 4)
◆ HUELSEN (CH.): *Le Chiese di Roma nel*

Medioevo, Cataloghi Ed. Appunti, Florence, 1927
◆ KRAUTHEIMER (R.), CORBETT (S.), FRANKI (W.), FRAZER (A.K.): *Corpus basillicarum christianarum Romae,* 6 vol., Vatican City, 1937–80 (Monumenti di antichita cristiana)
◆ KRAUTHEIMER (R.): *Rome, Profile of a City,* 312–1308, Princeton, 1980
◆ *Le Fortificazioni medievali a Roma. La Torre dei Conti e la Torre delle Milizie,* Fratelli Palombi Editori, Rome, 1991
◆ LLEWELLYN (P.): *Rome in the Dark Ages,* New York, 1971
◆ MASSIMI (G.): *La Chiesa di Santa Maria in Cosmedin,* Rome, 1989
◆ MATTHIAE (G.): *Le Chiese di Roma dal IV al X secolo,* Bologna, 1962 (Roma cristiana, 3)
◆ MATTHIAE (G.): *Mosaici medioevali delle chiese di Roma,* 2 vol., Rome, 1967
◆ MATTHIAE (G.): *Pittura romana del Medioevo* (prepared for publication by Andaloro (M.) and Gandolfo (F.), 2 vol., Rome, 1987–8
◆ OAKESHOTT (N.): *The Mosaics of Rome from the Third to the Fourteenth Century,* London, 1989
◆ *Roma nel Duecento l'arte nelia Citta dei papi di Innocenzo III a Bonifacio VIII,* ed. a cura di Angela Maria Romanini, Turin, 1991
◆ WALEY (D.): *The Papal State in the Thirteenth Century,* London, 1969

◆ RENAISSANCE AND MODERN ROME ◆

◆ ABRAMSON (M.C.): *Painting in Rome during the Papacy of Clement VIII: a Documented Study,* Garland, London and New York, 1981
◆ ARGAN (G.): *L'Architettura barocca in Italia,* Milan, 1957
◆ BARTONCCINI (F.): *Roma nell'Ottocento,* Bologna, 1985
◆ BELLIBARSALI (I.): *Conoscere le ville di Roma e del Lazio,* Rome, 1982
◆ BLUNT (A.): *Guide to Baroque Rome,* London, 1982
◆ BLUNT (A.): *Borromini,*

London, 1979
◆ BONNEFOY (Y.): *Rome 1630,* Paris and Milan, 1970
◆ BORSI (F.): *Le Bernin,* Hazan, Paris, 1984
◆ BÖSEL, *Jesuiten architektur in Italien 1540-1773,* Vienna, 1986
◆ BRANDI (C.): *La Prima Architettura barocca, Pietro da Cortona, Borromini, Bemini,* Bari, 1970
◆ BRIGANTI (G.), LAUREATI (L.), TREZZANI (L.): *The Bamboccianti. The Painters of Every Day Life in Seventeenth-century Rome,* Rome, 1983
◆ CARACCIOLO (A.): *Roma capitale dal Risorgimento alla crisi dello Stato liberale,* Rome, 1956
◆ CLARK (A.): *Studies in Eighteenth Century's Roman Baroque,* London, 1982
◆ D'ONOFRIO (C.): *Renovatio Romae, storia e urbanistica del Campidoglio all'EUR,* Rome, 1973
◆ EATON (C.): *Rome in the Nineteenth Century,* London, 1820
◆ ELLING (C.): *Rome, the Biography of its Architecture from Bernini to Thorwaldsen,* Tübingen, 1975
◆ ENGASS (R.): *Early Eighteenth Century Sculpture in Rome,* Pennsylvania State University Press, 1976
◆ FREEDBERG (S.L.): *Painting in Italy 1500-1600,* 2nd ed, London, 1983
◆ FROMMEL (C.L.): *Der Römische Palastbau der Hochrenaissance,* Tübingen, 1972
◆ HIBBERD (H.): *Carlo Moderno,* London, 1972
◆ HOOK (J.): *The Sack of Rome,* London, 1972
◆ HOWELLS (W.D.): *Roman Holidays,* London and New York, 1908
◆ INSOLERA (I.): *Roma, Immagini e realtà dal X al XX secolo,* Laterza, Rome-Bari, 1985
◆ KRAUTHEIMER (R.): *Rome, Profile of a City,* Princeton, 1980
◆ *Il Campidoglio e Sisto V,* Ed. Carte segrete, Rome, 1991
◆ KLACZKO (J.): *Rome and the Renaissance,* New York, 1926
◆ KOSTOF (S.): *The Third Rome, 1870-1950,* Berkeley, 1973
◆ *L'Accademia dei*

Lincei e la Cultura europea nel XVII secolo, Accademia dei Lincei, Rome, 1991

◆ *L'Accademia nazionale di San Luca*, Rome, 1974

◆ *La Galleria nazionale d'Arte antica*, Fratelli Palombi Editori, Rome, 1988

◆ *L'Arte degli Anni santi Roma, 1300–1875*, Rome, 1984–5

◆ *L'Arte per i papi e per i principi nella campagna romana: grande pittura del 600 et del 700*, Rome, 1990

◆ *La Villa de la Farnésine à Rome*, Ministero per i Beni culturali e ambientali, Rome, 1990

◆ *"La pittura del Cinquecento a Roma e nel Lazio"* in *La Pittura in Italia, Il Cinquecento*, Electa, 1987, Vol. II

◆ LEES-MILNE (J.): *St. Peter's*, London, 1967

◆ MAHON (D.): *Studies in Seicento Art and Theory*, London, 1947

◆ MALLORY (N.A.): *Roman Rococo Architecture from Clement XI to Benedict XIV*, New York, 1977

◆ MONELLI (P.): *Roma 1943*, Turin, 1945

◆ MONTAGU (J.): *Roman Baroque Sculpture*, London and New Haven, 1989

◆ MURRAY (P.): *Architecture of the Italian Renaissance*, London, 1960

◆ ORBAAN (J.A.F.): *Sistine Rome*, London, 1910

◆ PADULA (A.): *Roma e la regione nell'epoca napoleonica*, Rome, 1969

◆ PESCI (U.): *I Primi Anni di Roma capitale*, Florence, 1907

◆ *Piranesi e la veduta del Settecento a Roma*, Artemide Edizioni, Rome, 1989

◆ POLLAK (D.): *Die Kunsttätigkeit unter Urban VIII*, Vienna, 1927–31

◆ POPE-HENNESSY (J.): *Italian High Renaissance and Baroque Sculpture*, Vol. III, 3rd ed., Oxford, 1985

◆ PORTOGHESI (P.): *Rome of the Renaissance*, London, 1972

◆ PORTOGHESI (P.): *Baroque Rome*, London, 1970

◆ *Rome in Early Photographs, the Age of Pius IX, photographs 1846–78*, Copenhagen, Thorwaldsen Museum, 1977

◆ PRATESI (L.): *Via Giulia*, Itinerari d'Arte e di Cultura, Rome, 1989

◆ SAFARIK (E.A.): *Breve guida della galleria Doria Pamphili*, Fratelli Palombi Editori, Rome, 1991

◆ SALERNO (L.): *Pittori di paesaggio del Seicento a Roma*, Rome, 1977–80, 3 vol.

◆ SCHLEIER (E.): *"La pittura a Roma nel Seicento"* in *La Pittura in Italia, Il Seicento*, Electa, 1988, Vol. II

◆ SMITH (G.): *The Casina di Pius IV*, Princeton, 1977

◆ *Specchio di Roma barocca. Una guida inedita del XVII secolo* (presented by Connors (J.) and Rice (L.), Ed. dell'Elefante, Rome, 1991

◆ TITI (F.): *Studio di pittura, scultura et architettura nelle chiese di Roma, 1674–1763*, ed. comparata a cura di Contardo (B.) e Romano (S.), Florence, 1987

◆ TREVELYAN (R.): *Rome '44, the Battle for the Eternal City*, London, 1981

◆ TREVES (P.): *L'Idea di Roma e la Cultura italiana del secolo XIX*, Milan-Naples, 1962

◆ VENUTI (R.): *Descrizione topografica e istorica di Roma moderna*, Rome, 1964, reprinted 1977

◆ VANNELLI (V.): *Economia dell'architecttura in Roma liberale*, Ed. Kappa, Rome, 1979

◆ VOSS (H.): *Die Malerei des Barocks in Rom*, Berlin, undated. (1925)

◆ WATERHOUSE (E.): *Italian Baroque Paintings*, 2nd ed., London, 1976

◆ WITTKOWER (R.): *Art and Architecture of Italy, 1600–1750*, 3rd ed., 1973

◆ WITTKOWER (R.): *Studies in Italian Baroque*, London, 1975

◆ WITTKOWER (R.): *Gianlorenzo Bernini, the Sculptor of Roman Baroque*, 2nd ed., London, 1966

ROME ◆ TODAY

◆ ACCASTO (G.), FRATICELLI (V.), NICCOLINI (R.): *L'Architettura di Roma capitale, 1870-1970*, Rome, 1971

◆ *Art et fascisme* (under the direction of Milza (P.) and Roche-Pezard (F.), Complexe, Paris, 1989

◆ BENEVOLO (L.): *Roma oggi*, Laterza, Rome-Bari, 1977

◆ CEDERNA (C.): *Mussolini urbanistia*, Bari, 1983

◆ CHAMBERLAIN (E.R.): *Rome* (Time-Life Books), Amsterdam, 1976

◆ DE GUTTRY (I.): *Guida di Roma moderna dal 1870 ad oggi*, De Luca Ed d'Arte, Rome, 1989

◆ FRIEDMAN (J.): *Inside Rome*, London, 1993

◆ HOEFER (H.): *Rome* (Insight City Guides), London, 1988

◆ INSOLERA (I.): *Roma moderna*, Turin, 1962

◆ INSOLERA (I.): *Roma, immagini e realta dal X al XX*, Bari, 1980

◆ *L'Architettura del Ventennio a Roma*, Fratelli Palombi Editori, Roma, 1990

◆ *Museo del Folklore. Restauri e nuove acquisizioni*, Multigrafica Editrice, Rome, 1989

◆ QUARONI (L.): *Immagini di Roma*, Bari, 1949

◆ ROSSI (G.A.): *Rome from the Air*, London, 1989

◆ SAN FILIPPO (M.): *La Terza Roma*, Rome, 1993

◆ *The Vatican Collections, The Papacy and Art*, New York, Chicago and San Francisco, 1983

◆ REVUES ◆

◆ ARCHEO, attualità del passato, De Agostini, Rizzoli Periodici, Rome

◆ BELL'ITALIA, Mondadori

◆ *"BELLA ROMA"* numero speciale de Bell'Italia, No. 49, May 1990

◆ ROMA, ieri, oggi, domani, Newton Periodici, Rome

◆ *"ROMA"*, Meridiani, numero speciale September 1991

◆ ROME. En chair et en pierre, Autrement, hors-série No. 32, Paris, Juin 1988

MAPS ◆ AND PLANS ◆

◆ CARETTONI (G.), COLINI (A.M.), COZZA (L.), GATTI (G.): *La Pianta marmorea di Roma antica*, Rome, 1960

◆ DE ROSSI (G.B.): *Piante iconografiche e prospettiche di Roma anterio al XVI secolo*, Rome, 1879

◆ FRUTAZ (A.P.): *Le Piante di Roma*, Rome, 1962

◆ LANCIANI (R.): *Forma Urbis Romae*, Quasar, Rome, 1988

◆ LANCIANI (R.): *La Pianta di Roma antica e i Disegni archeologici di Raffaello*, in Rendic. Acc. Lincei, 1895, pp.791–804

◆ RAVAGLIOLI (A.): *Plan monumental et a vol d'oiseau du centre historique de Rome*, 1972

◆ PRESSOUYRE (S.): *Rome au fil du temps, Atlas historique d'urbanisme et d'architecture*, Bologna, 1973

◆ RODRIGUEZ ALMEIDA (E.): *Forma Urbis Marmorea Aggiornamento generale 1980*, Rome, 1980

◆ *Rome, archeological center (1/2000)*, édité par la Soprintendenza archeologica di Roma, en coll. avec l'Office de tourisme de Rome

TRADITIONS AND ◆ LIFESTYLE ◆

◆ CECCARELLI (L.): *Letture romane, Antologia di curiosità, personaggi e avvenimenti della città*, Fratelli Palombi Editori, Rome, 1989

◆ GRAF (A.): *Roma nella memoria e nelle immaginazioni del Medioevo*, Turin, 1915

◆ HARE (A.C.): *Walks in Rome*, London, 1887

◆ HUTTON (E.): *Rome*, London, 1909

◆ *I Mobili del Museo di Roma, Stilli, forme, tendenze dal XV al XIX secolo*, Fratelli Palombi Editori, Rome, 1979

◆ LEES-MILNE (J.): *Roman Mornings*, London, 1988

◆ *L'Ordine di Malta ieri e oggi*, Sovrano Militare Ordine Ospedaliero di San Viovanni di Gerusalemme detto di Rodi detto di Malta, Rome, 1992

◆ *La Rome pittoresque. Les aquarelles d'Ettore Roester-Franz*, Plurigraf, Narni-Terni, 1981

◆ *Lo Sport nel mondo antico*, Ed Quasar, Rome, 1987

◆ MORTON (H.V.): *A

Traveller in Rome, London and New York, 1957
◆ NAVAL (M.): *A Roma si racconta che... Leggende, aneddoti, curiosità*, Nuova Editrice Spada, Rome, 1978

LITERATURE:
◆ LATIN WRITERS ◆

◆ DAVENPORT (B.) (ED.): *The Portable Roman Reader*, Harmondsworth, 1979
◆ GRANT (M.): *Latin Literature, an Anthology*, Harmondsworth, 1978
◆ GRANT (M.) (ED.): *Roman Readings*, Harmondsworth, 1958
◆ GRANT (M.): *Roman Literature*, Harmondsworth, 1954
◆ AMMIANUS MARCELLINUS: *The Later Roman Empire* (tr. W. Hamilton), London, 1986
◆ LIVY: *History of Rome* (many translations)
◆ SUETONIUS: *The Twelve Caesars* (tr. R. Graves), Harmondsworth, 1957
◆ TACITUS: *The Histories* (several translations)
◆ TACITUS: *The Annals* (several translations)

LITERATURE:
◆ LATER WRITERS ◆

◆ BOWEN (E.): *A Time in Rome*, London and New York, 1966
◆ BROWNING (R.): *The Ring and the Book* (many editions)
◆ BYRON (LORD): *Childe Harold*, London 1812-17 (many editions)
◆ CELLINI (B): *Autobiography*, (tr John Addington Symonds), London 1925
◆ CHATEAUBRIAND (F.R. DE): *Memoirs* (tr. R. Baldick), London, 1961
◆ CLARK (E.): *Rome and a Villa*, Garden City, 1952
◆ CRAWFORD (F.M.): *Ave Roma Immortalis*, New York, 1898
◆ DICKENS (C.): *Pictures from Italy*, London, 1846
◆ DYER (J.): *The Ruins of Rome*, London, 1740
◆ EVELYN (J.): *Diaries* (many editions)
◆ GOETHE (J.W. VON): *Italian Journey* (tr. W.H. Auden and E. Mayer), London and New York, 1968
◆ GRAVES (R.): *I Claudius*, London, 1934
◆ JAMES (H.): *Daisy Miller*, London, 1879

◆ MONTAIGNE (M. DE): *The Journal of Montaigne's Travels in Italy*, London, 1903
◆ MORAVIA (A.): *Roman Tales* (tr. A. Davidson), London, 1956
◆ NIGHTINGALE (F.): *Florence Nightingale in Rome. Letters Written in the Winter of 1847-48*, Philadelphia, 1981
◆ ROGERS (S.): *Italy, a Poem*, London, 1830
◆ SHAKESPEARE (W.): *Julius Caesar*
◆ STENDHAL: *A Roman Journal* (tr. H. Chevalier), London, 1959
◆ STENDHAL: *Rome, Naples, Florence* (tr. R.N. Coe), London, 1959
◆ TAINE (H.): *Italy. Naples and Rome* (tr. J. Durand), London, 1867
◆ TWAIN (M.): *Innocents Abroad*, Hartford, Connecticut, 1869
◆ ZOLA (E.): *Rome* (tr. E.A. Vitzetelly), New York, 1896

◆ FILMOGRAPHY ◆

◆ *Accatone*, P.P. PASOLINI, 1961
◆ *Bellissima*, L. VISCONTI, 1951
◆ *The Belly of an Architect*, P. GREENAWAY, 1987
◆ *Ben Hur*, W. WYLER, 1959
◆ *Bicycle Thieves*, V. DE SICA, 1948
◆ *Cleopatra*, J.L. MANKIEWICZ, 1963
◆ *La Dolce Vita*, F. FELLINI, 1960
◆ *The Eclipse*, M. ANTONIONI, 1962
◆ *The Fall of the Roman Empire*, S. BRANSTON, 1964
◆ *Fellini Roma*, F. FELLINI, 1971
◆ *Fellini-Satyricon*, F. FELLINI, 1969
◆ *Julius Caesar*, J.L. MANKIEWICZ, 1953
◆ *Mamma Roma*, P.P. PASOLINI, 1962
◆ *Nights of Cabiria*, F. FELLINI, 1957
◆ *Quo Vadis?* M. LEROY, 1951
◆ *Roman Holiday*, W. WYLER, 1953
◆ *Roman Spring of Mrs Stone*, J. QUINTERO, 1961
◆ *Rome, Città aperta*, R. ROSSELLINI, 1945
◆ *La Storia*, L. COMENCINI, 1985
◆ *Sunday in August*, L. EMMER, 1949
◆ *Three Coins in a Fountain*, J. NEGULESCO, 1954

ACKNOWLEDGMENTS

Grateful acknowledgment is made to the following for permission to reprint previously published material:

◆ CURTIS BROWN LTD: Excerpt from *The Grand Tour of William Beckford*, edited by Elizabeth Mavor, © 1986 by Elizabeth Mavor. Reprinted by permission of Curtis Brown Ltd., London, on behalf of Elizabeth Mavor.

◆ GREENE & HEATON LIMITED: Excerpt from *Grand Tour Today*, by William Sansom, © 1968 by William Sansom, The Hogarth Press, London. Reprinted by permission of Greene & Heaton Limited, London.

◆ SIMON & SCHUSTER, INC.: Excerpt from *The Letters of John Cheever* by Benjamin Cheever, © 1988 by Benjamin Cheever. Reprinted by permission of Simon & Schuster, Inc.

◆ THAMES & HUDSON LTD: Diary entries of Oct. 31, 1950, and Nov. 7, 1952, from *The Passionate Sightseer* by Bernard Berenson, © 1960 by Thames & Hudson Ltd. Reprinted by permission of Thames & Hudson Ltd., London.

◆ LIST OF ILLUSTRATIONS

◆ LIST OF ILLUSTRATIONS

Firemen's Barracks, cl. *idem.*
406–407 Theater and Piazzale delle Corporazioni © ENIT.
407 *Roman ship with a cargo of wheat,* 3rd century, fresco, Bibl. Vaticana © Michael Dixon.
408 Mosaic showing the Ostia lighthouse, cl. A. de Luca.
408–409 General view and details of the Merchants' mosaics, cl. *idem.*
409 *Idem.*, details.
410 *Mithras killing the bull,* marble, Museo d'Ostia © Scala.
410–411 Model of an *insula,* Museo de la Civiltà Romana © Scala.
411 Bar decoration of the Thermopolium, 4th century AD, Museo di Ostia © Scala.
Via dei Molini, Casa di Diana and Forum, cl. A. de Luca.
412 Temple of Hercules, cl. A. di Luca.
Latrines, Temple of Rome and Augustus, pavement of colored marble in the Casa di Psiche e Amore and Casa degli Aurigi, cl. *idem.*
413 Terme dei Sette Sagi and the Serapeum, cl. A. de Luca.
Cupid and Psyche, statue, cl. *idem.*
Carnet d'Auguste © Bibl. nat., Paris.
414 Mithraeum of Felicissimus, cl. A. de Luca.
Fresco in the Insula degli Volte Dipinte, cl. A. de Luca.
Naval Combat, frieze of the Tomb of Cartilius Poplicola, bas-relief © Scala.
414–15 Horrea of Hortensius, cl. *idem.*
415 *Dyer's workshop,* engraving in *La Vie des Grecs et des Romains,* 1894, all rights reserved.
Campo Magna Mater, postcard, all rights reserved.
Fish market, cl. A. de Luca.
416 Castello di Giulio © ENIT. *Una Domenica in Agosto,* L. Emmer, 1949, private coll., Paris.
Lido d'Ostia, cl. S. Grandadan.
Via Severiana crossing the Isola Sacra © Luisa Ricciarini, Milan.
418 Ponte Sant'Angelo, cl. Marzi Morselli.
Piazza San Pietro © ENIT.
420 Aeroporti di Roma, cl. Gallimard.
424 Side of Roman bus, cl. M. Marzot.
425 Metro sign, cl. N. Pascarel.
426 Telephone, phone cards, letter box, cash dispenser, cl. Gallimard.
430 Caffè Settimiano, Via Garibaldi, cl. M. Marzot.
Hostaria Farnese, Via dei Baullari, cl. M. Marzot.
431 Antico Caffè Greco, Via dei Condotti, cl. G. Peyrot. Ice cream and drinks vendor, cl. Gallimard.
432 *La Dolce Vita,* F. Fellini, © Archivio S.A.C.
Accatone, P. P. Pasolini, *idem.*
Roma, Città Aperta, R. Rossellini, *idem.*
The Belly of an Architect, P. Greenaway, *idem.*
433 Theater show © ENIT. Teatro Eliseo, cl. G. Peyrot.
435 Water clock in Pincio Gardens, cl. G. Peyrot.
Villa Sciarra © ENIT, Paris.
436 Etruscan sarcophagus, National Museum, Palazzo Vitteleschi, Tarquinia, cl. G. Berengo Gardin © TCI.
437 Lid of sarcophagus, *idem.*
Man paying homage, fresco, Tomb of the Augurs, *idem.*
Winged horses, Museo Nazionale, Palazzo Vitteleschi, *idem.*
438 Villa Aldobrandini, Frascati, cl. J.-L. Malroux.
Lago di Albano, cl. Gallimard.
440 Lago di Nemi, cl. Gallimard.
Terminillo © ENIT.
442 Coliseum, cl. M. Marzot.
Dome of the Pantheon, cl. S. Bottani.
San Giovanni in Laterano, cl. *idem.*
Trajan's Column, cl. *idem..*
Piazza San Pietro, cl. G. Peyrot.
Piazza del Campidoglio © ENIT.
443 Roman Forum, cl. M. Marzot.
Arch of Constantine, cl. A. Idini.
Villa Adriana, cl. G. Peyrot.
Trevi Fountain, cl. J.-L. Malroux.
Piazza Navona (Fontana del Moro), cl. G. Peyrot.
Trinità dei Monti, cl. *idem.*
447 House of Livia, fresco, postcard, private coll.
Entrance to the Catacombs of San Callisto, cl. G. Peyrot.
450 Angel of Ponte Sant'Angelo, Bernini, cl. A. Idini.
San Carlo alle Quattro Fontane, Borromini, cl. A. Idini.
451 Ceiling of the Gesù, B. Gaulli, painted decoration © ENIT.
Sant'Andrea della Valle, cl. Gallimard.

List of illustrators:

Cover:
H. Dixon, J.-M. Guillou, R. Hutchins.
Nature:
16–17 : J. Chevallier, J.-M. Kacédan, P. Robin, F. Desbordes.
18–19 : F. Desbordes, J. Chevallier, C. Felloni.
20–1 : A. Bodin, J. Wilkinson, C. Felloni, J. Chevallier.
22–3 : F. Desbordes, J. Chevallier, C. Felloni.
24 : F. desbordes, C. Felloni, J. Wilkinson.
History:
35 : B. Lenormand.
38–9 : J.-P.Chabot.
Architecture :
59 : J.-C. Sené.
60–1 : O. Hubert.
62–3 : P. Poulain.
64–5 : C. Quiec.
66–7 : M. Sinier.
68–9 : P. Lhez.
70–1 : J.-C. Sené.
71 : Gallimard.
72–3 :J.-B. Héron.
74–5 : J.-M. Kacédan.
76–7 : P. de Hugo.
78–9 : T. Townsend.
80–1 : H. Dixon.
82 : R. Hutchins.
83 : T. Hill.
84–5 : N. Castle.
86–7 : M. Shoebridge, J.-M. Guillou.
88–9 : J.-M. Guillou.
90–1 : S. Doyle, M. Morlacchi.
92-93 : R. Hutchins, J.-M. Guillou, B. Lenormand.
94 : Philippe Mignon.
Itineraries:
136–7 : J.-P. Poncabare.
146–7 : B. Lenormand.
163 : J.-M. Guillou.
180 : C. Quiec.
189 : H. Goger.
192–3, 202, 205 : C. Quiec.
208 : T. Hill.
216–7 : O. Hubert.
234–5 : J.-P. Poncabare.
246, 251 : J.-M. Guillou.
394–5 : C. Quiec.
405 and 407 : P. Montagut.
Travel Notebook:
M. Pommier.
Maps:
The itinerary maps have been taken from the *Pianta monumentale di Roma,* Centro Culturale Cicerone, Roma © Armando Ravaglioli and Luigi Piffero, with the exception of the map of the area and the itinerary maps for the Via Appia, the Villas, Tivoli, Palestrina and Ostia, which are by Eric Gillion.

Computer graphics:
Olivier Brunot.
Emmanuel Calamy.
Paul Coulbois.
Nathalie Pujebet.

When the city is not mentioned, it is Rome except in the case of, ENSBA, ENIT, Gallimard, musée du Louvre, RMN for which it is Paris ; Giraudon à Vanves and TCI (Touring Club Italiano) for which it is Milan.

We would like to thank the following people for their help:
Mme G. de Aldécoat.
M. C. Bernoni.
Mme L. Bianciani (cons. Bibl. nat., Rome).
M. S. Bottani.
M. B. Brizzi.
M. L. Ceccarelli.
M. Hinard.
Mme A. Hubrecht (agence Giraudon).
M. Christian Landes (cons. Musée archéologique de Lattes)
M. J.-L. Malroux.
M. P. Pinon.
Mme Portelance (ENSBA).
Mlle N. Sassaro (ENIT).
Mme L. Schaetzel (Institut catholique).
M. L. Ugiano (Istituto Luce).

GLOSSARY AND
BIOGRAPHICAL INDEX

◆ GLOSSARY

◆ A ◆

◆ ACANTHUS: Classical ornament based on the stylized leaves of the acanthus plant which adorn the capitals of Corinthian columns.

◆ ACCOLADE: A curved ornamental molding, especially one having the shape of an ogee arch.

◆ AEDICULE: Small niche or alcove framed by two columns, originally used in classical architecture.

◆ AEDILE: Roman magistrate in charge of the city's administration.

◆ AISLE: Lateral division in a church parallel to the nave.

◆ AMBULATORY: Aisle for walking around the back of a church; also, the gallery of a cloister.

◆ ANNONA: Food supplies in ancient Rome.

◆ APOTHEOSIS: Ceremony elevating an emperor to the rank of a god (deification).

◆ APSE: Rounded end of a church nave or aisle, generally behind the choir or containing it.

◆ ARCH: Curve formed by a vault. The Roman arch is semicircular, as opposed to the pointed Gothic arch.

◆ ARCHITRAVE: Lowest level of an entablature which rests horizontally on columns.

◆ ARCHIVOLT: Curved arch resting on columns.

◆ ATLAS OR TELEMON: Sculpted male figure supporting an architectural element.

◆ ATRIUM: Entrance courtyard surrounded by a covered gallery.

◆ ATTIC: Topmost level of a classical building.

◆ B ◆

◆ BALDACCHINO: A canopy, supported by columns, over an altar.

◆ BARREL VAULT: Vault created by a round or Roman arch.

◆ BASILICA: Ancient Roman building, with nave and aisles, designed for commercial and legal activities. Its architecture served as a model for the first Christian churches.

◆ BASIN: Shallow stone bowl-shaped water container found in Roman baths; later used for fountains.

◆ BASKET OR BELL: the flared and decorated part of a capital.

◆ BOSSAGE: Construction technique using large rough-hewn blocks of stone.

◆ BUCRANE: Classical decorative motif based on an ox's head.

◆ C ◆

◆ CAMPANILE: Bell tower, not usually attached to the main part of a church.

◆ CAPITAL: Architectural element which crowns the shaft of a column. Each of the five architectural orders has its own style of capital. Three of these are classical: Doric, Ionic and Corinthian.

◆ CAPITOLINE TRIAD: A group of three gods, Jupiter, Juno and Minerva, which replaced the triad of Jupiter, Mars and Quirinus and was worshipped on all the capitols throughout the whole Roman world.

◆ CARTOON: From cartone, meaning large sheet of paper. A full-size preparatory drawing for a painting or a fresco.

◆ CARYATID: Sculpted female figure used as a supporting column.

◆ CELLA: Innermost space in a temple which enclosed the statue of the divinity.

◆ CHANCEL: Part of a church containing the altar, sanctuary and choir, usually separated from the nave by an arch.

◆ CHEVET: The extremity of an apse.

◆ CIBORIUM: A baldacchino covering the tabernacle of a high altar.

◆ CISTA: A casket or basket used to store ritual objects.

◆ COFFER: An ornamental sunk panel in a ceiling.

◆ COMITIA: Assemblies of the Roman people, of which there were three types: curiata, centuriata and tributa.

◆ COMPOSITE: Architectural order of columns combining the Ionic and the Corinthian.

◆ CONFESSIO: Tomb of a martyr, or an altar built over a tomb of a martyr. Also used to refer to the altar of a basilica.

◆ CONSULS: Two magistrates vested with supreme power under the Republic.

◆ CORBELING: Projecting or overhanging piece or part of a building.

◆ CORINTHIAN: One of the three classical orders of columns, characterized by sculpted acanthus leaves on the capital.

◆ CROSSING: The space created by the intersection of the nave and the transept in a church.

◆ CRYPT: Underground chapel, usually containing the tomb of a saint.

◆ CRYPTOPORTICUS: Vaulted subterranean corridor.

◆ CUL-DE-FOUR: Vault in the shape of half a cupola.

◆ D ◆

◆ DAMNATIO MEMORIAE: Measures taken by the Senate to punish crimes against the state, especially "bad" emperors. Included erasing names from inscriptions and refusing apotheosis.

◆ DICTATOR: Roman magistrate vested with supreme powers for a fixed length of time.

◆ DORIC: One of the three classical orders of columns. It does not have a base, the shaft is sometimes fluted and the capital is a geometric shape, suggesting a corbeling.

◆ DRUM: Cylindrical base of a cupola.

◆ E ◆

◆ EMBRASURE: Oblique or splayed opening of a bay or window.

◆ ENTABLATURE: Combination of the main components of a classical façade supported by columns (architrave, frieze and cornice).

◆ EXEDRA: A semi-rotunda, usually with bench or seats.

◆ EXTRADOS: External or covering surface of a vault or cupola.

◆ F ◆

◆ FASCES: An axe bound by a bundle of rods; it was a symbol of a Roman magistrate's power. The fasces were carried by the lictor.

◆ FATHERS OF THE CHURCH: Early theologians who established the doctrine of the Church.

◆ FORUM: Public space designed for major activities in a Roman town (religion, trade, justice and politics).

◆ FRIEZE: Horizontal decorative band between the cornice and the architrave of a classical façade.

◆ G ◆

◆ GROTESQUES: Mural decorations composed of plants and mythical figures.

◆ GROUND PLANS OF CHRISTIAN CHURCHES: Basilical plan, with a nave and two or more aisles; Greek-cross plan, with four equal branches; Latin-cross plan, with two shorter transversal branches (transepts).

◆ H ◆

◆ HARUSPEX: A priest, originally of an Etruscan priesthood, who specialized in divination using the entrails of sacrificed animals.

◆ HERM: A sculpted male figure used instead of a column to support an architectural element.

◆ HILLS: According to tradition Rome was built on top of seven hills (the Capitol, Palatine, Aventine, Coelian, Quirinal, Viminal and Esquiline).

◆ HOLY YEAR: A Jubilee Year celebrated by the Roman Catholic Church every 25 years since the time of Pope Paul II. Pilgrims from all over the world visit the holy places in Rome, particularly the four major basilicas whose Holy Doors, normally bricked up, are opened.

◆ HYPOGEUM: Underground burial chamber.

◆ I ◆

◆ IDES: The 15th day of March, May, July and October and the 13th day of the other months in the Roman calendar.

◆ IMPERIUM: Sovereign, civil and military power which belonged to superior magistrates (praetors and consuls) and to the emperor in Imperial times.

◆ IONIC: One of the three classical orders of columns. The capital has symmetrical volutes on either side.

◆ J ◆

◆ JUBILEE: Plenary indulgence granted by the pope during Holy Year to the faithful who accomplish certain acts of devotion.

◆ K ◆

◆ KALENDS: 1st day of the Roman month.
◆ KEYSTONE: Central stone at the top of an arch.

◆ L ◆

◆ LARARIUM: Altar or shrine dedicated to the *lares*, household gods.

◆ M ◆

◆ MAGISTRATES: Generic term for the political leaders of Rome who had a variety of specialized and collegial duties. In ascending order of seniority they were: quaestor, aedile, praetor and consul. There were also the censors, in charge of the census, and the tribunes of the people (defenders of the plebs).
◆ MANDORLA: Almond-shaped medallion in which Christ and sometimes Mary are portrayed triumphant.
◆ MANES: Spirits of the dead which became the object of a Roman cult.
◆ MAUSOLEUM: A large stately tomb.
◆ METOPE: Square space in Doric friezes, often plain but sometimes decorated with a bucrane or other ornamental motif.
◆ MOLDINGS: Reliefs on the façade of a building.

◆ N ◆

◆ NARTHEX: Vestibule or entrance hall of a Christian basilica.
◆ NAVE: The main elongated space inside a church.
◆ NONES: The 7th day of March, May, July and October and the 5th day of the other months of the Roman calendar.
◆ NYMPHAEUM: Natural or artificial grotto decorating a garden, usually with a fountain.

◆ O ◆

◆ OCULUS: Round opening in a wall or cupola.
◆ ORDERS: The architectural system of antiquity. The term is also used to refer to the elements which make up a column (base, shaft and capital) and the entablature (architrave, frieze and cornice). There are five architectural orders of columns: the three classical orders (Doric, Ionic and Corinthian) and the Tuscan and Composite.
◆ OVOLO MOLDINGS: An oval decorative motif used in the Doric order.

◆ P ◆

◆ PENDENTIVE: Vaulted surface between the rectangular wall and the domed cupola.
◆ PERISTYLE: Colonnade surrounding a building or courtyard.
◆ PIER: Rectangular pillar that bears the weight of a cupola.
◆ PILASTER: Visible part of a column attached to a wall.
◆ PODIUM: Stone platform of a Roman temple.
◆ POMERIUM: Furrow or trench marking the sacred boundary of the city, within which the army, the dead and temples of foreign gods were not allowed.
◆ PONTIFF: Minister of the Roman cult and member of the college of priests, headed by the high priest (*pontifex maximus*). In Imperial Rome the emperor was the supreme pontiff.
◆ PORTICO: Generally a covered passage with columns. The term is also used with reference to a porch supported by columns in front of a building.
◆ PRAETOR: Magistrate in charge of justice.
◆ PRONAOS: The space in classical temples, between the entrance colonnade and the actual sanctuary (*cella*).
◆ PUTTO (PLURAL, PUTTI): Naked child, without wings.

◆ Q ◆

◆ QUAESTOR: Magistrate in charge of public funds.
◆ QUIRITES: Another name for the citizens of Rome.

◆ R ◆

◆ RAISED ARCH: An arch, the height of which is greater than half the span.
◆ RETICULAR OR RETICULATED: Laid out in the form of a net.
◆ RIBBED DOME: A dome with projecting bands on the underside of the vault or ceiling.
◆ ROMAN PAINTING: Roman mural paintings are generally classified under four distinct styles according to criteria established by the excavations in Pompeii. The first style (2nd century and early 1st century BC) is essentially architectural and of Greek influence. The second style (end of the Roman Republic) is characterized by the use of trompe l'oeil (vanishing perspectives and false architecture). In the third style (period of Augustus and Claudius) decorative motifs are depicted against solid backgrounds on which small framed motifs are set. Finally, in the fourth style (period of Nero to 79 AD), the painting becomes more "impressionistic" in its brush strokes and introduces more imaginary elements.
◆ ROSTRA: Podium or platform for speakers in the Roman Forum.

◆ S ◆

◆ SACRISTY: Side-room in a church where religious objects such as chalices and vestments are kept.
◆ SALII: Salian priests of Mars and Quirinus whose ceremonies opened the warring season (in March) and closed it (in October).
◆ SCHOLA CANTORUM: The school of choristers of a church, or the choir itself as an architectural or musical ensemble.
◆ SENATUS CONSULTUM: Decision of the Roman Senate.
◆ STEREOBATE: An undecorated platform of masonry forming the foundation of a colonnade.
◆ STUCCO: A mixture of plaster and marble dust used to decorate surfaces; the term also refers to the decorative motifs made from the mixture.
◆ STYLOBATE: A molded platform of masonry forming the foundation of a colonnade.
◆ SUBSTRUCTION: A term, derived from Latin, used specifically with reference to classical architecture, to define the supporting structures of theaters and temples.
◆ SUOVETAURILE: Sacrifice of a pig (*sus*), a ram (*ovis*) or a bull (*taurus*).
◆ SURBASED ARCH: An arch, the height of which is less than half the span.

◆ T ◆

◆ TABERNACLE: A small ornamented cupboard or box placed in the center of the altar containing the Blessed Sacrament.
◆ TERM OR TERMINAL FIGURE: A sculpted belted and banded limbless figure or animal on top of a pillar.
◆ TITULUS: Place of Christian worship in a private dwelling.
◆ TRIBUNE: Apse of a Christian church containing the bishop's throne. In ancient Rome the term referred to a person elected to represent the people (plebs).
◆ TRIFORIUM: Upper arcaded gallery over the nave, choir or transept of a church, originally a triple-arched window.
◆ TRIUMPHAL ARCH: Monumental gate. Also, in Christian basilicas the arch separating the narthex from the nave.
◆ TYMPANUM: In temples it is the surface enclosed by the cornices of a pediment, particularly ones that are a triangular shape; in churches it is the surface enclosed by the lintel and the archivolt of a portal.

◆ V ◆

◆ VAULTING: Curved surface or element of an arch or a vault.
◆ VENT: Manhole or gauge in a pipe or aqueduct.
◆ VOLUTE: Ornamental spiral.

ARTISTS AND ◆ ARCHITECTS ◆

INDEX

STREET MAPS OF
CENTRAL ROME

The maps

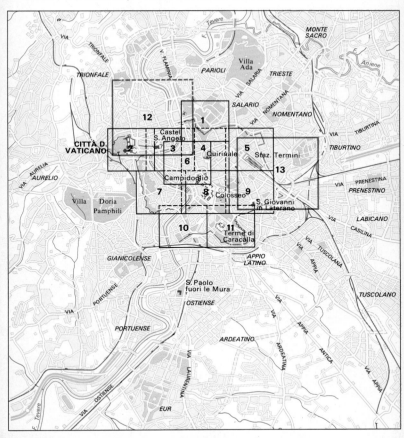

Key to symbols used

	Ruins		Gardens
	Palazzi, museums		Cemeteries
	Public buildings		Main roads
	Churches		Railway lines
	Synagogues	Ⓜ COLOSSEO	Subway
	Mosques	a▢ ꞏr	Hotels; restaurants
	Apartment buildings		Scale: 1:7,500 (1 in. = 625 ft) Scale: 1:12,500 (1 in. = 1,042 ft)

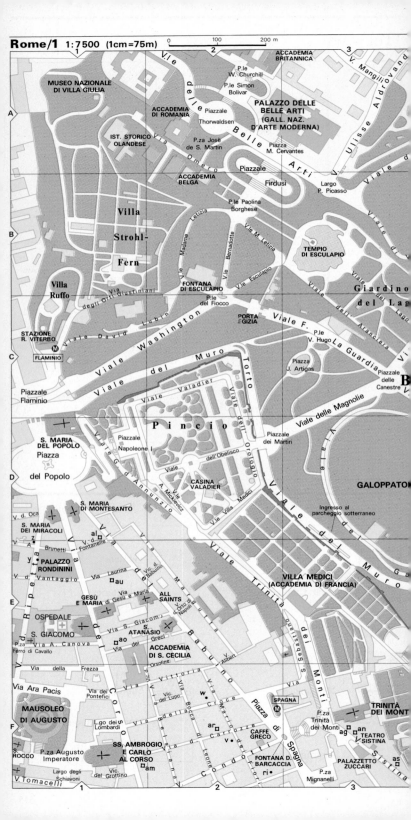

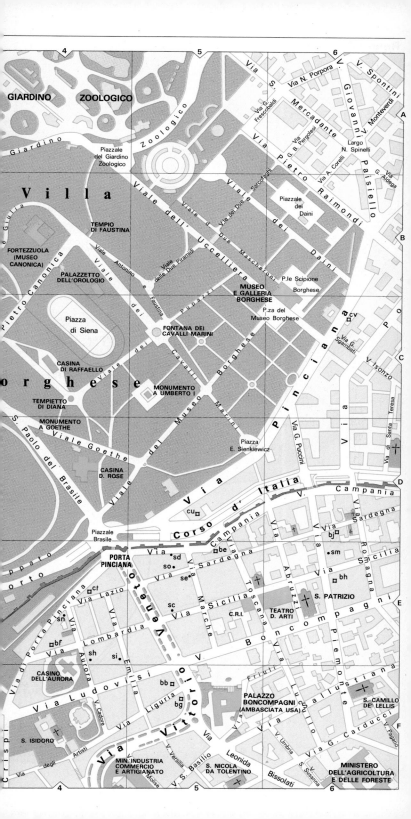

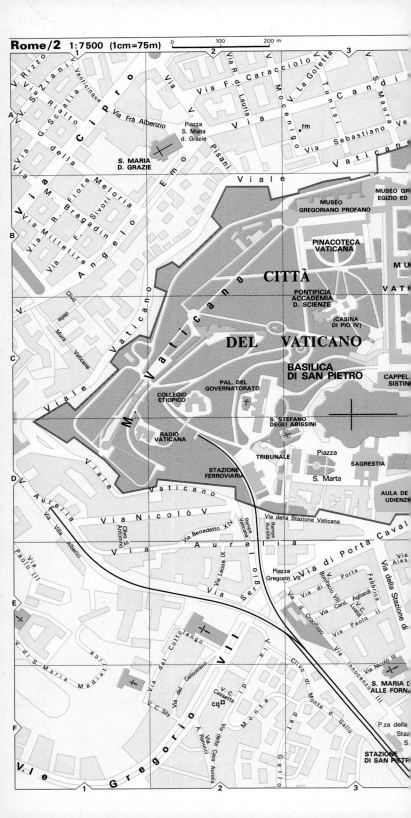

Rome/2 1:7500 (1cm=75m)

0   100   200 m

A

V. Rizzo
V. Ziani
V. S. Scalto
V. G. Rialto
V. della
Via Cipro
Venticinque
Via Frà Albenzio

Via
Via F. d. Caracciolo
Via R. Lauria
V. V. Mocenigo
V. La Goletta
Tunisi
Via S. Maura
V. C. a. n. d. i.
Ve

Piazza
S. Maria
d. Grazie

•tm

Via Sebastiano

Via   Vaticano

**S. MARIA
D. GRAZIE**

B

Via M. Fiore Meloria
Via R. Bragadin
Via F. Sivori
Via Millelire
Via Angelo
Emo Pisani

Viale

**MUSEO
GREGORIANO PROFANO**

**MUSEO GR
EGIZIO ED**

**PINACOTECA
VATICANA**

CITTÀ

**MU
VAT**

V.
Clivo
delle
Mura Vaticane

**PONTIFICIA
ACCADEMIA
D. SCIENZE**

C

M. Vaticano

Viale Vaticano

**(CASINA
DI PIO IV)**

DEL VATICANO

**BASILICA
DI SAN PIETRO**

**CAPPEL
SISTIN**

**PAL. DEL
GOVERNATORATO**

**COLLEGIO
ETIOPICO**

**S. STEFANO
DEGLI ABISSINI**

**RADIO
VATICANA**

Viale

TRIBUNALE

Piazza

SAGRESTIA

**STAZIONE
FERROVIARIA**

Via Vaticano

D

V. Aurelia
Via Villa Alberici

Via Nicolò V

Clivo S. Antonino

Via della Stazione Vaticana

Rampa Vaticana
Rampa Aurelia

S. Marta

**AULA DE
UDIENZI**

Via di Porta Caval
Via Ales

E

Via Paolo III

Via Aurelia

Via Serg

Via Leone IX

Piazza
Gregorio VII

Via di Porta
V. Bonifacio VIII
V. Card. Agliardi
V. C. Luaglia
Fabbrica
Via della Stazione di

Via d. Crocifisso
Via Paolo II

Via Innocenzo III

Via Nicolò III

V. di S. Maria Mediat
Via del Cottolengo

Via del Gelsomino

V. C. Sily
V. C.
Cassetta
cq□

Via Monte d. Gallo
Via della Cava Aurelia
A. Ranucci

Clivo di Monte d. Gallo

**S. MARIA D
ALLE FORN**

P.za della
Staz
S

F

V.le Gregorio VII

Gallo

**STAZIONE
DI SAN PIETR**

1   **2**   **3**

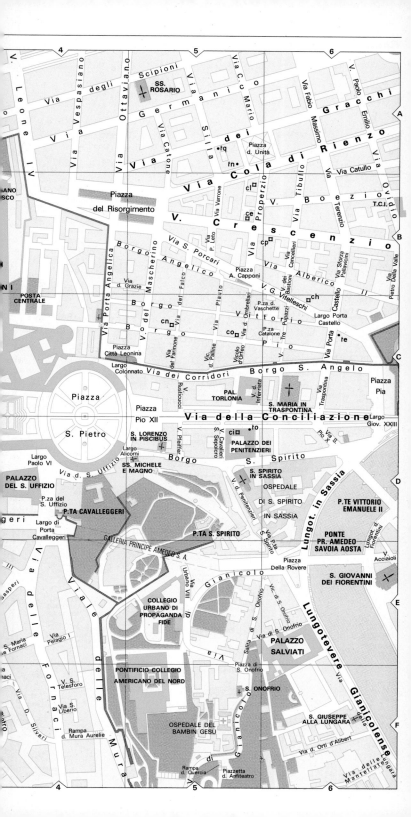

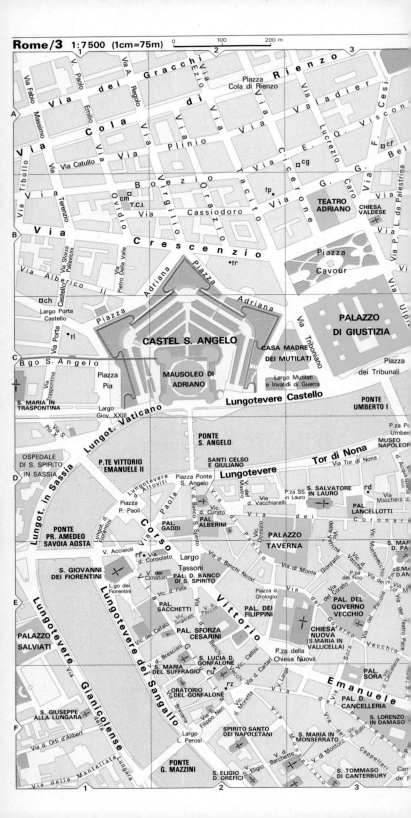

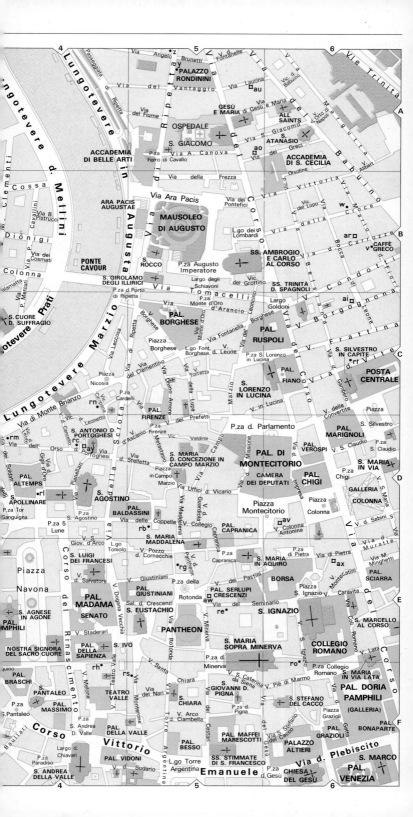

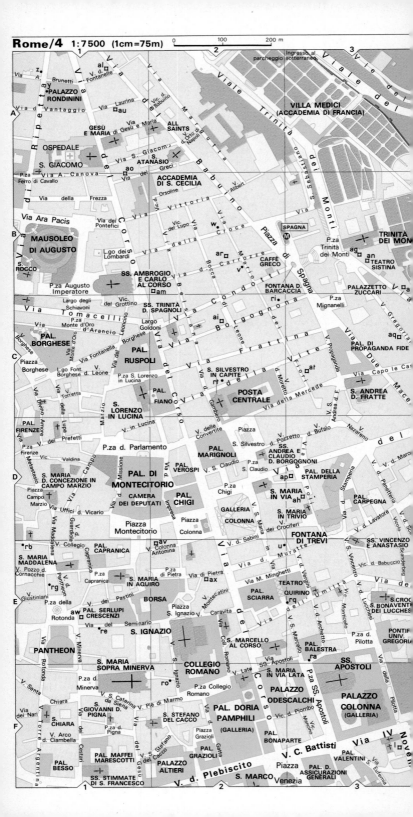

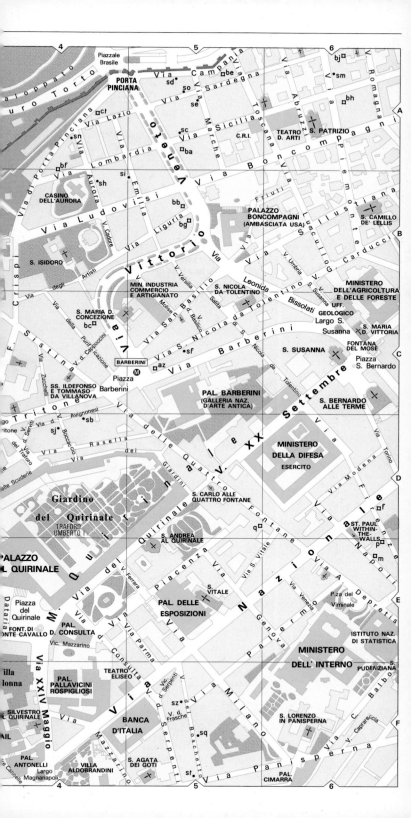

Rome/5   1:7500 (1cm=75m)

0 — 100 — 200 m

A

Via Romagna

Via Sicilia

Via Puglie

Via Lucania

Via Calabria

bj □ ✛

□ sm

□ bh

bl •

• sl

Piazzale di
Porta Pia

VILLA
PAOLINA

PORTA PIA

V. Belisario

V. Cadorna

S. CUORE
DI GESÙ

Via Boncompagni

Via Collina

Via Piave

Nerva

Via Piemonte

bd □

sg □   bi □

Piazza
Sallustio

B

Via Sallustiana

Via Aureliana

V. S. Spaventa

V. Flavia

V. Tullio

sa •

Via Settembre

Via Bezzecca

• r

Via Montebello

S. CAMILLO
DE' LELLIS

MIN. D.
LAVORO

Via Pagano

✛✛

**MINISTERO
DEL TESORO
E DEL BILANCIO**

**SS. ROSARIO
DI POMPEI**

Via Goito

Via Castelfidardo

Via G. Carducci

Via Salandra

Via Via

Via Cernaia

V. Macao

**MINISTERO
DELL'AGRICOLTURA
E DELLE FORESTE**

**UFF.
GEOLOGICO**

Largo S.
Susanna

Via Pastrengo

Piazza
delle Finanze

Via Volturno

V. Calatafimi

ab □

**Piazza
Indipenden**

C

S. SUSANNA

Piazza
S. Bernardo

S. MARIA
D. VITTORIA

FONTANA DEL MOSÈ

V. E. V. Orlando

a □

Via Parigi

Romita

**SALA DELLA
MINERVA**

✛

V. Curtatone

Piazz

**S. BERNARDO
ALLE TERME**

Barberini

**S. MARIA
D. ANGELI**

**TERME
DI DIOCLEZIANO**

L.go G. Monte
Martini

Via Solferino

A.C.I.

Galli

Caracciolo

M REPUBBLICA

P.za della

(DIPARTIM. EPIGRAFICO)

Viale E. De Nicola

e □

**SACRO
CUORE DI
GESÙ**

D

Via Nazionale

Via Modena

**FONTANA
DELLE NAIADI**

Repubblica

Viale L. Einaudi

Terme di
Diocleziano

L.go Villa
Peretti

Piazza

dei   Cinquecento

**MURA
SERVIANE**

Via V. E.

Via F

b □

f □

**ST. PAUL
WITHIN-
THE-WALLS**

**TEATRO
DELL'OPERA**

Via d. Dioclezia

**MUSEO NAZ. ROMANO
(EX COLLEGIO MASSIMO)**

M TERMINI

E

Via Napoli

p □

m □

P.za
B. Gigli

• s

c □

Via Viminale

bx □

Via Azeglio

Via Cavour

Via Amendola

Via Gio

Via Gi

Via A.

P.za del
Viminale

De Pretis

Balbo

Via Torino

d □

d □

bt □

br □

bp □

bm □

bq □

Via Principe

Via Daniele Manin

**ISTITUTO NAZ.
DI STATISTICA**

Via Cesare

V. Capreccia

V. Rosmini

Via Farini

Via Giolitti

cr □

**MINISTERO
DELL'INTERNO**

**S.
PUDENZIANA**

✛

BAMBIN GESÙ

V. Ruinaglia

Piazza d.
Esquilino

V. d. Esquilino

Via Napoleone III

• t

af □

Piazza
M. Fanti

Via Urbana

**S. MARIA
MAGGIORE**

✛

Via Liberiana

**S. ANTONIO
ABATE**

✛

Carlo

**EX
ANTIQUARIO
ROMANO**

F

V. Capocci

Via S. M. Maggiore

Via Paolina

Piazza
S. M. Maggiore

Via

1   **2**   **3**

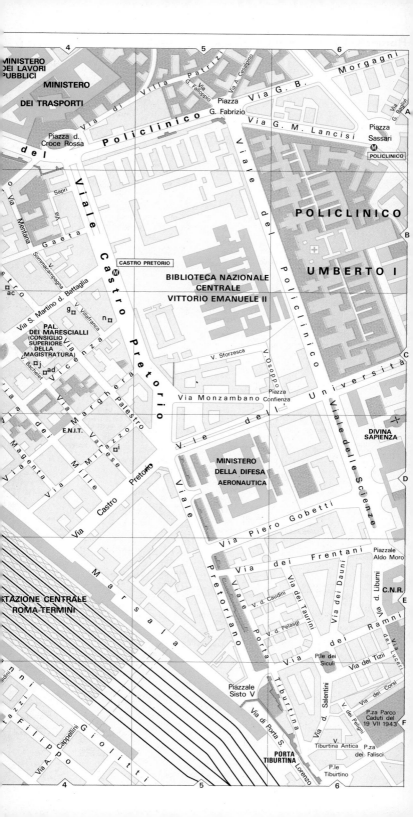

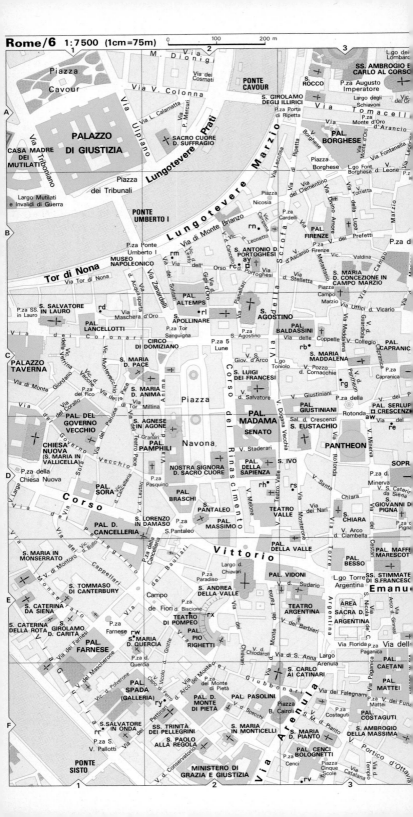

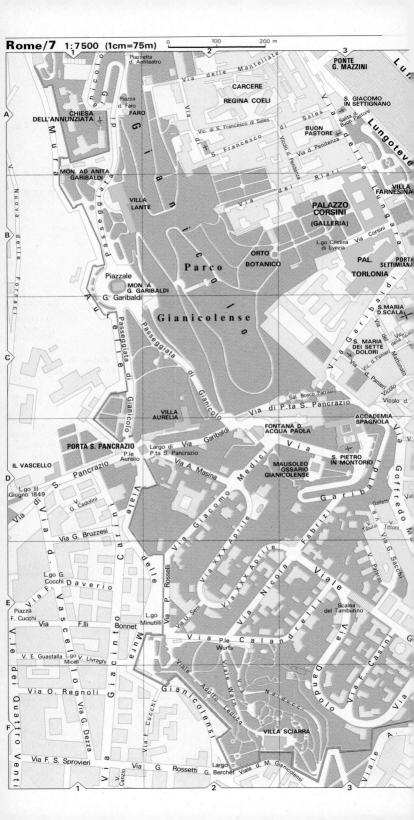

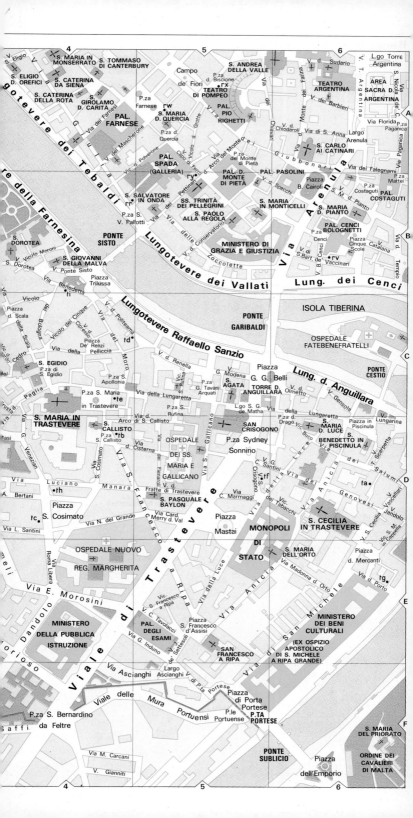

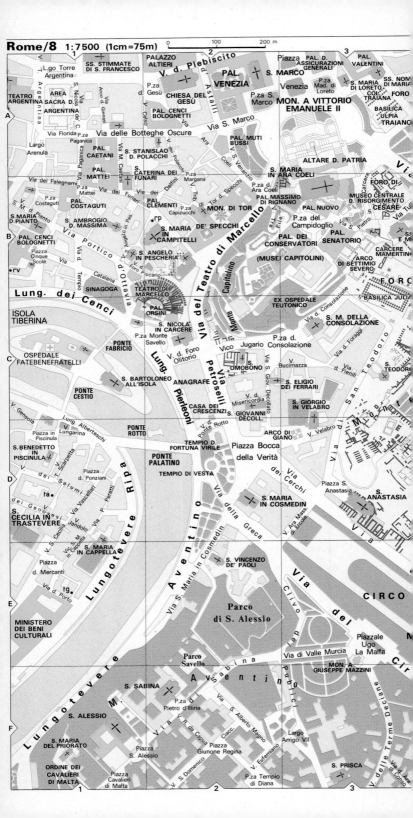

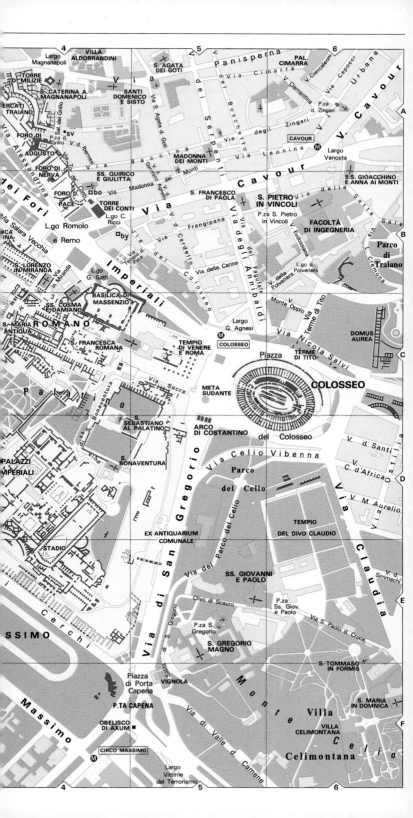

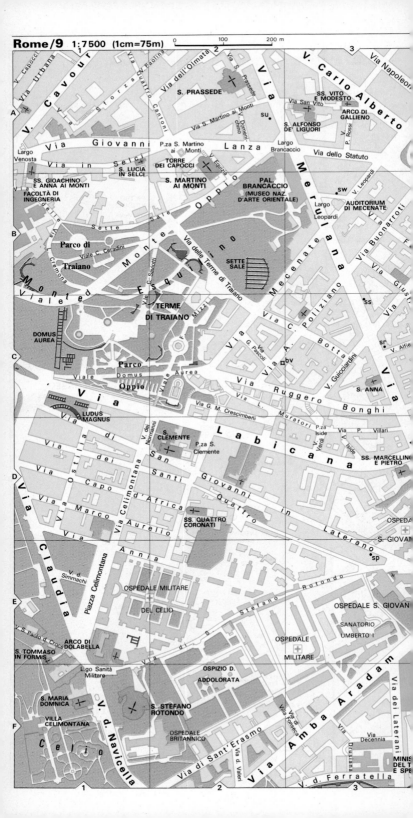

Rome/9 1:7500 (1cm=75m)

0   100   200 m

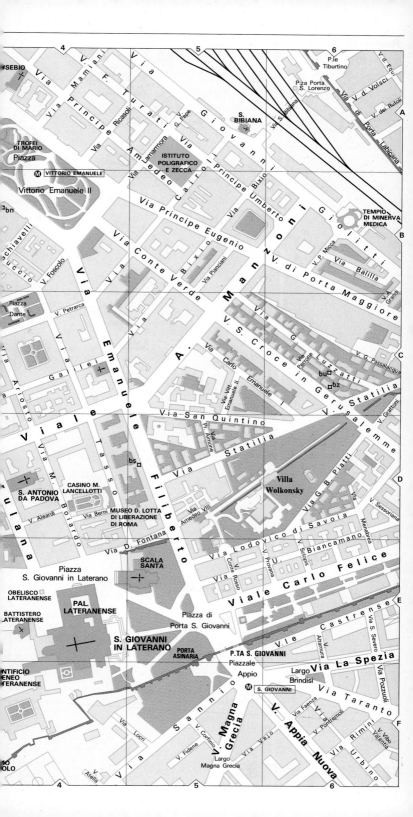

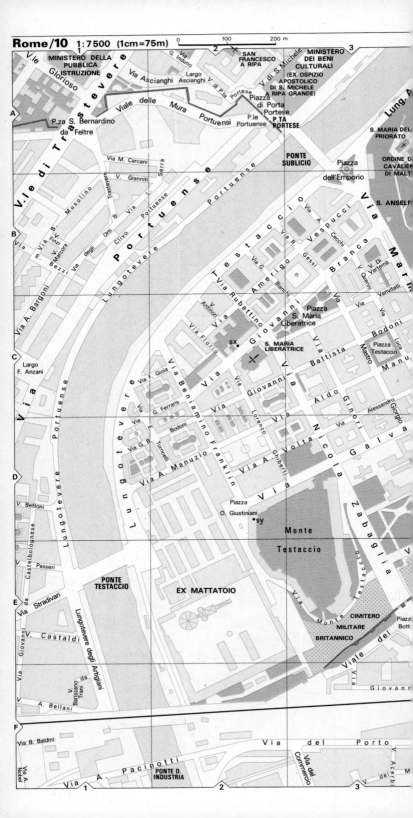

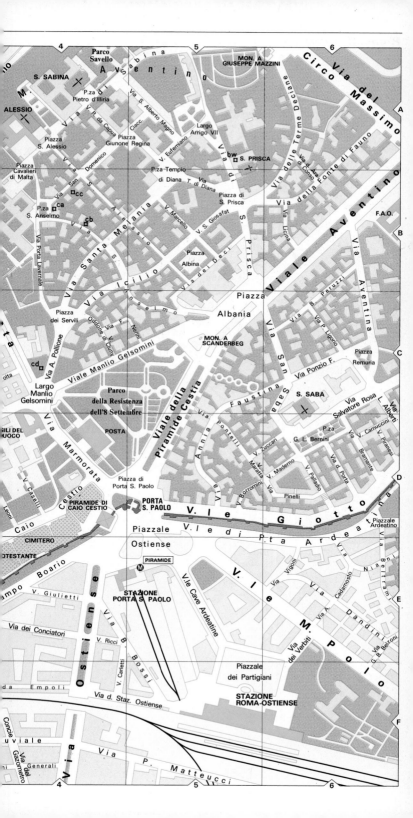

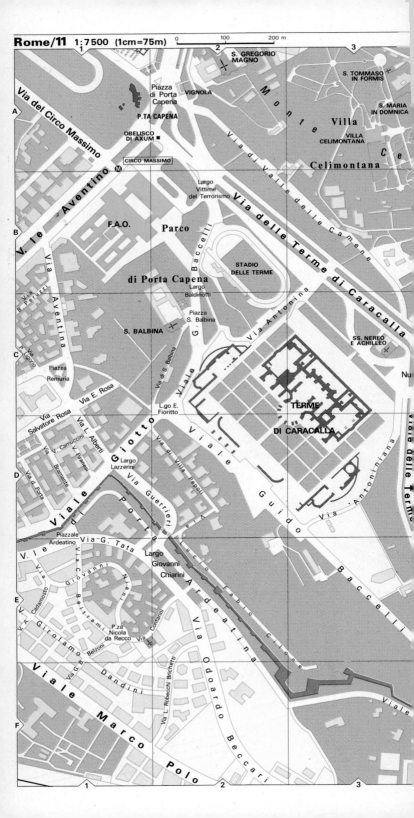

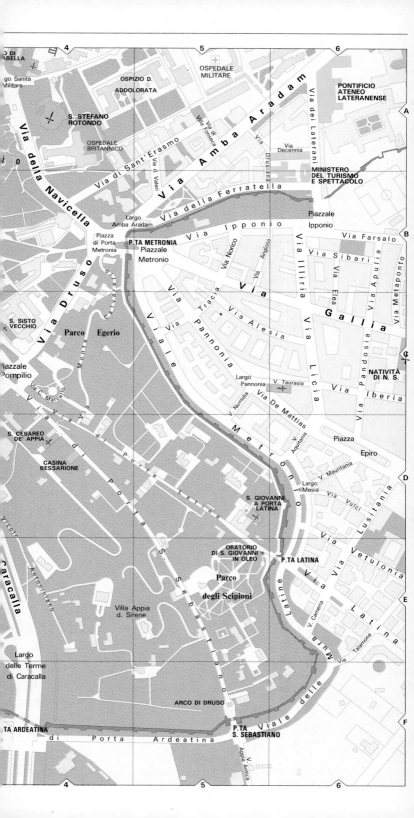

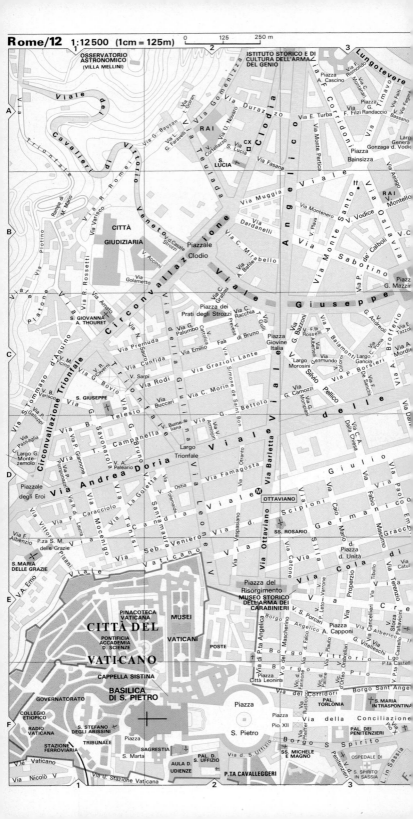

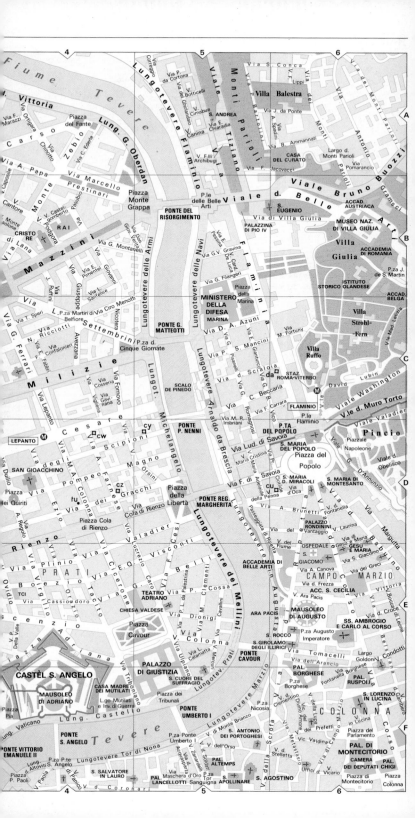

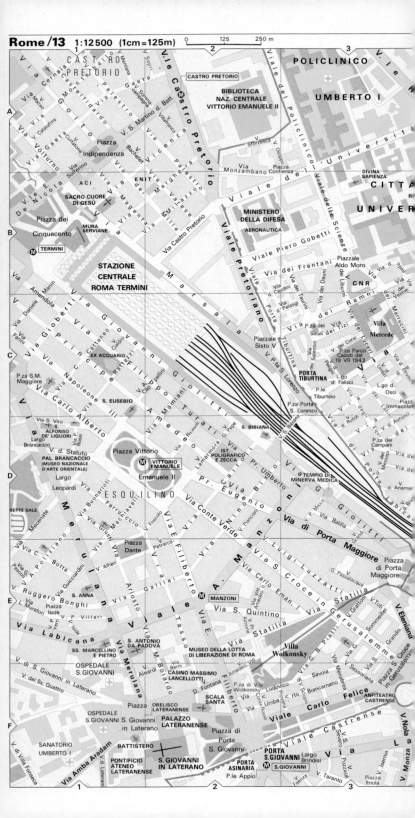

◆ MAP INDEX

550

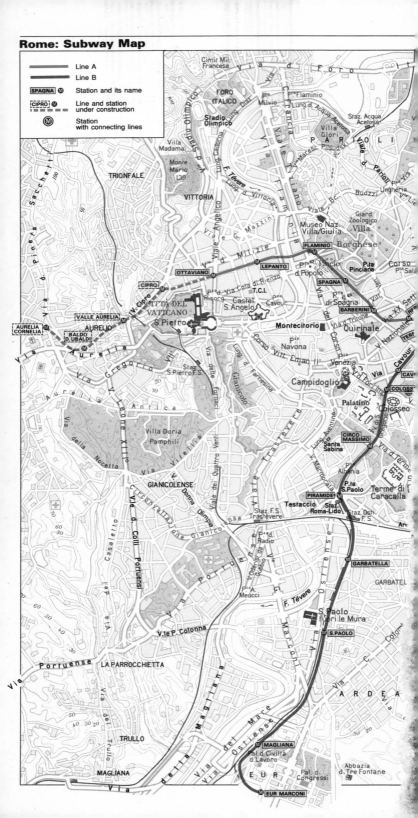